Mortality in an International Perspective

European Studies of Population

The book series *European Studies of Population (ESPO)* aims at disseminating population and family research, with special relevance for Europe. It may analyse past, present and/or future trends, as well as their determinants and consequences.
The character of the series is multidisciplinary, including formal demographic analyses, as well as social, economic and/or historical population and family studies.
The following types of studies are of primary importance: (a) internationally relevant studies, (b) European comparative studies, (c) innovative theoretical and methodological studies, and (d) policy-relevant scientific studies. The series may include monographs, edited volumes and reference works.
The book series is published under the auspices of the *European Association for Population Studies (EAPS)*.

For further volumes:
http://www.springer.com/series/5940

Jon Anson • Marc Luy
Editors

Mortality in an International Perspective

Springer

Editors
Jon Anson
Social Work
Ben-Gurion University of the Negev
Beer Sheva
Israel

Marc Luy
Vienna Institute of Demography
of the Austrian Academy of Sciences
Vienna
Austria

ISSN 1381-3579
ISBN 978-3-319-03028-9 ISBN 978-3-319-03029-6 (eBook)
DOI 10.1007/978-3-319-03029-6
Springer Dordrecht Heidelberg New York London

Library of Congress Control Number: 2014932985

Printed on acid-free paper

Springer is part of Springer Science+Business Media (www.springer.com)

All who live must die
We study when and why so
All may live longer

Contents

Contributors

Jon Anson Department of Social Work, Ben-Gurion University of the Negev, Beer Sheva, Israel

O. M. Antonova Russian State Statistics Service, Moscow, Russia

Aina Faus Bertomeu Universidad Nacional de Educación a Distancia—UNED, Departamento de Servicios Sociales y Fundamentos Histórico-Jurídicos, Madrid, Spain

Latrica E. Best Department of Pan-African Studies and Department of Sociology, University of Louisville, Louisville, KY, USA

Eleonora Soledad Rojas Cabrera Centro de Investigaciones y Estudios sobre Cultura y Sociedad, Consejo Nacional de Investigaciones Científicas y Técnicas, Universidad Nacional de Córdoba, Córdoba, Argentina

Dora Estela Celton Centro de Investigaciones y Estudios sobre Cultura y Sociedad, Consejo Nacional de Investigaciones Científicas y Técnicas, Universidad Nacional de Córdoba, Córdoba, Argentina

Peter Congdon Department of Geography and Centre for Statistics, Queen Mary University of London, London, UK

Eileen M. Crimmins Andrus Gerontology Center, University of Southern California, Los Angeles, CA, USA

Esther María León Díaz Retired Researcher, Centro de Estudios de Población y Desarrollo, Oficina Nacional de Estadísticas e Información, Havana, Cuba

G. N. Evdokushkina Department of Health Statistics, Federal Research Institute for Health Organization and Informatics of Ministry of Health of the Russian Federation, Moscow, Russia

N. S. Gavrilova Center for Demography and Economics of Ageing, NORC at the University of Chicago, Chicago, IL, USA

Juan Manuel García González Universidad Nacional de Educación a Distancia—UNED, Departamento de Servicios Sociales y Fundamentos Histórico-Jurídicos, Madrid, Spain

Anne Herm IACCHOS, Université catholique de Louvain, Louvain-La-Neuve, Belgium

Estonian Institute for Population Studies, Tallinn University, Tallinn, Estonia

A. E. Ivanova Department of Health Statistics, Federal Research Institute for Health Organization and Informatics of Ministry of Health of the Russian Federation, Moscow, Russia

Jung Ki Kim Andrus Gerontology Center, University of Southern California, Los Angeles, CA, USA

İsmet Koç Institute of Population Studies, Hacettepe University, Altindag Ankara, Turkey

Katalin Kovács Demographic Research Institute, Budapest, Hungary

Madelín Gómez León Centre d'Estudis Demogràfics, Universitat Autònoma de Barcelona, Bellaterra (Barcelona), Spain

Marc Luy Vienna Institute of Demography of the Austrian Academy of Sciences, Vienna, Austria

S. Yu Nikitina Russian State Statistics Service, Moscow, Russia

María Marta Santillán Pizarro Centro de Investigaciones y Estudios sobre Cultura y Sociedad, Consejo Nacional de Investigaciones Científicas y Técnicas, Universidad Nacional de Córdoba, Córdoba, Argentina

Michel Poulain IACCHOS, Université catholique de Louvain, Louvain-La-Neuve, Belgium

Estonian Institute for Population Studies, Tallinn University, Tallinn, Estonia

Rosa Gómez Redondo Universidad Nacional de Educación a Distancia—UNED, Departamento de Servicios Sociales y Fundamentos Histórico-Jurídicos, Madrid, Spain

T. P. Sabgayda Department of Health Statistics, Federal Research Institute for Health Organization and Informatics of Ministry of Health of the Russian Federation, Moscow, Russia

V. G. Semyonova Department of Health Statistics, Federal Research Institute for Health Organization and Informatics of Ministry of Health of the Russian Federation, Moscow, Russia

Jeroen J. A. Spijker School of Social and Political Studies, University of Edinburgh, Edinburgh, UK

V. I. Starodubov Academy of Medical Sciences, Federal Research Institute for Health Organization and Informatics of Ministry of Health of the Russian Federation, Moscow, Russia

Ahmet Sinan Türkyılmaz Institute of Population Studies, Hacettepe University, Altindag Ankara, Turkey

Edward Jow-Ching Tu National Centre for Epidemiology and Population Health, College of Medicine, Biology & Environment, Australian National University, Canberra, Australia

Sarinnapha Vasunilashorn Division of General Medicine and Primary Care, Beth Israel Deaconess Medical Center, Harvard Medical School, Brookline, MA, USA

İlknur Yüksel-Kaptanoğlu Institute of Population Studies, Hacettepe University, Altindag Ankara, Turkey

Zhongwei Zhao Australian Demographic and Social Research Institute (Coombs Building), Research School of Social Sciences, College of Arts and Social Sciences, The Australian National University, Canberra, Australia

Jiaying Zhao Canberra, Australia

Chapter 1
Introduction: Recent Themes in Mortality Research

Jon Anson and Marc Luy

Abstract There has been a recent resurgence in mortality studies, and the annual, or biannual meetings of the EAPS Health, Morbidity and Mortality Working Group have become an important venue for European and other researchers to meet, share and discuss their findings. This introductory chapter presents a brief overview of some of the main themes in current mortality research, and discusses such questions as the meaning of published mortality measures and the relationship between period and cohort life tables. In the second part, we present a summary discussion of the 12 papers in the current volume.

Keywords Overview · Life tables · Period and cohort · Summary

Research in mortality has experienced an impressive resurgence in the past few years. Harris (2010) in her Presidential Address to the 2009 PAA reported that "[o]ver the past 7 years, submissions to Health and Mortality have increased by 50 %" and we are feeling a similar upsurge in Europe. Whether this is due to the encouraging increase in life expectancy, at least in the developed world, to the growing availability of good data, software and hardware for analysis or merely to the growth of a new generation of demographers is hard to say. Whatever the reason, the result is a rapid increase in the number of on-going studies in mortality, leading to a situation in which many scholars work on similar topics, often unaware of similar research conducted by other researchers at other places. The present volume presents work from a cross section of the major themes of this research, and in this introduction we shall attempt to locate these themes within the broader context of recent writings in the field.

One thing is clear. The mortality situation in the world has improved tremendously over the past half century, and continues to do so. In the past 50 years world life expectancy has risen from 52.6 years in 1960 to 69.6 years in 2010, a cumulative rise

J. Anson (✉)
Department of Social Work, Ben-Gurion University of the Negev,
84105 Beer Sheva, Israel
e-mail: anson@bgu.ac.il

M. Luy
Vienna Institute of Demography of the Austrian Academy of Sciences,
Wohllebengasse 12-14, 6th floor, 1040 Vienna, Austria
e-mail: mail@marcluy.eu

J. Anson, M. Luy (eds.), *Mortality in an International Perspective*,
European Studies of Population 18, DOI 10.1007/978-3-319-03029-6_1,

of over 3 years per decade[1]. This rise, however, has not been uniform: in general, the countries with the lowest life expectancy have gained life-years faster than have those with a higher life expectancy. In the Middle East and North Africa the average gain has been over 5 years per decade, whereas in the high income countries the rise has been little over 2 years per decade. This general convergence in life expectancy has been offset, on the one hand, by the slow rise in life expectancy in Sub-Saharan Africa and on the other by the decline, followed by a rise, in life expectancy in the ex-Communist countries of Central and Eastern Europe. In Sub-Saharan Africa, which in any case started off with very low life expectancies, life expectancies have risen by only 1.28 years per decade, and in Eastern Europe, average male life expectancy effectively stagnated between 1960 and 1990 and in some cases, such as Russia, has yet to recover its earlier level.

The resurgence in mortality studies has focussed on a number of themes. The following review is not meant to be exhaustive, but rather to give a sense of the range of current concerns addressed by the mortality literature, mainly based on articles published in five major journals[2] over the years 2010–2011. Several of the articles are mainly descriptive, setting out how a particular population fares, with the articles' main purpose being to bring together various incomplete parts of the data puzzle in order to present an intelligent assessment. Some of these articles are historical, such as Dalla-Zuanna's two articles on nineteenth century infant mortality in the Austrian Empire (Dalla-Zuanna and Rossi 2010) and in North Eastern Italy (Dalla-Zuanna and Rosina 2011), and Thornton and Olson's (2011) study of the interplay of material and cultural effects in nineteenth century Montreal, though most are contemporary (Kohler and Preston 2011; Saikia et al. 2011). Although these articles do not generally present a theoretical question, and their main purpose is descriptive rather than analytical, most do, nonetheless, have important insights which go beyond their presentation of the mortality data: thus Patterson (2010), comparing mortality rates in and out of prison in the United States finds that mortality rates for incarcerated Afro-Americans are considerably lower than for the non-prison black population. For whites, by contrast, mortality rates in prison are similar to those for black prisoners, and considerably higher than for the appropriate non-prison population. As they note (p. 603), "Such findings speak to the depth of deprivation some groups suffer in U.S. society—a place with such deprivation that prison, in some cases, is a lesser enemy in life." Guyarvarch et al. (2010), comparing mortality in different ecological regions in Senegal, point out that the mortality risk of snake bite in the savannah region of Bandafassi (13.4/100,000) in 2002 was about the same as that for road accidents in France; Désesquelles et al. (2010) bring out the importance of looking at multiple cause patterns of mortality, and Banks et al. (2010) and Shkolnikov et al. (2011) both identify differences in the pattern of mortality between the United States on one hand, and England and Wales on the other, and suggest explanations in terms of differences in the pattern of medical and social services in these two countries.

[1] http://data.worldbank.org/indicator/sp.dyn.le00.in.

[2] Demography; Demographic Research; European Journal of Population; Population and Development Review; Population Studies.

A second group of analyses seek to explain patterns of mortality and their differences rather than just to describe them, and they are as interesting for what they do not present as for what they present. Social inequalities and gender as explanations for mortality differences have almost disappeared, or, to be precise, are taken as given rather than being the focus of the analysis (but see Schumacher and Vilpert 2011). Instead researchers are now asking how social differences translate themselves into mortality differences and the answer, almost invariably, is in the way people smoke, eat and drink themselves to death. Thus Crimmins et al. (2010) look at the way biodemographic markers can help us understand the relation between SES, health and mortality and Rogers et al. (2010) do the same for sex differences; Guillot et al. (2011) explain what they term the Russian mortality paradox, whereby Moslems have lower material welfare than ethnic Russians but nonetheless live longer, in terms of alcohol consumption; Monteverde et al. (2010) look at the different effects of obesity in the US and Mexico; Pampel and Demney (2011), Rostron and Wilmoth (2011) and Staetsky (2011b) look at the deleterious effects of smoking (but see also Ho and Preston (2010)); Rendall et al. (2011) look at the benefits of marriage, though sadly they do not consider the effects of cohabitation, and Staetsky (2011a) explains the lower mortality of Jews in the UK as being due to their healthier lifestyle. In its essence, the paradigm most of these articles are working with is:

Social conditions (inequality) –>
behaviour (smoking, drinking, diet, exercise) –>
bio-markers (e.g. high blood pressure, cholesterol, obesity) –>
mortality.

We seem to be saying that, true, nothing will make us live forever, but if we lead a healthy life, cut out smoking, drink responsibly and in moderation, eat a balanced diet, and make full use of the services that the medical profession provides, we can go a long way to living out our maximum potential life span. The root causes of premature mortality may be poverty, deprivation and social inequality, but the relation is far from deterministic, and the way in which people respond to these conditions has an important role to play. Tapia Granados and Ionides (2011) even go so far as to suggest that the lengthening of the life span is a secular trend which is actually held back by economic booms, and that mortality, in fact, progresses procyclically, going up in good times and down in bad times.

This is not to say there are no papers looking at social conditions in and of themselves, such as Anson (2010) on the importance of household structures, Kuhn's (2010) reworking of Caldwell's (1986) now classic paper on the routes to low mortality, and Zheng et al.'s (2011) focus on the importance of macro social and economic factors in increasing survivorship in the population. Grigoriev et al. (2010) look at differences in mortality increases and recovery in Belarus, Lithuania and Russia, pointing out the different routes these three countries have taken to a market economy and the way these may have affected their mortality experiences, an issue that has recently been hotly debated in the Lancet (see, e.g. Stuckler et al. 2009; Earle and Gehlbach 2010; Stuckler et al. 2010). There are also papers presenting intriguing findings which have yet to be fully explained: Drefahl (2010) shows that we are better off with a younger spouse—men in particular; and Jin et al. (2010) argue that an unbalanced sex ratio is detrimental to the sex which is over-represented, mainly, they suggest, through the limitations this imbalance places on access to the marriage market.

As we move into finer and finer analyses of the burgeoning micro-data sets which are becoming available, we are more and more focussing on individual behaviour and responsibility. What is missing, in large part, is an appreciation of what sociologists call the questions of structure and agency: why do people (apparently) act irresponsibly; is this behaviour necessarily irrational, that is, does not make sense given the social condition in which they live their lives, and would mortality differences disappear if everyone did act in a so-called responsible manner? Under what conditions do people develop the sort of resilience which enables them to live longer and healthier lives (Shen and Zheng 2010)? There is an appealing immediacy in the micro-study of individuals and their specific mortality risks as a function of their personal characteristics and behaviours, but unless and until we place these within the context in which people actually live their lives, we are left without an explanation for the apparently *irresponsible* behaviour of so many individuals.

There have been a number of articles looking at the relation between cohort and period mortality, and the explanatory weight that should be given to each. While some authors do show a clear relation between in utero or childhood events and elder health and mortality (McEniry and Palloni 2010; Wen and Gu 2011) or between the timing of birth in the economic cycle and length of life (van den Berg et al. 2011), others suggest that the mortality effects on a cohort of shocks in early life are minimal (Cohen et al. 2010; Myrskylä 2010a, 2010b) and that the predominance of cohort effects is less robust than is often assumed (Murphy 2010). The secular decline in mortality is undoubtedly a wave, or series of waves, that the various cohorts ride, each in its turn, but cohorts, too, are heterogeneous. In a changing world, the experiences of each cohort are unique, but even such major events as wars, natural disasters, technological advances or dramatic changes in social policy will affect different subgroups in different ways, just as period effects will. It is thus unlikely that there will be one simple formula relating period and cohort effects for all time—it is much more likely that the relationship will be cohort- and period-specific.

The relation between period and cohort mortality patterns is closely related to the search for the "true" measure of underlying mortality conditions. Lay people may take a period measure of life expectancy at face value, as indicating, in some sense, the average age at which people die. As demographers we are too aware of its limitations. The age specific mortality rates from which life expectancy is derived touch on different cohorts whose susceptibility, as we saw, may be tempered by their past experiences, and in any case the rates are constantly changing so that what is true in one year will no longer be true as the various cohorts age by the next year. We are therefore impatient to draw up a mortality schedule which will allow for changes. Even if we can't draw up a cohort life table until all, or most of the cohort, are departed, at least we can get an insight into the cohort's probable life expectancy. Missov and Lenart (2011), for instance, suggest that, under appropriate circumstances, a 2.5 year increase in period life expectancy per decade will translate, approximately, into a 3.3 year increase in cohort life expectancy per decade. Guillot and Kim (2011) argue that the true underlying measure of mortality is the Cross-sectional Average Length of life (CAL), based not on the synthetic number of survivors to each age (l_x) but rather on the proportion of each cohort who have survived to each age; and Denton and Spencer (2011) propose a dynamic extension of the period life table that draws out the implications, for survivorship and life expectancy, of observed rates of change of death probabilities. All of these approaches try to form a bridge between the level (or should we say, levels) of mortality observed at any point in time, and the mortality experiences of the various cohorts. Yet the ontological gap between the period and the cohort life table is not something that can be bridged by dint of technical adjustment. The cohort life table is a historical record, and to the extent that the cohort is closed to migration, it represents the true life (and death) experience of the cohort as it lives out is life-span. The period life table, by contrast, is strictly synthetic. It brings together the mortality rates, by age, for a particular year, or even a few consecutive years, and from these it derives "the probabilities of dying and their implications for survivorship, including the expected years of life remaining at different ages." (Denton and Spencer 2011, p. 832). Long before we had computer spreadsheets or simulations, the life table presented an exercise in "what if…" age specific mortality rates stay constant over the lifetime of people born at the time of the life table. So (period) life expectancy is not anyone's average, or expected, age at death, it is merely a weighted average of the reciprocals of the observed rates, with the weights being given by the survivorship curve implied by these rates (Cohen 2010).

This is not to say that the measured period life expectancy is not meaningful. On the contrary—it is extremely meaningful for what it is, a reflection of the average level of mortality in a population at any given time, an average which in no way depends on the particular age structure of the population, or on arbitrary decisions made by the researcher in choosing a standard population to control different age distributions. However, no amount of juggling will turn this synthetic measure into a true measure of lifetime mortality. The period life table is built on a certain number of premises, and we can adjust these in order to obtain tempo-adjusted mortality rates; dynamically changing mortality rates; cohort-dependent survivorship probabilities etc., but the ontological status will remain that of a synthetic model, which may or (most probably) may not match the actual mortality experience of a specific cohort. As Denton and Spencer (2011, p. 833) point out, we remain in the world of "what if". Whether the adapted life table does, or does not, represent the true underlying mortality better than the standard life table, of course, depends on the point of view of the evaluator, but in order to obtain a model which is agreed upon by all, or most, practitioners, we need first to define a bit more clearly what we mean by the true underlying level of mortality. At the very least, such adaptations of the life table should be presented with some kind of reflection of the bounds of credibility, such as the fan charts proposed by Dowd et al. (2010).

A fourth major avenue of research focusses on the mathematics of the life table. This includes the fine collection in the Demographic Research series on formal relations (Cohen 2010; Vaupel 2010; Vaupel and Zhang 2010; Wagner 2010; Cohen

2011; Missov and Lenart 2011) but there are many research articles whose main focus is on methods. Some of these concern the construction of various life table forms, such as Cai et al. (2010) on the estimation of multi-state life table functions, Lynch and Brown (2010) on estimating healthy life expectancies using partial information, and Luy et al. (2011) on the use of indirect estimates of mortality to estimate mortality differences by socioeconomic status in Italy. A number of papers consider the variability of life table estimates and mortality projections (Cohen 2011; Dowd et al. 2010; Scherbov and Ediev 2011; Shang et al. 2011) and Rostron (2010) extends previous methods for estimating smoking-attributable deaths in the population. In this context, we should not forget Poulain's (2011) timely reminder that no analysis can be better than the data on which it is based.

Finally, we should note the growing attention being given to the internal structure of the life table and the measures that may be used to compare life tables, other than by life expectancies. These include comparisons of the three central measures of longevity (Canudas-Romo 2010), the crossover point when e_0 (i.e. life expectancy at birth) equals, and then overtakes life expectancy at age 1, e_1 (Canudas-Romo and Becker 2011), the implications of the rate of mortality increase in later life (Thatcher et al. 2010; Tuljapurkar and Edwards 2011) and the way mortality changes at various ages affect life disparity—the compression or expansion of the mortality curve (Wagner 2010). We should also include in this group the continuing analyses of e-dagger ($e^{\dagger}$) and its usefulness in comparing life tables of different populations (Vaupel and Canudas-Romo 2002; Shkolnikov et al. 2011).

The European Working Group on Health, Morbidity and Mortality was established to bring together mortality researchers from every part of Europe (and beyond) in annually or biannually held workshops to exchange findings and discuss on-going work. The variety of topics coming up in this interdisciplinary research area is enormous and the possibilities to create inner- and inter-disciplinary research and collaborations are not exhausted by these workshops. This is why we decided to present a collection of such works in this book; works which also exemplify some of the major themes in the current mortality literature.

The present volume grew out of a meeting of the Working Group held at the Vienna Institute of Demography in September, 2011, and by bringing together, in print, a broad selection of the papers presented at that meeting we hope to further this dialogue. After an initial screening of papers submitted for this volume, each paper was reviewed, anonymously, by two other contributors, and the authors revised the papers in the light of the reviews. The papers present a cross-section of the work and concerns of mortality researchers across the continent, ranging from London and Madrid in the west to Moscow in the east, with a few additions from further afield. Although most of the papers are focussed on a particular population, the range of the papers is broad, covering the measurement and evolution of mortality over time; changes in the cause patterns of mortality; changes in mortality patterns at different ages, and specific analyses of mortality in particular countries.

We commence with two chapters focussing on macro trends in mortality, the one looking at counties of the United States, the other at European countries. In both, there is a close attention to methodological issues in order to improve on the reliability of the substantive conclusions. Congdon ("Estimating Life Expectancy in Small Areas, with an Application to Recent Changes in Life Expectancy in US Counties") analyses life expectancies at birth and at 65, and 30-year survivorship from age 45, for 3,139 US counties. Such estimation can be problematic when population sizes are small and there are liable to be small or even zero numbers of deaths in some age groups, and as Congdon notes, amalgamating units is likely to create its own problems when contiguous, but unlike, units are amalgamated. Instead, he proposes a "borrowing from strengths" approach, using spatial correlations between adjacent counties, and temporal correlations between adjacent age groups in order to stabilise the estimates of the age-specific mortality rates. The result is a model in which the values for these rates are not fixed, but drawn from a larger population of random effects, so that there are actually considerably fewer parameters than would be needed if each rate were estimated directly from the local numbers of deaths and population sizes. Looking at life tables in relation to income levels at three time points, 1995–1998, 1999–2002 and 2003–2006 he concludes that:

1. Life expectancy has been static over time in poorer counties but rising in richer counties, so that mortality inequality has been growing;
2. The male-female gap is wider in lower income counties. Furthermore, the gap has been growing in lower income counties and narrowing in higher income counties;
3. Mortality levels are strongly clustered by region, and in particular, there is an ever coalescing cluster of counties with a life expectancy deficit in the South Eastern United States.

In the second chapter in this section, Spijker ("Socioeconomic determinants of mortality in Europe: Validation of recent models using the latest available data and short-term forecasts") considers the evolution of mortality in the last two decades of the twentieth century in Eastern and Western Europe, modelling the change in standardised mortality rates for nine major causes and for total mortality and producing forecasts for two causes of death and total mortality. By his model the level of mortality for any year depends on mortality in the previous year and various economic, social and behavioural (epidemiological) variables, suitably lagged to allow for their effects to operate. Males and females are modelled separately, as are Eastern and Western Europe, in order to allow for their different stages in the epidemiological transition and the models are then projected forward to 2009, updating the appropriate epidemiological variables, for validation, and then to 2020. The major predictors of mortality level are GDP per capita and the proportion of the population employed in the industrial (secondary) labour force (essentially an indicator of social development) with lesser effects for levels of education, divorce rates, smoking and alcohol use. His major conclusions are that mortality will continue to decline. In the West this decline will be faster for males than for females, leading to a narrowing of the gender difference in mortality, a pattern that will not be seen in the East. There are also important differences in the evolution of particular causes: for instance, whereas levels of lung cancer mortality are converging in the West as male levels decline and female levels rise to a peak, this is not occurring in the East where female levels have traditionally been low, and male levels do not yet show signs of decline.

Our second set of papers focusses on analyses of mortality at the national level, with particular attention to specific risk profiles and causes of death. Kovacs ("Social Disparities in the Evolution of an Epidemiological Profile: Transition Processes in Mortality between 1971 and 2008 in an Industrialized Middle Income Country: The Case of Hungary") looks at trends in mortality inequalities by education in Hungary for a number of causes of death. She begins with a detailed discussion of the evolution of the concept of the Epidemiological Transition. What began as one transition has become a number of different transitions, depending on circumstances, and has even been broken down into cause-specific transitions, such as those pertaining to cancer or circulatory causes. Nonetheless, it largely remains, in the literature, a linear, unidirectional process—raising the possibility that we should be talking of epidemiological profiles rather than stages on the road to modernisation. At the same time, we need to consider parallel transitions such as that of nutrition, as the content, quality and variety of food changes with increasing wealth and awareness. Looking at Hungary, and carefully splicing together trends from three different ICD classifications, Kovacs identifies a number of different cause-specific patterns which have emerged over time. Overall, mortality levels for low and high education groups have bifurcated since the 1970's, so that whatever common process across the whole of the Hungarian population there may have been has now separated into two sub-populations with very different epidemiological profiles.

At the opposite end of the spectrum, Vasunilashorn et al. ("Predicting Mortality from Profiles of Biological Risk and Performance Measures of Functioning") consider not what people die of, but who is at greater risk of dying. Taking data for over 3,000 people aged 60 and above, they construct latent-class profiles based on 10 physiological and 5 performance measures. On the basis of these profiles they group the sample into four risk groups, those with no risk, high inflammation, high blood pressure and high frailty. Controlling for sex, education and ethnicity, the three latter groups were two to three times as likely to die over the 5 years of follow-up as were the no-risk group. A major strength of their approach is that it underscores the internal consistency of various physiological and performance risks, as reflected in the correlations between them. The latent classes were constructed without reference to the outcome measure, mortality, so this is not just a validation of previously identified risk factors, but an independent identification of particular patterns of risk.

Moving to the analysis of a specific cause, Semyonova et al. ("Approaches to the assessment of alcohol-related losses in the Russian population") present an estimate of the total level of alcohol related mortality in the Russian Federation. They show that over time the aetiology of alcohol-related deaths has changed from alcohol poisoning to somatic causes deriving from alcohol abuse (mental disease; diseases of the nervous system; cardiomyopathy and alcoholic liver disease). They suggest, therefore, that a reliance on data relating to alcoholic poisoning alone is misleading. Analysis by regions enables comparisons between geographical gradients in alcohol-related deaths, as compared with overall mortality, but also highlights data reliability problems as administrators try to underplay the role of alcohol in their causes of death.

Our third group of reports relate to deaths at specific ages. Starting with infancy, Santillán Pizarro et al. ("Infant mortality measurement and rate of progress on international commitments: a matter of methods or of guarantees of rights? Some evidence from Argentina") considers changes in the level and distribution of infant mortality in Argentina over the past 20 years. Infant mortality is a critical measure not only of welfare but also of social justice and Argentina has committed itself to meeting a number of international criteria, both in the decline of infant mortality at the national level and in the distribution of infant mortality among its different regions and social groups. The authors show that while infant mortality has, indeed, halved over this period, this has not been sufficient to meet the international standards to which Argentina has committed itself. Furthermore, regional mortality differences have not diminished over this period. This is particularly troubling as it indicates that while preventable infant mortality has declined, its relative incidence in the disadvantaged regions remains as high, or even higher, than it was.

Yüksel-Kaptanoğlu et al. ("Avoidable Factors Contributing to Maternal Deaths in Turkey") look at another important indicator of living standards and social justice, that of maternal mortality. Turkey, with a maternal mortality ratio of 29/100,000 is intermediate between the Commonwealth of Independent States and East Asia on the one hand, and the More Developed Countries on the other. In the absence of reliable register data, the article reports on a survey conducted in 2005 in a sample of 29 of Turkey's provinces, covering about 54 % of the country's population. They conclude that women who die as a result of childbirth are typically from eastern, rural districts, are younger and are less educated than the general population. By their estimate, a half to three-quarters of maternal deaths are from avoidable causes, in particular post-partum haemorrhaging. Following analysis of clinical records and verbal autopsies, they suggest the major institutional causes are to be found at the household and community level (prevention of unwanted pregnancies, use of ante-natal services, identification of critical symptoms and timely referral to medical assistance) but also at the level of the supply of adequate health facilities.

Two articles look at mortality at later ages. Gomez Redondo et al. ("Changes in mortality at older ages: The case of Spain, 1975–2006") look at the evolution of mortality at ages 65 and above over 30 years, from 1975 to 2006. Spanish mortality is among the lowest in Europe, with an average life expectancy of over 80 years. The three major causes of death at older ages are circulatory and respiratory diseases, both of which have been declining, and malignant tumours, the rate of which has been increasing. Men are particularly over-represented in the respiratory and malignant causes. There have been few changes in external causes of death, though their specific composition varies by age and sex. Over time there has been an increase in the risk of death due to mental illness and nervous diseases, and here women tend to be slightly over-represented. The authors note that given these variations by age and sex, the epidemiological profile offers important insights for understanding future trends. From a very different angle, Herm et al. ("Excess mortality risks in institutions: The influence of health and disability status") look at the effects of institutionalisation on the risk of dying. Using data for the entire Belgian population over age 65 at the 2001 census, and controlling for age, sex and health status, they show that those living in an institution have a greater risk of dying than those living independently, whether singly or as a couple. This disadvantage does, however, diminish with age, so that by age 90 there is no difference between the mortality risks in the different living arrangements.

Our fourth section provides "thick descriptions" of three particular countries and regions. Gomez and Léon ("Life expectancy differences in Cuba. Are females losing their advantages over males?") summarise mortality changes in Cuba over 30 years, between 1987 and 2005. They note that whereas mortality declined steadily from the 1930's to the 1970's, the decline slowed during the economic crisis of the 1980's and 1990's before picking up again in the twenty-first century. They use decomposition analysis, by cause and age, to ascertain the specific changes in mortality at 10-yearly intervals, and the differences between male and female mortality. Cuba is at an advanced stage of the demographic transition with low mortality and fertility, an ageing population, and most deaths coming from chronic and degenerative diseases. It also has a comparatively low sex difference in mortality, with a consistent life expectancy gap of about 4 years, though men were more affected by the crisis than women.

Moving on to a broader canvas, Sabgayda et al. ("Variable scales of avoidable mortality within the Russian population") seek to explain Russia's high level of mortality in comparison with Western Europe by looking at mortality variations within the Russian Federation. The variation is far greater for men than for women, and most of it is attributed to avoidable mortality, deaths that should not occur given the current state of medical knowledge, but nonetheless do occur either because of the lack of primary prevention (lifestyles leading to premature death); secondary prevention (a lack of early detection and diagnosis, particularly of various cancers); or tertiary prevention (a lack of adequate treatment and care). These preventable deaths, of which the most prevalent are in Group 1 (lifestyle-related) are closely correlated with the levels of overall mortality and with the levels of poverty and socio-economic development. The major explanation for avoidable mortality—and hence for super-mortality in general—is to be found in the social and political upheavals, rather than in the level of health expenditures. These, the authors argue, are a function of local political decisions rather than economic development and, in any case, are not directly related to the level of mortality.

In our final paper, Zhao et al. ("Long-term mortality changes in East Asia: Levels, age patterns, and causes of death") compare the pace and pattern of mortality decline in East Asia and in Western Europe. The decline in East Asia was particularly rapid after the Second World War, as these countries moved beyond the 50 years of life expectancy at birth mark. The rate of decline was considerably faster in the East than in the West, but the basic pattern of decline was quite similar: the major decline started among children aged 1–14, followed by the decline among infants and younger adults, then the middle aged, and finally the elderly. In East Asia, however, the time lag between declines at different ages was shorter, with a greater degree of simultaneity between the different age groups as the whole time frame of decline was compressed. The age pattern of decline was directly related to the Epidemiological Transition in causes of death: the decline in infectious diseases and the transition to CVD as the major cause of death, so that current mortality declines are mainly attributable to declines, or delays, in CVD mortality. They suggest that the rapid mortality decline was achieved through a combination of rapid economic growth on the one hand, combined with good health care and effective public health policies on the other.

Mortality is an ever-topical subject of research and the current volume presents a cross-section of the concerns with which demographers are grappling at the present moment. In bringing these studies together, we hope to offer a basis for future cooperation and cross-fertilisation of ideas between demographers, in Europe and beyond. This is also an opportunity to thank, once again, The Vienna Institute of Demography for hosting the workshop, and in particular Ms. Sylvia Trnka and all the staff who made the workshop possible.

References

Anson, J. (2010). Beyond material explanations: Family solidarity and mortality, a small area-level analysis. *Population and Development Review, 36,* 27–45.

Banks, J., Muriel, A., & Smith, J. P. (2010). Disease prevalence, disease incidence, and mortality in the United States and in England. *Demography, 47*(Supplement), S211–S231.

Cai, L., Hayward, M. D., Saito, Y., Lubitz, J., Hagedorn, A., & Crimmins, E. (2010). Estimation of multi-state life table functions and their variability from complex survey data using the SPACE Program. *Demographic Research, 22,* 129–158.

Caldwell, J. C. (1986). Routes to low mortality in poor countries. *Population and Development Review, 12*(2), 171–220.

Canudas-Romo, V. (2010). Three measures of longevity. Tine trends and record values. *Demography, 47,* 299–312.

Canudas-Romo, V., & Becker, S. (2011). The crossover between life expectancies at birth and at age one: The imbalance in the life table. *Demographic Research, 24,* 113–144.

Cohen, J. E. (2010). Life expectancy is the death-weighted average of the reciprocal of the survival-specific force of mortality. *Demographic Research, 22,* 115–128.

Cohen, J. E. (2011). Life expectancy: Lower and upper bounds from surviving fractions and remaining life expectancy. *Demographic Research, 24,* 251–256.

Cohen, A. A., Tillinghas, J., & Canudas-Romo, V. (2010). No consistent effects of prenatal or neonatal exposure to Spanish flu on late-life mortality in 24 developed countries. *Demographic Research, 22,* 579–634.

Crimmins, E., Kim, J. K., & Vasunilashorn, S. (2010). Biodemography: New approaches to understanding trends and differences in population health and mortality. *Demography, 47,* S41–S64.

Dalla-Zuanna, G., & Rosina, A. (2011). An analysis of extremely high nineteenth-century winter neonatal mortality in a local context of northeastern Italy. *European Journal of Population, 27,* 33–55.

Dalla-Zuanna, G., & Rossi, F. (2010). Comparisons of infant mortality in the Austrian Empire Länder using the Tafeln (1851–54). *Demographic Research, 22,* 813–862.

Denton, F. T., & Spencer, B. G. (2011). A dynamic extension of the period life table. *Demographic Research, 24,* 831–854.

Désesquelles, A., Salvatore, M. A., Frova, L., Pace, M., Pappagallo, M., Meslé, F., & Egidi, V. (2010). Revisiting the mortality of France and Italy with the multiple-cause-of-death approach. *Demographic Research, 23,* 771–806.

Dowd, K., Blake, D., & Cairns, A. J. G. (2010). Facing up to uncertain life expectancy: The longevity fan charts. *Demography, 47,* 67–78.

Drefahl, S. (2010). How does the age gap between partners affect their survival? *Demography, 47,* 313–326.

Earle, J. S., & Gehlbach, S. (2010) Did mass privatisation really increase post-communist mortality? *Lancet, 375,* 372.

Granados T. J. A., & Ionides, E. L. (2011). Mortality and macroeconomic fluctuations in contemporary Sweden. *European Journal of Population, 27,* 157–184.

Grigoriev, P., Shkolnikov, V., Andreev, E., Jasilionis, D., Jdanov, D., Meslé, F., & Vallin, J. (2010). Mortality in Belarus, Lithuania, and Russia: Divergence in recent trends and possible explanations. *European Journal of Population, 26,* 245–274.

Guillot, M., & Kim, H. S. (2011). On the correspondence between CAL and lagged cohort life expectancy. *Demographic Research, 24,* 611–632.

Guillot, M., Gavrilova, N., & Pudrovska, T. (2011). Understanding the "Russian Mortality Paradox" in Central Asia: Evidence from Kyrgyzstan. *Demography, 48,* 1081–1104.

Guyavarch, E., Pison, G., Duthé, G., Marra, A., & Chippaux, J.-P. (2010). Mortality due to external causes in three rural areas of Senegal. *European Journal of Population, 26,* 483–505.

Harris, K. M. (2010). An integrative approach to health. *Demography, 47,* 1–22.

Ho, J. Y., & Preston, S. H. (2010). US mortality in an international context: Age variations. *Population and Development Review, 36,* 749–773.

Jin, L., Elwert, F., Freese, J., & Christakis, N. A. (2010). Preliminary evidence regarding the hypothesis that the sex ratio at sexual maturity may affect longevity in men. *Demography, 47,* 579–586.

Kohler, I., & Preston, S. H. (2011). Ethnic and religious differentials in Bulgarian mortality, 1993–98. *Population Studies, 65,* 91–113.

Kuhn, R. (2010). Routes to low mortality in poor countries revisited. *Population and Development Review, 36,* 655–692.

Luy, M., Di Giulio, P., & Caselli, G. (2011). Differences in life expectancy by education and occupation in Italy, 1980–94: Indirect estimates from maternal and paternal orphanhood. *Population Studies, 65,* 137–155.

Lynch, S. M., & Brown, J. S. (2010). Obtaining multistate life table distributions for highly refined subpopulations from cross-sectional data: A Bayesian extension of Sullivan's method. *Demography, 47,* 1053–1077.

McEniry, M., & Palloni, A. (2010). Early life exposures and the occurrence and timing of heart disease among the older Puerto Rican population. *Demography, 47,* 23–43.

Missov, T. I., & Lenart, A. (2011). Linking period and cohort life expectancy linear increases in Gompertz proportional hazards models. *Demographic Research, 24,* 455–468.

Monteverde, M., Noronha, K., Palloni, A., & Novak, B. (2010). Obesity and excess mortality among the elderly in the United States and Mexico. *Demography, 47,* 79–96.

Murphy, M. (2010). Re-examining the dominance of birth cohort effects on mortality. *Population and Development Review, 36,* 365–390.

Myrskylä, M. (2010a). The effects of shocks in early life mortality on later life expectancy and mortality compression: A cohort analysis. *Demographic Research, 22,* 289–320.

Myrskylä, M. (2010b). The relative effects of shocks in early- and later- life conditions on mortality. *Population and Development Review, 36,* 803–829.

Pampel, F. C., & Denney, J. T. (2011). Cross-national sources of health inequality: Education and tobacco use in the world health survey. *Demography, 48,* 653–674.

Patterson, E. J. (2010). Incarcerating death: Mortality in U.S. state correctional facilities, 1985–1998. *Demography, 47,* 587–607.

Poulain, M. (2011). Exceptional longevity in Okinawa: A plea for in depth validation. *Demographic Research, 25,* 245–284.

Rendall, M. S., Weden, M. M., Favreault, M. M., & Waldron, H. (2011). The protective effect of marriage for survival: A review and update. *Demography, 48,* 481–506.

Rogers, R. M., Everett, B. G., Saint Onge, J. M., & Krueger, P. M. (2010). Social, behavioral, and biological factors, and sex differences in mortality. *Demography, 47,* 555–578.

Rostron, B. (2010). A modified new method for estimating smoking attributable mortality in high-income countries. *Demographic Research, 23,* 399–420.

Rostron, B. L., & Wilmoth, J. R. (2011). Estimating the effect of smoking on slowdowns in mortality declines in developed countries. *Demography, 48,* 461–479.

Saikia, N., Jasilionis, D., Faujdar, R., & Shkolnikov, V. M. (2011). Trends and geographic differentials in mortality under age 60 in India. *Population Studies, 65,* 73–89.

Scherbov, S., & Ediev, D. (2011). Significance of life table estimates for small populations: Simulation-based study of standard errors. *Demographic Research, 24,* 527–550.

Schumacher, R., & Vilpert, S. (2011). Gender differences in social mortality differentials in Switzerland (1990–2005). *Demographic Research, 25,* 285–310.

Shang, H. L., Booth, H., & Hyndman, R. J. (2011). Point and interval forecasts of mortality rates and life expectancy: A comparison of ten principal component methods. *Demographic Research, 25,* 173–214.

Shen, K., & Zeng, Y. (2010). The association between resilience and survival among Chinese elderly. *Demographic Research, 23,* 105–116.

Shkolnikov, V. M., Andreev, E. M., Zhang, Z., Oeppen, J., & Vaupel, J. W. (2011). Losses of expected lifetime in the United States and other developed countries: Methods and empirical analyses. *Demography, 48,* 211–239.

Staetsky, L. (2011a). Mortality of British Jews at the turn of the 20th century in a comparative perspective. *European Journal of Population, 27,* 361–385.

Staetsky, L. (2011b). The role of smoking in the explanation of the Israeli Jewish pattern of sex differentials in mortality. *Population Studies, 65,* 231–244.

Stuckler, D., King, L., & McKee, M. (2009) Mass privatisation and the post-communist mortality crisis: A cross-national analysis. *Lancet, 373,* 399–407.

Stuckler, D., King, L., & McKee, M. (2010). Did mass privatisation really increase post-communist mortality?—Authors' reply. *Lancet, 375,* 372–374.

Tapia, G., José, A., & Ionides, E. L. (2011). Mortality and macroeconomic fluctuations in contemporary Sweden. *European Journal of Population, 27,* 157–184.

Thatcher, A. R., Cheung, S. L. K., Horiuchi, S., & Robine, J.-M. (2010). The compression of deaths above the mode. *Demographic Research, 22,* 505–538.

Thornton, P., & Olson, S. (2011). Mortality in late nineteenth century Montreal: Geographic pathways of contagion. *Population Studies, 65,* 157–181.

Tuljapurkar, S., & Edwards, R. D. (2011). Variance in death and its implications for modeling and forecasting mortality. *Demographic Research, 24,* 497–526.

van den Berg, G. J., Doblhammer-Reiter, G., & Christensen, K. (2011). Being born under adverse economic conditions leads to a higher cardiovascular mortality rate later in life: Evidence based on individuals born at different stages of the business cycle. *Demography, 48,* 507–530.

Vaupel, J. W. (2010). Total incremental change with age equals average lifetime change. *Demographic Research, 22,* 1143–1148.

Vaupel, J. W., & Canudas-Romo, V. (2002). Decomposing change in life expectancy: A bouquet of formulas in honor of Nathan Keyfitz's 90th birthday. *Demography, 40*(2), 201–216.

Vaupel, J. W., & Zhang, Z. (2010). Attrition in heterogeneous cohorts. *Demographic Research, 23,* 737–748.

Wagner, P. (2010). Sensitivity of life disparity with respect to changes in mortality rates. *Demographic Research, 23,* 63–72.

Wen, M., & Gu, D. (2011). The effects of childhood, adult, and community socioeconomic conditions on health and mortality among older adults in China. *Demography, 48,* 153–181.

Zheng, H., Yang, Y., & Land, K. C. (2011). Heterogeneity in the Strehler-Mildvan general theory of mortality and aging. *Demography, 48,* 267–290.

Chapter 2
Estimating Life Expectancy in Small Areas, with an Application to Recent Changes in Life Expectancy in US Counties

Peter Congdon

Abstract Analysis of small area mortality contrasts via life tables, and estimation of functions such as life expectancies, raises methodological issues regarding a suitable model for the mortality data. Methodological assumptions may be relevant to assessing whether there are changes in spatial clustering or in spatial inequalities in life expectancy. Virtually all analyses of US small area mortality use conventional life table analysis, which takes no account of similarities between mortality rates for adjacent areas or ages, and is subject to potential instability of mortality rates involved in deriving life tables. The alternative strategy used here involves a statistical model that "borrows strength" by using random effects to represent correlations between adjacent ages and areas. The smoothed mortality rates from the model are used to derive male and female life expectancies in US counties for three periods: 1995–1998, 1999–2002 and 2003–2006. Changes in inequality measures (e.g. the concentration index) show an increase in income related inequality in county expectancies, while local spatial correlation indices show an enhancement of low expectancy clusters in the South Eastern USA.

Keywords Life expectancy · Spatial inequality · Clustering · Borrowing strength · Random effects · Bayesian

2.1 Background

Analysis of small area mortality variations raises questions about suitable techniques for estimating life table functions such as life expectancies. Conventional fixed effects methods for life tables are problematic for small areas (with under 10,000 population, and especially under 5,000 population), potentially resulting in implausible or even infinite life expectancy estimates, even with data pooled over a number of years.

P. Congdon (✉)
Department of Geography and Centre for Statistics,
Queen Mary University of London, Mile End Rd, London E1 4NS, UK
e-mail: p.congdon@qmul.ac.uk

J. Anson, M. Luy (eds.), *Mortality in an International Perspective*,
European Studies of Population 18, DOI 10.1007/978-3-319-03029-6_2,

Conventional life table analysis is subject to variance instability in estimated age-area specific mortality rates, leading on to wide confidence intervals for summary measures such as life expectancy (Anselin et al. 2006; Toson and Baker 2003). This issue is relevant to US counties, some of which have small populations: around 300 have populations under 5,000, and 700 (just under a quarter of all US counties) have populations under 10,000. Methodological choices are relevant to assessing growing spatial inequalities in life expectancy, and changes in spatial clustering of lower than average life expectancy.

Recent research points to widening geographic inequalities in US mortality (e.g. Murray et al. 2006; Ezzati et al. 2008) but, with the exception of Kulkarni et al. (2011), uses conventional life table analysis and various amalgamations of areas to alleviate the instability inherent in such analysis. The implicit statistical model for conventional life tables applied to areas involves a heavily parameterized fixed effect approach (i.e. NX parameters for N areas and X age groups), that ignores high correlations between mortality rates for adjacent ages, and spatial clustering in mortality risk (McLaughlin et al. 2007). As to amalgamation strategies, Ezzati et al. (2008), Murray et al. (2006) and Kulkarni et al. (2011) amalgamate the original 3141 US counties to 2068, 2072 and 2357 areas respectively. The area amalgamation approach may affect inferences regarding differentials in expectancies: for example, smaller counties in the US tend to be in rural areas, so amalgamation may affect inferences regarding the urban-rural gradient in expectancy.

The present analysis accordingly adopts a "structured effects" statistical model to estimate mortality rates, and hence life expectancies, in US counties between 1995–1998, 1999–2002 and 2003–2006. The original areas are retained, and a borrowing strength approach adopted for age and area mortality parameters, via random effects methods that recognize correlations between adjacent ages and areas (e.g. Jonker et al. 2012; Chambers et al. 2009). Bayesian estimation is used, with parameter estimates based on iterative Monte Carlo Markov Chain (MCMC) techniques, implemented via the WINBUGS program (Lunn et al. 2009). The effective number of parameters involved is considerably fewer than under conventional fixed effects approaches (Spiegelhalter et al. 2002; Zhu et al. 2006). The model includes spatial random effects that account for spatial clustering in high mortality (and low expectancy) (McLaughlin et al. 2007). A recent paper by Kulkarni et al. (2011) recognizes benefits from random effects borrowing of strength but adopts an area random effect which is not spatially configured.

Once stabilized estimates of life expectancy are obtained from the statistical model, the extent of spatial inequality and clustering is considered, both cross-sectionally and through time. Before this analysis of trends, a sensitivity analysis compares the structured effects model against the conventional life table approach, and other "non-conventional" smoothing methods for life tables, albeit within a Bayesian framework. Specifically a spatial version of the Heligman-Pollard model (Heligman and Pollard 1980), involving county specific parameters is considered, and a spatial adaptation of the relational model (Brass 1974).

2.2 Methods: Structured Effects Mortality Model

Studies applying conventional life tables to analyse area mortality use moment estimates of central death rates to derive life table schedules such as death probabilities q_{cx}, (for areas $c = 1, \ldots, N$; ages $x = 1, \ldots, X$), and average years of life remaining at exact age x, E_{cx}. Although the underlying statistical model is typically not made explicit, it has important limiting features. Assuming an underlying binomial sampling model for deaths y_{cx} in relation to populations at risk, P_{cx}, namely

$$y_{cx} \sim Bin(P_{cx}, m_{cx}),$$

then conventional life table involves as many fixed effect parameters (central mortality rates) m_{cx} as there are data points, namely *NX*. Moment maximum likelihood estimates of these parameters under the conventional life table method are simply, $\hat{m}_{cx} = y_{cx}/P_{cx}$. For the US application with $N = 3139$ counties (in 2003–2006) and $X = 13$, there are 40807 parameters (i.e. mortality rate estimates) under the fixed effects model, providing a large model dimension.

This drawback is combined with potentially unstable estimates of rates under the conventional life table estimation approach, with rates for smaller areas showing most variability (Anselin et al. 2006; Riggan et al. 1991), leading on to wide confidence intervals for life expectancies in each area. A related feature is that no account is taken of similarities in mortality between areas or ages, so each parameter is estimated separately without reference to those for other ages or areas. The conventional life table estimation procedure has particular drawbacks including potential overestimation of life expectancy for small populations, and problems (infinite left expectancies) produced by zero death rates in the final age interval in a particular area, which can only be remedied by ad hoc devices (e.g. replacing the zero death rate by the national death rate for the final age interval) (Eayres and Williams 2004).

By contrast, the pooling strength approach views effects for particular ages or areas as drawn from a larger population of random effects, following a particular overarching density. Additionally these effects may be *structured* to reflect real world correlations between mortality at adjacent ages and in neighbouring areas. Thus in the model for age-county mortality rates in Eq. (2.1) below, the county parameters γ_c represent smoothly varying effects of spatially correlated unobserved risk factors. The underlying spatially smooth process represented by these effects straddles arbitrary county boundaries which are unrelated to the underlying continuous spatial process (Best 1999; Fotheringham et al. 2002).

Spatial dependence in the γ_c follows a conditional autoregressive form (Besag et al. 1991),

$$\gamma_c | \gamma_{[-c]} \sim N\left(\frac{1}{\sum_d w_{cd}} \sum_{d \neq c} w_{cd}\gamma_d, \frac{\delta_\gamma}{\sum_d w_{cd}}\right),$$

where w_{cd} represents spatial interaction between counties c and d, and δ_γ is a variance parameter. Suppose $w_{cd} = 1$ if counties c and d are contiguous, and $w_{cd} = 0$

otherwise, let m_c be the number of counties contiguous to county c, and let A_c denote the neighbourhood of county c (namely the set of counties adjacent to it). Then this spatial scheme (implemented as the car.normal density in WINBUGS) becomes

$$\gamma_c|\gamma_{[-c]} \sim N\left(\frac{1}{m_c}\sum_{d\in A_c}\gamma_d, \frac{\delta_\gamma}{m_c}\right).$$

Other spatial schemes may be used, such as neighbourhoods including second order as well as first order neighbours (see Appendix 1); however, the above scheme is much the most commonly used for human health applications. For age effects, life table death rates typically display very high correlation between rates for adjacent ages, and a scheme representing such dependence is provided by a local level or random walk model (Durbin and Koopman 2001)

$$\alpha_x \sim N(\alpha_{x-1}, \delta_\alpha), \qquad x > 1$$

with the initial age effect α_1 modelled separately.

However, heterogeneity among individuals within age-area units implies that age and area effects alone may not account for extra-binomial variation (Appendix 2). So the model also includes unstructured random effects u_{cx} specific to area-age combinations, with the full model being

$$logit(m_{cx}) = \lambda + \alpha_x + \gamma_c + u_{cx} \tag{2.1}$$

This is subsequently denoted as the "structured effects model", which is later compared with spatially adapted versions of the Heligman-Pollard and relational models. It is likely that heterogeneity is greater in some age bands than others, so it is assumed that $u_{cx} \sim N(0, \phi_x)$. In model (2.1), gamma priors are adopted for $1/\delta_\gamma$ and $1/\delta_a$, and for the age-specific precisions $1/\phi_x$, with index and shape parameters equal to 1. A $N(0, 100)$ prior is used for λ.

Let age group x have interval length n_x, and denote the average fraction of the interval survived as a_x. Then life table death probabilities by area and age may be estimated (Bell and Miller 2005) from the smoothed m_{cx} as

$$q_{cx} = n_x m_{cx}/(1 + n_x(1 - a_x)m_{cx}).$$

From these one may estimate the survivorship and years-lived functions l_{cx} and L_{cx}, and in turn the average number of years of life E_{cx} remaining at exact age x. The case study below considers expectancies at birth, E_{c0}, and expectancies at age 65, E_{c65}, but other functions can be obtained such as survivor probabilities over particular age spans, such as the county specific probability of surviving from age 45 to 75, ${}_{30}p_{c,45} = 1 - {}_{30}q_{c,45} = l_{c,75}/l_{c,45}$.

As part of the MCMC sampling output, one may obtain full posterior densities for the life table functions in each county. This is not possible using conventional life table methods, which provide variance estimates using large sample approximations. One may also assess interval hypotheses on life table functions, for example the probability that the life expectancy in a particular county, E_{c0}, is below the US wide average, $\overline{E}_0$. This involves using indicator functions, such as $I(E_{c0} < \overline{E}_0)$, and totalling MCMC iterations where the condition in the indicator function is satisfied. Additional advantages are the greater precision (narrower confidence intervals) of this method compared to conventional methods, especially in areas with relatively small populations. Furthermore the borrowing strength method provides sensible estimates for small counties with small observed death totals. Examples are King County in Texas with 5 male deaths and a male population-years total of 655 in 2003–2006, and Arthur County (Nebraska) with 14 male deaths and a population-years total of 757. Conventional methods give implausible life expectancies under 40 for these counties. Bayesian methods avoid the *ad hoc* adjustments needed for conventional life tables when there are zero deaths in the last age interval, such as using national death rates instead.

It may be noted that in addition to small US counties, there are also many large counties in the data used, with large within-area samples of deaths and large populations at risk. The idea behind borrowing strength methods is to use information on mortality provided by all counties to provide stabilized estimates for small counties where within-area samples are relatively small. The large observation sample across areas, both in terms of over 3000 counties over 4 year periods, and around 10 million deaths (for males and females combined) in each 4 year period, will both assist in providing stabilized estimates for small areas and ensure that the data will dominate any prior assumptions. For example, borrowing of strength applied to the common age structure effects α_x will combine information about the mortality age gradient over all counties, so providing precise estimates. Similarly, the borrowing of strength random effects approach to estimate county-age interactions u_{cx} penalizes extreme parameter values that can occur under fixed effects methods.

2.3 Sensitivity Analysis: Comparison with Other Models for Smoothing Mortality and Conventional Life Tables

Other approaches have been used to smooth irregular mortality data. One widely used approach is to use parametric equations to smooth mortality rates, as in the eight parameter Heligman-Pollard model. Expressed in terms of odds of death rates, this model is

$$\frac{m_x}{1-m_x} = A^{(x+B)^C} + Dexp\left[-E\left\{\log\frac{x}{F}\right\}^2\right] + GH^x = R_{1x} + R_{2x} + R_{3x} = R_x.$$

The three components represent respectively child mortality, young adult mortality and mature-age mortality. The application here generalizes this parametric model to explain age-county mortality rates m_{cx}, and allows spatial variation in particular parameters. To this end, one may represent the level of child mortality as $A = \exp(\omega)$, and the level of young adult mortality as $\log(R_{2x}) = \eta_1 + \eta_2(\log x - \log F)^2$. Furthermore one may write the third component as

$$logit(R_{3x}) = \beta_1 + \beta_2 x,$$

since

$$R_{3x} = \frac{e^{\beta_1} e^{\beta_2 x}}{1 + e^{\beta_1} e^{\beta_2 x}} = \frac{GH^x}{1 + GH^x} (with\ G = e^{\alpha}, H = e^{\beta}).$$

Then spatial variation, following the same conditional autoregressive scheme as discussed above, involves the model

$$\begin{aligned} \frac{m_{cx}}{1 - m_{cx}} &= A_c^{(x+B)^C} + D_c\, exp\left[-E\left\{ \log \frac{x}{F} \right\}^2 \right] + G_c H_c^x \\ &= R_{1cx} + R_{2cx} + R_{3cx} = R_{cx}, \end{aligned}$$

and four sets of spatial effects, $\{s_{1c}, \ldots, s_{4c}\}$, which are centred to have average zero:

$A_c = exp\,(\omega + s_{1c})$ (varying child mortality level);
$D_c = exp\,(\eta_1 + s_{2c})$ (varying young adult mortality level);
$G_c = exp\,(\beta_1 + s_{3c})$ (varying mature adult mortality level);
$H_c = exp\,(\beta_2 + s_{4c})$ (varying mature adult mortality slope).

Then

$$logit(m_{cx}) = \log\,(R_{cx}) + u_{cx}, \tag{2.2}$$

where the $u_{cx}$are unstructured county-age random effects, as in the structured effects model of (2.1).

Another widely used approach to smoothing mortality data involves the use of standard age schedules in relational models (e.g. Himes et al. 1994), and relational models have also been applied to smoothing fertility and migration rates (e.g. De Beer 2011). Here logits of county-age model death rates for period t are related to US-wide logit death rates in period $t - 1$, so avoiding double use of the same data. Thus, for a county mortality model in 2003–2006, the standard (m_{sx})is provided by US-wide death rates in 1999–2002. Additionally intercepts and slopes $\{\alpha_c, \beta_c\}$ in the relational model are taken to vary by county, and be spatially structured (according to the above conditional autoregressive scheme). Then one has

$$\begin{aligned} y_{cx} &\sim Bin(P_{cx}, m_{cx}), \\ logit(m_{cx}) &= \alpha_c + \beta_c\, logit(m_{sx}) + u_{cx}, \end{aligned} \tag{2.3}$$

where the u_{cx} are county-age random effects, as discussed above, to account for extra-binomial variation.

The structured effects model (2.1) is compared to these alternative borrowing strength specifications (2.2) and (2.3), and to conventional life table methods, using male deaths and populations $\{y_{cx}, P_{cx}\}$ for counties $c = 1, \ldots, N$, and ages $x = 1, \ldots, X$ in 2003–2006. There are $N = 3139$ counties, excluding Clifton Forge (Virginia), and amalgamating two very small counties, namely Kalawao (Hawaii) with Maui, and Loving (Texas) with Winkler (Texas). There are $X = 13$ age groups as provided at the CDC Wonder site (http://wonder.cdc.gov/), namely, under 1, 1–4, 5–9, 10–14, 15–19, 20–24, 25–34, 35–44, 45–54, 55–64, 65–74, 75–84 and 85 +.

The conventional life table method involves unrelated fixed effects and is operationalized by assuming Beta(1,1) (i.e. uniform) priors on the death rates m_{cx}. Additionally for the conventional life table approach, if there are zero deaths in the final age interval, the national death rate for over 85's is substituted as the estimate for m_{cX}, in order to avoid infinite life or implausibly large life expectancies.

A particular focus is on the extent of differences between the four methods in estimates of life expectancies at birth and of probabilities of surviving from age 45 to 75. Aspects of sensitivity considered are the similarity/dissimilarity (inter-method correlation) across the 3139 counties; the precision of the estimates, with more precise estimates preferred; and model fit, assessed using the log pseudo marginal likelihood, abbreviated as LPML (Christensen et al. 2011; Kim et al. 2012). Precision is based on the total of posterior variances of the parameter estimates over the counties, which has been used by some analysts as a measure of model complexity (Gelfand and Ghosh 1998, p. 5).

An important additional aspect is the extent of spatial correlation (global and local) in county life table functions. For example, let $z_c = E_{c0} - \overline{E}_0$ be deviations in posterior mean life expectancies at birth in county c from the US wide average. Then a global measure of spatial correlation is provided by the Moran index,

$$I = \frac{N}{S_0} \sum_c \sum_d w_{cd} z_c z_d \Big/ \sum_c z_c^2,$$

where $S_0 = \sum_c \sum_d w_{cd}$. The localised version of this index (Anselin 1995) is

$$I_c = \frac{z_c}{m_2} \sum_d w_{cd} z_d,$$

where $m_2 = \sum_c z_c^2 / N$. For considering spatial patterning, an additional perspective using conventional methods is provided by the standard mortality ratio (SMR): the ratio of deaths in a county to expected deaths in the county population if US-wide age-specific death rates prevailed.

Inferences are based on the second halves of two chain runs of 10,000 iterations from dispersed initial values, with convergence achieved before iteration 5,000 using Brooks-Gelman criteria (Brooks and Gelman 1998). Table 2.1 shows that the best fitting approach is the relational model, but that more precise estimates of life expectancies and of 45–75 survival probabilities are obtained under the structural effects model. In fact, there is a very high correlation (over 0.99) between life expectancies and survival probabilities under these two methods (see panel B in Table 2.1), such that in practical terms they are effectively interchangeable. A slightly worse fit is obtained for the spatial Heligman-Pollard model, with correlations of 0.94–0.95 between its life expectancy estimates and those of the relational and structural effects models.

Table 2.1 Sensitivity analysis according to method, male mortality, 2003–2006

(A) Precision, Fit and Distributional Aspects

	Structural Effects	Spatial-Relational	Spatial Heligman-Pollard	Conventional (Fixed Effects)
Precision of Estimates (total posterior variances over all counties)				
Life Expectancies, age 0	1649	1965	3139	9044
Probability of surviving from 45 to 75	1.066	1.121	1.553	2.721
Measures of Fit				
LPML	-119482	-118207	-121510	-140793
Distributional features: Expectancies at Birth				
Mean	74.28	74.19	74.44	72.34
1st percentile	68.31	67.51	68.63	57.87
5th percentile	69.99	69.43	70.31	65.95
95th percentile	78.20	78.32	78.46	77.76
99th percentile	79.69	79.76	81.09	79.22
Distributional features: survival probabilty ${}_{30}p_{45}$				
Mean	0.625	0.623	0.624	0.618
5th percentile	0.519	0.517	0.515	0.493
95th percentile	0.717	0.717	0.723	0.731

(B) Correlations between Life Table Functions

Life Expectancies, age 0	Structural Effects	Spatial-Relational	Spatial Heligman-Pollard
Spatial-Relational	0.994		
Spatial Heligman-Pollard	0.953	0.942	
Conventional (Fixed Effects)	0.541	0.558	0.433

Survival probabilty ${}_{30}p_{45}$	Structural Effects	Spatial-Relational	Spatial Heligman-Pollard
Spatial-Relational	0.997		
Spatial Heligman-Pollard	0.978	0.977	
Conventional (Fixed Effects)	0.936	0.939	0.943

(C) Spatial Sensitivity

Global Moran Spatial Correlation	E_0, Structural Effects	E_0, Spatial-Relational	E_0, Spatial Heligman-Pollard	E_0, Conventional (Fixed Effects)	SMR
	0.66	0.65	0.54	0.41	0.51

Correlation between Local Moran Statistics	E_0, Structural Effects	E_0, Spatial-Relational	E_0, Spatial Heligman-Pollard	E_0, Conventional (Fixed Effects)
E_0, Spatial-Relational	0.985			
E_0, Spatial Heligman-Pollard	0.886	0.853		
E_0, Conventional (Fixed Effects)	0.188	0.206	0.172	
SMR	0.935	0.931	0.885	0.168

Fig. 2.1 Estimated life expectancies, males 2003–2006, structural effects method

The conventional fixed effects approach has a markedly worse fit, and correlations only around 0.5 between its life expectancy estimates and those obtained under the three borrowing strength models, though its survival probability estimates are closer to those under other methods. It may be noted that in some counties with small death totals and populations at risk, the conventional method provides estimated life expectancies under 50 (in 16 counties), the lowest expectancies being for King County (Texas) and Arthur County (Nebraska).

Panel C of Table 2.1 considers global and local Moran spatial correlations for life expectancy estimates. It shows that higher (but similar) global Moran coefficients of around 0.65 are obtained under the structural effects and spatial-relational methods. The Moran coefficient for the SMR is slightly lower at around 0.51, though still indicates strong spatial clustering. There is also a high concordance in local Moran coefficients in terms of correlation between the local Moran coefficients over the 3139 counties. The correlation between the SMR-based local Moran coefficients and the local coefficients obtained using the structural effects model is around 0.94. Life expectancies estimated by the conventional life table method show a relatively low concordance with other methods in terms of localised spatial patterning.

Figure 2.1 shows estimated life expectancies under the structural effects method, and Fig. 2.2 shows local clustering coefficients. The latter have high values in regions with concentrations of adjacent high expectancies (e.g. in northern parts of the mid-West), and also in regions with concentrations of adjacent low expectancies (e.g. in Mississippi and Louisiana). Figure 2.3 shows local clustering coefficients based on standard mortality ratios, which show a similar pattern to Fig. 2.2. Table 2.2 includes results from the structural effects model applied to both males and females in 2003–2006, and shows the concentrations of low expectancies at birth in states of the mid-South and South-East USA.

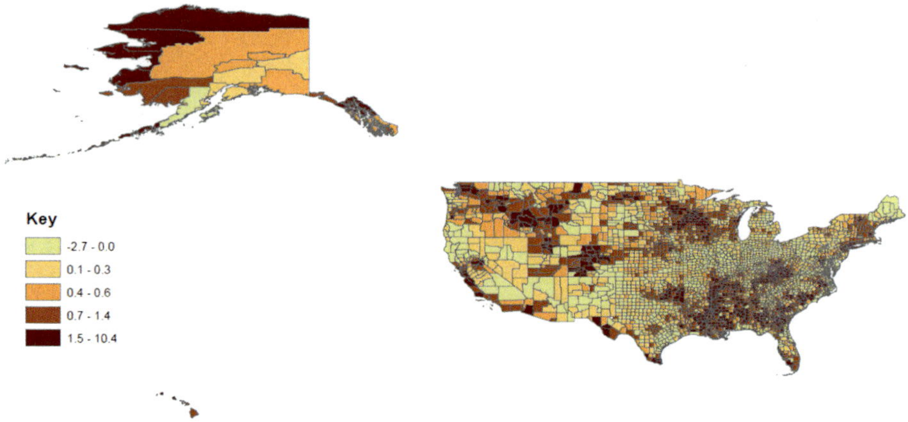

Fig. 2.2 Local Moran statistics, male expectancies 2003–2006, structural effects method

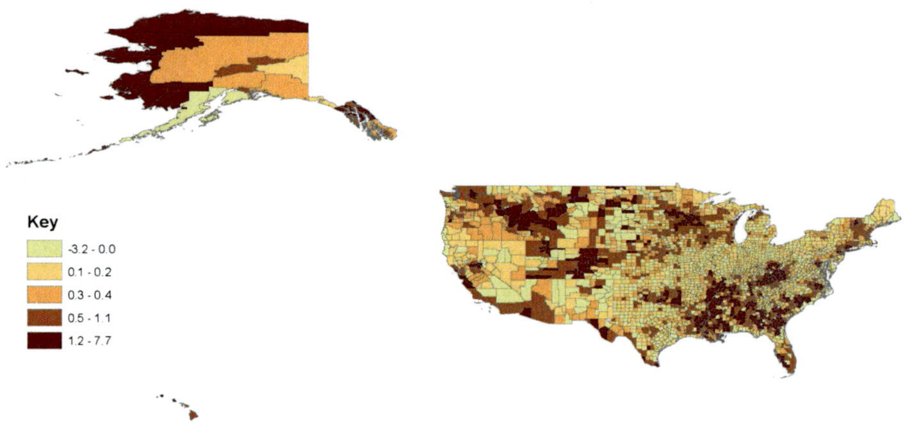

Fig. 2.3 Local Moran statistics, male SMRs 2003–2006

2.4 Assessing Trends in Inequality and Spatial Clustering

The previous analysis has shown the utility of the structured effects model and this model is now applied to assessing trends in spatial inequality. Using estimates of county life expectancy based on smoothed estimates of mortality rates, m_{cx}, one may assess changes in life expectancy gradients. We consider life expectancy at birth and at age 65. Three periods are considered: 1995–1998, 1999–2002, and 2003–2006, with data from the CDC Wonder site (http://wonder.cdc.gov/) – see Appendix 3 for details of areas.

One approach to assessing inequality is in terms of measures of area socioeconomic status, such as county average household income. Then inequality measures of social-group disparity are relevant (Harper and Lynch 2005), such as the slope

Table 2.2 Total counties within each state below national life expectancy 1st quartile, or above national 3rd quartile (2003–2006). Structural effects model

		Males		Females	
	Total counties	Below US 1st quartile	Above US 3rd quartile	Below US 1st quartile	Above US 3rd quartile
Alaska	27	7	13	3	13
Alabama	67	54	0	52	0
Arkansas	75	38	2	35	1
Arizona	15	3	6	1	7
California	58	2	28	2	26
Colorado	64	0	43	0	42
Connecticut	8	0	7	0	6
Dist of Columbia	1	1	0	0	0
Delaware	3	0	0	0	0
Florida	67	14	18	18	20
Georgia	159	112	6	108	5
Hawaii	4	0	4	0	4
Iowa	99	0	59	0	73
Idaho	44	0	26	0	19
Illinois	102	8	17	10	14
Indiana	92	11	7	13	4
Kansas	105	5	32	3	32
Kentucky	120	62	1	71	1
Louisiana	64	50	0	51	0
Massachusetts	14	0	9	0	10
Maryland	24	2	5	1	3
Maine	16	1	6	0	4
Michigan	83	2	22	5	19
Minnesota	87	0	64	0	79
Missouri	115	24	6	28	5
Mississippi	82	68	0	51	0
Montana	56	3	25	4	11
North Carolina	100	38	5	32	6
North Dakota	53	2	26	1	45
Nebraska	93	1	51	0	59
New Hampshire	10	0	8	0	9
New Jersey	21	1	12	3	9
New Mexico	33	5	8	2	13
Nevada	17	2	2	5	2
New York	62	0	26	0	14
Ohio	88	12	8	15	6
Oklahoma	77	43	2	49	1
Oregon	36	0	13	3	4
Pennsylvania	67	4	13	1	16
Rhode Island	5	0	3	0	4
South Carolina	46	27	1	21	1
South Dakota	66	7	27	2	47
Tennessee	95	67	1	71	1
Texas	253	44	39	46	43
Utah	29	0	20	2	10
Virginia	134	39	23	35	12
Vermont	14	0	10	0	12
Washington	39	0	24	1	19
Wisconsin	72	1	45	0	48
West Virginia	55	24	2	36	0
Wyoming	23	1	10	1	6
US	3139	785	785	782	785

index of inequality and the concentration index (Wagstaff et al. 1991). Let E_j be average life expectancy in $j = 1, \ldots, J$ ranked socioeconomic categories (e.g. $J = 10$ for counties arranged into income deciles), p_j be population shares with $\sum_{j=1}^{J} p_j = 1$, and $R_j = \sum_{k=1}^{j} p_k - p_j/2$ denote category ranks (in terms of cumulative population share). Assuming an approximately linear relationship between socioeconomic category and life expectancy, and defining average life expectancy as $E_a = \sum_j p_j E_j$, a disparity measure including information across all categories is provided by weighted linear regression of E_j/E_a on R_j (with weights p_j), with slope S providing the slope index of inequality (Kakwani et al. 1997; Low and Low 2004). The concentration index (Kakwani et al. 1997) for socio-economically grouped data is given by

$$C = \frac{2}{E_a}\left[\sum_{j=1}^{j} p_j R_j E_j\right] - 1.$$

If the health index is a positive measure of health, such as life expectancy (since higher expectancies denote better health), and if socioeconomic categories are ranked in ascending SES order from 1 (lowest income, or highest poverty) to J (highest income or lowest poverty), then a positive value of S or C "indicates that health is distributed in favour of the rich, and a negative one that it is distributed in favour of the poor" (Erreygers 2009).

Of interest also for assessing spatial health equity are changes in the extent of spatial clustering of estimated county life table functions. These are measured using global and local versions of the Moran index as discussed by Anselin (1995). Of major interest in equity terms is spatial clustering of areas with below average expectancy, which may be denoted "expectancy deficit" clustering. For example, Fig. 2.1 shows low life expectancies in the South East USA in 2003–2006, and Fig. 2.2 shows the high local clustering coefficients in this region. It is therefore pertinent to consider whether this results from an intensification of expectancy deficit clustering.

Table 2.3 considers life expectancies at birth and age 65 across the three periods, expressed in terms of population weighted averages of county expectancies within county income deciles. These deciles are based on county median income estimates in 2005, 2001 and 1997. Certain features are apparent, such as faster improvement in male expectancy, at least when all counties are considered (Arias 2006).

In terms of income related contrasts, Table 2.3 shows that life expectancies at birth are static in the lowest income areas, but consistently improving in higher income areas. Increases in male life expectancy at age 65 are also more marked in higher income counties. This widening is confirmed by inequality indices. For life expectancy at birth, the interdecile gap, and inequality measures for grouped data (the concentration index, C, and the slope index, S), show widening inequality between area income deciles between 1995–1998 and 2003–2006. For expectancy at 65, a widening is especially apparent in the contrast between 1995–1998 and 1999–2002.

Table 2.3 Trends in inequality of life expectancies by county income deciles

	Males			Females			Male-Female contrast		
	1995–1998	1999–2002	2003–2006	1995–1998	1999–2002	2003–2006	1995–1998	1999–2002	2003–2006
(A) Life expectancies at birth									
Decile 1 (Low income)	71.5	71.8	71.8	78.9	78.4	78.7	7.4	6.6	6.9
Decile 2	70.7	70.9	71.9	78.0	77.6	78.5	7.2	6.7	6.6
Decile 3	71.0	72.4	73.2	78.0	78.6	79.4	7.0	6.2	6.2
Decile 4	71.2	73.1	73.0	78.1	79.1	78.9	6.9	5.9	5.9
Decile 5	72.5	73.2	73.9	79.1	78.8	79.6	6.6	5.7	5.7
Decile 6	72.9	73.5	74.0	79.2	79.0	79.6	6.4	5.6	5.5
Decile 7	72.7	73.7	74.5	79.0	79.2	79.9	6.3	5.5	5.4
Decile 8	73.3	73.5	75.3	79.4	79.0	80.6	6.1	5.5	5.3
Decile 9	73.5	74.6	75.7	79.4	79.9	80.6	5.9	5.2	4.9
Decile 10 (High income)	75.3	76.2	77.4	80.4	80.6	81.5	5.1	4.4	4.2
All counties	73.5	74.4	75.3	79.4	79.6	80.4	6.0	5.2	5.1
Interdecile gap	3.8	4.4	5.5	1.5	2.3	2.8			
Concentration index, C	0.0099	0.0105	0.0116	0.0047	0.0056	0.0061			
Slope index of inequality, S	0.062	0.066	0.0725	0.029	0.035	0.038			
(B) Life expectancies at Age 65									
Decile 1 (Low income)	15.2	15.4	16.2	19.2	18.8	19.5	4.0	3.4	3.3
Decile 2	15.2	15.2	16.1	18.9	18.5	19.4	3.7	3.3	3.3
Decile 3	15.0	15.9	16.8	18.7	19.1	19.9	3.7	3.2	3.1
Decile 4	15.1	16.0	16.4	18.8	19.2	19.4	3.7	3.2	3.0
Decile 5	15.6	15.8	16.9	19.3	18.9	19.8	3.6	3.1	3.0
Decile 6	15.6	16.0	16.9	19.2	19.1	19.7	3.6	3.1	2.8
Decile 7	15.6	16.2	17.0	19.2	19.2	19.9	3.6	3.0	2.9
Decile 8	16.0	16.0	17.5	19.4	19.0	20.2	3.3	3.0	2.8
Decile 9	16.0	16.6	17.5	19.3	19.5	20.1	3.3	2.8	2.6
Decile 10 (High income)	16.4	17.0	17.9	19.6	19.6	20.3	3.1	2.6	2.4
All counties	15.9	16.4	17.4	19.3	19.3	20.1	3.4	2.9	2.7
Interdecile gap	1.2	1.5	1.7	0.4	0.8	0.8			
Concentration index, C	0.0139	0.0159	0.0160	0.0055	0.0074	0.0065			
Slope index of inequality, S	0.087	0.100	0.100	0.034	0.047	0.041			

Table 2.4 Trends in spatial correlation

(A) Global Moran indices				
		1995–1998	1999–2002	2003–2006
Expectancy at birth	Males	0.650	0.662	0.659
	Females	0.673	0.709	0.695
Expectancy at age 65	Males	0.638	0.645	0.585
	Females	0.637	0.668	0.613

(B) Totals of low expectancy counties where local spatial correlation is high and increasing				
	E0 (Males)	E0 (Females)	E65 (Males)	E65 (Females)
Alabama	24	33	18	32
Arkansas	3	1	1	2
Georgia	33	42	29	36
Illinois	1	0	1	0
Indiana	0	0	0	1
Kansas	0	0	0	1
Kentucky	22	20	15	17
Louisiana	25	29	14	22
Missouri	6	4	3	2
Mississippi	16	9	11	5
North Carolina	0	3	0	3
Nevada	0	0	0	1
Ohio	3	0	1	0
Oklahoma	22	27	18	21
South Carolina	2	3	2	0
Tennessee	24	27	16	24
Texas	7	2	0	1
Virginia	10	8	12	11
West Virginia	9	15	4	15
USA	207	223	145	194

A further feature is a wider male-female expectancy gap in low income areas than in higher income areas. Moreover, the male-female gap in life expectancy at birth in the lowest income counties widened between 1999–2002 and 2003–2006, whereas the gap in most other counties lessened through all three periods. For example, in the highest income counties, the gap fell from 5.1 (1995–1998) to 4.2 in 2003–2006.

Table 2.4 shows that global indices of spatial correlation (calculated over all counties using posterior mean expectancies) are broadly stable, though generally peaking in 1999–2002. However, trends in local Moran indices can provide more information on the extent and location of increased clustering in counties with an expectancy deficit.

To assess this, the following criteria are used to select counties: (a) the county expectancy in 2003–2006 is below the US average; (b) the local Moran index for the county is in the top quartile of all local index values in 2003–2006, so that the county is at the centre of a cluster of low expectancy counties, and (c) the local Moran index in 2003–2006 exceeds the local index in the two earlier periods. For example, Butler County in Alabama has a male expectancy in 2003–2006 of 69.0, its local Moran in 2003–2006 is 3.03 (higher than the US wide third quartile of 0.98 for all local Moran indices), and its 2003–2006 local Moran value exceeds the earlier local Moran indices of 2.58 (1999–2002) and 2.53 (1995–1998). In all there are 207 counties across the USA which conform to this pattern for male life expectancy at birth.

Panel B of Table 2.4 considers trends in local spatial correlation patterns across all four expectancy outcomes, and contains only states with one or more county showing increased clustering and an expectancy deficit. Table 2.4 shows that such counties are predominantly in states of the South East USA, though a few are also located in the rust belt states. For example, states with the highest proportion of counties with intensified deficit clustering in male expectancy at birth are Louisiana (25 of 64 counties), Alabama (24 of 67 counties), Oklahoma (22 of 77 counties) and Tennessee (24 of 95 counties). These four states account for half of all counties showing increased spatial clustering in below average male expectancy at birth, and also for around a half of all counties showing increased spatial clustering in below average female expectancy at birth, in below average male expectancy at 65, and in below average female expectancy at 65.

2.5 Discussion

Much of the recent literature on inequalities in US mortality is ecological in nature in the sense of focusing on variations in area mortality. Different area frameworks have been used, some studies using US states (Shi et al. 2005; Kawachi et al. 1997), or US metropolitan areas (Cooper et al. 2001; Lobmayer and Wilkinson 2002), while a number of studies use various aggregations of US counties. Aggregation approaches introduce an additional methodological complication, for example, which areas to amalgamate, whether clusters can include originally non-adjacent areas or are based on originally adjacent areas, choice of formal agglomeration method or ad hoc grouping, and what population threshold to decide that areas need to be aggregated.

The present paper seeks to retain a small area focus as far as possible, using US counties as the unit of analysis. When the set of areas under consideration includes small areas, techniques for modelling the mortality data become especially relevant to estimating life table functions such as life expectancies. Whereas existing ecological analyses of US life expectancies use conventional life table analysis, the strategy here "borrows strength" by using random effects methods that recognize correlations between adjacent ages and areas. As McLaughlin et al. (2007) state, "the strong spatial patterning of mortality rates further indicates the need for attention to spatial relationships and more sophisticated statistical modelling". In particular, random effects smoothing methods are used to estimate life expectancies by county, sex and 4 year period (2003–2006, 1999–2002, 1995–1998). A structural effects method, as in Eq. (2.1), is compared to other borrowing strength methods, and is found to have strong consistency in estimated life table functions with a spatial adaptation of the relational model.

The broad spatial pattern of the resulting county life expectancy estimates shows low expectancies to be concentrated in South East US, while the west coast, northern parts of the Mid West, and most of New England have relatively high expectancies. Formal inequality measures applied to the three sub-periods show an increase in inequality in life expectancy over county income deciles: whereas there is little gain in life expectancy in the lowest income counties, high income counties showed expectancy improvements exceeding the US wide average (see Table 2.3). An analysis of local spatial correlations (Table 2.4) shows that counties with below average expectancy and increased spatial concentrations of such low expectancy are concentrated in the south east USA.

These are potential avenues for further research such as the potential impact of different forms of spatial interaction. The analysis here nevertheless illustrates the potential of a random effects based model of mortality, and the use of the small area expectancy estimates so derived in adding to an understanding of trends and variations in area mortality.

Appendix 1 Spatial Dependence

Apart from neighbourhood adjacency, there are a number of other potential spatial interaction schemes that could be used, and inferences in some applications may be sensitive to the form of spatial interaction (Earnest et al. 2007; Watson 2008). As well as first order neighbours, one may widen adjacency to include neighbours of neighbours (second order neighbours) or even third order neighbours (Duczmal et al. 2006). Spatial weights based on inter-area distances D_{cd} may be used, such as inverse power distance decay schemes,

$$w_{cd} = D_{cd}^{-\alpha},$$

where $\alpha > 0$. Earnest et al. (2007) consider alternatives $\alpha = 1, \alpha = 2$, and $\alpha = 3$. Watson (2008) also considers exponential distance decay weighting schemes, such as

$$w_{cd} = \exp(-\alpha D),$$

where $\alpha > 0$.

Appendix 2 Age-County Effects and Binomial Deviance

Inclusion of the u_{cx} effects is needed to ensure the expected posterior saturated binomial deviance is approximately equal to number of observations, namely $NX =$

$3139 \times 13 = 40807$ (Knorr-Held and Rainer 2001, p. 114). Denote predicted deaths from the model as $\nu_{cx} = P_{cx}m_{cx}$, and the deviance as $DV = 2\sum_{c}\sum_{x} e_{cx}$, where

$$e_{cx} = y_{cx}\log\left(\frac{y_{cx}}{\nu_{cx}}\right) + (P_{cx} - y_{cx})\log\left(\frac{P_{cx} - y_{cx}}{P_{cx} - \nu_{cx}}\right).$$

Then one may monitor DV through the MCMC sequence to ensure it is approximately equal to NX.

Appendix 3 Area Specifications

Counties with missing data, because the county has been abolished, or not yet created, are excluded from the period concerned, and counties with exposed (gender-specific) populations under 500 (over 4 year periods) are amalgamated with neighbours. For 2003–2006 there are then 3139 counties, excluding Clifton Forge (Virginia), and amalgamating Kalawao (Hawaii) with Maui, and Loving (Texas) with Winkler (Texas). In 1999–2002, there are the same number of counties, but excluding Denali (Alaska) and including Clifton Forge, and with amalgamations as in 2003–2006. For 1995–1998, an additional exclusion is Broomfield (Colorado), so that N = 3138.

References

Anselin, L. (1995). Local indicators of spatial association—LISA. *Geographical Analysis*, 27, 93–115.

Anselin, L., Lozano, N., & Koschinsky, J. (2006). Rate transformations and smoothing. GeoDa Center Research Report, http://geodacenter.asu.edu/learning/tutorials. Accessed 23rd October 2012

Arias, E. (2006). United States life tables, 2003. *National vital statistics reports: From the Centers for Disease Control and Prevention, National Center for Health Statistics, National Vital Statistics System, 54*(14), 1–40.

Bell, F., & Miller, M. (2005). *Life tables for the United States social security area 1900–2100.* Actuarial Study No. 116, US Social Security Administration.

Besag, J., York, J., & Mollié, A. (1991). Bayesian image restoration with, two applications in spatial statistics. *Annals of the Institute of Statistical Mathematics, 43,* 1–59.

Best, N. (1999). Bayesian ecological modelling. In A. Lawson, A. Biggeri, D. Böhning, E. Lesaffre, J.-F. Viel, & R. Bertollini (Eds.), *Disease mapping and risk assessment for public health* (pp. 194–201). New York: Wiley.

Brass, W. (1974). Perspectives in population prediction: Illustrated by the statistics of England and Wales. *Journal of the Royal Statistical Society A, 137*(4), 532–583.

Brooks, S., & Gelman, A. (1998). General methods for monitoring convergence of iterative simulations. *Journal of Computational and Graphical Statistics, 7,* 434–445.

Chambers, R., Tzavidis, N., & Salvati, N. (2009). *Borrowing strength over space in small area estimation: Comparing parametric, semi-parametric and non-parametric random effects and M-quantile small area models*. Univ. Wollongong, Centre for Statistical & Survey Methodology, Working Paper.

Christensen, R., Johnson, W., Branscum, A., & Hanson, T. (2011). *Bayesian ideas and data analysis: An introduction for scientists and statisticians*. Boca Raton: Chapman & Hall/CRC Press.

Cooper, R., Kennelly, J., Durazo-Arvizu, R., Oh, H., Kaplan, G., & Lynch, J. (2001). Relationship between premature mortality and socioeconomic factors in black and white populations of US metropolitan areas. *Public Health Reports, 116*, 464–473.

De Beer, J. (2011). A new relational method for smoothing and projecting age-specific fertility rates: TOPALS. *Demographic Research 24*, 409–454. http://www.demographic-research.org/volumes/vol24/18/.

Duczmal, L., Patil, G., Tavares, R., & Cancado, A. (2006). *Detection of spatial clusters in maps equipped with environmentally defined structures*. Center for Statistical Ecology and Environmental Statistics (Penn State University) Technical Report 2006-0527. Available at http://sites.stat.psu.edu/~gpp/technical_reports.htm. Accessed 23rd October, 2012

Durbin, J., & Koopman, S. (2001). *Time series analysis by state space methods*. Oxford: Oxford University Press.

Earnest, A., Morgan, G., Mengersen, K., Ryan, L., Summerhayes, R., & Beard, J. (2007). Evaluating the effect of neighbourhood weight matrices on smoothing properties of conditional autoregressive (CAR) models. *International Journal of Health Geographics, 6*, 54. (2007 Nov 29).

Eayres, D., & Williams, E. (2004). Evaluation of methodologies for small area life expectancy estimation. *Journal of Epidemiology & Community Health, 58*, 243–249.

Erreygers, G. (2009). Correcting the concentration index. *Journal of Health Economics, 28*, 504–515.

Ezzati, M., Friedman, A., Kulkarni, S., & Murray, C. (2008). The reversal of fortunes: Trends in county mortality and cross-county mortality disparities in the United States. *PLoS Medicine, 5*(4), e66. doi:10. 1371/journal.pmed.0050066.

Fotheringham, A., Brundson, A., & Charlton, M. (2002). *Geographically weighted regression: The analysis of spatially varying relationships*. Chichester: Wiley.

Gelfand, A., & Ghosh, S. (1998). Model choice: A minimum posterior predictive loss approach. *Biometrika, 85*, 1–11.

Harper S., & Lynch, J. (2005). *Methods for measuring cancer disparities: Using data relevant to healthy people 2010 cancer-related objectives. NCI Cancer Surveillance Monograph Series, Number 6*. Bethesda: National Cancer Institute.

Heligman, L., & Pollard, J. (1980). The age pattern of mortality. *Journal of the Institute of Actuaries, 107*(1), 49–82.

Himes, C., Preston, S., & Condran, G. (1994). A relational model of mortality at older ages in low mortality countries. *Population Studies, 48*(2), 269–291.

Jonker, M., van Lenthe, F., Congdon, P., et al. (2012). Comparison of Bayesian random effects and traditional life expectancy estimations in small area applications. *American Journal of Epidemiology* (forthcoming).

Kakwani, N., Wagstaff, A., & van Doorslaer, E. (1997). Socioeconomic inequalities in health: Measurement, computation and statistical inference. *Journal of Econometrics, 77*, 87–103.

Kawachi, I., Kennedy, B., Lochner, K., & Prothrow-Stith, D. (1997). Social capital, income inequality, and mortality. *American Journal of Public Health, 87*(9), 1491–1498.

Kim, S., Sundaram, R., Louis, G., & Pyper, C. (2012). Flexible Bayesian human fecundity models. *Bayesian Analysis, 7*(2), 771–800.

Knorr-Held, L., & Rainer, E. (2001). Projections of lung cancer mortality in West Germany: A case study in Bayesian prediction. *Biostatistics, 2*(1),109–129.

Kulkarni, S., Levin-Rector, A., Ezzati, M., & Murray, C. (2011). Falling behind: Life expectancy in US counties from 2000 to 2007 in an international context. *Population Health Metrics 2011, 9*, 16.

Lobmayer, P., & Wilkinson, R. (2002). Inequality, residential segregation by income, and mortality in US cities. *Journal of Epidemiology & Community Health, 56*, 183–187.

Low, A., & Low, A. (2004). Measuring the gap: Quantifying and comparing local health inequalities. *Journal of Public Health & Medicine, 26,* 388–396.

Lunn, D., Spiegelhalter, D., Thomas, A., & Best, N. (2009). The BUGS project: Evolution, critique and future directions. *Statistics in Medicine, 28,* 3049–3067.

McLaughlin, D., Shannon Stokes, C., Johnelle Smith, P., & Nonoyama, A. (2007). Differential mortality across the U.S.: The influence of place-based inequality. In L. Lobao, G. Hooks, & A. Tickamyer (Eds.), *The sociology of spatial inequality* (pp. 141–162). Albany: SUNY Press.

Murray, C., Kulkarni, S., Michaud, C., Tomijima, N., & Bulzacchelli, M. (2006). Eight Americas: Investigating mortality disparities across races, counties, and race-counties in the United States. *PLoS Medicine, 3,* e260. doi:10.1371/journal.pmed.0030260.

Riggan, W., Manton, K., Creason, J., Woodbury, M., & Stallard, E. (1991). Assessment of spatial variation of risks in small populations. *Environmental Health Perspectives, 96,* 223–238.

Shi, L., Macinko, J., Starfield, B., Politzer, R., & Xu, J. (2005). Primary care, race, and mortality in US states. *Social Science and Medicine, 61,* 65–75.

Spiegelhalter, D., Best, N., Carlin, B., & van der Linde, A. (2002). Bayesian measures of model complexity and fit. *Journal of the Royal Statistical Society: Series B, 64,* 583–639.

Toson, B., & Baker, A. (2003). *Life expectancy at birth: Methodological options for small populations*. Office of National Statistics, National Statistics Methodological Series No. 33.

Wagstaff, A., Paci, P., & van Doorslaer, E. (1991). On the measurement of inequalities in health. *Social Science & Medicine, 33,* 545–557.

Watson, H. (2008). *Extensions of spatial statistical methods to incorporate spatial dependency and time constraints with application to breast cancer incidence data in New York state*. Ph.D Thesis, New York University.

Zhu, L., Gorman, D., & Horel, S. (2006). Hierarchical Bayesian spatial models for alcohol availability, drug "hot spots" and violent crime. *International Journal of Health Geographics, 5,* 54. (2006 Dec 7).

Chapter 3
Socioeconomic Determinants of Mortality in Europe: Validation of Recent Models Using the Latest Available Data and Short-Term Forecasts

Jeroen J. A. Spijker

Abstract Mortality is forecast for total mortality, lung cancer and circulatory system diseases excluding stroke for 21 countries. The forecasts are produced from models that include non-demographic variables in their model formulation and a time lag of 0–15 years between the exogenous variables and mortality. Separate time-series models are first constructed for men, women, Eastern and Western Europe and 11 causes of death using data for the period ± 1980 to 2000. The three cause-of-death models are then validated by comparing modelled with observed standardised death rates up to 2005–2009, depending on the country, before two short-term forecasts are made up to 2020. The first forecast is called the constant scenario as all exogenous variables are held constant after the year 2009. The second is the convergence scenario as values are set to converge by a certain year. Results showed that in most Western European countries the observed decline in total mortality since the late 1970s is set to continue in the near future for men, but is likely to level off for women. The mortality decline since the mid- to late 1990s in most Eastern European countries is predicted to continue. One important advantage of short-term forecasts is that values of the exogenous variables are already known for those variables for which a time lag has to be incorporated, meaning that both total mortality and specific causes of death can be accurately estimated for about 10–15 years ahead. This should of course be of great interest to policy makers.

Keywords Cause-specific mortality · Forecasts · Time series · Socioeconomic factors · Eastern Europe · Western Europe

---

J. J. A. Spijker (✉)
School of Social and Political Studies, University of Edinburgh, Room 5.05, Chrystal Macmillan Building, 15a George Square, Edinburgh EH8 9LD, UK
e-mail: j.spijker@ed.ac.uk

J. Anson, M. Luy (eds.), *Mortality in an International Perspective*, European Studies of Population 18, DOI 10.1007/978-3-319-03029-6_3,

3.1 Introduction

The main purpose of this chapter is to produce short-term total and cause-specific mortality forecasts from time-series models that include non-demographic variables as part of the model specification for a selection of European countries. The methodology employed was developed as part of a PhD research whose main objective was to "assess the importance of socioeconomic factors on mortality differences across Europe over time and between countries or regions to determine which factors should be incorporated into future mortality scenarios" (Spijker 2004, p. 7). Accordingly, other factors are only of interest if they intervene in the association between socioeconomic factors and mortality, or if their effect is considerable.

The data used to obtain the mortality models refer to $\pm$ 1980 to 1999. The interest of the research does not lie in the explanation of the disease processes leading to death (already covered by other disciplines), but to identify socioeconomic factors that cause international differences in mortality and changes over time. The research framework is thus set at the macro level, i.e. it entails aggregated mortality and exogenous data, not individual-level data that link mortality with specific characteristics of the deceased, although individual-level studies formed an important basis for the selection of exogenous variables. Separate time-series models were constructed for men and women and Eastern and Western Europe, in recognition of their different political and economic pathways. Using econometric model equations, mortality was subsequently forecast up to the year 2020.

3.2 Background

Since 1970 improvements in life expectancy in Western Europe have been mainly due to the rapidly declining death rates among the elderly, owing to the already low mortality levels at young ages. Many epidemiologists consider this period of change the fourth phase of the epidemiological transition, which some have labelled as the '*age of delayed degenerative diseases*'. The major causes of death have not changed significantly, but many of them are occurring at a later age (see, e.g Olshansky and Ault 1986). During this period, a cause-of-death shift also occurred within the group of degenerative diseases as the proportion of deaths from cancer slowly increased relative to circulatory system diseases. Although recent cause-specific mortality trends indicate that some Eastern European countries such as the Czech Republic have also entered the fourth phase (Spijker 2004, 2009), other Eastern European countries have remained in the third phase of the epidemiological transition (also known as the '*age of degenerative and man-made diseases*'). In these countries life expectancy at birth stagnated in the 1970's and 1980's and even showed periods of decline during the 1990's, especially among men (Meslé and Vallin 2002). This pertains, in particular, to countries of the former Soviet Union. As a result East-West life expectancy differences (both sexes combined) increased from 1.6 years in 1965–1970 to 10.3 years 35 years later (United Nations 2011, own calculations).

Analysing mortality by cause of death is also important for understanding mortality differences over time and space, as its aetiology (cause) provides us with some knowledge of the risk factors of the disease. For instance, reductions in behavioural risk factors and improvements in health care have been identified as the main determinants for the recent changes in mortality. Although the majority of the most prevalent causes of death have several risk factors in common, a change in one such risk factor does not affect each cause of death to the same degree. There may also be variations in time between exposure to a particular risk factor and its effect on different diseases. These are important considerations in both the analysis of mortality differences and in forecasts.

While the third and fourth stages of the epidemiological transition serve as the general context of the current mortality pattern in Europe, in order to obtain a clearer overview of the important factors that affect health, the analysis was set within the life course framework. The study is ecological in design, and it was assumed that determinants of health related to the life course could be identified at the population level, even if these do not serve to demonstrate the well-known causal relationships inferred from individual level studies (Gravelle 1998; Valkonen 1993). For instance, the propensity to smoke or other types of risk behaviour do not occur randomly, but are determined by a wide range of direct and indirect factors throughout life, including both socioeconomic and macroeconomic factors.

There are also important compositional effects. In Western countries, for instance, manual workers show more adverse risk behaviour and are expected to live shorter lives than non-manual workers. Therefore, a change or difference in the composition of the population in terms of economic structure is also likely to cause changes or differences in behavioural risk factors, which will be reflected in cause-specific mortality patterns, usually at some later period in time. This inherent time delay between the exposure (such as being unemployed) and its (indirect) association with mortality is also why the life course approach has been applied to this research, as the risk of exposure accumulates over time. It was considered that by calculating cause-specific time lags for each variable that was used in the analysis some of this time effect could be taken into account.

3.3 Previous Studies and Study Objective

In the field of mortality modelling, there has been a shift from the traditional trend-oriented approach to a more process-oriented one, that is, a change from inter- or extrapolation to one that uses disease processes and related risk factors in model formulation (Keilman 2003; Manton and Stallard 1984; Tabeau et al. 2001).

Traditional approaches tend to be aggregate models that describe the evolution over time of the mortality risk broken down by demographic variables (i.e. usually age and sex, often cause-of-death and occasionally other characteristics such as marital status as well). Perhaps the most widely used extrapolative mortality forecasting technique today is the Lee-Carter model. While "it makes no effort to incorporate knowledge about medical, behavioural, or social influences on mortality change. Its virtues are that it combines a rich yet parsimonious demographic model with statistical time series methods, it is based firmly on persistent long-term historical patterns and trends" (Lee and Carter 1992). The Lee-Carter method produces independent country-specific forecasts based on log-linear fixed age effects and additive normally distributed homoscedastic error terms over time. When forecasting a group of countries simultaneously, a common age parameter is fixed to ensure consistent forecasts for multiple countries (Li and Lee 2005). Variants and extensions of the Lee-Carter method have also been produced with varying success (e.g. Booth et al. 2006; Li and Lee 2005; Li et al. 2004).

Others have raised the need for incorporating uncertainty in population forecasts (e.g. Alho and Spencer 1985; Keilman 2001). As a result, methods have been developed to calculate probabilistic forecasts that describe the uncertainty of future populations by relying on time series models, expert judgements or extrapolation of past forecast errors. The use of the Bayesian approach is well known, one which offers an explicit, coherent and transparent mechanism to include uncertainty in the data, the parameters of the model and the model itself, by using probability distributions, whereby the predictive distributions follow directly from the probabilistic model applied. As a result, probabilistic population forecasts, with more reliable and coherent estimates of predictive distributions, can be obtained. Together, these have the potential to improve the measurement of uncertainty in forecasts, and thus improve our potential for planning and understanding population change (Abel et al. 2010). Examples of papers on Bayesian estimation of mortality include Pedroza (2006), Girosi and King (2008), Abel et al. (2010) and Chunn et al. (2010).

Another approach in time-series models of mortality is to include, besides age and sex, also causes of death. This was done by Tabeau et al. (2001), who applied three different forecasting approaches: overall mortality by period, cause-specific period, and cohort. Not surprisingly, each approach produced a different level of mortality. When the two period approaches are compared, the overall approach resulted in higher female life expectancies than the cause-specific approach in the year 2020 for ages 40, 60 and 80 in all four Western European countries that were studied, but lower life expectancies for men, with one exception. Mortality projections from the cohort approach were not considered as a reasonable alternative to overall period or cause-specific period approaches as it overestimated future mortality as a result of difficulties encountered in formulating hypotheses for cohorts born after 1930. Instead, the cause-of-death approach was deemed the most encouraging of the three due to the simplicity of the parameterisation functions for mortality by cause, while epidemiological knowledge can also be used in formulating hypotheses for the future.

For this reason, epidemiological models have the potential to improve the projection of mortality as patterns of mortality (or morbidity) are primarily 'explained' by the distribution within populations of risk factors, such as smoking, dietary habits or physical inactivity (lifestyle), socioeconomic variables or environmental exposures (Van den Berg-Jeths et al. 2001). At the macro-level, these non-demographic models often take the form of statistical regression models. In a time-series or cross-sectional approach, mortality or morbidity indicators are selected as the dependent variable and linked to a number of covariates such as those just mentioned (Keilman 2003). A well-known example of this approach is the Global Burden of Disease Study by Murray and Lopez (1996), which projects, on the basis of socioeconomic covariates and behaviour life expectancy, mortality and Disability Adjusted Life Years for specific causes, and total population for macro regions and the world as a whole to the year 2020. An obvious advantage of this type of model compared to the trend-oriented approach is that the latency period of several decades between the start of smoking and the incidence of a smoking-related disease is explicitly modelled. Mechanical extrapolations based on the conspicuous trend in the 1960s and 1970s, but overlooking the trend in smoking during the last 20–25 years (decrease for men, increase for women), will yield projected lung cancer levels that are too high for men and too low for women (Keilman 2003). Other examples are epidemiological models that base their cause-specific or total mortality projections on past and projected behavioural risk factors (e.g. Van Genugten et al. 1997; Barendregt et al. 1998). At the micro-level, stochastic models have been developed for ageing and disease processes for individuals, that include frailty models, physiological ageing models, and models for DNA repair (see Yashin 2001). Although models that incorporate age-dependent frailty have considerable potential for mortality forecasting because they enable researchers to model the impact of observed and unobserved stochastically changing covariates on individual chances of survival (Keilman 2003), such models have not yet been applied in mortality forecasting.

Finally, there are two related studies worth mentioning where contextual factors were used in a qualitative manner. The first study by Van Hoorn and De Beer (1998) produced three regional and national scenarios for the countries of the European Economic Area, where the value of future life expectancy at birth up to 2050 for both sexes in each country was determined by, among other ‘tools’, assumptions that were made regarding the development of country and gender differences in future life expectancies. In a similar study two scenarios for 33 European countries were produced that also covered the first half of the twenty-first century, but were based on the key question as to whether Europe will be characterised primarily by economic and cultural similarities, or by differences (Van Hoorn and Broekman 1999).

The above frame of thought has also been applied here, but in a quantitative manner by utilizing non-demographic macro models to produce cause-specific mortality forecasts. The premise for not relying on simple extrapolations of past mortality trends for forecasting is the large number of known health determinants whose patterns are neither static nor tend to have an immediate impact on mortality (e.g. smoking). With this in mind, two “what-if” forecast scenarios are made: one constant scenario where all exogenous variables are held constant after the year 2009; and one “convergence scenario” where values are set to converge by a certain year.

3.4 Data and Method

The main source for the national age-, sex- and cause-specific mortality data and age- and sex-specific population data was the *WHO Mortality Database* (WHO 2011b). Both mortality and population data were already in, or could be aggregated to, the

Table 3.1 Causes of death selected for analyses, their ICD codes and contribution to total male and female mortality in Western and Eastern Europe between around 1980 and 2000[a]

Cause of death	ICD-8	ICD-9	ICD-10	SDR per 100,000 (% of total mortality)			
				West		East	
				Male	Female	Male	Female
Total mortality	*000-E999*	*000-E999*	*A00-Y89*	*1,045.8*	*623.1*	*1,600.4*	*899.0*
Lung cancer	161–162	161–162	C32–C34	7.2 %	2.4 %	6.0 %	1.3 %
Prostate cancer (men only)	185	185	C61	2.8 %		1.1 %	
Breast cancer (women only)	174	174	C50		4.9 %		2.6 %
Remaining cancer	Rest of 140–239	Rest of 140–239	Rest of C00–D48	15.1 %	17.9 %	11.0 %	12.6 %
Stroke	430–438	430–438	I60–I69	9.4 %	13.2 %	13.9 %	19.4 %
Circulatory syst. dis. ex stroke	Rest of 390–458	Rest of 390–459	Rest of I00–I99	33.9 %	31.4 %	38.2 %	41.1 %
Respiratory system diseases	460–519	460–519	J00–J99	8.2 %	6.5 %	6.5 %	4.5 %
Chronic liver dis. & cirrhosis	571	571	K70–K76	1.8 %	1.2 %	1.9 %	1.2 %
Traffic accidents	E800–E845	E800–E848	V00–V99	2.2 %	1.2 %	2.1 %	1.2 %
Suicide	E950–R959	E950–R959	X60–X84	2.3 %	1.4 %	2.8 %	3.5 %

[a] See Appendix *Table* A.1 for the countries and years in each analysis

required 19 five-year abridged age intervals (0, 1–4, 5–9, 10–14, . . . , 80–84, 85 +). The dependent variable was the cause-specific age-standardised death rate (SDR), which was calculated using the 1970 WHO standard population for Europe. The mortality data contained causes of death that were coded according to the 8th, 9th or 10th revision of the International Classification of Diseases (ICD)[1] (see Appendix Table A.1). Causes of death were selected on the basis of their relative importance, the quality of their registration and the documented association with socioeconomic factors[2]. The nine that were eventually chosen covered 83.5 and 83.6 % of total male mortality in the selected Western and Eastern European countries, respectively, and 80.3 and 84.9 % of total female mortality (see Table 3.1). Due to international inconsistencies in the registration of ischaemic heart disease (IHD) (ICD-9 410-414) and other heart disease (ICD-9 415-429), a residual circulatory system disease category was formed by subtracting the cerebrovascular disease (stroke) deaths from the entire circulatory system disease category (labelled CIRC-ex-stroke from here on). A similar aggregation has also been done in the past (e.g. Law and Wald 1999; Murray

[1] ICD-8 pertains to the A list and the ICD-9 to the B-list or the country-specific codes for Switzerland and the New Independent States before they changed to the international coding system.

[2] This last criterion accords with the main objective of the research that this chapter is based on (see Introduction).

and Lopez 1996). The most important macro-determinants of the specific heart and CIRC-ex-stroke, as well as the symptoms and proximate causes (e.g. hypertension and smoking) are similar. Lung cancer and prostate cancer were subtracted from total cancer to create the category 'remaining cancer'. Although this remains a rather heterogeneous cause-of-death group, containing over 200 types of cancer, the disease process is the same—only the location varies. Moreover, they also share important disease determinants such as smoking, alcohol consumption and insufficient intake of fibre, fruit and vegetables.

Explanatory variables tested for their inclusion in the time-series models were selected on the basis of their established associations at the individual level with mortality, including socioeconomic, demographic, environmental, and health-care variables. The variables and data sources used are listed in Table 3.2 together with their expected association according to previous epidemiological studies (one well-known publication is provided for each exogenous variable tested in this study, but a more detailed account can be found in (Spijker 2004; Spijker and Van Wissen 2010). Data on pollution, unemployment, smoking, fruit and vegetable consumption and government health expenditure as a percentage of GDP were only available for Western Europe.

3.4.1 Pooled Cross-Section and Time-Series Analysis

Given the historical differences in economic development within Europe, it was decided to conduct separate analyses for men and women and Western and Eastern European countries (labelled 'West' and 'East'). Mortality was modelled for the period between around 1980 and 2000 (Table 3.3). Pooled cross-section and time-series analysis was employed to analyse the data, for which the statistical programme Eviews 3.1 was used (Quantitative Micro Software 1994). This tool pools the time-series data (T) for each country (N) in order to obtain a data set of N*T observations and allows the model to analyse the cross-country and inter-temporal variations in mortality simultaneously. Moreover, by treating time and space as one dimension a single effect for each independent variable is obtained. The basic time-series model is thus:

$$Y_{it} = \alpha + \beta X_{it} + \delta_i + \gamma_t + \varepsilon_{it}, \tag{3.1}$$

where Y_{it} is the dependent variable, i.e. the SDR, and $\mathbf{X}_{it}$ is a k-vector of regressors. ε_{it} are the error terms for $i = 1, 2, \ldots,$ I cross-sectional units (i.e. countries) observed for dated periods $t = 1, 2, \ldots,$ T. The α parameter represents the overall constant in the model, while the δ_i and γ_t represent cross-section or period-specific effects (random or fixed).

Table 3.2 Overview of exogenous variables and their sources

Variable	Abbreviation	Measured as	Source	Ass. with mortality
Per capita Gross Domestic Product (log)	GDPc	Log of Geary Khamis PPPs in 1990 US$	1	− a
Income inequality	GINI	A value between 0 and 1 indicating the distribution of income	2	+ b.
Education	EDU	Number of years of education	3	− c
Secondary sector employment	IND	% of the labour force employed in the secondary sector	4	+ c, d, e
Primary sector employment	AG	% of the labour force employed in the primary sector	4	+ and − d
Divorce	DIV	Divorce Rate per 100 marriages	5	+ f
Alcohol	ALC	Alcohol consumption—litres of pure ethanol per person per year (age 15 +)	6, 11	+ and − g
Pollution (log)	POL	Log of Sulphur Oxides (1,000 t) per km^2	7, 8	+ h
Urbanisation	URB	Percentage of the population resident in urban areas	9	i
Unemployment	UNEMP	Total unemployed as % of labour force	10	+ j
Smoking	TOBAC	Tobacco consumption—grams per person per year per sex (age 15 +)	11	+ k
Fruit	FRUIT	Average amount of fruits and vegetables available per person per year (kg)	12	− l
Cereals	CEREAL	Average amount of cereals available per person per year (kg)	12	− m
Health Care (GDP)	HCGDP	Governmental expenditure on health as a % of GDP	11	− n
Health Care (PPP)	HCPPP	Governmental expenditure on health in PPPs per capita	12	− n

Source: (1) The Conference Board (2011); (2) Mainly from WIDER (2008). Other sources include: for Switzerland, Flückiger (2002); for Norway, Statistics Norway (1999); for several Eastern European countries, Svenjar (2001); for Russia and the Ukraine, Gregory (1997); (3) Barro and Lee (2000, 2011). For most countries, the data covered the period 1960–2010 at 5-year intervals. The intermediate years were fitted by means of a first-and-second order function or linear interpolation; (4) European Commission (2011) and ILO (2002); OECD (1999, 2004a, 2011 b); for former Czecholovakia from (Federální Statistický Úřad various years); (Český Statistický Úřad various years); (5) For most countries, data were obtained from the European Commission (2011); for the USSR successor states, Czechoslovakia and West Germany, some data were obtained from the Council of Europe (2001) and CIS STAT (1998), (6) Tekin (2002), Treml (1997), OECD (2004b), OECD (2011a), WHO (2011a); (7) Lefohn et al. (1999); (8) European Commission (2011) and OECD (2004b); (9) United Nations (2010); (10) For Belarus, Bulgaria, the Czech Republic, Hungary, Latvia and the Slovak Republic registered unemployment; source Western Europe: Gärtner (2004); OECD (2011 b); source Eastern Europe: European Commission (2011); ILO (2002); OECD (2011 b); source Ukraine: CIS STAT (1998); (11) OECD (2001, 2011 b); (12) WHO (2002, 2011a)

Association with mortality: (a) Mackenbach and Looman (1994), although the association was considered 'weak' as urbanisation and industrialisation obscured the mortality- lowering effect; (b) Wilkinson and Pickett (2006); (c) Davey Smith et al. (1998); (d) Valkonen et al. (1993)—farmers tend to have mortality levels between those for manual and non-manual workers; (e) Kunst et al. (1998); (f) Hu and Goldman (1990); (g) Alcohol is considered to have a long-term negative association and short-term positive association with heart disease and total mortality and only positive to the other causes of death. See e.g. Hart et al. (1999) and Rimm et al. (1996); (h) Brook et al. (2004); (i) Only included as a control variable since it is associated with factors that are both positively and negatively associated with mortality (e.g. greater problems with drugs and contamination but better access to public health services and public transport); (j) Lundin et al. (2010); (k) Peto et al. (1992); (l) Artalejo et al. (1998); (m) Liu (2003); (n) Nolte and McKee (2003)

Table 3.3 Countries and period for which cause-specific mortality and population data were obtained for the model and validation analyses, as well as the time frame of the scenarios*

Western Europe	Model	Validation	Scenario	Eastern Europe	Model	Validation	Scenario
Austria	1977–1999	2000–2009	2010–2020	Belarus	1981–1999	2000–2007	2008–2020
Belgium	1977–1999	2000–2005	2006–2020	Bulgaria	1981–1999	2000–2008	2009–2020
Denmark	1977–1999	2000–2006	2007–2020	F. Czechoslovakia	1981–1985		
Former FRG	1977–1999			Czech Republic	1986–1999	2000–2009	2010–2020
Finland	1977–1999	2000–2009	2010–2020	Slovak Republic	1986–1999	2000–2009	2010–2020
France	1977–1999	2000–2007	2008–2020	Estonia	1981–1999	2000–2008	2009–2020
Greece	1977–1999	2000–2009	2010–2020	Former GDR	1981–1990		
Italy	1977–1999	2000–2007	2008–2020	Hungary	1981–1999	2000–2009	2010–2020
Netherlands	1977–1999	2000–2009	2010–2020	Latvia	1981–1999	2000–2009	2010–2020
Norway	1977–1999	2000–2009	2010–2020	Russia	1981–1998	2000–2006	2007–2020
Sweden	1977–1999	2000–2008	2009–2020	Ukraine	1981–1999	2000–2009	2010–2020
Switzerland	1977–1999	2000–2007	2008–2020				
United Kingdom	1977–1999	2000–2009	2010–2020				

* The Slovak data for 1986-91 were obtained by subtracting the number of deaths and population of the Czech Republic from the data that were available for Czechoslovakia. Data for 1983 and 1984 for Belarus, Estonia, Latvia and the Ukraine, 1991 for Belarus and 2000 for the United Kingdom were linearly interpolated from the surrounding years that were available (e.g. Belarus 1983 = 1982 + 1/3*(1985-1982). Population data were obtained for the same years as the mortality data.

To capture country-specific elements that are not covered by the exogenous variables, such as the effect of the Soviet political system on economic and educational factors in Eastern European countries and the former Soviet Union, or dietary factors other than the consumption of alcohol, fruit and vegetables, and cereals, country fixed effects (δ_i) are calculated. These fixed effects or country-specific intercepts make having an overall constant in the model redundant, while period-specific means are also removed from the dependent variable and exogenous regressors. Finally, perhaps the most important and influential independent variable included in each model is mortality at time $t - 1$. This is because it is assumed that natural death is a slow process and that therefore mortality rates are not completely independent from year to year. Although this makes model values a priori close to the observed ones, the analysis has not been performed from an explanatory perspective, but from a modelling one. Our model equation thus becomes:

$$Y_{it} = \delta_i + \rho y_{it-1} + \beta X_{it} + \varepsilon_{it}, \tag{3.2}$$

Where y_{it-1} is the lagged endogenous variable that corresponds to country i, i.e. mortality at time $t - 1$, in the period prior to the start of the forecast sample.

Cross-Section Heteroscedasticity and Testing for Serial Correlation

As it was assumed that cross-section heteroscedasticity was present (e.g. errors associated with high mortality may have larger variances) cross-section weights were included as they minimize the weighted sum-of-squared residuals.[3] Another important issue to consider in time-series modelling is the possible presence of a structural pattern (serial correlation) in the error-term of the model. One way to test for this is to include a first-order autoregressive (AR) term. If significant it means that the probability of a positive/negative error term at time t, following a positive/negative error term at time $t - 1$, is larger than that of an error term with a reversed sign. In the event of positive autoregression, an error-term at time t that is under- or over-estimated will be similarly under- or over-estimated at time $t + 1$ and negative autoregression indicates the opposite. However, results from the Durbin-Watson (DW) test, often used to test the presence of AR, which comes with the standard *Eviews* output, showed that no AR(1) term was required. The author supposes that the inclusion of mortality at time $t - 1$ may already account for much of the potential autocorrelation.

3.4.2 Elasticities

In order to compare the coefficients of the covariates, elasticities were calculated. Since mortality at time $t - 1$ was included, the models are dynamic ones and therefore

[3] The equation weights are the inverses of the estimated equation variances, and are derived from unweighted estimation of the parameters of the system (Quantitative Micro Software 1994)

both short- and long-term elasticities can be determined. Short-term elasticity is a form of standardised measure that estimates the relative change in the cause-specific mortality rate as a consequence of a relative change in a determinant. Since mortality at time *t* also depends on mortality at time $t-1$, and therefore in turn on $t-2$, $t-3$, etc., any independent variable also has long-term effects. For instance, an economic shock such as the sudden emergence of unemployment will effect mortality not only in year *t*, but also in years $t+1$, $t+2$, $t+3$, etc. The extent of the long-term effect depends on both the strength of the direct effect and the proximity of mortality at time *t* with that of the previous year. In case an exogenous variable has a large long term effect on a particular cause of death, this would be an important fact to consider when mortality is forecast.

3.4.3 Lags

Before starting the pooled cross-section and time series analysis, lags were calculated for the exogenous variables because it was considered that the influence on mortality patterns of economic and other variables is usually not contemporaneous, but the result of many years of exposure. A common example of this is smoking and lung cancer. Lags, however, are seldom incorporated in mortality analysis and, even when they are included, they do not always give the desired result (e.g. Judge 1995). The effect of smoking is better known, as it is a proximate risk indicator with a profound impact on population health. Epidemiological research has indicated that, for individuals, a substantial decline in smoking levels brings about a fall in IHD mortality approximately 15 years later, while for lung cancer the lag is approximately 30 years (Ruwaard and Kramers 1993). If *j* is the number of years variable $\boldsymbol{X}$ is lagged the time-series model equation thus becomes:

$$Y_{it} = \delta_i + \rho y_{it-1} + \beta X_{it-j} + \varepsilon_{it}, \tag{3.3}$$

Because lags vary according to the a priori outcome, i.e. the cause of death, establishing the correct time lags is a difficult process. This is why they were determined by a combination of theoretical reasoning (life course perspective and the aetiology of the disease), availability of time series and empirical tests. In most cases the method employed was to conduct a pooled cross-section and time-series analysis for a range of lags for each variable separately but that also included mortality at time t -1 and cross-section weights. The results were then compared and the lag corresponding to the highest model coefficient value was provisionally taken as the 'true' one. I say provisionally because some consistency between causes of death with a similar aetiology was desired. However, due to the rapid economic transformation and larger fluctuations in life expectancy in Eastern Europe, it was decided to conduct this lagging exercise separately for the two European analyses, although no further distinction was made between men and women. Lag values are given in Table 3.4 and variable averages (without lag) for both parts of Europe in Table 3.5.

3.4.4 Model Validation and Short-Term Forecasts

For the model validation exercise, two comparisons are made. Firstly between the actual and modelled SDR for the original time series; and secondly, by comparing the modelled values with the SDR that were calculated for the most recent years that the WHO Mortality Database have available (see Table 3.1). This second comparative analysis implicitly tests the predictive value of the models. Finally, two short-term forecasts are made up to the year 2020. The first is called the constant scenario as all exogenous variables are held constant after the year 2009. The second is the convergence scenario as values are set to converge by a certain year (see Table 3.5). In both cases, so-called "dynamic forecasting" is employed: *EViews* performs a multi-step forecast of SDR ($\hat{y}$), beginning at the start of the forecast sample. Thus, if S is the first observation for country i in the forecast sample,

$$\hat{y}_{Si} = \delta_i + \rho y_{Si-1} + \beta X_{Si-j} + \varepsilon_{Si}, \tag{3.4}$$

where y_{Si-1} is the country-specific value of the lagged endogenous variable in the period prior to the start of the forecast sample. This is the one-step-ahead forecast. Forecasts for subsequent observations use the previously forecasted values of y, i.e.:

$$\hat{y}_{Si+k} = \delta_i + \rho y_{Si+k-1} + \beta X_{Si-j+k} + \varepsilon_{Si+k}, \tag{3.5}$$

For the purpose of this chapter, only the results for total mortality, lung cancer and CIRC-ex-stroke are presented and discussed.

Although data for additional years had to be obtained for all variables to conduct the model validation exercise and make the short-term forecasts, future values were only required for the external cause of death models and several natural causes of death for Eastern Europe. In case no new data could be obtained or data for certain years were missing, own estimations were made (usually by simple linear extrapolation except for education where missing values were estimated using log-linear modelling).

Several adjustments also had to be made. Firstly, it was decided to employ the natural log of GDP per capita rather than the actual value, because it is generally considered that the additional health effect of a certain amount of income decreases with increasing income. Secondly, the smoking variable was not judged to be very accurate for modelling purposes, as the average level of tobacco consumption in a population included the non-smoking population, which does not represent life-time exposure as a period measurement. Moreover, sex-specific values had to be estimated from total consumption and male and female smoking prevalence rates. Although the introduction of time lags partly allowed for life-time exposure, the (often incomplete) smoking data did not go further back than 1960. This made estimating meaningful lags difficult. The observed lung cancer mortality rate was therefore considered to be a more appropriate smoking indicator (see also Barendregt et al. 2002) and was consequently used in the cause-of-death related models (see TOBAC column in Table 3.4). The exception was lung cancer itself for which the original tobacco

Table 3.4 Variable-specific lags (in years) applied to the variables in the pooled cross-country and time-series analyses[a]

	lnGDP –	GINI +	EDU –	IND +	AG	URB	DIV +	ALC +/–	UNEMP +	TOBAC +	POL +	FRUIT –	Hcgdp –
Western Europe													
Total	15	10	15	5	5	0	10	0/15	5	0[b]	15	5	1
Lung cancer	15	10	15	10	10	0	10	5	10	10	10	5	2
Prostate cancer (men)	15	10	15	10	10	0	10		10	0[b]		5	2
Breast (women)	10	10	15	10	10	0	10		10	0[b]		5	1
Other cancer	15	10	15	5	5	0	10	5	5	0[b]		5	2
CIRC-ex-stroke	15	10	15	5	5	0	10	0/15	5	0[b]	15	5	1
Cerebrovascular disease	15	10	15	5	5	0	10	0	5	0[b]		5	1
Respiratory system dis.	15	10	15	10	10	0	10	10	10	0[b]	15	5	1
Liver dis. and cirrhosis	3	5	15	5	5	0	10	0	5			5	1
Traffic accidents	0	0	0	0	0	0	1	0	0				1
Suicide	0	0	0	0	0	0	1	0	0				1
Eastern Europe													
Total	0	0	15	5	5	0	1	0	5	0[b]			
Lung	15		10	5	5	0	10	5	5				
Prostate cancer (men)	15		15	10	10	0	10			0[b]			
Breast cancer (women)	10		15	10	10	0	10			0[b]			
Other cancer	15		10	10	10	0	10	10		0[b]			
CIRC-ex-stroke.	0	0	15	5	5	0	1	0	5	0[b]			
Cerebrovascular disease	0	0	15	5	5	0	1	0	5	0[b]			
Respiratory system dis.	15	5	15	5	5	0	1	0	5	0[b]			
Liver dis. and cirrhosis	0	0	15	2	2	0	1	0	2				
Traffic accidents	0	0	0	0	0	0	1	0	0				
Suicide	0	0	0	0	0	0	0	0	0				

[a]The sign next to a variable indicates documented directions of association, as explained in Table 3.3, which also provided a key for the abbreviated variable names. The same lags were used for males and females

[b]Lung cancer SDR were used (see main text)

Table 3.5 Average first, last and convergence year value of the explanatory variables used in the modelling procedure and short term convergence scenario to the year 2020 for Western and Eastern Europe. (Source: See Table 3.3)

Variable	Western Europe		Eastern Europe		Convergence	
	1977	1999	1981	1999	Year	Value
Per capita GDP (GK US$)	13,025.9	19,591.7	7,054.0	8.7	2060	65,217.0
Income inequality (gini)	27.7	29.3	22.0	29.7	2030	30.0
Education (years of education)	7.7	9.5	8.8	10.6	2040	12.6
Secondary sector employment (% of total)	36.7	25.8	40.9	31.9	2050	18.8
Primary sector employment (% of total)	10.2	5.2	17.4	14.1	2050	1.4
Divorce (per 100 marriages)	25.2	42.5	34.2	53.7	2030	48.0
Alcohol (liters/person/year)	12.2	9.8	13.8	12.0	2040	6.0
Pollution (SO^2/km^2)	5,312.1	7.2			2050	1.0
Urbanisation (% urban)	74.4	79.5	66.0	68.3	a	a
Unemployment (%)	9.9	7.0	0.0	10.7	2030	5.0
Smoking—males (grams/person/sex/year)	3,411.7	2,317.4			2030	900.0
Smoking—females (grams/person/sex/year)	1,732.9	1,722.9			2030	900.0
Fruit and vegetables (grams/person/sex/year)	178.7	220.3			2050	400.0
Health Care (% of GDP)	7.0	8.6			2050	12.0

[a] For urbanisation the United Nations estimates were used

consumption variable was used, though only for the Western European models as data were not available for all Eastern European countries. Thus, using lung cancer as a proxy for smoking also provided the possibility to test the influence of tobacco on Eastern European mortality as well as to obtain more independent estimates of the effect of other mortality determinants known to be associated with lifetime smoking (e.g. secondary sector employment). The scenario estimates for lung-cancer were subsequently used to estimate the other smoking-related causes of death (including total mortality). Thirdly, with regard to total mortality and CIRC-ex-stroke, the protective and detrimental effects of alcohol were tested simultaneously, rather than choosing the more influential of the two as was done recently in (Spijker and Van Wissen 2010). Alcohol is thought to reduce the risk of the thickening of the arteries—a risk factor of IHD—in the long term (in the model it was lagged 15 years), while short-term detrimental effects of alcohol include the increased risk of sudden IHD and stroke (e.g. as a result of binge drinking), for which reason no lag was introduced. Finally, the same lags were used for unemployment and the two employment sector variables as they are all influenced by changes in (structural) employment.

Using the sample of countries and years, the data were modelled. Due to the correlation between related variables (e.g. between industrial employment and GDPc), the inclusion of one may make another variable insignificant. This was one reason why only the results of the "best models" rather than saturated models are provided. Moreover, for forecasts it makes little sense to include all variables when just a few are relevant. It is nevertheless important to bear in mind that what a variable "represents" is more general than the measurement itself. To give an example, the proportion of the workforce in secondary sector employment is not just a pure labour variable, but also represents other aspects, such as socioeconomic development (countries with a high proportion of industrial employment usually have a lower GDPc and a less well educated population than countries with a larger service sector), and even behaviour (manual labourers are generally less health conscious, as they smoke and drink more and eat less healthy food).

3.5 Results I: The Sex-Specific Cause-of-Death Models for Western and Eastern Europe

As the results in Tables 3.6 and 3.7 indicate, each model fits the data very well: the adjusted R^2 values range from 0.908 (West European female model for respiratory system diseases) to 0.999 (East European model for female remaining cancer). Mortality at time $t - 1$ seemed to best predict mortality. This is not surprising as most deaths are the result of lifetime accumulations of health risks and exposures and therefore the probability of death will not fluctuate that much from year to year. Its high predictive value in many of the models (the level of mortality for one particular year was up to 0.96 the value of the previous year) makes its inclusion in the model conclusive. Including exogenous variables contributed less to the overall fit, but nevertheless provided important parameters for forecasting as the elasticities in Appendix Table A.2 show. Finally, the high R^2 was also partly due to the inclusion of cross-country weights and fixed effects (i.e. country-specific intercepts) (see bottom of each table). One point to bear in mind when interpreting the results is that, in many instances, the exogenous variables have been lagged by different times, depending on the cause of death, and also by different amounts in Eastern and Western Europe. In regard to the latter, the effect on mortality of several of the variables appears to be more immediate in Eastern than in Western Europe. This is particularly the case with absolute and relative income and divorce.

Results showed that the natural log of GDP per capita (from here on GDPc) and the proportion of the workforce employed in the industrial sector are the variables that are significant most often. Divorce can be added to this for (especially West European) women, education for Eastern Europe and short-term detrimental effects of alcohol consumption and urbanisation for Eastern Europe. Finally, smoking, which was not tested in each model, was most often significant in the models for West European men (in all but prostate cancer).

3.5.1 The Effect of Absolute and Relative Income on Mortality

If we would consider the results in more detail, GDPc is significant in seven out of ten male and female models in Western Europe and in five and eight models in Eastern Europe, respectively. The short-term elasticity for total mortality was similar

Table 3.6 Results from the pooled model for the different causes of death: "West" analysis. (Data source: Mortality: WHO (2011a). See Table 3.3 for the definitions of the exogenous variables)

	Total	Lung cancer	Prostate c.	Other c.	Circ-stroke	Stroke	Respiratory	LDC	Traffc	Suicide
Men										
Cause at t-1	0.71***	0.96***	0.72***	0.78***	0.90***	0.83***	0.36***	0.89***	0.71***	0.84***
ln GDP	– 90.19***	– 3.59***	3.32***			– 8.06*	– 42.71***		– 3.44***	– 1.50***
GINI					0.61*		0.43**	0.08***		
EDU					– 3.12**					
IND	1.19*			0.23**	0.94***				0.17***	
AG		– 0.15 *	0.11 **	0.44 ***	– 0.79***		– 0.77 *		– 0.20 ***	– 0.06 ***
DIV			0.01 **			0.06 **	0.23***	0.005 *	0.01 **	
ALC_short	4.72***					0.65***	***	0.36***	0.16***	0.09**
ALC_long					– 0.68***		0.89			
ln POL	16.71***						1.95***			
URB							0.36**	0.03*	– 0.09***	– 0.11***
UNEMP				0.23***					– 0.14***	
TOBAC	1.20***	0.0004*		0.06***	0.15***	0.09***	0.21***			
FRUIT		– 0.01*	– 0.01*							
HCGDP		– 0.34**	– 0.14*	– 0.55**		– 0.54***			– 0.15*	
Fixed Effects										
Austria	936	40	– 22	20	14	81	375	– 4	42	26
Belgium	867	41	– 21	18	– 5	72	389	– 8	45	29
Switzerland	941	42	– 21	19	2	77	390	– 8	41	26
West Germany	912	41	– 22	22	7	80	380	– 7	40	26
Denmark	951	42	– 22	24	15	76	386	– 7	43	28
Finland	998	40	– 23	16	15	80	405	– 5	43	29
France	891	42	– 23	25	– 3	71	369	– 9	43	26
Greece	876	46	– 25	14	13	82	372	– 8	46	21
Italy	874	44	– 24	21	– 7	79	378	– 6	42	23
Netherlands	882	41	– 21	20	– 2	74	388	– 8	42	26
Norway	1,035	41	– 20	24	17	84	408	– 5	42	26
Sweden	1,038	40	– 21	20	18	83	391	– 6	46	27
United Kingdom	903	39	– 23	18	1	77	415	– 7	39	24

Table 3.6 (continued)

	Total	Lung cancer	Prostate/Breast c.	Other c.	Circ-stroke	Stroke	Respiratory	LDC	Traffc	Suicide
Durbin-Watson	2.427	2.538	2.241	2.390	2.372	2.397	2.285	2.163	2.150	2.192
R2 adj. Model	0.989	0.996	0.988	0.998	0.986	0.984	0.957	0.995	0.972	0.974
R2 adj. Model#	0.971	0.989	0.948	0.973	0.986	0.974	0.900	0.992	0.715	0.982
R2 adj. T-1 only#	0.971	0.988	0.945	0.972	0.985	0.975	0.891	0.992	0.715	0.982
R2 adj. IVs only#	0.590	0.484	0.635	0.571	0.740	0.325	0.444	0.544	0.192	0.117
Women										
Cause at t-1	0.70***	0.86***	0.90***	0.84***	0.88***	0.83*	0.34***	0.79***	0.57***	0.83***
ln GDP	− 71.82***	1.03***		− 2.33*		− 11.86***	− 22.38***		− 2.20***	− 0.60**
GINI							0.21**	0.03*		
EDU						1.51**				− 0.25***
IND	1.78***		0.15***	0.23***	0.63*	0.26**			0.10***	0.04*
AG		0.09***	− 0.06***	− 0.20**			− 0.22***		− 0.09**	0.07***
DIV	0.24*	0.01***	0.02***			0.05***	0.15***		0.01*	0.01***
ALC_short	2.03*							0.22*		0.06***
ALC_long				0.19***	− 0.29**		0.47***			
ln POL	14.39 ***									
URB		0.04 ***		− 0.09 **		− 0.18***		0.02***	− 0.04***	
UNEMP				0.12*			0.54***		− 0.07***	
TOBAC	1.19**	0.0005***				0.10**	0.56***			
FRUIT										
HCGDP			− 0.27***							
Fixed Effects										
Austria	723	− 12	− 0.82	36	6	113	204	− 2	25	8
Belgium	709	− 13	0.08	37	2	115	209	− 4	27	8
Switzerland	733	− 13	− 0.67	35	− 1	111	213	− 4	24	8
West Germany	705	− 13	− 0.91	38	2	114	210	− 4	24	7
Denmark	735	− 10	1.36	43	5	112	210	− 4	26	9
Finland	758	− 13	− 0.40	38	2	115	217	− 3	25	8
France	696	− 13	− 0.01	34	− 2	113	205	− 5	26	7

Table 3.6 (continued)

	Total	Lung cancer	Breast c.	Other c.	Circ-stroke	Stroke	Respiratory	LDC	Traffc	Suicide
Greece	725	− 13	1.35	35	7	119	205	− 4	26	8
Italy	700	− 12	0.21	35	0	116	204	− 3	25	6
Netherlands	714	− 13	0.33	39	2	116	210	− 5	25	8
Norway	775	− 12	0.02	40	2	114	226	− 3	24	8
Sweden	776	− 13	− 0.81	39	3	113	214	− 3	24	8
United Kingdom	702	− 10	− 0.91	37	0	112	229	− 4	23	7
Durbin-Watson	2.440	2.510	2.432	2.457	2.445	2.327	2.200	2.450	2.076	2.275
R2 adj. Model	0.986	0.995	0.996	0.998	0.989	0.987	0.908	0.991	0.966	0.972
R2 adj. Model#	0.966	0.985	0.955	0.973	0.978	0.982	0.894	0.972	0.838	0.972
R2 adj. T-1 only#	0.965	0.985	0.952	0.973	0.977	0.982	0.872	0.972	0.829	0.970
R2 adj. IV's only#	0.507	0.408	0.203	0.471	0.649	0.407	0.500	0.538	0.450	0.51

Method: GLS (Cross Section Weights)
Sample: 1977 1999; Total panel (unbalanced) observations: 290
* $p < 0.01$; ** $p < 0.05$; *** $p < 0.01$ (one sided)
# Model also excludes cross-section weights and fixed effects

Table 3.7 Results from the pooled model for the different causes of death: "East" analysis (Data source: Mortality: WHO (2011a). See Table 3.3 for the definitions of the exogenous variables)

	Total	Lung cancer	Prostate c.	Other c.	Heart dis.	Stroke	Respiratory	LDC	Traffic	Suicide
Men										
Cause at t-1	0.54***	0.84***	0.34***	0.53***	0.68***	0.68***	0.56***	0.72***	0.69***	0.62***
ln GDP	− 127.78***			− 8.55***	− 51.84*				7.82***	− 9.78***
GINI					1.11***		0.34*	0.23***	0.10**	
EDU		− 3.71***	1.68***		− 20.10**	− 4.83**	− 5.65***			
IND	11.22**		0.20**	1.51***		1.54***	0.46*	0.31***	0.23***	0.41***
AG	9.82***	0.16*	0.15**					0.14***		0.33***
DIV			0.02**	0.22***			0.17***	0.04***		0.25***
ALC_short	23.80***				6.47***	2.36***	1.96***	0.49 ***	0.44 **	0.62***
ALC_long		0.91***		0.27**						
URB	21.86***	0.86***	0.14***	− 0.57**	5.66***	2.07***	− 2.38***	0.20***	0.83***	
UNEMP						0.67**		0.08**		
TOBAC	1.56***			0.37**	0.39***		0.31***			
Fixed Effects										
Bulgaria	− 761	− 32	− 25	75	283	− 116	166	− 34	− 132	58
Belarus	− 596	− 20	− 28	91	340	− 113	187	− 35	− 127	65
Czech Republic	− 966	− 26	− 20	94	253	− 153	166	− 35	− 143	59
Czechoslovakia	− 787	− 21	− 22	82	289	− 137	171	− 33	− 139	61
East Germany	− 821	− 35	− 22	98	259	− 170	199	− 32	− 143	68
Estonia	− 698	− 31	− 18	94	266	− 127	142	− 39	− 135	67
Hungary	− 683	− 21	− 14	98	258	− 130	141	− 15	− 131	69
Latvia	− 645	− 28	− 19	94	260	− 109	145	− 38	− 127	67
Russia	− 714	− 25	− 29	91	262	− 104	185	− 39	− 135	67
Slovak Republic	− 571	− 14	− 20	88	359	− 133	140	− 26	− 124	62
Ukraine	− 659	− 22	− 29	84	309	− 105	184	− 34	− 128	59
Durbin-Watson	1.635	2.146	2.000	2.250	1.797	1.903	2.054	1.674	1.708	1.929
R2 adjusted	0.996	0.998	0.994	0.999	0.996	0.986	0.936	0.965	0.929	0.972
R2 adj. Model#	0.875	0.959	0.943	0.981	0.730	0.949	0.909	0.966	0.783	0.945
R2 adj. T-1 only#	0.854	0.952	0.943	0.976	0.696	0.202	0.309	0.964	0.775	0.931
R2 adj. IVs only#	0.566	0.271	0.372	0.930	0.118	0.950	0.905	0.367	0.224	0.701

Table 3.7 (continued)

	Total	Lung cancer	Breast c.	Other c.	Heart dis.	Stroke	Respiratory	LDC	Traffic	Suicide
Women										
Cause at t-1	0.58***	0.95***	0.73 ***	0.54***	0.66***	0.74***	0.40***	0.66***	0.61***	0.64***
ln GDP	−28.53*	1.62***	−2.48***	−8.69***	−37.41*		7.78**	0.85***	2.26***	
GINI	1.67**							0.08***	0.03***	
EDU	−24.33***	−0.57***	0.96***		−16.64**	−5.06***	−1.43***			−0.39***
IND	1.16***			0.84***		0.21*	0.30**	0.10***	0.04***	0.03***
AG				0.68***			0.32**	0.11***		0.05***
DIV			0.08***					0.04***		0.04***
ALC_short	7.74***				2.07***	1.18***		0.23***	0.21***	0.05***
ALC_long		0.05***		0.53***						
URB	8.69***		0.12***		2.59***	1.20***	−2.94***	0.15***	0.21***	
UNEMP					0.78***					
TOBAC				0.84***						
Fixed effects										
Bulgaria	62	−10	12	2	388	−14	146	−27	−36	2
Belarus	109	−9	8	9	409	−13	147	−27	−34	2
Czech Republic	−14	−8	10	25	377	−32	162	−28	−38	2
Czechoslovakia	66	−9	12	24	394	−21	160	−27	−38	2
East Germany	−11	−9	9	24	394	−48	180	−26	−38	6
Estonia	−9	−10	11	19	369	−26	138	−30	−36	2
Hungary	68	−8	13	36	381	−27	142	−19	−36	5
Latvia	15	−10	10	21	357	−14	137	−29	−34	2
Russia	38	−9	8	15	382	−2	164	−28	−36	3

Table 3.7 (continued)

	Total	Lung cancer	Breast c.	Other c.	Heart dis.	Stroke	Respiratory	LDC	Traffic	Suicide
Slovak Republic	129	−9	13	26	428	−25	122	−23	−34	1
Ukraine	99	−9	9	9	410	−7	147	−27	−35	2
Durbin-Watson	1.803	2.381	2.276	2.153	1.999	1.863	1.961	2.073	1.887	2.194
R2 adj. Model	0.994	0.993	0.996	0.999	0.992	0.988	0.949	0.956	0.931	0.981
R2 adj. Model#	0.757	0.979	0.945	0.972	0.693	0.964	0.918	0.951	0.502	0.935
R2 adj. T-1 only#	0.742	0.978	0.942	0.972	0.690	0.964	0.911	0.948	0.418	0.934
R2 adj. IVs only#	0.214	0.166	0.059	0.643	0.047	0.279	0.443	0.320	0.236	0.436

Method: GLS (Cross Section Weights)
Sample: 1981 1999; Total panel (unbalanced) observations 243
* $p < 0.10$; ** $p < 0.05$; *** $p < 0.01$ (one-sided)
# Model also excludes cross-section weights and fixed effects

in all four models (see Appendix Table A.2). Given that GDPc was in fact its natural log, it implies that more extra wealth is required in Western Europe for the same relative health gains. In Eastern Europe, results also show that GDPc is significant in CIRC-ex-stroke (both sexes) and suicide (men). Conversely, in Western Europe GDPc, considered an indicator of absolute wealth, is only significant in suicide, while income inequality as measured by the Gini coefficient appears to play a similar role in both parts of Europe. The association between GDPc and traffic accidents is positive rather than negative in Eastern Europe, suggesting that car ownership and the ensuing mortality risk was, at least for the period that was modelled (1981–1999), positively associated with welfare. GDPc also shows a positive association with lung cancer for women in both parts of Europe (although in the East elasticities were much higher), thus indicating that it is still a welfare disease for them. Regarding income inequality, it was significant for chronic liver disease and cirrhosis (LDC) in both parts of Europe and for both sexes and in all but East European women in the case of respiratory system diseases. In terms of time changes and country-differences in total mortality, however, its effect was rather limited, although for the Eastern Europe analysis this was expected as there were few international differences in income inequality during the socialist period. On the other hand, the results for LDC and respiratory system diseases shows that it takes little time before a sudden rise in income inequality affects mortality from these causes.

3.5.2 The Effect of Labour Force Indicators on Mortality

In both parts of Europe and for men and women, the proportion of industrial employment in the workforce is an important explanatory factor for total mortality, remaining cancer and traffic accidents, showing a detrimental effect, also after including other risk factors like smoking or alcohol consumption. Indeed, for East European men, the variable was significant in all but lung cancer and CIRC-ex-stroke. Although the effect of improved occupational safety standards, independent of the employment structure could not be tested, it seems plausible that improvement in wealth emanating from an increasing share in service sector industries is associated with health more than factors inherent to social class differences in health. This is because on the two occasions when industrial employment was not significant it occurred after introducing GDPc into the model (this also occurred in other models like that of female respiratory system diseases in Western Europe). Finally, short-term elasticities of industrial employment are quite high in the Eastern European models (up to 0.5 %), and the long-term effect on mortality rises up to 1.4 % (LDC in the model for men).

When agricultural employment was significant, the association was usually negative with mortality in Western Europe (a notable exception being female lung cancer) and positive in Eastern Europe (see for instance, the results for suicide). Rural life therefore seems to benefit particularly people in Western Europe while conditions may be harsher in Eastern Europe.

At the population level the effect of unemployment on mortality was minor. This can be explained by the fact that at the low levels of unemployment typical of Western European countries (after lagging the variable 10 years, the average for the studied countries and period was just 4 %) a very high relative risk is needed to have some bearing on international mortality differences or changes over time. However, given the increases in unemployment since the 1980s and its recent emergence in Eastern Europe, unemployment is likely to become a more important factor.

3.5.3 The Effect of Education on Mortality

The importance of education as an independent health-promoting factor associated with the acquisition of knowledge related to health-damaging behaviours rather than just economic development was only really evident in Eastern Europe as in most West European models it was not significant. This was because in the male and female models GDPc often showed a significant protective effect instead. Education would usually have been significant if GDPc were excluded, including in the model for total mortality. The only significant associations between education and mortality are found in the analyses of male CIRC-ex-stroke as well as in female suicide and stroke mortality. With regard to the latter the association was positive. This is still a plausible result given that cerebrovascular disease is a common cause of death among elderly and education is positively association with old-age survival (i.e. there is likely to be a selection effect). In the case of Eastern Europe, there are a number of models, especially among women, where besides GDPc, education is also significant. This suggests that health-related knowledge, both in terms of behaviour and the ability to optimise the use of health services, might be indispensable in the fight against these diseases (and that education is not just an indicator of welfare). Indeed, the fact that the association with breast and prostate cancer is positive suggests that more education may not only lead to earlier diagnosis but also (and subsequently) to higher mortality as a result of higher rates of detection of a tumour that would have gone undiagnosed among less educated populations.

3.5.4 The Effect of Divorce on Mortality

The only social factor that was tested was divorce. While mortality declined in Western Europe between the late 1970s and late 1990s, the level of divorce has steadily increased and, indeed, divorce appears to have a significant counter effect on this trend for several of the selected causes of death, particularly for women. A future consequence may therefore be that in those countries where divorce is still a recent or minor phenomenon (particularly in southern Europe) continued increases in divorce are likely to have an impact on future levels of mortality. Results of the analysis also showed that the magnitude of the effect of divorce was larger in Eastern

Europe than in the West and larger for men than for women, which may be due to higher general levels of stress (see Kristenson et al. 1998). The literature also clearly suggests that divorce is more detrimental to the health of men than that of women (Joung 1996). Our results also confirm this at the population level as the elasticities are higher for men than for women for the same cause of death, especially in Eastern Europe where elasticities reach a maximum of 0.23 (short-term) and 0.60 (long-term) for male suicide.

3.5.5 *The Effect of Behavioural Factors on Mortality*

The models also included several behavioural factors. The results show that at the population level, two types of associations exist between the consumption of alcohol and mortality: negative in the long term in Western Europe with regard to total mortality and CIRC-ex-stroke (both sexes) as well as a positive (i.e. detrimental) short/intermediate term effect for most causes of death, especially in Eastern Europe. The positive short-term association with both total and circulatory system disease mortality in Eastern Europe is possibly because of traditions of "binge drinking" that are known to elevate the risk of sudden IHD. The effect of smoking was measured by the association of lung cancer mortality with the specific cause of death category (except for lung cancer itself, of course, in which case the less reliable tobacco consumption variable was used for Western Europe; there was no data for Eastern Europe). Results show that smoking has a large impact on differential mortality for West European men, being significant for all natural causes of death for which it was tested except prostate cancer. For East European men, results are quite similar with the elasticity for total mortality being equal, as for West European men. Smoking is also significant in all models for respiratory system diseases except for East European women. However, among West European women, it particularly lacks an association with circulatory system diseases. Although most countries had their smoking peak around 1980, towards the end of the 1990's country differences were just as large as in 1960. Given the time delay that it takes for smoking to have a fatal impact on health, it is expected that smoking will continue to be an important factor in mortality differences between countries in Europe well into the twenty-first century, particularly for women where the effect is just being felt. As to the effect of fruit and vegetable consumption, it could only be tested for Western Europe. However, significant effects for men were only found regarding prostate and remaining cancer. Still, as the West and North of Europe still lag behind in consumption levels compared to Southern Europe more health gains can still be made there. This of course applies even more to Eastern Europe and the former Soviet Union. Due to insufficient data government health expenditure could only be tested for Western Europe, where it had a small but significant effect on mortality from most natural causes at the population level for men and for breast cancer in the case of women.

3.5.6 *The Effect of Environmental Factors on Mortality*

The last two variables that were tested were urbanisation and pollution. Pollution could only be tested in Western Europe and proved to be statistically significant for total mortality among both sexes and for male respiratory system diseases, though elasticities were very low. Lastly, urbanisation was significant in over 20 models, but was only considered as a control variable due to its association with a number of factors that are both positively and negatively associated with mortality. For instance, while there may be greater access to public health services and medical technology in urban areas (which in itself may produce higher levels of mortality for a specific disease due to higher rates of detection), such areas are also characterised as having more people suffering social isolation and greater problems with drugs and alcohol. The latter is perhaps best exemplified by the results for LDC as urbanisation was significant in all four LDC models. Although in aetiological terms alcohol is its most important direct determinant (and indeed, average population-level alcohol consumption was significant in each model), it suggests that European urban environments also entail greater exposure to certain risky behaviour.

3.6 Results II: Model Validation and Short-Term Scenarios for Total Mortality, Lung Cancer and Circulatory System Diseases Excluding Stroke

The time series models were validated by comparing the observed with the estimated SDR for each country and year that the models were based on. Taking the example of standardised male cancer mortality in Eastern Europe we know from equation 3 that $Y_{it} = \delta_i + \rho y_{it-1} + \beta X_{it-j} + \varepsilon_{it}$. Considering the model results in Table 3.7, male lung cancer mortality (SDR_{lung}) in Eastern Europe can be estimated using the following econometric model equation:

$$\begin{aligned}\mathrm{SDR}_{lung,t,i} &= \alpha_i + 0.843^{*}\mathrm{SDR}_{lung,t-1,i} - 3.714^{*}\mathrm{EDU}_{t-10,i}\\ &\quad + 0.157^{*}\mathrm{AG}_{t-5,i} + 0.906^{*}\mathrm{ALC}_{t-10,i} + 0.859^{*}\mathrm{URB}\end{aligned}$$

We can now estimate the lung cancer mortality rate in one of the modelled countries for any of the years during the study period (except the first year) using the known observed level of the year before and the specified exogenous characteristics at time t – lag j. For instance, the modelled lung cancer rate for the Ukraine in 1999 would be:

$$\begin{aligned}\mathrm{SDR}_{lung,1999,UA} &= -21.91 + 0.843^{*}84.58 - 3.714^{*}9.91 + 0.157^{*}21.76\\ &\quad + 0.906^{*}10.34 + 0.859^{*}68.42 = 84.12\end{aligned}$$

The actual value equalled 82.51, which amounts to a difference (ε, the disturbance) of + 1.61 deaths per population of 100,000 or + 1.9 %. Average model deviances

Table 3.8 Model validation: Maximum difference (absolute value) between observed and predicted SDR for total mortality, lung cancer and heart disease for the period from 2000 to 2005–2009 for men and women in 21 European countries. (Data source: Mortality: WHO (2011a). Note: Three-year moving averages were calculated from the modelled results in order to eliminate the most erratic residuals)

	Total mortality				Lung cancer				CIRC-ex-stroke			
	Male	Per cent	Female	Per cent	Male	Per cent	Female	Per cent	Male	Per cent	Female	Per cent
Western Europe												
Austria	19	2.2	7	1.4	3	5.1	1	3.8	14	5.5	9	6.2
Belgium	29	3.5	6	1.2	2	2.1	1	5.4	6	2.9	2	1.2
Switzerland	9	1.2	5	1.0	1	2.8	1	4.6	6	3.2	2	2.2
Denmark	23	2.8	22	3.7	2	2.9	2	4.7	17	8.5	11	10.0
Finland	28	3.5	26	5.7	2	4.2	1	4.5	4	1.4	7	5.5
France	29	3.6	31	6.8	1	1.4	1	3.5	3	1.8	3	4.0
Greece	24	3.3	20	4.1	1	1.2	1	4.8	8	4.0	5	3.4
Italy	14	1.8	8	1.7	2	2.4	1	4.3	15	8.5	10	8.6
Netherlands	32	3.8	30	5.4	2	2.3	2	9.9	4	2.0	5	4.3
Norway	40	5.4	9	2.0	2	4.1	1	5.4	18	9.0	10	8.5
Sweden	47	7.1	20	4.5	2	6.1	1	6.2	10	4.1	6	4.9
UK	21	2.7	18	3.4	3	5.4	1	2.2	10	4.8	7	6.1
Eastern Europe												
Bulgaria	39	2.8	48	6.1	6	8.5	2	14.5	19	2.9	12	3.3
Belarus	51	2.8	82	9.8	4	5.3	0	4.3	37	4.9	21	6.7
Czech Repub.	70	7.0	57	9.6	3	4.8	1	4.9	22	5.0	14	5.8
Estonia	133	9.2	35	6.6	12	13.1	2	14.4	44	8.1	25	11.4
Hungary	89	6.3	63	8.7	10	8.6	3	9.4	32	6.8	23	7.5
Latvia	165	10.4	46	6.4	4	4.7	1	13.8	50	8.6	28	10.0
Russia	164	7.5	45	4.3	4	4.6	0	1.5	54	6.9	14	3.6
Slovak Repub.	249	20.1	26	3.6	7	8.5	2	14.0	44	8.2	18	4.9
Ukraine	79	4.2	52	5.6	4	6.3	1	9.0	50	5.8	20	4.0

for each country for total mortality, lung cancer and CIRC-ex-stroke are given in Table 3.8.

A more useful way to validate the cause-specific mortality models would be to model mortality for several years beyond the sample range of the explanatory model. Here this was done for up to a decade, i.e. to the latest year for which the WHO had mortality data available (Table 3.1). One should bear in mind that this also requires the acquisition of additional years of data for the exogenous variables (up to the same year as the mortality data if no time lag is used). Model validation is nothing more than producing short-term forecasts by introducing the required variable values into the earlier-made models. To illustrate this with the same example as before, the observed lung cancer rate for the Ukraine in 2009 was 62.74. According to the model results the SDR was:

$$\begin{aligned} \mathrm{SDR}_{lung,2009,UA} &= -21.91 + 0.846^{*}63.57 - 3.714^{*}10.52 + 0.157^{*}23.85 \\ &\quad + 0.906^{*}11.43 + 0.859^{*}68.39 = 65.60 \end{aligned}$$

Considering that the variable coefficients are derived from a model that includes a total of 9 countries, that in the Ukraine agricultural employment actually increased between 1989 and 1999 and alcohol consumption increased more than the Eastern European average (both variables were lagged 10 years), the fact that lung cancer mortality declined more during the first decade of the twenty-first century than what was estimated by the model suggests a slight underspecification of the model. It may be partly because the effect of smoking could not be directly tested, only indirectly through the known educational, occupational and urban-rural differences in smoking. Nevertheless, as we shall see, for both total mortality and the two causes of death investigated, the differences between the modelled and actual values are generally very small.

Regarding the two short-term scenarios from the mid-to-late 2000s to 2020 based on the model results that used data from around 1980 to 1999, but including the latest (i.e. 2000 to 2005–2009) SDR for the mortality at time $t-1$ variable, the plausibility of the results is mixed. In the majority of cases the projected trend is a continuation of current mortality levels. Male levels of lung cancer mortality are in most instances quickly approaching the levels for women, as male rates have been declining since the 1980s or 1990s (depending on the country), and female rates have been increasing since the 1970s (especially in Western Europe), although they are set to level off in the near future. With regard to total and non-stroke circulatory system disease mortality in both Western Europe and the Czech Republic, rates have been declining over the last three decades, but this decline has been more pronounced among men and is predicted to continue. In fact, some countries show the unlikely scenario that men will have lower mortality than women by the year 2015 (Belgium, France, the Netherlands in CIRC-ex-stroke and the Czech and Slovak Republics in total mortality). On several other occasions the projected trend is opposite to the trend according to recent observations (e.g. lung cancer in Belarus and the Ukraine is set to increase after 10–15 years of continuing decline), but this is likely to be due to less credible projected values for some of the exogenous variables. In addition, while disturbances were most often small as the model includes mortality in the previous year, when they were large and fluctuated from being positive to negative this was in part due to large yearly fluctuations in mortality and/or in the exogenous variables. This applied particularly to Eastern European countries. The main findings may be summarised as followed.

3.6.1 *Total Mortality*

Although the modelled values for the West European countries appear to coincide almost perfectly with the observed ones within the range used to construct the models, this is not entirely the case, as the scaling of the graphs obscures some of the differences (Fig. 3.1). The maximum deviance that was recorded was around 3.7 % for men (Dutch males, 1978), equivalent to about 27 deaths per population of 100,000, and 4.4 % for women (French women, 1999), equivalent to about 20 deaths population

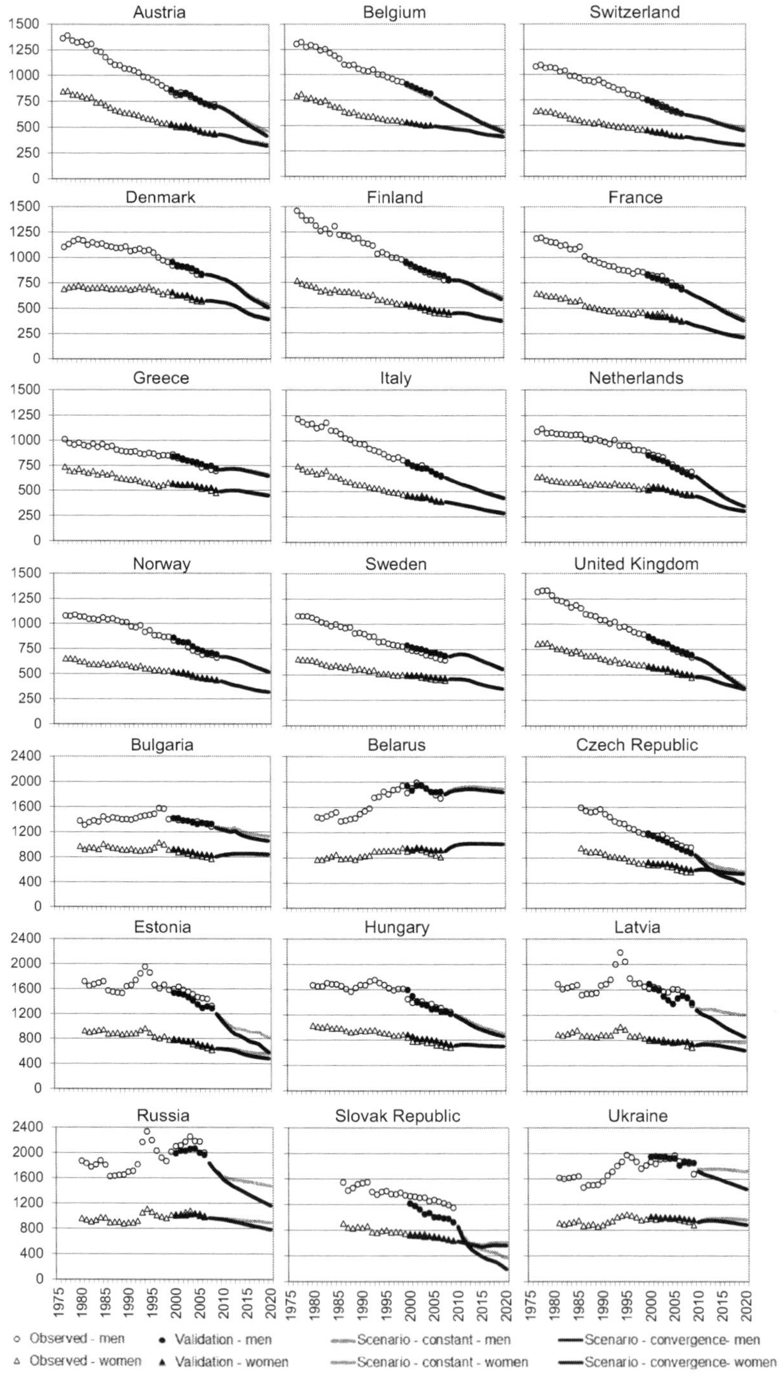

Fig. 3.1 Observed and modelled total mortality rate for a selection of Western and Eastern European countries, 1977/81–2020

of 100,000. Differences were also quite limited with regard to the 6–10 additional years that were used to validate the models (see Table 3.8). The most obvious discrepancies were for French women (lower decline than predicted) and Swedish men (higher decline than predicted). By contrast, there were larger differences between the observed and modelled values for Eastern Europe. Maximum relative differences were 7.8 % for Russian men (1993) and 5.0 % for Estonian women (also 1993), exactly when mortality was at its highest point. Absolute differences were therefore much higher than observed for Western Europe (in these two cases respectively 164 and 47 deaths per population of 100,000). As one of the most important variables used to predict mortality for one year was the mortality rate of the year before, this difference is not so surprising when there are large annual changes in the mortality rate as was the case here. For this reason the predicted levels of mortality for the latest available years were also different from the observed levels when there was a sudden trend break, although the modelled values generally followed the same trend as observed, albeit with a year's delay and a less acute mortality change. See, for instance, the result for Russian men. With respect to the forecasts, male total mortality in Western Europe is set to continue its decline as observed since the late 1970s. In some instances, this decline in the short term may be accelerated (e.g. in Austria, the Netherlands and the UK) or continue at a slower pace (e.g. Greece). Female mortality is less likely to decline very rapidly and its current trend may level off (Greece). With respect to Eastern Europe most countries in the sample have clearly recovered from the mortality crisis of the 1990s, although in about half the countries their mortality levels are still above that of the mid-1980s. Nevertheless, predictions are that most mortality levels will continue to decline at a similar pace. Exceptions are Belarus, where only a slight decline has taken place, but levels are predicted to increase slightly until the early 2010s (both sexes); and Bulgaria, Czech Republic, Hungary and Latvia where the decline observed during the last decades is predicted to come to a halt. Finally, the large sex-differences that exist in the absolute level of total mortality in Eastern Europe are set to decline or even disappear as the predicted relative mortality change until 2010 is larger for men than for women. Exceptions are Belarus under both scenarios, as well as Latvia, Russia and the Ukraine under the constant scenario.

3.6.2 Lung Cancer

Although the quality of the smoking variable in the Western European analysis for lung cancer was not optimal, the absolute difference between the observed and modelled values was never more than 3 deaths per population of 100,000 for men and 2 for women, although due to the very low level of mortality among women in most countries, relative differences were usually larger than observed for men (a maximum of 9.5 % in Norway, in 1978) (Fig. 3.2). Even though no smoking data were used to model the Eastern European data, the modelled rates were also very similar to what was observed with maximum differences of 6 deaths per 100,000 for men

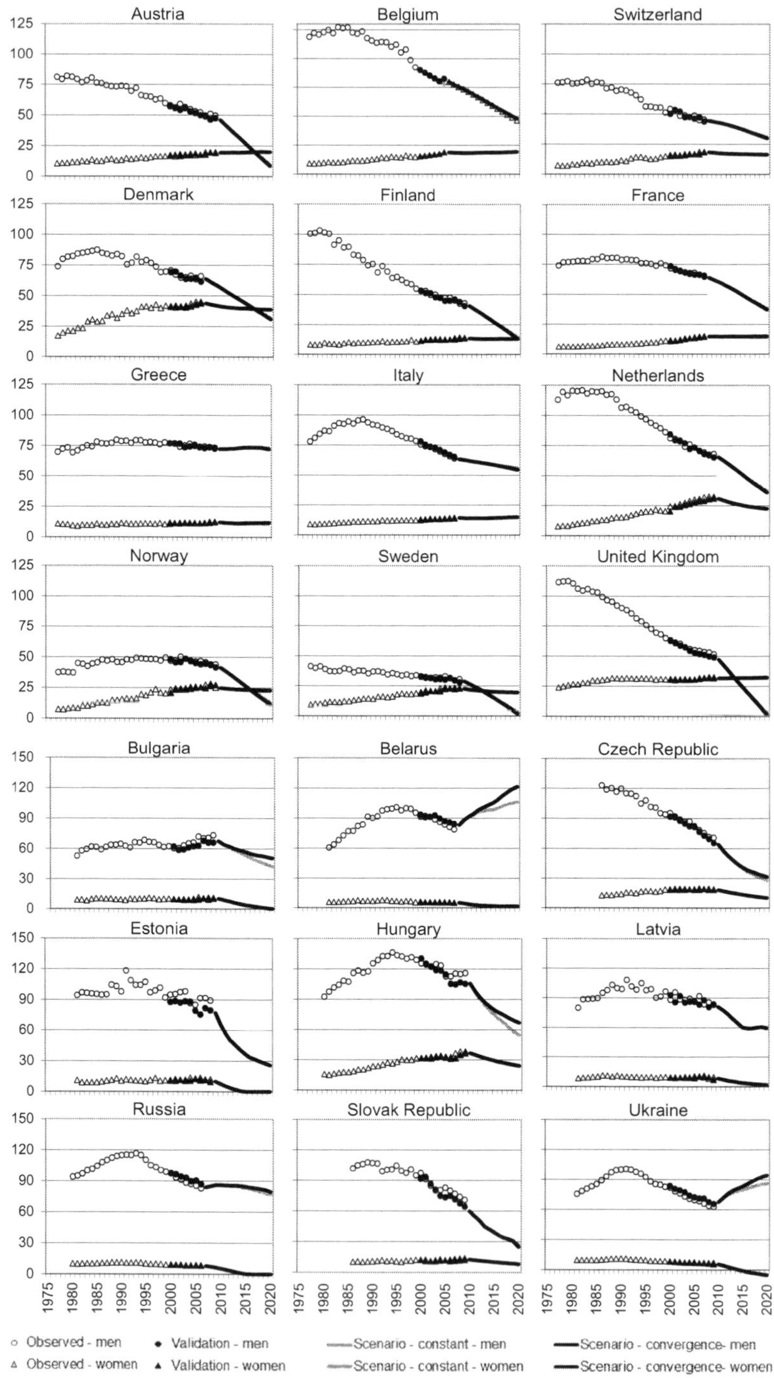

Fig. 3.2 Observed and modelled lung mortality rate for Western and Eastern European countries, 1977/81–2020

(Latvia, 1984) and 1.3 per 100,000 for women (Estonia, 1983), when the lung cancer mortality rate was between 60 and 130 for East European men and 5 and 30 for East European women. During the 1990s most West European countries began to see a drop in male lung cancer mortality. According to the forecasts, this is set to continue in the same linear fashion in the second half of the current decade. In Norway, where mortality levels between the late 1980s and early 2000s was stable at just under 50 deaths per population of 100,000, the recent decline that can be observed is set to intensify during the forecast period. West European women experienced a different smoking pattern than did men, as smoking was popularised much later. For this reason, lung cancer mortality levels are still increasing in most countries, although a levelling off has either been recently observed or is predicted for the near future. For Denmark, Sweden and the Netherlands a small decline is even predicted. While gender differences were very large for some countries in the beginning of the sample period, up to more than 100 deaths per population of 100,000 for Belgium, Finland and the UK, 30 years later this difference is decreasing fast and in the case of Norway, Sweden and the UK, is set to converge between 2010 and 2015. In Eastern Europe, the male lung cancer epidemic was at its height somewhat later and with generally higher levels than in Western Europe. Predictions are diverse: In Russia a levelling off in the recent decline is suggested, while in the Ukraine and Belarus an increase is predicted (although this may be due to model misspecification). In the remaining countries it is predicted that the declining trend will continue. Female mortality levels are generally lower in the East than in the West and for most countries the current and predicted trend suggests a levelling off of the increase or even a slight decline in the mortality rate. In fact, with the exception of the two anomalous countries, the pattern (but not absolute levels) of the current and predicted lung cancer mortality rate is very similar for men and women.

3.6.3 Circulatory System Diseases Excluding Stroke

What is striking with regard to the trend in CIRC-ex-stroke within Western Europe from the late 1970s until the latest available year (about 2009), with the exception of Greece, is the uniformity (i.e. continual decline) not only between the countries, but also between men and women. The difference between the observed and predicted values was therefore usually no more than a few percentage points and the model fitted the data for the additional years very well (Fig. 3.3). For example, the absolute difference in Finland for the additional ten years that were obtained to validate the model was never more than 4 deaths per population of 100,000 (or 1.4 %) among men or 7/100,000 (or 5.5 %) among women. In Eastern Europe, some countries (e.g. Estonia and Latvia) have shown signs of recovery over the last decade after the abrupt increases in the early 1990s. In others (e.g. Russia) mortality continued to increase until the mid-2000s, while in the Czech and Slovak Republics and Hungary circulatory system diseases have steadily declined since the mid-1980s. Due to the different patterns, the differences between the observed and modelled

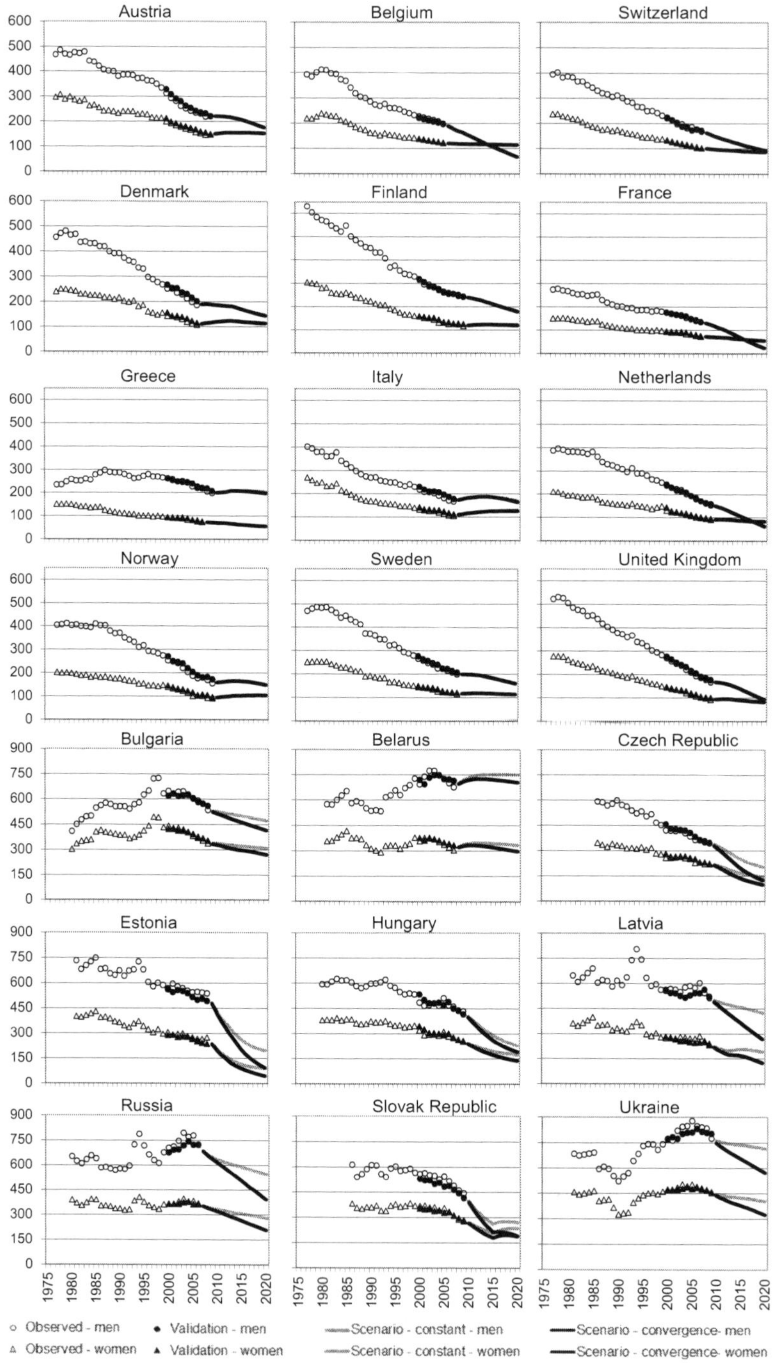

Fig. 3.3 Observed and modelled mortality from circulatory system diseases without stroke rate for Western and Eastern European countries, 1977/81–2020

rates are larger than in Western Europe, although there are no great deviations from the general mortality trend. Differences are largest around the period of sudden increases or decreases in mortality when the modelled trend tends to lag a year behind the observed trend. Only with regard to Latvian and Ukrainian men did the observed morality rate for the validation years not quite follow the modelled rate.

With regard to the projected rates, there are basically three trends. The first is a continuation of the decline that was observed throughout the entire study period in most of the Western European countries. The second observed trend is a levelling off in the rate of decline. In the case of Italy, where current rates are already low, this may suggest that, at least in the short term, possible further gains in survival from this disease are limited. In the case of Austria and Denmark this appears to be the effect of smoking, which hampers further decline. With regard to Belarus, where this trend is also predicted even though current levels are still relatively high, it may suggest that the social and economic conditions are still not such as to allow circulatory system diseases to continue their rapid decline. This is also reflected in the differences that are observed between the static and convergence scenarios (this also applies to several other countries): according to the static scenario the exogenous variables remain at the same level throughout the predicted period while in the convergence scenario conditions will become more similar to the best performing European country, so that mortality will also be lower. The third observed trend is the sudden decline that is predicted in most East European countries, where the mortality rate has only recently shown signs of recovery or which will take place during the predicted period. Again, while absolute sex differences in mortality from CIRC-ex-stroke are large, the observed and proposed trends for men and for women are similar.

3.7 Summary and Conclusion

The main purpose of this chapter was to test cause-specific mortality models that were based on both mortality indicators and exogenous variables. These time series models were adapted from earlier research that assessed the importance of socioeconomic and other factors on mortality differences across Europe over time and between countries to determine which factors should be incorporated into future mortality scenarios (Spijker 2004). The time frame of the explanatory analysis was from 1977 (Western Europe)/1981(Eastern Europe) to 1999, with forecasts to 2020 for which the period 2000 to 2005–2009 (depending on the country) served to validate the models. Model validation was done by constructing econometric model equations based on the model results, estimating mortality for the validation period and comparing these with the observed SDR for the same years. The required mortality and population data were obtained from the WHO Mortality Database. Subsequently, two types of short-term scenarios were produced on the basis of the results of the same models, although the observed 2000 to 2005–2009 SDR were used as input for the mortality at time $t - 1$ variable. The first scenario was based on the premise that the values of the exogenous variables would not change after 2009 and the second that levels would converge between countries. Western and Eastern Europe and men and women were analysed separately. Because of the time lag between exposure and health effects of a particular variable, which, in the case of most causes of death is often a matter of years, few differences were observed for the two scenarios. The exception was several Eastern European models as fewer variables were lagged.

Besides total mortality, causes of death were also analysed: nine groups of causes for the modelling exercise and two, i.e. lung cancer and heart disease, for the model validation and short-term scenarios. The reason for studying causes of death is that they provide knowledge of disease determinants and can therefore be considered as the first step towards possible explanation for mortality differences. For projection purposes, too, cause-specific rather than total mortality trends have been preferred in the past, particularly for short-term forecasting, because of the simplicity of the parameterisation functions for mortality by cause and also the fact that epidemiological knowledge can be used in formulating hypotheses (Tabeau et al. 2001).

Another important aspect of the analysis was pooling the countries. Due to the different political and economic histories of Eastern and Western Europe, several exogenous variables were not considered as being comparable, and the analysis was therefore split into two. For a future analysis that uses more recent data for the modelling component, however, Eastern Europe could also be split into a Central European and a former Soviet Union cluster as mortality trends, especially in Russia and the Ukraine, have diverged from the rest of Eastern Europe since the early 1990s when mortality first increased more acutely and its recuperation since then has been slower. Another option worth looking at is to model countries that have experienced sudden health and economic changes separately. However, further clustering Western Europe would lead, perhaps, to groups of countries which are so homogeneous that certain variables will become unimportant in explaining within-cluster differences even though they are known to cause international mortality differences (e.g. dietary factors when only analysing Mediterranean countries).

One important contribution of this chapter, and is one that is worth exploring in more detail, is the use of lung cancer mortality as an indicator for life-time smoking exposure for the modelling and projection of total mortality and smoking-related causes of death. Although this meant that the coefficient for tobacco consumption in the lung cancer model could not be compared with the other models, it was considered to be a more reliable smoking indicator than when annual tobacco consumption data are used. Another contribution was the simultaneous testing of the positive long-term and negative short-term health effect of alcohol for total mortality and circulatory system diseases excluding stroke, although on no occasion were both significant in the same model.

Regarding the results, the most important independent variable is mortality at time $t-1$. It was a conscious decision to include this as one of the explanatory variables given that under normal conditions mortality does not change radically from one year to the next, because intrinsically, the timing of death is determined by a multitude of factors across the life course, some of which originate even before birth and which cannot be unveiled with cross-sectional population-level data. On the other hand, it was thought that the yearly fluctuations in mortality or gradual changes could be modelled by non-demographic variables, as these would be the result from more short-term economic, social and behavioural changes. Thus it was not surprising to see that the variable lag times that were calculated for the Eastern European models were often shorter than in Western Europe due to the economic, political and social uncertainties there in the 1990s. This particularly pertained to the economic variables, GDPc and income inequality, the latter of which even had an impact on total mortality among women, even though income inequality has only been high in recent years. This said, the direct association (i.e. without a time lag) during the 1980s and 1990s in Eastern Europe between macro-economic indicators and mortality is likely to change in future if both mortality and the independent variables change less abruptly over time. In contrast, with the economic crisis that has hit much of Europe since 2008 it would be interesting to see if certain macro-economic indicators now have a direct effect on specific causes of death in Western Europe. Indeed, if GDPc has both short- and long-term effects on health and mortality, the econometric model equation used for forecasting should incorporate GDPc twice: lagged and not lagged.

With regard to the models, each exogenous variable was significant in one or more of the cause-specific models, thus indicating that not only economic factors play a role in explaining mortality differences over time and between countries, but also social, environmental and behavioural factors. This is true not only for men, but also for women, and in different types of political and economic settings.

For total mortality, lung cancer and heart disease, model values were tested against the data stretching from 1977/1981 to 1999, as well as up to the most recently available data in order to ascertain if the models could also be applied beyond the sample range. For total mortality differences there were no more than 86 deaths per population of 100,000 (6.6 %) in the West European sample countries (men, Finland 1985), though larger discrepancies between the observed and modelled values were observed for several of the East European countries (e.g. 259 deaths/100,000 or 12.0 % in 1993 for Russian men). This was particularly the case around the years of mortality crisis and recovery, although only in terms of the magnitude and timing of the mortality change, as in general the modelled mortality trend was in the right direction. Results showed that in Western Europe, male mortality is set to continue its decline as observed since the late 1970s at about the same speed or at a slightly slower pace, while the current decline in female mortality may level off in some countries or, as in the case of Greece, mortality may even increase.

In Eastern Europe total mortality is predicted to continue its decline since the mid- to late 1990s, with Belarus, Hungary and Russia as exceptions. Overall, there is still little sign of a narrowing of the sex difference in total mortality in Eastern Europe as is the case in Western Europe, even for the forecast period. With respect to lung cancer, the most obvious result was that sex differences in mortality have already narrowed drastically in most West European countries and are predicted to converge in Austria, the Scandinavian countries and the UK, as male mortality continues to decline and female mortality continues to rise or level off. In Eastern Europe, lung cancer mortality is still a relatively unimportant cause of death among women, while male levels are generally higher than in Western Europe, and show little sign of declining in the near future. Also with regard to heart disease there were few differences between the modelled and observed mortality rates for the Western European models. The declining trend that is observed for most countries is set to continue, albeit at a slower pace in those countries with already low levels, particularly among women. Results could indicate a minimum level of about 75 deaths per population of 100,000 in the future, at least for women, although male levels are slowly converging. The latter also applies to Eastern Europe, but levels are still much higher there. Nevertheless, unlike total mortality, a continuation of the current decline is projected for all countries and for both men and women.

The aim now is to seek ways to further improve the methodology of modelling cause-specific mortality with non-demographic variables and to integrate the results into a multidisciplinary population projection. It may be that the models are too general, as we know from the concept of competing causes of death and the associated problem of inaccuracies of the cause-of-death statistic, that particularly at very old ages, the underlying cause of death is less the result of a clearly-defined aetiological (causal) path than the random result of a more generalised deterioration of the capacity for life (Rosenberg, 1993). Therefore, because mortality from chronic diseases increases with age and in an ageing population such as that of Europe, most mortality occurs at old age, it may be preferable to exclude deaths above the age of 85 or 90 and model only all-cause mortality for the oldest-old. Other age-groups should also be modelled separately, such as ages 0, 1–24, 25–64, 65–84, as the models include exogenous variables and a variable will not have the same association with each age, e.g. unemployment has little relevance for the non-working age population, or the meaning of the association changes with age, e.g. industrial employment for infant mortality may be an indicator of the parental socioeconomic context, while for adults this may indicate their own socioeconomic context. Other robustness tests, such as splitting up the modelled period, should also be performed.

Mortality trends usually don't fluctuate from year to year, which is why the level of mortality in the previous year was the most important variable in the time series models. Although trend extrapolation is often used in mortality forecasts, health-related exogenous variables have not been used for modelling short-term mortality forecasts. Yet process-oriented forecasts would seem a more valid form than standard practice. Furthermore, the modelled results from the 5–10 year validation period proved to be very accurate in most cases and the short-term scenarios up to about 2015 plausible for most countries. Indeed, one important advantage of short-term forecasts is that values of the exogenous variables are already known for those variables for which a time lag has to be incorporated, meaning that both total mortality and specific causes of death can be accurately estimated for about 10–15 years ahead. This should, of course, be of great interest to policy makers concerned with public health and medical care, although models constructed for future forecasts should really be based on the latest available data rather than having a "validation period" of up to a decade as presented here (as this study is principally methodological) as well as including some measure of uncertainty. Modelling up to an earlier period can then be done to develop and test the model. Thus, in order to obtain plausible results for all of the studied countries and causes of death, some fine tuning is still required.

Appendix

Table A.1 Countries and years for which cause-specific mortality and population data were obtained[a]

	77	78	79	80	81	82	83	84	85	86	87	88	89	90	91	92	93	94	95	96	97	98	99	00	01	02	03	04	05	06	07	08	09
Western Europe																																	
Austria	8	8	8	9	9	9	9	9	9	9	9	9	9	9	9	9	9	9	9	9	9	9	9	*9*	*9*	*10*	*10*	*10*	*10*	*10*	*10*	*10*	*10*
Belgium	8	8	9	9	9	9	9	9	9	9	9	9	9	9	9	9	9	9	9	9	9	10	10	*E*	*E*	*E*	*E*	*10*	*10*				
Denmark	8	8	8	8	8	8	8	8	8	8	8	8	8	8	8	8	8	10	10	10	10	10	10	*10*	*10*	*10*	*10*	*10*	*10*	*10*			
FRG	8	8	9	9	9	9	9	9	9	9	9	9	9	9																			
Finland	8	8	8	8	8	8	8	8	8	8	9	9	9	9	9	9	9	9	9	10	10	10	10	*10*	*10*	*10*	*10*	*10*	*10*	*10*	*10*	*10*	*10*
France	8	8	9	9	9	9	9	9	9	9	9	9	9	9	9	9	9	9	9	9	9	9	9	*10*	*10*	*10*	*10*	*10*	*10*	*10*	*10*		
Greece	8	8	9	9	9	9	9	9	9	9	9	9	9	9	9	9	9	9	9	9	9	9	9	*9*	*9*	*9*	*10*	*10*	*10*	*10*	*10*	*10*	*10*
Italy	8	8	9	9	9	9	9	9	9	9	9	9	9	9	9	9	9	9	9	9	9	9	9	*9*	*9*	*9*	*10*	*E*	*E*	*10*	*10*		
Netherlands	8	8	9	9	9	9	9	9	9	9	9	9	9	9	9	9	9	9	9	10	10	10	10	*10*	*10*	*10*	*10*	*10*	*10*	*10*	*10*	*10*	*10*
Norway	8	8	8	8	8	8	8	8	8	9	9	9	9	9	9	9	9	9	9	10	10	10	10	*10*	*10*	*10*	*10*	*10*	*10*	*10*	*10*	*10*	*10*
Sweden	8	8	8	8	8	8	8	8	8	8	9	9	9	9	9	9	9	9	9	9	10	10	10	*10*	*10*	*10*	*10*	*10*	*10*	*10*	*10*	*10*	
Switzerland	8	8	8	8	8	8	8	8	8	8	8	8	8	8	8	8	8	8	10	10	10	10	10	*10*	*10*	*10*	*10*	*10*	*10*	*10*	*10*		
UK	8	8	9	9	9	9	9	9	9	9	9	9	9	9	9	9	9	9	9	9	9	9	9	*E*	*10*	*10*	*10*	*10*	*10*	*10*	*10*	*10*	*10*
Eastern Europe																																	
Belarus					9	9	E	E	9	9	9	9	9	9	E	9	9	9	9	9	9	9	9	*9*	*9*	*10*	*10*	*E*	*E*	*E*	*10*		
Bulgaria					9	9	9	9	9	9	9	9	9	9	9	9	9	9	9	9	9	9	9	*9*	*9*	*9*	*9*	*E*	*10*	*10*	*10*	*10*	
Czechoslovakia					9	9	9	9	9	9	9	9	9	9	9																		
Czech Rep.										9	9	9	9	9	9	9	9	10	10	10	10	10	10	*10*	*10*	*10*	*10*	*10*	*10*	*10*	*10*	*10*	*10*
Slovak Rep.										E	E	E	E	E	E	9	9	10	10	10	10	10	10	*10*	*10*	*10*	*10*	*10*	*10*	*E*	*E*	*10*	*10*

Table A.1 (continued)

	77	78	79	80	81	82	83	84	85	86	87	88	89	90	91	92	93	94	95	96	97	98	99	00	01	02	03	04	05	06	07	08	09
Estonia					9	9	E	E	9	9	9	9	9	9	9	9	9	9	9	9	10	10	10	*10*	*10*	*10*	*10*	*10*	*10*	*10*	*10*	*10*	
GDR					9	9	9	9	9	9	9	9	9	9																			
Hungary					9	9	9	9	9	9	9	9	9	9	9	9	9	9	9	10	10	10	10	*10*	*10*	*10*	*10*	*10*	*10*	*10*	*10*	*10*	*10*
Latvia					9	9	E	E	9	9	9	9	9	9	9	9	9	9	9	10	10	10	10	*10*	*10*	*10*	*10*	*10*	*10*	*10*	*10*	*10*	*10*
Russian Fed.					9	9	9	9	9	9	9	9	9	9	9	9	9	9	9	9	9	9	10	*10*	*10*	*10*	*10*	*10*	*10*	*10*			
Ukraine					9	9	E	E	9	9	9	9	9	9	9	9	9	9	9	9	9	9	9	*9*	*9*	*9*	*9*	*9*	*10*	*10*	*E*	*10*	*10*

[a]In the "year" columns, "8", "9", and "10" refer to the mortality data that were classified according to the ICD-8 (A-list), ICD-9 (B-list and country-specific codes for Switzerland and the New Independent States), and ICD-10 revisions. The Slovak data for 1986–91 were obtained by subtracting the number of deaths and population of the Czech Republic from the data that were obtained for Czechoslovakia. For these years, Czechoslovakia was excluded from the main analysis. Data for missing years were interpolated when data for surrounding years were available (e.g. Belarus 1983 $= 1982 + 1/3^*(1985 - 1982)$). Up to 1999 the data were used for the construction of the cause-of-death models while the years in italics were used for the validation analysis. Population data were obtained for the same years as the mortality data. E = estimated

Table A.2 Short- and long-term elasticities for male and female cause-specific mortality in Western and Eastern Europe[a]

	Total mortality	Lune cancer	Prostate Cancer	Other cancer	CIRC-ex stroke	Stroke	Respiratory	LDC	Traffic accidents	Suicide
Western Europe, men										
lnGDP	−0.09/−0.29	−0.05/−1.13	0.11/0.41			−0.08/−0.48	−0.50/−0.78		−0.15/−0.51	−0.06/−0.41
GINI					0.05/0.48		0.14/0.23	0.11/1.01		
EDU					−0.06/−0.64					
IND	0.04/0.13			0.05/0.22	0.09/0.87				0.22/0.77	
AG		−0.02/−0.46	0.04/0.13	0.02/0.11	−0.02/−0.19		−0.09/−0.14		−0.06/−0.22	−0.02/−0.11
DIV			0.01/0.04			0.02/0.09	0.07/0.11	0.01/0.06	0.02/0.06	
ALC no lag	0.05/0.17					0.07/0.42		0.20/1.81	0.08/0.26	0.04/0.26
ALC lagged					−0.02/−0.21		0.12/0.19			
POL	0.02/0.07						0.03/0.04			
URB							0.32/0.50	0.13/1.14	−0.29/−1.01	−0.35/−2.24
UNEMP				0.01/0.04					−0.04/−0.13	
TOBAC	0.09/0.31	0.02/0.45		0.03/0.13	0.03/0.33	0.07/0.42	0.20/0.31			
FRUIT		−0.04/−0.88	−0.04/−0.13							
HCGDP		−0.03/−0.83	−0.04/−0.13	−0.03/−0.12					−0.05/−0.18	
Western Europe, women										
lnGDP	−0.12/−0.38	0.07/0.49		−0.02/−0.13		−0.14/−0.85	−0.55/−0.83		−0.31/−0.71	−0.07/−0.40
GINI							0.15/0.23	0.13/0.60		
EDU						0.14/0.80				−0.24/−1.41
IND	0.10/0.32		0.17/1.69	0.07/0.43	0.11/0.90	0.11/0.62			0.44/1.01	0.13/0.79
AG		0.06/0.38	−0.02/−0.19	−0.02/−0.1			−0.05/−0.08		−0.09/−0.21	−0.06/−0.35
DIV	0.01/0.03	0.02/0.12	0.02/0.18			0.02/0.09	0.09/0.14		0.05/0.11	0.03/0.20
ALC no lag	0.04/0.12							0.32/1.53		0.07/0.41
ALC laeeed				0.02/0.12	−0.02/−0.14		0.13/0.20			
POL	0.02/0.08									
URB		0.22/1.53		−0.06/−0.4		−0.17/−1.00		0.26/1.22	−0.43/−0.99	
IJNEMP				0.01/0.04			0.06/0.08		−0.07/−0.15	
TOBAC	0.03/0.09	0.06/0.42				0.02/0.10	0.20/0.30			
FRUIT										
HCGDP			−0.07/−0.69							

Table A.2 (continued)

	Total mortality	Lune cancer	Prostate Cancer	Other cancer	CIRC-ex stroke	Stroke	Respiratory	LDC	Traffic accidents	Suicide
Eastern Europe, men										
lnGDP	− 0.08/− 0.18			− 0.05/− 0.10	− 0.08/− 0.27				0.23/0.76	− 0.22/− 0.57
GINI					0.05/0.14		0.08/0.17	0.20/0.71	0.08/0.25	
EDU			0.78/1.19		− 0.27/− 0.84	− 0.18/− 0.56	− 0.44/− 1.00			
IND	0.28/0.61		0.45/0.68	0.34/0.73		0.28/0.87	0.17/0.40	0.39/1.43	0.26/0.85	0.35/0.91
AG	0.11/0.23	0.03/0.18	0.16/0.24					0.08/0.28		0.12/0.30
DIV			0.04/0.07	0.04/0.09			0.07/0.16	0.05/0.20		0.23/0.62
ALC no lae	0.18/0.40				0.13/0.41	0.13/0.41	0.23/0.53	0.20/0.71	0.16/0.53	0.17/0.44
ALC laeeed		0.12/0.77		0.02/0.04						
URB	0.93/2.04	0.61/3.87	0.52/0.80	− 0.22/− 0.47	0.63/1.98	0.63/2.00	− 1.55/− 3.53	0.44/1.58	1.67/5.48	
UNEMP						0.004/0.01		0.01/0.03		
TOBAC	0.09/0.21			0.20/0.43	0.06/0.19		0.28/0.64			
Eastern Europe, women										
lnGDP	− 0.03/− 0.08	0.14/2.61	− 0.11/− 0.39	− 0.08/− 0.17	− 0.10/− 0.30		0.19/0.32	0.08/0.23	0.25/0.64	
GINI	0.05/0.11							0.20/0.57	0.09/0.22	
EDU	− 0.23/− 0.56	− 0.43/− 7.91	0.33/1.22		− 0.37/− 1.07	− 0.24/− 0.91	− 0.29/− 0.48			− 0.34/− 0.95
IND	0.05/0.12			0.30/0.64		0.05/0.18	0.30/0.50	0.38/1.10	0.17/0.43	0.11/0.32
AG				0.11/0.25			0.14/0.23	0.17/0.50		0.07/0.21
DIV			0.11/0.39					0.17/0.48		0.15/0.41
ALC no lae	0.11/0.25				0.07/0.20	0.08/0.32		0.26/0.77	0.28/0.72	0.06/0.16
ALC laeeed		0.05/0.99		0.06/0.13						
URB	0.66/1.56		0.33/1.23		0.48/1.39	0.47/1.79	− 4.93/− 8.26	0.98/2.85	1.62/4.10	
UNEMP					0.003/0.01					
TOBAC				0.09/0.18						

[a] See Table 3.3 for the definitions of the exogenous variables and Tables 3.6 and 3.7 for the model coefficients

References

Abel, G. J., Bijak, J., Forster, J. J., Raymer, J., & Smith, P. W. F. (2010). What do Bayesian methods offer population forecasters? Centre for population change working paper 6/2010. ESRC Centre for Population Change, University of Southampton.

Alho, J. M., & Spencer, B. D. (1985). Uncertain Population Forecasting. *Journal of the American Statistical Association, 80*(390), 306–314.

Artalejo, F. R., Guallar-Castillon, P., Banegas-Banegas, J. R., de Andres-Manzano B., & del, Rey-CaleroJ. (1998). Consumption of fruit and wine and the decline in cerebrovasuclar disease mortality in Spain (1975–1993). *Stroke; a journal of cerebral circulation, 29,* 1556–1561.

Barendregt, J. J., Van Oortmarssen, G. J., Van Hout, B. A., Van Den Bosch, J. M., & Bonneux, L. (1998). Coping with multiple morbidity in a life table. *Mathematical Population Studies, 7*(1), 29–49. doi:10.1080/08898489809525445.

Barendregt, J. J., Looman, C. W. N., & Brom-Hansen, H. (2002). Comparison of cohort smoking in Denmark and The Netherlands. *Bulletin of the WHO, 80*(1), 26–32.

Barro, R. J., & Lee, J.-W. (2000). International data on educational attainment: Updates and implications. CID Working Paper 42. Boston MA, USA.

Barro, R. J., & Lee, J.-W. (2011). Educational Attainment for Total Population, 1950–2010. v. 1. 2, 09/11 http://www.barrolee.com. Accessed 27 Dec 2011.

Booth, H., Hyndman, R. J., Tickie, L., & De Jong, P. (2006). Lee-Carter mortality forecasting: A multi-country comparison of variants and extensions. *Demographic Research, 15,* 289–310.

Brook, R.D., B. Franklin, W. Cascio, Y. Hong, G. Howard, M. Lipsett, R. Luepker, M. Mittleman, J. Samet, S.C. Smith Jr, and I. Tager. (2004). Air pollution and cardiovascular disease: a statement for healthcare professionals from the Expert Panel on Population and Prevention Science of the American Heart Association. Circulation 21(109):2655–2671.

Český Statistický Úřad. (various years). Statistická ročenka České Republiky. CSO, Prague.

Chunn, J. L., Raftery, A. E., & Gerland, P. (2010). Bayesian Probabilistic Projections of Mortality. Paper presented at the Annual Meeting of the Population Association of America, Washington, D.C.

CIS STAT. (1998). CD-ROM 1998-3: Official Statistics of the Countries of the Commonwealth of Independent States. CIS STAT.

Council of Europe. (2001). *Recent demographic developments in Europe 2000.* Strasbourg: Council of Europe Publishing.

Davey Smith, G., Hart, C. L., Hole, D. J., MacKinnon, P., Gillis, C., Watt, G., Blane, D., & Hawthorne, V. M. (1998). Education and occupational social class: Which is the more important indicator of mortality risk? *Journal of Epidemiology and Community Health, 52,* 153–190.

European Commission. (2011). Eurostat database http://epp.eurostat.ec.europa.eu/portal/page/portal/statistics/search_database. Accessed 27 Dec 2011.

Federální Statistický Úřad. (various years). Statistická ročenka Československé Socialistické Republiky. CSO, Prague.

Flückiger, Y. (2002). Gini coefficents for Switzerland 1967–1991. Personal communication. Used with permission.

Gärtner, M. (2004). EUR macro data http://www1.fgn.unisg.ch/eurmacro1st/macrodata/datamtrx.html. Accessed 10 Jan 2006.

Girosi, F., & King, G. (2008). *Demographic forecasting.* Princeton: Princeton University Press.

Gravelle, H. (1998). How much of the relation between population mortality and unequal distribution of income is a statistical artefact? *British Medical Journal, 316*(7128), 382–385.

Gregory, P. R. (1997). Russia and the Ukraine. Policy innovations. http://www.policyinnovations.org/ideas/policy_library/data/01121. Accessed 30 Oct 2008.

Hart, C. L., Davey Smith, G., Hole, D. J., & Hawthorne, V. M. (1999). Alcohol consumption and mortality from all causes, coronary heart disease, and stroke: Results from a prospective cohort study of Scottish men with 21 years of follow up. *British Medical Journal, 318*(7200), 1725–1729.

Hu, Y., & Goldman, N. (1990). Mortality differentials by marital status: An international comparison. *Demography, 27*(2), 233–250.
ILO. (2002). Labour statistics database. http://laboursta.ilo.org. Accessed 15 Dec 2011.
Joung, I. M. A. (1996). Marital status and health: Descriptive and explanatory studies. Ph.D Thesis, Erasmus University Rotterdam, Rotterdam.
Judge, K. (1995). Income distribution and life expectancy: A critical appraisal. *British Medical Journal, 311*(7015), 1282–1285.
Keilman, N. (2001). Demography. Uncertain population forecasts. *Nature, 412*(6846), 490–491.
Keilman, N. (2003). Types of models for projecting mortality. In T. Bengsston & N. Keilman (Eds.), *Perspectives on mortality forecasting 1. Current practice*. Stockholm: Swedish National Social Insurance Board.
Kristenson, M., Kucinskienë, Z., Bergdahl, B., Calkauskas, H., Urmonas, V., & Orth-Gomér, K. (1998). Increased psychosocial strain in Lithuanian versus Swedish men: The LiVicordia study. *Psychosomatic Medicine, 60,* 277–282.
Kunst, A. E., Groenhof, F., Mackenbach, J. P., health Ewgosii. (1998). Occupational class and cause-specific mortality in middle aged men in 11 European countries: Comparison of population bases studies. *British Medical Journal, 316*, 1636–1642.
Law, M., & Wald, N. J. (1999). Why heart disease mortality is low in France: The time lag explanation. *British Medical Journal, 318*(7196), 1471–1480.
Lee, R. D., & Carter, L. R. (1992). Modeling and forecasting the time series of U.S. mortality. *Journal of the American Statistical Association, 87*(419), 659–671.
Lefohn, A. S., Husar, J. D., & Husar, R. B. (1999). Estimating historical anthropogenic global sulfur emission patterns for the period 1850–1990. *Atmospheric Environment, 33*(21), 3435–3444.
Li, N., & Lee, R. (2005). Coherent mortality forecasts for a group of populations: An extension of the Lee-Carter method. *Demography, 42*(3), 575–594.
Li, N., Lee, R., & Tuljapurkar, S. (2004). Using the Lee-Carter method to forecast mortality for populations with limited data. *International Statistical Review, 72*(1), 19–36.
Liu, S. (2003). Is intake of breakfast cereals related to total and cause-specific mortality in men? *American Journal of Clinical Nutrition, 77*(3), 594–599.
Lundin, A., Lundberg, I., Hallsten, L., Ottosson, J., & Hemmingsson, T. (2010). Unemployment and mortality—A longitudinal prospective study on selection and causation in 49321 Swedish middle-aged men. *Journal of Epidemiology & Community Health, 64,* 22–28.
Mackenbach, J. P., & Looman, C. W. N. (1994). Living standards and mortality in the European Community. *Journal of Epidemiology and Community Health, 48,* 140–145.
Manton, K. G., & Stallard, E. (1984). *Recent trends in mortality analysis*. London: Academic Press.
Meslé, F., & Vallin, J. (2002). Mortality in Europe: The divergence between East and West. *Population-E, 57*(1), 157–198.
Murray, C. J. L., & Lopez, A. D. (1996). Estimating causes of death: New methods and global and regional applications for 1990. In C. J. L. Murray & A. D. Lopez (Eds.), *Global burden of disease and injury series: Volume I: The global burden of disease: A comprehensive assessment and disability from diseases, injuries, and risk factors in 1990 and projected to 2020*. Cambridge: Harvard University Press.
Nolte, E., & McKee, M. (2003). Measuring the health of nations: Analysis of mortality amenable to health care. *British Medical Journal, 327*(7424), 1129–1132.
OECD. (1999). *Historical statistics 1960/97 (1999 Edition)*. Paris: OECD Publications.
OECD. (2001). OECD health data 2001. http://www.oecd.org. Accessed 19 April 2002.
OECD. (2004a). *Labour force statistics 1983–2003*. Paris: OECD Publications.
OECD. (2004b). OECD health data 2004 (3rd ed.). http://www.oecd.org. Accessed 20 June 2005.
OECD. (2011a). OECD health data 2011. http://www.oecd.org. Accessed 22 Dec 2011.
OECD. (2011b). OECD stat extracts: Labour force statistics and health expenditure and financing. http://stats.oecd.org. Accessed 18 Dec 2011.
Olshansky, S. J., & Ault, A. B. (1986). The fourth stage of the epidemiologic transition: The age of delayed degenerative diseases. *The Millbank Memorial Fund Quarterly, 64*(3), 353–391.

Pedroza, C. (2006). A Bayesian forecasting model: Predicting U.S. male mortality. *Biostatistics (Oxford, England), 7,* 530–550.

Peto, R., Lopez, A. D., Boreham, J., Thun, M., & Heath C. Jr. (1992). Mortality from tobacco in developed countries: Indirect estimation from national vital statistics. *Lancet, 339*(8804), 1268–1278.

Quantitative Micro Software. (1994). *Eviews user's guide*. California: QMS, Irvine.

Rimm, E. B., Klatsky, A., Grobbee, D., & Stampfer, M. J. (1996). Review of moderate alcohol consumption and reduced risk of coronary heart disease: Is the effect due to beer, wine, or spirits? *British Medical Journal, 312,* 731–736.

Ruwaard, D., & Kramers, P. G. N. (Eds.). (1993). *Volksgezondheid Toekomst Verkenning: De gezondheidstoestand van de Nederlandse bevolking in de periode 1950–2010*. The Hague: Sdu Uitgeverij.

Spijker, J. J. A. (2004). Socioeconomic determinants of mortality differentials in Europe. PhD Thesis. University of Groningen, Groningen.

Spijker, J. J. A. (2009). Explanations for the age, sex, spatial, and temporal structure of Czech mortality for the period 1987–97. *Environment and Planning A, 41*(3), 682–702.

Spijker, J. J. A., & Van Wissen, L. J. G. (2010). Socioeconomic determinants of male mortality in Europe: The absolute and relative income hypotheses revisited. *Genus LXVI,* (1), 37–61.

Statistics Norway. (1999). Income distribution survey: Recent trends in income inequality in Norway. Statistics Norway, Oslo. http://www.ssb.no/english/subjects/05/01/incdist/main.html. Accessed 1 May 2003.

Svenjar, J. (2001). Transition economies: Performances and challenges. vol William Davidson Working Paper Number. University of Michican, Ann Arbor, MI.

Tabeau, E., Ekamper, P., Huisman, C., & Bosch, A. (2001). Predicting mortality from period, cohort or causespecific trends: A study of four European countries. In E. Tabeau, A. Van den Berg-Jeths, & C. Heathcote (Eds.), *Forecasting mortality in developed countries: Insights from a statistical, demographic and epidemiological perspective* (pp. 159–187). Dordrecht: Kluwer Academic Publishers.

Tekin, E. (2002). Employment, wages, and alcohol consumption in Russia: Evidence from panel data. Discussion Paper, Vol 432. Institute for the Study of Labour (IZA), Bonn.

The Conference Board. (2011). The Conference Board Total Economy Database, September 2011. http://www.conference-board.org/data/economydatabase/. Accessed 22 Dec 2011.

Treml, V. G. (1997). Soviet and Russian statistics on alcohol consumption and abuse. In J. L. Bobadilla, C. A. Costello, & F. Mitchell (Eds.), *Premature death in the new independent states* (pp. 220–238). Washington, DC: National Academy Press.

United Nations. (2010). *World urbanization prospects: The 2009 revision*. New York: UN Department of Economic and Social Affairs/Population Division.

United Nations. (2011). *World population prospects*. New York: UN Department of Economic and Social Affairs/Population Division.

Valkonen, T. (1993). Problems in the measurement and international comparisons of socioeconomic differences in mortality. *Social Science and Medicine, 36*(4), 409–418.

Valkonen, T., Martelin, T., Rimpelä, A., Notkola, V., & Savela, S. (1993). *Socioeconomic mortality differences in Finland, 1981–90. Population* (Vol. 1). Helsinki: Statistics Finland.

Van den Berg-Jeths, A., Hoogenveen, R. T., de Hollander, A. E. M., & Tabeau, E. (2001). A review of epidemiological approaches to forecasting mortality and morbidity. In E. Tabeau, A. Van den Berg-Jeths, & C. Heathcote (Eds.), *Forecasting mortality in developed countries: Insights from a statistical, demographic and epidemiological perspective* (pp. 33–56). Dordrecht: Kluwer Academic Publishers.

Van Genugten, M. L. L., Hoogenveen, R. T., & de Hollander, A. E. M. (1997). Scenario's voor de sterfte aan longkanker en coronaire hartziekten. In A. Van den Berg-Jeths A (Ed.), *Gezondheid en zorg in de toekomst: Volksgezondheid toekomst verkenning deel VII. RIVM* (pp. 128–135). Bilthoven: Elsevier/De Tijdstroom.

Van Hoorn, W., & Broekman, R. (1999). Uniformity and diversity scenarios for mortality. In J. De Beer, L. J. G. Van Wissen (Eds.), *Europe: One continent, different worlds: Population scenarios for the 21st century, vol European Studies of Population* (Vol. 7, pp. 71–90). Dordrecht: Kluwer Academic Publishers.

Van Hoorn, W., & de Beer, J. (1998). Long term mortality scenarios for the countries of European economic area. Eurostat Working Paper 3/1998/E/n8. Eurostat, Luxembourg.

WHO. (2002). Health for all database. http://data.euro.who.int/hfadb/. Accessed 26 April 2002.

WHO. (2011a). Health for all database. http://data.euro.who.int/hfadb/. Accessed 22 Dec 2011.

WHO. (2011b). WHO mortality database, 25 March 2011 update. http://www.who.int/healthinfo/morttables/en/. Accessed 8 Nov 2011.

WIDER. (2008). World income inequality database. http://www.wider.unu.edu/research/Database/en_GB/database/. Accessed 20 April 2009.

Wilkinson, R. G., & Pickett, K. E. (2006). Income inequality and health: A review and explanation of the evidence. *Social Science and Medicine, 62,* 1768–1784.

Yashin, A. (2001). Mortality models incorporating theoretical concepts of ageing. In E. Tabeau, A. Van den Berg-Jeths, & C. Heathcote (Eds.), *Forecasting mortality in developed countries: Insights from a statistical, demographic and epidemiological perspective* (pp. 261–280). Dordrecht: Kluwer Academic Publishers.

Chapter 4
Social Disparities in the Evolution of an Epidemiological Profile: Transition Processes in Mortality Between 1971 and 2008 in an Industrialized Middle Income Country: The Case of Hungary

Katalin Kovács

Abstract The present paper seeks to understand the transformation of mortality patterns in Hungary, by which mortality inequalities by education began to appear in the early 1980s, continued to grow in the following 25 years, and now seem to be stabilising. The first part of this paper overviews the theoretical innovations of the last decades regarding the interpretation of cause-specific mortality dynamics, often referred to as epidemiological transitions theories, and their relevance for the analysis of mortality inequalities. The paper then analyses the cause-specific trends of mortality for two educational classes between 1971 and 2008. The trends were corrected for changes in the coding system and divided into linear (stagnating, increasing or decreasing) periods. Causes of death were grouped according to the relationship between the sequences of these periods for the two educational classes. The 57 causes of death were finally clustered into six groups. One group, which is dominated by nutrition-related and cardiovascular diseases, is largely responsible for the onset of mortality inequalities in 1980. The results imply that the quality of nutrition has diverged for the educational classes since 1980, and this fact has left its footprint on the pattern of mortality. The history of food production and availability seems to be in line with nutrition-related mortality, and it is argued that nutrition transition theory provides a very plausible explanatory framework for the growth of mortality inequalities.

Keywords Epidemiological transition · Hungary · Inequality · Historical development

Supported by the Hungarian Scientific Research Found (OTKA 59063).
The author is grateful for one of the anonymous reviewers for providing outlines for the graph that appears in the text as Fig. 4.4.
A previous version of the first part of this article was published in Hungarian in Demográfia, 2012/1, pp. 5–43.

K. Kovács (✉)
Demographic Research Institute, Budapest, 1–3 Buday L. u., H-1024, Hungary
e-mail: kovacs@demografia.hu

J. Anson, M. Luy (eds.), *Mortality in an International Perspective*,
European Studies of Population 18, DOI 10.1007/978-3-319-03029-6_4,

4.1 Introduction

Countries in Central and Eastern Europe (CEE) experienced rapid industrialisation under equalising state-controlled regimes, and entered into the globalising international economy two decades ago. Their transformation into service economies is still an on-going process. Over the past 20 years social inequalities have increased sharply, reaching medium-level income inequalities in an EU context, which is considered high by the citizens of these countries. In the present paper I look at the implications these changes have had on the level and distribution of mortality in Hungary, as an example of this group of countries.

All-cause mortality is considerably higher in CEE countries than in the rest of the European Union, but it was recently shown to correspond to the income level of these countries (Spijker and von Wissen 2010). On the other hand, inequalities in mortality by education have been found to be extremely high in all of these countries (Mackenbach et al. 2008). So far the explanation for these developments has only been provided within a larger context that applies to the whole of the Eastern European region, including not only CEE and Baltic countries but also countries like Russia, Belarus and Ukraine. One of main conclusions has been that they have not so far undergone the healthier life style changes that have occurred in Western Europe, and this has resulted in a "reversed epidemiological transition", in which an elevated burden of cardiovascular diseases dominates the pattern of mortality (Vallin and Meslé 2004). Is this framework applicable to Central and Eastern Europe and does it explain the evolution of their cause of death pattern and high level of inequalities? If so, what role did income play in these processes and what are the specific social processes that triggered these developments?

In Hungary, inequalities in all-cause mortality were negligible during the 1970's and widened during the 1980's. The next one and a half decades brought a further, dramatic, increase in inequalities, which appear to have stabilised at this very high level for the past half a decade (Fig. 4.1). As regards broad groups of causes of death, the data suggest that the apparent similarities in all-cause mortality during the 1970s might be attributable to causes other than the lack of inequalities in living conditions between people with different education. This period was characterized by the over-mortality of the less educated from cardiovascular diseases and the over-mortality of the more educated from malignant tumours (Fig. 4.2 and 4.3). An explanation is called for which will look at the historical development of cause-specific mortality within the framework of the epidemiological transition. In this paper I shall review recent developments in epidemiological transition theory, and test the applicability of some of these theories to the evolution of cause- and education-specific mortality inequalities in Hungary between 1971 and 2008.

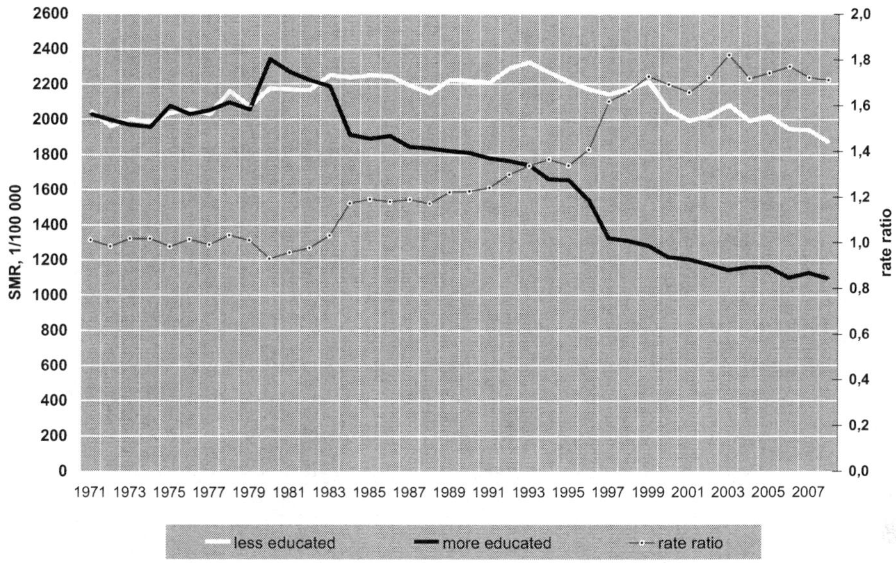

Fig. 4.1 Total mortality by education between 1971 and 2008, Hungarian population aged 30 and over

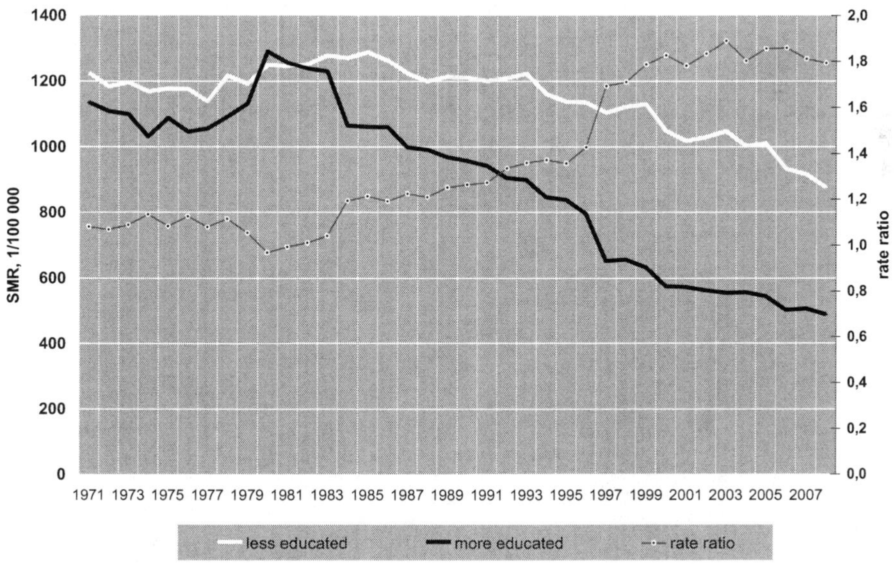

Fig. 4.2 Cardiovascular mortality by education between 1971 and 2008, Hungarian population aged 30 and over

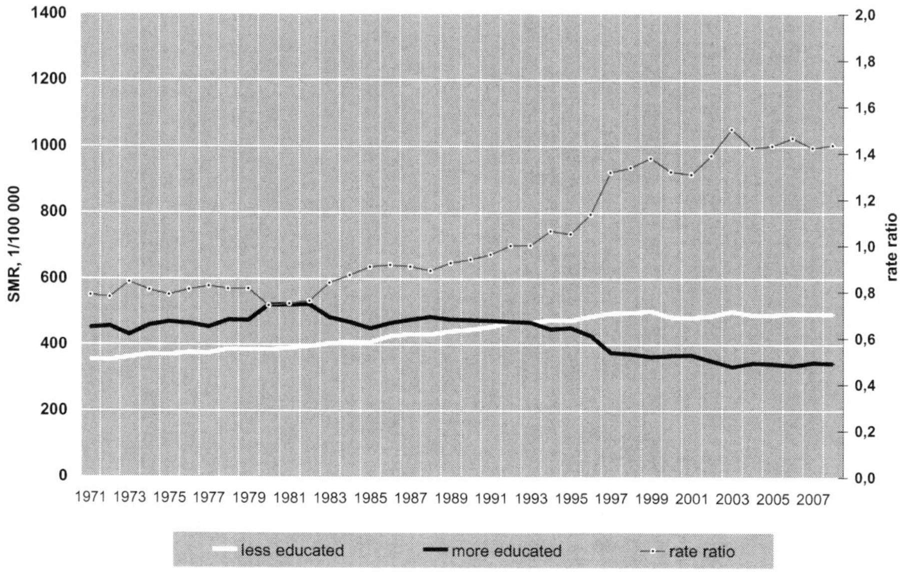

Fig. 4.3 Mortality due to cancer by education between 1971 and 2008, Hungarian population aged 30 and over

4.2 Understanding Changing Disease Patterns Over Time: The Epidemiological Transition Theory

Long-term mortality trends are commonly interpreted within the framework of epidemiological transition theory, outlined 40 years ago by Omran (1971). The original statements of the theory on mortality, fertility and population growth have already been tested, analysed, criticised and modified. By now, epidemiological transition theory and demographic transition theory have split: the first one has gradually shifted towards a focus on cause- and age-specific mortality patterns, while the second is now far more concerned with patterns of fertility and family formation.

The original postulates of Omran are, without doubt, of a heuristic nature: based on limited empirical basis (in its original form it was based on the long-term cause-specific mortality trends of just six countries), it provided a comprehensive picture of the evolution of cause-of-death patterns throughout the history of mankind. In a rather vague division of human history, three transitional phases were distinguished: the 'age of pestilence and famine', the 'age of receding pandemics', and the age of 'degenerative and man-made diseases' (Omran 1971). Stages were differentiated on the basis of average life expectancy, and age- and cause-specific mortality. During the first phase, which encompassed most of human history (the "pre-industrial period", Omran 1998), mortality due to chronic malnutrition, endemic infectious diseases, and high prenatal and maternal mortality shaped the overall high level of mortality, which was further increased by epidemics, famine and wars in the "peak years".

In the second stage, which started in the eighteenth or nineteenth century in Western societies, mortality declined considerably, mainly due to factors other than medical interventions: improved nutrition, improvement of personal cleanliness, ecological recession of certain diseases, better housing conditions and the start of using contraceptive methods. The cause-of-death pattern was less and less characterized by diseases caused by pandemics but communicable diseases—tuberculosis in particular—were still dominant. The third stage is characterised by the dominance of non-communicable diseases, such as diseases of the circulatory system and different types of cancer. From the perspective of the future development of the theory, the additional characteristics of the stages are less important, though Omran's approach, which has been modified several times by himself and others over the past 30 years, remained complex and aimed at explaining the whole of population dynamics.

The evidence which accumulated subsequent to Omran's original article, coming mainly from countries of the Americas, shows little correspondence with this original framework and offers an amazing variety of cause-specific mortality patterns and their changes over time (Albala and Vio 1995; Castillo-Salgado et al. 1999; Costello and Osrin 2005; Hill et al. 2007; Huicho et al. 2009; Marshall 1991; Vigneron 1989; Vigneron 1993). This evidence was incorporated into the original model as three models, the Classic, the Delayed and the Accelerated models (Omran 1983). Later on this was expanded to six models, the Classical Western Model, the Semi Western Model and four Non-Western Models: the Rapid, the Upper Intermediate, the Lower Intermediate and the Slow (Omran 1998). Other authors suggested a different classification of countries (Frenk et al. 1991) in order to incorporate new evidence that did not fit into the original sorting in the first form of the epidemiological theory. From the perspective of countries in Latin America, the concept of an epidemiological *transition* was in sharp contrast to the mortality experience of many countries of the region, which were characterized by a sharp divide between the mortality patterns of different population groups within one country. This experience questioned the choice of countries as the units of analysis, and even raised doubts about the usefulness of the whole concept of an epidemiological transition. Apart from total refutation, the experience of Latin American countries are best summarized as a "patchwork pattern" in which different social groups are often segregated geographically, and display diverse mortality patterns corresponding to different stages of the epidemiological transition. In other words, "different epidemiological worlds" live next to each other. For industrialised countries, on the other hand, a large collaborative study of WHO did confirm the previously proposed trend of age-specific death rates for two broad groups of causes of diseases in the last half of the twentieth century (Salomon and Murray 2002).

The more and more sophisticated classification, however, did not help to overcome one of the major theoretical drawbacks of the original theory. Despite the very complex, and somewhat apocalyptic, view of the future presented by Omran in his last article (1998), epidemiological transition theory presents a linear view of changes in mortality patterns, according to which more developed stages follow less developed ones, alongside with the course of 'modernisation'. This process may take place slowly or quickly, and with some variations, but it also follows a linear route. In this respect, epidemiological transition theory does not differ from theories of modernisation propounded in the 1970's (Carolina and Gustavo 2003) and is very similar to the dominant view of demographic transition theories (Melegh and Őri 2003).

The theory of an epidemiological transition was attractive not only for public health researchers, it can also be viewed as a major contribution to the on-going debate of historians and historical demographers centred around the nature of mortality changes in the last centuries. In countries with a long history of collecting detailed mortality data, the distinctive phases of receding epidemics and the death toll of infectious diseases in general could be identified. Due to the great variability within the regions of one single country (for Sweden: Rogers and Nelson 1997), this further classification, unlike the contribution coming from the discipline of gerontology, has not become a commonly accepted modification of the original epidemiological transition theory. Olshansky and Ault (1986) carried out a detailed examination of the age-specific death rates of the US and pointed to the onset of an epidemiological phase that differs from the one specified as the third stage of the epidemiological transition in the original form of the theory. This fourth stage, they suggested, is characterized by the dominance of the same major causes of death as the third stage but with a continuing delay in mortality from some of these causes, leading to a further significant improvement in life expectancy. The new stage, called the 'age of delayed degenerative and man-made diseases' has become a standard part of the most commonly accepted form of the epidemiological transition theory.

Anthropology or 'evolutionary biology' has also made its contribution to refining epidemiological transition theory by adding a new transition stage, thus refining how the original theory divided up the other end of the historical time-scale (Armelagos et al. 2005). The addition of the "baseline" mortality pattern, called the 'Palaeolithic stage', however, is less relevant from the perspective of the current research. The approach of evolutionary medicine, which emphasises the links between the specific nature of human production, diet and other aspects of living conditions, and cause-specific mortality, can, however, be beneficial in interpreting contemporary mortality trends as well.

Another major discipline contributing to the further refinement of epidemiological transition theory was epidemiology itself. Recent trends in epidemiological research clearly exhibit some fragmentation. Epidemiology was first concerned with certain diseases in detail but recently more comprehensive approaches have emerged. Alongside the continuing research of the risk factors associated with specific diseases, trends in mortality due to major groups of diseases have also been studied and the results and hypotheses presented in the framework of "sub-transition models" such as cancer transition and cardiovascular transition (also known as the cardiovascular revolution).

The cancer transition is an extension of the classic transition theory that takes into account new discoveries on the role of infections in the development of certain types of cancers. The discovery of the presence of bacteria in the majority of stomach cancer cases promoted the recognition of how important infections are in cancer in general, though the infectious origin of certain other cancers (such as cancer of the cervix, testicular cancer and certain lymphomas) was already well-known. New discoveries triggered the formulation of "cancer transition theory" (Gerstein and

Wilmoth 2002), according to which there is a definitive restructuring process in operation within cancer mortality: those with an infectious origin lose their importance and other non-infection-related cancers emerge.

Most cancers, however, are known to be influenced by some major risk factors such as non-appropriate diet, smoking and excessive alcohol consumption. These well-known risk factors are now more and more closely linked to societal transformation processes, mostly of a global nature. From among these theoretical frameworks we note in particular the theory of a nutritional transition (Popkin 2006, Popkin and Mendez 2007). In this framework, major features of food production, distribution and several other characteristics of living conditions are connected to mortality patterns. Nutritional transition theory, just like epidemiological transition theory, divides human history into five distinctive patterns, out of which the fourth corresponds to the living conditions of contemporary CEE countries. The fifth profile describes the living conditions and dietary habits of the most health-conscious members of the most affluent countries. Labelling the phases not as stages but as profiles obscures the fact that these patterns are arranged in historical order so that they also represent some "developmental route". The patterns, however, are connected with a large number of dimensions of actual living conditions. As regards the transition to the fourth ("obesity characterized") profile, several processes, such as "supermarketisation", are connected to several social processes like the demand for safer food, the changing opportunity cost of females' time, technological changes, and changes in logistics and production systems. Altogether this transition is technically characterized by the growing importance of edible oil and animal products in human diet. Additionally sugar consumption is on the rise, often in the form of consuming sweetened beverages. The shift from high fibre intake to refined grains and additionally declining fruit and vegetable intake is also documented in many countries (Popkin 2006). Transition theories regarding other risk factors are less developed at the moment, but the term "smoking epidemic" is also in use and the influence of strong economic forces has already been recognised (Yach et al. 2007).

Regarding the other dominant groups of diseases, cardiovascular mortality has always been regarded as being strongly related to the epidemiological transition. Ischemic heart disease in particular often serves as a "marker disease" that indicates a country's position in the phases of the epidemiological transition (Heuveline et al. 2002). Based on the observations of the contemporary occurrence and frequency of different cardiovascular diseases in different regions of the world, a complete framework for "cardiovascular transition" has gained popularity in the past few years. This framework provides a correspondence between particular cardiovascular diseases and stages of the epidemiological transition (Califf et al. 2010). The linearity of the occurrence of the stages is not stated but it is inherent in the logic of this scheme. The 'pestilence and famine' stage, with life expectancy around 35 years, is characterized by a modest share of CVDs in total mortality (5–10 %) and the dominant forms of cardiovascular mortality are rheumatic heart disease and other infection-related diseases of the circulatory system, cardiomyopathy in particular. The latter disease may also be connected to malnutrition. In the second stage the proportion of deaths caused by CVD grows to 15–35 % and cardiovascular mortality is dominated by rheumatic valve disease, ischemic heart disease and haemorrhagic stroke. In this stage life expectancy reaches about 50 years. In the third stage, in which life expectancy reaches 60 years, the proportion of deaths due to cardiovascular diseases is greater than 50 %. The dominant causes of death within CVDs are ischemic heart disease, and ischemic and haemorrhagic stroke. In the stage of 'delayed degenerative diseases' the proportion of CVDs among all deaths falls below 50 % and life expectancy exceeds 70 years. Major cardiovascular causes of death are the same as in the previous stage, with the addition of congestive heart failure. Another important observation not exactly linked to stages is a major shift between stroke types: haemorrhagic stroke declines while ischemic stroke emerges (Lawlor et al. 2002).

A fourth stage also appears in some variations of the "cardiovascular transition" schemes. In some cases (Yusuf et al. 2001a) a stage of 'health regression and social upheaval' is visualised, characterised by the re-emergence of rheumatic heart disease and a new increase in ischemic heart disease due to increasing alcoholism. In the increasingly unregulated social environment, violence also becomes more common and hypertensive disease—which is otherwise characteristic of stage 2 according to these authors—also re-emerges. This visualisation, of course, relies heavily on recent Russian mortality trends. Other authors have predicted the emergence of heart failure as the main characteristic of a future scenario for CVD mortality (Bonnux et al. 1994; Gaziano et al. 2006).

Risk factors for cardiovascular diseases were found similar to the ones identified for cancers but the linkage between the single diseases and the exact role of single risk factors is less clear, with some exceptions. For two major different stroke types, for instance, different set of risk factors had already been identified (O'Donnall et al. 2010), though inappropriate diet, smoking and excessive intake of alcohol play an important role in the development of all cardiovascular diseases.

Predictions on the future trends of mortality and cause-specific mortality are not restricted to the field of cardiovascular diseases. In his last publication Omran (1998) also outlined a fifth stage, the 'age of aspired quality of life with paradoxical longevity and persistent inequalities'. In this he expressed his hope for a future decrease of inequalities in survival, together with an expectation that there was a high probability of the re-emergence of infectious diseases. Nevertheless, the 'invisible perils' in the future of mankind are considered by Omran as well, such as the possibility of the evolution of an (airborne) virus with abilities similar to those of HIV; the potential misuse of atomic bombs; and high, uncontrolled population growth.

Omran's view on the unpredictable role of infectious diseases is not unique. Several other authors foresaw the future emergence of new diseases and the re-emergence of "old" infectious diseases that were previously believed to have been controlled by medical interventions. Notable examples are the emergence of multi-drug resistant tuberculosis and avian flu. Following the emergence of the HIV/AIDS pandemic, the fear of new infectious diseases is spreading. Scientific examination reveals, however, that the majority of the emerging and newly recognised diseases are in fact not new but were known only in some peripheral regions of the world and have reached the consciousness of the wealthy only recently (Farmer 1996). A closer examination of

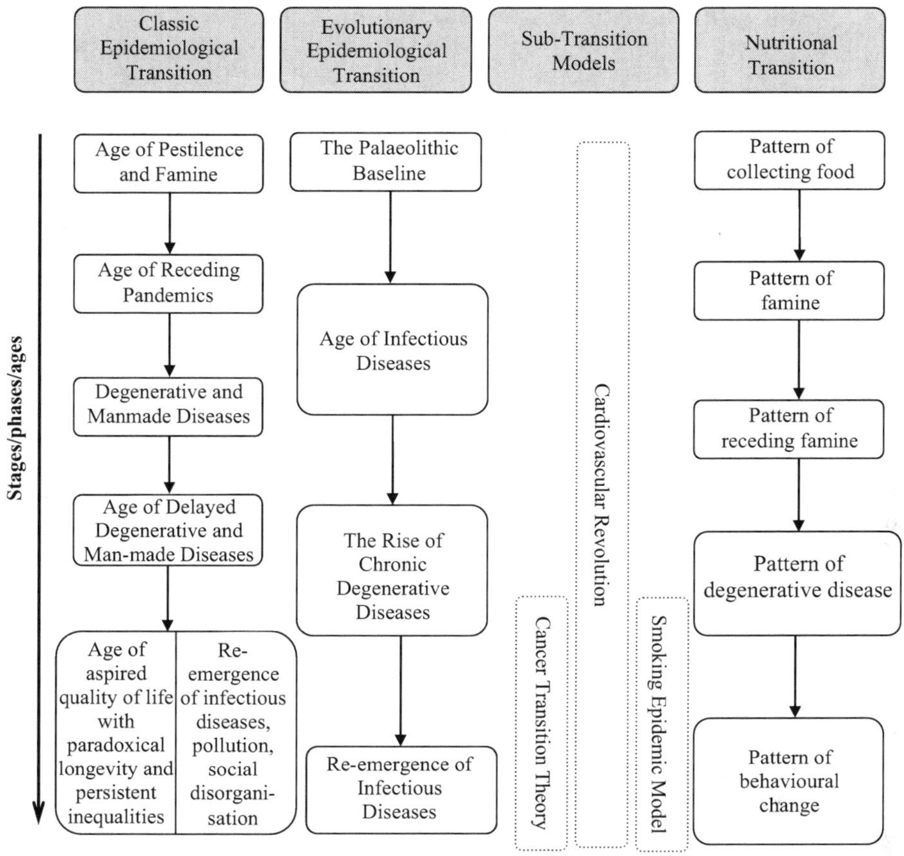

Fig. 4.4 Outline of the major variations of the epidemiological transition theory

the circumstances of the onset of 29 "newly identified" diseases during the 1990s pointed out that human activity played a triggering role in the majority of the cases.

In the integrated view of evolutionary medicine that divides human history only into three epidemiological transitions, the "third transition" is the new era of emerging and re-emerging infectious diseases (Harper and Armelagos 2010). The "end of the antibiotic era", as this approach calls it, results mostly from the intensification of the globalisation process, especially that of the transportation system, which serves as a 'virtual superhighway' for pathogens.

Figure 4.4 outlines the theories providing a comprehensive explanation for changes in patterns of mortality and their phasing. While many epidemiological transition theories cover the whole of the history of mankind, others refer only to developments in the latest centuries, or even just decades. Most of them inherently treat the process of change in mortality patterns as "development", i.e. as a linear, and in some respect hierarchical process. Possible reverses and uncertainties mostly appear regarding the latest stages—which is probably due to empirical observations being more numerous and diverse regarding the near past.

4.3 Understanding Social Disparities in Cause-of-Death Patterns

The issue of social disparities is present in nearly all approaches to the epidemiological transition. In most cases social inequalities in mortality or diverse mortality patterns that are characteristic of social classes, strata or groups are discussed in relation to major drivers (or causes) of the epidemiological transition. In some cases drivers or causes are stated only in general, like modernisation, industrialisation and urbanisation. In other cases propositions are well-formulated and corroborated by some empirical evidence. Omran, starting from his very first publication, continuously mentioned social disparities in mortality as well as the driving forces listed above but he did not provide a theoretical framework for the application of these in connection with particular mortality or disease patterns specific for single countries or population sub-groups.

McKeown (1976a, b, 2009; McKeown and Record 1962) studied the disappearance of infectious diseases in industrialising England and formulated his famous nutrition hypothesis. Detecting a time-lag between the almost complete disappearance of numerous infectious diseases, and a very notable drop in tuberculosis mortality, before the discovery of the appropriate treatment methods (mostly antibiotic drugs), he concluded that the major cause of decreasing mortality was the improvement in the living conditions and, in particular, the nutritional status of the population during the nineteenth century. The nutritional thesis provides an obvious explanation for social disparities in mortality, whose modified versions later appear in recently developed explanatory approaches.

Evolutionary medicine, with its anthropological orientation, considers the "Palaeolithic" baseline to have been free from social hierarchies in early human communities (Harper and Armelagos 2010). Notably they also focus on dietary habits. They suggested that there was a low mortality period before human communities settled down, as a result of their varied diet as well as small population size. Mortality started to grow when diet became heavily reliant on crops, which were unequally distributed across population strata. In parallel, the growth of average community size led to new, infectious, diseases becoming the leading causes of death. Based on this approach one can conclude that unequal access to food results in unequal resistance to diseases, thus inevitably leading to inequalities in mortality.

Historians and historical demographers, however, present a rather different picture of those centuries of human history which can be characterised by the dominance of infectious diseases. They suggest that some of the infectious diseases exhibit a "discriminative" nature: there is a long incubation period between the moment of infection and the development of the disease and the resistance of the host matters during the process of battling with these diseases. Other infections, by contrast, are "quick" enough not to allow time for the host (the human body) to develop resistance and they kill in a short time; consequently, they can be considered "non-discriminative". Several infectious diseases, such as smallpox and mumps, have been observed to change over the centuries, as their originally "non-discriminative" nature turned into "discriminative". It is still unclear if the changing nature of some formerly fatal diseases is due to increased community-level resistance to those diseases or merely to the changing nature of the disease-scape. However, the disappearance of some infectious diseases, notably the plague, is still explained in several alternative ways (Slack 1981).

During early modern times, when infectious diseases dominated mortality, the excess mortality of those in disadvantaged social positions was likely to be more pronounced in those causes of death that were connected with epidemics and pandemics. According to historical demographers, excess deaths were indeed connected to the availability of food, though this relationship was largely influenced by the effectiveness of supportive networks (Bengtsson et al. 2004), which helped to mitigate the effect of economic hardships (e.g. famine). Regarding the plague outbreaks in London, it was observed that the locus of epidemics moved from the central, relatively wealthy parishes to the poorer suburban ones during the seventeenth century. Overall, it is likely that social disparities existed in the era of infectious diseases, though their importance might have changed over time, partly due to factors that operated independently of social organisation and human activity and partly due to greater awareness and ability to cope among the wealthy (Slack 1989; Hall 2008).

The early industrial era inevitably brought large mortality inequalities, which are well documented for some countries. Time series of mortality data by social groups, however, are not available for many countries. Studies using time series on income inequality for industrialised countries have suggested that mortality inequalities were narrowing from the first years of the twentieth century until about 1970, and widening afterwards. Detailed British data (Pamuk 1985) has reinforced this view. This process probably took place in varying ways in different regions: in Sweden no sign of the emergence of social inequalities in mortality was found till the 1950s (Bengtsson and Dribe 2011).

Theoretical explanations for modern inequalities have emerged in the fields of both epidemiology and sociology. In the epidemiology of cardiovascular diseases a particular "disease mobility" was observed first: in the beginning of the twentieth century myocardial infarction used to be the disease of the affluent in developed North American and European countries, but in the 1960s and the 1970s mortality rates due to infarction started to decline earlier and more rapidly among the better educated and the better off (Marmot et al. 1991; Kaplan and Keil 1993). These experiences led to the formulation of the social "following pattern" of diseases. Based on the concept of the diffusion of innovation, Pearson (2003) suggested an "adoption theory": population groups with higher education and/or better income adopt new ideas, products and behavioural patterns more readily. Once a risk factor is recognised, it first becomes public knowledge among those with higher social status, mediated by health education or mass media. The messages reach the poorer and/or less educated groups of societies later.

The life course perspective for understanding the occurrence of chronic diseases also originates from cardiovascular epidemiology (Forsdahl 1978; Kuh and Ben-Shlomo 1997). Its scope, however, is much wider, identifying risk factors that act during the *in utero* period and early childhood, risk factors which are associated with the social position of the parents (Davey-Smith and Hart 2002). From the point of view of social sciences, these findings call for integrating intergenerational mobility into epidemiological transition models that are used to understand the particular mortality patterns of single countries.

In the social sciences the "fundamental causes" concept was introduced in order to understand the relationship between socio-economic status and disease. These fundamental causes do not refer to causes of death but to dimensions of social position which are causally linked to resources that can be used to avoid risk or to minimize the consequences of diseases once they occur. Resources include money, knowledge, power, prestige and interpersonal relationships. Fundamental causes act, according to the proponents of this idea, when new diseases, new risk factors or new knowledge on risk factors emerge or new medical technologies are introduced (Link and Phelan 1995). In these cases living conditions and access to resources act directly to grant or restrict different groups' access to, and application of, the new technology. Social position, therefore, is the fundamental cause of a disease (or death) and not a "proxy", as it was previously treated in epidemiological research.

The concept of fundamental causes has only recently been applied to the analysis of cause-of-death patterns (Miech et al. 2011). The examination of education-specific mortality inequalities and their dynamics over the last decades of US history aimed at testing the fundamental cause hypothesis. A large number of causes of death (85) were included in this examination. In accordance with the concept of fundamental causes, the analysis found increasing inequalities for most "emerging" causes, e.g. those whose overall rate was in an increase.

Omran's classic paper on the epidemiological transition (1971) positioned Hungary together with the rest of "Eastern Europe", in the same model as Japan. Mortality developments have diverged significantly since then. The latest additions to the concept of epidemiological transition provide no direct guidance for understanding overall mortality trends and educational inequalities in mortality. Detailed knowledge has accumulated on the changes in mortality profiles in developed high-income countries. Mortality trends, especially the burden of infectious and non-communicable diseases, are widely discussed with regard to low income countries. Industrialized middle-income countries seem to be neglected in the discussion of the epidemiological transition. In order to fill this gap, first we examine the applicability of one of the previously outlined theories that focus primarily on other regions of the world: the plausible "following" hypothesis. The higher overall level of mortality as well as the cause of death patterns in Hungary (and other CEE counties), often referred to as "lagging behind" those of Western Europe, might be interpreted as the mortality pattern of a society in which large population segments who are "lagging behind" produce an overall "delayed" cause-of-death pattern and large mortality inequalities at the same time. If this proposal were true and meaningful, one would observe the same mortality dynamics for the more and the less advantaged segments of the population but with some time lag regarding the latter group. Existing data allow us to examine these processes by education only: I shall therefore compare the mortality development of the less and the more educated Hungarian adults. As a contrast I also examine the applicability of another popular branch of theories known as risk behavioural factor approaches, in particular, the possible role of nutrition in shaping cause-of-death pattern differences.

4.4 Data and Methodology

Mortality data for Hungary, by education, are available from 1971. For the period between 1971 and 2008 we calculated age-standardized cause-specific mortality rates by education for the population aged 30 and above. Cause-specific death rates were also calculated for the whole population and by education groups. Data on the number of deaths by education is provided by the mortality register of the Hungarian Central Statistical Office. Corresponding population estimates and forecasts were prepared by László Hablicsek, based on census data from 1970, 1980 and 1990 (Hablicsek and Kovács 2007). Underlying causes of death were included in the analysis. Education level was dichotomized: high (completed 12 years and passed the Matura exam) and low. These two groups will be referred to as the less and the more educated.

Selecting the relevant causes of death was a multi-stage process. First we selected causes cited in discussions of the epidemiological transition theory that linked their theoretical considerations to empirical analysis. The starting point, however, was the broad categorization into the two distinctive groups of causes of death which came out of the WHO Global Burden of Diseases study (Salomon and Murray 2002). Group 1 included the infectious diseases; diseases of the pulmonary system and several diseases connected to malnutrition and maternal mortality. Group 2 encompassed all other diseases, except the external causes: injuries, homicide and suicide. Looking at a large number of countries over shorter or longer observational periods (from 1950 to 2000) and taking into account total mortality and wealth (as measured by GDP), Salomon and Murray (2002) found no consistent relationship between external causes and total mortality or wealth, and we decided therefore to leave them out of the present analysis.

The next step in selecting the causes of death was based on those considerations which have been summarized in the introduction. Additional results from studies that analysed time trends for a number of diseases in specific countries with regard to the epidemiological transition were also included, particularly studies on the epidemiological transition in the Netherlands (Wolleswinkel-van den Bosch 1996; Wolleswinkel-van den Bosch et al. 2007) and in Canada (Lussier et al. 2008). For Group 1 causes, the identification of nutrition-related, pulmonary or maternal causes of death is not problematic. The large group of 'infectious and parasitic diseases', as the International Classification of Diseases calls it, was much more difficult to break down into smaller and meaningful causes of death, because if anything is clear from the literature, it is that infectious diseases are generally declining but they still vary significantly by country. Therefore we decided to select all those causes for which more than 100 cases were found for each year during the period between 1971 and 2008. This procedure resulted in a list of one disease: tuberculosis. We also added the "new diseases" such as HIV/AIDS and newly recognised and antibiotic-resistant infectious diseases. These categories turned out to be almost empty. In practice, the study also includes a number of infectious diseases which are traditionally classified under pulmonary diseases (such as influenza, pneumonia) or other major disease groups (peptic ulcer, appendicitis), or whose coding in some periods overlaps other broad cause-of-death groups (meningitis, enteritis).

Group 2 included different types of cancers and cardiovascular diseases, divided up according to those "sub-theories" of the epidemiological transition which we briefly introduced earlier. For cardiovascular diseases, the categorisation was based on the list of diseases that appear in different versions of the "cardiovascular transition". Apart from these, some other distinctions were also made according to major coding categories such as chronic and acute ischemic heart diseases. Among cancers, we distinguished in particular all those cancer types with are connected with infections. A further distinction was made by major risk factors, including not only smoking, excessive drinking and obesity, but also environmental and occupational exposures (for a short summary see Table 4.1). This categorisation, however, does not lead to easy interpretation, due to the pervasive and complex nature of the everyday operation of risk factors. Some other diseases, specifically discussed by certain authors with respect to the epidemiological transition, such as Alzheimer and Parkinson's Disease, were also added. The list of the causes of death that we selected for analysis is included in the Appendix, together with the coding used. Age-specific death rates by the selected causes of death (where possible) were used to create standardized mortality rates using the European standard population.

Mortality trends, resulting from the standardisation process, did not form continuous time series in most cases, as illustrated in Fig. 4.5. There were three different ICD coding versions in operation during the observed period, and in addition, "automatic coding" was introduced in 2005, which again affected the structure of the (underlying) causes of death, as if another new ICD version had been introduced. ICD-9 was introduced in 1979 and ICD-10 in 1996. First we fitted the different versions of ICD codes, often with the help of literature, in order to achieve the same content for each disease over time. When code-fitting was not obvious, we relied on code-fitting used by others (Wolleswinkel-van den Bosch et al. 1996; Wolleswinkel-van den Bosch et al. 1998; Hashibe et al. 2009; Lawlor et al. 2002). The resulting time series called "original values" still did not construct continuous curves in this study.

There are three known methods to deal with the changes of ICD coding system. The first one, the "double or bridge coding" would require coding death in a certain period according to both the outgoing and the new coding systems. This task was carried out only in 2005 for the Hungarian mortality data. The second method follows the exact matching of the disease categories by four-digit coding (Meslé and Vallin 1996). This method was partly used in this study but only for some specific causes of death. After establishing the coding we followed a third method of fitting the curves (Janssen and Kunst 2004) but applying a simpler method than they did. First the obvious outliers were excluded from the original time series, judged by visual observation. Then, based on standardized values presented in 2000, 2001, 2002, 2003 and 2004, a linear prediction for 2005 was compared with the actual value for each analysed cause of death. The ratio of these two values provided a coefficient with which we fitted the values for the period between 1996 and 2004 in order to have a continuous time trend. This procedure was repeated twice to fit the values taken in the period between 1971 and 1978 and between 1979 and 1995. The fitted curve can be rather different from the one based on the original values, as demonstrated by Fig. 4.5, and should be treated as an estimation for the period between 1971 and 2004.

Table 4.1 Major risk factors for selected cancer types. (Source: Parkin 2006; Dalton-Griffin and Kellam 2009; Calle and Kaaks 2004; Anand et al. 2008; Bofetta and Nyberg 2003)

Cancer type	Infections		Obesity		Smoking		Alcohol	Environmental factors			
	Strongly related to infections	Some connection to infections	High (≥ 2) relative risk for obese people	Moderate relative risk between 1 and 2	Strongly connected	Moderately connected		Asbestos	Air pollution	Drinking water with high arsenic content	Chlorate and nitrate in drinking water
Oral		X			X						
Oesophagus		X		X			X				
Stomach	X			X							
Colorectal		X	/X/			X				(x)	
Liver	X			X		X	X			(x)	
Gallbladder			X								
Pancreas			X			X					
Larynx					X		X				
Lung					X			X	X	X	
Melanoma											
Other skin										X	
Mesothelioma								X			
Breast cancer				X							
Cervix	X					X					
Uterus			X								
Ovary											
Kidney				X							
Bladder		X				X				X	X
Non-Hodgkin disease		X									
Leukaemia		X									

X Well established association, *(x)* Less established association, /x/ different risk profiles for men and women

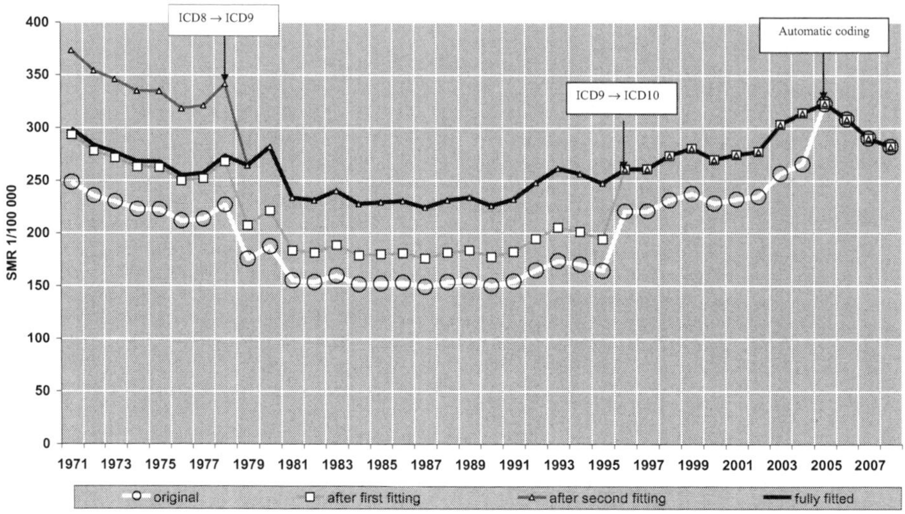

Fig. 4.5 Estimating the real value of mortality from chronic ischemic heart diseases: the fitting procedure

Fitting coefficients were calculated by causes of death, but always for the entire population. The same coefficients were used to fit curves for those with lower and higher educational background. The values of the coefficients, listed in the Appendix, provide an overview about the reliability of the estimated time series : the closer the coefficients are to 1, the higher the reliability. No fitting was applied in the case of those causes which were too small to calculate standardized rates or for those which showed outliers "too often", such as influenza. Overall mortality trends were similarly not fitted (Fig. 4.1).

We now turn to consider the relation between the two estimated mortality time series for groups with lower and higher education. For certain causes of death, almost exclusively in those years when the annual number of deaths is very low, it was not possible to determine definitive relations since the low number of deaths did not allow for standardisation, so fitting was also not applied. Therefore the general trends of overall mortality due to these causes are difficult to establish. This fact is well illustrated in the case of obesity. From this cause less than 20 deaths were reported annually between 1979 and 2004, but about 200 in the following 4 years. As for inequalities, a clearer picture emerges from the distribution of the number of deaths: most of them appeared among the less educated. Deaths due to nutritional anaemia, malnutrition and obesity, as well as maternal death almost exclusively happened among those with lower education.

For other rare causes of death such as HIV/AIDS and "newly emerging infectious diseases", however, no such pattern evolves. HIV/AIDS mortality was the highest in 1994, when 32 deaths were attributed to this disease. The number of cases declined afterwards and people with lower and higher educational attainment seem to be equally affected. Among the newly emerging diseases only 61 deaths were reported from 2009, again distributed proportionally between the educational classes.

After disregarding the above-mentioned causes of death, we categorized the remaining causes by the relationship between the two mortality time series displayed by the groups with lower and higher education. The classification of the relations rested on a simplified view of the time series. Given that we worked with estimated values in the classification, the dynamics represented by the time series were the focus. The time series were broken down to linear (growing, stagnating or declining) phases and the classification was based on the relationship between the sequences of these phases by causes of death, presented by the two mortality time series. Time series were broken down into phases using join-point regression analysis, with software provided by the National Cancer Institute of the United States.[1] This regression is for analysing trends and the software fits data in the simplest possible sequence of linear trends which are connected by the join-points. First a linear trend for the overall period is fitted, then trends with a growing number of joint-points are also fitted and their significances are tested against the Null-hypothesis (e.g. having 0 join-points). The tests of significance are based on a Monte Carlo permutation test. The breakdown of the time series was successful in most of the cases, though the method applied involves some uncertainties. The location of the join-points is provided together with confidence intervals, which were often very wide, covering even 8–10 years. In the following classification only those periodicities were considered when confidence intervals for the joint points were shorter than 8 years. Uncertainties were taken into account in all those cases when confidence intervals were wider than 3–4 years. The sequences of linear trends and the corresponding set of join-points by cause of death are not given here but are available from the author.

To examine the "follow-up" hypothesis, first one has to give a clear definition of a follow-up pattern of two curves. The method chosen for this analysis was not to construct a general definition but first to regard the estimated mortality time series for the two educational groups, then to classify them by their type of relation and then to examine the possible interpretations of their being "follow-up" by type.

4.5 Results

The application of this method resulted in six different groups of diseases, according to the relationship between the mortality trends estimated for the more and the less educated. This classification allows us to investigate the possibility of providing a proper definition of follow-up. In the case of diseases with strongly declining mortality (Type I) the definition of follow-up is not obvious at all. The dynamics of decline did not provide any meaningful definition of follow-up, since for the major diseases of this category (pulmonary tuberculosis, haemorrhagic stroke and cancer of the stomach) the timing of strongly declining and the less strongly declining periods, represented by the mortality of the less and more educated, mostly coincide (Fig. 4.6). The existence of sequences of declines with a different pace also means

[1] http://surveillance.cancer.gov/joinpoint/.

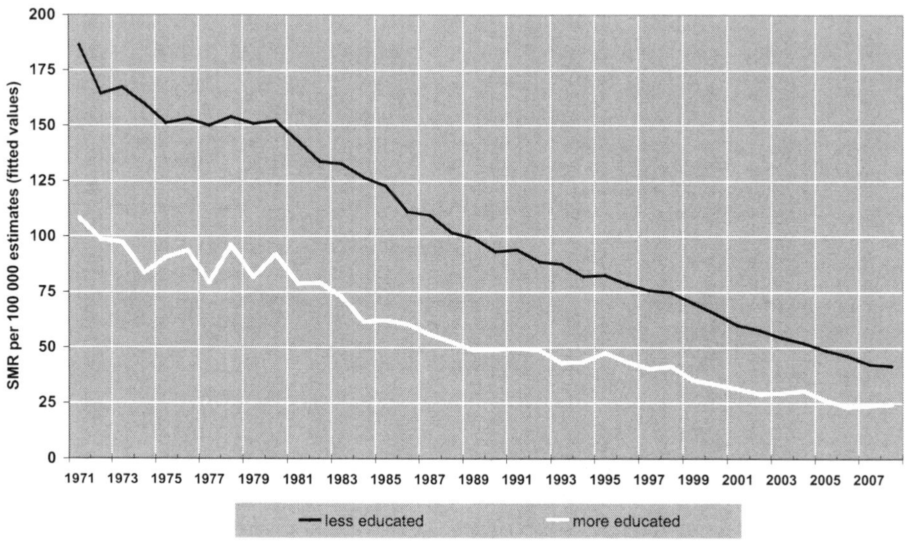

Fig. 4.6 Mortality due to haemorrhagic stroke by education 1971–2008, Hungarian population aged 30 and over, representing type I causes of death

that a definition based simply on when mortality of the less educated reached the mortality level of the better educated also gives no clear-cut answer: for instance, the value of tuberculosis mortality of the more educated in 1983 was reached 2 years later by the less educated, but the values for the more educated in 1988 or in 1996 were reached, by the less educated, only 12 or 9 years later, respectively. In the case of influenza, the level of fluctuation highly exceeds the level of inequalities. For rarer diseases that also belong to this class of causes of death, temporal but irregular high peaks of mortality among the better educated would make it difficult to define a follow-up pattern (Table 4.2).

In the case of some other diseases, mortality of the less and the more educated also shows similar sequences of periods of linear trends, but the overall trends are not declining (Type II, Fig. 4.7). Inequalities change little or not at all over time and the mortality of the more educated never (in "regular" cases such as the hypertensive diseases of the circulatory system or cervical cancer) or just in exceptional years (in the case of mesothelioma and epilepsy) reaches the level of the less educated. Providing any follow-up definition seems meaningless in these cases (Table 4.2). In a number of diseases, however, the sequences of the linear periods of different types are also similar for the less and the more educated, but the overall dynamics of the curves turn to be very different. For these causes of death mortality levels are quite similar at the beginning of the period considered here, but at a certain point of time mortality of the two groups starts to diverge quite distinctly (Type III, Fig. 4.8).

Regarding most diseases in the class of Type III mortality, negligible differences in mortality characterise the beginning of the observed period and then the same types of linear trends apply to both educational groups, but the levels of mortality

Table 4.2 Types of relation between the mortality of the less and more educated

Type	Sub-type	Cause of death	Possibilities to interpret the relation of the two mortality time series as follow up	Other relevant information regarding the relation of the two mortality time series
I. Diseases with strongly declining mortality in both educational groups	Continuously higher mortality for less educated but narrowing inequalities	Pulmonary tuberculosis	NOB	
		Hemorrhagic stroke (*see Fig.* 4.6)	NOB	
		Cancer of the stomach	NOB	
	Slight irregularities in the declining pattern	Other tuberculosis	NOB	
		Rheumatic heart disease	NOB	
	Fluctuating mortality	Influenza	NOB	
	The more educated had occasionally higher mortality	Appendicitis	NOB	
		Multiple sclerosis	NOB	
		Hodgkin disease	NOB	
II. Parallel sequences of growing, stagnating or declining periods of mortality from these diseases for more and less educated with stable mortality differences favouring the more educated	Regular	*Hypertensive diseases of the circulatory system* (*see Fig.* 4.7)	NAT	
		Cancer of cervix uteri	NAT	
	Irregular in terms of mortality differences: more educated have occasionally higher mortality	Mesothelioma	NAT	
		Epilepsy	NAT	

Table 4.2 (continued)

Type	Sub-type	Cause of death	Possibilities to interpret the relation of the two mortality time series as follow up	Other relevant information regarding the relation of the two mortality time series
III. Parallel sequences of growing, stagnating or declining periods of mortality among more and less educated with little or no over-mortality of the less educated at the start, then inequalities widen dramatically to the benefit of the better educated	Confirmed by the joint-point analysis	Meningitis	NOB	1982 (W)
		Pneumonia	M	1985 (W)
		Chronic bronchitis	C	1980 (W)
		Emphysema	NOB	1980 (W)
		Chronic ischemic heart disease (see Fig. 4.8)	M	1980 (W)
		Cardiomyopathy	M	1980(W)
		Arrhythmias	M	1979–80 (W)
		Heart failure	M	1983 (W)
		Non-rheumatic valve disease	M	1990 (W)
		Atherosclerosis	NOB	1983 (W)
		Other disease of the veins	NOB	
		Cancer of the oesophagus	M	1986 (W)
		Gallbladder cancer	NOB	1982–92 (W)
		Melanoma	M	1981 (W)
		Other skin cancer	M	1982 (W)
		Diabetes	M	1983 (W)
		Cirrhosis of the liver	M	1977 (W)
		Cancer of uterus[a]	M	1980 (W)
		Mental disorders	M	1982 (W)
	With some irregularities	Cancer of larynx	M	1989(W)[b]

Table 4.2 (continued)

Type	Sub-type	Cause of death	Possibilities to interpret the relation of the two mortality time series as follow up	Other relevant information regarding the relation of the two mortality time series
	Confirmed only by visual inspection	Pulmonary heart diseases	M	1983 (W)
IV. The two educational groups start with the same type (inclining, declining or stagnating) of trend and mortality from the disease is higher for the better educated. Mortality of the better educated changes its trend in a certain year for the better and finally huge over-mortality of the less educated is present	Only mortality of the better educated shows major trend change during the period resulting in higher mortality among the less educated by the end of the period	Enteritis	C min 23y	1985 (T)
		Cancer of the colon	C min 15y	1993 (T)
		Cancer of rectum	C min 27y	1981 (T)
		Cancer of the liver[c]	M	1982 (T)
		Cancer of the pancreas	C min 18y	1990 (T)
		Cancer of bronchus and the lung (*see Fig.* 4.9)	C min 19y	1989 (T)
		Cancer of kidney	C min 19y	1989 (T)
		Cancer of the bladder	C min 14y	1994 (T)
		Ovarian cancer	C min 6y	2002 (T)
		Cancer of the brain	C min 29y	1979 (T)
		Leukaemia[d]	C min 28y	1980 (T)
		Diseases of the digestive system other than cirrhosis	C min 23y	1983 (T)

Table 4.2 (continued)

Type	Sub-type	Cause of death	Possibilities to interpret the relation of the two mortality time series as follow up	Other relevant information regarding the relation of the two mortality time series
	Both educational mortality curves change trends significantly during the period	*Acute ischemic heart disease* (*see Fig.* 4.10)	Y, Follow-up time: 17y	1981 and 1998 (T)
		Ischemic stroke	Y, Follow-up time: 17y	1980 and in 1997 (T)
		Breast cancer	Y, Follow-up time: 7y	1992 and in 1999 (T)
V. Steady but profoundly different trends are shown by the two educational groups during the whole period starting with higher mortality of the better educated	Mortality levels are similar at the end	Aortic aneurysm	M	
		Cancer of the oral cavity	M	
		Cancer of thyroid	M	
		Prostate cancer (*see Fig.* 4.11)	M	
		Non-Hodgkin disease	M	
	Mortality is much higher for the less educated at the end	Peptic ulcer	M	
VI. Not classified		Parkinson disease		
		Asthma		

NOB Not obvious, *NAT* Not at all, *C* Only with compromises, *Y* Yes, *M* Meaningless, *W* Calendar year from which mortality of less and more educated start to diverge, *T* Calendar year from which major changes in trend(s) appear—coinciding with a join-point follow-up time in years

[a] Mortality of the less educated is higher at the start of the period, too

[b] In some sense, 1982 can be also a turning point

[c] Trend-change appeared in the mortality of less educated

[d] Mortality reaches about the same level in both educational groups by the end of the period

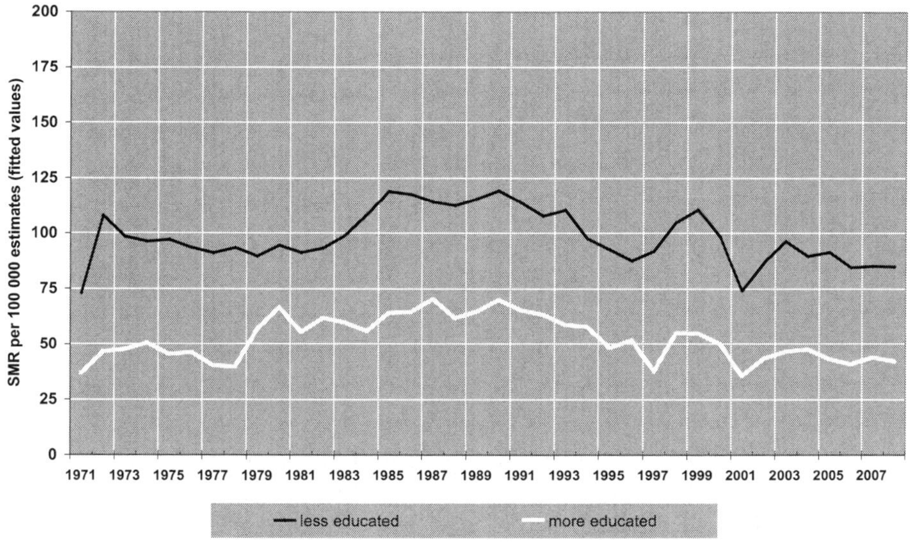

Fig. 4.7 Mortality due to hypertensive diseases of the circulatory system by education 1971–2008, Hungarian population aged 30 and over, representing type II causes of death

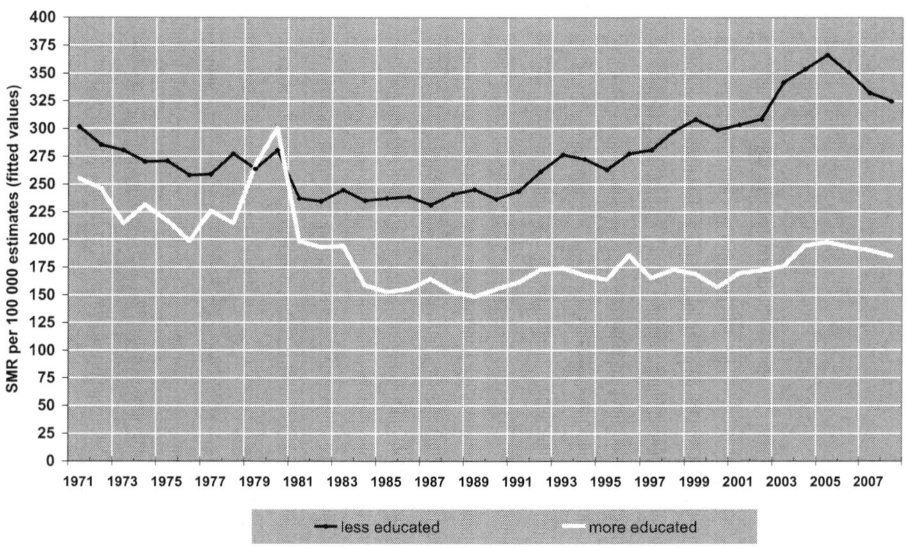

Fig. 4.8 Mortality due to chronic ischemic heart disease 1971–2008, Hungarian population aged 30 and over, representing type III causes of death

become more and more different. Some vague meaning can be given to a possible follow-up pattern only in those cases where the common trend is a decline (meningitis, emphysema, atherosclerosis, other diseases of the veins, and cancer of the

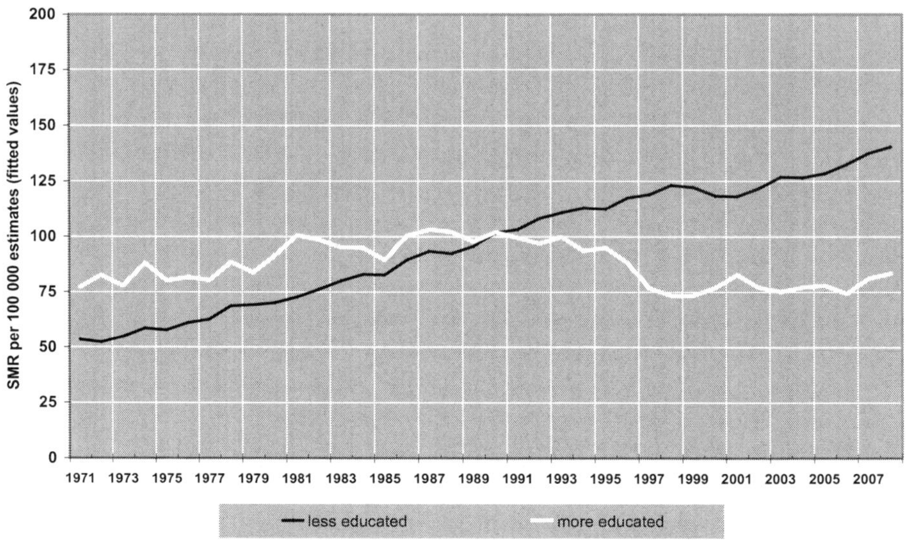

Fig. 4.9 Mortality due to cancer of the trachea, bronchus and the lung by education 1971–2008, Hungarian population aged 30 and over, representing type IV causes of death

gallbladder), similar to the one we give for Type I diseases. In other cases, however, when the mortality of both educational classes increases, there is no sign that mortality of the less educated would follow that of the more educated by any means. It is more plausible that "the same story is played out" for both of the educational groups concerning risk factors or general conditions of life but with very different risk levels.

For Type IV causes of death (Fig. 4.9), the less educated population is characterised by growing mortality, while the mortality of the better educated changed from a growing to a declining trend. Similar trend changes can be expected in the future for the mortality of the less educated, but this change will appear later than the end of our observation period. Approximate minimum time-lags for the onset of this change are given in Table 4.2. In practice these time lags can also be a bit longer, since we cannot be sure if the last couple of years of the observation period represented the beginning of a new type of trend or not.

Altogether, a clear follow-up pattern was detected only for three—though very important—causes of death (Fig. 4.10). As regards acute ischemic heart disease, ischemic stroke and breast cancer, the sequences of the rising and declining periods are similar for the less and the more educated with a time-lag, so the mortality of the less educated seems to follow the mortality of the more educated. Though it is impressive that the estimated follow-up time is the same for ischemic heart disease and ischemic stroke, it is important to mention that these "scenarios" are also "played out" at different mortality levels. At their maximum values, breast cancer and ischemic stroke mortality of the better educated is 20 % higher and that of acute ischemic heart disease is 40 % higher than those of the less educated, suggesting that follow-up type explanations need to be supplemented for a full understanding.

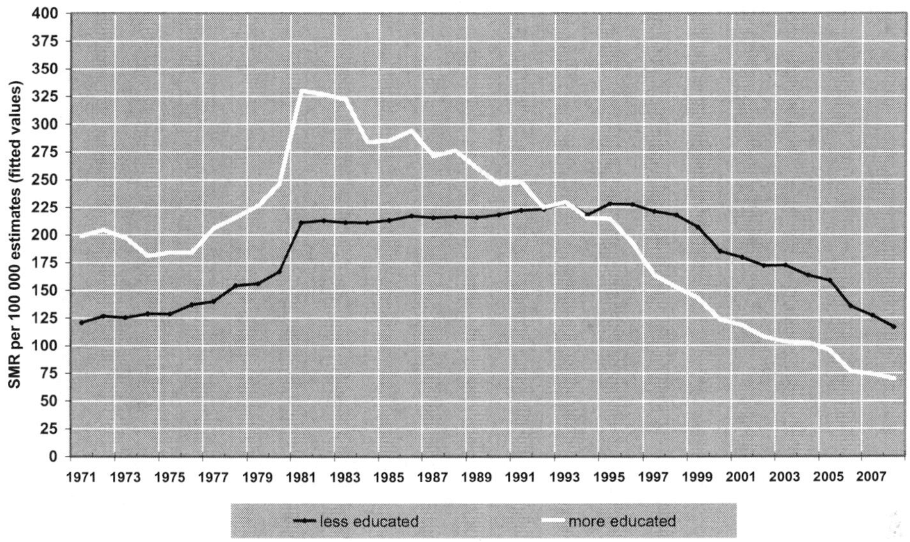

Fig. 4.10 Mortality due to acute ischemic heart disease by education 1971–2008, Hungarian population aged 30 and over, representing type IV causes of death and a follow-up pattern

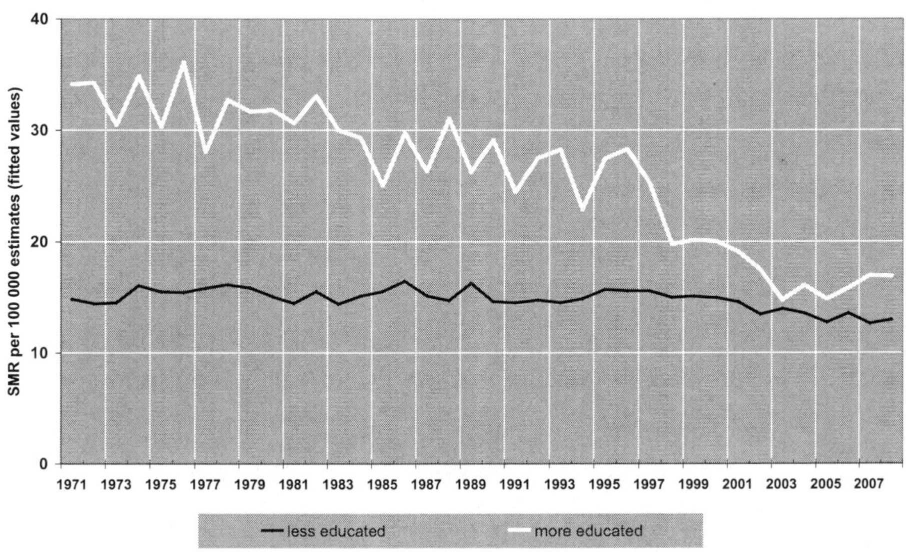

Fig. 4.11 Mortality due to prostate cancer by education 1971–2008, Hungarian population aged 30 and over, representing type V causes of death

Type V causes of death are characterized by different trends for the two educational groups for the whole of the period (see Fig. 4.11). For some, the mortality of the less educated increases and that of the more educated decreases (aneurysm); for

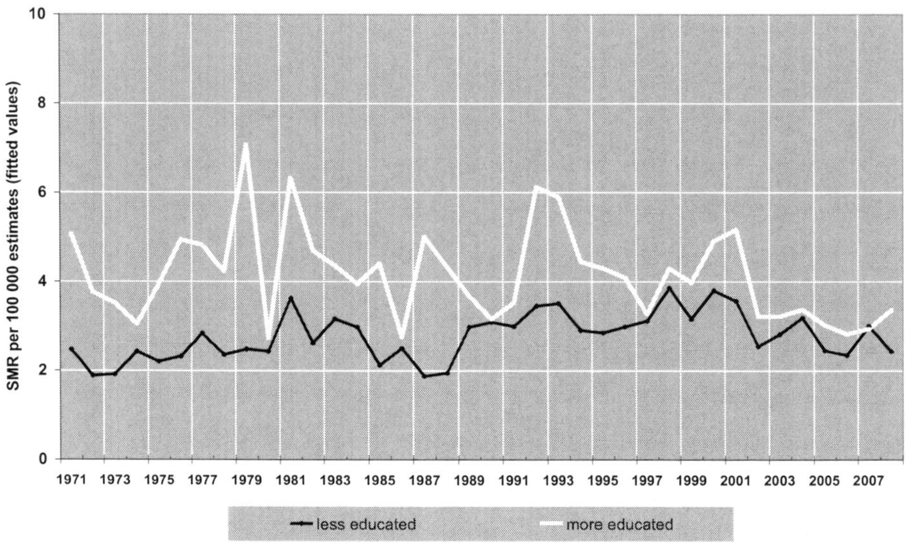

Fig. 4.12 Mortality due to Parkinson disease by education 1971–2008, Hungarian population aged 30 and over, representing type VI causes of death

others, both are in increasing but with different intensity (cancer of the oral cavity, non-Hodgkin disease) or the mortality of the better educated is declining while the mortality of the less educated is stagnating (cancer of thyroid, prostate cancer, peptic ulcer). The possibility that these diseases start to decline or strongly decline among the less educated can certainly be hoped for, but the follow-up time would be longer in these cases than our observation period. There is thus no point in laying down a definition for the purpose of this study. Some diseases, typically rare causes of death, could not be classified into the previous types and they are placed into Type VI, represented by Fig. 4.12.

Though a clear follow-up pattern was identified for only three causes of death, there is evidence of some kind of follow-up for a large number of diseases but it is not easily identified. Time lags are usually long, exceeding more than one or two decades, so that while follow-up may provide a vague and partial explanation for mortality developments and the development of inequalities for the chosen relatively short time period, it certainly does not a provide a full picture. Taking a closer look at the onsets of trend changes, it is quite obvious that they cluster in time. Most of the changes occurred in the very first years of the 1980s and around 1990. Both these periods were important turning points, and the two clusters can thus be interpreted as indicators of two diverging trends in living conditions, in the widest possible sense of the term.

In the first cluster we find, surprisingly, a number of nutrition-related causes of death: diabetes, other endocrine diseases, and two strongly nutrition-related cancers (cancer of the uterus and gallbladder cancer). Trends of mortality by education diverge from about the same point of time for a number of causes of death related to the circulatory system: chronic ischemic heart disease, arrhythmias, heart failure, atherosclerosis, other diseases of the veins and arteries and pulmonary heart disease. Causes of death which are possibly nutrition-related, such as cancer of the rectum, acute ischemic heart disease and ischemic stroke, also show signs of changing mortality relations by education between 1980 and 1983. Some other causes of death, which are clearly not nutrition-related, such as meningitis, cancer of the liver, cancer of the brain, melanoma, other skin cancer and leukaemia, join this cluster. The most likely interpretation of the existence of this cluster is that these changes reflect the widening inequalities in the quality of diet for the two social groups distinguished by educational level. Alternatively, within the risk-factor oriented explanatory framework, one can argue that all these changes are attributable to diverging trends of excessive alcohol consumption, noting that cirrhosis of the liver, the only cause of death which is clearly related to alcohol consumption, started to emerge a couple of years earlier. Alcohol-related changes are known to have an immediate mortality impact but some possible effects of the divergence in alcohol consumption cannot be ruled out. Altogether, divergence in nutrition seems to provide a more suitable explanatory framework.

The second cluster includes causes of death with important trend changes between 1989 and 1993. Smoking-related causes, such as cancer of the larynx and cancer of the trachea, bronchus and lung, clearly dominate this cluster, joined by some other diseases such as colon, pancreas, kidney and bladder cancer and valve diseases with other than rheumatic origin. Attributing the evolution of this cluster to the appearance of the divergence in smoking habits in the two educational classes, it is to be noted that this divergence point seems to be more diffused in time than the one related to the divergence in nutrition: trends of important smoking-related causes of death (cancer of the oesophagus) started to diverge a year earlier than 1989, though this cancer type is also influenced by nutrition.

4.6 Discussion

To explain the rise of mortality inequalities between the less and the more educated from the very beginning of the 1980s in Hungary, one might turn towards basic sociological approaches which would focus on the changing relations of education and income, assuming that the relationship between the two was non-existent in the 1970s and became gradually stronger over the period between 1981 and 2008. From a simplified point of view on the former state socialist states that assumes that these countries had no income inequalities at all, the onset of mortality inequalities during the 1980s must be a mystery.

In fact, income inequalities were already present and connected to educational levels during the 1970s in Hungary. Even after taking compensation in-kind into account—since a large share of incomes was undoubtedly distributed in this form—the income of those with higher education can be estimated as being twice as high as that of people without this qualification (Pető and Szakács 1985). During the

1980s the maturation of the "second economy" partly confused this relationship. In this period the state made some form of economic activities free from its direct control; therefore, in this sector (especially in agriculture) a limited market economy developed. Social status was distributed along two axes: in the formal economy, in which income and education were correlated, creating very mild income inequalities, and in the informal economy, in which education and income did not correlate strongly (Kolosi 1987). Since the emergence of the free market economy following 1990, the correlation of income and education has become stronger and stronger, just as in most European countries (Tóth 2005). This, coupled with the lack of a significant improvement in GDP, led to widening social inequalities and the extension of poverty.

The changing relation between income and education therefore plays a certain role in explaining widening mortality inequalities, but it cannot explain the negligible mortality inequalities which existed during the 1970s nor their revival during the 1980s. We should look, therefore, at nutrition-related risk factors.

The food supply in Hungary was mostly based on domestic production during the 1970s and 1980s. Limited exchange with other state socialist countries existed but imports were mainly limited to a small amount of tropical fruits. Domestic products, however, were satisfactory for domestic demand. Agriculture had developed into one of the leading ones in Europe and from the 1960's there was no food shortage in Hungary. The distribution of food was rather even and quality differences by education hardly existed. During the 1980s, with the growth of the "second economy", food provision varied and prices were already partly market-driven. The better-off could use their resources to purchase better quality food and these provisions were available to a large share of the population, but obviously not for everyone. Low food prices, together with energy prices which were still subsidized, made it possible for a larger proportion of the population to buy food of satisfactory quality. In the countryside, "around-the-house" agricultural activity was widespread, producing mostly for the household (occasionally producing for the market, too). During the 1980's the proportion of food grown "around-the-house" was estimated at 40 % of the overall food consumed (KSH 2009).

From the 1990s the food supply and the price system of the country were placed into a global context. Open trade relations provided a great variety of available food, while domestic production, including around-the house output, started to decline. Food prices relative to income represented a greater and greater share of household expenditure and competed with rising energy costs. Around-the-house agricultural production, which had been characteristic for many households for decades, halved in less than a decade: its share in overall food consumption of 20 % in 2000 had shrunk to 10 % by 2008 (KSH 2009). As a result of these processes, the availability of quality food has been shrinking for an ever growing proportion of the population. Domestic agricultural production, however, started to recover in the last years of our observation period, as the states that joined the European Union in 2004 came to benefit from the unified European Agricultural Policy.

The history of food production and food availability seems to run in parallel to the inequalities in nutrition-related mortality, so this narrative provides a very plausible explanatory framework for our findings. If this framework is supported by similar findings from other countries, then we can conclude that the mortality of the middle income industrialised countries, with moderate income inequalities, is still strongly determined by nutritional differences and by the lack of availability of quality food for large proportions of their populations.

Social differences in food intake have been described both in wealthy and poorer countries and are usually discussed in connection with obesity. Major changes in human nutrition have also been described, characterized by a growth in sugar and animal source food intake (Popkin 2006). In the context of wealthier countries, the poorer nutritional habits of the less educated is usually understood in the context of lack of knowledge, forced habits by tradition or lack of awareness due to putative or real economic interests. In the case of poor countries the phenomena is understood in the context of absolute deprivation and poverty. Several facts indicate that none of these scenarios are appropriate for middle income countries. Hungarian household surveys, for instance, indicate that the amount of sugar and sweetened beverages consumed is much lower in low income households than in households with higher income. The difference in this respect between the lowest and the highest income quintile households was fivefold in 2008[2]. Some features of the differences in food consumption, however, run parallel with the pattern of the Western countries, such as the similar levels of pork consumption of households with different income and the large gaps in poultry, fruit and vegetable consumption. Relatively high pork intake is the only fact which would suggest that tradition also plays some role in forming nutrition patterns. Differences in fruit and vegetable consumption fluctuate and depend on yearly prices (Polgár 2005; KSH 2009) so there is good reason to attribute these differences to the decline of around the house production and the lack of financial resources. Food intake differences by education can largely be explained by rising poverty among the less educated and the changes in the system of food production and pricing.

As a generalisation of our findings, we note that the nutritional elements of living conditions are rarely measured in Europe and they are usually restricted to the poorest countries. In the first relevant Eurobarometer survey, however, less than 15 % of the West European population answered "yes" to the question if paying for food causes any (some or serious) problem, and the corresponding proportion was between 23 and 46 % for Central, Eastern and Baltic countries (not including the Czech Republic and Slovenia). These data refer to the years around 1990. Publicly available raw data of the second European Quality of Life Survey[3] (2007) indicate that the question of food quality is still relevant in CEE and Baltic countries. For the only directly food-related question ("Can you afford a meal with meat, chicken or fish every second day if you want it?") no more than 10 % of the population gave a negative answer in West European countries, whereas this proportion was around 25 % in most CEE and Baltic countries and in Greece, and even higher in some countries such as Slovakia,

[2] http://www.ksh.hu/docs/hun/xtabla/haztfogy/tablhf10_05_04.html Az egy főre jutó éves kiadások részletezése COICOP-csoportosítás szerint, 2010 [Detailed annual household spending on food per capita by COICOP classification, by income quintiles, 2010]

[3] http://www.eurofound.europa.eu/areas/qualityoflife/eqls/2007/index.htm.

Bulgaria and Hungary (31, 38 and 42 %, respectively)[4]. The same question was included in the same year in the European Statistics on Income and Living Condition survey and released results (Ward et al. 2009) suggest that that survey yielded a similar picture: no more than 12 % of the population in Western Europe was affected and 15 %–37 % in Central and Eastern Europe and in the Baltic countries (except for Estonia, Romania and Bulgaria).

Data indicate that even if starvation-related mortality is negligible in lower-middle income European countries, there are good reasons to assume that the quality of nutrition is still not satisfactory for large proportions of the populations in these countries, and leaves its footprint on their mortality pattern. As far as the history of the Hungarian food provision regime is concerned, some of its elements can be regarded as similar to other countries of the region, while some other elements are certainly different.

The above-mentioned developments in income inequalities and food provision in the 1970s are probably similar in all CEE countries, while the introduction of the second economy was unique to Hungary. The development of free market conditions from the 1990s and the degree of exposure to the global competition varied over time and between the countries, as did the role of around-the-house agricultural production. Rising income inequalities and the application of a global pricing system, however, seem to lead to similar levels of mortality inequalities in these countries, though the composition of over-mortality by cause differs (Leinsalu et al. 2009). CEE and Baltic countries, therefore, probably share more common features than differences in this respect. The generalization of the findings for the whole region of "Eastern Europe", however, seems less fruitful, allowing for the fact that the CEE and Baltic countries have had consistently lower income inequalities than countries of the Former Soviet Union other than the Baltic countries. Several other aspects of household economy, such as the overwhelming role of energy expenditure in CEE countries, are not present in the same way.

4.7 Limitations and Shortcomings of the Study

The analysis of cause-specific mortality is a challenging task. These studies typically go beyond the time periods of consistent registration systems of causes of death and creating credible time series is demanding. The solution chosen in this paper can be criticized and other alternatives of code bridging should be considered in further research. The classification of causes of death by their relation to mortality developments between the more and the less educated can also be questioned and other alternatives should also be regarded. The method followed by this paper was to decompose the overall time series to sequences of linear trends and there is no doubt that other than linear approximate trends could also have been considered. Moreover, the linear approximation itself was carried out with a high level of uncertainty: the

[4] http://www.eurofound.europa.eu/areas/qualityoflife/eqls/eqls2007/2eqls_07_05.htm.

exact point of time when trends changed was hard to establish, which introduces some uncertainties about the findings.

The changing composition of the population over time is an inherent problem of studies examining long term developments. In our case the share of the population aged 30 years or more with less than secondary school graduation was 87 % in 1971 and 63 % in 2008. A more detailed educational classification of the population would have been desirable but was impossible to carry out with consistency due to major changes in the schooling system during the observed period.

In our discussion we deliberately avoided some important issues which might naturally be regarded as good candidates for explaining mortality inequalities, such as health care provision and differences in health care utilization. The reason for this neglect was the lack of space to cover all elements of cause-specific mortality inequalities in one paper. Instead, we aimed at identifying some general driving forces contributing to widening inequalities. Setting up an accurate statistical record of the different health services, which would have been necessary to evaluate their role, was beyond the possibilities of this study. Similarly, we had to disregard other, similarly important elements of welfare policy, except for some aspects of income distribution.

Our discussion addresses only some of all the arguments raised in different theoretical approaches to the epidemiological transitions theory. We limited the scope of the paper to looking at the role of nutrition in the long term development of mortality and mortality inequalities. The intention of providing an explanation for the observed mortality trends in connection with the social processes of Hungary in the last four decades has left little space for discussing the applicability of other, similarly attractive, explanatory frameworks that undoubtedly have high potential.

Appendix

Cause of death	ICD 8 coding (1971–1978)	ICD 9 coding (1979-1995)	ICD 10 coding (1996–2008)	Fitting coefficients for 1978, 1996 and 2005
Diarrhoea, dysentery, enteritis	006–009, 561–563, 004, 532	006–009, 555–558, 004, 532, 562	A06–A09, K50–K55, A03, A04, K26, K65, K67	1.17; 0.85; 0.84
Septicaemia caused by other agents than streptococcus or staphylococcus	38	38	A41.40–A41.90	Small case number
Tuberculosis	010–018	010–018	A15–A19, B90	1.00; 0.91; 1.00
Pulmonary tuberculosis	010–012	010–012	A15–A16	0.94; 0.79; 0.89
Other tuberculosis	013–018	013–018	A17–A19, B90	1.23; 1.55; 1.42
HIV/AIDS	–	042–044, 279.5	B20–B24	Small case number
SARS and other new diseases with unknown aetiology and disease caused by antibiotic resistant bacteria	–	–	U00–U99	Small case number
Viral hepatitis	070	070	B15–B19	Small case number
Syphilis	090–097	090–097	A50–A53	Small case number
			G22, I98.00	
Encephalitis, meningitis	045–046	036	A85–A89	1.10, 1.27, 1.17
	062–066	046–049	G00–G06	
	036	062–064	G37.30–G37.40	
	320–324	320–326	A17.00, A39, A81, A83, A94	
			G08, G09, G92, G36.10	
Influenza	470–474	487	J10–J11	Not fitted
Other acute upper respiratory infections	460–466, 034.0	460–465, 034.0	J00–J06	Small case number
Pneumonia	480–486	480–486	J12–J18	0.91, 0.76, 0.76
Chronic bronchitis	490, 491	490.00		
		491, 494.00	J40–J42, J47	0.82, 1.23, 2.16
Emphysema	492	492	J43	1.05, 1.12, 1.19
Asthma	493	493	J45	0.89, 0.58; 0.94

Cause of death	ICD 8 coding (1971–1978)	ICD 9 coding (1979-1995)	ICD 10 coding (1996–2008)	Fitting coefficients for 1978, 1996 and 2005
Other diseases of the pulmonary system	460–519	460–519	J20–J30, J44, J46–J99	Small case number
Appendicitis	540–543	540–543	K35–K38	1.22; 1.27; 1.17
Peptic ulcer	533–534, 531	531, 533–534	K25, K27–K28	0.68; 0.76; 0.90
Nutritional anomies	280–281	280–281	D50–D53	Small case number
Diabetes	250	250	E10–E14	1.24; 1.38; 1.40
Malnutrition, nutritional deficiencies	260–269	260–268	E40–E64	Small case number
Obesity	277–278	278	E65–E68	Small case number
Diseases of the endocrine system other than diabetes, malnutrition or obesity	240–246, 251–259, 270–273, 275–279	240–246, 251–259, 270–273, 275–277	E00–E07 E15–E35, E70–E90	Small case number
Cirrhosis of the liver	571	571	K70, K71.30–K71.80, K72.10, K73, K74, K76	0.71; 0.65; 0.95
Diseases of the digestive system other than cirrhosis	520–570, 572–577	520–570, 572–579	K00–K67, K71.00–K71.20, K72.00, K72.30–K72.90, K75, K77–K93	0.84; 0.91; 0.95
Parkinson disease	342	332.00	G20	1.20; 1.46; 1.43
Alzheimer disease	290	290.1, 331	F00–F03, G30	Small case number
Multiply sclerosis	340	340	G35	1.09; 0.81; 0.92
Epilepsy	345	345	G40, G41.00–G41.10	1.57; 1.31; 1.32
Maternal mortality	630–678	630–679	O00-O99	Small case number
Mental disorders	*290–315*	*287.80–319*	*F00–F99*	*2.01; 1.23; 2.14*
Cancer of the oral cavity	140–149	140–149	C00–C14	1.14; 0.88; 0.97
Cancer of oesophagus	150	150	C15	0.91; 0.85; 0.89
Cancer of the stomach	151	151	C16	0.84; 0.85; 0.91
Cancer of the colon	153	153	C18	0.87; 0.93; 0.99

Cause of death	ICD 8 coding (1971–1978)	ICD 9 coding (1979-1995)	ICD 10 coding (1996–2008)	Fitting coefficients for 1978, 1996 and 2005
Cancer of the rectum, rectosigmoid junction, anus and anal canal	154	154	C19–C21	0.84; 0.79; 0.85
Cancer of the liver	155	155	C22	0.84; 0.79; 0.85
Cancer of the gallbladder	156	156	C23–C24	0.89; 0,91; 0.85
Cancer of pancreas	157	157	C25	1.00; 0.93; 0.93
Cancer of larynx	161, I46.80	161, I46.50	C32	0.88; 0.91; 0.98
Cancer of trachea, bronchus and the lung	162	162	C33–C34	0.92; 0.92; 0.91
Melanoma	172	172	C43	0.92; 0.91; 0.91
Other skin cancer	173	173	C44	0.68; 1.00; 0.76
Mesothelioma	*158.90, 163.00, 163.10*	*163.00–163.90, 158.80,–164.10, 171.40–171.60*	*C45*	*0.22; 0.21; 0.60*
Breast cancer	174	174	C50	0.89; 0.90; 0.91
Cancer of the vulva	184	184	C51–C52	Small case number
Cancer of the cervix	180	180	C53	1.00; 0.87; 0.86
Cancer of uterus	*182*	*182, 179*	*C54, C55*	*0.60; 0.60; 0.66*
Cancer of ovary	181, 183	181, 183	C56, C57, C58	0.97; 0.90; 0.90
Cancer of penis	187.0	187.00–187.41	C60	Small case number
Cancer of prostate	185	185	C61	0.96; 0.90; 0.90
Cancer of testicle	186	186	C62	Small case number
Cancer of kidney	189.00–189.10	189.00–189.10	C64, C65	0.93; 1.12; 0.98
Cancer of bladder	188, 189.20–189.90	188, 189.20–189.90	C66, C67, C68	0.98; 0.90; 0.91
Cancer of the brain and other part of the nervous system	190.00–192.30	190.00–192.30	C69–C72	1.03; 0.90; 0.93
Cancer of thyroid	193	193	C73	1.16; 1.18; 1.35
Hodgkin disease	201	201	C81	1.72; 0.68; 0.79
Non-Hodgkin disease	200, 202	200, 202	C81–C82	0.65; 0.83; 0.89
Leukaemia	203–209	203–209	C90–C97	0.98; 0.86; 0.85
Rheumatic heart disease	*390–398*	*390–398*	*I00–I09*	*0.90; 0.31; 0.31*
Acute rheumatic heart disease	390–392	390–392	I00–I02	Small case number

Cause of death	ICD 8 coding (1971–1978)	ICD 9 coding (1979-1995)	ICD 10 coding (1996–2008)	Fitting coefficients for 1978, 1996 and 2005
Chronic rheumatic heart disease	*393–398*	*393–398*	*I05–I09*	*0.79, 0.28; 0.31*
Rheumatic valve disease	*394.0, 395.0, 396.0*	*394.0–397.0*	*I05–I08*	*1.03, 0,15, 0.25*
Hypertensive diseases	400-404	401-405	I10-I15	0.84; 1.34; 1.42
Ischemic heart disease	410–414	410–414	I20–I25	0.89; 1.11; 1.12
Chronic ischemic heart disease	412	414	I25	1.20; 1.50; 1.18
Acute ischemic heart disease	410–411, 413–414	410–413	I20–I24	0.64; 0.80; 0.99
Pulmonary heart diseases	426, 450	415–417	I26–I28	1.20; 1.28; 1.45
Other heart diseases	420–425, 427–428	420–429	I30–I52	1.97; 1.08; 1.03
Valve heart disorders with no rheumatic origin	*424.0–424.1*	*424.00–424.30*	*I34–I37*	*0.42; 1.00; 0.88*
Acute endocarditis	421	421	I33, I39.8	Small case number
Acute myocarditis	422	422	I40-41	Small case number
Cardiomyopathy	425	425	I42-I43	3.35; 1.11; 0.88
Arrhythmias	*427*	*427*	*I46-I49*	*0.34; 1.12; 0.78*
Heart failure	*427–428*	*428*	*I50*	*0.36; 5.08; 4.38*
Cerebrovascular diseases	430–438	430–438	I60–I69	1.01; 0.91; 0.88
Hemorrhagic stroke	430–431	430–432	I60–I62	0.96; 0.88; 0.90
Ischemic stroke[a]	432–435, 437	433, 434, 436	I63–I66	0.64; 0.79; 0.75
Diseases of the arteries and the veins	*432–448*	*440–444, 447–448*	*I70–I79*	*0.23; 0.81; 0.84*
Atherosclerosis	440	440	I70	0.76; 0.79; 0.86
Aortic aneurysm	441	441	I71, I72.00	0.77; 1.15; 1.13
Other disease of the arteries and the veins	442–448	450–458	I80–I89	1.04, 0.73; 0.68

Cursive Uncertain estimates

[a] Several variations of coding this disease are in use

References

Albala, C., & Vio, F. (1995). Epidemiological transition in Latin America the case of Chile. *Public Health, 109,* 431–442.

Anand, P., Kunnumakara, A. B., Sundaram, C., Harikumar, K., Tharakan, S. T., Lai, O. S., Sung, B., & Aggarwal, B. B. (2008). Cancer is preventable disease that requires major lifestyle changes. *Pharmaceutical Research, 25*(9), 2097–2116.

Armelagos, G. J., Brown, P. J., & Turner, B. (2005). Evolutionary, historical and political economic perspectives on health and disease. *Social Science and Medicine, 61*(4), 755–765.

Bengtsson, T., & Dribe, M. (2011). The late emergence of socioeconomic mortality differentials: A micro-level study of adult mortality in southern Sweden 1815–1968. *Explorations in Economic History, 48,* 389–400.

Bengtsson, T., Cameron, C., & Lee, J. Z. (Eds.). (2004). Life under pressure. Mortality and living standards in Europe and Asia, 1700–1900. Cambridge: The MIT Press.

Boffetta, P., & Nyberg, F. (2003). Contribution of environmental factors to cancer risk. *British Medical Bulletin, 68,* 71–94.

Bonnux, L., Barendregt, J. J., Meeter, K., Bonsel, G. J., & van der Maas, P. J. (1994). Estimating clinical morbidity due to ischemic heart failure: The future rise of heart failure. *American Journal of Public Health, 84*(19), 20–28.

Calle, E. E., & Kaaks, R. (2004). Overweight, obesity and cancer: Epidemiological evidence and proposed mechanism. *Nat Rev Cancer, 4,* 579–591.

Califf, R. M., Armstrong, P. W., Granger, C. B., Harrington, R. A., Lee, K., Simes, R. J., van de Werf, F., Wallentin, L., & White, H.D., for the Virtual Coordinating Centre for Global Collaborative Cardiovascular Research (VIGOUR) organization. (2010). Towards a new order in cardiovascular medicine: re-engineering through global collaboration. European Heart Journal. doi:10.1093/eurheartj/ehp550.

Carolina, M. S., & Gustavo, L. F. (2003). Epidemiological transition: Model or illusion? A look at the problem of health in Mexico. *Social Science & Medicine, 57,* 539–550.

Castillo-Salgado, C., Mujica, O., & Loyola, E. (1999). A subregional assessment of demographic and health trends on the Americas: 1980–1998. *Statistical Bulletin (Metropolitan Life Insurance Company),* 80(2), 2–12.

Costello, A., & Osrin, D. (2005). Epidemiological transition, medicalisation of childbirth, and neonatal mortality: Three Brazilian birth-cohorts. *The Lancet, 365*(March 5), 825–826.

Dalton-Griffin, L., & Kellam, P. (2009). Infectious causes of cancer and their detection, Mini review. *Journal of Biology, 8,* 67.

Davey-Smith, G., & Hart, C. (2002). Life-course socioeconomic and behavioural influences on cardiovascular disease mortality: The collaborative study. *American Journal of Public health, 92*(8), 1295–1298.

Farmer, P. (1996). Social inequalities and emerging infectious diseases. *Emerging Infectious Diseases, 2*(4), 259–269.

Forsdahl, A. (1978). Living conditions in childhood and subsequent development of risk factors for arteriosclerotic heart disease. The cardiovascular survey in Finnmark 1974–75. *Journal of Epidemiology and Community Health, 32,* 34–37.

Frenk, J., Frejka, T., Bobadilla, J. L., Stern, C., Lozano, R., Sepúlveda, J, & Jose, M. (1991). Health transition in middle income countries. New challenges for health care. *Health Policy and Planning, 4*(1), 29–39.

Gaziano, T., Reddy, S. K., Paccaud, F., & Chatuverdi, V. (2006). Cardiovascular Disease. In D. T. Jamison, J. G. Breman, A. R. Measham, G. Alleyne, M. Claeson, D. B. Evans, P. Jha, A. Mills, & P. Musgrove (Eds.), *Disease control priorities in developing countries* (2nd ed.) *The Word Bank.* Washington DC, P 645–662.

Gerstein, O., & Wilmoth, J. R. (2002) The cancer transition in Japan since 1951. *Demographic Research, 7,* 271–306.

Hall, A. (2008). Plague in London: A case study of the biological and social pressures exerted by 300 Years of Yersinia pestis, Thesis. Oregon State University.

Hablicsek, L., & Kovács, K. (2007). Az életkilátások differenciálódása iskolai végzettség szerint, 1971–2008, Kutatási jelentések, 84, KSH Népességtudományi Kutatóintézet, Budapest. 2007.

Hashibe, M., et al. (2009). Interaction between tobacco and alcohol use and the risk of head and neck cancer: Pooled analysis in the International Head and Neck Cancer Epidemiology Consortium. *Cancer Epidemiol Biomarkers Prev, 18,* 541.

Harper, K., & Armelagos, G. (2010). The changing disease-scape in the third epidemiological transition. *Int. J. Environ. Res. Public Health, 7,* 675–697.

Harper, S., Lynch, J., & Davey-Smith, G. (2011). Social determinants and the decline of cardiovascular diseases: Understanding the links. *Annu. Rev. Public Health, 32,* 39–69.

Heuveline, P., Guillot, M., & Gwatkin, D. R. (2002). The uneven tides of the health transition. *Social Science & Medicine, 55,* 313–322.

Hill, K., Vapattanawong, P., Prasartkul, P., Porapakkham, Y., Lim, S. S., & Lopez, A. D. (2007). Epidemiologic transition interrupted: a reassessment of mortality trends in Thailand, 1980–2000. *International Journal of Epidemiology, 36,* 374–384.

Huicho, L., Trelles, M., Gonzales, F., Mendoza, W., & Miranda, J. (2009). Mortality profiles in a country facing epidemiological transition: An analysis of registered data. *BMC Public Health, 9,* 47.

Janssen, F., & Kunst, A. E. (2004). ICD coding changes and discontinuities in trends in cause-specific mortality in six European countries, 1950–99. *Bulletin of the World Health Organization, 82*(12), 904–913.

Kaplan, G. A., & Keil, J. E. (1993). Socioeconomic factors and cardiovascular disease: A review of the literature. *Circulation, 88,* 1973–1998.

Kolosi, T. (1987). *Tagolt társadalom.* Budapest, Gondolat.

KSH. (2009). Zöldség és gyümölcsfogyasztás, Statisztikai Tükör, II. évfolyam 97. szám.

Kuh, D., & Ben-Shlomo, Y. (1997). *A life course approach to chronic disease epidemiology.* United States: Oxford University Press.

Lawlor, D. A., Davey-Smith, G., Leon, D. A., Sterne, J. A. C., & Ebrahim, S. (2002). Secular trends in mortality by stroke subtype in the 20th century: A retrospective analysis. *The Lancet, 360*(December 7), 1818–1823.

Leinsalu, M., Stirbu, I., Vågero, D., Kalédiené, R., Kovács, K., Wojtyniak, B., Wróblewska, W., Mackenbach, J. P., & Kunst, A. E. (2009). Educational inequalities in mortality in four eastern European countries: Divergence in trends during the post-communist transition from 1990 to 2000. *International Journal of Epidemiology, 38,* 512–525.

Link, B. G., & Phelan, J. (1995). Social conditions as fundamental causes of disease. *Journal of Health and Social Behaviour, 35* (Extra Issue), 80–94.

Lussier, M. H., Bourbeau, R., & Choiniére, R. (2008). Does the recent evolution of Canadian mortality agree with the epidemiologic transition theory? *Demographic Research, 18,* 531–568.

Marshall, M. (1991). The second fatal impact: Cigarette smoking, choric disease and the epidemiological transition in Oceania. *Social Science and Medicine, 33*(12), 1327–1342.

Mackenbach, J. P., Stirbu, I., Roskam, A. J., Schaap, M., Menvielle, G., Leinsalu, M., & Kunst, A. E., for the European Union Working Group on Socioeconomic Inequalities in Health. (2008). Socioeconomic Inequalities in Health in 22 European Countries. *New England Journal of Medicine, 358,* 2468–81.

Marmot, M. G., Stansfeld, S., Patel, C. F., North, M. B., Head, J., White, L., Brunner, E. A., Feeney, A. G., & Davey-Smith, G. (1991). Health inequalities among British civil servants: The Whitehall II study. *The Lancet, 337*(8754), 138–93.

McKeown, T. F. (1976a). *The modern rise of population.* London: Edward Arnold.

McKeown, T. F. (1976b). *The role of medicine–dream, mirage or nemesis*? London: Nuffield Provincial Hospital Trust.

McKeown, T. F. (2009). The epidemiologic transition: Changing patterns of mortality and population dynamics. *Am J Lifestyle Med, 3*(1 Suppl.), 19–26.

Mckeown, T. F., & Record, R. G. (1962). Reasons for the decline of mortality in England and Wales during the nineteenth century. *Population Studies, 16,* 94–122.

Melegh, A., & Őri, P. (2003). A második demográfiai átmenet elmélete. In Spéder Zs. (szerk.): Család és népesség – itthon és Európában, KSH NKI – Századvég Kiadó. Budapest, 495–623.

Meslé, F., & Vallin, J. (1996). Reconstructing long-tem seria of causes of death. The case of France. *Historical methods, 29*(2), 72–87.

Miech, R., Pampel, F., Kim, J., & Rogers, R. G. (2011). The enduring association between education and mortality. The role of widening and narrowing disparities. *American Sociological Review, 76*(6), 913–934.

O'Donnell, M. J., et al. (2010). Risk factors for ischemic and intracerebral haemorrhagic stroke study in 22 countries. *The Lancet, 376*(9735), 112–123.

Omran, A. R. (1971). The epidemiologic transition, a theory of the epidemiology of population change. *Milbank Memorial Fund Quarterly, 49,* 509–538.

Omran, A. R. (1983). The epidemiologic transition theory: A preliminary update. *Journal ofTropical Pediatrics, 29,* 305–316.

Omran, A. R. (1998). The epidemiologic transition theory revisited thirty years later. *World Health Statistics Quarterly, 51,* 99–119.

Olshansky, J., & Ault, A. B. (1986). The fourth stage of the epidemiological transition: The age of delayed degenerative diseases. *The Milbank Quarterly, 64,* 355–391.

Pamuk, E. (1985). Social class inequality in mortality from 1921 to 1972 in England and Wales. *Population Studies, 39*(1), 17–31.

Parkin, D. M. (2006). The global health burden of infection-associated cancers in the year 2002. *International Journal of Cancer, 118,* 3030–3044.

Pearson, T. A. (2003). Education and income: Double-edged swords in the Epidemiological Transition. *Ethnicity & Disease, 13*(Suppl. 2), S158–S163.

Pető, I., & Szakács, S. (1985). A hazai gazdaság négy évtizedének története, 1945–1985, Közgazdasági és Jogi Könyvkiadó, Budapest.

Polgár, Á. (2005). Élelmiszermérlegek és tápanyagfogyasztás, 2003, Budapest, 2005, Központi Statisztikai Hivatal.

Popkin, B. M. (2006). Global nutrition dynamics: The world is shifting rapidly toward a diet linked with non-communicable diseases. *Am J Clin Nutr, 84,* 289–298.

Popkin, B. M., & Mendez, M. (2007). The rapid shift of the nutrition. The global obesity epidemic. In I. Kawachi & S. Wamela (Eds.), *Globalization and Health* (pp. 68–97). Oxford: University Press.

Rogers, J., & Nelson, M. C. (1997). The epidemiologic transition revisited: Or what happens if we look beneath the surface? *Health Transition Review, 7*(2), 241–255.

Salomon, J. A., & Murray, C. J. L. (2002). The epidemiological transition revisited: Compositional models for causes of death by age and Sex. *Population and Development Review, 28*(2), 205–228.

Slack, P. (1981). The disappearance of plague: An alternative view. *The Economic History Review, New Series, 34*(3), 469–476.

Slack, P. (1989). The response to plague in early modern England: Public policies and their consequences. In J. Walter, R. Schofield (Eds.), *Famine. Disease and the social order in early modern society* (pp. 167–187). Cambridge: Cambridge University Press.

Spijker, J., & von Wissen, L. (2010). Socioeconomic determinants of male mortality in Europe: The absolute and relative income hypotheses revisited. *Genus LXVI*(1), 37–61.

Tóth, IGy. (2005). Income composition and inequalities in Hungary, 1987–2003, TÁRKI Social Report Reprint Series No. 3. Budapest, Tárki.

Vallin, J., & Meslé, F. (2004). Convergences and divergences in mortality. A new approach to health transition, Demographic Research. Doi: 10.4054/Dem.Res.2004.S2.2.

Vigneron, E. (1989). The epidemiological transition in an overseas territory: Disease mapping in French Polynesia. *Social Science and Medicine, 29*(8), 913–922.

Vigneron, E. (1993). Epidemiological transition and geographical discontinuities: The case of cardiovascular mortality in French Polynesia. *Social Science and Medicine, 37*(6), 77–790.

Ward, T., Lelkes, O., Sutherland, H., & Tóth, I. Gy. (2009). European inequalities. Social Inclusion and Income Distribution In the European Union, Tárki, Budapest.

Wolleswinkel-van den Bosch, J. (1996). The epidemiological transition in The Netherlands, Rotterdam: Erasmus University.

Wolleswinkel-van den Bosch, J., van Poppel, F. W. A., & Mackenbach, J. P. (1996). Reclassifying causes of death to study the epidemiological transition in The Netherlands, 1875–1992. *European Journal of Population, 12*(4), 327–361.

Wolleswinkel-van den Bosch, J., van Poppel, F. W. A., & Mackenbach, J. P. (1998). Mortality decline in the Netherlands in the period 1850–1992, a turning point analysis. *Social Science and Medicine, 47*(4), 429–463.

Yach, D., Wipfli, H., Hammond, R., & Glantz, S. (2007). Globalization and tobacco. In I. Kawachi, S. Wamela (Eds.), *Globalization and Health* (pp. 68–97). Oxford: University Press.

Yusuf, S., Reddy, S., Ôunpuu, S., & Anand, S. (2001a). Global burden of cardiovascular diseases Part I: General considerations, the epidemiologic transition, risk factors, and impact of urbanization. *Circulation, 104,* 2746–2753.

Yusuf, S., Reddy, S., Ôunpuu, S., & Anand, S. (2001b). Global burden of cardiovascular diseases Part II: Variations in cardiovascular disease by specific ethnic groups and geographic regions and prevention strategies. *Circulation, 104,* 2855–2864.

decline than reported in previous studies of summary measures using an equally weighted count of the total number of at-risk indicators of dysregulated systems. Using a similar computational method to examine change in summary measures over-time, Karlamangla et al. (2006) also found that individuals with an increased biomarker risk score had higher risk of all-cause mortality over a 7-year period compared to those who exhibited a decrease in allostatic load score.

Recursive partitioning (RP) of individuals into low, intermediate, and high allostatic load categories is another approach to creating a biomarker summary score. To perform this technique, a set of predictor biomarker variables is identified and a well-established outcome, such as mortality, is defined. Once these are established, the recursive partitioning algorithm searches among the predictor biomarker variables and their cutpoints to determine the best single predictor variable and its corresponding cutpoint. Individuals are then partitioned into two groups, with individuals on one side of the cutpoint predicted to be in one of the outcome categories while individuals on the other side of the cutpoint are predicted to reside in the alternate outcome category (Zhang and Singer 1999). Using the MacArthur Study of Successful Aging, Gruenewald et al. (2006) illustrated the utility of RP techniques to identify biomarker classifications predictive of 12-year mortality.

A fourth approach uses factor analysis to investigate the relationships among individual biomarkers by grouping markers into system-specific factors. For instance, Kubzansky et al. (1999) observed three general factors to which they termed metabolic dysregulation, cardiovascular function, and SNS activity, which they associated with low educational attainment and hostility. Using some similar and additional biomarkers, Nakamura and Miyao (2003) also detected three system-specific factors related to pulmonary function, hematology, and protein metabolism. Among insulin resistant individuals, Sakkinen et al. (2000) examined 21 biomarkers that were grouped into seven factors associated with insulin resistance syndrome: body mass, inflammation, Vitamin K dependent proteins, insulin/glucose, procoagulation, blood pressure, and lipids.

We propose to use latent class analysis, a potentially promising approach for considering multiple indicators collected at one timepoint. This is an appropriate method of classifying individuals based on multiple biological and functioning indicators that represent functioning across several physiological systems by identifying clusters of individuals who share similar biological and functioning profiles. The latent class approach also allows for consideration of a multi-physiological system without depending on a given outcome for categorization. This is in contrast to the recursive partitioning method that requires an outcome measure (e.g., mortality) to categorize individuals with a given biological profile (as used by Gruenewald et al. (2006)). In other words, the latent class approach instead groups people based solely on the independent variables (biomarker or functioning indicators) and does not require an outcome variable in its classification process. The latent class approach has been used to classify individuals on a variety of health risk measures, including childhood disadvantage (Hamil-Luker and O'Rand 2007; O'Rand and Hamil-Luker 2005) and health risk behaviors (Laska et al. 2009). No studies, to our knowledge, have used this approach to classify individuals based on their biological profiles.

As indicated above, health domains included in summary measures have generally included indicators of cardiovascular health, metabolic indicators, inflammatory markers and indicators of functioning of SNS and HPA. In addition to indicators of physiological state, markers of functioning have also been predictive of future adverse outcomes (Crimmins et al. 2010; Guralnik et al. 1989; Newman et al. 2006). Along with the biomarkers generally included in summary measures, indicators of cognitive, kidney, lung, and physical function were found to be predictive of 5-year mortality, particularly among older persons (Crimmins et al. 2010).

The purpose of this study is to investigate how biomarkers and performance measures of functioning can be used to classify individuals into risk profiles using the latent class approach. The latent classes determined by this approach will be used to determine the utility of this categorization to predict subsequent mortality. It is hypothesized that this approach to classifying individuals based on their at-risk biomarker and functioning indicator profiles will yield additional useful information about how to categorize and better understand the meaning of risk profiles. This would provide another analytic technique for operationalizing health using an individual's biological risk and frailty profile as a means of classification.

5.3 Materials & Methods

5.3.1 Study Population

Participants with linked mortality data from the National Health and Nutrition Examination Survey (NHANES) III [1988–1994] aged 60 and older were included in the study. The NHANES is designed to regularly monitor the health and nutritional status of the American noninstitutionalized population. Every year approximately 5,000 people undergo detailed interviews and medical examinations that include several physiological measures and laboratory tests. US counties are the primary sampling units for this survey, which uses a complex sampling design requiring that weights be applied in analysis to make the sample representative of the US population.

Individuals with follow-up mortality data for the 5-years after their examination in the NHANES survey were included in our analysis ($N = 3{,}120$). Mortality and cause-of-death information were accessed from data linked to the National Death Index (NDI). The NDI has been shown to have very high sensitivity and specificity and is regarded as the best source of mortality data for survey matching (Cowper et al. 2002). Since we are interested in the classification of biomarkers related to mortality among non-violent, non-accidental deaths, we excluded individuals with violent or accidental causes of death based on the International Classification of Diseases, Injuries, and Causes of Death (ICD-10) ($N = 16$). This includes individuals dying from motor accidents ($N = 5$), falls ($N = 5$), other non-transport accidents ($N = 1$), suicide ($N = 2$), homicide ($N = 3$), or medical/surgical care complications ($N = 1$). Given the small number of individuals who died of certain causes of death (e.g., 3 individuals died of nervous system related conditions [ICD-10 classifications: G00, G03, G20–G21, G30]), we do not present results for cause-of-death analysis.

5.3.2 Measures

Ten markers were examined that have generally been included in earlier analyses using summary measures. These include indicators of cardiovascular functioning, metabolic processes and inflammation: diastolic blood pressure, systolic blood pressure, albumin, C-reactive protein (CRP), fibrinogen, glycated hemoglobin, total cholesterol, high-density lipoprotein cholesterol (HDL), and body mass index (BMI) (high: very obese, and low: underweight). Additionally, five indicators of frailty and functioning were also examined: Cystatin C (an indicator of kidney function), score of cognitive functioning, 8-foot timed walk, timed test of balance (tandem stance), and lung function (forced expiratory volume in 1 s [FEV1]/forced expiratory vital capacity [FVC]). The indicator of cognitive functioning was determined using a scale based on 26 questions. The total number of incorrectly answered questions was summed to create a cognition score, with a higher score indicating worse functioning. The questions asked included: the current date and day of the week; repeat words (e.g., apple, table, and penny) on first, second, and third trial; five monetary subtraction questions; 12 questions pertaining to story recall (six questions asked about two stories).

At-risk levels of these measures have been associated with adverse outcomes, including mortality. To examine the relationship between the latent class risks of biological and functioning indicators to mortality, we used clinical cutpoints (where available). If clinical cutpoints were not available, we attempted to distinguish the top population-based quartile and classify this as the at-risk level to dichotomize individuals into higher-risk and lower-risk levels (Table 5.1).

Based on their reported association with mortality, we considered additional variables, including: age, sex, years of education, marital status (married [includes spouse living in the household or not, as well as self-report of "living as married"] or not married [includes separated, divorced, widowed, and never married]) (Berkman 2000; Elo and Preston 1996; Idler and Benyamini 1997; Verbrugge and Wingard 1987).

5.3.3 Statistical Analysis

Latent class analysis (LCA) was conducted to classify individuals based on their biomarker and functioning profiles. LCA can be used to characterize the structure of the latent classes by determining the conditional probabilities for each of the observed variables in each of the latent classes (Clogg and Goodman 1984, 1986). Using these resultant latent classes, logistic regression models were conducted to predict mortality within 5-years of the interview when the indicators were measured. Three

Table 5.1 Cutoff points indicating higher risk for 15 biological and functioning indicators

Indicator	At-risk cutoff	%
Systolic blood pressure	> 90 mmHg	38.54
Diastolic blood pressure	> 140 mmHg	4.79
Albumin	≤ 3.9 g/dl	16.23
C-reactive protein	> 0.3 mg/dl	35.21
Fibrinogen	> 400 mg/dl	13.19
Glycated hemoglobin	≥ 6.5 %	13.08
Total cholesterol	> 240 mg/dl	33.13
High-density lipoprotein cholesterol	< 40 mg/dl	22.86
High BMI/very obese	> 35 kg/m^2	6.42
Low BMI/underweight	< 18.5 kg/m^2	1.66
Cystatin C[a]	> 1.25 mg/dl	20.16
Cognition score[a]	> 15 (of 26)	4.37
8-ft timed walk[a]	> 4.6 m/s	17.09
Timed tandem stance[a]	< 10 s	30.56
Lung function (FEV$_1$/FVC)[a]	< 32.89885	26.05

[a]At-risk cutoff based on top 25 % of sample distribution
BMI body mass index

models were examined: Model I adjusts for age and sex; Model II adds education (≥ high school vs < high school), marital status (dichotomus variable), and ethnicity to Model I. Model III includes self-rated health in addition to Model II covariates. For these three models, the class categorized as "no high-risk" (described below in further detail) was the latent class referent group in the analyses predicting 5-year mortality. The final model (Model IV) considers the association between a simple summary measure of allostatic load (computed by adding the total number of at-risk biological and functioning indicators [possible range 0–15] and Model III covariates. These models enable us to consider the effect of sociodemographic factors in our examination of the biological and functioning latent class risk profiles to mortality. Formally, the fully adjusted model that includes the latent class risk profiles (Model III) can be written as follows:

$$logit(\pi) = \alpha + \beta_D D_D + \beta_H H_H + \beta_L L_L$$

where D denotes demographic controls (age, sex, education, ethnicity), H denotes self-rated health, and L denotes latent class risk profiles. We account for the complex sampling design of NHANES using surveylogistic in SAS. All analyses were conducted using SAS (SAS Institute, Inc., Cary, NC), with the exception of LCA which used Latent Gold 4.5.

5.4 Results

The proportion of the US age 60+ population with high-risk levels of biomarkers and functioning indicators are reported in Table 5.1. Nearly 40 % had elevated SBP and 35 % had high CRP, while 13 % exhibited high fibrinogen levels. More than 20 % had

Table 5.2 Study sample characteristics ($N = 3{,}120$)

	Mean (SD) or %
Age	68.82 (10.76)
Male (%)	41.68
Ethnicity (%)	
Non-Hispanic white	86.04
Non-Hispanic black	7.14
Hispanic	5.35
Other	1.47
Education (%)	
< High school (<12 years)	54.25
≥ High school (≥12 years)	45.75
Married (%)	61.71
Self-reported health status (%)	
Excellent	14.79
Very good	26.18
Good	33.91
Fair	19.83
Poor	5.28
Dead after 5-year baseline (%)	13.56

high-risk (measured low) levels of HDL and 33 % had high-risk total cholesterol. A lower proportion had extreme BMI levels: 6 % were very obese and 2 % were underweight. For the measures of functioning, about 20 % had high Cystatin C levels, 31 % had low performance on the timed tandem stance, and 26 % had low lung function as indicated by FEV_1/FVC.

Table 5.2 summarizes the characteristics of the study sample. The mean age of the study population was 68.8 years, with males comprising less than half of the population (41.7 %). Overall, 61.7 % were married, and the participants had an average of 11.3 years of education (data not shown). The majority were non-Hispanic whites (86 %), with 7.1 % non-Hispanic blacks, and 5.4 % Hispanics. Five years after the initial exam, 13.6 % were no longer living.

To determine the latent class profiles that group individuals based on their biomarker and frailty profiles, we first examined all potential baseline models for the study sample. Table 5.3 shows that the 4-class model is the best baseline model based on the size of the decrease in the likelihood-ratio G^2 relative to the decline in degrees of freedom (df), which dropped substantially with the addition of each latent

Table 5.3 Comparison of baseline models from LCA for Age 60 +

No. of classes	Likelihood ratio G^2	df	AIC	BIC
2	4376.89	32736	4438.89	4626.18
3	4087.43	32720	4181.43	4465.39
4	**3912.93**	**32704**	**4038.93**	**4419.56**
5	3815.48	32688	3973.48	4450.78
6	3735.92	32672	3925.92	4499.88

Boldface type indicates the optimal model.

LCA latent class analysis, *df* degrees of freedom, *AIC* Akaike's information criteria, *BIC* Bayesian information criterion

Table 5.4 Probability estimates of high-risk biomarkers and functioning indicators of the four latent classes: No high-risk, High inflammation, High blood pressure, and High frailty

Indicator	Latent classes			
	Class 1	*Class 2*	*Class 3*	*Class 4*
	No high-risk	High inflammation	High blood pressure	High frailty
Systolic blood pressure	0.27	0.32	**1.00**	**0.46**
Diastolic blood pressure	0.02	0.00	0.31	0.02
Albumin	0.09	0.35	0.15	0.23
C-reactive protein	0.18	**0.83**	0.40	0.38
Fibrinogen	0.03	**0.44**	0.10	0.17
Glycated hemoglobin	0.06	0.29	0.16	0.17
Total cholesterol	0.32	0.33	0.40	0.30
HDL cholesterol	0.17	0.38	0.29	0.17
High BMI/obese	0.02	0.13	0.10	0.13
Low BMI/underweight	0.01	0.01	0.02	0.04
Cystatin C	0.07	0.38	0.31	**0.43**
Cognition score	0.02	0.02	0.09	0.16
Timed walk	0.07	0.13	0.10	**0.87**
Tandem stance	0.20	0.30	0.33	**0.83**
Lung function	0.23	0.33	0.30	0.27
Class probability	*0.58*	*0.19*	*0.12*	*0.11*

Note: Some factors (e.g., cholesterol measures and lung function) do not distinguish classes.
Bold indicates >0.40
N = 3,120
HDL high-density lipoprotein, *BMI* body mass index

class (up to four classes). However, when up to five classes were added, the Bayesian information criteria (BIC) increased, thereby suggesting that, for this population, the 4-class model is best (Likelihood-ratio difference = 3912.93, df = 32704).

Table 5.4 shows the probability estimates of each high-risk level of biomarkers and functioning indicators for the four latent classes. These estimates indicate the probability that an individual, who has been grouped into a given latent class, will have an at-risk level of a given biomarker. The four latent classes were termed: (1) no high-risk [low probability (≤ 0.40) of having at-risk levels for any of the indicators]; (2) high inflammation [high probability (> 0.40) of having high-risk levels of CRP after fibrinogen); (3) high blood pressure [high probability of having high SBP]; and (4) high frailty [high probability of having at-risk SBP, Cystatin C, timed walk, and tandem stand]. More than half of the study sample (58 %) were classified as no high-risk; 19 % were grouped as high inflammation; 12 % as high blood pressure; 11 % as high frailty. LCA of subgroups of ethnic categories, less than high school vs at least high school education, and marital status (married vs not married) yielded substantively similar latent classes.

Using these latent classes, we determined the odds of mortality 5-years after examination (Table 5.5). After adjusting for age and sex, individuals classified as high inflammation, high blood pressure, or high frailty, had significantly higher

Table 5.5 Odds Ratios from logistic regression models predicting 5-year mortality with latent class risk profiles (Models I-III) of biological and functioning indicators and a summary measure of allostatic load (Model IV)

Baseline variables	Model I		Model II		Model III		Model IV	
	OR	(95 % CI)	OR	(95 % CI)	OR	(95 % CI)	OR	(95 % CI)
Age (years)	1.10	(1.07–1.12)	1.09	(1.07–1.12)	1.10	(1.08–1.12)	1.09	(1.07–1.12)
Women (vs men)	0.49	(0.37–0.65)	0.47	(0.34–0.64)	0.47	(0.34–0.65)	0.46	(0.34–0.63)
≥ High School (vs. < High School)			1.03	(0.77–1.37)	1.11	(0.82–1.51)	1.11	(0.82–1.50)
Married (vs. not married)			0.88	(0.63–1.22)	0.56	(0.62–1.19)	0.83	(0.60–1.13)
Ethnicity								
NH White + Other				Reference		Reference		Reference
NH Black			1.20	(0.86–1.66)	1.08	(0.77–1.53)	1.01	(0.72–1.43)
Hispanic			0.57	(0.31–1.06)	0.53	(0.29–0.98)	0.55	(0.30–1.00)
Self-rated health								
Excellent						Reference		Reference
Very Good					1.25	(0.74–2.11)	1.19	(0.71–2.00)
Good					1.17	(0.71–1.93)	1.04	(0.63–1.71)
Fair					1.13	(0.99–1.29)	1.11	(0.98–1.27)
Poor					3.66	(1.79–7.50)	3.15	(1.58–6.30)
Latent classes								
No High-risk		Reference		Reference		Reference		
High Inflammation	2.63	(1.83–3.80)	2.62	(1.81–3.80)	2.36	(1.61–3.45)		
High Blood pressure	1.91	(1.24–2.95)	1.81	(1.16–2.82)	1.67	(1.06–2.61)		
High Frailty	2.91	(1.94–4.37)	2.85	(1.87–4.36)	2.37	(1.56–3.61)		
Summary measure of allostatic load							1.30	(1.20–1.40)

Model I includes age, sex, and latent classes.
Model II includes Model I variables plus education, marital status, and ethnicity.
Model III includes Model II variables plus self-rated health.
Model IV includes age, sex, education, marital status, ethnicity, self-rated health, and summary measure of allostatic load.

risk of 5-year mortality compared to individuals classified in the no high-risk group (Model I). The high frailty class was almost three times as likely to die after 5 years than the no high-risk class (odds ratio [OR], 95 % confidence interval [CI] = 2.91, [1.94–4.37]). Individuals in the high inflammation class were 2.6 times as likely to die than the no high-risk class, while those in the high blood pressure class were nearly two times as likely to die than the no high-risk class (OR [95 % CI] = 1.91 [1.24–2.95]). The addition of years of education, marital status, and ethnicity in Model II, did not substantially change the magnitude or significance of the latent classes to predict 5-year mortality, with the three latent classes significantly predicting mortality relative to the no high-risk class. Including self-rated health into the model (Model III) attenuated the relationship between the latent class risk profiles and mortality although the significance remained. Model IV indicates that every point increase in the summary measure of allostatic load is associated with an increase in mortality risk (OR [95 % CI] = 1.30 [1.20–1.40]).

5.5 Discussion

This study finds that older American adults can be classified into four latent class risk profiles based on ten biological markers and five indicators of functioning. The four latent classes were named based on theoretically meaningful labels: no high-risk (not high on any of the measures), high inflammation (high on fibrinogen and CRP), high blood pressure (high SBP), and high frailty (low performance on walk and tandem stance tests and high SBP and Cystatin C). Using the four designated latent classes, we found that in comparison to people in the no high-risk class, individuals grouped in the high inflammation and high frailty class were about 2.5 times as likely to die after 5 years, and those classified in the high blood pressure class were 1.7 times as likely to die after 5 years.

These findings build on previous studies that have utilized other methods to categorize biological risk, ranging from a basic summation score of elevated risk (Seeman et al. 2001) to canonical correlation analysis (Karlamangla et al. 2002, 2006) to recursive partitioning of individuals (Gruenewald et al. 2006). The latent class approach employed in this study is a unique application for biomarker classification that categorizes individuals by their individual biological and functioning profiles. This approach extends initial attempts to consider multisystem functioning and suggests the utility of the latent class approach in characterizing individuals based on their profiles of physiological dysregulation. In comparison to initial attempts to consider multiple measures using a simple equi-weight summation method (e.g., Seeman et al. 2001) and to factor analysis (as used by Sakkinen et al. 2000), the latent class approach focuses on classifying groups of individuals within a population based on similarities of their biological and functioning profiles as opposed to focusing on the inter-relationships among individual biomarkers.

An additional strength of the latent class approach is that it allows for consideration of a multi-physiological system without depending on a given outcome for categorization. This is in contrast to the recursive partitioning method that requires an outcome measure (e.g., mortality) to categorize individuals with a given biological profile (e.g., Gruenewald et al. (2006)). Simply put, the latent class approach only uses information on the independent variables (biomarker or functioning indicators) and does not require an outcome variable in its classification process.

The approach used in the current study classifies individuals based on their system-wide underlying health status, which accounts for functioning across several physiologic subsystems without being outcome dependent. In utilizing this method, this study contributes to the current literature on population health and use of biological and functioning markers to better understand the risk profiles of some early signs of declining health in a nationally representative older population. These analyses identify differences in biomarker and functioning risk profiles among older adults and determine risk for mortality based on these classifications.

Some of our findings of increased risk of 5-year mortality among individuals having individual measures of high inflammation, high blood pressure, or high frailty have been reported in other studies. Individuals with elevated levels of inflammatory markers (including CRP and fibrinogen) have been associated with an increased risk of cardiovascular disease (Albert 2007; De Martinis et al. 2006; Kuller et al. 1996; Ridker et al. 1997; Rost et al. 2001; Tracy et al. 1997; Zakai et al. 2007), one of the leading causes of death among older US adults (Centers for Disease Control 2005). These indicators have also been predictive of both vascular and non-vascular mortality (Clarke et al. 2008) and were elevated in near-term death among older males (Jenny et al. 2007). Additionally, several population-based studies have consistently reported on the relationship between high blood pressure and increased incidence of cardiovascular disease, stroke, coronary heart disease, and mortality related to these causes (Lowe et al. 1998; National High Blood Pressure Education Program 1997; Stamler et al. 1998, 1999).

The concept of frailty, developed by geriatricians, focuses on the decline in several systems that represent increasing loss of reserves, declines in resilience, lack of energy and ability to function (Fried et al. 2001; Lunney 2003; Morley et al. 2002). Individuals classified as frail have previously been noted to have poorer health and to be at greater risk of mortality compared to non-frail individuals (Cawthon et al. 2007; Mitnitski et al. 2005). Typically included among indicators of frailty, and as examined here, are markers of system functioning (e.g., cognitive status) and performance measures (e.g., timed walk test and timed tandem stance) (Crimmins et al. 2010; Rothman et al. 2008). Understanding the links between these various dimensions and risk profiles of health and mortality will provide us with an improved understanding of the processes associated with aging and mortality.

Overall, this study has several strengths. First, it uses a nationally representative sample of the US population to investigate the relationship among various biomarkers to one another, as well as to mortality. Second, it utilizes mortality follow up data obtained through a reliable data source: the National Death Index. Third, this is the first study to our knowledge that methodologically examines the relationship of both biomarkers and indicators of functioning using the latent class approach.

Despite its strengths, our study also had limitations. For instance, we were limited to the use of logit models to investigate the relationship between the latent classes and 5-year mortality given that we only had information on survival status. This did not include date of death information, so we were unable to conduct more sophisticated analyses to model survival.

The latent class approach to classifying individuals based on their biological and functioning profiles was found to significantly predict 5-year mortality. More specifically, individuals with profiles that include high-risk levels of inflammation, blood pressure, and frailty were more likely to die than individuals classified as no high-risk. This methodological approach to using multiple indicators obtained at one time point seems an appropriate means to classifying individuals based on multiple biological and functioning indicators that represent functioning across several physiological systems. Our findings also suggest the importance of using these indicators to evaluate older adults at high-risk for these markers, in order to improve the health and years lived among older adults.

Acknowledgments This work was supported in part by the US National Institute on Aging Grants T32AG0037 and P30 AG17265. Merril Silverstein and Wonho Lee provided helpful suggestions on a previous draft of this manuscript.

Appendix

Table A.1 Percent with at-risk cutoff points for 15 biological and functioning indicators by marital status, education level, and ethnicity

Indicator		Marital status		Education		Ethnicity		
	At-risk cutoff	Married	Not Married	$<$ High school	$\geq$ High school	NH white[b]	NH black	Hispanic
Systolic blood pressure	$>$ 90 mmHg	40.82	49.04	46.6	41.02	42.32	48.69	45.43
Diastolic blood pressure	$>$ 140 mmHg	6.39	5.59	6.98	4.91	4.53	10.86	6.24
Albumin	$\leq$ 3.9 g/dl	15.75	20.13	18.27	16.48	15.72	24.34	16.55
C-reactive protein	$>$ 0.3 mg/dl	36.83	39.46	39.92	35.62	35.98	45.71	36.72
Fibrinogen	$>$ 400 mg/dl	14.85	16.53	16.85	13.96	14.02	19.79	16.11
Glycated hemoglobin	$\geq$ 6.5 %	17.3	16.21	20.11	13.04	11.89	25.39	23.22
Total cholesterol	$>$ 240 mg/dl	29.91	33.71	30.87	32.12	31.82	33.98	28.59
High-density lipoprotein cholesterol	$<$ 40 mg/dl	27.78	16.53	24.9	21.46	24.2	14.19	28.16
High BMI/very obese	$>$ 35 kg/m^2	6.12	7.19	8.10	4.70	5.28	10.16	7.26
Low BMI/underweight	$<$ 18.5 kg/m^2	0.69	2.80	1.24	1.68	1.76	1.58	0.87
Cystatin C[a]	$>$ 1.25 mg/dl	18.79	27.56	24.36	19.78	26.6	17.16	14.66
Cognition score[a]	$>$ 15 (of 26)	6.65	11.5	13.01	3.02	5.49	14.19	12.34
8-ft timed walk[a]	$>$ 4.6 m/s	18.47	32.67	31.11	15.85	19.94	29.42	31.2
Time tandem stance[a]	$<$ 10 s	29.54	44.49	40.04	30.01	37.05	33.63	32.95
Lung function[a]	$<$ 32.89885	25.12	22.92	24.72	23.63	27.61	21.72	17.13

BMI body mass index, *NH* non-hispanic

[a]Based on top 25 % sample distribution

[b]Includes "Other" ethnic groups not classified as NH White, NH Black, or Hispanic

References

Albert, M. A. (2007). Inflammatory biomarkers, race/ethnicity and cardiovascular disease. *Nutrition Reviews*, *65*, 234–238.

Berkman, L. F. (2000). Social support, social networks, social cohesion and health. *Social Work in Health Care*, *31*, 3–14.

Bernard, C. (1957). *An Introduction to the study of experimental medicine*. Mineola: Dover Publications.

Cawthon, P., Marshall, L. M., & Michael, Y., et al. (2007). Frailty in older men: Prevalence, progression, and relationship with mortality. *Journal of the American Geriatrics*, *55*, 1216–1223.

Clarke, R., Emberson, J. R., & Breeze, E., et al. (2008). Biomarkers of inflammation predict both vascular and non-vascular mortality in older men. *European Heart Journal*, *29*, 800–809.

Clogg, C. C., & Goodman, L.A. (1984). Latent structure analysis of a set of multideimensional contingency tables. *Journal of the American Statistical Association*, *79*, 762–771.

Clogg, C. C., & Goodman, L. A. (1986). On scaling models applied to data from several groups. *Psychometrika*, *51*, 123–135.

Cowper, D. C., Kubal, J. D., Maynard, C., & Hynes, D. M. (2002). A primer and comparative view of major vcUS mortality databases. *Annals of Epidemiology*, *12*, 462–68.

Crimmins, E. M., Johnston, M., Hayward, M., & Seeman, T. (2003). Age differences in allostatic load: An index of physiological dysregulation. *Experimental Gerontology*, *38*, 731–734.

Crimmins, E. M., Kim, J. K., & Vasunilashorn, S. (2010). Biodemography: New approaches to understanding trends and differences in population health and mortality. *Demography*, *47*, 41–64.

Crimmins, E., & Seeman, T. (2001). Integrating biology into demographic research on health and aging (with a focus on the MacArthur Study of Successful Aging). In C. Finch & J. Vaupel (Eds.), *Cells and surveys: Should biological measures be included in social science research?* (pp. 9–41). Washington, DC: National Academy Press.

Crimmins, E. M., & Seeman, T. E. (2004). Integrating biology into the study of health disparities. *Population and Development Review*, *30*, 89–107.

Crimmins, E. M., & Vasunilashorn, S. (2011). Links between biomarkers and mortality. In R. G. Rogers & E. M. Crimmins (eds.), *International handbook of adult mortality* (pp. 381–398). Springer.

Crimmins, E., Vasunilashorn, S., Kim, J. K., & Alley, D. (2008). Biomarkers related to aging in human populations. *Advances in Clinical Chemistry*, *46*, 161–217.

De Martinis, M., Franceschi, C., Monti, D., & Ginaldi, L. (2006). Inflammation markers predicting frailty and mortality in the elderly. *Experimental and Molecular Pathology*, *80*, 219–227.

Elo, I. T., & Preston, S. H. (1996). Educational differentials in mortality: United States, 1979–1958. *Social Science & Medicine*, *42*, 47–57.

Fried, L. P., Tangen, C. M., Walston, J., Newman, A. B., Hirsch, C., Gottdiener, J., Seeman, T., Tracy, R., Kop, W. J., Burke, G., & McBurnie, M. (2001). Frailty in older adults: Evidence for a phenotype. *Journal of Gerontology: Medical Sciences*, *56*, 146–156.

Goldman, N., Turra, C. M., Glei, D. A., Lin, Y. H., & Weinstein, M. (2006). Physiological dysregulation and changes in health in an older population. *Experimental Gerontology*, *41*, 862–870.

Gruenewald, T. L., Seeman, T. E., Karlamangla, A. S., & Sarkisian, C. A. (2009). Allostatic load and frailty in older adults. *Journal of the American Geriatrics Society*, *57*, 1525–1531.

Gruenewald, T. L., Seeman, T. E., Ryff, C. D., Karlamangla, A. S., & Singer, B. H. (2006). Combinations of biomarkers predictive of later life mortality. *Proceedings of the National Academy of Sciences U S A*, *103*, 14158–14163.

Guralnik, J. M., Branch, L. G., Cummings, S. R., & Curb, J. D. (1989). Physical performance measures in aging research. *The Journals of Gerontology Series A: Biological Sciences and Medical Sciences*, *44*, 141–146.

Hamil-Luker, J., & O'Rand, A. M. (2007). Gender differences in the link between childhood socioeconomic conditions and heart attack risk in adulthood. *Demography, 44*, 137–158.

Idler, E. L., & Benyamini, Y. (1997). Self-rated health and mortality: A review of twenty-seven community studies. *Journal of Health and Social Behavior, 38*, 21–37.

Jenny, N. S., Yanez, N. D., Psaty, B. M., Kuller, L. H., Mirsch, C. H., & Tracy, R. P. (2007). Inflammation biomarkers and near-term death in older men. *American Journal of Epidemiology, 165*, 684–695.

Karlamangla, A. S., Singer, B. H., & Seeman, T. E. (2006). Reduction in allostatic load in older adults is associated with lower all-cause mortality risk: MacArthur Studies of Successful Aging. *Psychosomatic Medicine, 68*, 600–507.

Karlamangla, A. S., Singer, B. H., McEwen, B. S., Rowe, J. W., & Seeman, T. E. (2002). Allostatic load as a predictor of functional decline MacArthur studies of successful aging. *Journal of Clinical Epidemiology, 55*, 696–710.

Karlamangla, A. S., Singer, B. H., & Seeman, T. E. (2006). Reduction in allostatic load in older adults is associated with lower all-cause mortality risk: MacArthur Studies of Successful Aging. *Psychosomatic Medicine, 68*, 500–507.

Kubzansky, L. D., Kawachi, I., & Sparrow, D. (1999). Socioeconomic status, hostility, and risk factor clustering in the Normative Aging Study: Any help from the concept of allostatic load? *Annals of Behavioral Medicine, 21*, 330–338.

Kuller, L. H., Tracy, R. P., Shaten, J., & Meilahn, E. N. (1996). Relation of C-reactive protein and coronary heart disease in the MRFIT nested case-control study. Multiple Risk Factor Intervention Trial. *American Journal of Epidemiology, 144*, 537–547.

Kulminski, A. M., Arbeev, K. G., Christensen, K., Mayeux, R., Newman, A. B., Province, M. A., Hadley, E. C., Rossi, W., Perls, T. T., Elo, I. T., & Yashin, A. I. (2011). Do gender, disability, and morbidity affect aging rate in the LLFS? Application of indices of cumulative deficits. *Mechanisms of Ageing and Development, 132*, 195–201.

Lanza, S. T., Collins, L. M., Lemmon, D. R., & Schafer, J. L. (2001). PROC LCA: A SAS procedure for latent class analysis. *Structural Equation Modeling, 14*, 671–694.

Laska, M. N., Pasch, K. E., Lust, K., Story, M. & Ehlinger, E. (2009). Latent class analysis of lifestyle characteristics and health risk behaviors among college youth. *Prevention Science, 10*, 376–386.

Lowe, L. P., Greenland, P., Ruth, K. J., Dyer, A. R., Stamler, R., & Stamler, J. (1998). Impact of major cardiovascular disease risk factors, particularly in combination, on 22-year mortality in women and men. *Archives of internal medicine, 158*, 2007–2014.

Lunney, J. R., Lynn, J., Foley, D., Lipson, S., & Guralnik, J. (2003). Patterns of functional decline at the end of life. *Journal of the American Medical Association, 289*, 2388–2398.

McEwen, B. S. (2000). Allostasis and allostatic load: Implications for neuropsychopharmacology. *Neuropsychopharmacology, 22*, 108–124.

McEwen, B. S. (2004). Protective and damaging effects of mediators of stress and adaptation: Allostasis and allostatic load. In J. Schulkin (Eds.), *Allostasis, homeostasis and the costs of physiological adaptation* (pp. 65–98). Cambridge: Cambridge University Press.

McEwen, B. S., & Stellar, E. (1993). Stress and the individual. Mechanisms leading to disease. *Archives of internal medicine, 153*, 2093–2101.

McEwen, B. S. (2002). Sex, stress and the hippocampus: Allostasis, allostatic load, and the aging process. *Neurobiology of Aging, 23*, 921–939.

McEwen, B. S., & Seeman, T. (1999). Protective and damaging effects of mediators of stress. Elaborating and testing the concepts of allostasis and allostatic load. *Annals of the New York Academy of Sciences, 896*, 30–47.

Mitnitski, A., Song, X., Skoog, I., Broe, G. A., Cox, J. L., Grunfeld, E., & Rockwood, K. (2005). Relative fitness and frailty of elderly men and women in developed countries and their relationship with mortality. *Journal of the American Geriatrics Society, 53*(12), 2184–2189.

Morley, J. E., Perry, H. M., & Miller, D. R. (2002). Editorial: Something about frailty. *Journal of Gerontology: Medical Sciences, 57*, M698–704.

Nakamura, E., & Miyao, K. (2003). Further evaluation of the basic nature of the human biological aging process based on a factor analysis of age-related physiological variables. *The Journals of Gerontology Series A: Biological Sciences and Medical Sciences*, *62*, 1096–1105.

National High Blood Pressure Education Program. (1997). The Sixth Report of the Joint National Committee on Prevention, Detection, Evaluation, and Treatment of high blood pressure. *Archives of internal medicine*, *157*, 2413–2446.

Newman, A. B., Simonsick, E. M., & Naydeck, B. L., et al. (2006). Association of long-distance corridor walk performance with mortality, cardiovascular disease, mobility limitation, and disability. *The Journal of the American Medical Association*, *296*, 2018–2026.

O'Rand, A. M., & Hamil-Luker, J. (2005). Processes of cumulative adversity: Childhood disadvantage and increased risk of heart attack across the life course. *Journals of Gerontology Series B Psychological Sciences and Social Sciences*, *60*, 117–124.

Ridker, P. M., Cushman, M., Stampfer, M. J., Tracy, R. P., & Hennekens, C. H. (1997). Inflammation, aspirin, and the risk of cardiovascular disease in apparently healthy men. *The New England Journal of Medicine*, *336*, 973–979.

Rost, N. S., Wolf, P. A., & Kase, C. S., et al. (2001). Plasma concentration of C-reactive protein and risk of ischemic stroke and transient ischemic attack: The Framingham Study. *Stroke*, *32*, 2575–2579.

Rothman, M. D., Leo-Summers, L., & Gill, T. M. (2008). Prognostic significance of potential frailty criteria. *Journal of the American Geriatrics Society*, *56*, 2211–2216.

Sakkinen, P. A., Wahl, P., Cushman, M., Lewis, M. R., & Tracy, R. P. (2000). Clustering of procoagulation, inflammation, and fibrinolysis variables with metabolic factors in insulin resistance syndrome. *American Journal of Epidemiology*, *152*, 897–907.

Seeman, T. E., & Crimmins, E. M. (2001). Social environment effects on health and aging: Integrating epidemiologic and demographic approaches and perspectives. *Annals of the New York Academy of Sciences*, *954*, 588–117.

Seeman, T. E., Crimmins, E., Huang, M. H., Singer, B. V., Bucur, A., Gruenewald, T., Berkman, L. F., & Reuben, D. B. (2003). Cumulative biological risk and socio-economic differences in mortality: MacArthur Studies of Successfual Aging. *Social Science & Medicine*, *58*, 1985–1997.

Seeman, T., Glei, D., Goldman, N., Weinstein, M., Singer, B., & Lin, Y. (2004). Social relationships and allostatic load in Taiwanese elderly and near elderly. *Social Science & Medicine*, *59*, 2245–2257.

Seeman, T. E., McEwen, B. S., Rowe, J. W., & Singer, B. H. (2001). Allostatic load as a marker of cumulative biological risk: MacArthur studies of successful aging. *Proceedings of the National Academy of Sciences U S A*, *98*, 4770–4775.

Seeman, T. E., Singer, B., Rowe, J. W., Horwitz, R., & McEwen, B. S. (1997). Price of adaptation –allostatic load and its health consequences. MacArthur Studies of Successful Aging. *Archives of internal medicine*, *157*, 2259–2268.

Seplaki, C., Goldman, N., Weinstein, M., & Lin, Y. H. (2004). How are biomarkers related to physical and mental well-being? The *Journals of Gerontology Series A: Biological Sciences and Medical Sciences*, *59*, 201–217.

Singer, B., Ryff, C., & Seeman, T. E. (2004). Operationationalizing allostatic load. In J. Schulkin (Ed.), *Allostasis, homeostasis, and the cost of physiological adaptation* (pp. 113–149). Cambridge: Cambridge University Press.

Stamler, J., Greeland, P., & Neaton, J. D. (1998). The established major risk factors underlying epidemic coronary and cardiovascuarl disease. *CVD Prevention*, *1*, 82–97.

Stamler, J., Stamler, R., Neaton, J. D., Wentworth, D., Daviglus, M. L., Garside, D., Dyer, A. R., Liu, K., & Greeland, P. (1999). Low risk-factor profile and long-term cardiovascular and noncardiovascular mortality and life expectancy. *The Journal of the American Medical Association*, *282*, 2012–2018.

Sterling, P., & Eyer, J. (1988). Allostasis: A new paradigm to explain arousal pathology. In S. Fisher & J. Reason (Eds.), *Handbook of life stress, cognition, and health* (pp. 629–649). New York: Wiley.

Tracy, R. P., Lemaitre, R. N., & Psaty, B. M., et al. (1997). Relationship of C-reactive protein to risk of cardiovascular disease in the elderly. Results from the Cardiovascular Health Study and the Rural Health Promotion Project. *Arteriosclerosis, Thrombosis, and Vascular Biology*, *17*, 1121–1127.

Turra, C. M., Goldman, N., Seplaki, C. L., Glei, D. A., Lin, Y. H., & Weinstein, M. (2005). Determinants of mortality at older ages: The role of biological markers of chronic disease. *Population and Development Review*, *31*, 677–701.

Verbrugge, L. M., & Wingard, D. L. (1987). Sex differentials in health and mortality. *Women Health*, *12*, 103–45.

Wadsworth, M. E. J. (1997). Health inequalities in the life course perspective. *Social Science & Medicine*, *44*, 859–869.

Wang, T. J., Gona, P., Larson, M. G., Levy, D., Benjamin, E. J., & Tofler, G. H., et al. (2007). Multiple biomarkers and the risk of incident hypertension. *Hypertension*, *49*, 432–438.

Wilson, P. W. R., D'Agostino, R. B., Levy, D., Belanger, A. M., Silbershatz, H., & Kannel, W. B. (1998). Prediction of coronary heart disease using risk factor categories. *Circulation*, *97*, 1837–1847.

Zakai, N. A., Katz, R., & Jenny, N. S., et al. (2007). Inflammation and hemostasis biomarkers and cardiovascular risk in the elderly: The cardiovascular health study. *Journal of Thrombosis and Haemostasis*, *5*, 1128–1135.

Zhang, H., & Singer, B. (1999). *Recursive partitioning in the Health Sciences*. New York: Springer.

Chapter 6
Approaches to the Assessment of Alcohol-Related Losses in the Russian Population

V. G. Semyonova, N. S. Gavrilova, T. P. Sabgayda, O. M. Antonova, S. Yu Nikitina and G. N. Evdokushkina

Abstract Until recently, the level of alcohol-related losses in Russia was assessed using mortality from accidental poisoning by alcohol. Our study shows that currently the alcohol-related losses in Russia are determined primarily by degenerative diseases of alcoholic etiology. We show that partitioning of alcohol-related deaths into poisoning and somatic pathology (causes due to degenerative diseases related to alcohol abuse) provides important insights into the patterns of alcohol-related mortality. In particular, it shows that the use of accidental alcohol poisoning alone as an indicator of alcohol-related mortality leads to a significant underreporting of alcohol-related losses in Russia during the first decade of the twenty-first century.

The study of alcohol-related mortality in the Russian regions revealed areas of high risk for alcohol deaths and regions where deaths from alcohol poisoning or from somatic pathologies of alcoholic etiology are systematically underreported. Furthermore, the regional analysis provided us with an opportunity to assess how complete are the official statistics of alcohol-related losses in the Russian population. The existing legal framework in Russia and current diagnostic practices allow regional administrations to underreport socially significant losses including losses related to alcohol. There is no doubt that the establishment of uniform country-wide standards for reporting alcohol-related mortality will lead to a substantial increase in the scale of losses caused by alcohol. These measures are a necessary first step for developing effective programmes for the reduction of alcoholism in Russia.

Keywords Russia · Alcohol · Cause of death · Regional differences · Gender differences

---

V. G. Semyonova (✉) · T. P. Sabgayda · G. N. Evdokushkina
Department of Health Statistics, Federal Research Institute for Health Organization and Informatics of Ministry of Health of the Russian Federation, 11, Dobrolubov St., Moscow 127254, Russia
e-mail: vika@mednet.ru

N. S. Gavrilova
Center for Demography and Economics of Ageing, NORC at the University of Chicago, 1155 E 60th Street, Chicago 60637, IL, USA

O. M. Antonova · S. Y. Nikitina
Russian State Statistics Service, 39, Miasnitskaya St., Bldg. 1, Moscow 107450, Russia

J. Anson, M. Luy (eds.), *Mortality in an International Perspective*, European Studies of Population 18, DOI 10.1007/978-3-319-03029-6_6,

Alcoholism has long been the most significant source of excess mortality in Russia (Nemtsov 1998, 2001, 2009; Starodubov et al. 2003; Ivanova and Semyonova 2005; Mckee et al. 2001; Leon et al. 2007, 2009). The role of alcohol consumption as a risk factor of mortality has been demonstrated in a number of publications including papers by Leon et al. (1997) and Mäkelä et al. (1997). After the initial period of increase in life expectancy in Russia (1984–1987), mainly due to Gorbachev's anti-alcohol campaign, life expectancy in Russia rapidly dropped during the period of economic and political reforms (1988–1994). In the beginning of the twenty-first century life expectancy in Russia stabilized and started to increase slowly after 2005. Taking into account these new patterns and trends in life expectancy, it is important to assess the contribution of alcohol consumption to these changes (as a substantial risk factor of mortality for the adult population).

Until recently, the level of alcohol-related losses was assessed using mortality from accidental poisoning by alcohol (Andreev and Zbarskaya 2010). Moreover, even now, administrative officials in Russian regions consider mortality from accidental alcohol poisoning to be the only indicator of alcohol losses. The ICD-10, however mentions 12 major causes of death with an alcoholic etiology:

1. mental and behavioral disorders due to alcohol (F10);
2. alcohol-related degeneration of the nervous system (G31.2);
3. alcoholic polyneuropathy (G62.1);
4. alcoholic myopathy (G72.1);
5. alcoholic cardiomyopathy (I42.6);
6. alcoholic liver disease (alcoholic cirrhosis, hepatitis, fibrosis) (K70);
7. alcoholic gastritis (K 29.2);
8. chronic pancreatitis with alcoholic etiology (K86.0);
9. fetal alcohol syndrome (Q86.0);
10. accidental poisoning (exposure) by alcohol (X45);
11. intentional self-poisoning and exposure to alcohol (X65);
12. exposure and poisoning by alcohol with undetermined intent (Y15).

Thus, a complete account of alcohol deaths is not limited to accidental alcohol poisoning. On the one hand, this category does not include all cases of alcoholic poisoning and on the other hand it overlooks alcohol-related losses due to various kinds of somatic pathology. This raises a number of questions, the most important of which is the extent of losses due to alcohol abuse in Russia. We tested the correctness of using deaths from accidental alcohol poisoning as a universal indicator showing the possible losses caused by alcohol. For this, we estimated total alcohol-related mortality (i.e. mortality from all alcohol-related causes) and conducted an analysis of its trends and structure in Russia and the Russian regions.

The study of alcohol-related mortality in the Russian regions reveals areas of high and low risk for alcohol deaths. In addition, the regional analysis provides us with an opportunity to assess how complete are the official statistics of alcohol-related losses in the Russian population.

6.1 Data and Methods

To estimate the extent of alcohol-related mortality, we used the Rosstat database of recorded deaths, with all personal identifiers removed. This database uses codes of ICD-10 for specific causes of death rather than the abbreviated list of causes adopted in Russia (used in the basic form of statistical reports on mortality C-51). Alcohol-related mortality was calculated using the automated information system "FAISS-Potential" (Ermakov et al. 1999). Mortality was standardized with the European age structure as a standard in order to make results comparable to the results obtained by other researchers on this topic. Analysis was performed separately for persons at young working ages (20–39 years), old working ages (40–59 years) and older ages (60 years and older) to identify the age characteristics of alcoholic mortality.

Among the 12 causes of death of alcoholic etiology identified in ICD-10, three causes belong to poisoning; one refers to mental illness; three to diseases of the nervous system; one to cardiovascular diseases; three to diseases of the digestive system and one to congenital malformations (fetal alcohol syndrome). For some specific nosologies with a very small numbers of cases, the analysis was conducted in the context of the classes of causes of death to which these causes belong. We used four groups of somatic causes of alcohol-related mortality: mental alcohol-related deaths, alcohol-related diseases of the nervous system, alcoholic cardiomyopathy and alcoholic liver disease. The death rate from alcohol poisoning was evaluated as the sum of three categories: accidental alcohol poisoning (X45), alcohol poisoning with undetermined intent (Y15), intentional self-poisoning and exposure to alcohol (X65).

We applied the term "somatic" to degenerative diseases, the origin of which lies in alcohol abuse, rather than external causes of death or poisoning. As we show later, dividing alcohol-related deaths into poisoning and somatic pathology is very informative for describing patterns of alcohol-related mortality in Russia during the first decade of the twenty-first century (2000–2009).

In the analysis of regional mortality we used rank correlations. We did not include data on alcohol consumption at the regional level, taking into account the opinion of experts that such data are not reliable and greatly underestimate alcohol consumption both in Russia as a whole and in the Russian regions (Nemtsov 2011). The analysis is conducted by age group, rather than for all age groups together, because age is the most important factor when studying poisoning and somatic causes. Because of the high level of alcohol-related mortality at ages 40–59 years, overall alcohol mortality is determined by this middle age group rather that by mortality among young adults and the elderly.

6.2 Alcohol-Related Mortality of the Adult Russian Population in 2000–2009

During the past decade, total alcohol-related mortality in Russia rose slightly, especially among the elderly. At the same time a decrease in mortality from alcohol poisoning was observed in all adult age groups. These opposite tendencies require more detailed consideration. Figures 6.1 and 6.2 show that among persons of younger

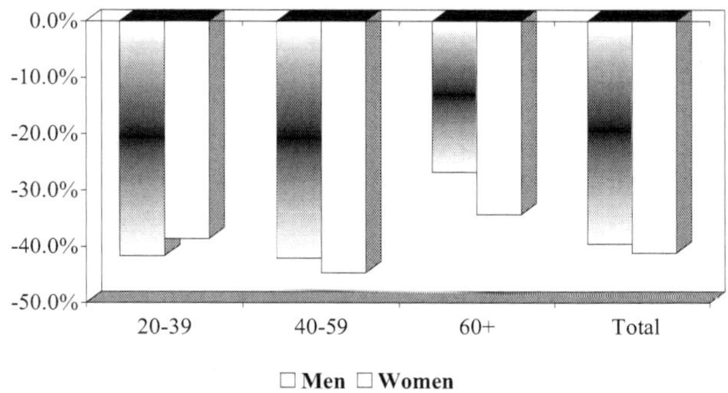

Fig. 6.1 Decline of mortality from alcohol poisoning among adult population in Russia from 2000 to 2009 (percent), by age and sex

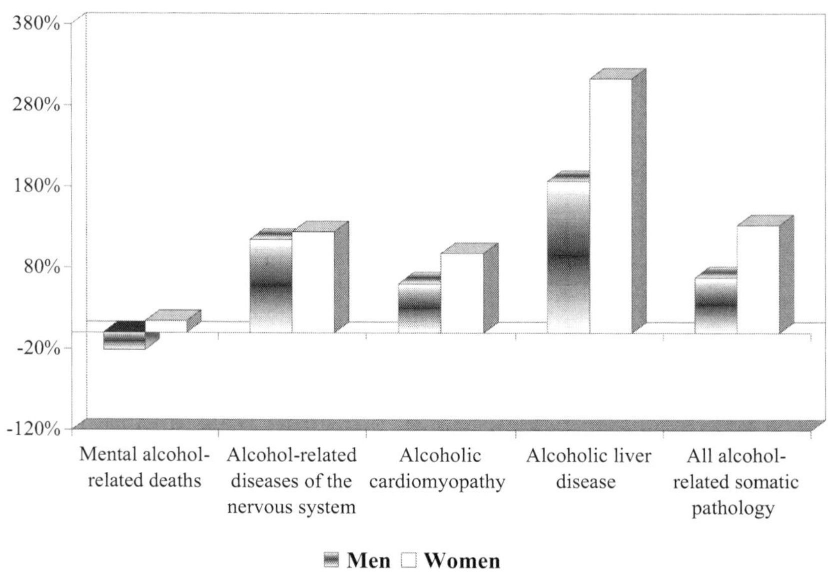

Fig. 6.2 Changes in mortality due to alcohol-related somatic pathology among population of younger working age (20–39 years) in Russia from 2000 to 2009 (percent), by sex and type of somatic pathology

working age (20–39) in 2000–2009 there was a decrease in mortality from alcohol poisoning by 41.7 % among men and 38.6 % among women, while deaths from alcohol-related somatic pathology increased by more than two thirds (68.3 %) for men and by 2.3 times for women (see Fig. 6.2).

The largest increases in 2000–2009 were observed for diseases of the digestive system caused by alcohol (2.9- and 4.1-fold increase, respectively) as well as alcoholic cardiomyopathy (an increase of 60.45 % and a 2-fold, respectively). Such negative trends are also noted for diseases of the nervous system caused by alcohol abuse (more than 2-fold increase among males and females). The male death rate from mental and behavioral disorders due to alcohol consumption (i.e., those states

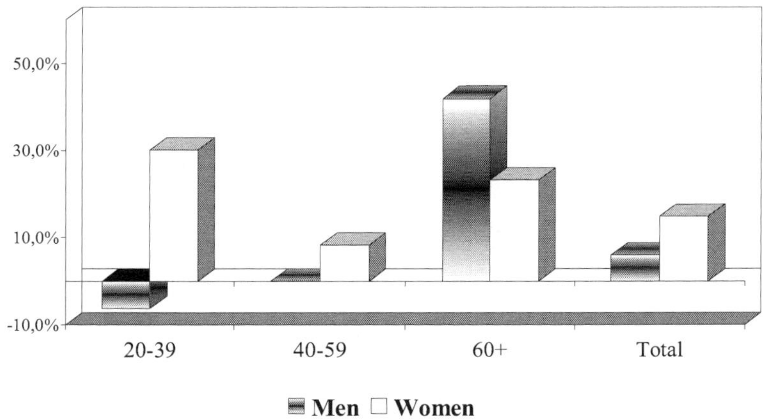

Fig. 6.3 Changes in total alcohol-related mortality of adult population in Russia in 2000–2009 (percent), by age and sex

of health termed chronic alcoholism) decreased by 21.4 % in 2000–2009, but female mortality from these causes grew by 14.3 %.

Because of these divergent trends (increase in mortality from somatic causes and reduction in alcohol poisoning), the results for 2000–2009 were significantly different for male and female populations. Figure 6.3 shows that the total alcohol-related mortality among men of younger working age decreased by 6.2 % for this period, while the mortality among women of this age increased by almost one third (30.2 %).

When discussing the changes in alcohol-related mortality over the past 10 years, we can consider two stages of mortality change for all age groups. During the first stage, until 2005, death rates were rising, and after 2005 (second stage) alcohol-related mortality began to decline. Figure 6.4 shows changes in total alcohol-related mortality among the younger working age population (20–39 years) in Russia from 2000 to 2009, in which we can see clearly these two divergent trends: growth in 2000–2005 and decline in 2005–2009.

The changes in total alcohol-related mortality and its components (external and somatic) during the period of declining mortality (2005–2009) are of particular interest. Figure 6.5 shows that the declines in both somatic mortality and in mortality from alcohol poisoning among the younger working age population accelerated dramatically in the last year of the period under study. There was a noticeable deceleration in the decline of total alcohol-related mortality in 2007–2008 compared with 2005–2007 (from 8.7 to 5.6 % among men and from 7.3 to 2.7 % among women) primarily due to an increase in somatic mortality (more than a two-fold reduction in the rate of decline among men and switch from a 6.0 % decrease to a 2.6 % growth in mortality among women). However, in 2009, the total alcohol-related mortality among men and women of younger working age fell by 11.1 and 14.2 % respectively as a result of 11.7 and 13 % reductions in somatic pathology and 10.3 and 17 % reduction in mortality from alcohol poisoning.

Similar trends were observed among the population of older working ages (40–59 years). Among men of this age group the total alcohol-related mortality in 2000

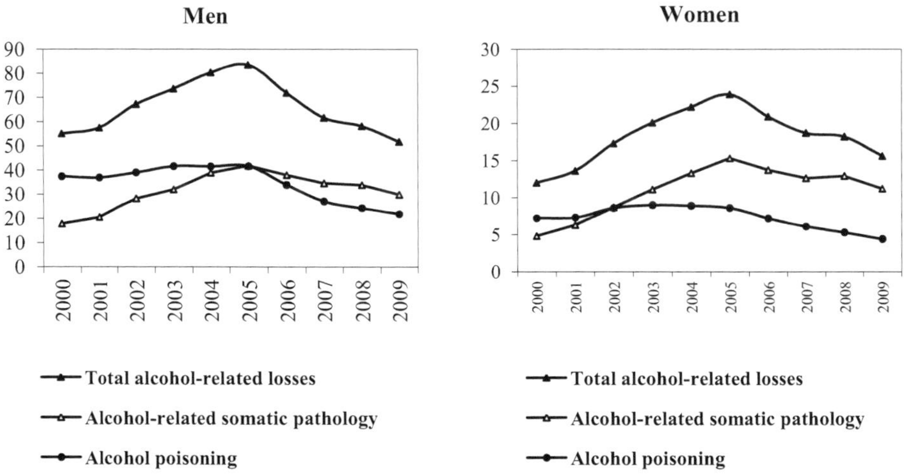

Fig. 6.4 Alcohol-related mortality among population of younger working age (20–39 years) in Russia in 2000–2009, by sex and type of alcohol-related losses (standardized rates per 100,000)

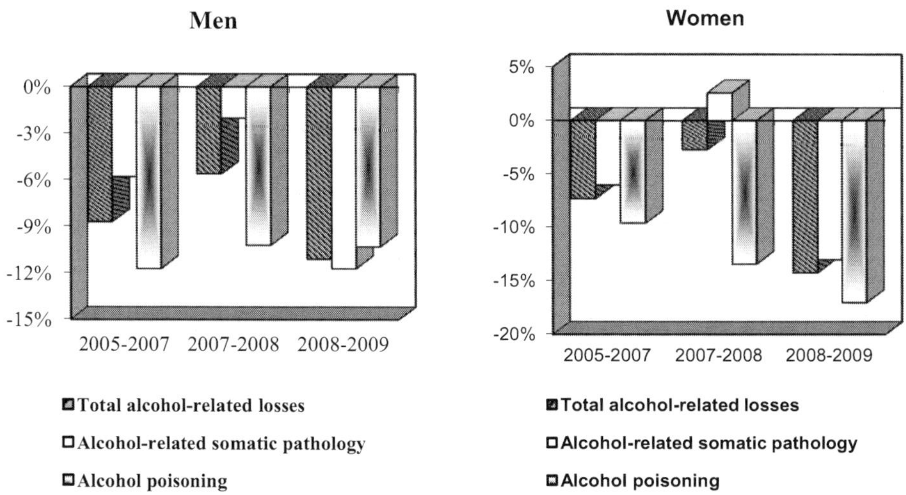

Fig. 6.5 Annual rates of changes in alcohol-related mortality among population of younger working age (20–39 years) in Russia, by sex, type of alcohol-related losses and calendar period (percent)

and 2009 was almost the same (166.2 and 166.4 per 100,000) and among women it increased by 8.3 %. Mortality from alcohol poisoning decreased by 42.1 % among men and by 44.7 % among women during this period while alcohol-related somatic mortality increased by 58.8 and 73.0 % respectively (Figs. 6.1, 6.3 and 6.6). Figure 6.6 shows changes in mortality due to alcohol-related somatic pathology among the population of 40–59-year olds in 2000–2009. Among the somatic causes of death, the worst tendencies were observed for mortality from diseases of the digestive

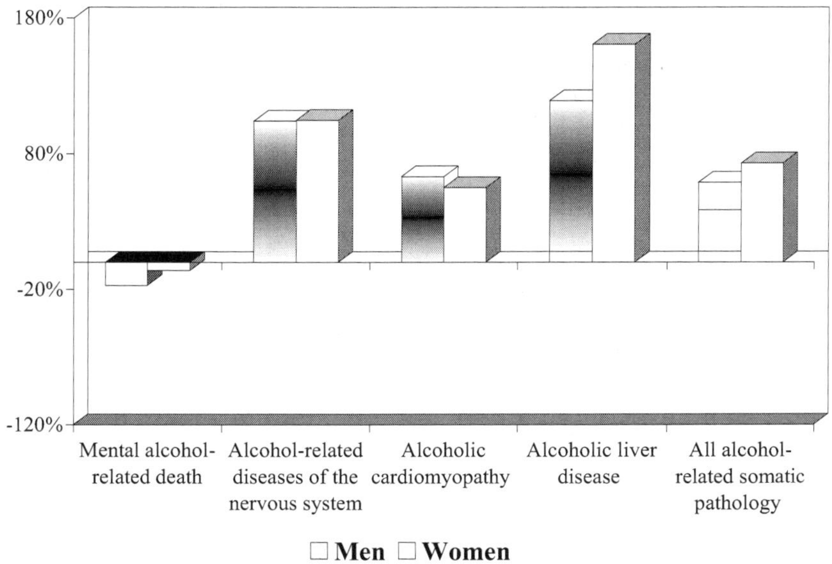

Fig. 6.6 Changes in mortality due to alcohol-related somatic causes among population of older working age (40–59) in Russia in 2000–2009 (percent), by sex and type of alcohol-related losses

system, which increased 2.2-fold for men and 2.6-fold for women. As in the younger age groups, mortality from these causes is predominantly determined by alcoholic liver cirrhosis, which comprises 66.6 % of all male deaths due to the diseases of the digestive system caused by alcohol, as well as 71.1 % of all such female deaths. Mortality due to diseases of the nervous system and sensory organs caused by alcohol (namely, the degeneration of the nervous system caused by alcohol—G31.2), had similar rates of growth for men and women (both showed a 2-fold increase). Also, mortality due to alcoholic cardiomyopathy had very similar rates of growth for men and women (63 and 55 % respectively).

The level of mortality from mental and behavioral disorders due to alcohol (F10), decreased by 17.2 % among men but only by 6.1 % among women in 2000–2009. As in the case of young working ages, during the last year of our study there is a noticeable improvement compared with the trends observed in 2005–2008: total alcohol-related mortality of 40–59-year olds declined by 11.8 % for men and by 10.9 % for women, which is close to the decline of mortality observed in 2005–2007 (10.4 and 11.1 % respectively).

These changes are particularly notable when compared with the 1—and 3.6 % growth rates of this indicator in 2007–2008 (Figs. 6.7 and 6.8). Figure 6.7 shows the dynamics of alcohol-related mortality among the population of older working age (40–59 years) in Russia since 2000 till 2009, and Fig. 6.8 shows the rates of change in such mortality from 2005 till 2009. Note that the change from a positive to a negative trend in 2008 was related to somatic causes (growth by 3.8 and 7.6 % as opposed to an annual decline of 9 and 10.1 % in 2005–2007). Mortality from alcohol poisoning continued to decline in 2007–2008, although the rates of improvement significantly

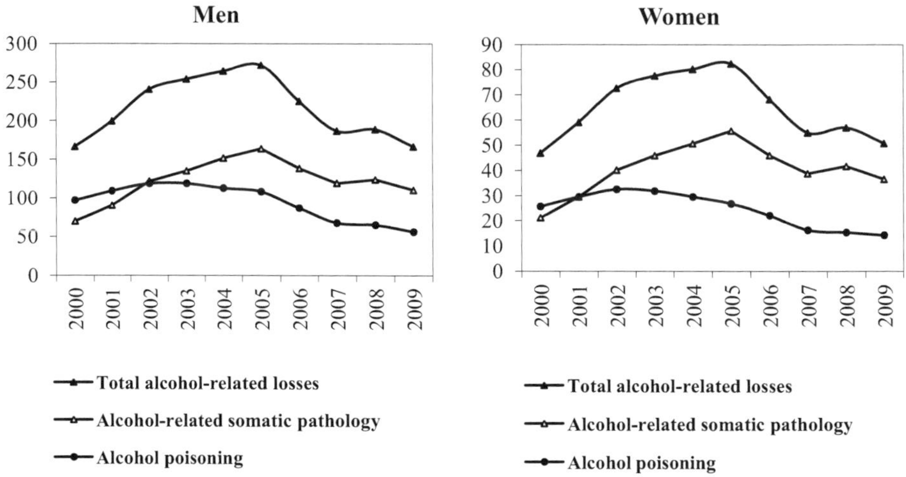

Fig. 6.7 Alcohol-related mortality among population of older working age (40–59 years) in Russia in 2000–2009, by sex and by type of alcohol-related losses (standardized rates per 100,000)

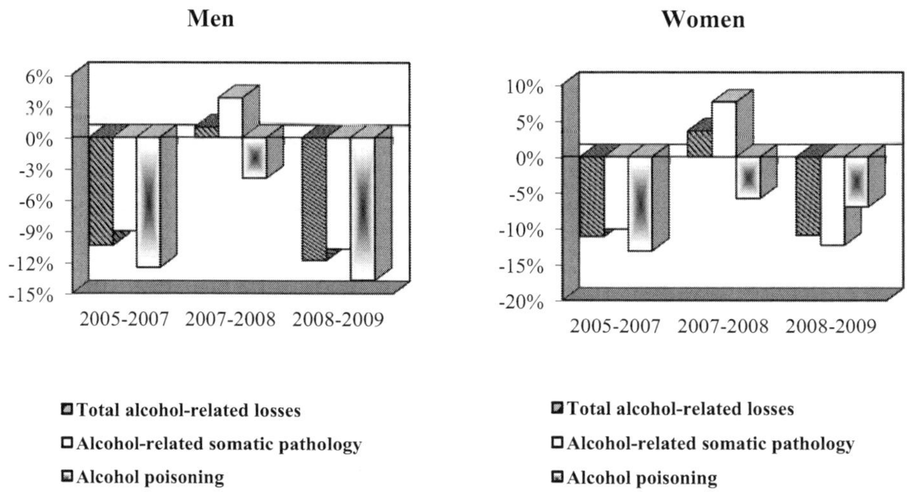

Fig. 6.8 Annual rates of change in mortality due to alcohol-related causes among population of older working age (40–59 years) in Russia, 2005–2009 (percent), by sex, type of alcohol-related losses and calendar period

decreased compared to 2005–2007 (3.9 and 5.8 % in 2007–2008 versus 12.5 and 13.1 % respectively). In 2009 there was a renewed decline in mortality due to alcohol poisoning, particularly among men (a decrease of 13.7 and 7.0 % respectively). Thus, as in the case of young working ages, the improvements in alcohol-related mortality observed in 2009 were determined by both alcohol poisonings and somatic alcohol-related causes.

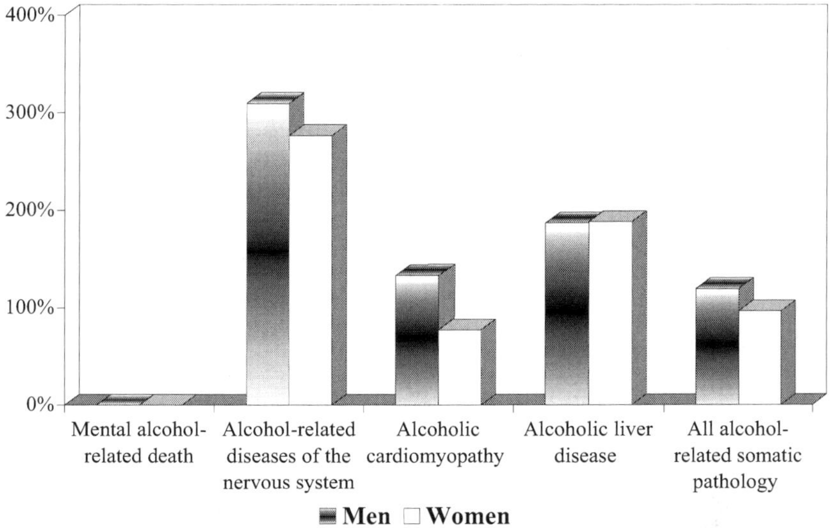

Fig. 6.9 Changes in mortality due to alcohol-related somatic causes among the elderly population (60 years and older) in Russia in 2000–2009, by sex and cause (percent)

Alcohol mortality in the elderly population (60 years and older) is characterized by trends which are similar to those observed at younger ages and here again the growth in death rates in 2000–2009, by 43.1 % among elderly men and by 23.2 % among women, was due to alcohol-related somatic pathology. Mortality due to somatic causes grew by 2.2 and 2 times among men and women respectively, compared with a 26.8 and 34.3 % decrease in mortality from alcohol poisoning (Figs. 6.1, 6.3 and 6.9). Figure 6.9 shows the rates of change in mortality due to alcohol-related somatic pathology among the elderly population in 2000–2009. The highest rate of increase (4.1-and 3.8-fold among men and women respectively) was observed for mortality due to diseases of the nervous system, almost all of which were due to alcoholic degeneration of the nervous system (G31.2). In the second place, in terms of mortality growth (2.9-fold for both older men and women), are diseases of the digestive system, among which alcoholic liver cirrhosis was the cause of death for over 70 % of men and 75 % of women. Mortality due to alcoholic cardiomyopathy increased 2.3-fold and by 77.4 % among elderly men and women respectively. Mental and behavioural alcohol-related disorders were the only causes of mortality which slightly declined in 2000–2009 (by 3.3 and 5.7 %).

Figure 6.10 shows the changes in alcohol-related mortality among the elderly Russian population from 2000 to 2009 and Fig. 6.11 shows the rates of change for this mortality from 2005 to 2009. It should be noted that the improvements in mortality in 2009 were minimal among the elderly population, although they are more noticeable compared to changes in 2007–2008. For example, in 2008–2009 total alcohol-related mortality decreased by 0.9 % among older men and by 5.5 % among older women versus a 5 and 0.5 % growth in 2007–2008. However, the rates of decline in 2009

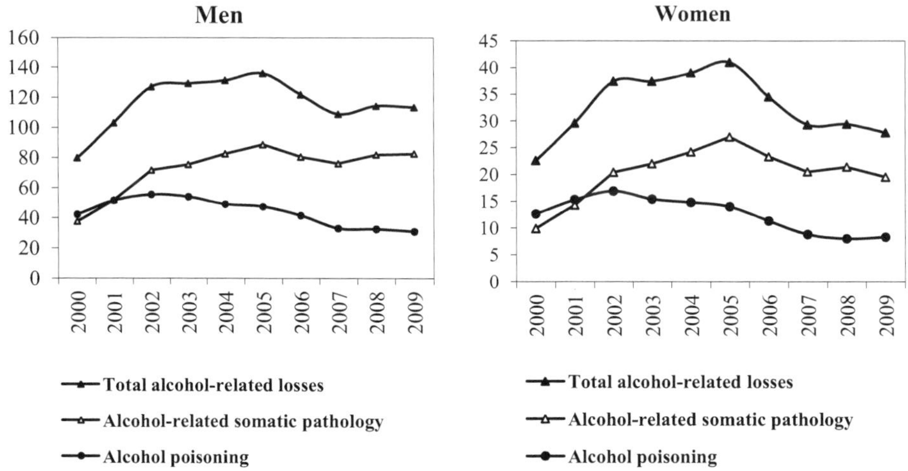

Fig. 6.10 Alcohol-related mortality among older (60+) population in Russia, 2000–2009, by sex and type of alcohol-related losses (standardized rates per 100,000)

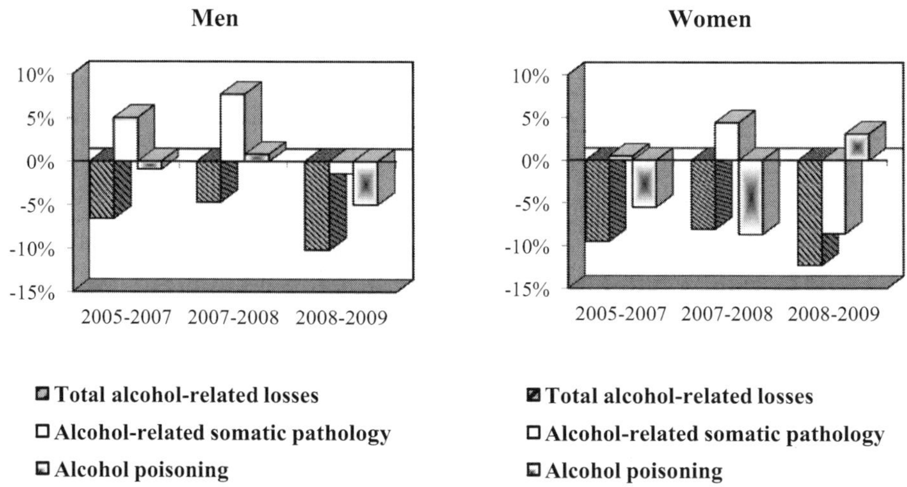

Fig. 6.11 Annual rates of change in mortality due to total alcohol-related causes among older population in Russia, 2005–2009, by sex and type of alcohol-related losses (percent)

were significantly lower than the annual rates of decline in 2005–2007, when they were 6.6 % among older men and 9.5 % among older women (Figs. 6.10 and 6.11).

We would like to note some gender differences in the trends of alcohol-related mortality among the elderly population in Russia, which appeared in the last year of the period under study. While the deterioration in alcohol-related mortality in 2007–2008 compared to 2005–2007 was due to somatic causes (growth by 7.7 % for older men and by 4.4 % for older women) with a very small improvement in mortality trends from alcohol poisoning, the trends of somatic mortality and mortality from alcohol poisoning for older men and women in 2009 showed opposite trends. For men, the improvement in mortality due to alcohol poisoning accelerated (a decrease in mortality by 5 %) while for women the prior decrease in mortality from alcohol poisoning changed to a 3.1 % increase in 2009. At the same time, there was a slight deterioration in alcohol somatic mortality (growth for men by 0.8 % and a change from growth to decline among women). The positive developments in alcohol-related mortality observed in 2009 among the older Russian population were determined by positive changes in mortality from alcohol poisoning for men and by positive developments in alcohol-related somatic pathology for women.

Summarizing the analysis of alcohol-related mortality among the three age groups of the Russian population it should be noted that the positive trends in mortality from alcohol poisoning began as early as in 2002–2003. However, the decline in mortality from alcohol-related somatic pathology began only in 2005, and during the same period one could observe positive trends for total alcohol-related mortality. Some gender differences here should be emphasized: for men, alcohol-related losses grew mainly among the elderly, while for women, the growth of losses occurred mainly at ages 20–39. Thus, we may conclude that women (and young women of reproductive ages in particular) are now in the risk group for alcohol-related mortality in Russia.

Tables 6.1 and 6.2 show the level and the structure of mortality among the adult Russian population (older than 20 years) due to alcohol-related somatic pathology over a 10-year period (2000–2009). It is clear from the tables that alcoholic cardiomyopathy is the dominant cause of alcohol somatic pathology during the study period. The share of alcoholic cardiomyopathy among alcohol somatic deaths slightly decreased for men of younger working age (from 58.2 to 55.5 %), and grew among people older than 40 years, most notably among the elderly (from 58.6 to 60.1 % among 40–59-year-olds and from 51.4 to 54.7 % among persons age 60 + years). Among women, by contrast, there was a decline in the share of alcoholic cardiomyopathy among women in all age groups above 20 years, particularly among young women (from 54.6 to 46.4 %). At the same time, there is a stable growth in the importance of alcohol-related diseases of the digestive system for both men and women. The contribution of these causes to alcohol-related somatic deaths rose from 17.3 to 29.4 % and from 22.6 to 40.2 % among 20–39-year-olds, from 17.1 to 23.6 % and from 24.6 to 37 % among 40–59-year-olds, from 20.2 to 26.4 % and from 25.2 to 36.9 % among older individuals[1]. We note that 2009 did not bring any changes to the 10-year evolution of the structure of somatic mortality of alcoholic etiology (Tables 6.1 and 6.2).

The condition of "chronic alcoholism" (F10) occupies the third place among alcohol-related somatic mortality, but its importance has declined by almost half over the study period comprising about 10 % in all the age-sex groups studied. The importance of degeneration of the nervous system caused by alcohol turned out to be minimal during the study period, and its changes showed fluctuations.

We can thus see a fundamental change in the pattern of alcohol-related mortality for the adult Russian population during the period of 2000–2009: on the one hand a

[1] Alcoholic cirrhosis of the liver dominated among the diseases of the gastrointestinal tract at any age.

Table 6.1 The nosology profile of mortality for the male Russian population aged 20 + years due to alcohol-related somatic pathology in 2000–2009 (standardized rates of mortality per 100,000 and contribution in percent)

Years	Mental alcohol-related causes		Alcohol-related diseases of the nervous system		Alcoholic cardiomyopathy		Diseases of digestive system		Alcohol-related somatic pathology	
	Mortality	Percent	Mortality	Percent	Mortality	Percent	Mortality	Percent	Mortality	percent
Males of 20–39 years old										
2000	3.6	20.0	0.8	4.4	10.3	58.2	3.1	17.3	17.8	100.0
2001	3.5	16.9	1.2	5.6	11.9	58.1	4.0	19.4	20.5	100.0
2002	4.3	15.1	1.4	5.1	17.0	60.3	5.5	19.6	28.2	100.0
2003	3.8	11.8	2.0	6.2	19.7	61.5	6.5	20.4	32.0	100.0
2004	3.9	9.9	2.4	6.1	24.0	61.7	8.7	22.3	38.9	100.0
2005	4.2	9.9	2.4	5.6	24.9	59.5	10.4	25.0	41.8	100.0
2006	3.8	10.1	2.0	5.3	22.1	58.3	10.0	26.3	38.0	100.0
2007	3.5	10.1	1.7	4.9	19.7	57.1	9.6	27.9	34.6	100.0
2008	3.6	10.6	1.7	5.1	18.8	55.5	9.8	28.8	33.9	100.0
2009	2.8	9.4	1.7	5.7	16.6	55.5	8.8	29.4	29.9	100.0
Males of 40–59 years old										
2000	13.7	19.6	3.3	4.7	40.7	58.6	11.9	17.1	69.5	100.0
2001	16.5	18.3	4.7	5.3	53.6	59.4	15.4	17.0	90.2	100.0
2002	18.0	14.8	7.1	5.9	76.5	62.9	20.0	16.4	121.6	100.0
2003	17.3	12.8	8.4	6.2	85.7	63.6	23.5	17.4	134.8	100.0
2004	16.5	10.9	9.8	6.5	97.3	64.3	27.7	18.3	151.3	100.0
2005	16.2	9.9	10.5	6.4	105.0	64.2	31.8	19.5	163.5	100.0
2006	13.6	9.8	8.5	6.1	86.9	62.9	29.2	21.1	138.1	100.0
2007	12.3	10.3	7.0	5.8	73.9	62.0	26.1	21.9	119.2	100.0
2008	13.4	10.8	7.3	5.9	75.4	61.0	27.6	22.3	123.7	100.0
2009	11.3	10.2	6.7	6.1	66.4	60.1	26	23.6	110.4	100.0

Table 6.1 (continued)

Years	Mental alcohol-related causes		Alcohol-related diseases of the nervous system		Alcoholic cardiomyopathy		Diseases of digestive system		Alcohol-related somatic pathology	
	Mortality	Percent	Mortality	Percent	Mortality	Percent	Mortality	Percent	Mortality	percent
Males of 60 years old and older										
2000	9.0	23.9	1.7	4.5	19.4	51.4	7.6	20.2	37.6	100.0
2001	10.0	19.3	2.7	5.3	28.2	54.6	10.7	20.8	51.7	100.0
2002	11.7	16.4	4.2	5.9	41.4	57.8	14.2	19.9	71.6	100.0
2003	11.0	14.6	4.6	6.1	44.3	58.8	15.4	20.5	75.3	100.0
2004	10.4	12.6	6.2	7.5	48.3	58.6	17.5	21.3	82.4	100.0
2005	10.1	11.4	6.8	7.6	52.2	59.0	19.5	22.0	88.6	100.0
2006	8.8	11.0	6.3	7.9	45.8	56.9	19.5	24.2	80.4	100.0
2007	8.7	11.5	5.8	7.7	41.8	54.9	19.7	25.9	76.0	100.0
2008	9.1	11.1	6.2	7.5	46.1	56.3	20.5	25.1	81.9	100.0
2009	8.7	10.5	6.9	8.4	45.1	54.7	21.8	26.4	82.5	100.0

Table 6.2 The nosology profile of mortality for the female Russian population aged 20 + years due to alcohol-related somatic pathology in 2000–2009 (standardized rates of mortality per 100,000 and contribution in percent)

Years	Mental alcohol-related causes		Alcohol-related diseases of the nervous system		Alcoholic cardiomyopathy		Diseases of digestive system		Alcohol-related somatic pathology	
	Mortality	Percent	Mortality	Percent	Mortality	Percent	Mortality	Percent	Mortality	percent
Females of 20–39 years old										
2000	0.9	18.2	0.2	4.6	2.6	54.6	1.1	22.6	4.8	100.0
2001	0.8	13.2	0.4	5.9	3.4	54.7	1.6	26.2	6.3	100.0
2002	1.0	11.1	0.4	4.7	4.9	56.6	2.4	27.5	8.7	100.0
2003	1.1	10.0	0.5	4.8	6.1	54.9	3.4	30.3	11.1	100.0
2004	1.2	8.7	0.6	4.8	7.1	53.7	4.4	32.8	13.3	100.0
2005	1.1	7.5	0.8	5.0	8.0	52.3	5.4	35.1	15.3	100.0
2006	1.0	7.3	0.7	4.8	7.0	51.1	5.0	36.8	13.7	100.0
2007	1.2	9.6	0.5	3.8	5.9	46.7	5.0	39.9	12.6	100.0
2008	1.3	9.9	0.0	0.1	6.1	47.7	5.0	38.9	12.9	100.0
2009	1	8.9	0.5	4.5	5.2	46.4	4.5	40.2	11.2	100.0
Females of 40–59 years old										
2000	3.4	16.2	0.8	3.9	11.7	55.4	5.2	24.6	21.1	100.0
2001	4.3	14.5	1.5	5.0	16.9	57.3	6.8	23.2	29.5	100.0
2002	4.3	10.8	2.1	5.3	23.9	59.7	9.7	24.2	40.1	100.0
2003	4.4	9.6	2.6	5.7	26.9	58.8	11.9	26.0	45.8	100.0
2004	4.2	8.4	2.8	5.5	29.0	57.3	14.6	28.8	50.6	100.0
2005	4.1	7.4	2.8	5.0	31.8	57.2	16.9	30.5	55.6	100.0
2006	3.7	8.1	2.0	4.3	25.2	54.8	15.1	32.8	45.9	100.0
2007	3.4	8.7	1.9	4.8	20.2	52.2	13.3	34.3	38.7	100.0
2008	3.4	8.2	1.8	4.3	21.7	52.2	14.7	35.3	41.6	100.0
2009	3.2	8.8	1.7	4.7	18.1	49.6	13.5	37.0	36.5	100.0

Table 6.2 (continued)

Years	Mental alcohol-related causes		Alcohol-related diseases of the nervous system		Alcoholic cardiomyopathy		Diseases of digestive system		Alcohol-related somatic pathology	
	Mortality	Percent	Mortality	Percent	Mortality	Percent	Mortality	Percent	Mortality	percent
Females of 60 years old and older										
2000	1.7	17.1	0.3	2.7	5.5	55.1	2.5	25.2	9.9	100.0
2001	2.1	14.7	0.5	3.6	7.9	54.9	3.8	26.8	14.3	100.0
2002	2.3	11.4	0.8	3.8	12.0	58.6	5.4	26.3	20.4	100.0
2003	2.2	9.9	0.8	3.7	13.1	59.5	5.9	26.9	22.0	100.0
2004	2.2	9.1	1.1	4.6	13.8	57.0	7.1	29.3	24.2	100.0
2005	2.1	7.7	1.3	5.0	15.1	56.0	8.5	31.3	27.0	100.0
2006	1.8	7.6	1.3	5.4	12.5	53.8	7.7	33.2	23.3	100.0
2007	1.7	8.1	1.1	5.4	10.0	48.9	7.7	37.6	20.5	100.0
2008	1.7	8.0	1.1	5.1	11.2	52.5	7.3	34.4	21.4	100.0
2009	1.6	8.2	1	5.1	9.7	49.7	7.2	36.9	19.5	100.0

Table 6.3 Dynamics of distribution of alcohol-related male mortality (percent) in Russia in 2000–2009, by age and type of pathology

Type of pathology	2000	2001	2002	2003	2004	2005	2006	2007	2008	2009
Males of 20–39 years old										
Alcohol poisoning	67.8	64.3	58.0	56.5	51.6	49.9	47.2	43.9	41.8	42.2
Alcohol-related somatic pathology	32.2	35.7	42.0	43.5	48.4	50.1	52.8	56.1	58.2	57.8
Total	100.0	100.0	100.0	100.0	100.0	100.0	100.0	100.0	100.0	100.0
Males of 40–59 years old										
Alcohol poisoning	58.2	54.7	49.4	46.8	42.7	39.8	38.6	36.2	34.4	33.7
Alcohol-related somatic pathology	41.8	45.3	50.6	53.2	57.3	60.2	61.4	63.8	65.6	66.3
Total	100.0	100.0	100.0	100.0	100.0	100.0	100.0	100.0	100.0	100.0
Males of 60 years old and older										
Alcohol poisoning	52.8	49.8	43.6	41.7	37.2	34.8	34.0	30.2	28.4	27
Alcohol-related somatic pathology	47.2	50.2	56.4	58.3	62.8	65.2	66.0	69.8	71.6	73
Total	100.0	100.0	100.0	100.0	100.0	100.0	100.0	100.0	100.0	100.0

growth in mortality from alcohol-related somatic causes and, on the other, a decline in mortality from alcohol poisoning. In 2000, the alcohol-related mortality of the adult population in Russia was determined predominantly by mortality from alcohol poisoning while by 2009 somatic causes had become the leading causes of alcohol-related mortality (and the contribution of somatic alcohol mortality increases with age for both men and women). Overall, almost two thirds of alcohol-related mortality among men and three quarters among women were determined by various types of somatic pathology (see Tables 6.3 and 6.4). Note, however, that the situation in 2009 is somewhat different from the general evolution of alcohol-related mortality in the last decade. For the first time during the study period, the significance of alcohol poisoning increased, albeit marginally, among 20–39-year-old men and among women older than 40 years. Right now it is difficult to predict whether this is a random event or the beginning of an inversion in the structure of alcohol-related mortality in these age groups.

Thus, we may conclude that during the last decade, the pattern of alcohol-related mortality in Russia was subjected to fundamental changes: in 2000, this mortality was determined predominantly by alcohol poisoning, while in 2009, it became determined mainly by somatic pathologies of alcohol etiology. For this reason, estimates of alcohol-related losses of population which are based on mortality from accidental poisoning by alcohol alone seriously underestimate the level of mortality from this cause: almost two thirds of male and three fourths of female alcohol-related mortality, which is determined by different kinds of somatic pathologies, remain in the "shadow".

We also should take into account another factor. According to the official statistics by Rosstat, the contribution of alcohol-related mortality to the total mortality of the working population in Russia does not exceed 10 % (Regions of Russia 2010). Meanwhile, according to the research by AV Nemtsov and coauthors (Nemtsov 2003,

Table 6.4 Dynamics of distribution of alcohol-related female mortality (percent) in Russia in 2000–2009, by age and type of pathology

Type of pathology	2000	2001	2002	2003	2004	2005	2006	2007	2008	2009
Females of 20–39 years old										
Alcohol poisoning	59.8	53.8	49.8	45.0	40.1	35.9	34.5	32.8	29.2	28.2
Alcohol-related somatic pathology	40.2	46.2	50.2	55.0	59.9	64.1	65.5	67.2	70.8	71.8
Total	100.0	100.0	100.0	100.0	100.0	100.0	100.0	100.0	100.0	100.0
Females of 40–59 years old										
Alcohol poisoning	54.9	50.0	44.8	41.0	36.8	32.5	32.5	29.5	26.8	28.0
Alcohol-related somatic pathology	45.1	50.0	55.2	59.0	63.2	67.5	67.5	70.5	73.2	72.0
Total	100.0	100.0	100.0	100.0	100.0	100.0	100.0	100.0	100.0	100.0
Females of 60 years old and older										
Alcohol poisoning	56.0	51.6	45.3	41.2	38.0	34.1	32.7	30.1	27.4	29.9
Alcohol-related somatic pathology	44.0	48.4	54.7	58.8	62.0	65.9	67.3	69.9	72.6	70.1
Total	100.0	100.0	100.0	100.0	100.0	100.0	100.0	100.0	100.0	100.0

2004, 2009; Nemtsov and Sudakov 2002) and Zaridze et al. (2009a, b), the alcohol component in the mortality of the Russian population is significantly higher than 10 % (according Zaridze's estimates for three Siberian cities, the share of alcohol-related deaths is equal to almost one half of mortality at working ages).

Such a situation may arise due to underreporting of losses due to alcohol abuse in the Russian regions. However, it is not clear whether the authors' conclusions about the high rates of alcohol-related mortality in the Siberian cities (Zaridze et al. 2009a, b) are applicable to other regions of Russia. To test this hypothesis, we conducted a regional analysis of alcohol-related mortality in 2009 in Russia[2].

6.3 Regional Specificity of Alcohol-Related Mortality Among the Adult Population of Russia

The regional distribution of alcohol-related mortality of the adult population in Russia (both total and cause-specific) does not show any marked age-specific pattern. This is evidenced by the high rank correlation coefficients for the main causes of death of alcoholic etiology between the regions for each age group (people of younger and older working ages, the elderly) and for the total male and female populations. Table 6.5 shows that in 2009 the correlation coefficients never dropped below 0.72 ($N = 83$, $p < 0.001$) for younger working-ages, below 0.97 ($N = 83$, $p < 0.001$) for older working-ages, and below 0.7 ($N = 83$, $p < 0.001$) for the elderly, which indicates a high degree of similarity between the regional distribution of rates among

[2] Republics of Ingushetia and Chechnya were excluded from the regional analysis due to insufficient reliability of mortality data in these regions.

Table 6.5 Coefficients of rank correlation for the main causes of death of alcoholic etiology between the regional mortality for three age groups (20–39, 40–59, 60 +) among men and women in 2009

Causes of death of alcoholic etiology	Men aged			Women aged		
	20–39	40–59	60 +	20–39	40–59	60 +
Mental alcohol-related death	0.72	0.98	0.88	0.87	1.00	0.97
Alcohol-related diseases of the nervous system	0.94	0.98	0.93	0.86	0.97	0.77
Alcoholic cardiomyopathy	0.91	0.99	0.91	0.94	0.97	0.96
Diseases of digestive system	0.84	0.97	0.79	0.79	0.97	0.84
Accidental alcohol poisoning	0.89	0.99	0.88	0.80	0.98	0.89
Alcohol poisoning with undetermined intent	0.99	1.00	0.99	0.96	0.99	0.89
Alcohol-related somatic pathology in total	0.90	0.98	0.90	0.93	0.99	0.95
Alcohol poisoning in total	0.92	0.99	0.91	0.79	0.98	0.88
Total alcohol-related mortality	0.89	0.99	0.89	0.93	0.99	0.94

people of all the studied age groups[3]. These results suggest that the patterns of alcohol-related mortality identified earlier for the total population can adequately characterize the regional profile of mortality among these three age groups of adult population.

Past studies of Russian mortality have revealed two regional gradients of mortality: life expectancy declines from the European West to the Asian East and life expectancy also declines from the European South to the European North. These regional gradients in mortality are well-established for Russia and have been described in detail elsewhere (Starodubov et al. 2003; Ivanova and Semyonova 2009). The most plausible explanation for these regional differences is an explanation based on living conditions and lifestyle (Starodubov and Ivanova 2012).

Tables 1A and 2A in the Appendix show a rather unexpected pattern of alcohol-related mortality: one of the Russian gradients ('good' West—'bad' East) is almost absent (particularly for men) and the other one ('good' European South—'bad' North) is well reflected in the data. The worst areas, the 10 regions with the highest level of alcohol-related mortality, are represented mainly by the European Northern regions, belonging to the Northwest and North Central federal districts (Novgorod and Vladimir regions, Chukotka Autonomous Okrug, as well as by men of Archangelsk, Tver, Yaroslavl, Lipetsk, Tula, Ivanovo and Amur regions, Buryatia republic, and by women of Tuva, Komi, Kaliningrad, Leningrad, Chita and Magadan regions). Thus, of the ten worst regions in terms of alcohol-related mortality only seven (two regions for men and five regions for women) are located in the Asian part of Russia. Yet, as recently as in 2004, the ten regions with the highest levels of alcohol-related mortality were all located in the Asian part of Russia (Nemtsov 2004).

The list of regions with the lowest alcohol-related mortality consists of the North Caucasian republics and Volga and the Southern regions. There is a greater gender conformity in this case. In 2009, the lowest alcohol-related mortality was observed in the republics of Dagestan, North Ossetia, Kalmykia, Bashkortostan and Tatarstan, and the Belgorod, Rostov and Kursk regions. Also, the lowest level of mortality was

[3] This pattern was also observed in 2008.

observed in Tomsk and the Tyumen regions for men and in Karachai-Cherkessia and Kabardino-Balkaria for women. Thus, in the Asian part of Russia only two regions were in the lowest mortality group (for men).

The less pronounced "East—West" gradient, together with a strong "European South—North" gradient, represents a specific pattern of regional distribution of alcohol-related mortality, which distinguishes it from the regional distribution of other leading causes of death. Also, in 2009, variations in total alcohol-related mortality in Russia reached 10.8 times for men (from 19.9 in Bashkortostan to 215.8 per 100,000 in the Amur region) and 63.5 times for women (from 2.4 in North Ossetia to 152.4 per 100,000 in the Chukchi Autonomous District). Female mortality in sparsely populated Chukotka exceeded mortality in the Tyva Republic (occupying the next position according to alcohol-related mortality) by 2.6 times. However, if we rely on data from the more populated regions, the variation in total alcohol-related mortality for the female population is reduced to 24.5-fold.

When we are talking about mortality from alcohol poisoning, it is impossible to avoid the problem of alcohol poisoning with undetermined intent (Y15). It is included in the group "lesions with undetermined intent" (Y10-Y34). According to ICD-10, this group includes "cases where the available information is not sufficient for medical and legal experts to conclude whether the incident was an accident, self-damage or violence with intent to kill or damage" (experts find it difficult to determine whether the alcohol poisoning was due to accident or suicide—X65). We should note that such an unusual method of suicide is extremely rare in Russia. In 2008, among nearly 40,000 suicides only 19 cases were reported under the category of X65. On the other hand, accounting for alcohol poisonings as "injuries with undetermined intent" substantially improves the statistics of such a socially important cause as alcohol poisoning for a particular region.

Mortality due to alcohol poisoning with undetermined intent was not registered in almost 40 % of Russian regions for men and in almost 60 % of regions for women. However, such mortality exceeded the country levels (2.2 for men and 0.5 for women per 100,000) in 22 and 17 regions respectively. In 2009, this latter group had a significant gender similarity. The list includes Khakassia, Stavropol Krai, Kursk, Orel, Ryazan, Tambov, Rostov, Volgograd, Nizhny Novgorod, Samara, Sverdlovsk, Omsk and Tomsk regions, Sakhalin and the Jewish autonomous region. This list is largely the same as in 2008, indicating a consistent pattern of underreporting of deaths due to alcohol poisoning. In some cases, there is gender specific registration of alcohol poisoning with undetermined intent, with the Amur region being the most striking example, where the level of male mortality due to this cause is the highest in Russia (88.9 per 100,000) although there are no cases of female mortality from this cause (see Tables 1A and 2A).

To demonstrate how easily and effectively the official statistics can be "improved" by using this uncomplicated technique, note, for example, that in 2009 the actual mortality rate from alcohol poisoning (overall mortality from accidental poisoning and poisoning with undetermined intent) exceeded the officially reported level of mortality from accidental poisoning by 3 times for males and 2.5 times for females in the Stavropol region, by 2.2 and 1.6 times in the Volgograd region, by 2.1 and 3.2

times in the Kursk region, by 2.8 and 2.5 times in the Rostov region, by 2.8 and 3.4 times in the Ryazan region, by 2.6 and 3.4 times in Sakhalin, by 1.5 and 1.8 times in the Tambov region, by 2.5 and 1, 8 times in the Tomsk region. In the Amur region the official death rate from alcohol poisoning for men was 2.4 times lower than the actual level. In Russia as a whole the real rate exceeded the officially reported one by almost 10 % (9.1 % for men and 8.3 % for women).

This practice is not specific to any one part of Russia. Among the regions "improving" the official indicators of mortality from alcohol poisoning there were regions belonging to all Federal districts (except for the North-West) as well as regions belonging to areas with both high and low life expectancy. Since the purpose of this study was an analysis of regional patterns of real levels of mortality from alcohol poisoning, the regional pattern of losses in this study is estimated using overall mortality from all poisoning causes regardless of the intent.

Mortality from alcohol poisoning in the Russian regions is characterized by significant variability: in 2009 there were 77-fold variations for male mortality (from 2.0 in the North Ossetia to 153.9 per 100,000 in the Amur region) and a 516-fold variation for female mortality. Mortality from alcohol poisoning in the region with the highest levels of this indicator was twice as high as mortality in the regions with the next highest level of alcohol poisoning (Tuva for men and Buryatia for women), but even if we exclude these extreme cases, the differences are 37.3 times for male and 223.0 times for female mortality.

In 2009, the ten areas with the lowest mortality rates from alcohol poisoning included Moscow, Dagestan, North Ossetia, Kabardino-Balkaria, Tatarstan, Murmansk and Rostov regions for both sexes, St. Petersburg, Bashkortostan, Kamchatka for men and Karachaevo-Cherkessia, Stavropol Krai, Khabarovsk Krai for women. The ten areas with the highest mortality rates from alcohol poisoning included the republics of Chuvashia, Altai, Buryatia and Tuva, the Kirov and Amur regions for both sexes, Arkhangelsk, Bryansk, Yaroslavl and Sakhalin regions for men, and the republics of Mari-El and Komi, Zabaikalsky Krai and Chukotka for women. Thus, the "East—West" gradient for mortality from alcohol poisoning is much clearer than the gradient for total alcohol-related mortality: the area of the highest mortality includes half of the Asian regions in the case of men and 60 % of the Asian regions in the case of women. At the same time, only one Asian region (Kamchatka for men and Khabarovsk Kraj for women) is in the list of regions with the lowest mortality from alcohol poisoning.

The variability of male mortality from alcohol-related somatic pathology is substantially smaller than that observed for mortality from alcohol poisoning. In 2009, variability was 24.6-fold for male mortality and 75-fold for female mortality. It is interesting that Tyva turned out to be a region with the lowest level of somatic alcohol mortality for men (7.7 per 100,000) while the lowest level of this mortality for women was observed in North Ossetia (1.8 per 100,000). The highest levels of mortality from somatic alcohol-related causes in 2009 were reported in the Chukotka Autonomous Area (189.5 for men and 135.1 for women per 100,000). If we remove the unreliable data of the Chukotka region from the list and use the data for the next region in the list, the Novgorod region (for male and female mortality), the ratio of maximum and minimum regional mortality rates would be close for men and women: 20.1 and 24.0 times respectively.

The list of regions with the lowest mortality from somatic pathology caused by alcohol abuse in 2009 included also the Republics of Dagestan and Bashkortostan, Altai Krai, Belgorod, Rostov, Ryazan, Samara and Tomsk regions, as well as the Jewish Autonomous Region for male mortality and Karachaevo-Cherkessia for female mortality. Note that despite the low somatic mortality from causes of alcoholic etiology in two regions (Tuva and the Ryazan region) the death rate from alcohol poisoning in these regions was high (Ryazan region was included in the 20 worst regions for this indicator). The list of regions with the highest mortality (besides those already mentioned) include Chukotka Autonomous Okrug and the Novgorod region, Vladimir, Ivanovo, Tula, Leningrad and Kamchatka regions, as well as Tver and Lipetsk regions for male mortality and Kaliningrad and Magadan regions, the republic of Komi for female mortality.

Thus, we may conclude that the "East—West" gradient is offset by counter-trends in somatic pathologies of alcoholic etiology. There were only two regions for men and three regions for women in the Asian part of Russia out of 10 regions with the highest levels of somatic alcohol mortality. On the other hand, there were four regions for men and two regions for women in the Asian part of Russia among the 10 regions with the lowest mortality. We should note that the offsetting of the 'good' West—'bad' East gradient is determined in the first place by the diseases of the digestive system of alcoholic etiology (mainly by alcoholic liver cirrhosis) (see Tables 1A and 2A).

It is fundamentally important to note the very poor similarity between regional patterns of mortality from somatic pathologies of alcoholic etiology. Even for such common pathologies as alcoholic cardiomyopathy and alcoholic liver cirrhosis the coefficient of rank correlation was equal to 0.42 ($N = 83$, $p < 0.001$) for men and 0.27 ($N = 83$, $p = 0.01$) for women. The similarity between mortality from alcohol poisoning and mortality from total alcohol-related somatic pathology is particularly low, with coefficients of rank correlation equal to 0.12 ($N = 83$, $p = 0.27$) for men and 0.23 ($N = 83$, $p < 0.05$) for women.

This a the most unexpected result, in our opinion: we would normally expect a common risk factor (alcohol abuse) to result in a similarity in the regional mortality patterns of mortality from major causes of alcoholic etiology. A high level of losses from alcohol poisoning cannot be accompanied by low level of mortality from somatic alcohol pathology (Ledermann 1956, 1964). There might be some exceptions to this rule. One example of such exceptions is France where a high level of alcohol consumption is accompanied with low level of cardiovascular mortality. Despite high levels of alcohol consumption, France has very low levels of mortality from alcohol poisoning, which is related to the manner in which alcohol products are consumed. Russia, on the other hand, is characterized by a different, "Northern" pattern of alcohol consumption, resulting in higher levels of alcohol poisonings and somatic diseases of alcohol etiology (Nemtzov 2011).

We thus suggest that using the regional rank conformity of mortality from alcohol poisonings and somatic causes as our criterion it is possible to identify regions where some components of alcohol mortality are underestimated (Semyonova et al. 2010). In order to avoid bias in making conclusions about systemic underestimation of mortality we used a difference of 30 points in both directions. This decision was determined by the scale of the study, which included data for 78 regions of the Russian Federation. The existing data do not allow us to determine what is the true reason for the lack of balance between external and somatic causes of alcohol mortality. It may happen because poisonings, or somatic causes, or both causes are underestimated. In our study we rely more on the data on mortality from alcohol poisoning because this diagnosis is based on the expertise of a medical examiner.

Based on the criterion of rank conformity by mortality from alcohol poisoning and somatic causes, we found that somatic alcohol-related mortality is underestimated in more than 15 % of Russian regions while mortality from alcohol poisoning is underestimated in more than 17 % of regions. Moreover, regions with a good match between external and somatic alcohol-related mortality (ranks differ by no more than 10 points) account for less than one third of all the Russian regions both for men and for women. A serious imbalance between two types of alcohol-related mortality (more than 30 points) was observed in almost one third of the Russian territories (see Tables 1A and 2A).

Our data suggest that a systemic undercount of alcohol poisonings (difference of 30 and more points in ranks between two types of alcohol-related mortality) is being practiced in such regions as Moscow and St. Petersburg, the Republic of Sakha (Yakutia), Krasnodar and Stavropol territories, Murmansk, Vladimir, Volgograd, Chelyabinsk, Magadan and Kamchatka regions, while underestimation of somatic alcohol-related mortality is practiced in the republics of Chuvashia, Altai, Tyva and Khakassia, Krasnoyarsk kraj, Bryansk, Ryazan, Samara, Kostroma and Tomsk regions. The largest imbalance reaches 65 points for men and 48 points for women in Kamchatka (poisonings). For alcohol-related somatic causes the largest imbalance is observed for men in Tyva (77 points) and women in Chuvashia (61 points).

6.4 Discussion

According to the official data, overall alcohol-related mortality in Russia in 2000–2009 comprised about 10 % of total mortality declining up to 1–2 % among the elderly. However, regional analysis of alcohol-related mortality allowed us to reveal serious imbalances between regional profiles of mortality from alcohol poisonings and alcohol-related somatic causes. These facts allowed us to suggest the existence of systematic underestimation of alcohol-related losses in a number of Russian regions including such large cities as Moscow and St Petersburg.

Using this approach we have been able to identify regions where the administrations systematically attempt to minimize alcohol-related losses in their statistical reports, either from alcohol poisonings or from alcohol-related somatic causes. We can use the very large differences in the ranks of regions by the levels of mortality from alcohol poisoning and alcohol-related somatic pathology as a criterion of systematic undercount of alcohol-related deaths. It is reasonable to suggest that a difference in 30 points in the study of 78 regions (i.e., one third of the list) in both directions is too big.

Also, it is possible to consider regions adjacent to the regions with mortality imbalances, which are similar in their level of economic development, culture, population health, etc. and hence in the structure of their causes of death. For example, in two neighboring regions (Sverdlovsk and Chelyabinsk oblasts) we observe an almost 1.5-fold difference in overall alcohol-related mortality for men (82.5 vs 121.7 per 100,000) and for women (22.9 vs 33.3 per 100,000). This difference occurs because of a twofold difference in mortality from alcohol cardiomyopathy (31.3 vs 64.7 and 8.3 vs 16.8 per 100,000) suggesting an underestimation of this type of alcohol-related mortality in Sverdlovsk region.

Our proposed approach based on conformity in the ranking of mortality from somatic and external causes of death should be considered as purely indicative, but it does allow researchers to identify regions with systematic and intentional underestimation of losses caused by alcohol. Further studies can provide more accurate estimates of alcohol losses and the extent of such underreporting in the identified regions. Our estimates of alcohol-related mortality do not agree with those reported by Andreev and Zbarskaya, who argue that the quality of alcohol-related statistics in Russia is acceptable (Andreev and Zbarskaya 2010). We believe that this estimate is too optimistic, and that the quality of data on alcohol-related losses in Russia is not as good as it is, for instance, in the U.S., France and Finland. The key difference between Russia and the developed countries is the way in which administrative resources are used when data on socially important causes of death (including deaths from alcohol-related causes) are reported. Unfortunately the attention paid by the Russian leaders to demographic problems often results in attempts to underestimate the scale of the problem by regional administrations—a phenomenon, which is unlikely to be observed in the US, Finland and France.

In fact, a more recent paper by Andreev and colleagues (Leon et al. 2011) makes a similar argument. In this article the authors present data about a sizeable alcohol component in mortality from coronary heart disease and cerebrovascular disease in Russia. We believe that the conclusions by Nemtsov and Zaridze about the underestimation of alcohol-related mortality in Russia and its regions look more reasonable, although a true extent of this undercount requires more research.

We suggest four major reasons for the undercount of alcohol-related deaths in Russia (Weissman et al. 2006):

- In the case of somatic causes of death it is possible to report an alcohol-related diagnosis in the death certificate in only two cases: if the deceased was registered in a narcotics dispensary, or in the presence of an expert in alcohol/drug dependence. Thus, the existing legal system does not prevent registration of deaths from alcohol poisoning as somatic deaths. It also gives an opportunity to undercount alcohol somatic deaths by using diagnoses not related to alcohol abuse (Weissman et al. 2006).
- Tests for alcohol in the blood, which are mandatory for forensic examinations, are not required during the postmortem studies conducted in the event of death from a non-external cause, including cardiovascular diseases and diseases of the digestive system.

- At present, it is the common practice in Russia to make 'alcohol' diagnoses as the diagnoses of the last resort in the case of no other possible options. For example, in the case of death due to a traffic accident, when the level of alcohol in the blood of the deceased is close to 5% (lethal dose), the medical death certificate would still indicate traffic accident as the cause of death. This situation may change after the adoption of new rules of testing for alcohol among drivers and stricter punishment for driving under the influence of alcohol, particularly in the case of traffic accidents involving victims.
- Requests from relatives to change 'compromising' diagnosis.
- The methods of data manipulation are specific to each region, so the regional analysis of alcohol-related mortality does not reveal uniform regularities in distribution of major alcohol-related deaths.
- A group of causes named "Symptoms, signs and ill-defined conditions" as well as other diffuse causes included in categories such as "Other," or "Unspecified" (in particular, alcoholic cardiomyopathy is often considered as cardiomyopathy unspecified) serve as a latent reservoir of alcoholic losses (both due to poisoning, and somatic pathology), An example of the reshuffling of deaths related to alcohol poisoning to deaths from injuries of undetermined intent ('alcohol poisonings of undetermined intent') mentioned earlier is the most obvious and the easiest way to reveal such manipulations. Taking into account that we consider here socially meaningful and socially conditioned causes of death, risks of data manipulations in order to minimize alcohol-related mortality may be particularly high.

6.5 Conclusion

The study showed that currently alcohol-related losses in Russia are determined primarily by degenerative diseases of alcoholic etiology rather than by alcohol poisoning. Therefore, we believe that the use of mortality from accidental alcohol poisoning as an indicator of alcohol-related mortality in Russia as well as in the Russian regions is not correct, because this approach may lead to a significant underreporting of alcohol-related losses.

The study also showed the existence of a specific group of regions where deaths from alcohol poisoning or from somatic pathologies of alcoholic etiology are systematically underreported. Overall, a significant underestimation of one or another component of alcohol-related mortality is practiced in one third of the Russian regions, including Moscow and St. Petersburg.

This situation follows from the existing legal framework in Russia and the current practice of diagnostics of alcohol-related deaths, which allows regional administrations to underreport socially significant losses including losses related to alcohol. There is no doubt that the establishment of uniform country standards of accounting for alcohol-related mortality will lead to substantial increase in the scale of losses caused by alcohol, but these measures can only be a first step for the developing of effective programs for alcoholism reduction in Russia.

Appendix

Table A.1 Regional distribution of male alcohol-related mortality (per 100,000) in Russia in 2009, by specific alcohol-related cause of death

Region	1	2	3	4	5	6	7	8	9
Russian Federation	5.2	3.4	29.8	13	24.1	2.2	51.4	26.3	77.7
Altay territory	1.7	1.1	6.2	4.7	29	0.1	13.7	29.1	42.8
Krasnodar territory	4.6	2.5	47	13.9	10.8	0	68	10.8	78.8
Krasnoyarsk territory	5.5	1.9	5.5	6.4	45.4	0.7	19.3	46.1	65.4
Primorye territory	1.1	1.1	10.9	6.4	10.8	19.5	19.5	30.3	49.8
Stavropol territory	1.3	1.4	49.7	6.5	4.4	8.9	58.9	13.3	72.2
Khabarovsk territory	2.8	0.4	13.1	6	5.5	14.7	22.3	20.2	42.5
Republic of Adygea	8.3	0.5	17.3	6.5	30.5	0	32.6	30.5	63.1
Republic of Altai	0.0	1	31.7	10.6	58.2	0	43.3	58.2	101.5
Republic of Bashkiria	0.0	0.1	6	3.6	10	0.2	9.7	10.2	19.9
Republic of Buryatia	0.0	1.6	45.4	25.5	64.2	0	72.5	64.2	136.7
Republic of Dagestan	4.3	0.8	0.9	11.6	2.9	0.3	17.6	3.2	20.8
Republic of Kabardino-Balkaria	6.1	0.4	18.5	12.8	3.1	0	37.8	3.1	40.9
Republic of Kalmykia	2.2	0	3.6	16.4	11.6	0.7	22.2	12.3	34.5
Republic of Karachaevo-Cherkessia	6.2	1	8.6	12.5	8.2	7.9	28.3	16.1	44.4
Republic of Karelia	7.9	11.5	25	9.4	34	1.3	53.8	35.3	89.1
Republic of Komi	12.8	3.8	20.1	33.8	51.2	0	70.5	51.2	121.7
Republic of Mari El	2.3	1.3	29.4	19.4	53.2	0	52.4	53.2	105.6
Republic of Mordovia	9.0	0.3	22.6	2.3	16.6	0	34.2	16.6	50.8
Republic of Saha (Yakutia)	3.9	2.1	57.6	18	10.7	0.8	81.6	11.5	93.1
Republic of Severnaya Ossetia	1.0	2	10	17.6	1.4	0.6	30.6	2	32.6
Republic of Tatarstan	0.5	1.3	14.2	8	6.9	2.7	24	9.6	33.6
Republic of Tyva	1.1	0	2.8	3.8	74.6	0	7.7	74.6	82.3
Republic of Udmurtia	3.3	10	41.9	35.5	41.4	0	90.7	41.4	132.1

Table A.1 (continued)

Region	1	2	3	4	5	6	7	8	9
Republic of Khakassia	3.1	2.6	8.9	5.3	33.7	2.5	19.9	36.2	56.1
Republic of Chuvashia	2.0	1.7	11.7	3.7	57.1	0	19.1	57.1	76.2
Amur region	2.7	1.9	38	19.3	65	88.9	61.9	153.9	215.8
Arkhangelsk region	5.2	7.6	57.6	15.3	63.9	0.1	85.7	64	149.7
Astrakhan region	0.4	5.1	14.9	2.6	22.4	0.7	23	23.1	46.1
Belgorod region	0.7	0.1	2.7	11.6	18.2	1	15.1	19.2	34.3
Bryansk region	2.8	11	24.9	14.2	64.7	1.4	52.9	66.1	119
Vladimir region	7.5	7.7	104.7	33.2	27.5	0	153.1	27.5	180.6
Volgograd region	0.6	1.8	59.3	9.4	4.8	5.7	71.1	10.5	81.6
Vologda region	3.8	2.2	31.7	16.9	31.7	0	54.6	31.7	86.3
Voronezh region	3.6	1.9	12.9	12.7	24.9	2.3	31.1	27.2	58.3
Ivanovo region	8.6	24.3	64.1	32.1	54.3	0	129.1	54.3	183.4
Irkutsk region	2.7	1.1	24.9	4.3	20.9	0.1	33	21	54
Kaliningrad region	5.7	2.7	56.3	12.4	48.4	0.5	77.1	48.9	126
Kaluga region	4.8	1.1	17.3	10.6	43.4	0	33.8	43.4	77.2
Kamchatka region	23.1	0	66	8.7	8.5	0	97.8	8.5	106.3
Kemerovo region	14.1	6.2	41.5	9.1	43.2	0	70.9	43.2	114.1
Kirov region	6.7	6.8	36.3	9.7	63.2	1.4	59.5	64.6	124.1
Kostroma region	7.0	1.3	15.2	17.1	50	0.6	40.6	50.6	91.2
Kurgan region	8.4	1.4	25.9	5.9	46.5	0	41.6	46.5	88.1
Kursk region	5.5	3.2	5.3	6.4	8.2	8.9	20.4	17.1	37.5
Moscow	8.1	6.1	15.3	15.9	2.8	0	45.4	2.8	48.2
St. Petersburg	3.0	7.6	50.8	4.4	10.1	0	65.8	10.1	75.9
Leningrad region	52.2	5.9	9.3	30.7	37.6	0.3	98.1	37.9	136
Lipetsk region	50.6	1.9	37.8	28.1	29.4	0	118.4	29.4	147.8
Magadan region	30.1	1.2	57.7	4.9	32.6	0	93.9	32.6	126.5
Moscow region	5.2	1.7	58.7	19.5	19.2	0	85.1	19.2	104.3
Murmansk region	6.1	5.9	36	10.9	3.7	0.9	58.9	4.6	63.5
Nizhny Novgorod region	5.0	4.2	44.2	25.7	41.5	4.2	79.1	45.7	124.8
Novgorod region	13.0	7.8	118.2	21.6	37.9	0.4	160.6	38.3	198.9

Table A.1 (continued)

Region	1	2	3	4	5	6	7	8	9
Novosibirsk region	0.1	1.6	33.1	9.4	26.5	0.1	44.2	26.6	70.8
Omsk region	1.6	6.5	30.2	9.8	38.5	7.3	48.1	45.8	93.9
Orenburg region	8.4	4.7	32	8.5	18.2	0	53.6	18.2	71.8
Orel region	2.0	2.6	17.3	18.8	42.5	9.6	40.7	52.1	92.8
Penza region	0.6	3.4	11	12.9	45.3	0	27.9	45.3	73.2
Perm region	3.8	4.2	25	16.8	40.2	0	49.8	40.2	90
Pskov region	2.5	2	25.3	26.3	19.4	0	56.1	19.4	75.5
Rostov region	4.2	0.6	2.8	4.6	3.7	6.6	12.2	10.3	22.5
Ryazan region	7.2	1	3.5	6.5	17.7	31.1	18.2	48.8	67
Samara region	0.5	2.1	5.5	10.1	24.9	9	18.2	33.9	52.1
Saratov region	3.5	1.6	11.4	10.5	35	0.1	27	35.1	62.1
Sakhalin region	2.6	0.8	36.6	18.9	22.3	35.7	58.9	58	116.9
Sverdlovsk region	0.3	2.2	31.3	14.4	27.7	6.6	48.2	34.3	82.5
Smolensk region	22.5	0.8	29.1	9.1	46.3	0	61.5	46.3	107.8
Tambov region	3.1	2.1	48.8	15.9	24.1	12.9	69.9	37	106.9
Tver region	2.1	8.3	83.6	8.5	56.5	0	102.5	56.5	159
Tomsk region	0.0	0.4	7.7	0.6	5.4	7.9	8.7	13.3	22
Tula region	3.7	9.5	77.1	30.1	37.3	0.3	120.4	37.6	158
Tyumen region	1.3	1.8	15.8	4.3	11.7	4.6	23.2	16.3	39.5
Ulyanovsk region	0.7	0.9	22.6	8	35.3	0.3	32.2	35.6	67.8
Chelyabinsk region	7.9	1.9	64.7	22.9	22.8	1.5	97.4	24.3	121.7
Trans-Baikal territory	4.2	1.4	62.6	9.4	42.2	0	77.6	42.2	119.8
Yaroslavl region	1.7	10	47.9	30.5	56.7	0.7	90.1	57.4	147.5
Jewish autonomous region	0.0	0	11.8	7	24	4	18.8	28	46.8
Chukotka autonomous area	59.6	0	110.1	19.8	16	0	189.5	16	205.5

1 psychiatric disorders caused by alcohol; *2* diseases of nervous system caused by alcohol; *3* alcohol cardiomyopathy; *4* diseases of digestive system caused by alcohol; *5* accidental poisoning by alcohol; *6* alcohol poisonings with undetermined intent; *7* somatic pathology caused by alcohol; *8* alcohol poisonings; *9* total mortality caused by alcohol

Table A.2 Regional distribution of female alcohol-related mortality (per 100,000) in Russia in 2009, by specific alcohol-related cause of death

Region	1	2	3	4	5	6	7	8	9
Russian Federation	1.4	0.8	7.9	6	6	0.5	16.1	6.5	22.6
Altay territory	0.7	0.2	1.8	1.7	8.4	0	4.4	8.4	12.8
Krasnodar territory	1.2	0.5	9.7	7	2.6	0	18.4	2.6	21
Krasnoyarsk territory	1.2	0.6	1.6	3.8	14.3	0.3	7.2	14.6	21.8
Primorye territory	0.1	0.2	3.5	4.1	2.9	0	7.9	2.9	10.8
Stavropol territory	0.3	0.5	9.5	2.5	0.8	1.2	12.8	2	14.8
Khabarovsk territory	0.9	0.5	6.3	2.8	1.6	0	10.5	1.6	12.1
Republic of Adygea	2.7	0	2.1	3.3	13	0	8.1	13	21.1
Republic of Altai	0.0	0	11.5	3.6	17.8	0	15.1	17.8	32.9
Republic of Bashkiria	0.1	0	1.9	1.8	2.6	0	3.8	2.6	6.4
Republic of Buryatia	0.0	0.4	17.7	13.4	22.3	0	31.5	22.3	53.8
Republic of Dagestan	1.2	0.1	0.7	1	0.1	0	3	0.1	3.1
Republic of Kabardino-Balkaria	0.6	0	3.6	1.8	0.6	0	6	0.6	6.6
Republic of Kalmykia	0.0	0	0.8	1.8	4.3	0	2.6	4.3	6.9
Republic of Karachaevo-Cherkessia	0.0	1.5	1.1	1.7	0.8	0	4.3	0.8	5.1
Republic of Karelia	5.1	4.8	12	7	7.5	0.2	28.9	7.7	36.6
Republic of Komi	2.5	1.4	5.9	24.9	19	0.2	34.7	19.2	53.9
Republic of Mari El	0.2	0.4	9.7	11.6	16.4	0	21.9	16.4	38.3
Republic of Mordovia	2.2	0	4	0.5	2	0	6.7	2	8.7
Republic of Saha (Yakutia)	0.8	0	17.8	6.6	5.9	0.2	25.2	6.1	31.3
Republic of Severnaya Ossetia	0.3	0	0.6	0.9	0.3	0.3	1.8	0.6	2.4
Republic of Tatarstan	0.1	0.2	4	2.6	1.1	0.3	6.9	1.4	8.3
Republic of Tyva	0.0	0	2.5	4.7	51.6	0	7.2	51.6	58.8
Republic of Udmurtia	1.2	2.6	10.4	16.7	12.2	0.1	30.9	12.3	43.2
Republic of Khakassia	2.6	0.6	3.6	4.6	8.4	2.3	11.4	10.7	22.1
Republic of Chuvashia	1.3	0.4	2.6	2.3	18.8	0	6.6	18.8	25.4

Table A.2 (continued)

Region	1	2	3	4	5	6	7	8	9
Amur region	0.9	0.6	10.8	10.5	17.3	0	22.8	17.3	40.1
Arkhangelsk region	1.4	1.9	17.1	7.7	15	0	28.1	15	43.1
Astrakhan region	0.0	1.3	2.7	2	6.9	0	6	6.9	12.9
Belgorod region	0.1	0.1	0.4	3.6	2.7	0.1	4.2	2.8	7
Bryansk region	0.2	0.9	3.2	4.7	10.6	0.2	9	10.8	19.8
Vladimir region	1.5	1.7	23.9	15.4	6.1	0	42.5	6.1	48.6
Volgograd region	0.3	0.3	14.5	4.1	1.4	0.9	19.2	2.3	21.5
Vologda region	0.7	0.4	4.9	5.7	6.5	0	11.7	6.5	18.2
Voronezh region	0.7	0.4	2.8	6.1	4.8	0.3	10	5.1	15.1
Ivanovo region	1.5	4.6	10.9	15	12.6	0	32	12.6	44.6
Irkutsk region	0.8	0.2	7	2.5	6.2	0	10.5	6.2	16.7
Kaliningrad region	1.9	1.8	27.4	11.1	16.1	0.2	42.2	16.3	58.5
Kaluga region	1.4	0.3	6.1	6	10.1	0	13.8	10.1	23.9
Kamchatka region	8.4	0.5	21.5	5.2	4.7	0	35.6	4.7	40.3
Kemerovo region	6.6	1.5	14.6	5.8	14.5	0	28.5	14.5	43
Kirov region	0.8	1.1	8.7	5.4	17.3	0.7	16	18	34
Kostroma region	0.7	0	2.2	10.4	11.3	0	13.3	11.3	24.6
Kurgan region	2.9	0.5	8.6	2.8	11.9	0	14.8	11.9	26.7
Kursk region	0.0	0.4	0.8	2.2	0.9	2	3.4	2.9	6.3
Moscow	2.3	1.3	4.1	6.8	0.8	0	14.5	0.8	15.3
St. Petersburg	0.8	2.1	12	1.7	2.2	0	16.6	2.2	18.8
Leningrad region	19.9	2	2.3	14.4	8.9	0.2	38.6	9.1	47.7
Lipetsk region	11.3	0.3	6.7	6.3	3.3	0	24.6	3.3	27.9
Magadan region	9.2	0	27.4	5.9	6	0	42.5	6	48.5
Moscow region	0.9	0.3	14.9	8.6	3.2	0	24.7	3.2	27.9
Murmansk region	2.9	3	10.1	4	0.9	0	20	0.9	20.9
Nizhny Novgorod region	0.8	0.6	11.7	11	7.5	0.9	24.1	8.4	32.5

Table A.2 (continued)

Region	1	2	3	4	5	6	7	8	9
Novgorod region	3.5	1.4	30.5	7.7	11	0	43.1	11	54.1
Novosibirsk region	0.1	0.3	9.7	4.9	5.9	0	15	5.9	20.9
Omsk region	0.8	0.6	10.6	3.4	11.4	1.2	15.4	12.6	28
Orenburg region	2.1	1	8.5	5.9	4.5	0	17.5	4.5	22
Orel region	0.4	0.4	4.2	7.5	7.3	2.5	12.5	9.8	22.3
Penza region	0.0	1	2.8	4.9	6.8	0	8.7	6.8	15.5
Perm region	1.3	1	8	11.4	11.4	0	21.7	11.4	33.1
Pskov region	1.0	0.7	5.4	12.9	3.5	0	20	3.5	23.5
Rostov region	0.6	0.2	0.8	1.2	0.8	1.2	2.8	2	4.8
Ryazan region	1.3	0.1	1	2.2	2.2	5.3	4.6	7.5	12.1
Samara region	0.2	0.4	1.2	2.6	6.2	1.8	4.4	8	12.4
Saratov region	0.5	0.3	1.9	4.4	6.8	0	7.1	6.8	13.9
Sakhalin region	0.6	0	14	13.1	5.5	10.4	27.7	15.9	43.6
Sverdlovsk region	0.0	0.4	8.3	7.1	5.9	1.2	15.8	7.1	22.9
Smolensk region	4.7	0	5.5	5.9	11.6	0	16.1	11.6	27.7
Tambov region	0.4	0.9	9.1	4.5	2.9	2.1	14.9	5	19.9
Tver region	1.1	1.8	22.4	4.7	12.2	0	30	12.2	42.2
Tomsk region	0.0	0.3	3.2	0.3	3.7	2.9	3.8	6.6	10.4
Tula region	1.2	2.2	23.6	14.1	5.4	0	41.1	5.4	46.5
Tyumen region	0.4	0.3	5.8	4.4	3.1	1.7	10.9	4.8	15.7
Ulyanovsk region	0.4	0.1	5.9	5	7.8	0.3	11.4	8.1	19.5
Chelyabinsk region	1.4	0.6	16.8	9.3	5	0.2	28.1	5.2	33.3
Trans-Baikal territory	0.9	0.2	21	7.8	16.8	0	29.9	16.8	46.7
Yaroslavl region	0.2	2.3	10.5	14.9	10.4	0	27.9	10.4	38.3
Jewish autonomous region	0.0	0	6.2	9.4	6	2.8	15.6	8.8	24.4
Chukotka autonomous area	41.3	0	86.5	7.3	17.3	0	135.1	17.3	152.4

1 psychiatric disorders caused by alcohol; diseases of nervous system caused by alcohol; *3* alcohol cardiomyopathy; *4* diseases of digestive system caused by alcohol; *5* accidental poisoning by alcohol; *6* alcohol poisonings with undetermined intent; *7* somatic pathology caused by alcohol; *8* alcohol poisonings; *9* total mortality caused by alcohol

References

Andreev, E., & Zbarskaya, I. (2010). Alkogol kak prichina smerti (Alcohol as a cause of death. Electronic Journal). *Demoskope Weekly, 425–426*. http://demoscope.ru/weekly/2010/0425/tema01.php (in Russian).

Ermakov, S. P., Antonyuk, V. V., Gavrilova, N. S., & Evdokushkina, G. N. (1999). Factographic automated information reference system (FAISS-"Potential"). In K. Peter (Ed.), *Proceedings of the international collaborative effort on automating mortality statistics* (Vol. 1, pp. 99–1252). Hyattsville: NCHS (DHHS Publication No. (PHS). 19-1-19-2).

Ivanova, A. E., & Semyonova, V. G. (2005). Smertnost: Faktory, gruppy riska, otsenka poter (Mortality: factors, risk groups, estimation of losses). In V. N. Kuznetsov & L. L. Rybakovsky (Eds.), *Strategiya demograficheskogo razvitiya Rossii* (pp. 21–38) (Strategy for demographic development of Russia). Moscow: CSP (in Russian).

Ivanova, A. E., & Semyonova, V. G. (2009). Tendentsii I territorialnye razlichiya smertnosti (Trends and regional differences in mortality). In L. L. Rybakovsky (Ed.), *Demographic profiles of Russian regions* (pp. 53–90). Moscow (in Russian).

Ledermann, S. (1956). *Alcohol, alcoholisme, alcoholisation*. Paris: Press Univ. de France.

Ledermann, S. (1964). Can one reduce alcoholism without changing total consumption in a population? 27th International Congress on Alcohol and Alcoholism. Frankfurt-am-Main.

Leon, D. A., Saburova, L., Tomkins, S., Andreev, E., Kiryanov, N., McKee, M., & Shkolnikov, V. M. (2007). Hazardous alcohol drinking and premature mortality in Russia: A population based case-control study. *The Lancet, 369,* 2001–2009.

Leon, D. A., Shkolnikov, V. M., & McKee, M. (2009). Alcohol and Russian mortality: A continuing crisis. *Addiction, 104,* 1630–1636.

Leon, D. A., Shkolnikov, V., McKee, M., Kiryanov, N., & Andreev, E. (2011). Alkogol i smertnost ot bolezney sistemy krovoobrascheniya (Alcohol and mortality from circulatory diseases. Electronic Journal). *Demoskop Weekly, 461–462*. http://demoscope.ru/weekly/2011/0461/tema05.php (in Russian).

Mäkelä, P., Valkonen, T., & Martelin, T. (1997). Contribution of deaths related to alcohol use to socioeconomic variation in mortality: Register based follow up study. *British Medical Journal, 315,* 211–216.

Mckee, M., Shkolnikov, V. M., & Leon, D. A. (2001). Alcohol is Implicated in the fluctuations in cardiovascular disease in Russia since the 1980s. *Annals of Epidemiology, 11*(1), 1–6.

Nemtsov, A. V. (1998). Tendentsii potrebleniya alkogolya i obuslovlennye alkogolem poteri zdorovya i zhizni v Rossii v 1946–1996 godi. (Trends in alcohol consumption and alcohol-related losses of health and life expectancy in Russia in 1946–1996 years). In A. K. Demin (Ed.), *Alkogol i zdorove naseleniya Rossii. 1900–2000* (pp. 98–107). (Alcohol and public health in Russia. 1900–2000). Moscow: Russian Association of Public Health (in Russian).

Nemtsov, A. V. (2001). *Alkogolnaya smertnost v Rossii, 1980–90-e godi* (p. 295). (Alcohol mortality in Russia, 1980–90s). Moscow: NALEX (in Russian).

Nemtsov, A. V. (2003). *Alkogolny uron regionov Rossii* (p. 136) (Alcohol damage to Russia's regions). Moscow: NALEX (in Russian).

Nemtsov, A. V. (2004). Kogda zhe zakonchitsya marafon alkogolnoy smertnosti? (When will the end of the alcoholic marathon of deaths? Electronic Journal). *Demoskope Weekly, 43–144*. http://demoscope.ru/weekly/2004/0143/tema01.php (in Russian).

Nemtsov, A. V. (2009). *Alkogolnaya istoriya Rossii: noveyshy period* (p. 320). (Alcohol history of Russia: The newest period). Moscow: Publishing house Librokom (in Russian).

Nemtsov, A. V., & Sudakov, S. A. (2002). Smerti pri otravlenii alkogolem v regionah Rossiyskoy Federatsii v 1991–1997 vody (Death by alcohol poisoning in Russia's regions in 1991–1997 years). *Voprosy narkologii* (Proceedings of Narcology), *5,* 65–70 (in Russian).

Regions of Russia. Socio-economic indicators. (2010). Rosstat website. http://www.gks.ru/bgd/regl/b10_14p/IssWWW.exe/Stg/d03/23-05.htm.

Semyonova, V. G., Antonova, O. I., Evdokushkina, G. N., & Gavrilova, N. S. (2010). Poteri naseleniya Rossii v 2000–2008gg., obuslovlennye alkogolem: masshtaby, struktura, tendentsii (Losses of Russian population in 2000–2008 due to alcohol: size, structure, trends). *Social Aspects of Public Health* (electronic edition), *2*(14). http://vestnik.mednet.ru/content/view/188/30 (in Russian).

Social Atlas of Russian regions. http://www.socpol.ru/atlas/overviews/demography/index.shtml.

Starodubov, V. I., Mikhailova, Yu V., & Ivanova, A. E. (Eds.). (2003). *Health of the Russian population in a social context of the 1990s: Problems and prospects* (p. 248). Moscow: Meditsina (in Russian).

Starodubov, V. I., & Ivanova, A. E. (Eds.). (2012). *Development of human potential in Russia and population health*. Moscow: Litterra (in Russian).

Weissman D., Dubrovina, E. V., & Redko, A. N. (2006). Informatsionnoe obespechenie issledovany po problemam smertnosti v Rossii (Information support for research on mortality in Russia). *Obschestvennoe zdorove i profilaktika zabolevany* (*Public health and disease prevention*), *6*, 31–38 (in Russian).

Zaridze, D., Maximovitch, D., Lazarev, A., Igitov, V., Boroda, A., Boreham, J., Boyle, P., Peto, R., & Boffetta, P. (2009a). Alcohol poisoning is a main determinant of recent mortality trends in Russia: evidence from a detailed analysis of mortality statistics and autopsies. *International Journal of Epidemiology, 38,* 143–153.

Zaridze, D., Brennan, P., Boreham, J., Boroda, A., Karpov, R., Lazarev, A., Konobeevskaya, I., Igitov, V., Terechova, T., Boffetta, P., & Peto, R. (2009b). Alcohol and cause-specific mortality in Russia: A retrospective case-control study of 48,557 adult deaths. *The Lancet*, *373,* 2201–2214.

Chapter 7
Infant Mortality Measurement and the Rate of Progress on International Commitments: A Matter of Methods or of Guarantees of Rights? Some Evidence from Argentina

María Marta Santillán Pizarro, Eleonora Soledad Rojas Cabrera and Dora Estela Celton

Abstract Infant mortality is considered to be one of the greatest expressions of social injustice. Thus, the Convention on the Rights of the Child (CRC) in 1989 urged adhering states to take the necessary steps to reduce it progressively and as a guarantee of equal opportunities. This objective was further supported by a series of subsequent international conferences, in which specific goals of reduction, both in the level as well as in the differences between social sectors, were laid down. Among them: The World Summit for Children in 1990, the International Conference on Population and Development in 1994, the Millennium Summit in 2000 and the Special Session on Children in 2002.

Argentina adheres to both the CRC and the subsequent conferences, adopting the goals concerning the levels of infant mortality as they were laid down internationally. However, in so far as the goals of inter-sector gaps reduction are concerned, it reduced their requirements. Results show that, from 1990, the country has managed to reduce the level of infant mortality, although it has not reached all the goals agreed upon with the international community. The situation regarding the fulfillment of the equality goals, however, is worse. According to the method and degree of disaggregation used results vary, showing, at times, that disparities, far from shrinking, have actually increased. This means non-compliance with the commitments agreed upon in the framework of children's rights, a situation that is aggravated, in particular, when the topic of preventable deaths is addressed.

Keywords Childhood · Human rights · Infant mortality · Inequality

M. M. Santillán Pizarro (✉) · E. S. Rojas Cabrera · D. E. Celton
Centro de Investigaciones y Estudios sobre Cultura y Sociedad, Consejo Nacional de Investigaciones Científicas y Técnicas, Universidad Nacional de Córdoba, Córdoba, Argentina
e-mail: mm_santillan@yahoo.com.ar

E. S. Rojas Cabrera
e-mail: eleonorarojascabrera@gmail.com

D. E. Celton
e-mail: dora.celton6@gmail.com

J. Anson, M. Luy (eds.), *Mortality in an International Perspective*,
European Studies of Population 18, DOI 10.1007/978-3-319-03029-6_7,

7.1 Introduction

The death of a child, in particular a preventable death, highlights the difficulties that some have in exercising their right to health, and, even more seriously, their essential right to life. The exercise of other rights too, inherent to both the child and to the home where it belongs, is at stake. Therefore, infant mortality is one of the greatest expressions of social injustice. The international community has addressed this issue in the Convention on the Rights of the Child (CRC) in 1989 and in several subsequent conventions (Ferrer, 2005; UNDP, 2006; IIDH-UNFPA, 2009). The CRC requires adhering states to take all necessary steps to reduce infant mortality progressively, and guarantee equal opportunities. This requirement was reiterated in the World Summit for Children in 1990, the International Conference on Population and Development (ICPD) in 1994, the Millennium Summit in 2000 and the Special Session on Children in 2002.

The CRC states that infant mortality must be reduced, but it does not say to what extent. The subsequent conferences, by contrast, specify both the extent of the reduction and the time frame for achieving it. Moreover, some of them, acknowledging the vulnerability of some children belonging to certain social, geographical and cultural sectors, assert that the reduction should be achieved with a simultaneous decrease in the gaps between the various sectors.

Argentina ratified the CRC in 1990[1] and adheres to the above-mentioned conferences, adopting the goals referring to the reduction in the general level of infant mortality as they were laid down internationally. Nevertheless, with regard to the equality goals, the country has taken a less strict stand, and incorporates a goal proposing a reduction of disparities to a lesser extent than that established in the framework of the conferences[2].

Furthermore, it needs to be borne in mind that the total number of deaths occurring during the first year of life, as well as those occurring at later ages, includes deaths due to causes that are difficult to prevent (according to the available technology and resources) and others that could have been avoided by means of preventive measures or prompt treatment. To the extent that these measures affect the sectors differently, the inequality in the exercise of the right to life is exposed.

In this context, the following questions arise:

> Has Argentina been able to reduce the level of infant mortality enough to comply with the commitments agreed upon?
> Is it making progress toward the reduction of existing inequalities in order to reach, at least, the goal laid down at the national level?
> Is it in a position to reach the goals set for future years?
> Can Argentina meet its commitments for the reduction of differences, if the analysis only takes into account those deaths which could have been avoided given the current level of available resources?

---

[1] http://treaties.un.org/Pages/ViewDetails.aspx?src=TREATY&mtdsg_no=IV-11&chapter=4&lang=en.

[2] Both the goals set in international conferences and the goal laid down at a national level in Argentina, will be conveniently stated explicitly in the following section.

In order to find an answer to these questions, we focus on the goals reached by the country and on pending issues relevant to fulfilling the commitments agreed upon before the international community. We note that, as no conference explicitly states the way in which the reduction of differences should be measured, the results may vary according to methodological criteria and the degree of disaggregation used to compare infant mortality levels, which can lead to different conclusions regarding progress made towards the guarantee of children's rights. Based on the foregoing goal, we present below a brief summary on infant mortality in Argentina in the light of the goals laid down at the international conferences, and the modifications introduced by Argentina. We then present criteria for assessing the fulfillment of the commitments concerning the reduction of mortality during the first year of life, the results and lastly, our conclusions.

7.2 The Intentions: Infant Mortality at the CRC and at International Conferences and its Incorporation by Argentina

As we noted in the introduction, infant mortality is a priority issue for several international organizations promoting human rights, to the extent that it is considered a violation of the rights to health and to life. For this reason, the Convention on the Rights of the Child (CRC) in 1989, born in the core of the United Nations, urges adhering states to take all necessary steps to reduce the number of deaths occurring during the first year of life (CRC, 1989, Section 24, Subsection 2). CRC is the first legally binding international instrument which takes into account the full range of human rights: civil, cultural, economic, political and social. Moreover, given its standing, non-compliance with the duties agreed upon by adhering states brings about the possibility that these duties can be judicially enforced, thus making the states liable before the international community (UNICEF, n.d.). Therefore, the incorporation of infant mortality among its postulates indicates not only the importance given to this issue but also the states' responsibility to make the necessary efforts to make progress on reduction.

The requirement to reduce the number of infant deaths was not only expressed in the CRC, but was later taken up and reiterated more explicitly at a series of international conferences based on human rights, including: The World Summit for Children in 1990; the International Conference on Population and Development (ICPD) in 1994; the Millennium Summit in 2000 and the Special Session on Children in 2002. These conferences, although not legally binding, take the intentions expressed at the CRC one step further, by laying down action plans for the states, with quantifiable goals[3] for the reduction in the level of mortality during the first year of life, as well as the in the differences between geographical and social sectors. The

[3] That is to say, the goals setting the magnitude of the reduction in a determined time frame.

latter are closely related to the principle of equality[4], fundamental in the framework of human rights.

Hence, by means of adhering to the CRC and to the following conferences, Argentina has committed itself to making all necessary efforts to respect, protect and guarantee, progressively and with equal opportunities, the effective exercise of the rights mentioned therein. As regards infant mortality, it means that the State must take all the necessary steps to reduce, gradually, the number of deaths occurring during this stage and to ensure that they do not increase over time. Furthermore, it means that the country must pay special attention to underprivileged sectors, in recognition of their being more exposed to risk as a result of the situations in which they live, in order that the aforementioned rights may be exercised universally and without discrimination. Figure 7.1 shows a summary adapted to the Argentinean situation with respect to the goals laid down at the international conferences in relation to the reduction of infant mortality. These goals are organized according to the deadline given to fulfill each one of them, not according to the year in which the conference in which they originated was held.

As can be seen in Fig. 7.1, the goals linked to the reduction in the level of infant mortality were accepted by Argentina just as they were set out in the international agreements. However, Argentina did not fully commit to meet the goals for the reduction in infant mortality differences between social sectors. The ICPD Action Plan called for the elimination of existing disparities between geographical and social sectors between 1990 and 2010, and the Regional Action Programme for Latin America and the Caribbean similarly stipulated a 50 % reduction of the differences within adhering countries between 1990 and 2000. Although Argentina accepted this programme, adhering to the Millennium Development Goals, it nonetheless established a national goal that promises a smaller reduction in the disparities and an extended deadline. This goal consists of reducing by 10 % the inequalities between provinces between 1990 and 2015.

7.3 Data and Methods

We used information produced since 1990 by the Statistics and Economic Information Department of the Ministry of Health of the Argentine Republic (*Dirección de Estadística e Información del Ministerio de Salud de la Nación Argentina*-DEIS) (DEIS, 1992; DEIS, 2001; DEIS, 2010). To verify that the goals associated with the reduction in infant mortality were fulfilled, we analysed mortality rates published from 1990. Due to restricted availability of information and its quality, the analysis

[4] In the case of CRC, this is expressed in Article 2, when referring to equal opportunities to exercise the rights acknowledged in its text, although without setting specific goals in that respect.

<table>
<tr><th>Conference</th><th>Resulting action plan</th><th>Summarized goal</th></tr>
<tr><td colspan="3">Goals related to the reduction of the general level or average of infant mortality</td></tr>
<tr><td>World Summit for Children (1990)</td><td>Action plan to enforce the World Declaration on the Survival, Protection and Development of Children in the 1990s (Article 5(a)) (United Nations, 1990)</td><td rowspan="3">To reduce infant mortality by one third between 1990 and 2000</td></tr>
<tr><td rowspan="2">International Conference on Population and Development (ICPD) (1994)</td><td>Action plan of the ICPD (Paragraph 8.16) (United Nations, 1994)</td></tr>
<tr><td>Regional Action Programme (RAP) for Latin America and the Caribbean (1996) (Paragraph 67.1) (ECLAC, 1996)</td></tr>
<tr><td>Special Session on Children (2002)</td><td>A World Fit for Children (Article 36.a) (United Nations, 2002)</td><td>To reduce infant mortality by at least one third between 2000 and 2010</td></tr>
<tr><td>Millennium Summit (2000)</td><td>Millennium Development Goals (Goal 5) (National Council for the Coordination of Social Policies, Presidency of the Argentine Republic, 2010)</td><td>To reduce infant mortality by two thirds between 1990 and 2015</td></tr>
<tr><td colspan="3">Goals related to the reduction in the differences between geographical and social sectors</td></tr>
<tr><td rowspan="2">International Conference on Population and Development (ICPD) (1994)</td><td>Action plan of the ICPD (Paragraph 8.16) (United Nations, 1994)</td><td>To eliminate (between 1990 and 2010) disparities within countries and between geographical regions, ethnic and cultural groups and socioeconomic groups.</td></tr>
<tr><td>RAP (1996) (Paragraph 67.5) (ECLAC, 1996)</td><td>To reduce (between 1990 and 2000) at least by 50 per cent the infant mortality differences between the different residence areas, geographical areas and social groups.</td></tr>
<tr><td>Millennium Summit (2000)</td><td>Millennium Development Goals (Incorporation by Argentina) (Goal 5, target 2) (National Council for the Coordination of Social Policies, Presidency of the Argentine Republic, 2010)</td><td>To reduce (between 1990 and 2015) by 10 per cent the inequalities between the provinces.</td></tr>
</table>

Note: The Regional Action Programme for Latin America and the Caribbean is developed by the Economic Commission for Latin America and the Caribbean (ECLAC), as an adaptation of ICPD to the regional context.

Fig. 7.1 Summary adapted to Argentina with respect to the goals laid down at international conferences related to the reduction of infant mortality and differences between social sectors. (Note: The Regional Action Programme for Latin America and the Caribbean is developed by the Economic Commission for Latin America and the Caribbean (ECLAC), as an adaptation of ICPD to the regional context. Source: Compiled by the authors)

of the reduction of differences between social, geographical and cultural sectors is limited to geographical disaggregation by region and province[5,6].

As regards methods, as there is no generally agreed method for measuring the difference in mortality between different sectors of the population, three strategies are followed: The first one consists in calculating the "absolute difference" between the sectors with the highest and the lowest levels of infant mortality of the country. In this way, an indicator is obtained, which shows how many more infants per 1,000 births die in one area than in another one. The second strategy consists in calculating the ratio between mortality rates in the sectors with the highest and the lowest levels, expressing the difference in relative terms. This indicates how many times the infant mortality of a sector is higher, equal, or lower than that of the other. When this indicator has a value of 1, the interpretation is that both sectors have the same level of mortality. When it reaches, for instance, a value of 2.4, it indicates that a sector's mortality equals 2.4 times that of the other sector, that is to say, that for every 10 children per 1,000 births who die in the second sector, 24 die in the first one.

The third method consists of calculating the Gini coefficient, with the adaptation used by the National Council for the Coordination of Social Policies of the Argentine Republic (*Consejo Nacional de Coordinación de Políticas Sociales de la Nación Argentina*) in the follow-up reports to the Millennium Development Goals, to measure inequalities in the distribution of infant deaths between different groups[7]. This coefficient is a number varying between 0 and 1, where 0 indicates perfect equality in the distribution of the attribute of interest, and 1 perfect inequality. Its advantage, relative to the other measures, is that it includes information for all sectors of interest, and not just the extreme values of the distribution.

For those cases for which no information is available for the years involved in the different goals, data from intermediate years were used, under the assumption that the expected annual reduction is proportional, that is to say, 5 % yearly in the case of the goals encompassed by the Action Plan of the ICPD and its adaptation to the Latin American context, and 0.4 % yearly for goals set at a national level in the framework of the Millennium Development Goals. For example, if one wants to do research on the fulfillment of the goals set at an international level, and if information for the years 1997 and 2000 is available, the gap between those years should show

[5] The territory of the Argentine Republic is divided in 24 political-administrative units called provinces. These are, in turn, grouped in regions: Center (consisting of: the Autonomous City of Buenos Aires and the Provinces of Buenos Aires, Córdoba, Santa Fe and Entre Ríos), Cuyo (Provinces of Mendoza, San Juan, San Luis and La Rioja), Northeast (Provinces of Corrientes, Misiones, Chaco and Formosa), Northwest (Provinces of Catamarca, Santiago del Estero, Tucumán, Salta and Jujuy) and South (Provinces of La Pampa, Neuquén, Chubut, Santa Cruz and Tierra del Fuego). To avoid confusion, all our analyses are based on the regional division used in the yearly publications by DEIS.

[6] Argentinan death records include information on the social group of the deceased (for instance, mother's age and educational level, marital status and membership in medical insurance or health care plan). Nevertheless, we decided not to use these data for this research because they have (serious) quality problems regarding the completeness of the information.

[7] For more information, it is advisable see National Council for the Coordination of Social Policies, Presidency of the Argentine Republic (2007, p. 13 and p. 32).

a reduction of 15 %, or, if information for the years 1990 and 2009 is available, the gap should decrease by 95 %. Likewise, if one wants to analyze the situation of the country in relation to the fulfillment of the national goal and there is information available for the years 1990 and 2009, the gap should decrease by 7.3 %, whereas, if there is information available for the years 1997 and 2009, the gap should decrease by 4.7 %.

Lastly, the causes of infant deaths were disaggregated into preventable and unpreventable deaths using the classification proposed by the Single Health System (SUS) of Brazil in the year 2007 (Carvalho Malta et al. 2007)[8]. This is based on the causes of mortality defined in the Tenth Edition of the International Classification of Diseases (ICD 10), and it classifies as preventable those infant deaths that could have been avoided by:

a. immune-preventive actions;
b. appropriate attention to the mother during pregnancy and at delivery, and to newborns;
c. adequate diagnosis and treatment; or,
d. adequate actions to promote health linked to adequate healthcare.

In Argentina, ICD 10 came into force in 1997, so that preventable mortality indicators are only available from that year on.

7.4 Results

7.4.1 The Level of Mortality

Argentina has managed to reduce significantly the infant mortality level since 1990, the year when it ratified the CRC[9]. Figure 7.2 shows that the infant mortality rate

[8] The choice of a classification designed in another country results from a series of trials based on different classifications for preventable deaths according to preventability criteria used in different Latin American countries, that is to say: Argentina, Chile and Brazil. Based on the results obtained, we decided to choose the classification used by SUS in Brazil, because it disaggregates child deaths to a greater extent according to the preventability criteria it takes into account; whereas the classification used in Argentina offers several preventability criteria, depending on whether the death occurred in the neonatal period or in the post-neonatal period, which, for example, does not allow for the association of a post-neonatal death to a criterion linked to the neonatal period. Likewise, the classification used in Chile places most deaths within the "preventable by means of mixed actions" criterion, which does not allow, per se, for inferring the exact combination of measures that would have prevented its occurrence.

[9] Population projections prepared by the National Institute of Statistics and Censuses (INDEC) of Argentina (in collaboration with the Latin American and Caribbean Demographic Center (CELADE)—Population Division of the Economic Commission for Latin America and the Caribbean (ECLAC)) show a declining trend in the level of infant mortality even in the decades before 1990. Indeed, infant mortality rate is 65.9 per thousand live births in 1950–55 and reaches 27.1 per thousand live births in 1985–90 (INDEC, CELADE/ECLAC 2004).

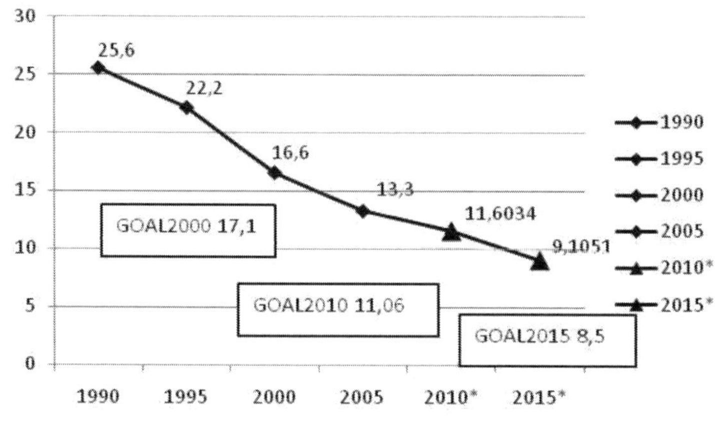

Fig. 7.2 Argentina. Evolution of the infant mortality rate and fulfillment of the goals to reduce the level of infant mortality. Per thousand live births. Period: 1990–2015. (Source: Compiled by the author using data published by DEIS)

dropped substantially, over 50 %, between 1990 and 2009, going from 25.6 to 12.1 per thousand live births. However, despite the efforts made, the gains were not sufficient to meet all of the goals agreed upon at the international conferences, namely, to reduce infant mortality by one third between 1990 and 2000 (GOAL 2000), by another third between 2000 and 2010 (GOAL 2010) and by two thirds between 1990 and 2015 (GOAL 2015).

GOAL 2000 called for the mortality of children under 1 year of age to reach a value equivalent to 17.1 per thousand live births, and, in fact, the rate in 2000 had a value of 16.6 per thousand live births (Fig. 7.2). The rate thus dropped at almost 4.5 % a year over this decade, surpassing the goal. Since then, however, the decline has been considerably slower. The information published until now by DEIS only extends to the year 2009[10], but it is possible, assuming a proportionate annual reduction, to approximate the progress towards the fulfillment of the goals set for the following years. Between 2000 and 2009 (nine years) the rate dropped at about 3.0 % a year to reach 12.1, with an expected level of 11.6 in 2010, as compared with the level of 11.06 set by GOAL 2010. At this rate, the expected level of infant mortality in 2015 will be under 10 (9.1/1,000), considerably higher than the rate of 8.5 called for in GOAL 2015. So, the country faces its first challenge: carrying out measures to speed up the drop in the mortality rate to fulfill all the commitments agreed upon (Fig. 7.2).

[10] Other information sources, such as the Latin American and Caribbean Demographic Centre (CELADE), offer future estimates regarding the infant mortality rate. Nonetheless, we decided not to use them for this research because our main interest is to show the capability of the information gathered in the country to monitor compliance with the commitments agreed upon concerning the reduction in the infant mortality level.

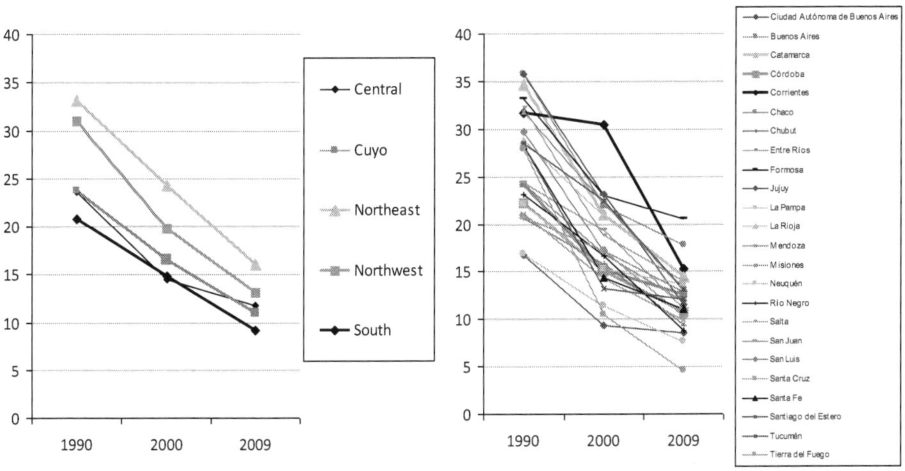

Fig. 7.3 Argentina. Evolution of the infant mortality rate at regional and provincial level. Per thousand live births. Period: 1990–2009. (Source: Compiled by the author using data published by DEIS)

7.4.2 Geographical Differences

As discussed on the methodological section, the analysis with respect the reduction of infant mortality differences between social, geographical and cultural sectors poses a very serious problem due to the quality of the available information for classification by social group (for example, the level of education reached by the mother of the deceased child). This prevents, at present, the calculation of specific indicators for social sector and the analysis is limited to the evolution of the rate of infant mortality from 1990 at a regional and provincial level. Figure 7.3 shows that the rates of infant mortality from 1990, in all regions, dropped significantly and consistently. The same figure shows, however, that throughout this period the Center and South had lower levels of infant mortality than did the rest of the provinces, in particular the Northeast and Northwest. The provinces, too, show a consistent decrease in the rate of infant mortality, but here, too, the disparities persist over time (Fig. 7.3).

Table 7.1 quantifies the disparities that can be seen in Fig. 7.3, as well as their evolution over time, based on the three methodological strategies proposed[11]. At the regional level it can be seen that the absolute gap drops gradually from 1990, although not enough to reach the goal set at RAP which requires a reduction by 50 % in the differences between geographical (and social) sectors in the 1990–2000 period[12]. Likewise, the value obtained in 2009 does not allow us to infer a reduction

[11] They are: Absolute and relative differences, and Gini coefficient (see above).

[12] The gap becomes narrower decreasing by 20.3 % going from 12.3 to 9.8 per thousand live births.

Table 7.1 Level and differences of infant mortality at regional and provincial level. Years 1990, 2000 and 2009. (Source: Compiled by the author using data published by DEIS)

Year	Region/province with highest infant mortality	Region/province with lowest infant mortality	Difference		
At regional level					
1990	Northeast	South	Absolute	Relative	Gini coefficient
	33.1	20.8	12.3	1.59	0.052
2000	Northeast	Center	Absolute	Relative	Gini coefficient
	24.3	14.5	9.8	1.68	0.072
2009	Northeast	South	Absolute	Relative	Gini coefficient
	16	9.2	6.8	1.74	0.045
At provincial level					
1990	Jujuy	Autonomous city of Buenos Aires	Absolute	Relative	Gini coefficient
	35.8	16.8	19	2.13	0.099
2000	Corrientes	Autonomous city of Buenos Aires	Absolute	Relative	Gini coefficient
	30.4	9.4	21	3.23	0.123
2009	Formosa	Tierra del Fuego	Absolute	Relative	Gini coefficient
	20.5	4.6	15.9	4.46	0.091

Mortality levels and absolute differences are in per thousand live births

of 95 % in the differences, as was laid down by the ICPD Action Plan[13], based on a proportional expected yearly reduction[14].

By contrast, the relative gap actually increases progressively over the years analyzed: For example, in 1990, for every 10 children dying in the South, 16 died in the Northeast; in 2009, this ratio increased to 17. Besides the non-fulfillment of the goals agreed upon at the conferences, this reveals a compromising situation for the country with respect to the progressive advance in the reduction of inequalities, a fundamental principle of human rights (Table 7.1). The trend in the Gini coefficient shows a similar problem, because it too increases between 1990 and 2000, and even though it decreases toward 2009, the goals set at the conferences, according to this method, are not reached (Table 7.1).

As regards the provinces, between 1990 and 2000, both the absolute gap and the Gini coefficient increased[15]. Nonetheless, both indicators decrease toward 2009, yielding values which, when compared to those calculated for 1990 (19 per thousand live births and 0.099), represent a decrease by 16.3 % (decreasing to 15.9 per thousand live births) and 8 % (reaching a value equal to 0.091), respectively. Although these levels are not enough to reach the goal set by the ICPD Action Plan[16], they would be enough to reach the goal set by the country. Again, supposing an expected yearly

[13] Which stipulates the elimination of the differences inside adhering countries by 2010.

[14] The gap becomes narrower decreasing by 44.7 % going from 12.3 to 6.8 per thousand live births.

[15] Needless to say that they would not reach the goal set by RAP.

[16] According to which, the differences must decrease by 95 % between the years analysed.

proportional reduction, which in this case would be of only 0.4 %, the goal requires a reduction by 7.6 % of interprovincial disparities between 1990 and 2009 (Table 7.1).

With respect to the evolution of the relative gap, the situation seen at the provincial level not only reproduces the trend at a regional level, but, what is worse, shows considerably higher values. So, for example, in 1990, for every 10 children who died in the City of Buenos Aires, around 21 died in Jujuy. In 2009, the gap showed a significant increase, for every 10 children dying in Tierra del Fuego, 45 died in Formosa (Table 7.1).

7.4.3 *Distribution of Mortality by Cause*

Even though the information currently available in Argentina does not allow for comparisons between social groups, it is possible, by classifying registered deaths by cause, to distinguish between those that could, and could not, have been prevented with the resources available in a given context. In this regard, it is the preventable deaths which effectively compromise the full exercise of human rights, because they can be controlled, unlike deaths deemed non-preventable, the occurrence of which cannot be prevented with the resources available at a given time.

In Argentina, preventable deaths account for a large proportion of infant deaths. In 1997, for example, approximately 64 of every 100 registered child deaths could have been prevented. In 2009, although the proportion decreases, still around 58 in every 100 child deaths are included in this category.

Table 7.2 compares the differences in the levels of infant mortality and preventable infant mortality, at a provincial level, in 1997, 2000 and 2009. In general, it can be seen that disparities in levels of mortality from avoidable causes increased during this period. Between 1997 and 2000 the absolute gaps in total and preventable infant mortality increased. Between 2000 and 2009 the absolute gaps decreased, but the reduction did not reach the 60 % required to reach the goal of the ICPD Action Plan[17]. It does, however, reach the goals of the national Millennium Development Goals Plan, where the required reduction is 4.8 %.

If we analyse the provincial differences using relative gaps, none of the goals are reached. In fact, there is a continued growth in relative difference between the best and the worst province, for both total and preventable infant mortality, with the latter being considerably higher. For example, while in 1997, for every 10 children dying in Tierra del Fuego, 27 died in Formosa; in 2009, said ratio increased to 10 and 45. If, on the other hand, only preventable deaths are considered, in 1997, for every 10 children dying in Tierra del Fuego, 32 died in Formosa; and in 2009, this ratio increases to 10:121[18] (Table 7.2).

[17] In fact, according to this strategy, gaps should be reduced by 14.5 % for total deaths and by 15.9 % for preventable deaths.

[18] In this case, it is worth pointing out that despite a decrease in mortality in Formosa, there was a significant reduction to 1.1 in Tierra del Fuego.

Table 7.2 Level and differences of infant mortality and preventable infant mortality at provincial level. Years 1997, 2000 and 2009. (Source: Compiled by the author using data published by DEIS based on the classification for preventable child deaths proposed by SUS)

Year	Province with highest infant mortality	Province with lowest infant mortality	Difference		
Infant mortality					
1997	Formosa	Tierra del Fuego	Absolute	Relative	Gini coefficient
	29.8	11.2	18.6	2.66	0.096
2000	Corrientes	Autonomous city of Buenos Aires	Absolute	Relative	Gini coefficient
	30.4	9.4	21	3.23	0.123
2009	Formosa	Tierra del Fuego	Absolute	Relative	Gini coefficient
	20.5	4.6	15.9	4.46	0.091
Preventable infant mortality					
1997	Formosa	Tierra del Fuego	Absolute	Relative	Gini coefficient
	22.1	7	15.1	3.15	0.114
2000	Corrientes	Tierra del Fuego	Absolute	Relative	Gini coefficient
	22.3	3.9	18.4	5.68	0.156
2009	Formosa	Tierra del Fuego	Absolute	Relative	Gini coefficient
	13.9	1.1	12.7	12.11	0.135

Mortality levels and absolute differences are in per thousand live births

The Gini coefficient, in both cases, increased between 1997 and 2000, but it decreased between 2000 and 2009. Although this decrease may be considered small, and insufficient to reach the goal of the ICPD Action Plan, for general child deaths it does fulfill the requirements of the national goal added to the Millennium Development Goals[19,20]. If, on the other hand, only those deaths that could have been prevented are considered, the trend of this coefficient does not show any of the goals being achieved (Table 7.2).

The situation appears even more difficult when we disaggregate preventable deaths by cause. Table 7.3 shows the interprovincial differences for five groups of preventable deaths in the period 1997–2009. For absolute gaps, the table shows that, regardless of the preventability criteria referred to, all but one of the interprovincial differences are reduced by amounts exceeding the 4.2 % reduction called for in the Millennium Development Goals. Nonetheless, only in the case of deaths "preventable by appropriate health promotion" is the goal of the ICPD Action plan[21] met, with disparities, in this case, decreasing by 68.7 %. By contrast, for "deaths preventable by appropriate diagnosis and treatment" the situation actually became worse and the absolute gap increased, indicating a regression in the guarantee of equal opportunities.

The trend in relative gaps, on the other hand, is far less encouraging, and they increase substantially over the period studied, as do the Gini coefficients. Once again

[19] For which the reduction of differences shows a value close to 5.2 %.

[20] It should be remembered that its expected reduction, in that period, is 4.2 %.

[21] Which proposes a 60 % reduction in the differences.

Table 7.3 Differences in infant mortality and preventable infant mortality at provincial level according to selected preventability criteria. Years 1997, and 2009. (Source: Compiled by the author using data published by DEIS based on the classification for preventable child deaths proposed by SUS)

Preventability criterion	Absolute difference		Relative difference		Gini coefficient	
	1997	2009	1997	2009	1997	2009
Deaths preventable by appropriate care to women during pregnancy	63.6	52.7	10.19	43.88	0.236	0.3
Deaths preventable by appropriate care to women at childbirth	22.8	17.3	5.89	21.38	0.19	0.268
Deaths preventable by appropriate care to newborns	83.5	63.8	5.51	22.1	0.143	0.183
Deaths preventable by appropriate diagnosis and treatment	30	35.9	7.75	–	0.222	0.29
Deaths preventable by appropriate health promotion, related to health care	61.4	19.2	23.37	–	0.319	0.331

Absolute differences are expressed by 10,000 live births

Given its small participation in the total preventable deaths, the calculation of the differences in the distribution of deaths linked to inappropriate immune-preventive actions is omitted

we have evidence of non-compliance with the commitments agreed upon both at a national and international level regarding human rights (Table 7.3).

7.4.4 Most Frequent Causes of Preventable Deaths

Lastly, it is interesting to analyze the differences found in the distribution of preventable deaths according to the most frequent causes. In Argentina, in 1997, deaths linked to shortness of breath in newborns are ranked first among deaths from preventable causes (17.1 % of total preventable deaths), followed by deaths attributed to conditions related to a short duration of gestation and low birth weight (15.5 %), and infections specific to the perinatal period (10.5 %). In 2009, the composition of the structure of mortality due to preventable causes underwent some modifications, although not substantial: deaths related to short duration of gestation and low birth weight took first place (22 % of preventable deaths), followed by those associated with shortness of breath in newborns (16.8 %) and infections specific to the perinatal period (10.9 %)[22].

Table 7.4 shows the inequalities existing at a provincial level concerning deaths due to the preventable causes mentioned above, between 1997 and 2009. We can see that the more disaggregated the information, the clearer becomes the persistence

[22] Although the causes mentioned before show a significant participation in the total preventable deaths, the mortality levels associated with them decrease between 1997 and 2009. In fact, the rate associated with shortness of breath in newborns decreases by 42.2 %, going from 20.6 to 11.9 per 10,000 live births; the rate linked to conditions related to short duration of gestation or low birth weight decreases by 17 % (going from 18.8 to 15.6 per 10,000 live births); and the rate linked to

Table 7.4 Argentina. Level and differences in infant mortality due to the three most frequent causes of preventable infant mortality. Years 1997 and 2009. (Source: Compiled by the author using data published by DEIS based on the classification for preventable child deaths proposed by SUS)

Year	Province with highest infant mortality	Province with lowest infant mortality	Difference		
Shortness of breath in newborns					
1997	Formosa	Neuquén	Absolute	Relative	Gini coefficient
	51	0.9	50.1	56.67	0.203
2009	San Luis	Salta	Absolute	Relative	Gini coefficient
	40.6	0.4	40.2	101.5	0.308
Conditions linked to short duration gestation and low weight at birth					
1997	Catamarca	Santiago del Estero	Absolute	Relative	Gini coefficient
	66.6	3.6	63	18.5	0.310
2009	Tucumán	San Luis	Absolute	Relative	Gini coefficient
	53.6	–	53.6	–	0.339
Infections specific to the perinatal period					
1997	Corrientes	Tierra del Fuego	Absolute	Relative	Gini coefficient
	31	–	31	–	0.246
2009	Chaco	Tierra del Fuego	Absolute	Relative	Gini coefficient
	26.7	–	26.7	–	0.303

Mortality levels and absolute differences are in per 10,000 live births

of inequalities over time and, more seriously, the more these inequalities increase. For absolute gaps, the three analyzed causes show a decrease, but one which is not enough to reach the goal laid down in the ICPD Action Plan. Nonetheless, they do meet the goal agreed upon at a national level, which called for a reduction of 4.2 % over the period in question (disparities decrease by 19.8 % in the case of deaths linked to shortness of breath in newborns, by 14.9 % in the case of deaths related to short duration of gestation and low birth weight, and by 13.9 % in the case of certain infections which are specific to the perinatal period) (Table 7.4). As in the previous paragraphs, however, the trends in relative gaps and in the Gini coefficient show a clear and consistent increase in disparities[23] (Table 7.4).

7.5 Conclusions

Argentina has reduced significantly the level of infant mortality since 1990. Nevertheless, the rate at which this decrease has occurred is not enough to meet all the goals set at international conferences, or even the less strict goals to which the country has

specific infections occurring during the perinatal period decreases by 38.9 % (from 12.6 to 7.7 per 10,000 live births).

[23] In fact, relative gap increase can only be seen in the first cause of death. For the rest of the causes, geographical differences observed are especially given that some provinces reach zero deaths in 1997 and 2009.

committed itself at a national level. Hence, this is the first challenge the country has to face: to take steps to speed up the reduction in this rate.

Evaluation of the reduction in infant mortality gaps between geographical and social sectors depends on the methodological criteria and the degree of disaggregation being used. In particular, if the focus is on relative (and not absolute) disparities between regions and provinces, then not only has the (less strict) goal set at the national level not been reached, but disparities have actually increased. The situation gets even worse when we consider only preventable deaths, in which case the differences not only become larger, they also increase more over time.

We have focused in our analysis on the distribution of a few specific causes for a number of reasons. Firstly, these causes make up a substantial proportion of preventable deaths, and they are therefore a key to reducing national levels of infant mortality, as well as regional disparities. Secondly, a detailed analysis of each cause separately shows that they respond to two clearly differentiated preventability criteria. Deaths due to shortness of breath in newborns, or to infections specific to the perinatal period can be reduced by means of appropriate measures of newborn health care. On the other hand, deaths linked to prematurity and low birth weight can be reduced or even eradicated by providing adequate care for women during pregnancy. Despite the reductions in the absolute levels of infant mortality, most recent data reflect the need for state intervention to guarantee the human rights, not only of children, but also of the homes to which they belong. This guarantee must begin by strengthening the capabilities of families to provide the protection and special care that children need from their conception on. At the same time, we have also seen the need for strengthening the healthcare system, so that all children may receive the care they need from the moment they are born.

The persistence of disparities at the level of infant mortality between different geographical areas is a reflection of inequalities in the exercise of the right to life. Thus, we are not only talking about reaching a specific goal, but also of making the necessary effort to achieve universality in the exercise of a fundamental right, one without which it is not possible to exercise any other right. At issue is the promotion of the well-being of all children and in particular in reducing the risks faced by those who belong to the most unprivileged sectors of society.

Lastly, it must be stressed that the fact that there is no accepted methodology for monitoring the commitments agreed upon concerning human rights can lead a country to use the most convenient strategy to submit its reports to the international community, and in this way to obtain a "tag" indicating that it has complied with its commitments to that community. The result is the playing down of a serious problem, that of the preventable death of a child, which, in the end, is one of the greatest violations of human rights.

References

American Commission on Human Rights (2008). *Lineamientos para la elaboración de indicadores de progreso en materia de derechos económicos y sociales*. At http://www.cidh.oas.org/pdffiles/Lineamientosfinal.pdf. Accessed 15 March 2008.

Bureau of Statistics and Information of the Argentine Ministry of Health. 1990, 2000 and 2009 yearbooks.

Bureau of Statistics and Information of the Argentine Ministry of Health. *Births and child death records. Years 1990, 1997, 2000 y 2009*.

Carvalho Malta, D., Duarte, E., Furquin de Almeida, M., Salles Dias, M., de Morais Neto, O., de Moura, L., Ferraz, W., & Marinho de Souza, M. (2007). Lista de causas de muertes evitables por intervenciones del Sistema Único de Salud de Brasil. *Epidemiol Serv Saúde Brasília, 16*(4), 233–244. (October–December).

DEIS (1992). *Statistical yearbook 1990*. Bureau of Statistics and Information of the Argentine Ministry of Health. Buenos Aires, Argentina.

DEIS (2001). *Statistical yearbook 2000*. Bureau of Statistics and Information of the Argentine Ministry of Health. Buenos Aires, Argentina. At http://www.deis.gov.ar/Publicaciones/Publicaciones.asp. Accessed 20 August 2010.

DEIS (2010). *Statistical yearbook 2009*. Bureau of Statistics and Information of the Argentine Ministry of Health. Buenos Aires, Argentina. At http://www.deis.gov.ar/Publicaciones/Publicaciones.asp. Accessed 14 April 2011.

ECLAC. (1996). Plan de Acción Regional Latinoamericano y del Caribe sobre Población y Desarrollo. Santiago de Chile. At http://www.eclac.org/_vti_bin/shtml.dll/celade/publica/lcg1920e/LCG1920e-todo.html/map. Accessed 8 Jan 2009.

Ferrer, M. (2005). La población y el desarrollo desde un enfoque de derechos humanos: intersecciones, perspectivas y orientaciones para una agenda regional. In *Serie Población y Desarrollo N° 60. CEPAL*. Santiago de Chile. At http://www.eclac.org/publicaciones/xml/6/23556/lcl2425-P.pdf. Accessed 15 March 2012.

IIDH—UNFPA. (2009). *Derechos humanos en la agenda de población y desarrollo. Vínculos conceptuales y jurídicos, estándares de aplicación*. Instituto Interamericano de Derechos Humanos y Fondo de Población de Naciones Unidas, San José de Costa Rica. At http://www.iidh.ed.cr/BibliotecaWeb/Varios/Documentos/BD_395509089/pobl-des.pdf. Accessed 4 May 2011.

INDEC, CELADE/ECLAC (2004). *Estimaciones y proyecciones de población. Total del país. 1950–2015*. Serie Análisis Demográfico N° 30. Buenos Aires, Argentina. Instituto Nacional de Estadísticas y Censos y Centro Latinoamericano y Caribeño de Demografia—División de Población de la Comision Economica para América Latina y el Caribe (CEPAL). At http://www.indec.mecon.ar/nuevaweb/cuadros/2/proyecyestimaciones_1950-2015.pdf. Accessed 11 July 2012.

INSTITUTO NACIONAL DE ESTADÍSTICAS Y CENSOS Y CENTRO LATINOAMERICANO Y CARIBEÑO DE DEMOGRAGRAFÍA—DIVISIÓN DE POBLACIÓN DE COMISIÓN ECONÓMICA PARA AMÉRICA LATINA Y EL CARIBE. (2004). Estimaciones y proyecciones de población. Total del país. 1950–2015. In *Serie Análisis Demográfico N° 30*. Buenos Aires, Argentina. At http://www.indec.mecon.ar/nuevaweb/cuadros/2/proyecyestimaciones_1950-2015.pdf. Accessed 11 July 2012.

Inter-Agency Network for Health Information—Organization. (2002). *Derechos del Niño. Seguimiento de la Aplicación de la Convención sobre los Derechos del Niño*. Buenos Aires, Argentina.

Inter-Agency Network for Health Information—Organization. *Un mundo apropiado para los niños y las niñas*.

Inter-Agency Network for Health Information—Organization. (2008). *Convención sobre los Derechos del Niño: Aplicación*. At http://www.unicef.org/spanish/crc/index_30208.html. Accessed 2 Feb 2008.

National Council for the Coordination of Social Policies, Presidency of the Argentine Republic. (2007). *Objetivos de Desarrollo del Milenio. Metadata. Argentine Adaptation.*

National Council for the Coordination of Social Policies, Presidency of the Argentine Republic. (2010). *Informe Objetivos de Desarrollo del Milenio 2010.*

PLAN DE ACCIÓN PARA LA APLICACIÓN DE LA DECLARACIÓN MUNDIAL SOBRE LA SUPERVIVENCIA, LA PROTECCIÓN Y EL DESARROLLO DEL NIÑO EN EL DECENIO DE 1990.

UNICEF. Convention on the Rights of the Child. A legally binding instrument. At http://www.unicef.org/crc/. Accessed 3 March 2010.

United Nations. (1989). Convention on the rights of the child.

United Nations. (1990). World declaration on the survival, protection and development of children. World Summit for Children. New York. At http://www.unicef.org/wsc/declare.htm. Accessed 9 March 2008.

United Nations (1990). Plan of Action for Implementing the World Declaration on the Survival, Protection and Development of Children in the 1990s. At http://www.unicef.org/wsc/plan.htm. Accessed 16 April 2010.

United Nations (1994). International Conference on Population and Development - ICPD - Programme of Action. At http://www.un.org/popin/icpd2.htm. Accessed 19 April 2010.

United Nations (2002). A world fit for children. A/RES/S-27/2. Twenty-seventh special session.

United Nations—Information Centre. (1994). Report from the International Conference on Population and Development, El Cairo, from 5th to 13th September, 1994. At http://www.cinu.org.mx/temas/desarrollo/dessocial/poblacion/icpd1994.htm. Accessed 7 March 2008.

UNDP. (2006). Human rights and millennium development goals. Establishing a relationship. Oslo, Norway. At http://www.undp.org/oslocentre/docs08/mdg_spanish_web.pdf. Accessed 27 Oct 2008.

Chapter 8
Avoidable Factors Contributing to Maternal Deaths in Turkey

İlknur Yüksel-Kaptanoğlu, Ahmet Sinan Türkyılmaz and İsmet Koç

Abstract Women's deaths during pregnancy or 42 days after the termination of pregnancy are called maternal deaths. For developing countries, maternal deaths continue to be significant in number. This study represents the avoidable factors contributing to maternal deaths in Turkey using the results of the National Maternal Mortality Study conducted in 2005. According to this nationally representative study, the maternal mortality ratio is 29 per 100,000 live births which is lower than for all regions of the developing world, and at about the same level as those of the Commonwealth of Independent States (CIS) and East Asia. In this study, avoidable factors are categorized into four groups: *household and community factors*, *health service provider factors*, *health service supply factors* and *other avoidable factors*. The results indicate two striking findings. Firstly, the significant impact of household and community level factors on maternal mortality compared to the impact of health service providers and health supply factors. This finding indicates that women's position in their community and in their household is the most problematic issue when it comes to preventing maternal deaths. The second striking result of this study is that there exists a clear need to adopt different strategies for the elimination of maternal deaths in different localities and regions. Although the impact of health service supply factors on maternal mortality were limited among the avoidable factors, the problems of reaching health facilities due to a lack of transportation and long distances between home and the health facility were frequently mentioned obstacles in rural areas.

Keywords Maternal mortality · Turkey · Survey · Risk factors · Death register

8.1 Introduction

For developing countries, maternal deaths continue to be significant in number. The "*death of a woman while pregnant or within 42 days of termination of pregnancy, irrespective of the duration and site of the pregnancy, from any cause related to or*

İ. Yüksel-Kaptanoğlu (✉) · A. S. Türkyılmaz · İ. Koç
Institute of Population Studies, Hacettepe University, Sihhiye Kampusu D Blok 5.kat, 06100 Altindag Ankara, Turkey
e-mail: ilknury@hacettepe.edu.tr

J. Anson, M. Luy (eds.), *Mortality in an International Perspective*, European Studies of Population 18, DOI 10.1007/978-3-319-03029-6_8,

aggravated by the pregnancy or its management but not from accidental or incidental causes" is defined as a maternal death by the World Health Organization (WHO 1992). According to recent global estimates, 358,000 maternal deaths occurred worldwide in 2008, and developing countries constituted 99 % of these mortalities (WHO et al. 2010). Reducing maternal deaths and improving the reproductive health of women, particularly in developing countries, are among the priorities of national governments as suggested in the Millennium Development Goals (MDGs). However, most developing countries do not have accurate and reliable data about maternal mortality.

As in many developing countries, Turkey's vital registration system is not well established and maternal mortality levels are estimated using various other data sources. The recent National Maternal Mortality Study (NMMS) studied all deaths of women of reproductive ages between 2005 and 2006, across 29 provinces, in an attempt to estimate maternal mortality levels, causes of maternal deaths and contributing factors. The survey combined a mortality study of women of reproductive ages, verbal autopsy and a review of records in health facilities, and estimated the maternal mortality ratio in Turkey to be 29 per 100,000 live births for the year 2005. Using these most recent comprehensive data, our aim is to contribute to maternal mortality studies in Turkey by presenting key avoidable factors which have not been previously examined. We have categorized these avoidable factors as *household and community factors*; *health service provider factors*, *health service supply factors* and *other risk factors*. In addition, avoidable factors by region as well as urban and rural residence were examined.

8.2 Measuring Maternal Mortality Levels

A nation's level of maternal mortality is often used as a multi-dimensional indicator of overall health and development. Maternal mortality levels are measured by the maternal mortality ratio, the maternal mortality rate and life time risks. Among these indicators, the maternal mortality ratio (the number of deaths per 100,000 live births) is the indicator most often used. According to the WHO, UNICEF, UNFPA and the World Bank's joint assessment, the maternal mortality ratio has shown a global decline since the 1990's (Hogan et al. 2010; WHO et al. 2010). The numbers point to a 34 % decline from 1990 levels. According to the figures for 2008, the maternal mortality ratio is 260 per 100,000 live births globally. Sub-Saharan Africa has the highest ratio with 640 per 100,000, followed by South Asia (280), Oceania (230), South-East Asia (160), North Africa (92), Latin America and the Caribbean (85), West Asia (68), and East Asia (41) (Table 8.1).

Another indicator of maternal health is the lifetime risk[1] of dying from a maternal cause, defined as the accumulated risk by the end of the reproductive period. One woman out of 140 will die due to maternal causes globally, while one out of

[1] The lifetime risk of maternal mortality is calculated with the following equation suggested by WHO et al. (2010): $1/(1-(1-\text{MMRatio})^{\text{TFR}})$.

Table 8.1 Maternal mortality estimates by the WHO, UNICEF, UNFPA and the WB and NMMR estimates for Turkey. (Source: WHO et al. 2010; HUIPS 2006)

Region	Maternal mortality ratio	Number of maternal deaths	Life time risk
World total	260	–	140
Developed regions	14	1,700	4,300
Countries of the Commonwealth of Independent States (CIS)[a]	40	1,500	1,500
Developing regions	290	355,000	120
Africa	590	207,000	36
North Africa	92	3,400	390
Sub-Saharan Africa	640	204,000	31
Asia	190	139,000	220
East Asia	41	7,800	1,400
South Asia	280	109,000	120
South-East Asia	160	18,000	260
West Asia	68	3,300	460
Latin America & the Caribbean	85	9,200	490
Oceania	230	550	110
Turkey (Only maternal deaths)	29	*387*[b]	*1,536*
Turkey (All pregnancy related deaths)	38	*520*[b]	*1,142*

[a] The CIS countries are Armenia, Azerbaijan, Belarus, Georgia, Kazakhstan, Kyrgyzstan, Tajikistan, Turkmenistan, the Republic of Moldova, the Russian Federation, and Uzbekistan

[b] The number of pregnancy related deaths and maternal deaths obtained from NMMR are inflated to give an estimate for the whole of Turkey

1,536 women will die of maternal causes in Turkey. Both the lifetime risk and maternal mortality ratio of Turkey are at about the same level as those of the Commonwealth of Independent States (CIS) and of East Asia. Table 8.1 indicates that the maternal mortality ratio for Turkey is lower than estimates for all regions of the developing world, although it remains 40 % higher than estimates for the maternal mortality ratio in developed regions and over 80 % higher than the lifetime risk of dying from a maternal cause as estimated for these countries. Matching the CIS and East Asia would confirm the transitional status of Turkey in terms of maternal mortality indicators (Table 8.1).

As is well known, identifying the cause of death is not possible in most developing countries, due to the absence of high quality vital registration and death certification systems. Misclassification and misreporting of deaths are some of the more common statistical problems. Therefore, different data sources and various methodologies such as Reproductive-Age-Mortality-Studies (RAMOS), sisterhood indirect method and verbal autopsy are used to overcome such measurement problems. Obtaining accurate, complete and continuous information about mortality has not been possible from the registration system in Turkey. In an attempt to address the above mentioned problems, a dual-record design was used in the first national study between 1974 and 1975, and the maternal mortality ratio was then estimated as 208 per 100,000 live births (State Institute of Statistics 1978). In 1989, research that used the sisterhood indirect estimation method estimated the maternal mortality ratio as 132 per 100,000 live births (SIS 1993). Another study based on hospital records estimated the maternal mortality ratio as 49 per 100,000 births for 1997–1998 (Akin et al. 2000; Biliker 2005). Moreover, in estimates based on mathematical models, maternal mortality ratios were estimated at 180 in 1990, 70 in 2000 and 44 in 2005 per 100,000 live births (WHO 1996; WHO 2004; Turkyilmaz et al. 2009). The lack of comprehensive data about maternal mortality and the confusion resulting from the different methodologies being used in the above mentioned studies clearly requires additional surveys on the national level.

The most recent survey on maternal mortality, the National Maternal Mortality Study was carried out between July 2005 and June 2006 in 29 provinces and the national maternal mortality ratio was estimated at 29 per 100,000 live births for the year 2005. The survey used burial data, which is considered highly comprehensive when compared with other sources in the country. The reliability of this method has been confirmed by many independent studies.

8.3 The Death Registration System in Turkey

It is useful to take a closer look at the death registration system in Turkey. Death registration is recorded by the General Directorate of Population and Citizenship Affairs of the Ministry of the Interior. Procedures for the reporting and registration of deaths are as follows: The health facility where a death has occurred, or the authority issuing burial permits in urban areas, is required to report the death to the *District Directorate of Population* of the district where the death has been certified. In some cases, relatives of the deceased may obtain the death report from the medical facility and personally take it to the population district for registration in order to facilitate the process. In rural areas, village headmen are required to report deaths to the District Directorate of Population. No medical documentation is sought for the registration of death in such cases.

In both rural and urban areas, deaths must be reported within 10 days of occurrence of the event. Delay in reporting is subject to penalties, albeit not heavy. The Ministry of the Interior and the Population Districts take a passive role in the registration of deaths. No systematic analysis or effort is made to ensure that deaths are registered. A death can only be registered if the deceased appears in a family ledger, therefore birth registration is a prerequisite for death registration. The identity card of the deceased is sent (by the health facility) or brought (by the village headman) to the District Directorate of Population of the particular authority reporting the death; the identity card is then destroyed and the record of the person is ultimately deleted ("closed") from the family ledger. A death certificate is issued by the population district where the death has been reported, which may or may not be the district where death has occurred, where the deceased had been living, or where the family ledger of the deceased appears.

In cases when death is reported by the headman, the cause of death is not recorded. In cases when a health facility reports the death, the cause of death is recorded according to the ICD-10, but such information is considered to be of very low quality.

Analyses of the reported numbers of deaths have also revealed that there exists a gross underreporting of deaths, particularly for women. According to the Ministry of the Interior, 340,015 deaths were reported in 2005. Even if one assumes a crude death rate of 6 per thousand, this implies an under-reporting of 22 %. The magnitude of under-reporting appears to be larger for infants and females.

8.4 Factors Contributing to Maternal Deaths

Identifying the causes of maternal deaths and other influencing factors has played an important role in eliminating maternal deaths. International campaigns and conferences, such as the Safe Motherhood Initiative in 1987, the Cairo Population and Development Conference in 1994, the Beijing Conference in 1995, and the Millennium Development Goals in 2000 have long called for the need to recognize the leading factors of maternal deaths and each campaign has suggested action plans to avoid them. These conventions have also highlighted the importance of social and economic factors and improvements in the health system (WHO 2004). Moreover, it has been shown that not only technical improvements are needed, but also social interventions are necessary for improving health systems (Berer 2007).

Maternal death is an "individual tragedy for a woman, her partner, her children and her family", and the main causes of deaths are generally known. More than 80 % of these deaths could be prevented through effective and affordable actions even in poor countries (WHO 2004). The literature about maternal mortality indicates that the majority of maternal deaths could have been prevented with timely medical care. In this regard, the frameworks developed by Thaddeus and Maine (1994) and McCarthy and Maine (1992) are useful tools for analysing the determinants of maternal deaths. McCarthy and Maine proposed a three-delay approach: reducing the likelihood that a woman will become pregnant, reducing the likelihood that a pregnant woman will experience a serious complication of pregnancy or childbirth, and improving the outcomes for those women with complications. Accordingly, family planning programmes, safe abortion services to reduce the risk of complications and improvements in labour and delivery services are suggested as means to reduce maternal deaths (McCarthy and Maine (1992).

In the three delay model presented by McCarthy and Maine, delays in the decision to seek care, delays in arrival at a health facility and delays in the provision of adequate care were the factors used in the analysis of maternal deaths. Delays in seeking medical care due to individual, family or community related problems, or difficulty reaching the health facility, as well as receiving inadequate medical care at that health facility, are the factors most often mentioned as contributing to maternal deaths (Thaddeus and Maine 1994; Barnes-Josiah et al. 1998; WHO 2004).

A multitude of factors can contribute to maternal deaths and most of them go hand in hand. Cultural factors, a family's socio-economic level, the education and occupation of women, and women's status within the family and community are all important factors in determining the level of medical care. The distance between home and the health facility as well as the number of health facilities, cost of treatment and the quality of care are among the obstacles faced when accessing health services.

In seeking medical care, cultural factors and perceptions about health and illness are among the determining factors. In Haiti, for example, perceptions about inadequate and ineffective health care are presented as the leading factor for not seeking help from hospitals. If women in Haiti perceived health care services as incompetent, costly, unpleasant or dangerous they did not use the services. However, more indirect factors such as the loss of domestic labour, transportation costs or the emotional stress of travel may also result in not seeking medical care (Barnes-Josiah et al. 1998).

Another example of the influence of the overall perception of care on maternal deaths comes from Northern Nigeria, the country with highest maternal mortality ratio in the world. In Nigeria, the primary cause of maternal deaths is eclampsia[2], and local perceptions about the cause of eclampsia are related to the 'evil spirit' of the patient. This perception influences the way treatment is sought, and Nigerians generally seek out traditional healers instead of finding medical care from health facilities (WHO 2003; Adamu et al. 2003).

Similarly, in rural Gambia, the results of a qualitative study indicate cultural factors and the relations between health staff and patients as the primary reasons for not seeking medical care. Patients' underestimation of the severity of their complications, reluctance to challenge traditional wisdom about pregnancy and childbirth issues, previous negative experience with the health staff or negative hearsay about services at the facility, as well as lack of funds, are underlying reasons. In the same study, lack of transportation, prolonged voyages or presenting to more than one medical facility, are also mentioned. Conditions at the hospital, such as lack of blood transfusions, are the most frequent reasons cited among the avoidable factors (Cham et al. 2005). Improving conditions at these facilities and improving the quality of training for health care staff are significant issues. In Uganda, for example, inadequate antibiotic supply, poor access to family planning services, the long distances to available health services, a poor referral system, the use of traditional medicine and the poor gathering of obstetric history are the primary causes of maternal deaths. This study suggests increasing resources for health services, improving roads in rural areas, as well as better informing people about family planning services (Mbonye 2001). In addition, another hospital based study in Pakistan highlights the importance of skilled care at all levels of pregnancy, including the prenatal and postnatal periods to reduce maternal deaths (Bano et al. 2011).

Previous studies conducted in developing countries point to the disadvantaged position of women in all social areas, including health. Women and children are the most disadvantaged groups in countries where patriarchal values are high and women's status is low (Santow 1995; Caldwell 1986; Bloom et al. 2001). Maternal death levels are one of the indicators of women's status (WHO 2004). International documents and national studies have emphasized the effects of gender relations in reducing maternal deaths. In Tunisia, credit for improvements in maternal mortality

[2] Eclampsia is usually a consequence of pre-eclampsia consisting of central nervous system seizures which often leave the patient unconscious; if untreated it may lead to death.

ratio goes to a voluntary political commitment on gender related concerns, including access to family planning; legalization of abortion; the creation of the National Board for Family and Population, and the Tunisian Safe Motherhood initiative in 1999 (Farhat et al. 2011).

8.5 Methodology

Quantitative data of NMMS carried out in 29 provinces in Turkey were used in this article. The data were collected by a RAMOS type of survey design[3] and information about deceased women between 12 and 50 years of age was obtained from burials. Cemetery officials in urban areas and village headmen in rural areas are the primary informants for the burials and they were asked to collect age and sex distribution of all burials. After registering women's deaths, information about the cause of death as well as other background characteristics of the deceased women was gathered in two different forms. If the maternal death occurred at a health facility, the records of the facility were reviewed with the help of Health Facility Record Review Form. If the women died outside of a health facility, a Verbal Autopsy Form was carried out at the household level to determine and classify the cause-of-death (Walraven et al. 2000). Finally, the cause of the maternal death was decided by a Central Review Committee, after reviewing all the forms and information[4].

Verbal autopsy as a "method of finding out the cause of a death based on an interview with next of kin or other caregivers" was performed with the assumption that "each cause of death investigated has a set of observable features which can be recalled during a verbal autopsy interview" (WHO 2010). This method has been used for more than two decades and is now employed widely to provide information on medical, as well as nonmedical causes of maternal death. In these verbal autopsies, interviews are conducted with the surviving spouse or family members in order to learn the signs and symptoms of the illness leading to death (Fortney et al. 1986; Geynisman et al. 2011).

In NMMS, the verbal autopsy form referred to as the Women's Death Questionnaire was developed, based primarily on a validated verbal autopsy instrument of adult deaths (Chandramohan et al. 1998) used for indirect causes of maternal deaths and for non-pregnancy-related female deaths. It was also based on two verbal autopsy instruments developed by Campbell as a part of two studies in Egypt. Other

---

[3] RAMOS type of data collection has been used to identify and investigate the causes of deaths of women in reproductive ages. There have been successful implementations of this method mainly in low-resource countries such as Surinam, Tanzania, Ghana, Gambia, Mozambique, Taiwan, Brazil and Jordan (Mungra et al. 1998; Zahr and Royston 1991; Kao et al. 1997; Walraven et al. 2000; Songane and Bergstrom 2002; Olsen et al. 2002 cited in Geynisman et al. 2011; Alves 2007; Amarin et al. 2010).

[4] This committee consisted of 7 obstetricians, 5 mid-career/senior public health experts/epidemiologists. Moreover, four medical doctors worked on a part-time basis to examine the burial forms, verbal autopsy reports, and health facility records.

documents such as the 2003 Demographic and Health Survey, the Bangladesh Maternal Health Services and Maternal Mortality Survey of 2001, the WHO manual of verbal autopsies for maternal mortality (Campbell and Ronsman 1995) and other WHO documents were reviewed for the development of verbal autopsy forms. In these interviews, the basic characteristics of the deceased woman and her husband were recorded, and information about the disease, treatment and manifestations of the woman's illness was obtained.

Health Facility Record Review Forms were used to identify sub-standard care and ascertain the cause of death, and information about basic characteristics of the women as well as treatments within the health facility was gathered. This form was developed after a study of a number of patient files in several hospitals throughout the country, in addition to reviewing the above mentioned documents. The form provides information in particular on the causes of death and treatment procedures, as well as the necessary background characteristics of the women. Information on 75 maternal deaths was obtained from verbal autopsy, 37 were from health facility review records and 106 cases were obtained by both instruments, to give a total of 218 maternal deaths.

8.5.1 Sampling

The sample design of NMMS was a weighted, stratified probability sample. The organizational requirements of the fieldwork meant that we needed to work at the provincial level and that once a province was selected *all* districts within the province and *all* settlements within these districts were part of the sample. Unlike the standard multistage sampling which is often used in household surveys, the only sampling unit was provincial in scope and the greatest challenge was to select a representative sample from among the 81 provinces that could yield national, urban/rural and 12 NUTS-1 regional estimates[5]. The 29 selected provinces included 16,139 urban (285) and rural (15,854) settlements with a population size of 39 million, thus covering 54 % of the country. The field work of the study was completed at the end of 2005.

Weighting, adjustment, and correction procedures were applied due to the disproportionate sample selection, incompleteness in sending of monthly-based forms and underreporting of deaths. The weighting factor ensured the sample was weighted to rescale the disproportionate allocation of the selected provinces. A "non-sending adjustment" was used to correct for the fact that not all settlements sent data each month. Correction factors were calculated for all project provinces with the help of a standard demographic technique—the Bennet and Horiuchi technique (Arriaga 1994). The factor required for the underreporting adjustment was 1.35, implying a

[5] According to a new system of regional breakdown Turkey is divided, for statistical purposes, into three administrative levels of *Nomenclature of Territorial Units of Statistics regions* (NUTS). The 81 provinces are designated as *NUTS-3 regions;* they can be aggregated into 26 *NUTS-2 regions*, which can in turn be aggregated into 12 *NUTS-1 regions*.

completeness rate at the level of 74 %. The level of underreporting was assumed to be the same for all provinces. Such correction factors have been previously used when maternal mortality is measured in the census (Stanton et al. 2001).

8.6 Results

8.6.1 *Profile of Maternal Deaths*

A total of 218 maternal deaths were recorded in the 29 provinces. The majority (70 %) of maternal deaths took place in health facilities. The mean age of the deceased women was 31.1 years; 7 % of deaths were adolescent mothers, and 32 % were in the 25–29 age groups. Almost all the women (98 %) were married at the time of death (HUIPS 2006). Although only a quarter of the country's population resides in rural settlements, the majority of the maternal deaths (56 %) took place in rural areas. In line with this finding, 45 % of all maternal deaths occurred in the eastern part of the country, which is the least developed region of Turkey. One third of the deceased women had not completed primary level education or had no education and only 15 % of them had education beyond the secondary level. These results clearly show that the women who died due to maternal causes were typically of a more rural origin, younger and less educated than the general population of the same age group.

The National Maternal Mortality Study results indicate that the reproductive behaviour of the deceased women was significantly different from that of women aged 15–49 in the general population. Among maternal deaths, only 24.7 % of women had previously used modern contraceptive methods and 26.9 % of this number experienced contraceptive failure[6], resulting in a pregnancy that led to their death. According to the 2003 Turkey Demographic and Health Survey (TDHS-2003)[7], 42.5 % of ever married women used modern contraceptives and 22.1 % of those women experienced contraceptive failure in the last pregnancy. Among women who died due to maternal causes, relatives of the deceased reported that approximately 31.0 % of pregnancies were unwanted compared to 20.1 % unwanted pregnancies in the TDHS-2003 (Table 8.2).

The survey results indicated that 78.8 % of women had been given antenatal care, but only 31.9 % of them visited antenatal care services four times or more during their pregnancy. Both the proportion in antenatal care and the number of antenatal care sessions taken by the deceased women were lower when compared to women in the comparison group. The number receiving antenatal care was found to be

[6] Contraceptive failure is calculated as the percentage of contraceptive users who become pregnant accidently within 12 months following the initiation of a contraceptive method.

[7] TDHS is a nationally representative sample survey designed to provide information on levels and trends on fertility, infant and child mortality, family planning and maternal and child health. Survey results are presented at the national level, by urban and rural place of residence, and for each of the five regions in the country.

Table 8.2 Comparison of certain characteristics of deceased women in NMMS, and non-deceased women in Turkey Demographic and Health Survey 2003. (Source: HUIPS 2004, 2006)

Variables	National maternal mortality study 2005		2003 Turkey demographic and health survey		
	Percent	Number of cases	Percent	95 % CI	Number of cases
Mean age	31.1	218	33.9	33.65–34.17	8,075
Married	97.6	218	98.8	97.2–99.5	7,686
No education/incomplete primary level	31.8	218	21.8	20.3–23.5	8,075
East	45.0	218	16.2	15.4–17.0	8,075
Urban	43.5	218	71.2	69.9–72.5	8,075
Modern method use	24.7	218	42.5	41.2–43.7	7,686
Method failure	26.9	218	22.1	NA	7,686
Unwanted pregnancy	31.0	218	20.1	NA	7,686
No antenatal care	21.2	218	18.6	16.8–20.6	3,356
Four or more antenatal care visits	31.9	218	53.9	51.6–56.3	3,356
Antenatal care provided by health staff	71.0	218	80.9	78.9–82.8	3,356

81.4 % in 2003, and the percentage visiting the health facilities four times or more was 53.9 % according to the results of 2003 Turkey Demographic and Health Survey. Similarly, the percentage receiving antenatal care from qualified health staff was also lower for women who died due to maternal causes. Seventy-one percent of deceased women took at least one antenatal care visit from trained health personnel during the pregnancy, while this percentage was 81 % for women in the comparison group. These comparisons confirmed that the deceased women had received less antenatal care from the trained health staff.

8.6.2 Avoidable Factors for Maternal Deaths

Several issues contribute to maternal deaths and most of them can be eliminated (WHO et al. 2010). The cause of death patterns varies among countries and within countries. For example, haemorrhage is the leading cause in Africa and Asia, while hypertensive disorder is the highest cause of death in Latin America and the Caribbean (Khan et al. 2006). In Turkey, an Asian country, the primary cause of maternal deaths is postpartum haemorrhage (21 %), followed by oedema, proteinuria and hypertensive disorders (18 %) and antepartum, intra-partum and postpartum deaths (16 %) due to other causes (HUIPS 2006).

Even though many studies have been carried out, particularly in developing countries, to eliminate maternal deaths, there is no standardized approach for the study of avoidable factors (WHO 2004). In fact, the avoidable factors of maternal mortality in Turkey have not been looked at in the limited number of previous studies. In this article, we study the avoidable factors by categorizing them into four groups: *household and community factors*, *health service provider factors*, *health service supply factors* and *other avoidable factors*. The percentage and number of avoidable factors for urban/ rural residence and regions were presented in Table 8.3.

According to the results of the National Maternal Mortality Study, 134 (61.6 %) maternal deaths could have been avoided among the 218 deaths in the country as a whole. Avoidable maternal deaths were higher in rural areas ($n = 78$) than in urban areas ($n = 56$), and these proportions were also different across regions. Avoidable factors in the regions of Central East Anatolia, South East Anatolia, North East Anatolia, Black Sea and Central Anatolia were above the national average. Among the avoidable factors, *household and community factors* constituted the highest percentage on the national level, including rural and urban areas, followed by health *service provider factors,* and other factors. Interestingly, the *health service supply factors* were found as the least frequent contributing factors for maternal deaths. Even though few maternal deaths were observed in the Central Anatolia regions, it could be said that most of the maternal deaths in those regions could be attributed to household and community factors. Only in the East Marmara region is the proportion of avoidable factors lower than 10 % (Table 8.3). The detailed information about these avoidable factors on the national level as well as urban and rural residence are shown in Table 8.4.

8.6.2.1 Household and Community Factors

The household and community factors include delays in recognizing medical problems, delays in seeking medical care, not using contraceptives even where there was no desire for another child, as well as not seeking antenatal care. Knowing the reasons behind these delays, as has been stated in many studies, is essential in order to understand the relationship between the community and the health-care system, as well as to shed light upon women's status within the community. Nationally, delays in recognizing medical problems (89.2 %) and delays in seeking medical care (80.4 %) are the most frequent avoidable factors. Even though the real causes of delays could not be known without information about lifestyle and perceptions of the health care system by the deceased woman and her family, the explanations in a verbal autopsy give some clues.

In one case, for example, a woman had a difficult and long delivery with the help of a traditional birth attendant at home. However, her family took her to a hospital only after a delay of 10 days, where a rupture of the uterus was diagnosed, but could no longer be treated. Similarly, a woman died because of postpartum haemorrhage 13 days following her delivery at home. Another woman died due to neglect of puerperal sepsis 10 days after the birth. In some other cases, women and their families refused treatment or refused to stay at the hospital, or they ignored the risk of being pregnant in cases of chronic heart problems or epilepsy. Sometimes, too, families lacked adequate economic resources to provide medical care from health facilities. In one urgent case, for example, an ambulance team demanded money before transport of the patient to the hospital. In addition to delays in recognizing the medical problem, there were some cases of not recognizing women's psychological problems. One

Table 8.3 Maternal mortality ratio and percent distribution of avoidable factors for maternal deaths by regions in Turkey

Variables	Maternal mortality ratio	Number of cases (n)	Household and community factors (%)	Health service provider factors (%)	Health service supply factors (%)	Other risk factors (%)	Percentage of avoidable factors (%)	Number of cases (n)
Place of residence								
Urban	20.7	123	32.9	16.4	0.8	8.4	58.6	56
Rural	40.3	95	38.6	11.5	2.8	10.6	63.6	78
12 regions								
Istanbul	11.0	11	24.0	4.4	–	8.7	37.1	4
West Marmara	42.1	8	43.1	2.5	0.9	–	46.4	4
Aegean	31.5	26	44.0	16.0	0.8	3.9	64.8	17
East Marmara	21.7	11	8.8	18.5	1.9	26.4	55.6	6
West Anatolia	7.4	5	20.7	31.0	1.5	–	53.2	3
Mediterranean	25.1	26	26.5	16.9	2.5	3.9	49.8	13
Central Anatolia	11.9	6	69.0	5.2	–	–	74.2	4
West Black Sea	26.8	11	59.4	16.7	–	–	76.1	9
East Black Sea	68.3	17	14.9	2.4	–	11.9	29.2	5
Northeast Anatolia	68.3	25	29.8	17.9	6.5	19.9	74.1	19
Central East Anatolia	36.9	23	50.6	13.2	3.8	8.8	76.4	17
Southeast Anatolia	38.9	49	41.4	16.6	1.6	12.3	71.8	34
Total	*28.5*	*218*	*36.2*	*13.7*	*2.1*	*9.6*	*61.6*	*134*

Table 8.4 Number of avoidable factors by type of settlement in Turkey. (Source: HUIPS 2006)

Avoidable factors	Urban % (*n*)	Rural % (*n*)	Turkey % (*n*)
Household and community factors	*56.1(31)*	*60.7(47)*	*58.8(79)*
Unwanted pregnancy but not using contraceptives	12.6(7)	30.7(24)	23.7(32)
Delay in recognizing problem	98.8(55)	83.0(65)	89.6(120)
Delay in seeking care	73.7(41)	85.7(67)	80.4(108)
No antenatal care	39.6(22)	43.4(34)	41.4(55)
Health service provider factors	*28.0(16)*	*18.1(14)*	*22.2(30)*
Poor quality antenatal care	48.56(27)	30.7(24)	38.3(51)
Midwife failed to diagnose	21.5(12)	26.9(21)	24.2(32)
Midwife failed to manage	21.5(12)	24.2(19)	23.1(31)
General Practitioner failed to diagnose	25.1(14)	19.2(15)	21.6(29)
General Practitioner failed to manage	19.8(11)	14.0(11)	16.7(22)
Obstetrics team failed to diagnose	53.9(30)	19.2(15)	33.6(45)
Obstetrics team failed to manage	55.6(31)	34.6(27)	43.7(59)
Provider failed to refer	5.5(3)	2.5(2)	3.9(5)
Obstetrician/medical team failed to diagnose	12.6(79	–	5.5(7)
Obstetrician/medical team failed to manage	16.2(9)	10.2(8)	12.5(17)
Health service supply factors	*1.5(1)*	*4.4(4)*	*3.4(4)*
Lack of surgical staff	–	3.8(3)	6.0(8)
Lack of anesthesia staff	–	2.5(2)	1.6(2)
Lack of nursing staff	–	3.8(3)	2.4(3)
Lack of blood	–	2.5(2)	1.3(2)
Lack of drugs	–	1.3(1)	0.8(1)
Lack of equipment	–	5.2(4)	3.2(4)
Lack of medical supplies	–	2.5(2)	1.6(2)
Operating theatre not available	–	1.3(1)	0.8(1)
Lack of back-up facilities	5.5(3)	5.2(4)	4.5(6)
Lack of anesthesia facilities	–	2.5(2)	1.6(2)
Lack of transportation between home and health facility	–	10.2(8)	6.0(8)
Lack of transportation between health facilities	–	–	–
Long distance to nearest hospital	10.8(6)	16.7(13)	14.1(19)
Health service communication breakdown	3.6(2)	5.2(4)	4.2(6)
Other risk factors	*14.3(8)*	*16.7(13)*	*15.6(21)*
Percentage of avoidable maternal deaths	*58.6(56)*	*63.6(78)*	*61.6(134)*

woman had attempted to commit suicide 1 month before her delivery; however her husband and her family did not realize the extent of her depression.

Recognizing medical complications is more common in urban than in rural areas, whereas a delay in seeking medical care is more often found in rural areas. Household and community factors are the most frequent factors in the Central East Anatolia (76.4 %), North East Anatolia (74.1 %), South East Anatolia (71.8 %), Central Anatolia region (69.0 %), followed by West Black Sea (59.4 %) and Central East Anatolia (50.6 %) (Table 8.3). Failure to use preventive measures, in particular use of contraception to prevent unwanted pregnancy (23.7 %) and absence of antenatal care (41.4 %) are the other leading significant factors. Both unwanted pregnancies and lack of antenatal care are more frequent in rural areas. Even though the number of cases is limited, household and community factors are significant in Central

Anatolia, West Black Sea and Central East Anatolia regions where the percentage of avoidable factors is higher than the country average.

8.6.2.2 Health Service Provider Factors

After reaching the health facility, failures in diagnosing or managing the problems by obstetricians, general practitioners, medical teams or midwife and poor quality of antenatal care are all factors related to the health service providers that are recognised as indicators of quality of provision. Twenty two percent of maternal deaths were attributed to these factors, and their proportion was higher in urban areas (28 %) than in rural (18.1 %). Among these factors, inadequate management by obstetricians, poor quality of antenatal care and lack of early diagnoses contributed more to maternal deaths than other health service providers. Within Turkey's health system, general practitioners and midwives are responsible for providing primary care. Sub-standard care given at the primary level contributed 16–24 % of maternal deaths nationally. In these primary care services, the typical and most often mentioned problem is the failure to manage chronic heart diseases, even when antenatal care was frequently sought. Moreover, signs and symptoms of imminent suicide were not recognized. In some of the cases, the woman and her family refused to undergo treatment or stay at the hospital. Misdiagnosis (33.6 %) and mismanagement (43.7 %) at the secondary care level were found to be high when compared to the third care level, where these contributions were 5.5 and 12.7 %, respectively. Failure to diagnosis eclampsia and consequently delaying caesarean section, early post-partum discharge even in the presence of hypovolemia, post operative abdominal abscess and an unrecognized perforation of the uterus during dilation and curettage were examples of insufficient or sub-standard care.

Among the health service provider factors, referral of patients to other health facilities (3.9 %) was the least contributing factor for maternal deaths. Both referrals from primary to secondary care level, and from secondary to third care levels were expedient and there was no communication problem among the health facilities during these referrals. However, in some emergency situations, patients were transferred to third level care facility even when the necessary comprehensive emergency obstetric care facilities existed in the secondary level.

More than one emergency medical transfer between the health facilities resulted in maternal deaths. In one case, a woman was referred because of post-partum haemorrhage to a mother-child hospital from a government hospital where she had had a difficult vaginal delivery. She was then referred to a university hospital on suspicion of a ruptured uterus instead of being given an urgently needed blood transfusion and she died on the way to the university hospital.

8.6.2.3 Health Service Supply Factors

The results of this survey indicate that several *health service supply factors*, such as adequate number of healthcare staff, sufficient equipment for diagnostic and treatment facilities, and availability of pharmaceuticals and medical supplies, played a relatively minor role (3.4 %) in contributing to maternal deaths. In fact, it was surprising to learn how, in many cases of eclampsia, a brain computer tomography or magnetic resonance tomography was readily available for the diagnosis of an intra-cerebral bleeding. Lack of back-up facilities contributed to 4.5 % of maternal deaths. Long distance to the nearest hospital was the most important supply factor (14.1 %), followed by lack of transportation between home and the health facility (6.0 %) and lack of surgical staff (6.0 %). In rural areas, all health service supply factors contributed significantly more than those in urban areas.

8.6.2.4 Other Avoidable Factors

Other factors that contributed to maternal deaths are births at home with the help of a traditional birth attendant, economic problems of the family affecting their ability to reach a health facility and also lack of social security, the latter of which is a major obstacle in seeking medical care. In 15.1 % of cases, some of these factors were responsible for maternal deaths. These factors were found to be higher than the health supply provider factors, especially in rural areas. The percentage where '*other factors*' were most significant in causing maternal mortality was highest in the Northeast Anatolia region that is one of the lesser developed regions of the country. The results also confirm that the differences among the regions are parallel to their development level.

8.7 Discussion and Conclusion

Our main goal in this article has been to provide information to policy makers about which avoidable factors are most important for the elimination of the maternal deaths in Turkey. Using the results of National Maternal Mortality Study carried out to estimate the level of maternal deaths in the country we categorized the avoidable factors into four groups. The result of this study indicates two striking findings: Firstly, the significant roles of household and community level factors are observed clearly among the avoidable factors when compared to the influence of *health service providers* and *health supply factors*. This finding indicates that the status of women in their community and in their household is the most problematic issue when it comes to preventing maternal deaths. Delays in recognizing medical problems and delays in seeking medical care constituted the main reasons behind maternal mortality, which in turn gives an indication of the importance of society's approach to diseases and overall health care systems, as well as women's position in the household and in the greater community.

Of course, our point is not to blame the individuals and community, but rather to highlight the importance of women's status and of community dynamics as important tools in the battle to eliminate maternal mortality. Even though there are no legal barriers to women's participation in education, labour force and political life, there are many problems in practice because of cultural values and patriarchal social structures. The educational level of women and their participation in the labour force lag behind men. At the household level, for example, there is gap between spouses in terms of age and educational level, particularly for women who are living in rural areas and less developed regions, and for less educated women. Sixty-two percent of women who have 5 or more children are less educated than their husbands. Similarly, the education gap increases in rural areas and less developed regions of the country (HUIPS 2009).

Some studies in Turkey also point to the importance of power relations within the family, beliefs that diseases come from God, and a lack of women's autonomy when it comes to seeking health care (Akşit 1993). According to a qualitative study, the decisions for seeking medical care and antenatal care were made by the mother-in-law, and these interventions influenced women's behaviour when seeking help (Conseil Sante et al. 2007). Although levels of coverage of antenatal care have been increasing and according to the last two demographic and health surveys, attendance was found as 81 % in 2003 and 92 % in 2008, there is still variation by women's education level and household wealth status.

In a similar vein, the number of visits and timing of antenatal care has been increasing nationally. Three quarters of women had attended antenatal care sessions four times or more, there are still regional and urban/rural variations. Women's empowerment and participation in the decision making processes at the household level were influenced by their autonomy within the family. However at the country level, the decisions for marriage, timing and number of children were mainly taken by the community instead of being individual decisions. For example, only 42 % of women choose their husband by themselves.

Additionally, one in four women had faced at least one controlling behaviour by their husbands, and 37 % of women's husbands insisted upon knowing where she was all the time (HUIPS 2009). These controlling behaviours and women's traditional gender roles may result in their neglecting to seek health care for themselves in some cases. The perceptions of home deliveries as "natural" also affected women's and community tendencies not to seek out a health facility until an emergency situation occurred. The results of the study indicate the importance of women's empowerment through increasing their education and awareness not only in health related matters, but also in other social areas.

The second striking result of this study is that there is a need to provide different strategies in the elimination of maternal deaths according to urban/rural residence and regions. Although the *health supply provider factors* were limited among the avoidable factors, the problems of reaching health facilities due to a lack of transportation and long distance between the home and the health facility were frequent obstacles in rural areas. Moreover, women in rural areas were more likely to give birth at home. Therefore, increasing the number of health facilities in rural areas and improving the ways to seek medical care should be taken into consideration by policy makers. These issues appear to be common across all regions, but particularly in less developed ones where maternal deaths and total fertility rates were higher than in the western parts of the country.

In conclusion, to eliminate maternal deaths, special efforts should be made to provide safe motherhood programmes, and in these programmes gender equality issues as well as the many cultural factors that prevent a woman from seeking medical care should be considered.

Acknowledgement The author(s) disclosed receipt of the following financial support for the research, authorship, and/or publication of this article: This study was conducted by the consortium of ICON-Institute Public Sector GmbH, Hacettepe University Institute of Population Studies (HUIPS), and BNB Consulting Ltd. Co., with the financial support of the European Commission. The research team consisted of the key experts Rudolf Schumacher, İsmet Koç, Oona Campbell and A.Sinan Türkyılmaz.

References

Adamu, Y. M., Salihu, H. M., Sathiakumar, N., & Alexander, G. R. (2003). Maternal mortality in Northern Nigeria: A population-based survey. *European Journal of Obstetrics and Gynecology and Reproductive Biology, 109,* 153–159.

Akin, A., Dogan, B., & Mıhcıokur, S. (2000). *Survey on causes of maternal mortalities from the hospital records in Turkey*, report submitted to the Ministry of Health General Directorate of mother and Child Health and Family Planning.

Aksit, B. (1993). Rural health seeking: Under fives in Sivas, Van and Ankara. In P. Stirling (Ed.), *Culture and economy: Changes in Turkish villages* (pp. 156–171). England: The Eothen Press.

Alves, S. V. (2007). Maternal mortality in Pernambuco, Brazil: What has changed in ten years? *Reproductive Health Matters, 15*(30), 134–144.

Amarin, Z., Khader, Y., Okour, A., Jaddou, H., & Al-Qutob, H. (2010). National maternal mortality ratio for Jordan, 2007–2008. *International Journal of Gynecology and Obstetrics, 111,* 152–156.

Arriaga, E. E. (1994). *Population analysis with microcomputers* (Vol. 1, p. 153). New York: Bureau of Census, USAID and UNFPA.

Bano, N., Chaudhri, R., Yasmeen, L., Shafi, F., & Ejaz, L. (2011). A study of maternal mortality in 8 principal hospitals in Pakistan in 2009. *International Journal of Gynecology and Obstetrics, 114*(2011), 255–259.

Barnes-Josiah, D., Myntti, C., & Augustin, A. (1998). The 'three delays' as a framework for examining maternal mortality in Haiti. *Social Science and Medicine, 46*(8), 981–993.

Berer, M. (2007). Maternal mortality and morbidity: Is pregnancy getting safer for women? *Reproductive Health Matter, 15*(309), 6–16.

Biliker, M. A. (2005). Maternal mortality in Turkey. *Journal of Perinatal Medicine, 31*(5), 380–385.

Bloom, S. S., Wypij, D., & Das Gupta, M. (2001). Dimensions of women's autonomy and the influence on maternal health care utilization in a North Indian city. *Demography, 38*(1), 67–78.

Caldwell, J. C. (1986). Routes to Low mortality in poor countries. *Population and Development Review, 3,* 137–157.

Campbell, O., & Ronsman, C. (1995). Report of a WHO workshop on verbal autopsy. WHO Document. World Health Organization Geneva.

Cham, M., Sundby, J., & Vangen, S. (2005). Maternal mortality in the rural Gambia, a qualitative study on access to emergency obstetric care. *Reproductive Health, 2*(3), 1–8.

Chandramohan, D., Maude, G. H., Rodriguez, L. C., & Hayes, R. J. (1998). Verbal autopsies for adult deaths: Their development and validatıın in a multicentre stduy. *Tropical Medicine and International Health, 3*(6), 436–446.

Conseil Sante, Sofreco, & Eduser. (2007). *Sağlık Araştırma Davranışı Araştırması (Health Seeking Behaviour Research).* Sağlık Bakanlığı Ana Çocuk Sağlığı ve Aile Planlaması Genel Müdürlüğü ve Avrupa Komisyonu Türkiye Delegasyonu, Ankara.

Farhat, E. B., Chaouch, M., Chelli, H. F., Gara, M., Boukraa, N., Garbouj, M., Hamrouni, M., Fourati, A., Calvez, T., & Thonneau, P. (2011). Reduced maternal mortality in Tunisia and voluntary commitment to gender-related concerns. *International Journal of Gynecology & Obstetrics*, doi:10.1016/j.ijgo.2011.10.010.

Fortney, J. A., Sussanti, I., Gadalla, S., Saleh, S., Rogers, S. M., & Potts, M. (1986). Reproductive mortality in two developing countries. *American Journal of Public Health, 76*(134), 38.

Geynisman, J., Latimer, A., Ofosu, A., & Anderson, F. W. J. (2011). Improving maternal mortality reporting at the community level with a 4-question modified reproductive age mortality survey (RAMOS). *International Journal of Gynecology and Obstetrics, 114*(2011), 29–32.

Hogan, M. C., Foreman, K. J., Naghavi, M., Ahn, S. Y., Wang, M., Makela, S. M., Lopez, A. D., Lozano, R., & Murrap, C. J. L. (2010). Maternal mortality for 181 countries, 1980–2008: A systematic analysis of progress toward Millennium Development Goal 5. *Lancet, 375*(9726), 1609–1623.

Kao, S., Chen, L. M., Shi, L., & Weinrich, M. C. (1997). Under-reporting and misclassification of maternal mortality in Taiwan. *Acta Obstetricia et Gynecologica Scandinavica, 76*(7), 629–636.

Khan, S. K., Wodlyla, D., Say, L., Gulmezoglu, A. M., & Van Look, P. F. (2006). WHO analysis of causes of maternal deaths: A systematic review. *Lancet, 367,* 1066–1074.

Hacettepe University Institute of Population Studies (HUIPS). (2004). *2003 Turkey demographic and health survey*. Ankara: Hacettepe University Institute of Population Studies, Ministry of Health, General Directorate of Mother and Child Health and Family Planning, State Planning Organization and European Union.

Hacettepe University Institute of Population Studies (HUIPS). (2009). *2008 Turkey demographic and health survey*. Ankara: Hacettepe University Institute of Population Studies, Ministry of Health, General Directorate of Mother and Child Health and Family Planning, State Planning Organization and TUBITAK.

Hacettepe University Institute of Population Studies (HUIPS), & ICON-INSTITUT Public Sector GmbH and BNB Consulting. (2006). *National maternal mortality study 2005*. Ministry of Health, General Directorate of Mother and Child Health and Family Planning and Delegation of European Commission to Turkey.

McCarthy, M., & Maine, D. (1992). A framework for maternal mortality. *Studies in Family Planning, 23,* 23–33.

Mungra, A., van Bokhoven, S. C., Florie, J., Van Kanten, R. W., van Roosmalen, J., & Kanhai, H. H. H. (1998). Reproductive age mortality survey to study under-reporting of maternal mortality in Surinam. *European Journal of Obstetrics & Reproductive Biology, 77,* 37–39.

Mbonye, A. K. (2001). Risk factors associated with maternal deaths in health units in Uganda. *African Journal of Reproductive Health/La Revue Africaine de la SantéReproductive, 5*(3), 47–53 (Published by: Women's Health and Action Research Centre).

Olsen, B. E., Hinderaker, S. G., Lie, R. T., Bergsjø, P., Gasheka, P., & Kvåle, G. (2002). Maternal mortality in northern rural Tanzania: Assessing the completeness of various information sources. *Acta Obstetricia et Gynecologica Scandinavica, 81*(4), 301–307.

Santow, G. (1995). Social roles and physical health: The case of female disadvantage in poor countries. *Social Science and Medicine, 40,* 147–161.

Songane, F. F., & Bergstrom, S. (2002). Quality of registration of maternal deaths in Mozambique: A community-based study in rural and urban areas. *Social Science and Medicine, 54*(1), 23–31.

Stanton, C., Hobcraft, J., & Hill, K., et al (2001). Every death counts: Measurement of maternal mortality via a census. *Bulletin of the World Health Organization, 79*(7), 657–664.

State Institute of Statistics (SIS). (1978). Turkish demographic survey 1974–1975, State Institute of Statistics, Prime Ministry of Republic of Turkey, SIS Publication No. 841, Ankara.

State Institute of Statistics (SIS). (1993). *1989 Turkish demographic survey*. State Institute of Statistics, Prime Ministry of Republic of Turkey, Ankara.

Thaddeus, S., & Maine, D. (1994). Too far to walk: Maternal mortality in context. *Social Science and Medicine, 38*(8), 1091–1110.

Turkyılmaz, A. S., Koç, I., Schumacher, R., & Campbell, O. M. R. (2009). The Turkey national maternal mortality study. *The European Journal of Contraception and Reproductive Health Care, 14*(1), 75–82.

Walraven, G., Telfer, M., Rowley, J., & Ronsmans, C. (2000). Maternal mortality in rural gambia and contributing factors. *Bulletin of the World Health Organization, 78*(5), 603–613.

World Health Organization (WHO). (1992). *International Statistical Classification of Diseases and Related Health Problems. Tenth Revision*. Vol (1): Tabular list. Vol (2): Instruction manual. Geneva.

World Health Organization (WHO). (1996). *Revised 1990 estimates of maternal mortality: A new approach by WHO and UNICEF*. World Health Organization and United Nations Children's Fund, Geneva.

World Health Organization (WHO). (2003). *Global burden of hypertensive disorders of pregnancy in the year 2000, prepared by Carmen Dolea and Caelo AbouZahr*. Geneva: World Health Organization.

World Health Organization (WHO). (2004). *Beyond the numbers: reviewing maternal deaths and complication to make pregnancy safer*. Geneva: World Health Organization. http://whqlibdoc.whoint/publications/2004/9241591838.pdf (Accessed 25.01.2012).

World Health Organization (WHO), UNICEF, & UNFPA. (2004). *Maternal mortality in 2000: Estimates developed by WHO, UNICEF and UNFPA*. Department of Reproductive Health and Research. Geneva: World Health Organization. http://www.who.int/reproductive-health/publications/maternal_mortality_2000/mme.pdf (Accessed 25.01.2012).

WHO, UNICEF, UNFPA, & The World Bank. (2010). *Trends in maternal mortality: 1990–2008*. Geneva: World Health Organization (Accessed 03.12.2011).

Zahr, A. C., & Royston, E. (1991). *Maternal mortality: A global factbook*. Geneva: WHO. ISBN 92-4-159001-7.

Chapter 9
Changes in Mortality at Older Ages: The Case of Spain (1975–2006)

Rosa Gómez Redondo, Juan Manuel García González and Aina Faus Bertomeu

Abstract Recent decades have witnessed the rise of a new and growing demographic group: the old people. This remarkable historical phenomenon is the direct result of an increase in survival rates, with more and more men and women celebrating their 85th birthday every year. As death rates fall and people live longer, the frequency distribution of age at death has shifted towards the more advanced groups, affecting a greater proportion of the population as a whole while the maximum lifespan has continued to rise. It should be emphasized that the number of octogenarians in wealthy countries grew over the course of the twentieth century, paralleled by a rise in the age of death among the very old. In the case of Spain, this trend did not happen until the 1970's. This paper analyses the impact of mortality and the evolution of the main causes of death among Spanish old people. Special attention is paid to variations in gender-specific trends over the last three decades, looking for the most relevant causes of death. Our work focuses on three different age groups: 65–79; 80–89 and 90 older, to distinguish the diversity of trends among older people. This research has also profited from the increase in the availability of official data on both mortality and the living population at advanced ages in recent years.

Keywords Mortality · Causes of death · Elderly and oldest-old · Differences by sex · Differences by gender · Spain

9.1 Introduction[1]

In Spain, two basic longevity indicators, the modal and the median age at death, reached a value of 80 years for men and over 85 years for women in 2004 (Gómez Redondo et al. 2007). This represents a milestone in the evolution of the Spanish population because it is an indication that Spanish men and women will both soon

[1] This work was supported by Grant CSO2010–18925 from the Spanish Ministry of Science and Innovation.

R. Gómez Redondo (✉) · J. M. García González · A. Faus Bertomeu
Universidad Nacional de Educación a Distancia—UNED, Departamento de Servicios Sociales y Fundamentos Histórico-Jurídicos. C/ Obispo Trejo, 2. 28040 Madrid, Spain
e-mail: rgomez@poli.uned.es

J. Anson, M. Luy (eds.), *Mortality in an International Perspective*,
European Studies of Population 18, DOI 10.1007/978-3-319-03029-6_9,

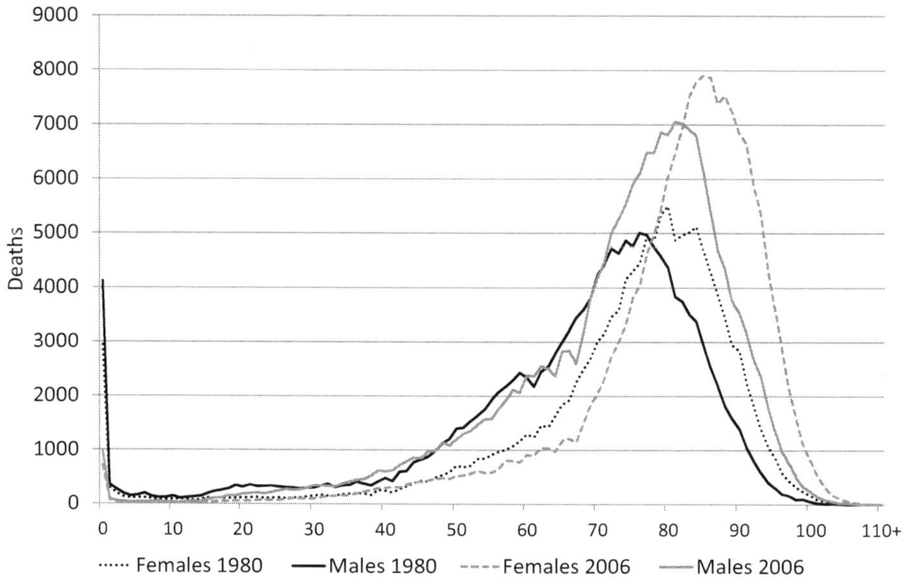

Fig. 9.1 Compression and shift of deaths. Men and women in 1980 and 2006. (Source: Own elaboration with data from the HMD and the INE)

attain a life expectancy of 85 years, a "mythical" age considered by many authors to be the maximum achievable life expectancy (Fries 1980, 1989; Olshansky et al. 1990, 2001; Coale and Guo 1991; Hayflick 2000). Another interesting aspect of recent Spanish longevity is that there is a quarter of a century gap between women's and men's indicators: women's modal and median ages at death in 1980 were only reached by men 25 years later, around 2006 (Figs. 9.1 and 9.2).

The structure of Spanish mortality has profoundly changed over the twentieth century: the mortality rate has fallen sharply, and during the second half of the twentieth century Spain joined the select group of countries with the highest level of human survival ever attained (Fig. 9.2). The whole Spanish population has undergone significant improvements throughout this period: life expectancy at birth exceeded 80 years for the first time in 2004, when it reached a value of 80.28 years for the general population (76.84 for men and 83.51 for women; Human Mortality Database). Since then, Spanish life expectancy has continued to rise steadily, reaching 80.94 years in 2006. Women, in particular, have experienced a rapid gain, with a life expectancy of 84.07 years in 2006, compared to 77.58 years among men, a difference of nearly 7.5 years.

A key moment in this process of change and advancement in Spanish mortality took place in the early 1970s. At that time, the increase in life expectancy was given a significant boost by the adult and elderly age groups, whose mortality continued to decline, especially among the female population, and has done so until today (Gómez Redondo 1995; Gómez Redondo and Boe 2005; Canudas et al. 2008). The resultant dynamics brought about a growing compression and a shift in mortality (Wilmoth 1997; Wilmoth and Horiuchi 1999; Robine 2001; Meslé and Vallin 2003), which in the last instance may be said to have led to an "aging" of the age of death, raising every longevity indicator, and bringing about a rectangularization of the survival curve.

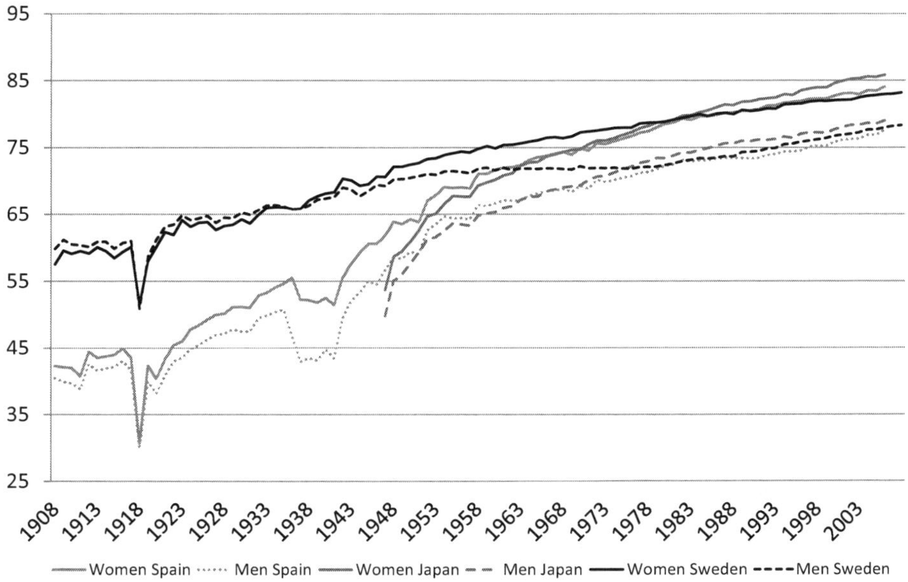

Fig. 9.2 Life expectancy at birth, 1908 to 2008, Men and women, Spain, Japan and Sweden. (Source: Own elaboration with data from the HMD)

The overall aim of this article is to analyze the evolution of mortality by cause of death between 1975 and 2006 among Spaniards over the age of 65. We distinguish three large age groups: those aged 65–79, to whom we will refer as the "young old"; those aged 80–89, referred as "old people"; and those aged 90 and older, referred as the "elderly". The analysis is carried out by gender.

First, we will focus on those sets of causes that weigh more heavily on the mortality of Spanish old people. Second, we will analyze those causes of death that show some signs and/or evidence of changing trends which might be relevant for the future convergence of men's and women's mortality (López 1983; Vallin 2006). Nevertheless, this division is difficult to maintain in practice, as the chapter also has a transverse axis, that is, a comparative analysis of the evolution of mortality by cause between men and women during the last three decades.

We have to take into account that at the end of the twentieth century the gender difference in life expectancy for children and young people began to change, but this change cannot be extrapolated to the older old population during the period under study. The difference between the life expectancy at birth for men and women has decreased during the last few years, as well as for young adults, but in the population older than 65 years we only see a small slowing down of the divergent trend, something which was already happening during the past century. During the first decade of the twenty first century, and always within the framework of the attained stabilization, it is possible to detect small decrements in the gender difference in younger old people. Nevertheless, it is not possible at the moment to claim that it a convergent trend is emerging. This is the reason why we pay special attention to the differences between men and women for certain causes of death which, in our study, show signs of change.

Since this general process cannot be understood outside the framework of the health transition and epidemiological theory (Vallin and Meslé 2004), our goal here is to continue our analysis of the changes in the Spanish epidemiological pattern over a period of only thirty years (Omran 1971), keeping close track of society's response to these important transformations (Frenk et al. 1991).

Old age has clearly come to be the indisputable locus of mortality in recent decades. This is true to such an extent that mortality trends among the elderly determine thc mortality trends of the Spanish population as a whole. Since the older population suffers increasingly from chronic and degenerative diseases, these are, at present, the most prevalent causes of death among the elderly (Meslé 2006a) and, consequently, among the Spanish population at large.

9.2 Sources and Methodology

The data on deaths by cause that were used in this analysis refer to the *de facto* population and derive from the micro data published by the *Instituto Nacional de Estadística* (INE, Spanish Statistics Institute) for the period 1975–2001, while the data for the period 2002–2006 were extracted from the INE website via INEBase (http://www.ine.es). Population data for the whole period 1975–2006 were taken from the Human Mortality Database (HMD). To define the denominator, we have used the population's exposure to risk of death, which is more appropriate than the population size since the former includes a correction that reflects the timing of deaths during the interval.

Given that this study covers a broad time period (longer than 30 years) and that the age structure of the population changed over this time, it was deemed appropriate to calculate age-standardized death rates by cause of death. The advantage of this approach is that these rates eliminate the effect of the age structure on mortality among the elderly—who have experienced an "aging of the aged" process since 1975– and thus allows us to discern the evolution of mortality trends in this specific population. The standard population we have used is the total (men plus women) Spanish population exposed to risk of death in 1991 as taken from the HMD, since that year falls in the middle of the period under study and also coincides with a census year. The age-standardized death rate by cause (TE_c) is obtained by adding up the product of the specific death rate for each age x and cause c and the standard population at each age x, and dividing this sum by the total standard population (men plus women):

$$\mathrm{TE}_c = \sum m_{x,c} P_x^{st} / P^{st}$$

where m corresponds to the age-specific death rates by cause c in age group x, p_x^{st} corresponds to the standard population in age group x, and P^{st} to the total standard population. These age-standardized rates by cause of death have been calculated for each sex and for three age groups: 65–79, 80–89, and 90+. They are expressed per 100,000 inhabitants.

Population and number of deaths by single age have been used. We have data from 65 until 100+ years old, but we suspect that population and deaths belonging to the group 90 + years may be exaggerated. This last open age group includes all people over 90 years old for both the standard population and deaths by cause, neither of which have an open-ended age group. Thus, the potential effect of changing age population structure during the analyzed period is somehow reduced.

The analysis is carried out by using cross-sectional data. It should be noted that the division of the 65 + population into three large age groups provides an analytical advantage, since it allows us to observe significant differences between the mortality trends and their strength in these three groups, given each one's distinctive health pattern. In addition, we are able to see a cohort effect on the impact of mortality. Generations born in 1910 (that reached the age of 65 in 1975) share the scene with those generations born at the end of the nineteenth century, who have emerged as today's supercentenarians. It is possible to standardize the population, but not the life stories, life conditions and health experienced by the members of these generations before they reached old age. Both the stories and the conditions will be reflected in the intensity of mortality, and this intensity will always be related to the social and technological context in which people lived. Furthermore, as is well known, there has been a substantial change in the mortality structure of Spanish women during this period. This transformation may have a certain impact on the evolution of differential mortality trends by sex.

In Spain, the information about causes of death is taken from the *Estadística de Defunciones según la Causa de Muerte*[2] (Statistics of Deaths by Cause). This database used to be part of the *Estadísticas del Movimiento Natural de la Población* (Vital Statistics), but in 1987 the INE decided to make the former a separate entity owing to the health nature of the information compiled in it.

The International Classification of Diseases and Causes of Death (ICD) has undergone three revisions during the period 1975–2006: the 8th Revision (1975–1979), the 9th Revision (1980–1998), and the 10th Revision (1999–2006). While the 8th and 9th Revisions presented only minor changes, the 10th Revision introduced substantial modifications. It allowed greater specificity, since it incorporated an alphanumerical system that doubled the number of existing codes. ICD10 also introduced several modifications in one of the coding rules for determining the basic cause of death, and provided more information for the codification of neoplasms (Audicana et al. 1998; Segura and Martínez 1998; Cirera 2006).

Research on death by cause involves several methodological difficulties that can be summarized into two essential problems:

1. the complexity of managing and standardizing the successive revisions of the ICD (Segura and Martínez 1998), while the required reconstruction of long time series of deaths by causes[3] (Vallin and Meslé 1988) is still in progress; and

[2] The available data on causes of death only refer to the basic cause of death, which is the one reported by the corresponding INE statistics. According to the World Health Organization (WHO), the basic or fundamental cause of death is "(a) the disease or lesion that initiated the change of pathological events leading directly to death, or (b) the circumstances surrounding the accident or violence produced by the fatal lesion" (WHO 1997).

[3] An ongoing project using methodology by Vallin and Meslé (1988).

2. errors on certification of cause of death may seriously compromise the quality of the analysis, although the quality of the data has notably improved over the course of the period under study.

The European Shortlist for Causes of Death (Eurostat 1998; Eurostat 2004) is the standard list used in this work, since it establishes a correspondence between the three ICD revisions made in the period 1975–2006 for 65 causes of death[4] (see Annex). These 65 causes of death include the most relevant causes within the current patterns of mortality and the mortality trends and projections of the European Union. In the absence of a reconstruction of time series of mortality by cause, this common list eliminates the discrepancies between the different ICD revisions. In this study, six large sets of causes are considered: diseases of the circulatory system, diseases of the respiratory system, malignant neoplasms, diseases of the nervous system and the sense organs, mental and behavioral disorders, and external causes of injury and poisoning. However, we will focus more specifically on those causes within these six large sets that have the greatest impact on mortality among the elderly: cerebrovascular diseases; ischemic heart diseases; malignant stomach, colon, larynx and trachea/bronchus/lung, breast, prostate and bladder neoplasms; diabetes mellitus; influenza; pneumonia; chronic lower respiratory diseases; suicide and intentional self-harm.

9.3 The Five Pillars of The Evolution of Mortality in Old Age

This analysis will consider the impact of the most important causes of death on the older population, depending on whether the men and women who make up the population are at the beginning or the end of this phase of their life cycle. Our comments are based on the figures representing annual series for each age group by causes of death.

The results obtained are basically related to five groups of causes that in our opinion are the pillars of the recent evolution of mortality. The importance of the decline in mortality from circulatory and respiratory diseases, which we will study closely later on, is matched by only one other set of causes in this period: that of the ill-defined diseases (see methodology). Nevertheless, and contrary to common understanding, the most important causes of death in Spain, and those whose decline has contributed most to the increase in life expectancy, are well defined. Death from diseases of the circulatory system accounted in 1975–79 for 58.6 % of the total deaths among women aged 90 + (53.0 for men aged 90 +), while the proportion was 44.6 % (36.9 for men) in 2005–2006. If we now add deaths from malignant tumors, we find that these two causes of death represented more than two-thirds of all deaths (71.6 % for women aged 90 + and 68.2 for men the same age) in 1975–79, while their weight lessened by the end of the period (58.1 % for women aged 90 + and 57.3 for men in the same age group). Finally, if we include deaths caused by diseases of the respiratory system we obtain 78.9 % for women aged 90 + (75.0 for men aged also 90 +) in 1975–79 and 64.9 % for women the same age (70.1 for men) in 2005–06.

[4] This shortlist was conceived as a useful and necessary tool for the carrying out of international comparisons of mortality data, both on a regional scale and in retrospective studies and projections.

Therefore, these three large sets of causes alone largely explain the epidemiological profile of the elderly population in Spain, and the changes it has undergone. On the other hand, we have also considered two additional causes because of their rapid increase over the course of recent years, especially taking into account their potential and important health, economic and social consequences in aged societies. We refer to mental illnesses and pathologies of the nervous system.

9.3.1 The Role of Diseases of the Circulatory System in the Decline of Mortality in the Population Over the Age of 65

Overall mortality at age 90 + shifted from 26,221 deaths per 100,000 inhabitants in 1975–79 to 20,904 in 2005–06 for women aged 90 + (29,744 and 24,418, respectively, for men aged 90 +). For women aged 80–89, it decreased from 11,677 to 6,964 (15,034 to 10,058 for men aged 80–89). And for the 65–79 age group, women's rates fell from 2,927 to 1,353 (4,870 to 2,893 for men aged 65–79). During this period we see an improvement in the trends of only two sets of causes: diseases of the circulatory system and diseases of the respiratory system. Tumors, mental disorders and diseases of the nervous system moved in the opposite direction. At much lower levels, we also find endocrine and digestive diseases, to mention just the main ones.

Cardiovascular diseases are certainly the true motor and main component of the decrease in mortality during the last quarter of the century. By contrast, the main brake to the continuous decrease is the tumor group. Figure 9.3 shows mortality from diseases of the circulatory system. We can observe a significant fall in overall mortality from this set of causes, with a clear declining trend for both sexes. The reduction in the number of deaths due to this type of disease is in line with what we know about the cardiovascular revolution in Western societies, although it is taking place with a certain delay (Caselli et al. 1995; Meslé and Vallin 2002). The greatest differences between men and women are found in the 65–79 age group. The trends by sex are closer in the 90 + age group, where women show higher mortality.

Among the population aged 65–79, female mortality shows a higher percentage decrease than male mortality, although the decrease of the standardized death rate (SDR) is smaller, since it dropped from 1,555 deaths per 100,000 inhabitants in 1975–79 to 425 in 2005–2006 for women aged 65–79, and from 2,276 to 810 deaths for men aged 65–79. The decrease is also clear for the 80–89 age group (from 7,166 to 2,869 deaths among women and from 8,163 to 3,352 among men) and the 90 + age group (from 15,351 to 9,313 deaths in the case of women and from 15,765 to 9,000 in that of men). Nevertheless, the weight of this cause of death on the overall male mortality is less than on the overall female mortality at the end of this period (Meslé 2006b).

It is worth noting that, for this set of causes, both the trends and the levels are very similar for both sexes, which means that the observable differences in overall mortality by sex are due to causes other than those associated with circulatory diseases. Mortality from this group of diseases has experienced a huge decline, having been reduced by over half its value in the course of these three decades. Nonetheless, and in line with what we know from previous studies (Gómez Redondo 1995; Blanes 2007;

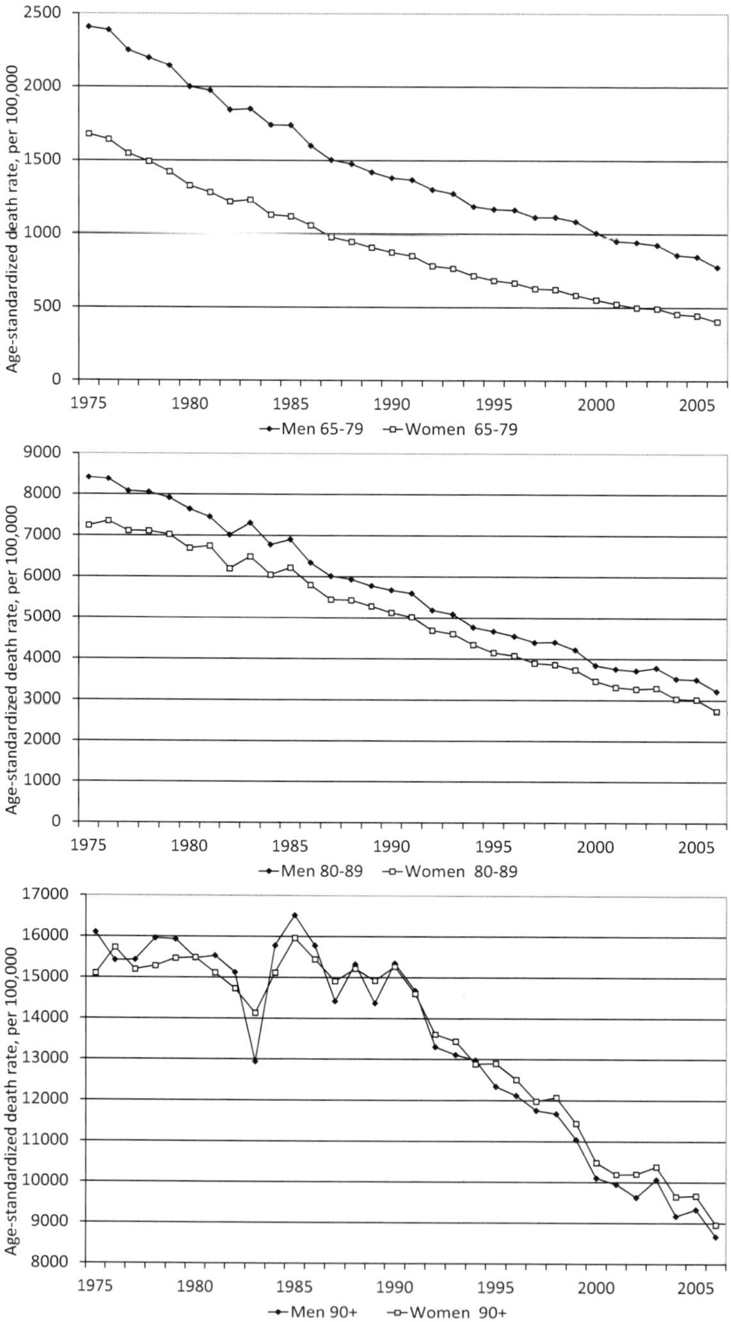

Fig. 9.3 Mortality from diseases of the circulatory system. Men and women. 65–79, 80–89, and 90+ years. 1975–2006. (Source: Own elaboration with data from the HMD and the INE)

Robles 2009; Gómez Redondo et al. 2010), diseases of the circulatory system still represent the main cause of death among the Spanish elderly population, because of the late arrival of the cardiovascular revolution in Spain (during the 1970s and 1980s). Indeed, mortality from this type of disease among the older population is more than double that caused by tumors, the next most important group. Mortality caused by the whole group of tumors was stable for most of this period, especially among men under 80, and it even experienced a slight decrease in the last few years. For those aged 65–79 mortality caused by the tumor group is comparable to that due to circulatory system diseases. This is the reason we discuss tumor-related mortality later on. Tumors are very heterogeneous, and each specific cause follows a particular trend affecting men and women differently. Let us only mention here that some are declining causes of death (prostate and stomach tumors) while some are increasing (bladder, colon and breast tumors). Within the 65–79 age group, the drop is from 530 deaths per 100,000 inhabitants in 1975–79 to 479 deaths in 2005–2006 for women aged 65–79, while there is a slight increase (from 1,096 to 1,115 deaths) among men aged 65–79. Therefore, diseases of the circulatory system have a greater impact on women than on men—and greater as well on the 90 + age group than on the 65–79 one.

Within this large set of causes, we can disaggregate two main causes of death, namely ischemic and cerebrovascular diseases (Figs. 9.4 and 9.5), both of them enormously important. Clearly the most salient result of this analysis is the great fall in mortality from cerebrovascular diseases throughout the period in question, regardless of the age group considered. A clearly declining linear trend can be observed for both sexes, to a point where mortality from ischemic diseases, which had distinctly lower levels in earlier years, now exceeds mortality associated with cerebrovascular diseases, at least among octogenarian men and women and among men aged 65–79. On the other hand, the reduction of mortality caused by ischemic diseases is not so marked among those older than 80 years, but is clearly observable among the younger-old since the early 1990s (Fig. 9.5). With regard to differences by sex, the incidence of death from cerebrovascular diseases is almost identical in men and women belonging to the 80–89 and 90 + age groups throughout this period, but higher among men than among women in the 65–79 age group. At the same time, in the case of ischemic diseases, a marked male over-mortality can be observed among this younger-old population, but showing a slow tendency to decline both in men and in women, a fact that might indicate an incipient tendency towards convergence.

Considering the magnitude of the decline in mortality from circulatory diseases, it makes sense to ask what factors are responsible for this trend. From a medical point of view, the answer is complex and would have to take into account at least three factors (Vallin and Meslé 2006). In the first place, we should mention the improvements in medical technology that have opened the door to a number of different therapeutic and surgical treatment strategies, such as the use of anti-coagulants, beta-blockers, pacemakers and bypass coronary surgery. In the second place, we should refer to the organization of emergency medical services, which play a key role in preventing many deaths by providing immediate attention. Finally, we should call attention to prevention. Since the aim of prevention is to monitor certain risk factors that can only be modified through the interaction between health policies and individual behavioral changes—the latter being very difficult to gauge—it is not easy to achieve. In this

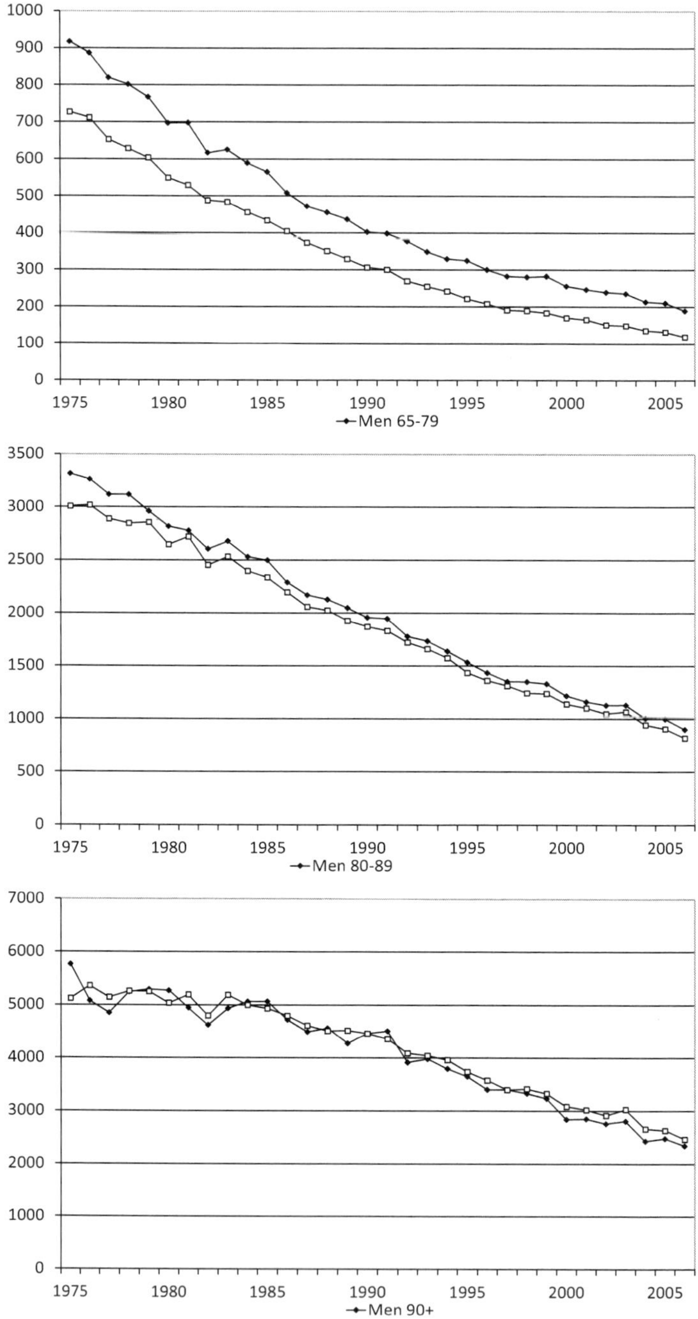

Fig. 9.4 Mortality from cerebrovascular diseases. Men and women. 60–79, 80–89 and 90 + years. 1975–2006. (Source: Own elaboration with data from the HMD and the INE)

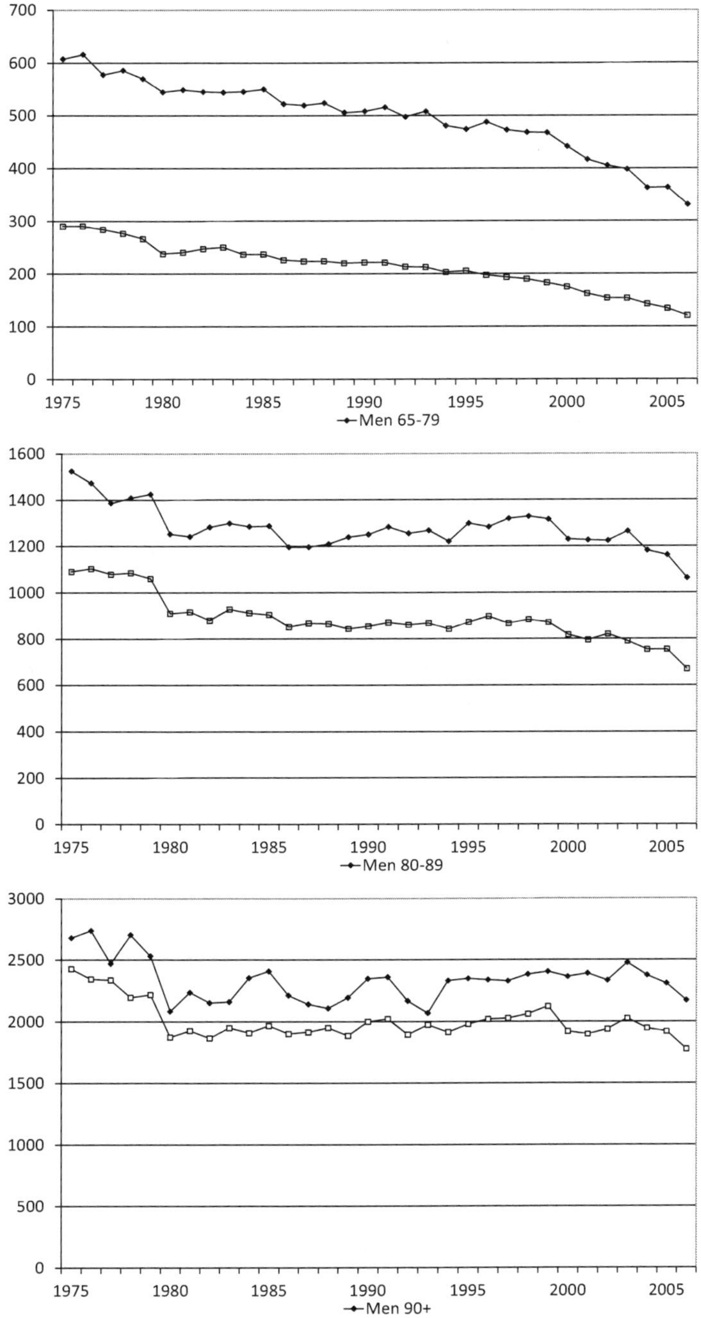

Fig. 9.5 Mortality from ischemic heart diseases. Men and women. 60–79, 80–89 and 90 + years. 1975–2006. (Source: Own elaboration with data from the HMD and the INE)

sense, awareness of the importance of the risk factors linked to different patterns of behavior is probably the crucial element in Spain's current healthcare transition stage.

An interesting result of this analysis is the similarity between the Spanish pattern of mortality from cerebrovascular and ischemic diseases among the elderly and that of Japan. In both cases, mortality from cerebrovascular diseases was higher during the period under study than in other Western countries, where the opposite situation was common and where cerebrovascular diseases represented the driving force behind the cardiovascular revolution. In the case of Japan and Spain, the new tendencies point to the pharmacological control of hypertension and to changes in eating habits as the main factors behind the reductions among older adults and the elderly in recent years. With regard to the reduction of mortality discussed above, it is important, on the one hand, to underline the role played by the health centers, which have proactively worked to prevent hypertension and diabetes. On the other hand, the strong political drive to reduce hypertension through information and prevention in the community sphere should also be acknowledged (Yoshinaga and Une 2005).

9.3.2 A Basic Factor in the Increment of Mortality in Old Age: Tumors

Tumors and diseases of the respiratory system represent the two other main sets of mortality causes among the elderly in Spain and in other countries in Spain's immediate vicinity. Figure 9.6 shows the progressive increment in mortality associated with the whole group of tumors—for women aged 90+, the rate rose from 1,128 deaths per 100,000 inhabitants in 1975–79 to 1,419 in 2005–06 (2,022 to 3,116 for men aged 90+). Differences by sex are very interesting within this set of causes, with male mortality being much higher than female mortality, indicating that the overall higher male mortality shown in Fig. 9.6 is related to the higher values of male mortality caused by these illnesses. In women, we can observe stabilization in mortality from tumors with a slight tendency towards decline within the 65–79 age group, something that is also evident in the case of men of the same age in the final years of this period. The percentages of malignant neoplasms in relation to the total number of deaths increased remarkably in these 30 years, among both women and men. The prevalence is much higher in the 65–79 age group—where malignant neoplasms represent more than one third of the total number of deaths—than in the 80–89 age group, where they only account for 20 % of deaths, or the 90+ age group, where cancer is responsible for less than 10 % of deaths. Furthermore, the prevalence of cancer is much higher in men than in women, especially within the 65–79 age group.

The rise of mortality by cancer is in line with the current epidemiological transition in which we currently find ourselves. Its incidence can be seen to rise as aging progresses. Aging raises the probability of death, since cells display greater somatic mutations and chromosomal abnormalities—many of which may cause cancer—leading to the increase of tumors among the longer-lived populations of today. In addition to these biological factors which are linked to the greater longevity of the

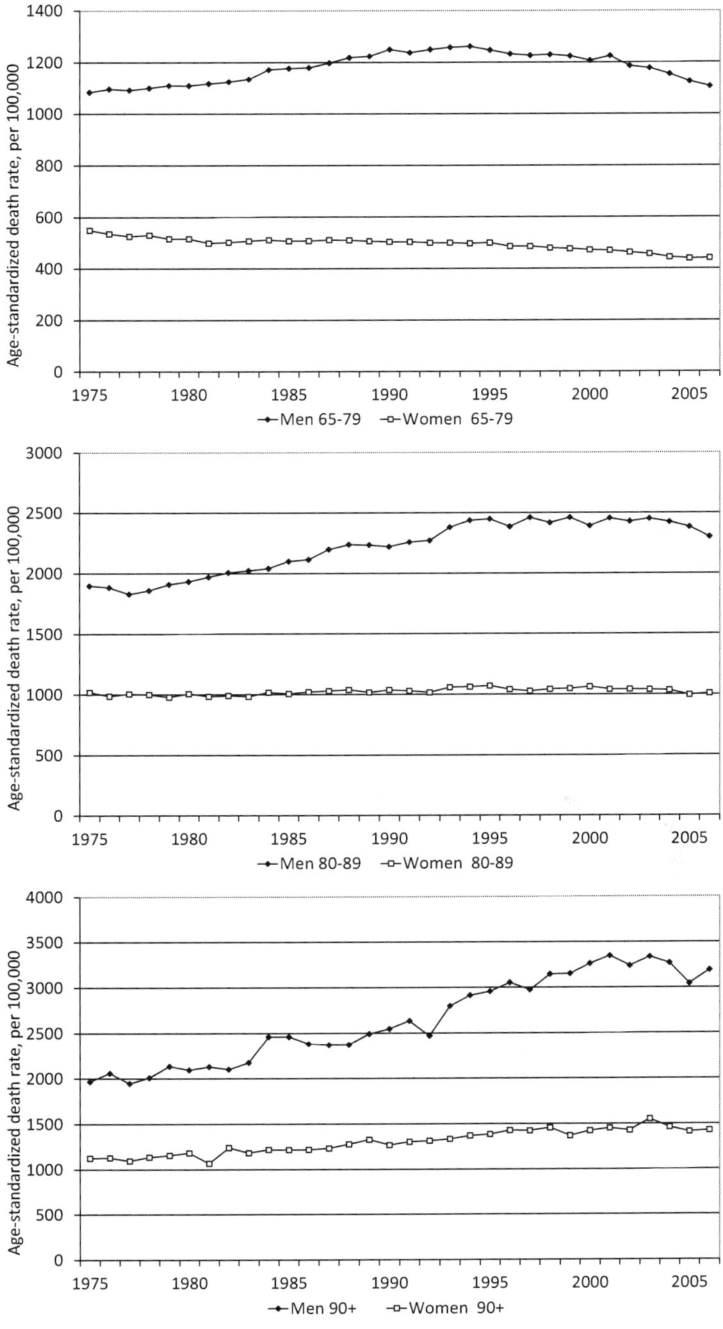

Fig. 9.6 Mortality from malignant neoplasms. Men and women. 65–79, 80–89, and 90 + years. 1975–2006. (Source: Own elaboration with data from the HMD and the INE)

human species, the rising incidence of cancer is also due to the growing prevalence of certain habits that interfere with health—such as smoking and alcohol consumption—and are associated with changes in diet and lifestyle, and to the exposure to carcinogenic agents (Waldron 1983). In this sense, one goal of the growing research in this field should be to differentiate—depending on the type of cancer to which we are referring—between, on the one hand, behavioral and societal factors and, on the other, the advent of genomic and proteomic technology (at a cellular and molecular level). These types of factors will both shape the future panorama concerning the prevention of these diseases.

It is essential to describe the distribution by age and sex of malignant neoplasms, although the evolution of mortality from certain tumors has followed different, and even disparate, trends Although our main objective is not to analyze each one cause making up this wide group, but rather to concentrate on those exhibiting higher divergence by sex, it is necessary to highlight here some other causes which have shown a relevant development. Deaths from stomach cancer dropped over the course of this period, as happened also in other countries (Klenk et al. 2007), while malignant colon neoplasms notably increased from 1975–79 to 2006, both by sex and age. Both sexes share the same pattern, although this kind of tumor has a lower prevalence among women than among men. Studies carried out in other countries reveal a similar mortality pattern for cancer, both as concerns the decrease in mortality caused by stomach cancer and in relation to the rise in mortality associated with colon neoplasms.

This tumor is a special case, since it seems to be more prevalent in the Spanish population than in other countries. Mortality caused by colon tumors has had a very peculiar evolution, since at the beginning of the period the rates were very similar for men and for women, but male mortality attributable to this cause "took off" starting in the 1980s and rates more than tripled over the course of the three decades analyzed. Mortality from this cause also increased among women, coming to exceed breast cancer by the beginning of the 1990s[5].

9.3.3 An Element of Circumstantial Irregularity in the Decreasing Trend of Mortality: Respiratory System Diseases

Diseases of the respiratory system have been the other traditional group of diseases causing higher mortality in Spain. Figure 9.7 shows the fairly irregular decline of mortality from respiratory diseases. This irregular decline in the incidence of death from respiratory diseases leads to a net result in 2006 that reverses the 1975–79 situation, with tumors coming to represent the second leading cause of death among the elderly, displacing respiratory diseases to a third position. This erratic trend is similar in men and in women, and for all age groups.

[5] Mortality due to pancreas, rectum, anus, bladder and lymphatic cancers also increased, although their respective levels are much lower than those discussed above.

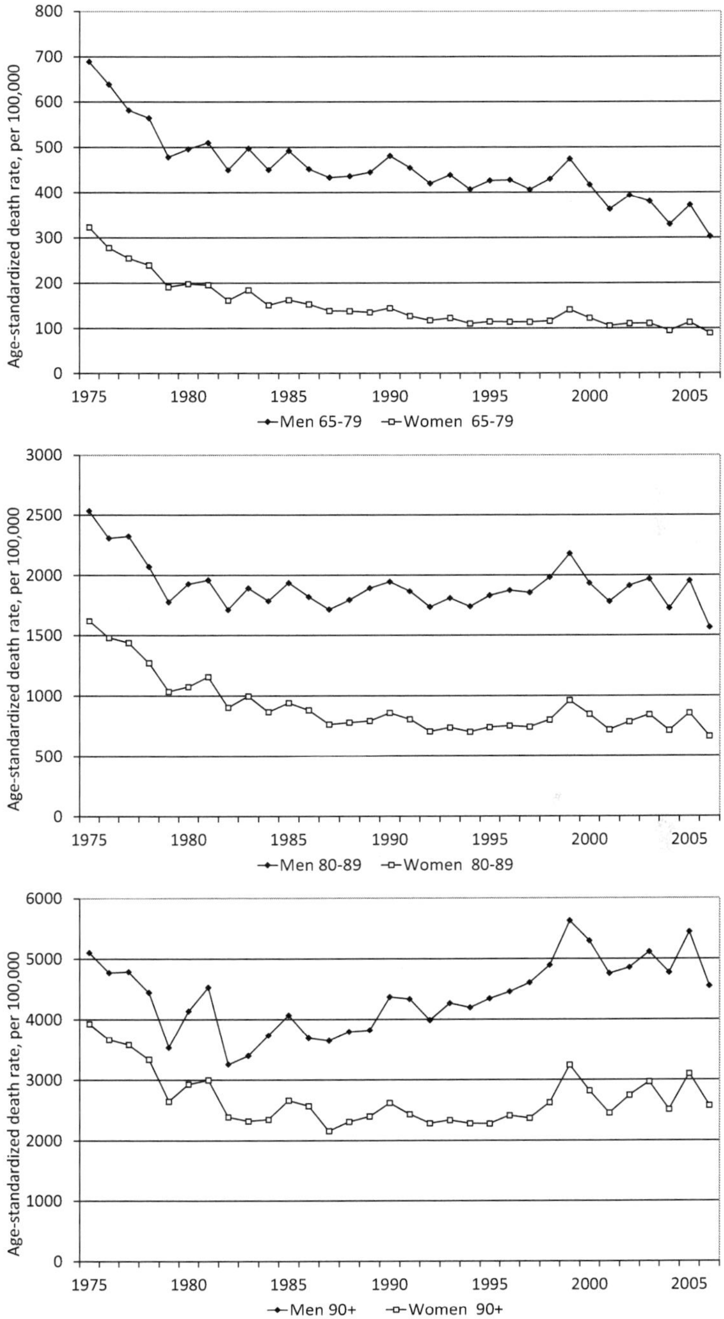

Fig. 9.7 Mortality from diseases of the respiratory system. Men and women. 65–79, 80–89, and 90 + years. 1975–2006. (Source: Own elaboration with data from the HMD and the INE)

Fluctuations, which respond to epidemic patterns associated with influenza or other related illnesses such as pneumonia or broncho-pneumonia, characterize the evolution of the prevalence of respiratory diseases. These illnesses have a high incidence among the elderly, who are very vulnerable to them (Horiuchi 2006). Focusing on this elderly group, it should be noted that a recent increase in mortality rates from respiratory diseases in both sexes has recently followed the previous decline. In addition, a certain number of causes in this set show a very marked seasonal pattern during both the winter and summer months, punctuated by episodes such as the heat wave of 2003. The evolution of two main causes of death in this set (pneumonias and chronic diseases of the lower respiratory system), evidences a very high male over-mortality. This is especially true of chronic lower respiratory diseases, which are closely associated with both prolonged tobacco consumption and with exposure to toxic substances linked to certain occupations.

9.3.4 A Brake on the Extension of Life Without Disability: Mental Disorders and Nervous System Diseases

Mortality by sex from mental disorders and diseases of the nervous system shows the greatest proportionate increase during the period under study. The great interest of these two causes stems from their impact on disability conditions among the elderly population, from the creation of dependency and also from the fact that they are the only two causes of death that present female over-mortality at older ages.

The introduction of the ICD-10 in 1999 gave rise to a diagnostic shift away from mental disorders and behaviors and towards diseases of the nervous system (Ruiz et al. 2002). In fact, dementias of the Alzheimer type, which were previously included in the group of organic senile and pre-senile psychoses, "left" the category of mental disorders and, together with Alzheimer, joined the category of nervous system diseases, causing a decline in the former and a progressive rise in the latter over the course of recent years. In this analysis, we consider both causes as a source for the potential growth of poor health and dependency at the end of the life cycle among the elderly. This is the reason why we describe these sets of causes as pillars in the recent evolution of mortality. At the same time, we believe that these causes show evidence of future changes in Spanish mortality, with a very possible convergence of mortality among older men and women. Due to their specific relevance, we postpone the analysis of these two sets of causes to the next section of this work.

9.4 Specific Signs of Changes Towards Convergence

In this section we shall analyze some causes of death that show indications of changing trends that might become important factors in the future evolution of differential mortality in Spain, something we already outlined above.

9.4.1 *The Impact of Changing Habits: Tobacco Consumption*

Malignant larynx and trachea/bronchus/lung neoplasms We find a significant increase in mortality caused by cancer of the larynx and trachea/bronchus/lung [6], the type of tumor that has contributed most heavily to the overall mortality from this type of disease (Fig. 9.8). Malignant larynx and trachea/bronchus/lung neoplasms have a much higher incidence among men (basically associated with tobacco consumption) than among women at these ages (Peto and López 1994). The prevalence of this type of cancer increased during the period studied, although this tendency shifted during the 1970s and only recently experienced a slight reduction. The magnitude of this increase is so great that the incidence of this kind of tumor has come to exceed that of prostate cancer, by far the most prevalent kind of cancer among men, as we will see later.

In the near future, we could expect a trend towards convergence of male and female mortality caused by tumors associated with tobacco consumption. Larynx and lung tumors are two significant examples. Figure 9.8 shows that there is an emerging trend among men to reduce their mortality from this cause—a trend that is well known to be linked to the prevention of unhealthy habits (tobacco). This has been especially evident within the 65–79 age group during the last years under study. We might already be experiencing a slight decrease a result of the expansion of preventive behaviors and the giving up of this habit.

On the other hand, there is not yet any convergence in the levels of male and female mortality associated with these types of cancer (Peto and Lopez 1994; Pampel 2002a, b), despite the currently high tobacco consumption habit of Spanish women, which, however, did not exist in the past among those cohorts making up the older population today. Women's adoption of certain masculine habits that had been traditionally absent among women in the past occurred in Spain with a certain delay as compared to other countries and, thus, no indications of its possible effects and consequences are yet noticeable, at least among the cohorts included in the age groups under study.

9.4.2 *Changing Trends Associated with Social and Health Prevention*

Diabetes

Diabetes is another cause for which prevention through medical care, pharmacological treatments, periodic controls, a healthy diet and habits are important. Diabetes is a traditional cause of female over-mortality; however, its evolution benefited women

[6] In the Eurostat classification larynx neoplasm is always linked to trachea/bronchus/lung neoplasms.

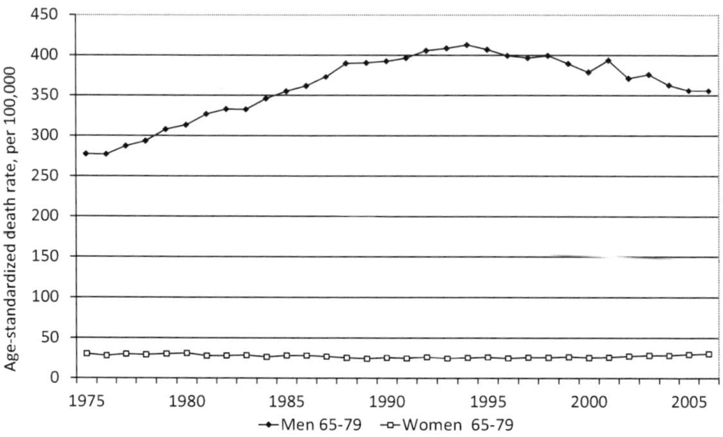

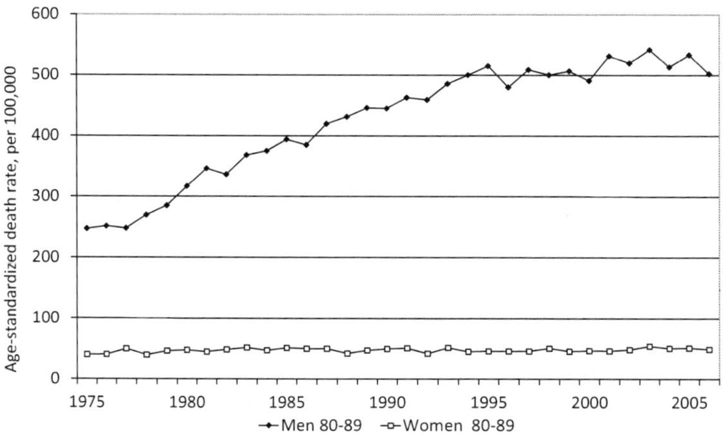

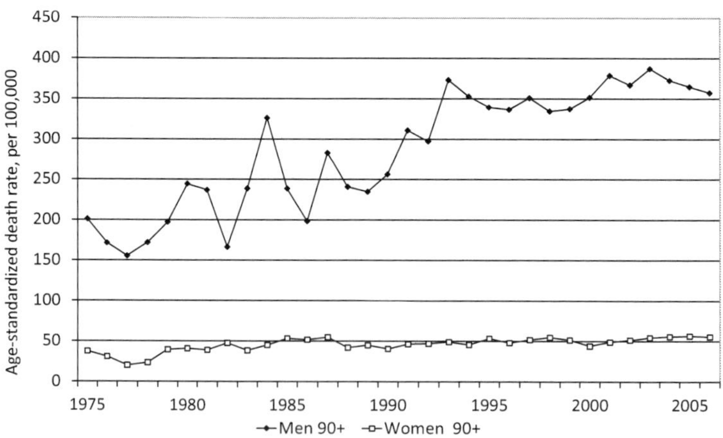

Fig. 9.8 Mortality from malignant larynx and trachea/bronchus/lung neoplasms Men and women 65–79, 80–89, and 90 + years. 1975–2006. (Source: Own elaboration with data from the HMD and the INE)

aged 65–79 during the 1980s, leading to a lower level of female mortality as compared to men from the middle of the 1990's (Fig. 9.9). This is evident among younger old women, but not in the other two age groups. As we know from health surveys, women are more willing to contact family doctors and carry out periodic controls and prescriptions than men are. Since the 1980's, diet care, medication and diabetes control are widespread among the older Spanish population.

Malignant Prostate and Breast Neoplasms

There are two sex-specific causes of death, breast and prostate cancer that, although they have quite different etiology and treatment, are both very sensitive to early detection. Thus, prevention plays an important role in reducing mortality from these causes. Improvements in the diagnosis and specific therapies to treat these two types of tumors have had different effects on each age group, although the evolution of the overall impact is similar in older male and female populations.

Breast cancer is one of the diseases with a very high impact on women's health. For this reason, the European Union Expert Committee recommended launching programs for the early diagnosis of gynecologic cancers as the best option, considering the impossibility to act on most of the risk factors (age, family genetics, premature menarche and delayed menopause, late pregnancy and absence of offspring, etc.). Current medical knowledge, as applied in these programs and in high quality therapies, guarantees a significant decrease of mortality. These programs were adopted regularly in Spain in 1993 (González et al. 2007).

In the case of breast tumors, there has been a clear decrease from the middle of the 1990's within the younger old women group, turning around the increasing trend from previous decades. On the other hand, mortality among women aged 80 and older does not show such a trend, although in the last years there is evidence within the 80–89 age group that points to stabilization (Fig. 9.10). These results reflect the fact that the early diagnosis programs were first implemented in women aged 50 to 65 years. Later on, they were extended to women aged 40–50, but up to the present no general protocol for periodic gynecologic controls has been implemented in older Spanish women, especially in those over 80 years. Even with this limitation, survival from this tumor in Spain is high, and it keeps improving (Alcaraz 2002).

In the case of prostate cancer, both its easy detection (although the generalization of the diagnostic test is still under way) and the availability of outpatient treatment have also led to a mortality decrease since the 1990s, particularly among men aged 65–79 (Fig. 9.11)

Diseases of the Respiratory System

Better living conditions at home and in residential areas, as well as the availability of medical treatments for diseases of the respiratory system (a major cause of death) have allowed a reduction in mortality from this cause among the older population. Prevention and pharmacological therapies have also played an important role here: this is first seen in the decrease of deaths due to pneumonia (Fig. 9.12), followed later

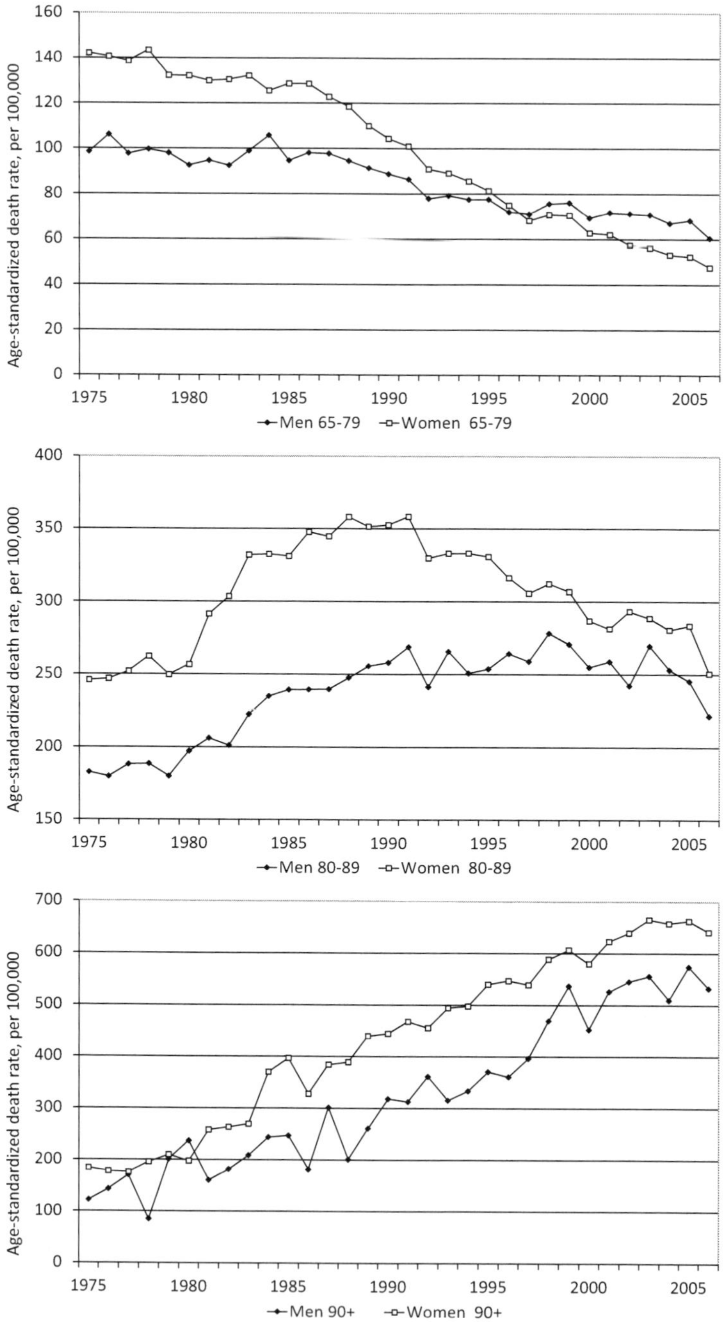

Fig. 9.9 Mortality from diabetes. Men and women 65–79, 80–89, and 90+ years. 1975–2006. (Source: Own elaboration with data from the HMD and the INE)

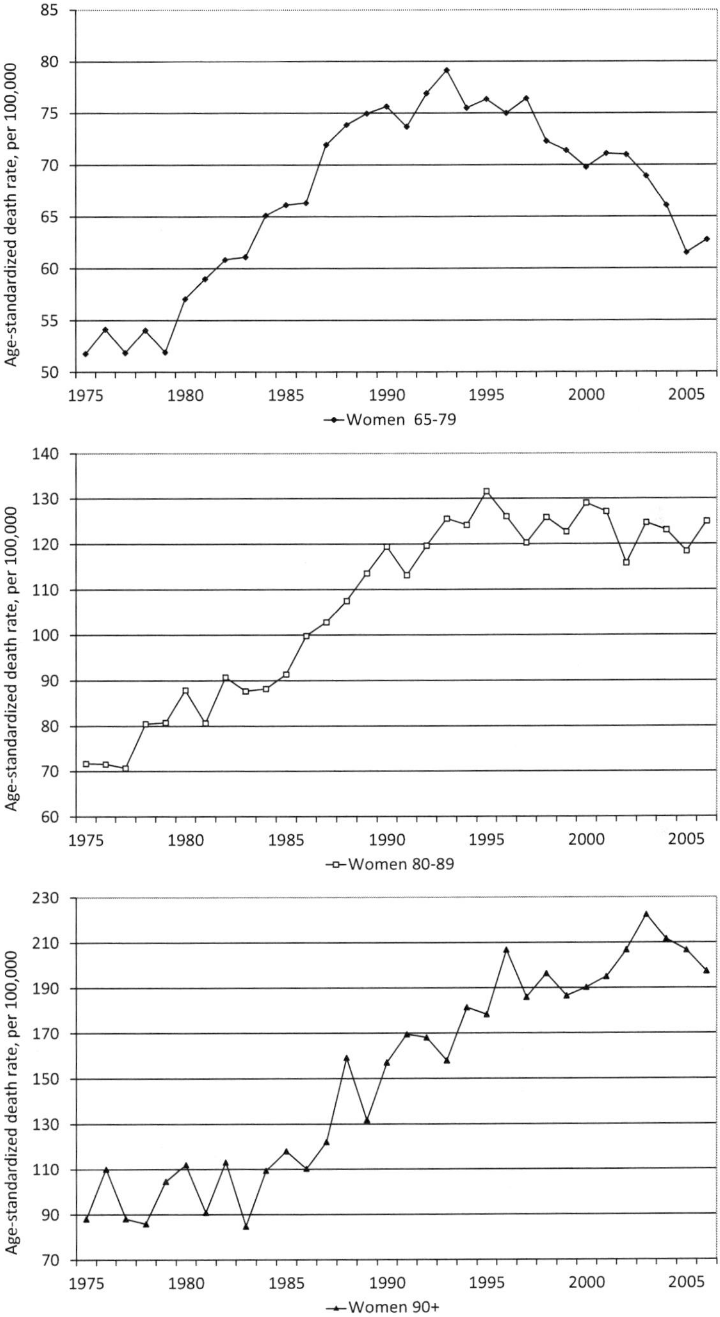

Fig. 9.10 Mortality from malignant breast neoplasms. Men and women. 65–79, 80–89, and 90 + years. 1975–2006. (Source: Own elaboration with data from the HMD and the INE)

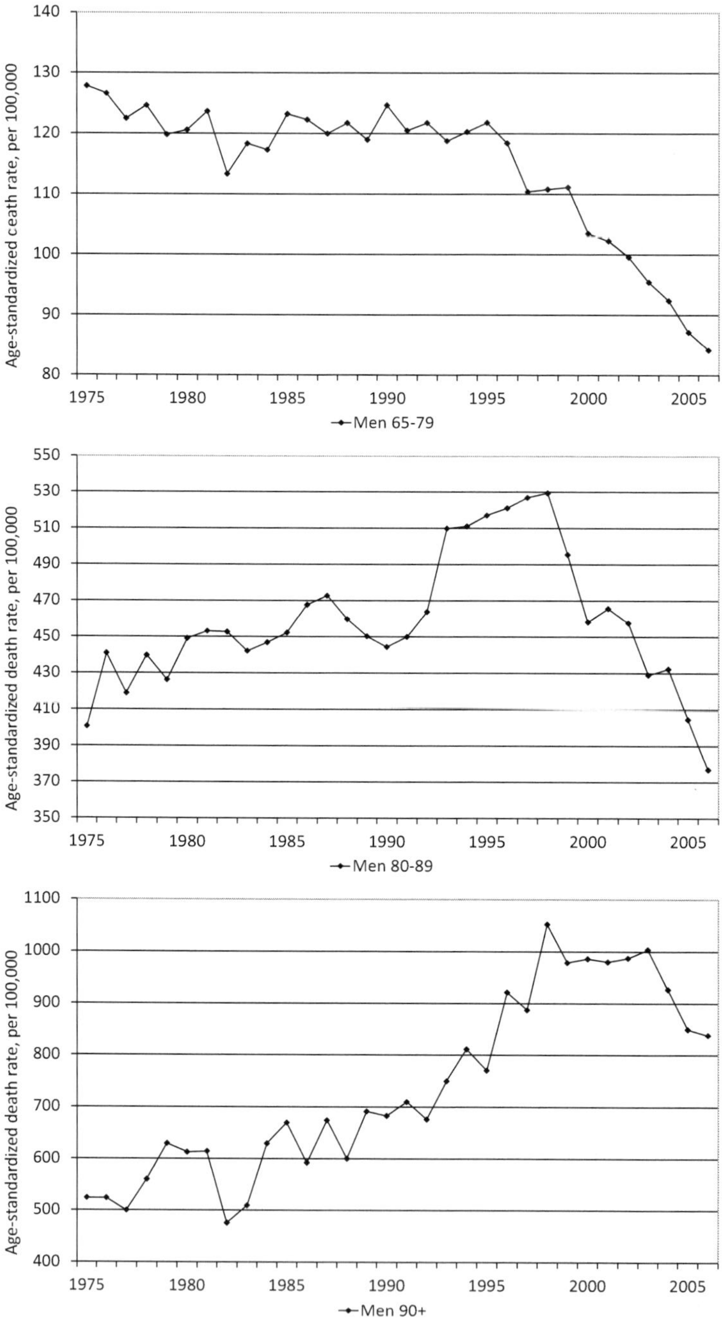

Fig. 9.11 Mortality from malignant prostate neoplasms. Men and women. 65–79, 80–89, and 90 + years. 1975–2006. (Source: Own elaboration with data from the HMD and the INE)

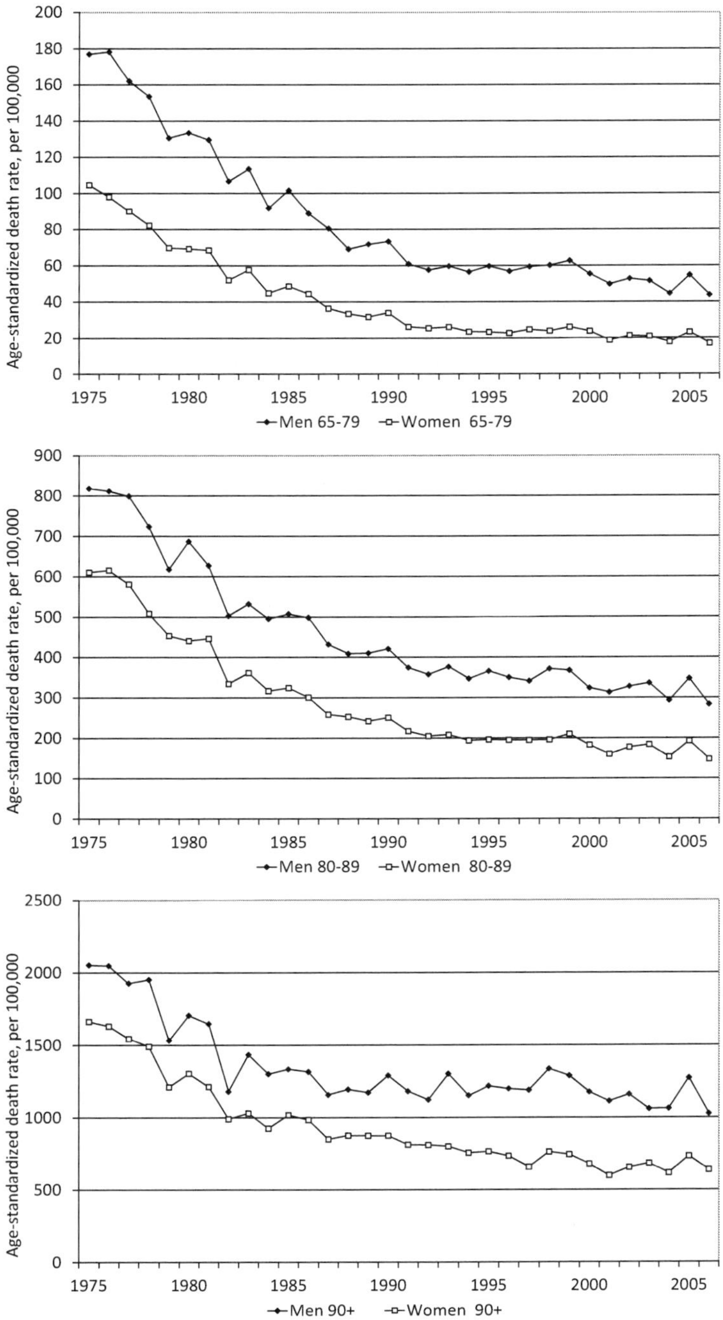

Fig. 9.12 Mortality from pneumonia. Men and women. 65–79, 80–89, and 90 + years. 1975–2006. (Source: Own elaboration with data from the HMD and the INE)

by the prevention of influenza (Fig. 9.13). Vaccination campaigns for the second age group, together with appropriate medicines, have had a great effect on the survival of the most fragile population.

Differences between men and women are evident in chronic lower respiratory diseases, but the mortality trend for these illnesses during this period shows an overall stabilization (Fig. 9.14). Men's over-mortality, partially caused by tobacco consumption, might explain the relative stagnation of mortality due to this cause observed in every age group during the last years.

9.4.3 The Impact of Differential Behavior in External Causes of Death

In 2006, deaths caused by external causes amounted to 4 % of the total number of deaths (14,830), and to more than 2 % of the deaths among those over 65 years (4,577). Since 1975, mortality from these causes has not experienced any clear and substantial improvement. Due to the heterogeneity of the different causes included in this set (car accidents, suicide, self-harm, homicides, accidental poisoning and falls), there are important divergences between their mortality rates by age and sex (Fig. 9.15).

Despite the fact that improvement in prevention[7] as well as in the quality of the physical and social environment are of special relevance in the evolution of mortality from most of these causes, deaths due to them have not experienced a clear decrease during this period. An example of this are deaths by accidental falls (Rubenstein 2006), a major source of disability and death among the elderly. On the other hand, within the global set of external causes of death, sex-related differences in mortality are evident in any age group, and we have only detected a slight decrease of mortality due to these causes among the younger old.

9.4.4 The Impact of Demographic Structure: Age and Sex

Mental disorders and nervous diseases Mental disorders and nervous diseases are the only ones showing an important increase during this period, especially at more advanced ages and during the past few years. The increasing trend of mental disorders throughout almost the entire period is also evident in the case of nervous diseases, although at a smaller rate, especially during the last years. This is of major importance due to the consequences it has for the quality of life of the older people and of ageing societies as a whole.

---

[7] These factors have improved in Spain during the last years through the proper design and implementation of architectural barriers, both at home and outside, as well as by increasing home support services for older people. In addition, health assistance in general, including surgical interventions for the elderly, has also been improved.

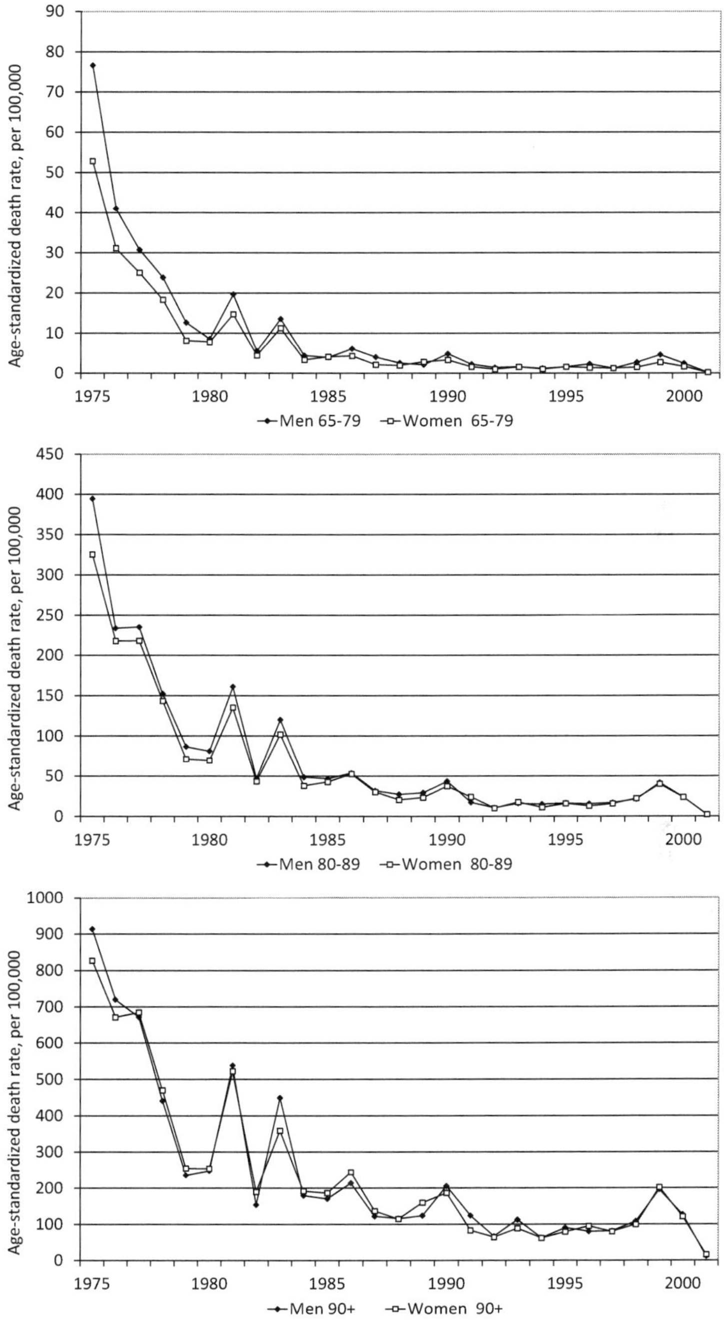

Fig. 9.13 Mortality from influenza. Men and women. 65–79, 80–89, and 90 + years. 1975–2006. (Source: Own elaboration with data from the HMD and the INE)

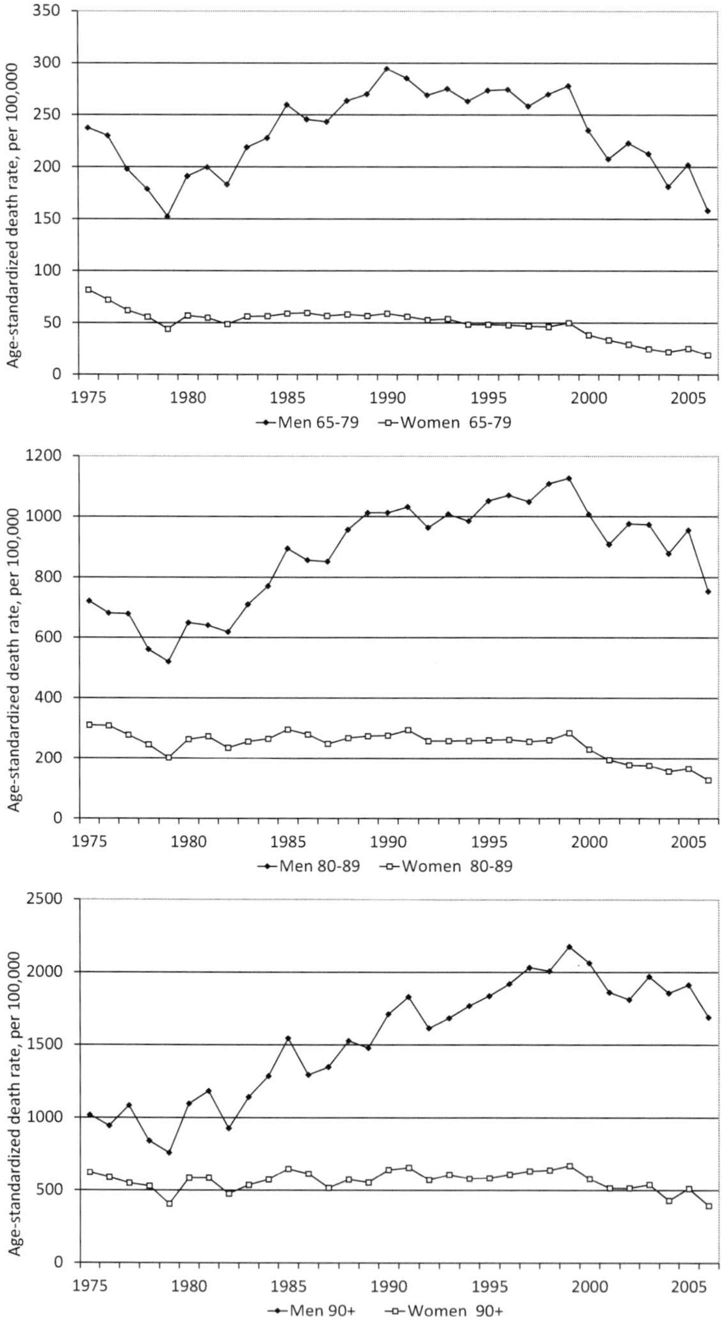

Fig. 9.14 Mortality from chronic lower respiratory diseases. Men and women. 65–79, 80–89, and 90 + years. 1975–2006. (Source: Own elaboration with data from the HMD and the INE)

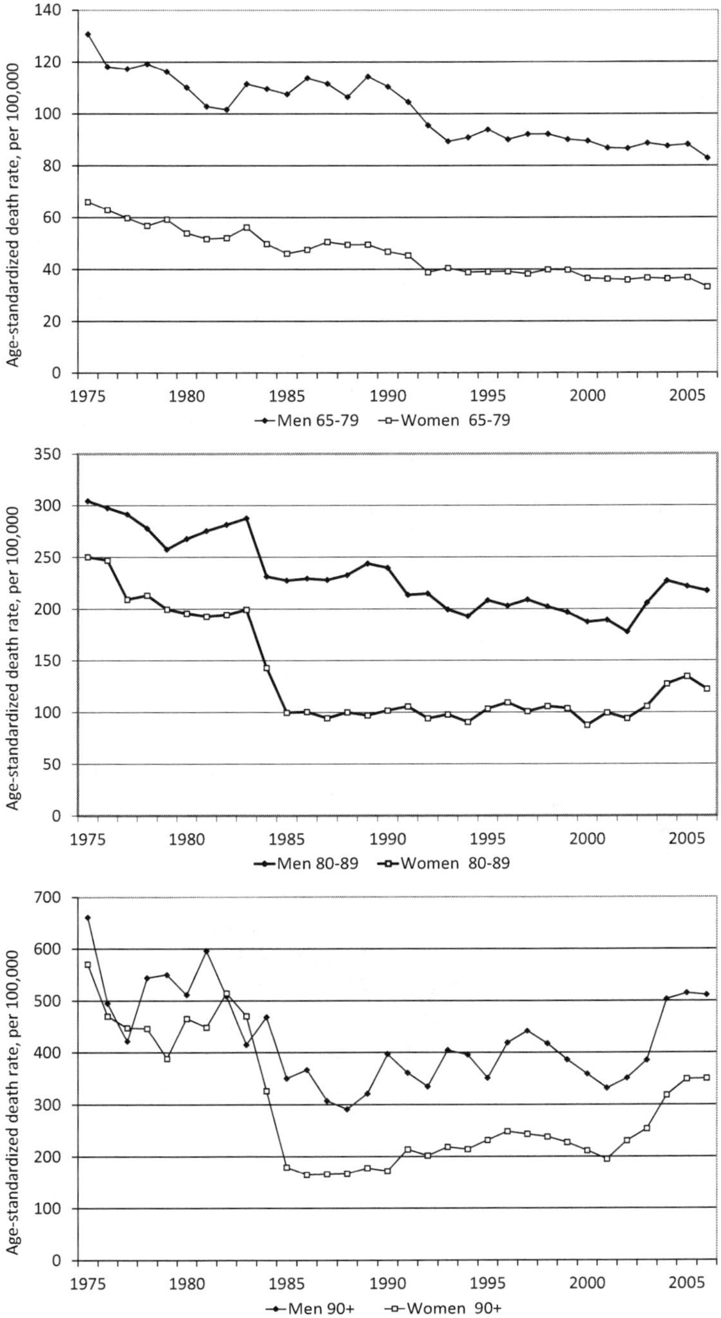

Fig. 9.15 Mortality from external causes. Men and women. 65–79, 80–89, and 90 + years. 1975–2006. (Source: Own elaboration with data from the HMD and the INE)

The data series on nervous diseases and mental disorders are affected by the introduction of the ICD10. We will study them in parallel in order to allow the detection of potential diagnostic transfers between them. It is worth pointing out here that one of the most relevant among nervous system diseases, Alzheimer, determines the evolution of the whole group.

In the last few years there has been a trend towards the stabilization of mortality caused by mental disorders but this, in turn, has been counterbalanced by an increase in the number of deaths caused by nervous system diseases during the same period. Although the stabilization of mortality from mental diseases may be influenced by the above mentioned revision of the ICD, we cannot eliminate the possibility that improved medical care and therapies that affect the quality of life of old people suffering from mental disorders could have a certain impact on their health conditions. In any case, the situation is quite different from the one these age groups experienced in the past (Figs. 9.16 and 9.17). Regarding these two sets of causes, there is a slight over-mortality among men in the younger age group (65–79). Nevertheless, there are almost no differences between men and women at more advanced ages, although a slight women's over-mortality has been observable during the last years, contributing to a certain convergent trend.

All in all, in elderly populations such as the Spanish one, it is not necessary to insist on the importance of the rise in morbi-mortality associated with this kind of illness, due to the growing longevity of the Spanish population (Puga and Abellán 2004) these illnesses generate a longstanding dependency among the elderly, and this should be a main target when setting the corresponding public policies.

These two sets of causes constitute a potential brake on the extension of healthy life and on the achievement of the final objective of demographically advanced societies, which is to live longer without disability. The existence of long-lived populations in the absence of disability may represent a new stage in the mortality transition (Vallin and Meslé 2004), but this stage may not be reached if mental and nervous diseases continue to spread in aged societies. On the other hand, if that happens, the feminization of disability will also continue to rise as a result of the existing sex-based differences in mortality and disability. It is for this reason, and because their evolution in recent years will play a determining role in the existing relationship between the extension of the median life span once old age has been reached and the extension of the period of social dependency at the end of the life cycle, that we have paid special attention to these two causes of death.

9.5 Discussion

Understanding the epidemiological profile of the elderly population today is essential in order to estimate the evolution of future life expectancy. In this sense, in order to contribute to the theoretical framework of the health transition in Spain, it is necessary both to follow the evolution of the main causes of death determining survival and to focus on those causes that show signs of changing trends.

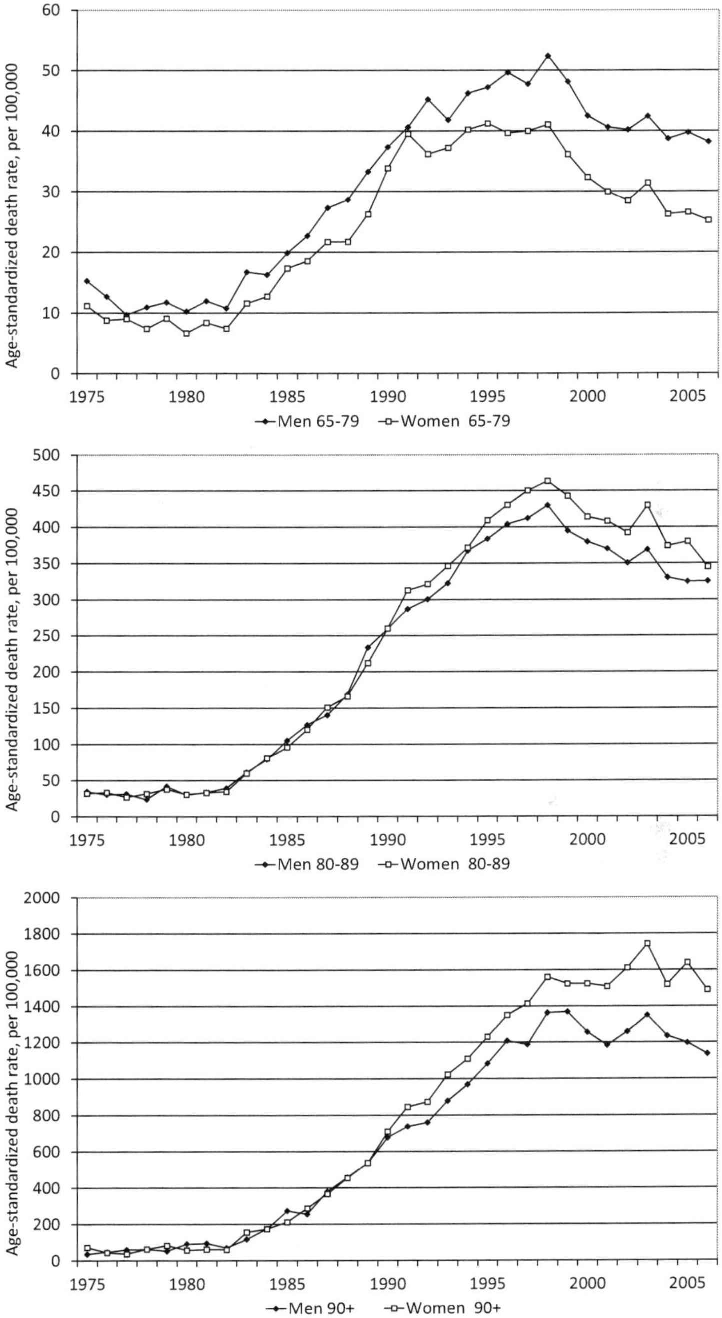

Fig. 9.16 Mortality from mental disorders. Men and women. 65–79, 80–89, and 90 + years. 1975–2006. (Source: Own elaboration with data from the HMD and the INE)

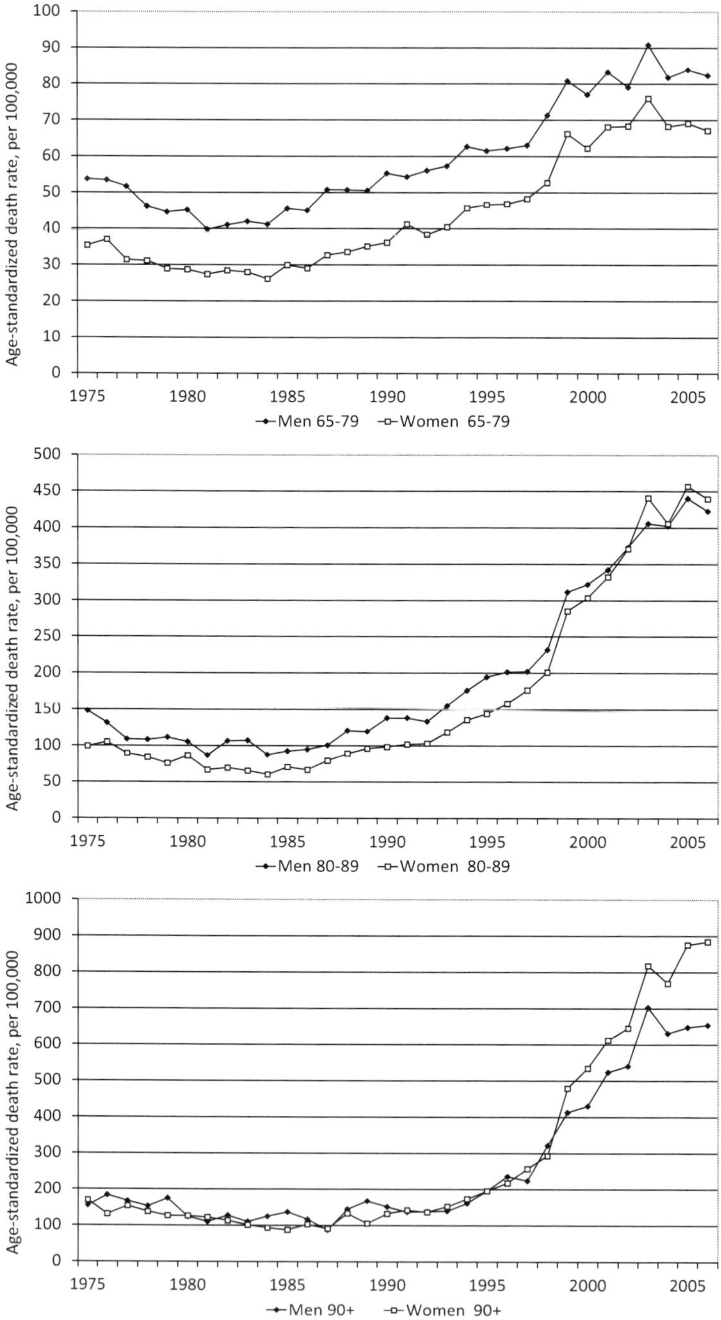

Fig. 9.17 Mortality from diseases of the nervous system. Men and women. 65–79, 80–89, and 90+ years. 1975–2006. (Source: Own elaboration with data from the HMD and the INE)

Our results confirm that the significant decrease in mortality among the elderly population during the period under study was largely driven by a decline in circulatory diseases, especially cerebrovascular illnesses. This constant fall in mortality is a trend induced by an authentic cardiovascular revolution—the main agent behind the observed increase in longevity among Spaniards. While the decrease of mortality from respiratory diseases also contributed to this decline, it did so to a much lesser extent and its contribution was more irregular.

On the other hand, within the group of death-causing diseases that grew in prevalence over the course of these three decades, the key role is played by tumors (mortality from stomach and liver cancer was the only tumor-induced mortality to decline during this period). Without a doubt, the evolution of mortality caused by malignant tumors will determine the rise or stabilization of life expectancy in upcoming years, given its enormous importance in relation to overall mortality.

Regarding sex differences, the maintenance of important sex-based differences is mainly due to higher male mortality, caused, first of all, by tumors and, secondly, by respiratory diseases. The differential evolution of these causes has led to the existence of a 25 year lag in men's, as compared to women's, longevity.

After defining the evolution of the main causes of death, we have focused especially on those causes which have affected men and women differentially. Our results show that some of them (basically tumors) show indications of potentially convergent trends. These signs are more prominent in the case of larynx, trachea, bronchus and lung tumors, which are decreasing among men aged 65–70. Consequently, this might contribute to men's mortality approaching the demographic position of women in the future.

In the case of Spanish old women, and taking into account the cohort factor, we have not yet detected the effects of the younger generations' changing unhealthy habits and behaviors during the last decades. This might be an additional potential convergence factor between male and female mortality, although empirical evidence must still be obtained. Also, advances in the treatment of prostate tumors have guaranteed an increase in the life span of men below 89 years. Nevertheless, the disappearance of women's over-mortality due to diabetes is no less relevant, just as much as the decrease of breast cancer among women aged 65–79 years. Regarding the privileged situation of women, we observe a single exception to traditional male over-mortality: the diseases of the nervous system and mental disorders at very old ages.

In conclusion, we have found that, while the general decreasing trend in mortality is maintained, several recent changes in the Spanish older population may be pointing to modifications in the known trends of differential sex mortality. The final balance must take into account the new signs of convergence, but also the foreseeable obstacles for the increase of the life span of both men and women.

Acknowledgments This work was supported by Grant CSO2010–18925 from the Spanish Ministry of Science and Innovation. We would like to acknowledge the former members of the group for their past contributions to our previous project SEJ2006–10972. We especially want to express our recognition to Elena Robles for her contribution to the database of causes of death which was developed in the previous research project.

9.6 Annex. Causes of death. European Shortlist. Eurostat

Nr	All causes of death			ICD–10 code	ICD–9 code	ICD–8 code
				A00–B99	**001–E999**	**000–E999**
01	*Infectious and parasitic diseases*			A00–B99	001–139	000–136
02		Tuberculosis		A15–A19,B90	010–018,137	010–019
03		Meningococcal infection		A39	036	036
04		AIDS (HIV-disease)		B20–B24	042–044	–
05		Viral hepatitis		B15–B19	070	070
06	*Neoplasms*			C00–D48	140–239	140–239
07		Malignant neoplasms		C00–C97	140–208	140–209
08			of which malignant lip, oral cavity, pharynx neoplasms	C00–C14	140–149	140–149
09			of which malignant esophagus neoplasms	C15	150	150
10			of which malignant stomach neoplasms	C16	151	151
11			of which malignant colon neoplasms	C18	153	153
12			of which malignant rectum and anus neoplasms	C19–C20–C21	154	154
13			of which malignant liver and intrahepatic bile ducts neoplasms	C22	155	155
14			of which malignant pancreas neoplasms	C25	157	157
15			of which malignant larynx and trachea/bronchus/lung neoplasms	C32–C34	161–162	161–162
16			of which malignant skin melanoma	C43	172	172
17			of which malignant breast neoplasms	C50	174–175	174
18			of which malignant cervix uteri neoplasm	C53	180	180
19			of which malignant neoplasms of other parts of uterus	C54–55	179,182	182
20			of which malignant ovary neoplasms	C56	183.0	183.0

Nr	All causes of death			ICD–10 code	ICD–9 code	ICD–8 code
				A00–B99	**001–E999**	**000–E999**
21			of which malignant prostate neoplasms	C61	185	185
22			of which malignant kidney neoplasms	C64	189.0	189.0
23			of which malignant bladder neoplasms	C67	188	188
24			of which malignant neoplasms of lymph./hematopoietic tissue	C81–C96	200–208	200–209
25	*Diseases of the blood(-forming organs), immunologic disorders*			D50–D89	279–289	280–289
26	*Endocrine, nutritional and metabolic diseases*			E00–E90	240–278	240–279
27		Diabetes mellitus		E10–E14	250	250
28	*Mental and behavioral disorders*			F00–F99	290–319	290–315
29		Alcohol abuse		F10	291,303	291,303
30		Drug dependence, toxicomania		F11–F16,	304–305	304–305
31	*Diseases of the nervous system and the sense organs*			G00–H95	320–389	320–389
32		Meningitis (other than 03)		G00–G03	320–322	320
33	*Diseases of the circulatory system*			I00–I99	390–459	390–444.1
34		Ischemic heart diseases		I20–I25	410–414	410–414
35		Other heart diseases		I30–I33,	420–423,	420–423,
36		Cerebrovascular diseases		I60–I69	430–438	430–438
37	*Diseases of the respiratory system*			J00–J99	460–519	460–519
38		Influenza		J10–J11	487	470–474
39		Pneumonia		J12–J18	480–486	480–486

Nr	All causes of death			ICD–10 code	ICD–9 code	ICD–8 code
				A00–B99	**001–E999**	**000–E999**
40		Chronic lower respiratory diseases		J40–J47	490–494,496	491–493,518
41			Of which asthma	J45–J46	493	493
42	*Diseases of the digestive system*			K00–K93	520–579	520–577,444.2
43		Ulcer of stomach, duodenum and jejunum		K25–K28	531–534	531–534
44		Chronic liver disease		K70,K73–74	571.0–571.9	571.0–571.9
45	*Diseases of the skin and subcutaneous tissue*			L00–L99	680–709	680–709
46	*Diseases of the musculoskeletal system/connective tissue*			M00–M99	710–739	710–738
47		Rheumatoid arthritis and osteoarthrosis		M15–M19	714–715	712–713
48	*Diseases if the genitourinary system*			N00–N99	580–629	580–629,792
49		Diseases of kidney and ureter		N00–N29	580–594	580–594
50	*Complications of pregnancy, childbirth and puerperium*			O00–O99	630–676	630–678
51	*Certain conditions originating in the perinatal period*			P00–P96	760–779	760–779
52	*Congenital malformations and chromosomal abnormalities*			Q00–Q99	740–759	740–759

Nr	All causes of death			ICD–10 code	ICD–9 code	ICD–8 code
				A00–B99	**001–E999**	**000–E999**
53		Congenital malformations of the nervous system		Q00–Q07	740–742	740–743
54		Congenital malformations of the circulatory system		Q20–Q28	745–747	746–747
55	*Symptoms, signs, abnormal findings, ill-defined causes*			R00–R99	780–799	780–782.3, 782.5–791, 793–796
56		Sudden infant death syndrome		R95	798.0	–
57		Unknown and unspecified causes		R96–R99	798.1–9,799	795–796
58	*External causes of injury and poisoning*			V01–Y89	E800–E999	E800–E999
59		Accidents		V01–X59	E800–E929	E800–E929, E940–E942
60			Of which transport accidents	V01–V99	E800–E848	E800–E845
61			Of which accidental falls	W00–W19	E880–E888	E880–E887
62			Of which accidental poisoning	X40–X49	E850–E869	E850–E877
63		Suicide and intentional self-harm		X60–X84	E950–E959	E950–E959
64		Homicide, assault		X85–Y09	E960–E969	E960–E969
65		Events of undetermined intent		Y10–Y34	E980–E989	E980–E989

References

Alcaraz, M. (2002). "Estudio de la no participación en el programa de prevención de cáncer de mama en la ciudad de Valencia". *Rev. Gaceta Sanitaria, 16*(3), 230–235.

Audicana Uriarte, C., Cirera Suárez, Ll., & Augusto Becker, R. (1998). "Caracterización de la 10ª Revisión de la Clasificación Internacional de Enfermedades (CIE-10). Principales diferencias con la 9ª en su aplicación a la mortalidad". In Ll. Cirera Suárez & E. Vázquez Fernández (Eds.), *La implantación en España de la 10ª revisión (CIE-10)* (pp. 55–69). Santiago de Compostela: Sociedad Espaola de Epidemiología.

Blanes, J. (2007). *La transición epidemiológica en España. Perfiles edad-causa de la mortalidad e impacto sobre la esperanza de vida.*, PhD Thesis.

Canudas-Romo, V., Glei, D., Gómez Redondo, R., Coelho, E, & Boe, C. (2008). "Mortality Changes in the Iberian Peninsula in the Last Decades of the Twentieth Century". *Population (English Edition), 63*(2), 319–344.

Caselli, G., Meslé, F., & Vallin, J. (1995). *Le triomphe de la médecine. Évolution de la mortalité en Europe depuis le début de siècle.* INED Dossiers et Recherches No. 45, Paris.

Cirera, Ll., et al. (2006). "Correspondencias entre CIE-10 y CIE-9 para las listas de causas de muerte del Instituto Nacional de Estadística y de la Región de Murcia". *Rev Esp Sal Pública, 80*(2), 157–175.

Coale, A., & Guo, G. (1991). "The use of new model life tables at very low mortality in population projections". *Population bulletin of the United Nations, 30,* 1–22.

Eurostat. (1998). "Causes of Death—ShortList". http://forum.europa.eu.int/Public/irc/dsis/health/library?l=/methodologiessandsdatasc/causessofsdeath/shortslistpdf/_EN_1.0_&a=d.

Eurostat. (2004). Base de Datos "New Chronos", European Comission, 2004. http://europa.eu.int/comm/eurostat.

Frenk, J., Bobadilla, J. L., Stern, C., Frejka, T., & Lozano, R. (1991). "Elements for a theory of the health transition". *Health Transition Review, 1*(1), 21–38.

Fries, J. F. (1980). "Aging, natural death, and the compression of morbidity". *New England Journal of Medicine, 303*(3), 130–135.

Fries, J. F. (1989). "The Compression of Morbidity: Near or Far?". *The Milbank Quarterly, 67*(2), 397–419.

Gómez Redondo, R. (1995). "Vejez prolongada y juventud menguada. Tendencias en la evolución de la esperanza de vida de la población espaola, 1970–1990". *REIS, 71,* 79–108.

Gómez Redondo, R., & Boe, C. (2005). "Decomposition analysis of Spanish life expectancy at birth: Evolution and change in the components by sex and age". *Demographic Research, 13*(20), 521–546. http://www.demographic-research.org/volumes/vol13/20/.

Gómez Redondo, R., Gènova, R., & Robles, E. (2007). "Envejecimiento, longevidad y salud. Bases demográficas en España". In S. Ballesteros (Ed.), *Envejecimiento saludable: Aspectos Biológicos, Psicológicos y Sociales* (pp. 41–76). Madrid: UNED.

Gómez Redondo, R., Robles, E., García, J. M., & Faus, A. (2010). "Recent trends on mortality by cause of death among the elderly in Spain and potential demographic sources for their study". In Expanding the Human Mortality Database: Data by Cause and Region. INED, June 17–19, Paris.

González, A., & González, M. J. (2007). "Programas de protección precoz del cancer de mama en España". *Psicooncología: investigación y clínica biopsicosocial en oncología, 4*(2–3), 249–263.

Hayflick, L. (2000). "The future of aging". *Nature, 408,* 267–269.

Horiuchi, S. (2006). "Causes of death among the oldest-old: Age related changes in the cause of death distribution. In J-M. Robine, E. M. Crimmins, S. Horiuchi, & Y. Zeng (Eds.), *Human Longevity, Individual Life Duration and the Growth of the Oldest-Old Population* (pp. 215–235). The Netherlands: Springer.

Klenk, J., Rapp, K., Büchele, G., Keil, U., & Weiland, S. (2007). "Increasing life expectancy in Germany: quantitative contributions from changes in age- and disease-specific mortality". *European Journal of Public Health, 17*(6), 587–592.

Lopez, A. (1983). "The sex mortality differential in developed countries". In A. Lopez, & L. Ruzicka (Eds.), *Sex differentials in mortality: trends, determinants and consequences. Selection of the paper presented at the ANU/UN/WHO meeting held in Canberra on 17 December 1981* (pp. 53–120).

Meslé, F. (2006a). "Medical Causes of Death". In G. Caselli, J. Vallin, & G. Wunsch (Eds.), *Demography: Analysis and Synthesis. Vol. II* (pp. 29–44). USA: Elsevier Academic Press.

Meslé, F. (2006b). Recent Improvements in life expectancy in France: Men Are Starting to Catch Up". *Population (English Edition), 61*(4), 365–387.

Meslé, F. & Vallin, J. (2002). "Mortality in Europe: The divergence between East and West". *Population (English edition), 57*(1), 157–197.

Meslé, F., & Vallin, J. (2003). "Increase in life expectancy and concentration of ages at death". In J-M. Robine, C. Jagger, C. D. Mathers, E. M. Crimmins, & R. M. Suzman (Eds.), *Determining Health Expectancies* (pp. 13–34). Chichester: John Wiley & Sons Ltd.

Meslé, F., & Vallin, J. (2006). "The Health Transition: Trends and Prospects". In G. Caselli, J. Vallin, & G. Wunsch (Eds.), *Demography: Analysis and Synthesis. Vol. II* (pp. 247–259). USA: Elsevier Academic Press.

Olshansky, S. J., Carnes, B. A., & Cassel, C. (1990). "In search of Methuselah: Estimating the upper limits to human longevity". *Science, 250*, 634–640.

Olshansky, S. J., Carnes, B. A., & Désesquelles, A. (2001). "Prospects for Human Longevity". *Science, 291*(5508), 1491–1492.

Omran, A. R. (1971). "The epidemiologic transition: a theory of the epidemiology of population change". *Milbank Mem Fund Q, 49,* 509–583.

Pampel, F. C. (2002a). "Cigarette use and the narrowing sex differential in mortality". *Population and Development Review, 28*(1), 77–104.

Pampel, F. C. (2002b). "Inequality, diffusion and the status gradient in smoking". *Social Problems, 49*(1), 35–57.

Peto, R., & Lopez, A., et al. (1994). *Mortality from smoking in developed countries 1950–2000: Indirect estimates from national vital statics* (pp. 103–553). Oxford: Oxford University Press.

Puga González, M. D., Abellán García, A. (2004). *El proceso de discapacidad. Un análisis de la encuesta sobre discapacidades, deficiencias y estado de salud*, Fundación Pfizer, Alcobendas (Madrid).

Robine, J-M. (2001). "Redefining the Stages of the Epidemiological Transition by a Study of the Dispersion of Life Spans: The Case of France". *Population: An English Selection, 13*(1), 173–194.

Robles, E. (2009). "¿De qué mueren los ancianos en España?". *Estudios Geográficos, LXX*(267), 567–598.

Rubenstein, L. Z. (2006). "Falls in older people: Epidemiology, risk factors and strategies for prevention". *Age Ageing, 35* (Suppl. 2), S37–S41.

Ruiz, M., et al. (2002). "Comparabilidad entre la novena y la décima revisión de la Clasificación Internacional de Enfermedades aplicada a la codificación de la causa de muerte en España". *Gaceta Sanitaria, 16*(6), 526–532.

Segura, A., & Martínez Navarro, F. (1998). "Las clasificaciones de enfermedades y causas de muerte y su evolución". In Ll. Cirera Suárez & E. Vázquez Fernández (Eds.), *La implantación en España de la 10ª revisión (CIE-10)* (pp. 17–38). Santiago de Compostela: Sociedad Espaola de Epidemiología.

Vallin, J. (2006). "Mortality differences by sex among the oldest-old". In J-M. Robine, E. M. Crimmins, S. Horiuchi, & Y. Zeng (Eds.), *Human Longevity, Individual Life Duration and the Growth of the Oldest-Old Population* (pp. 333–352). The Netherlands: Springer.

Vallin, J., & Meslé, F. (1988). *Les causes de décès en France de 1925 a 1978.* Institut National d'Études Démografiques. Presses Universitaires de France.

Vallin, J., & Meslé, F. (2004). "Convergences and divergences in mortality. A new approach to health transition". *Demographic Research, Special Collection,* 2(2), pp. 11–44. http://www.demographic-research.org.

Vallin, J., & Meslé, F. (1988a). *Les causes de decès en France de 1925 a 1978*. INED, Presses Universitaires de France.

Vallin, J., & Meslé, F. (1988b). "Evolution sociale de la mortalité, conquète et reconquète d'un avantage fèminin", Paris, Institut d'Ètudes Démographiques, Dossiers et recherche, 17.

Waldron, I. (1983). "Sex differences in human mortality: the role of genetic factors", *Social Science & Medicine, 17*, n 6, 321–333.

Wilmoth, J. R. (1997). "In search of limits". In K. W. Wachter & C. E. Finch (Eds.), *Between Zeus and Salomon: the biodemography of longevity*, National Research Council (Committee on Population) (pp. 38–64). Washington DC: National Academy Press.

Wilmoth, J. R., & Horiuchi, S. (1999). "Rectangularization revisited: Variability of Age at Death within Human Populations". *Demography, 36*(4), 475–495.

World Health Organization. (1997). *International classification of diseases, 1975 revision. Vol.1*, Geneva.

Yoshinaga, K., & Une, H. (2005). "Contributions of mortality changes by age group and selected causes of death to the increase in Japanese life expectancy at birth from 1950 to 2000". *European Journal of Epidemiology, 20,* 49–57.

Chapter 10
Excess Mortality Risks in Institutions: The Influence of Health and Disability Status

Anne Herm, Michel Poulain and Jon Anson

Abstract Mortality in the institutionalized aged population is generally recognized as being considerably higher than among those living independently; whereas among those living independently, there is a greater risk of mortality among those living alone than among those living with other adults (generally with spouse and/or children). However, given that the institutionalized population is liable to be poorer, and in poorer health than the independent-living population, it is unclear whether the higher mortality risk among the institutionalized population results from their poorer health, or from other causes associated with institutionalization. The Belgian Census of 2001, coupled with a near-complete follow-up of deaths over the subsequent year (2002), enables us to compute a reasonable measure of health at the time of the census and thus separate out the effects of health status and living conditions on mortality. Taken across the entire population of Belgian nationals resident in Belgium and aged 65 and above at the time of the census ($N = 1.64$ million cases with full data), and controlling for background characteristics, we find that except at very old ages, those living in old age homes have a higher risk of mortality than those living in private housing, *irrespective of health status*. We conclude that while much of the apparently higher mortality of the institutionalized aged population may be attributable to the generally poorer health of those living in institutions, there is nonetheless a salutogenic effect of living independently in private housing, whatever the individual's health status.

Keywords Belgium · Old age · Ill-health · Institutionalisation · Gender differences

J. Anson (✉)
Department of Social Work, Ben-Gurion University of the Negev,
84105 Beer Sheva, Israel
e-mail: anson@bgu.ac.il

A. Herm · M. Poulain
IACCHOS, Université catholique de Louvain, Place Montesquieu 17,
1348 Louvain-La-Neuve, Belgium

Estonian Institute for Population Studies, Tallinn University,
P.O. Box 3012, 10504 Tallinn, Estonia

J. Anson, M. Luy (eds.), *Mortality in an International Perspective*,
European Studies of Population 18, DOI 10.1007/978-3-319-03029-6_10,

10.1 Introduction

Mortality of the institutionalized elderly population is generally recognized as being considerably higher than that of those living in private households; and among the latter group, there is a greater risk of mortality among those living alone than among those living with other adults (generally with spouse and/or children). Given that the institutionalized population is liable to be in poorer health than the independent-living population, it is still unclear whether the higher mortality risk among the institutionalized population results from their poorer health, or from other causes associated with institutionalisation. This contribution will address this question by analysing the way mortality risks vary by age, sex and living arrangement, controlling for the impact of health status (disability) and education.

10.2 Living Arrangements, Health and Mortality Risks

A large number of studies have investigated the links between marital status and mortality and have underlined the protective role of marriage (Manzoli et al. 2007; Rendall et al. 2011). Mortality risks differ also by living arrangement when comparing persons living alone, in married couple with or without children, in cohabitating non-married couples or with other persons (Davis et al. 1997; Koskinen et al. 2007). Nevertheless most studies comparing the effect of living arrangements on mortality do not include in their analysis those living in collective households or in institutions. On the other hand, several studies have investigated the mortality risks in nursing homes, with the date of entry as starting point, but without comparing the mortality levels in institutions with those observed in private households (Breuer et al. 1998; Cohen-Mansfield et al. 1999; Dale et al. 2001; Kiely and Flacker 2002; Raines and Wight 2002; Flacker and Kiely 2003; Hjaltadattir et al. 2011). The only attempt at comparing the two main types of living arrangement, private or collective household, that we are aware of, is by Grundy (2010) who used the Office for National Statistics Longitudinal Study to study transition to institutions and the 4.5-year survival rates at the end of three decades, 1981, 1991 and 2001. Her findings show that mortality was higher for the institutionalised population than for those living alone (incidence risk ratio in 2001–2005 of 2.85 for women and 2.80 for men, difference between the sexes not significant). The incidence risk ratios were significant in each of the three periods studied, and increased between 1981–1985 and 2001–2005. Although Grundy did not study health status specifically, she did note that the mortality risk was higher for those who had moved into an institution during the previous decade.

Obviously the role of health as an intermediate variable is important (Lillard and Panis 1996; Molloy et al. 2009). Mortality risks are correlated with health status, the latter often being estimated using the Self-Rated Health Index (SRH) (Idler and Benyamini 1997). Among others, Zunzunegui et al. (2001) showed that the SRH is lower among elderly people living alone and lacking emotional support, while Murphy (1995) investigated the link between private living arrangements and health. But none of these authors included collective households or institutions in their analysis. Yet, as several authors have demonstrated, health is an important determinant for the choice of living arrangement (Börsch-Supan et al. 1996).

As health status deterioration is often the main reason for entering an institution (Klein 1996; Nihtila and Martikainen 2008), health status is found to be generally worse for those living in institutions compared to those living in private households. Accordingly, the question arises whether the difference in health status observed for those in different living arrangements could explain the differences in mortality risk between them. In other words, is the heightened mortality of those living in institutions merely a reflection of residents' poorer health, or is there a direct impact of living arrangements on mortality, even when controlling for health status? That question is of particular importance when considering the setting of policy in this field, and the relative desirability of different options.

10.3 Data

Data from the Belgian census of 2001 provide the opportunity to investigate more closely the impact of health on the difference in mortality risk by living arrangement. Our analysis focusses on all Belgian nationals aged 65 and above, enumerated as resident in Belgium on the 1st October, 2001 and who were still alive on 1st January 2002, according to the continuous population registration system. A total of 1,743,785 persons aged 65 and above are considered. Information on these individuals was derived from two sources:

a. Personal status information was derived directly from the population register: sex, date of birth and household characteristics, to identify living arrangements as of 1st January 2002;
b. Other personal information as reported by the individual in the 2001 census form was used to assess the individual's health status and level of education. In the population under study 30,672 (1.76 %) did not return a census form and only population registration data is available[1];
c. For living arrangements, we limited our investigation to three main groups: those living with others, those living alone and those living in nursing homes (*maisons de repos*). We excluded 32,307 (1.85 %) individuals whose living arrangements could not be determined unambiguously. These were individuals resident in non-nursing home institutions (mainly convents, monasteries, mental health institutions and prisons) or registered as living independently in nursing homes. Accordingly, our results concerning mortality risks in institutions only refer to nursing homes and cannot necessarily be generalised to other forms of institution.

[1] Presumably most of these people did not return the census form due to incapacity, and indeed the mortality risk for this group was very high, bearing out this assumption. However, given the small number of non-returns we decided it was preferable to avoid such assumptions and to exclude this group from the analysis.

d. We used level of education as a proxy measure of social status. Of the various questions relating to education, we focus on the distinction between those who continued education beyond their 15th birthday versus those who did not. Compared to questions on highest diploma obtained or years of schooling, this is probably the least given to different interpretations by respondents. As far as possible, missing data were supplemented by cross referencing the data from the 1991 census. Nonetheless, data were missing for a further 63,746 individuals. However, for almost half of these, information was available on whether they did, or did not, complete elementary school, and their educational level was imputed accordingly, as High, or Low, respectively. As a result, the number of missing cases was reduced to 32,710 (1.88 %) on this variable.

Removing all cases with missing values thus leaves us with 1,648,096 persons alive on the 1st January 2002, or 94.5 % of the original population under study. Of these, 41.6 % were men and 58.4 % women. The outcome variable, whether the individual survived or died during the year 2002, is also taken from the continuous population registration system. Of the total population analysed, 72,071 persons died during 2002, giving a crude death rate of 44.7/1,000[2].

We are treating personal characteristics as fixed at the census, though some changes in living arrangement and health status naturally did occur during 2002. Living arrangements may have changed, in particular moving from independent to institutionalised living arrangements, especially following widowhood; and health may have deteriorated. Although we do not have data on changes during the year of analysis, we may assume that such changes, where they occurred, will generally have been *into* an institution, and thus in the direction of a greater mortality risk, so that by fixing individual characteristics of health and living arrangements as they were at the time of the census or on 1st January, we are in fact introducing a bias disfavouring our hypothesis of higher mortality in ill health and in institutions. It is unlikely, therefore, that confirmatory evidence for our hypotheses can be attributable to changes in living arrangements that occurred during the year of follow-up.

Our Health Status indicator is based on four census questions, self-rated health status (SRH), disability status (disabled or not) and, for the disabled only, the impact of their disability on daily activities, and the extent to which they are bedridden. The census questions are the following:

1. SRH (on a five point scale from 'Very Good' to 'Very Poor').
2. Does the respondent suffer from any chronic disease or disability? This was a filter question ('Yes' or 'No') and those that answered affirmatively were asked:
   a. To what extent they were limited in their daily activities, on a three point scale from 'Little' to 'Severely'. Nevertheless one third of respondents who answered 'Yes' to question 2 did not answer question 2a.
   b. To what extent were they bedridden, again on a three point scale from 'Never or rarely' to 'Permanently'. As for daily activities, about one third of the respondents who answered 'Yes' to the filter question, did not answer this question.

---

[2] $CDR = \frac{Deaths}{Population - 0.5 \cdot Deaths}$.

We thus have three separate health questions: Self Rated Health (SRH); Limitations to daily activities (L) and being Bedridden (B). The filter question on chronic diseases is included in the last two questions, as all those who reported having no chronic disease were automatically classified in the null category on the last two questions.

In order to consider the relation between the three health questions we performed a Joint Correspondence Analysis (JCA) (Greenacre and Blasius 2006; Nenadic and Greenacre 2007). JCA is an extension of the two-way Correspondence Analysis (CA) that seeks to represent graphically the conditional distributions within each category of the different variables. Each variable is divided into categories, and in each category there is a distribution of the categories of all the other variables. The categories that have similar distributions of the other variables will be proximately located in the plot and those that have dissimilar distributions will be further apart. Figure 10.1 presents the JCA plot for this analysis. The three variables present three overlapping scales running from left to right on the first dimension, with good health on the left and poor health on the right. The three categories of non-response are located in the middle of this scale, but are placed off the scale on the second dimension. Nonetheless, this location does suggest that, *on average*, the non-responses should be regarded as being of average condition, and cannot be supposed to be people in particularly bad health. JCA also locates the cells of the cross-tabulation of the three variables on the same set of axes as the category labels (marked with a cross), thus enabling us to locate each cell in relation to the scale generated by the location of the category labels.

We treat the first dimension of the JCA plot as the value of this scale, ordinally locating the category labels, and therefore the cells, in relation to each other, and we may thus assign a scale value to each cell. Of the 150 possible combinations (6 categories of SRH $\times$ 5 categories each of Disability and Bedridden) there were 102 actual cells, and these were assigned raw scores ranging from -1.231 (no reported health problems) to 1.842 (extremely poor health).

For each cell, composed of 3 to 417,300 individuals, we computed the probability of dying during the year 2002. Figure 10.2 plots these probabilities against the scale value, with points sized relative to the square root of the number of people in the cell. The relationship between the two is clearly monotonic, but curvilinear. The line gives the binomial regression of the proportion dying against the exponential of the scale. There is, as can be seen, a good fit (pseudo-$R^2 = 0.793$) between the scale value and the proportion dying, thus giving *prime facie* validity to this index. Finally, we exponentiated the scale (for linearity) and, for ease of interpretation, we rescaled to create a Disability Index with values from 0 (no disability) to 100 (severe disability). This scale has a median of 13.0 and a mean of 21.8, indicating a skewed distribution with a heavy concentration of individuals without disability. It is to be noted that this index of disability was defined *without* reference to the proportion dying by level of the scale, and these proportions were used only for validation and for a monotonic, and hence order maintaining, transformation of the scale.

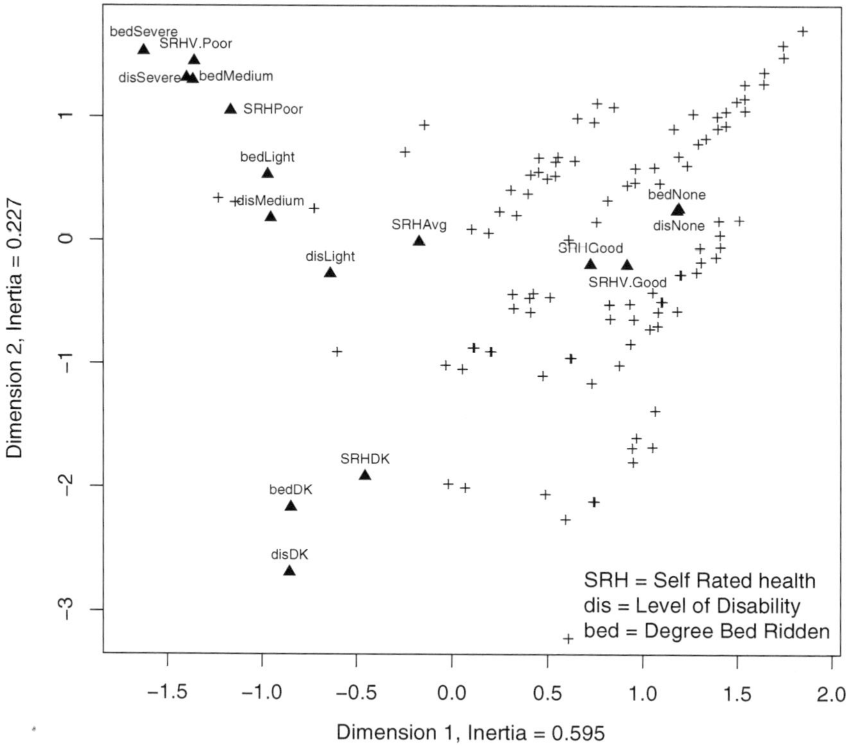

SRH (Self Rated Health): V.Good; Good; Average; Poor; V.Poor; DK (no response)

dis (Disability): Severe; Moderate; Light; None; DK (no response)

bed (Bedridden): Severe; Moderate; Light; None; DK (no response)

Axes scaled relative to inertia

+ indicate response cells

Fig. 10.1 Multiple correspondence analysis of health variables

10.4 Results

The data set outlined above was linked to the outcome variable: survival status at the end of the calendar year 2002, and our analysis focuses on the probability of dying during that year. We commence by considering how sex, age, education and living arrangements observed on 1st January 2002 influence the probability of dying during the year 2002, and then we will consider multivariate models predicting the probability of dying during the year, including the health indicator.

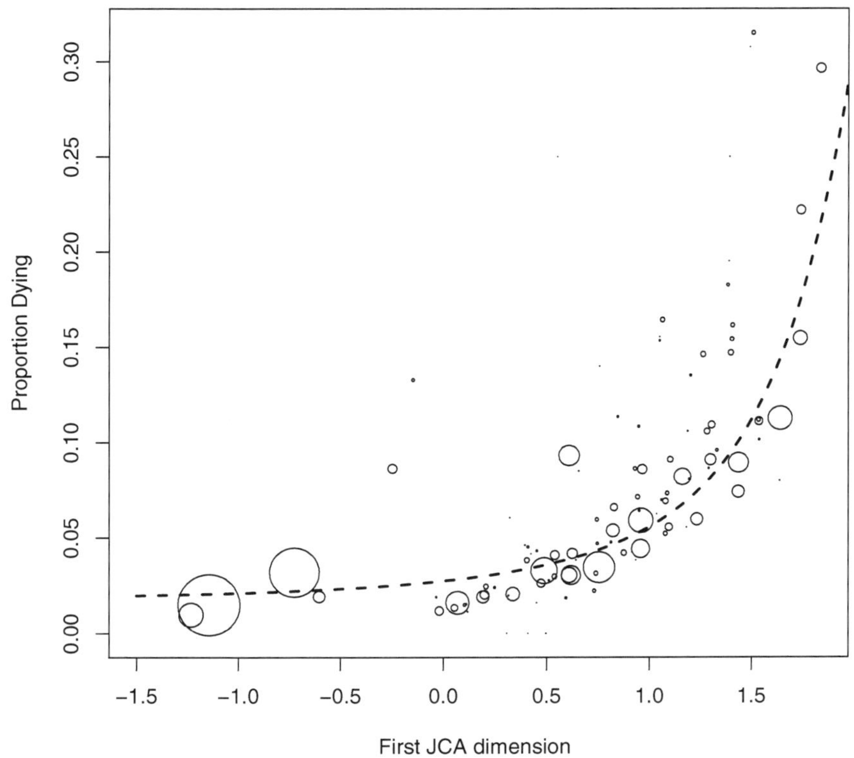

Notes: Point sizes relative to square root of group size
— = Binomial regression fit, proportion dying by index

Fig. 10.2 Proportion died by first JCA dimension

10.4.1 Age, Sex, Living Arrangement and Education

The proportion dying during 2002 increased from 18/1,000 for men aged 65 at the beginning of the year to 509/1,000 for men aged over 100, and from 9/1,000 to 375/1,000 for women. The logit probability of dying, by age, followed a linear increase. At all ages men maintained mortality rates considerably higher than those of women (Fig. 10.3). More than two-thirds of the population (67.4 %) were living with others in private households; over a quarter (28.5 %) were living alone, and the remaining 4 % were classified in the population register as living in institutions (collective non-private households). As shown in Fig. 10.3 and the Appendix, the mortality risk for both men and for women was higher among those living in institutions than among those living independently, in particular at younger ages. At the oldest ages, over age 90, the mortality risks converge and it is those living alone who are at the highest risk. In similar fashion, the relative risk of dying for those with higher education, controlling for age, is about 75 % the risk of those with lower education (details not shown).

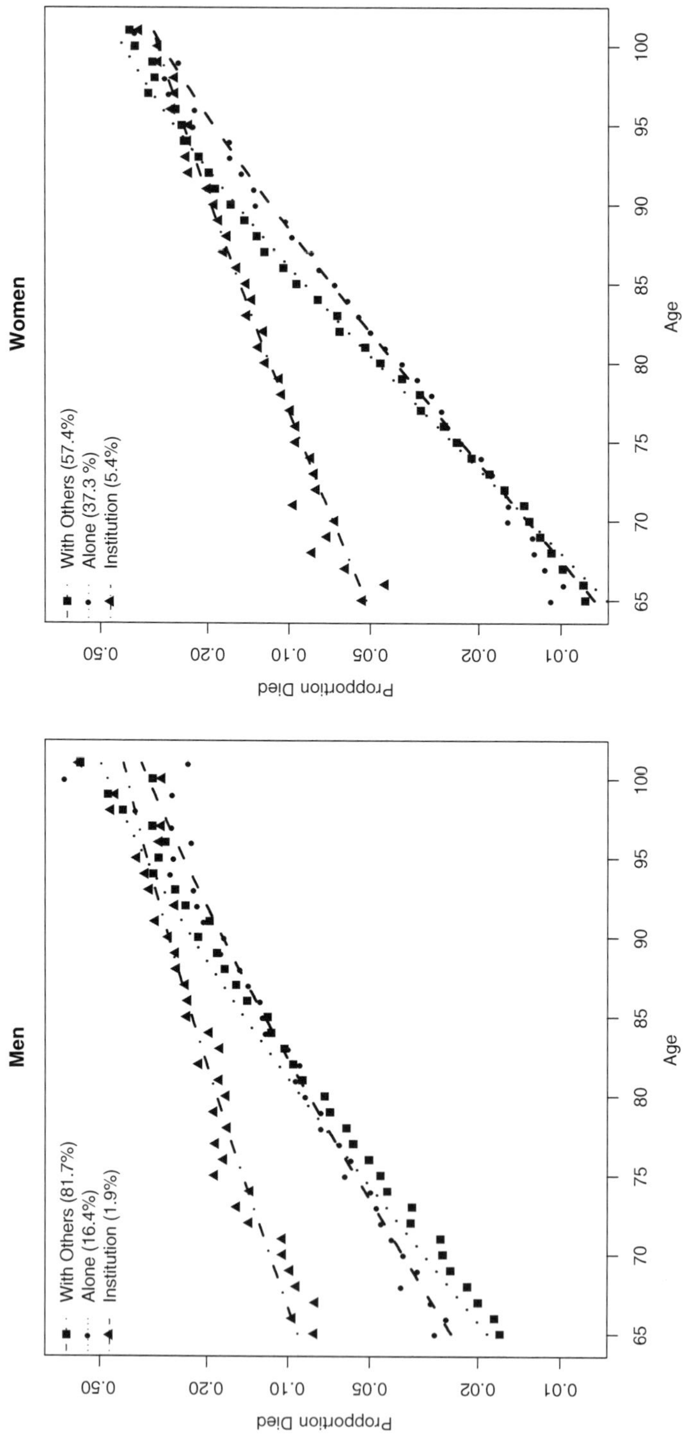

Fig. 10.3 Mortality risk during the year 2002 by sex, age and living arrangement

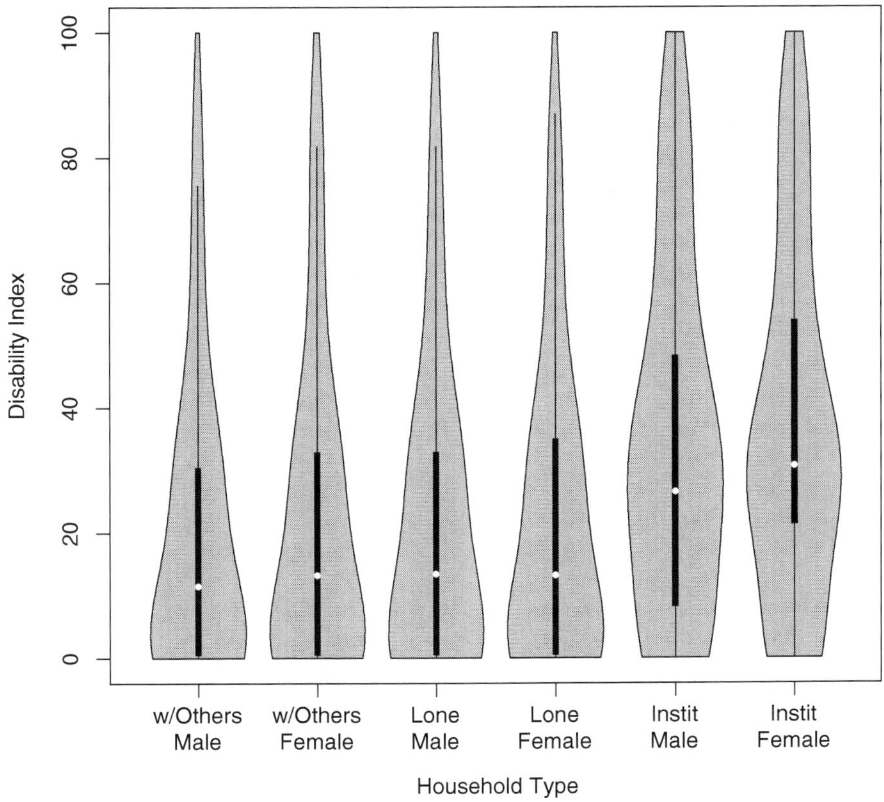

Fig. 10.4 Violin plot of health index by sex and living arrangements

10.4.2 Inter-Correlations

Given the above estimates of mortality risks, there must certainly be close correlations between the various independent variables. Women survive longer than men, and the over-representation of women increases with age. Similarly, those living in institutions will have been selected on the basis of health, amongst other considerations, so that any attempt to identify the effect of one of these variables must take into account, and control for, the effects of other variables. To see the inter-correlations between these variables, Fig. 10.4 presents a violin plot (Hintze and Nelson 1998; Adler 2005) of the disability index by sex and living arrangements. This is an extension of the standard boxplot (Tukey 1997), with the width of the "violin" reflecting the relative frequency of cases at the different levels of the dependent variable in each group. The distribution of the disability measure is similar in the two independent living arrangements, with a heavy concentration at the low (healthy) end and very few people at the high disability end of the spectrum. Men living with others are the healthiest and have the lowest median level of disability (11.5), while women living with others have a slightly higher median level (13.0), the same as that for men and

Table 10.1 Direct effects of sex, living arrangements, age, education and disability on mortality: binomial (logistic) regression for probability of dying during 2002

Variable	e^b (Relative risk)	z-value	CI (99.9 %, one tailed)
Intercept	0.0105	− 417	< 0.109
Sex (Male)	1		
Sex (Female)	0.493	− 83.0	< 0.508
Living with others	1		
Living alone	1.047	4.85	> 1.013
Institutionalised	1.892	46.6	> 1.804
Age (65 = base)	1.101	170	> 1.099
Education (Low)	1		
Education (High)	0.911	− 11.3	< 0.938
Disability	1.022	166	> 1.022
Null deviance = 115,531	Null df = 24,303	df gain = 6	
Model deviance = 31,443	Model df = 24,297	Deviance gain = 84,088	
Pseudo-R^2 = 0.728			

Base age = 65
For intercept, reported value is inverse logit of coefficient

women living alone. Those living in institutions present a very different pattern. The median level of disability is intermediate (26.0 for men, 30.1 for women), reflecting the presence of people in extremely poor health as well as a relatively large number of people in good health. However, although those in institutions have, on the average, a greater degree of disability, the main difference between those in independent and institutional living arrangements is in the spread of the health conditions. The institutionalised population shows a far more rectangular distribution, which includes all health conditions, whereas for those living alone or with others the modal condition is one of good health, and it is rare for them to be in very poor health.

10.4.3 Modelling Mortality

Table 10.1 presents the main effects binomial regression model of the probability of dying during 2002, as a function of age, sex, education, disability and living arrangements. As we have a clear directional hypothesis concerning the effect of each variable, we present one-tailed confidence intervals for the exponentiated coefficients, all of which are significant at $p < 0.001$. The underlying risk, for men aged 65, in good health, with low education and living with others, is 0.0105 (10.5/1,000). The risk is about a half this value for women, is about 5 % higher for those living alone, about 10 % lower for those with a higher level of education, and is about double for those living in institutions. Judging by the probability (z) values, however, the main effects are undoubtedly those of age and health. Mortality increases by about 10 % for each year of age, and increases by about 2.2 % for each unit increase in the disability index. Our first conclusion, then, is that institutionalisation and ill-health operate independently to increase the probability of dying, with institutionalisation doubling the mortality risk, and ill health (100 on the disability index) increasing the risk by a factor of almost 12 (0.976^{-101}) relative to best health (0 on the disability index).

Table 10.2 presents a model with interactions, nesting age, education and health within sex and living arrangements. The coefficients are identical to those obtained from six separate regressions, one for each combination of sex and living arrangements, but enabling statistical comparison between the columns. Intercepts refer to men or women, living with others, alone or in institutions, at age 65, with low education and at the lowest level of disability (best health).

1. The baseline values indicate a clear advantage for men and for women living with others over those living alone, and an even greater disadvantage for those living in institutions. For women living independently the mortality risk is less than half that for men in a similar situation, though their advantage when living in institutions is considerably less.
2. The effects of age (at disability index = 0) are greater for women than for men, and greater for those living independently and with others. Age has a smaller effect when the baseline risk is high so that at higher ages the differences between living arrangements effectively disappear.
3. As health declines the mortality risk increases at a similar rate for men as for women. As with age, the risk increases faster the lower the baseline condition, again partially offsetting the advantages noted above.
4. Those with higher education have a lower mortality risk, under all circumstances, than those with low education, and for men this advantage may tend to increase as we move from living with others through living alone to institutionalised, but note the overlap in the confidence intervals. For women there is no such trend, and all the confidence intervals overlap.

To bring out the interaction between age, disability and living arrangements, Fig. 10.5 presents the predicted probability of dying as disability increases, at ages 65, 80 and 95. At all ages, mortality is lowest amongst those living with others at low levels of disability, but the increase by disability level is greater for this group so that at high levels of disability the mortality risk is slightly lower for those living by themselves. Those living in nursing homes have a consistently higher mortality risk when disability is low, but this relative disadvantage disappears at higher levels of disability, especially at older ages. At age 65 there remains a considerable institutional disadvantage, even at high levels of disability. At age 80 the disadvantage remains, but it is considerably reduced. At age 95, by contrast, there appears to be no institutional disadvantage for those with high levels of disability. These results are the same for men as for women, though women do maintain a consistently lower level of mortality than men, at all ages, living conditions and levels of disability.

10.4.4 Partition Tree Analysis

The regression analysis above explores the contribution of each of the included variables to explaining the outcome variable (mortality) by positing a particular form

Table 10.2 Age and health nested within sex and living arrangements: binomial (logistic) regression for probability of dying during 2002

Variable	Men			Women		
	Living w/others	Living alone	Institutionalised	Living w/others	Living alone	Institutionalised
Intercept	0.00892	0.0170	0.0599	0.00409	0.00504	0.0342
	(0.00844, 0.00944)	(0.0153, 0.0188)	(0.0478, 0.0745)	(0.00381, 0.00440)	(0.00461, 0.00550)	(0.0293, 0.0397)
Age	1.0994	1.0834	1.0564	1.117	1.111	1.0612
	(1.0958, 1.1031)	(1.0776, 1.0893)	(1.0460, 1.0670)	(1.113, 1.121)	(1.107, 1.116)	(1.0547, 1.0678)
Health	1.0261	1.0187	1.0134	1.0241	1.0189	1.012
	(1.0254, 1.0269)	(1.0172, 1.0201)	(1.0109, 1.0160)	(1.0231, 1.0250)	(1.0179, 1.0199)	(1.0106, 1.0134)
Education	0.953	0.878	0.825	0.897	0.944	0.883
	(0.911, 0.996)	(0.808, 0.954)	(0.703, 0.966)	(0.845, 0.951)	(0.886, 1.004)	(0.806, 0.967)
Deviance	Null	1,808,209	Df	24,304	Pseudo-R^2	0.519
	Age × sex model	60,968		24,300		
	Model	29,339		24,280		
	Gain	*31,629*		*20*		

Values are exponentiated coefficients (inverse logit in Intercept row)
(Values in parentheses are 99.9 % confidence intervals)
Age × sex model is a baseline model of age nested in sex with no living arrangement, disability or education components
Pseudo-R^2 is the reduction in Deviance in the final model, relative to the baseline age × sex model

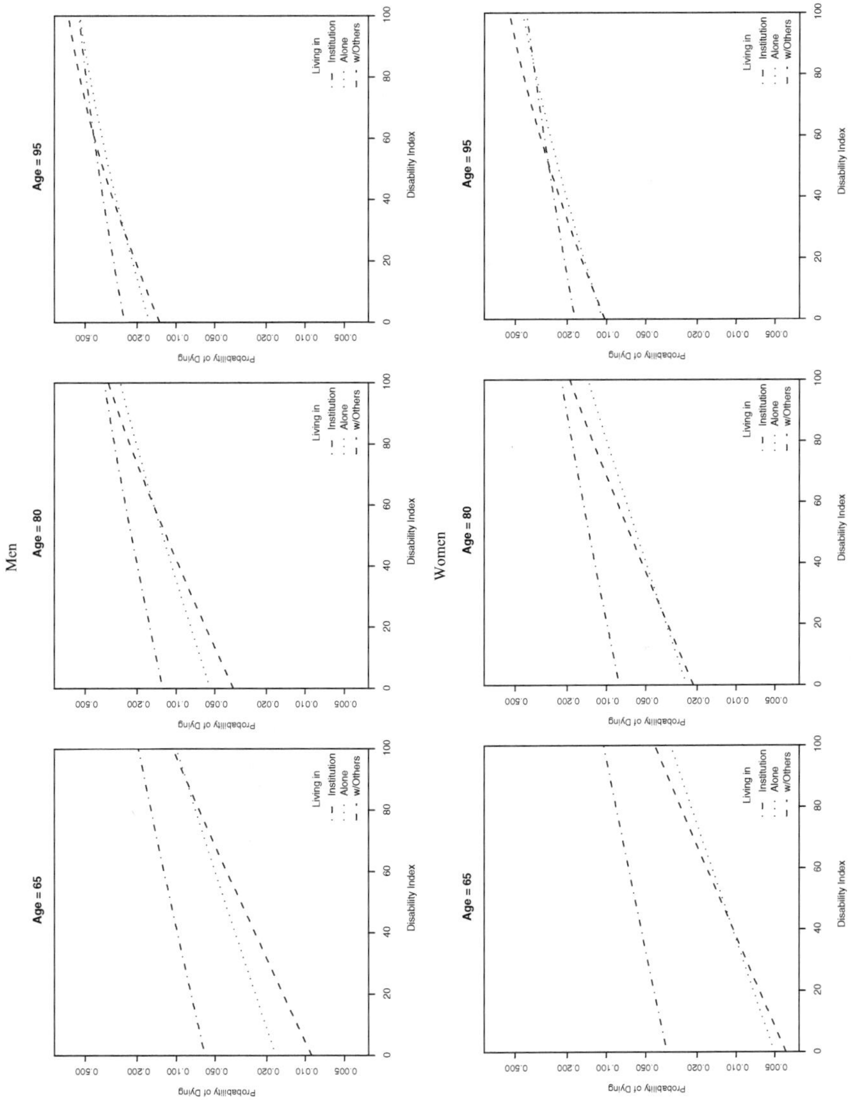

Fig. 10.5 Predicted mortality probabilities, by sex, living arrangements and level of disability, at selected ages

of this relationship (linear logistic), estimating the strength of this relationship (the coefficient) and testing for the statistical significance of each variable's contribution. An alternative approach, proposed by Breiman et al. (1984) and implemented by Therneau and Atkinson (2011), is to partition the data into subsets so as to maximize the differences between them, in terms of the mortality risk, and minimize differences within each subset. At each stage the data are divided according to the breakpoint of the variable that best partitions the data, that is, the one that maximally reduces the unexplained variation in the dependent variable. Each subset is in turn partitioned, and so on until an optimal division of the cases is reached. However, while the purpose of these partitions is variance reduction, this procedure is a data-mining procedure based on the evaluation of all possible partitions, and thus is not amenable to statistical induction (Strobl et al. 2009).

Figure 10.6a presents the partition tree of the probability of dying, by age, education, health, living arrangements and sex. The heights of the branches are proportional to the variance reduction entailed. The partition rule is indicated at each node, cases which match the rule (True) are in branches to the left of the node (lower mortality), those which do not (False) are to the right (higher mortality). The first node partitions by age, distinguishing between the lower risk of the younger population, aged 83 or younger, and the higher risk of the older population. The second partition is by disability, for both age groups, distinguishing between the lower risk of those with a score of less than 38.66 and the higher risk of those with a score of 38.66 and above. The longer length of the second partition arms on the left hand side indicates that for the younger population health has a greater effect on the mortality risk than it does for the older population. The third level of partitions is also in terms of age and health: for both the younger and the older population the risk is subdivided by age for those who are healthy. For the disabled there is a distinction between the mildly disabled and the very disabled. Living arrangements only become important at level 4, for those aged 76.5–89.5, in which group mortality is lower for those living independently than for those in institutions. At levels 5 and 6 there are minor partitions by age and sex (women < men). Finally, for each subset we see the actual probability of dying: thus for those aged 76 and under, with low disability, 0.015 (15/1,000) of the population died during the year. By contrast, amongst those aged 84 and over and at high disability (89.94 and above) 0.354 (354/1,000) died during the year.

The overall pattern is thus very clear, and closely matches that presented in the regression analysis: the major factors affecting the mortality risk are age and health, followed by living arrangements, with independent living being better than institutionalisation, in particular at low levels of disability and below the extremely old ages. Figure 10.6b presents group sizes and risks for the different leaves of the analysis. The groups are in the same order as the leaves of the partition tree, and are defined by the partition decisions. From this we can see there are three major mortality clusters: the relatively young and healthy, internally distinguished by age, living arrangements and sex; the relatively young but not so healthy, internally distinguished by disability, sex and age; and the older population, distinguished by disability, age and sex.

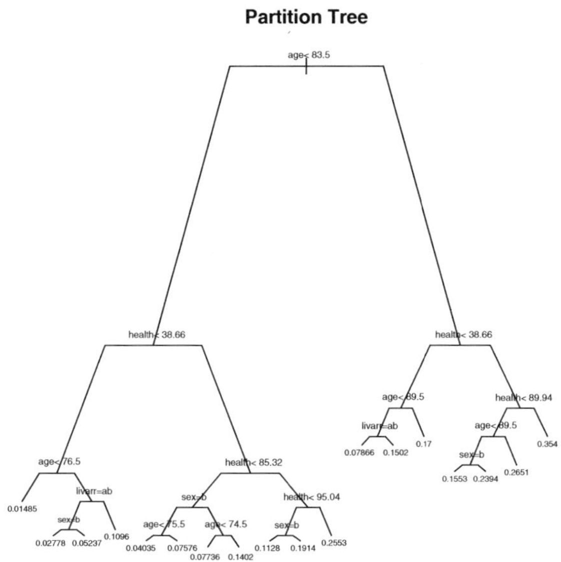

a

Notes: Nodes indicate partition rule, cases matching rule on the left(lower mortality), those not matching rule on . the right (higher mortality
Values under leaves are mortality probabilities
Disab = Disability index (low = good health)
Living Arrangements: a = with others, b = Alone, c = Institution
Sex: a = Male, b = Female

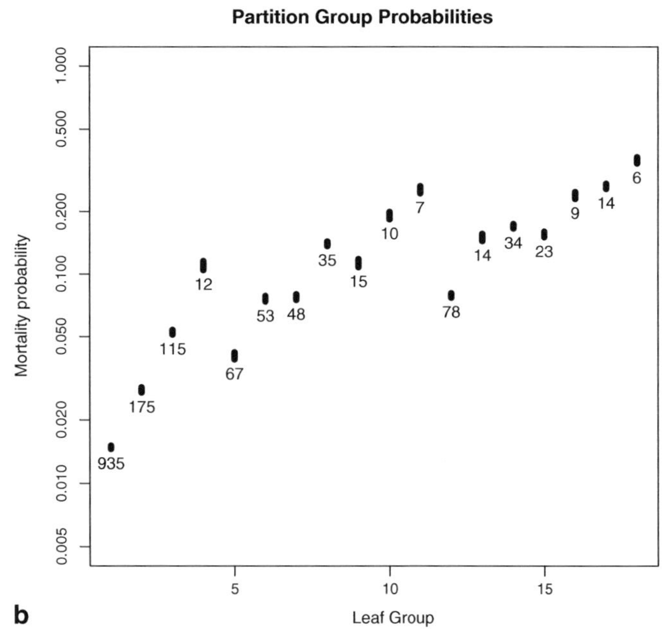

b

Notes: Points with confidence intervals,
numerical values are group sizes, in thousands
Groups are ordered by order in tree, left

Fig. 10.6 Partition tree of mortality risk, by age, disability, sex and living conditions

10.5 Discussion

In the population under study, for people aged 65 years and over, the two most important predictors of mortality are age and health status, with approximately equal contribution to the fit of the general model. These two variables are strongly correlated even though a certain mortality risk does exist even for those who are still relatively young and in apparently good health. Women experience half the risk of dying compared to men (0.493).

Our aim in this analysis was to consider the effects of living arrangements on this risk: to what extent does the probability of dying vary by living arrangement, controlling for the effects of sex, age, education and health? Even when controlling for these variables, living arrangements maintain some explanatory power, showing a slightly higher risk of dying for those living alone (5 % higher than those living with others), and almost double the risk for those living in institutions (1.892). These results indicate that there is a clear relative disadvantage to living in an institution, in particular for the younger population (below age 90) and for those who are not seriously disabled. We thus conclude that previously reported enhanced mortality risks for those living in institutions cannot be explained only in compositional terms and in particular, the greater mortality of the institutionalised population cannot be explained strictly in terms of this population's older age or greater level of disability.

However, as with all administrative prospective studies, this one too is limited by having one-time information on health status and living arrangements, as recorded at the census, with no follow-up information on deterioration of health or subsequent institutionalisation. In particular, we have not included information on widowhood, a major event that changes living arrangements and may lead to an augmented risk of death (Lusyne et al. 2001; Manor and Eisenbach 2003). However, given that transitions both in health and in living arrangements tend to be unidirectional, from good to poor health and from independent to institutional living, we suggest that these shortcomings will, if anything, lead to an underestimation of the effects we have been looking at in this study. Focussing on a relatively short time period of 1 year does limit the study, as it reduces the actual number of deaths, but this is offset by the size of the population analysed and it has the advantage that it reduces to a minimum the possibility of large scale changes in health and living arrangements.

Another shortcoming of this study is the very limited consideration of socio-economic variables. The data we have on the level of education is a dichotomous division between those who stopped their education early, and those who continued to higher levels of education. From the information we have it is clear that mortality is lower among the higher educated, but this does not appear to be directly related to living conditions or ill health, though it is possible that over a lifetime both disability and independent living may be conditioned on the level of education. We should also bear in mind that neither independent, nor institutional, living arrangements are homogeneous, and their quality will improve as material resources increase. However, we have no reliable information on such resources, including various insurance arrangements that pensioners may have, and level of education must stand as a very crude proxy for these.

Nevertheless these first results have important implications for the direction of policy for the elderly. Our results indicate very clearly that, except at very old ages, it is preferable for people to remain at home—either living with others or living alone—where a network of support services could enable them to maintain as normal a life as possible in their natural surroundings. These support services would include the provision of hot meals, home cleaning and personal help, an emergency help line and nursing and physician services for cases in need. We note (Figs. 10.3 and 10.5) that even at the highest ages, and in conditions of worst health, that is, even under conditions where the institutions may be expected to offer the greatest advantage for survival, there is little *advantage* to living in institutions, though we may assume that the institutionalised are those with least access to family and other communally based services.

Definitive answers concerning the advantages and disadvantages of living in institutions will await a far more thorough investigation, with a long term follow up on health and disability status as it evolves over time and over changes in living arrangements. On the basis of the data available for this study, there does clearly appear to be *prima facie* evidence that living independently, either alone or with other adults, significantly increases survival chances, in particular amongst all but the oldest-old, for whom we may say that living independently does not impair the chances of survival.

Acknowledgements The article has benefited from the support of research theme SF0130018s11 by the Estonian Ministry of Education and Science and ETF grants no. 8325 and 8904

10.6 Appendix: Cell Sizes and Mortality Risks, Sex by Age by Education by Living Arrangements

Sex	Age	Education	Living arrangements	Survived	Died	Rate/1,000
Men	65–84	Low	w/others	242,679	11,511	45.3
Men	65–84	Low	Alone	48,841	3,212	61.7
Men	65–84	Low	Instit	4,240	887	173.0
Men	65–84	High	w/others	276,888	9,944	34.7
Men	65–84	High	Alone	46,684	2,333	47.6
Men	65–84	High	Instit	2,640	463	149.2
Men	85+	Low	w/others	8,956	2,129	192.1
Men	85+	Low	Alone	5,780	1,210	173.1
Men	85+	Low	Instit	2,164	910	296.0
Men	85+	High	w/others	6,592	1,310	165.8
Men	85+	High	Alone	3,542	654	155.9
Men	85+	High	Instit	1,126	349	236.6
Women	65–84	Low	w/others	271,614	7,134	25.6
Women	65–84	Low	Alone	168,603	5,178	29.8
Women	65–84	Low	Instit	14,975	2,017	118.7
Women	65–84	High	w/others	241,566	4,185	17.0
Women	65–84	High	Alone	137,668	3,218	22.8
Women	65–84	High	Instit	7,653	864	101.4
Women	85+	Low	w/others	16,312	3,234	165.5
Women	85+	Low	Alone	25,864	3,385	115.7
Women	85+	Low	Instit	15,099	3,962	207.9
Women	85+	High	w/others	7,223	1,152	137.6
Women	85+	High	Alone	13,311	1,523	102.7
Women	85+	High	Instit	6,005	1,307	178.7

References

Adler, D. (2005). *Vioplot: Violin plot. R package version 0.2.* http://wsopuppenkiste.wiso.uni-goettingen.de/~dadler. Accessed 9 Feb 2011.

Börsch-Supan, A., Mcfadden, D., & Schnabel, R. (1996). Living arrangements, health and wealth effects. In D. Wise (Ed.), *Advances in the economics of aging* (pp. 193–218). Chicago: University of Chicago Press.

Breiman, L., Friedman, J. H., Olschen, C. J., & Stone, R. A. (1984). *Classification and regression trees*. Monterey: Wadsworth.

Breuer, B., Wallenstein, S., Feinberg, C., Camargo, M.-J. F., & Libow, L. S. (1998). Assessing life expectancies of older nursing home residents. *Journal of the American Geriatrics Society, 46*(8), 954–962.

Cohen-Mansfield, J., Marx, M. S., Lipson, S., & Werner, P. (1999). Predictors of mortality in nursing home residents. *Journal of Clinical Epidemiology, 52*(4), 273–280.

Dale, M. C., Burns, A., Panter, L., & Morris, J. (2001). Factors affecting survival of elderly nursing home residents. *International Journal of Geriatric Psychiatry, 16*(1), 70–76.

Davis, M. A., Moritz, D. J., Neuhaus, J. M., Barclay, J. D., & Gee, L. (1997). Living arrangements, changes in living arrangements and survival among community dwelling older adults. *American Journal of Public Health, 87*, 371–377.

Flacker, J. M., & Kiely, D. K. (2003). Mortality-related factors and 1-year survival in nursing home residents. *Journal of the American Geriatrics Society, 51*(2), 213–221.

Grennacre, M., & Blasius, J. (2006). *Multiple correspondence analysis and related methods* (Statistics in the Social and Behavioral Sciences). NY: Chapman & Hall.

Grundy, E. (2010). Household transitions and subsequent mortality among older people in England and Wales: Trends over three decades. *Journal of Epidemiology & Community Health, 65,* 353–359.

Hintze, J. L., & Nelson, R. D. (1998). Violin plots: A box plot-density trace synergism. *The American Statistician, 52*(2), 181–184.

Hjaltadattir, I., Halberg, I. R., Ekwall, A. K., & Nyberg, P. (2011). Predicting mortality of residents at admission to nursing home: A longitudinal cohort study. *BMC Health Services Research*, 11 (Article number 86, pages 1–11.).

Idler, E. L., & Benyamini, Y. (1997). Self-rated health and mortality: A review of twenty-seven community studies. *Health and Social Behavior, 38*(1):21–37.

Kiely, D. K., & Flacker, J. M. (2002). Common and gender specific factors associated with one-year mortality in nursing home residents. *Journal of the American Medical Directors Association, 3*(5), 302–309.

Klein, T. (1996). Determinants of institutionalization in old age. In R. Eisen & F. A. Sloan (Eds.), *Long-term care: Economic issues and policy solutions* (pp. 103–112). Boston: Kluwer Academic Publishers.

Koskinen, S., Joutsenniemi, K., Martelin, T., & Martikainen, P. (2007). Mortality differences according to living arrangements. *International Journal of Epidemiology, 36*(6), 1255–1264.

Lillard, L. A., & Panis, C. W. A. (1996). Marital status and mortality: The role of health. *Demography, 33*(3), 313–327.

Lusyne, P., Page, H., & Lievens, J. (2001). Mortality following conjugal bereavement, Belgium 1991–96: The unexpected effect of education. *Population Studies, 55*(3), 281–289.

Manor, O., & Eisenbach, Z. (2003). Mortality after spousal loss: Are there socio-demographic differences? *Social Science and Medicine, 56*(2), 405–413.

Manzoli, L., Villari, P., Pirone, G. M., & Boccia, A. (2007). Marital status and mortality in the elderly: A systematic review and meta-analysis. *Social Science and Medecine, 64,* 77–94.

Molloy, G. J., Stamatakis, E., Randall, G., & Hamer, M. (2009). Marital status, gender and cardiovascular mortality: Behavioural, psychological distress and metabolic explanations. *Social Science & Medicine, 69*(2), 223–228.

Murphy, M. (1995). Assessing the link between household and family living arrangements and health. In G. Wunsch & A. Hancioglu (Eds.), *Morbidity and mortality data: Problems of comparability*. Proceedings of the European Association for Population Studies and the Hacettepe Institute of Population Studies Workshop, Ürgüp, Turkey, 18–20 October 1995.

Nenadic, O. & Greenacre, M. (2007) Correspondence Analysis in R, with two- and three-dimensional graphics: The ca package. *Journal of Statistical Software* 20(3):1–13.

Nihtila, E., & Martikainen, P. (2008). Why older people living with a spouse are less likely to be institutionalized: The role of socio-economic factors and health characteristics. *Scandinavian Journal of Public Health, 36*(1), 35–43.

Raines, J. E., & Wight, J. (2002). The mortality experience of people admitted to nursing homes. *Journal of Public Health Medecine, 24*(3), 184–199.

Rendall, M. S., Weden, M. M., Favreault, M. M., & Waldron, H. (2011). The protective effect of marriage for survival: A review and update. *Demography, 48*(2), 481–506.

Strobl, C., Malley, J., & Tutz, G. (2009). An introduction to recursive partitioning: Rationale, application, and characteristics of classification and regression trees, bagging, and random forests. *Psychological Methods, 14*(4), 323–348.

Therneau, T. M., & Atkinson, B. (2011). Rpart: Recursive Partitioning. R package version 3.1–49. R port by Brian Ripley. http://CRAN.R-project.org/package=rpart. Accessed 8 May 2011.

Tukey, J. W. (1997). *Exploratory data analysis*. Reading: Addison.

Zunzunegui, M. V., Beland, F., & Otero, A. (2001). Support from children, living arrangements, self-rated health and depressive symptoms of older people in Spain. *International Journal of Epidemiology, 30,* 1090–1099.

Chapter 11
Life Expectancy Differences in Cuba: Are Females Losing Their Advantage Over Males?

Madelín Gómez León and Esther María León Díaz

Abstract Cuba is a developing country at an advanced stage of ageing, with a population growth rate around zero since 2006. The Cuban population shows a high life expectancy (77 years in 2007) and low infant mortality (below 5 per thousand births). Nonetheless, it has maintained a small sex gap (around 4 years) in life expectancy at birth over the last century. This paper examines the evolution of life expectancy at birth, and trends in specific causes of death. The differentials in life expectancy by sex and across time are examined in order to shed light on the narrower sex gap that Cuba shows compared to other countries. Data on population and specific death rates published by the National Statistics and Information Office and Public Health Ministry of Cuba are used. We decompose the mortality rates to determine the impact of age- and cause- specific death rates on the sex differential at three points in time; and on the life expectancy of each sex, from 1987 to 1995, and 1995 to 2007. Our results show that Cuba presents a mix of mortality patterns, with most of the deaths attributable to chronic or degenerative diseases. However, there is also a sizeable proportion of avoidable deaths such as those due to external causes, respiratory diseases or diabetes. Differences between periods are clear. During the economic crisis, male survivorship was seriously constrained while females barely kept their advantage of half of a year; but, in the recovery period, males recovered faster than females.

Keywords Life expectancy · Causes of death · Decomposition method · Cuba

M. Gómez León (✉)
Centre d'Estudis Demogràfics, Edifici E2, Campus de la Universitat Autònoma de Barcelona, 08193 Bellaterra (Barcelona), Spain
e-mail: mgomez@ced.uab.es

E. M. León Díaz
Retired Researcher, Centro de Estudios de Población y Desarrollo, Oficina Nacional de Estadísticas e Información, Havana, Cuba
e-mail: techy.emld@gmail.com

J. Anson, M. Luy (eds.), *Mortality in an International Perspective*, European Studies of Population 18, DOI 10.1007/978-3-319-03029-6_11,

11.1 Introduction

During the last century, most of the developed world experienced a steady increase in life expectancy at birth. From the beginning of the Twentieth century until the sixties, when it was overtaken by Sweden, the record life expectancy was held by the Netherlands. Since the end of the seventies Japan has been in the lead, with a life expectancy reaching 83 years in 2009 (Human Mortality Database: www.mortality.org). This substantial increase in longevity has been accompanied by a widening of the gap in life expectancy between males and females: females have consistently had a life expectancy advantage of between 3 and 8 years.

These two phenomena have been extensively studied. The first one, the increase in life expectancy at birth, depends directly on mortality patterns. The rise of this indicator was due to the mortality decline, firstly for age group 1–4, and then an overall decline in infant mortality. As life expectancy at birth is a measure of mortality averaged over all ages, once infant mortality reaches very low levels, the gains in life expectancy depend more on mortality rates at older ages (Christensen et al. 2009). Moreover, whenever there is an abrupt increase or decrease in mortality, we need to turn to an analysis of its components, that is, mortality at various ages, in order to understand the changes (Bongaarts and Feeney 2002; Oeppen and Vaupel 2002).

Epidemiological Transition Theory elaborates upon the changes in mortality patterns, and affirms that mortality shows several stages in its evolution: from an early stage characterized by infections and parasitic diseases it has evolved into one where chronic and degenerative conditions predominate (Omran 1971). Other studies (Nathanson 1984; Rogers and Hackenbert 1987) have emphasized that risk behaviour and lifestyle are linked to death in contemporary high income countries. This implies a mix of mortality patterns from different stages, as has also been argued in the convergence-divergence approach on countries' life expectancies (Meslé and Vallin 2004).

The second phenomenon, the increase of the sex differential in life expectancy at birth, has been observed all over the world, although developed countries account for its highest growth. Nevertheless, in some of these countries such as Sweden, Spain and France, the sex gap stagnated or even declined at the end of the century. Trovato (2005) has shown that the decline in the sex gap is due to convergence in the main causes of death. There have been fewer men's deaths due to accidents, violence, lung cancer and suicide, with a consequent improvement in male's survival. Moreover, this narrowing of the sex gap has also been associated with changes in life style, education and, in general, with the convergence of attitudes and behaviours of both sexes (Annandale and Hunt 2000).

Although this pattern of increasing life expectancy was first observed in the developed world, it has extended to other, less developed countries. According to United Nations Prospect 2007, developed regions had 76.5 years of life expectancy at birth in 2005–2010, while the less developed regions had 65.4 years (11 years less). Most developing countries follow this pattern but, nonetheless, there are some that are already catching up with the group of developed countries. For instance, Barbados, Brunei, Chile, Costa Rica, Cuba and Kuwait are developing countries with more than 77 years of life expectancy at birth in 2005–2010.

Cuban life expectancy increased rapidly until it reached 70 years in 1970. Subsequently, the improvement in life expectancy slowed down but has continued to rise, reaching 77 years in 2000 (30 years later), and 77.97 in the last period for which data is available (2005–2007). Hernández (1986) and Albizu-Campos (2002) have described this evolution as steady over time, but with two periods of slowdown: first during the first two decades of Twentieth century, and between 1985 and 1995.

The improvement in life expectancy over the Twentieth century has been linked to several factors. In particular, there has been a change in mortality patterns, from predominantly infectious diseases (higher for women), to non-infectious diseases, especially since the mid-twentieth century. It is noteworthy that, despite the high life expectancy at birth observed in Cuba, the difference between male and female life expectancies at birth has never exceeded 4 years (González and Ramos 1996).

The focus of our paper is on the changes in life expectancy at birth in Cuba, describing the mortality transformations that have shaped this indicator and the differences between males and females. Cuba's life expectancy stagnated at the end of the Twentieth century and beginning of the Twenty-First century, with growth being lowest during the nineties (which coincided with an economic crisis in Cuba after the fall of the Soviet Union). We analyse the changes in life expectancy in Cuba at three points in time (1987, 1995 and 2007) looking at the contribution of mortality patterns by age and sex to the sex differential in life expectancy at birth. We also look at trends for each sex through the period 1987–1995 and 1995–2007. In particular, we ask if the narrowing of the sex gap in this period was because males were doing better and catching up with females, or because females were doing worse.

We structure the contents of this article as follows: after describing the data and methods used in the analysis (Sect. 2), the evolution of life expectancy for several countries over the Twentieth century will be analysed in Sect. 3. Section 4 describes the main characteristics of Cuban population and mortality patterns during the three periods. We finish our analysis by decomposing the effect of age-specific causes of death over the sex differential in life expectancy at birth, looking at changes in time and also for each sex (Sect. 5). The final sections present the conclusions, references and annex (Sects. 6 to 8).

11.2 Data and Method

Data on population were acquired from the National Statistic and Information Office of Cuba (Demographic Yearbooks: 2006, 2008 and 2010). Deaths by age, sex, year of death and cause of death come from the Public Health Ministry of Cuba. Mortality data is on a yearly basis and correspond to years 1987, 1995 and 2007. Official Life Tables calculated by the National Statistic Office are used in this study, using those nearest to the years selected, which are: 1986–1987, 1994–1995 and 2005–2007. As we are working with official data, and did not have access to the primary databases, we could not use the corresponding yearly life tables that match the mortality rates. Moreover, for the trends in life expectancy and sex differentials in Cuba, we only have data grouped for 3 or 5 years, so the comparison with yearly data of other countries should be treated with caution.

During the time period covered, deaths were classified according to the International Classifications of Diseases (ICD), ICD-9 until year 2000 and ICD-10 from 2001 onwards. Changes in cause-of-death classification did not have any significant effect on the mortality trend of the relevant causes of death used in our research. Selected causes of death and corresponding ICD codes are given in Annex 1.

To understand the changes in life expectancy and the sex gap we need to look deeply into the mortality patterns and particularly into the contribution of the different causes of death over the life span of each sex. In order to do that, we will apply the decomposition method of Shkolnikov et al. (2001) to determine the impact of age and cause specific death rates on the difference in male and female life expectancy at three points in time, and for each sex at two periods in time.

The difference between two life expectancies may be expressed as:

$$e_x^2 - e_x^1 = \sum_{y=x}^{W} {}_n\varepsilon_y \tag{11.1}$$

where ε is the contribution to the difference between the life expectancies of population 2 and population 1 produced by the difference in mortality in age groups y to $y+n$. ε is obtained from:

$$\begin{aligned} {}_n\varepsilon_y = & \frac{1}{2l_x^1}\left[l_y^1\left(e_y^1 - e_y^2\right) - l_{y+n}^1\left(e_{y+n}^1 - e_{y+n}^2\right)\right] \\ & -\frac{1}{2l_x^2}\left[l_y^2\left(e_y^2 - e_y^1\right) - l_{y+n}^2\left(e_{y+n}^2 - e_{y+n}^1\right)\right] \end{aligned} \tag{11.2}$$

where x is the initial age group; y are exact ages; n is the length of the age interval; W the last age and l_x are the survivors at each age. Cause-specific mortality rates (j) are also decomposed and multiplied by equation [11.2], resulting in a matrix with the contribution of ages (rows) and causes of death (columns):

$${}_n\varepsilon_{y,j} = \frac{{}_nM_{y,j}^1 - {}_nM_{y,j}^2}{{}_nM_y^1 - {}_nM_y^2} \times {}_n\varepsilon_y \tag{11.3}$$

where ${}_nM_{y,j}$ is the central death rate in the population (1 or 2) for the age group y, y + n and the cause of death j; and ${}_nM_y$ is the central death rates for the total causes of death in the age group y, y + n.

The method allows us to divide up the difference between life expectancies. In our case, we are going to analyse differences between females and males for 1987, 1995 and 2007; and differences between 1987–1995 and 1995–2007 for each sex.

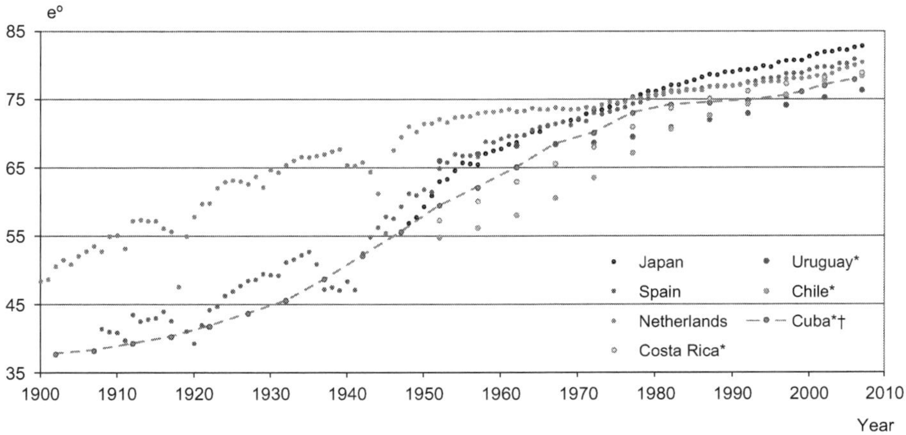

Fig. 11.1 Evolution of Life Expectancy at Birth (in Years) in selected countries. 1900–2008. (Sources: Human Mortality Database (HMD); Latin American and Caribbean Demographic Centre (CELADE); National Statistics Office (ONE), Cuba. *Five-year averages, † Three-year averages for the last 3 years)

11.3 Trends in Life Expectancy Over the Past Century

Trends in life expectancy during the twentieth century for specific countries are shown in Fig. 11.1. Although data for different countries do not always coincide in time the overall trends are clear. In the case of Japan, Spain and The Netherlands figures are expressed on a yearly basis, while for Costa Rica, Uruguay, Chile and Cuba they are in five-year intervals, with the exception of the last three years for Cuba that are in a three-year average.

As shown in Fig. 11.1, life expectancy at birth experienced the largest improvements during the first half of the twentieth century (with the exception of the World War periods, when it showed a strong drop). For instance, life expectancy in The Netherlands increased by 23 years, while in countries like Spain and Cuba the increase reached around 20 years. This progress was mainly due to scientific discoveries such as antibiotics, sulphas, etc., along with advances in the health and living conditions of the population. It enabled the control and eradication of many infectious and parasitic diseases, and increased infant and children's survival.

In the second half of the twentieth century, there was a slowdown in the increase of survival in many industrialized countries. Some countries experienced large improvements (around 20 years), catching up with those in the group with the highest levels, like Spain and even surpassing them, like Japan, which has held the record life expectancy at birth since 1972. Furthermore, some developing countries such as Chile, Costa Rica, Uruguay and Cuba had significant increases in this period. From the last part of the twentieth century until the present the indicators have been converging, so that the gap between the countries with the highest and lowest levels, which was almost 20 years in 1950, had been reduced to less than 10 years by 2008.

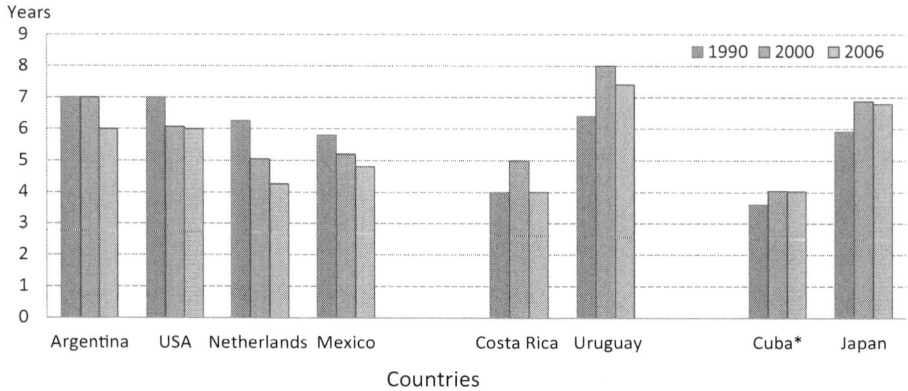

Fig. 11.2 Sex differential of life expectancy at birth for selected countries in 1990, 2000 and 2006. (Sources: Human Mortality Database (HMD); Latin American and Caribbean Demographic Centre (CELADE); National Statistics Office (ONE), Cuba. *Closest life table: 1986–1987, 1998–2000 and 2005–2007)

In the case of Cuba, the trend shows a continuous increase in life expectancy at birth, with the largest improvements between the 1930s and late seventies, when it was very close to that of the countries with the highest levels. However, during the eighties and nineties there was a slowdown in the pace of improvements, which did not recover until the beginning of the twenty-first century. It is this change in the trend of life expectancy that we address in the present paper. By analysing the evolution of mortality differences between and within sexes, we will address the issue of increases in life expectancy, as well as the observed decrease in the pace of improvements.

As life expectancy at birth is markedly different for each sex, we first look at them by analysing the sex differential of life expectancy for selected countries in 1990, 2000 and 2006. We grouped them according to three different behaviours of the sex gap: those that show a continuous decline; a second group where the gap fluctuates; and a third group where the gap first rises and then levels off (Fig. 11.2).

In the first group (formed by Argentina, USA, The Netherlands and Mexico) the gap ranges from 6 to 7 years in the first observation, and then declines between 4 and 6 years. The second group (Costa Rica and Uruguay) shows a rise and afterwards a drop. Note that although both are developing countries, the sex gap in life expectancy in Uruguay is almost double that in Costa Rica. The last group includes Japan and Cuba. Despite being at different levels, they experienced a similar development: an increment in the gap followed by a levelling off, at around 4 years in the case of Cuba and almost 7 years for Japan.

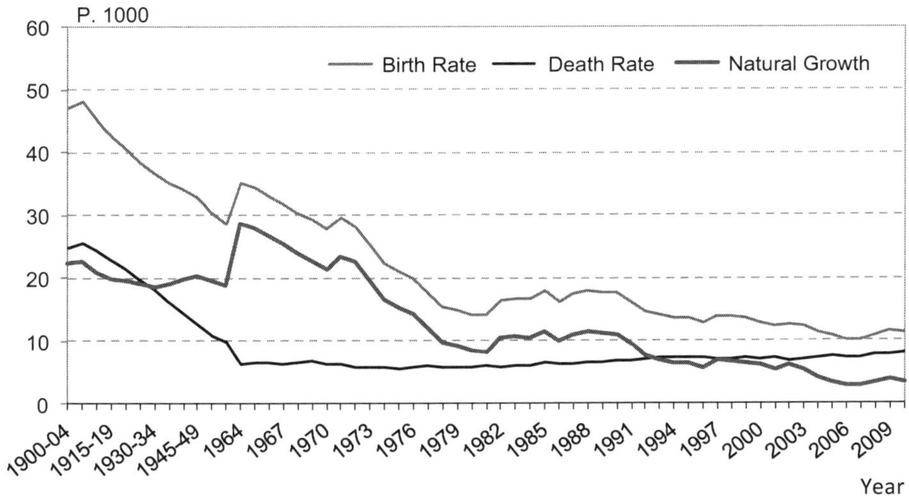

Fig. 11.3 Evolution of the growth rate and its components, Cuba 1900–2010 (per 1000 inhabitants). (Source: Cuban Demographic Yearbooks [2006, 2008 and 2010], Oficina Nacional de Estadísticas (2007, 2009, 2011))

11.4 The Case of Cuba

11.4.1 Population Trend

According to the classification of Latin-American countries presented by Chackiel (2004), Cuba has been in the Third Stage of the Demographic Transition since 1985–1990. Death rates have remained almost constant (varying within a narrow range of 5 to 7 per thousand), the population growth rate has started to decline and aging has become a major concern. In Fig. 11.3 we show the evolution of the natural growth rate and its components. The first four observations correspond to the initial 50 years of the century (only 5-year grouped data were available), so although there is a decline in the birth and death rates, it is not as steep as it seems due to this fact. Births increased during the sixties, corresponding to the baby boom but, by 1978, Cuban fertility fell below replacement level (less than 2.1 children per woman). This indicator has not recovered the replacement level, achieving the lowest levels in the nineties with a Total Fertility of 1.30, and then slightly increasing to 1.59 in 2008.

Regarding mortality, we observe that death rates declined until the beginning of the sixties, when they levelled off at very low levels (around 8 per thousand inhabitants). The mortality trend from 1902 (after the war and the establishment of the Republic of Cuba) starts to decline, especially due to improvements in health and economic and political conditions, but this did not reach the entire society (in particular not the lowest classes and rural areas). Different studies (Albizu-Campos 2003; Riverón and Azcuy 2001; UNICEF 1995) pointed out the impact of the Revolution in 1959, when health and education programmes were universalized in Cuba, spreading the

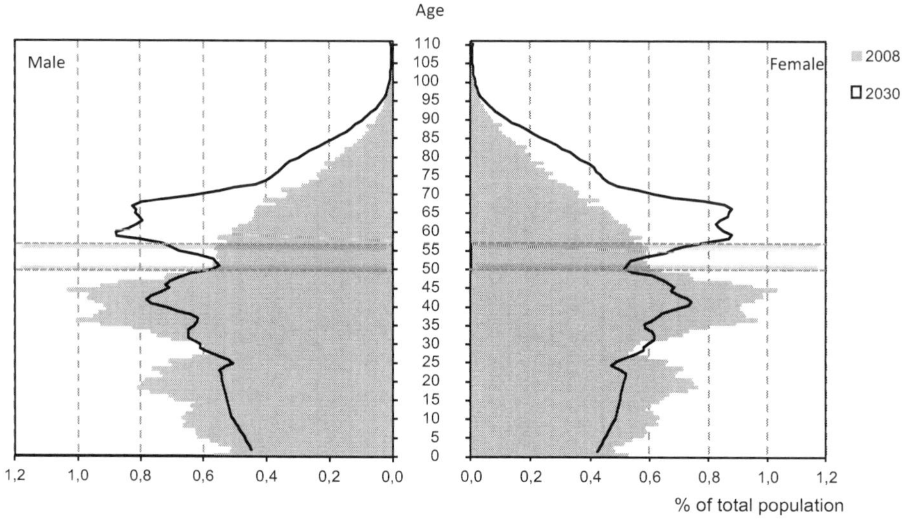

Fig. 11.4 Population pyramids for Cuba in 2008 and 2030* (Source: Data of population for 2008 comes from Oficina Nacional de Estadísticas (2009), Cuba. *Own projection of 2030 assuming fertility, mortality and migration constant based on 2008 official data; Total Fertility Rate (TFR): 1.59)

supply of health care to all areas (urban and rural) and without limitations, and thus increasing the health and living conditions of the population.

Since the last two decades of the twentieth century there has been a steady but slow increase in mortality, which is due to the population's age structure. As the Cuban population ages, and mortality becomes concentrated at older ages, it is expected that this trend will continue. The combination of mortality and fertility results in a declining rate of population growth, which depends markedly on what occurs with births and migration, but mortality has less impact given its steady trend. Thus, as a result, in 2006 the total growth rate fell below zero and has been fluctuating around that level until the present.

This evolution has led to a change in the structure of the population. With fewer new-borns and people living longer, the population has aged, as can be seen in the population pyramids (Fig. 11.4). Pyramids of 2008 and the projection for 2030 were calculated in single ages, from 0 to 110 and above. Although they appear unnaturally symmetric for both sexes, possibly due to data management, we can see the transformation of the pyramid's structure. The 2008 pyramid has a considerably reduced base at age 0 (compared to what had been in the past, for instance in 1966, people aged 42 years in 2008) as a result of the decline in fertility (since 1978, TFR dropped from 1.98 to 1.30). In the projections of 2030 the large generations of the past are gradually increasing the weight of every age they pass through, and therefore shrinking the base. We can also see the abrupt discontinuities between cohorts due to the impact of migration. Particularly important were the four outmigration waves which occurred during the second half of the 20th century in Cuba: 1959–1962; 1965–1972; 1980 and 1994, with a total population loss in these periods of 703,900

Table 11.1 Sex differential in life expectancy at birth for selected periods, Cuba. (Source: National Statistic Office, Cuba)

Periods	Males	Females	Differential
1955–1960	60.80	64.20	3.40
1969–1971	68.55	71.82	3.27
1986–1987	72.74	76.34	3.60
1994–1995	72.94	76.90	3.96
1998–2000	74.20	78.23	4.03
2001–2003	75.13	78.97	3.84
2005–2007	76.00	80.02	4.02

people, making up 65 % of the total migration for the period 1959–1999 (Aja 2000, 2002).

An extraordinary example of this impact can be seen in the pyramid of 2008, at ages 49 to 57 (those born between 1951 and 1959), where, instead of a gap, it looks like a vertical cut of the population. One of the reasons for this shape (apart from the effect of subsequent migration waves) is a particular migration pattern experienced by this generation in the period 1960–1962, when 14,000 children (5 % of total migrants of the period) migrated to the United States without their parents, a migration flow called the Peter Pan Operation (Torreira and Buajasan 2000). Another important aspect of the change in the population structure is the increase in the proportion of people over age 60. According to the population projection, by 2030 the elderly population will reach 31 %, twice the percentage in 2008.

Cuba began the twentieth century with a total life expectancy of 37.7 years (1900–1904) and a differential by sex of 3.96 years (González and Ramos 1996; López et al. 2005). For the second half of the century, the sex gap fluctuated between 3 to 4 years (Table 11.1). Several factors, biological, socio-economic and behavioural, affected this trend. After the Cuban Revolution in 1959 women took an active role in the transformation of society, increasing their labour force participation and educational attainment, among others. These changes led women to share similar behaviours and risk factors with men, for instance smoking tobacco (which increased especially among women until 2006, with 16 and 14 % of women and men smoking, respectively). These factors could possibly lead to a worsening in female's survival for causes that previously did not affect them, while at the same time, the improvements in the health system could have a positive effect on men's survival. Results from López et al. (2005) support this interpretation. They show that there was more progress in males' survival compared to females until the nineties, which helped to maintain the lower sex differential observed before. We shall check, below, whether this trend holds into the first decade of the twenty-first century, and what causes of death are responsible for it.

11.4.2 The Evolution of Mortality in Recent Decades

The age schedule of mortality in Cuba has changed considerably in the past 20 years (Fig. 11.5), from 1987, represented by the darkest blue line, until 2007, the lime

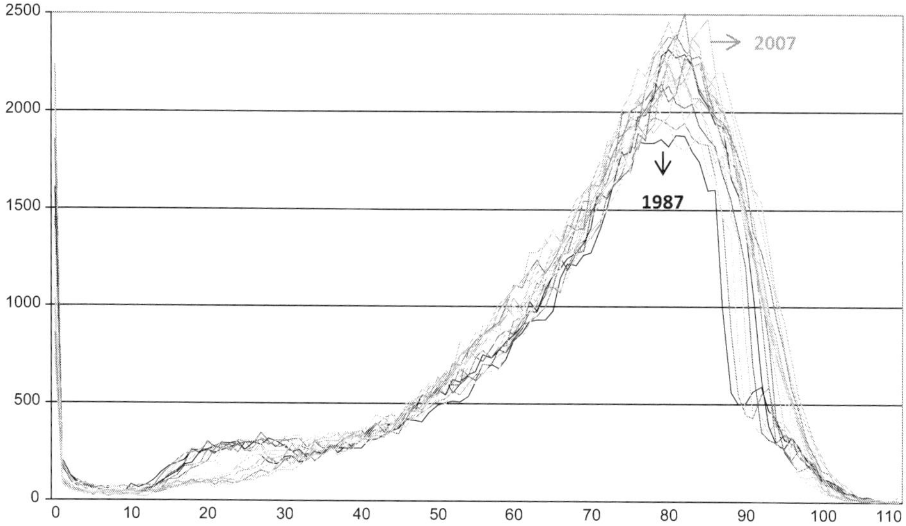

Fig. 11.5 Number of deaths by age from 1987 to 2007, Cuba. (Source: Taken from *Esperanza de vida Cuba y provincias, 2005–2007. Cálculos por sexo y edades*. Pp. 22, Gráfico 2. Cuba. 1987–2007. Número de defunciones por edad. Oficina Nacional de Estadísticas, 2008)

colour. There is a marked drop in mortality below age one and for younger adults there is a flat peak around age 25, followed by a decline in the number deaths in the surrounding ages until 2007. Later there is an appreciable increase in the number of deaths after age 70, with a peak around age 81 which is the modal age at death in 1987 (first line in dark blue). The modal age at death continues to shift to the right and the number of deaths around the mode increases until 2007 (upper line in lime colour). This shift towards older ages at death supports the idea that the Cuban population is extending its lifespan by delaying mortality at older ages.

Before analysing the effect of different causes of death on the differences in life expectancy, we will describe the pattern of mortality for the specific years that will be used later on. Mortality curves follow the regular U shape, describing a low infant mortality (reduced over time); a slight hump at younger adult ages (from age group 15–19 to 30–35); and an increment in mortality rates as age increases (Fig. 11.6). The differences by sex can also be seen, with lower mortality rates for females over all ages, although the smallest differences by sex are before age 5, and at older ages. The most significant changes over time can be seen at age 0, with an important reduction of mortality, and at younger ages (15–30), where the hump has been considerably reduced.

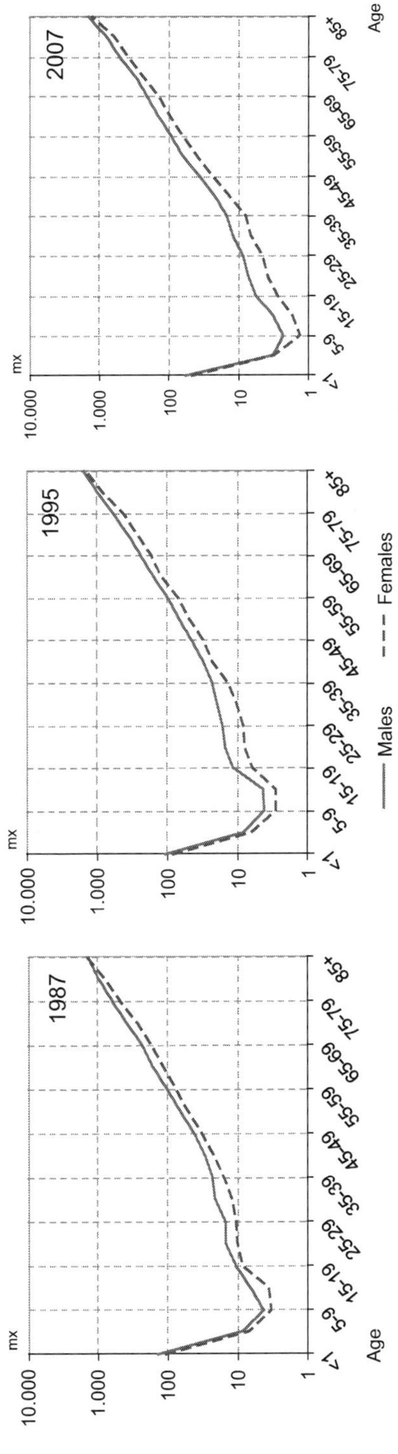

Fig. 11.6 Mortality pattern by sex and age groups. Years 1987, 1995 and 2007. (Source: Calculations based on data from National Statistic Office and Public Health Ministry of Cuba)

As previously mentioned, the first three principal causes of death in Cuba are non-infectious diseases. As early as 1970, heart disease, cancer (lung, colon and lymphoma) and cerebrovascular disease were the leading causes of death (Fernández 2006; Oficina Nacional de Estadísticas 2010). In this study, we will use the following 11 causes of death groups:

1. Heart diseases
2. Cancer
3. Cerebrovascular diseases
4. External causes (Accidents, Violent deaths and Suicide)
5. Respiratory diseases (including Influenza)
6. Artery and arterioles
7. Diabetes
8. Liver, Kidney and Obstruction
9. Congenital Malformation
10. Mental disorders (including Alzheimer disease)
11. Other causes

Given the impact of these causes in specific age groups and their evolution over time, we have grouped them into 6 patterns of mortality. Below are shown patterns of mortality due to Cancer, External Causes, Respiratory Diseases, Other Causes and Diabetes (other causes can be found in the Annex, sects. 2 to 7).

The first pattern of mortality affects especially adult life (cancer; heart diseases and liver, kidney and obstruction). Mortality due to cancer is depicted in Fig. 11.7. Over time the number of deaths below age 30 declines, but they increase appreciably above that age. Between the ages of 30 and 50 there are more female than male deaths, while men have more deaths at older age. Over the period studied, 1987 to 2007, the mortality rate for men increases faster with age than does the rate for women.

Figure 11.8 depicts the second pattern of mortality, that of external causes, one which affects all ages, especially younger adults. It shows a minimum at younger ages (0–14) and a maximum at young adult ages (20–30). By sex, males have a disadvantage at almost all ages and there is an increase of deaths in 1995 compared to 1987, particularly for younger adults, and then a decrease, especially for women. It is worth noting the rise in mortality rates at older ages and, in particular for the last two age-groups, the rise in the number of female deaths and rates, which surpass those of males.

The third pattern of mortality corresponds to the impact of respiratory diseases (also cerebrovascular diseases; and artery and arterioles), showing a gradual increase in mortality from age forty onwards. Both sexes experienced an increase in the number of deaths over time; however, the mortality rates of women decreased (Fig. 11.9).

The fourth pattern of mortality can be observed only for diabetes, where mortality is higher for females at almost all ages (Fig. 11.10). It affects mainly adult and older ages, and female deaths are almost double those of males. Over time, there was an increase in 1995, but the number of deaths then fell to its previous level, while mortality rates decreased, particularly for females, falling to half their value in previous observations.

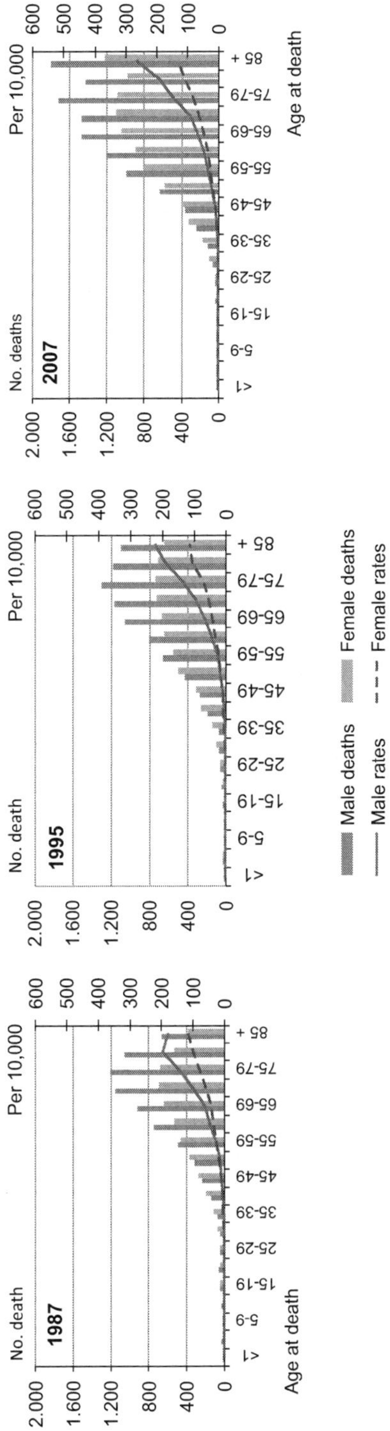

Fig. 11.7 Number of deaths and age-specific death rates of Cancer in 1987, 1995 and 2007, Cuba. (Source: Calculations based on data from Public Health Ministry of Cuba)

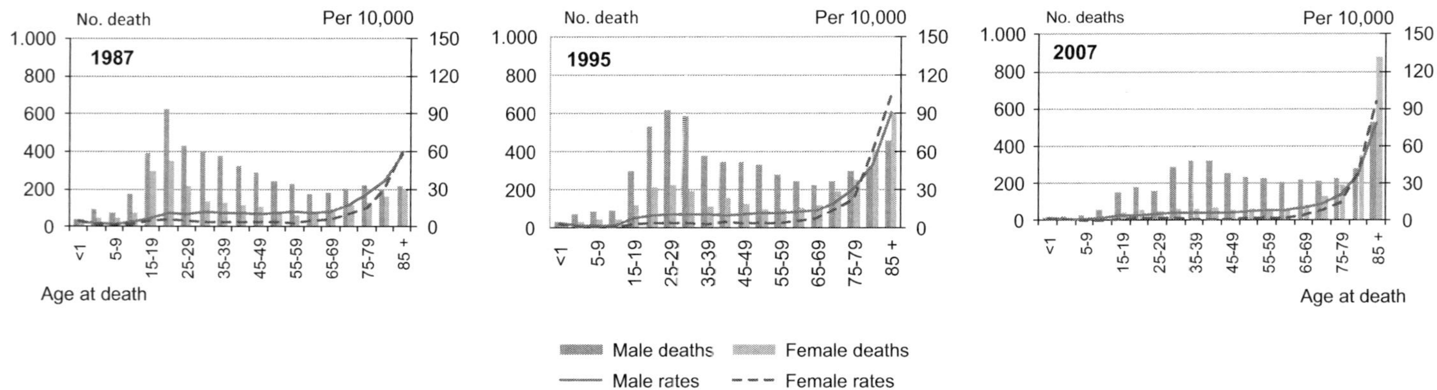

Fig. 11.8 Number of deaths and age-specific death rates of External Causes in 1987, 1995 and 2007, Cuba. (Source: Calculations based on data from Public Health Ministry of Cuba)

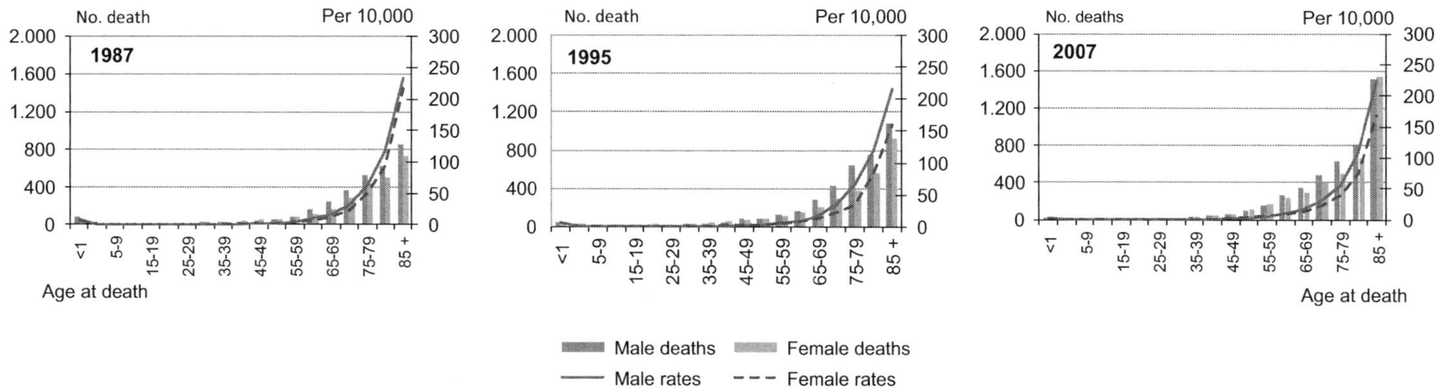

Fig. 11.9 Number of deaths and age-specific death rates of Respiratory Diseases in 1987, 1995 and 2007, Cuba. (Source: Calculations based on data from Public Health Ministry of Cuba)

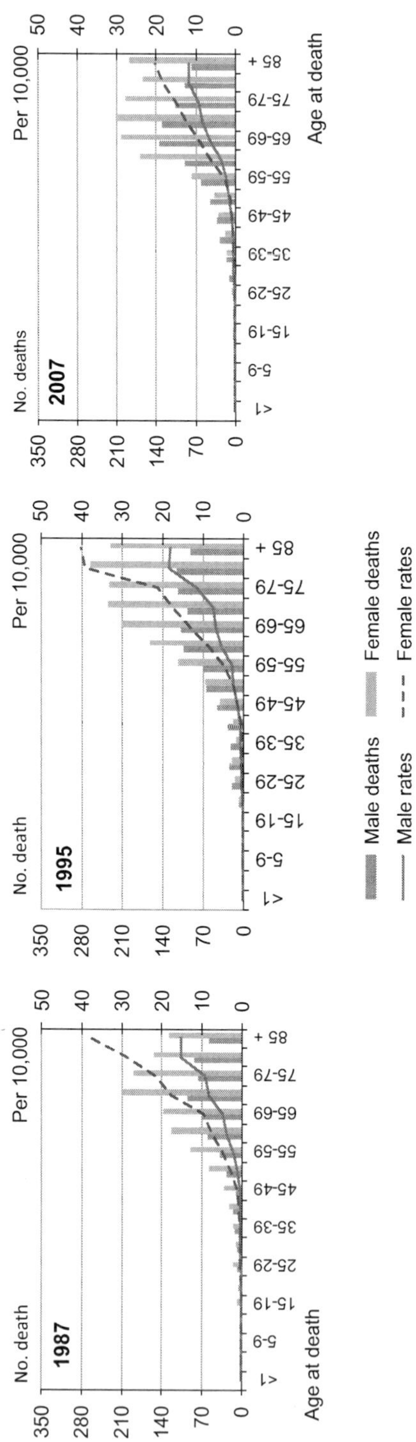

Fig. 11.10 Number of deaths and age-specific death rates of Diabetes Mellitus in 1987, 1995 and 2007, Cuba. (Source: Calculations based on data from Public Health Ministry of Cuba)

The fifth pattern describes the effect of mortality at two opposite ends of the life cycle: congenital malformations (Annex 6) which account for the majority of deaths in the first year of life, and which show a considerable decrease over time; and mental disorders (Annex 7), concentrated at the end of life, in particular after age 75, which affect females in particular, and which have been increasing over time.

The rest of the causes of death are grouped into other causes, forming the last pattern of mortality (Fig. 11.11). This group affects all ages, although there has been a considerable reduction from infancy through to young adult ages over time. In 2007, for age group 85 and above, females had more deaths from other causes than did males, but also with a reduction in death rates for both sexes.

11.5 Decomposition of Life Expectancy Differences at Birth

So far, we have shown that Cuba is at an advanced stage of the demographic transition, with low levels of fertility and mortality, and a death distribution that is concentrated at older ages. We now decompose the effect of age and specific-causes of death which account for differentials in life expectancy at birth. This will be done firstly for the sex differential in 1987, 1995 and 2007; and then, for each sex, to see the changes between the two periods (1987–1995 and 1995–2007).

The evolution of mortality trends has led to an increasing life expectancy at birth over time, and this improvement now depends mainly on gains in terms of survival at older ages. Furthermore, there are clear differences by sex in the mortality patterns, as was shown in the last section. The changing sex gap in life expectancy is made up of the relative age- and cause-specific gains and losses of each sex, and of the distinct way in which different causes of death affect each sex. In this section we will address the following questions: To what extent are these gains higher for females or males? What causes of deaths are responsible for gains or losses in survival?

11.5.1 Sex Differential in Life Expectancy at Birth

Figure 11.12 depicts the contribution of each age group to the sex-difference in life expectancy for the three years of observation. As we can see, all contributions are positive, meaning that at all ages, females gain more years of life than males. The life expectancy differential between females and males was 3.60 years in favour of females in 1986–1987 (green bars). There is a large contribution of infant mortality and a very low contribution at younger adult ages. The difference starts to increase from age group 20–24 onwards, with the highest contributions being at age groups 60–64 and 70–74.

In 1994–1995 (yellow bars), the differential was 3.96, higher than before, but contributions by age were different. Infant mortality decreased in importance, given the small proportions of deaths that occurred at age 0 in this period, but there was

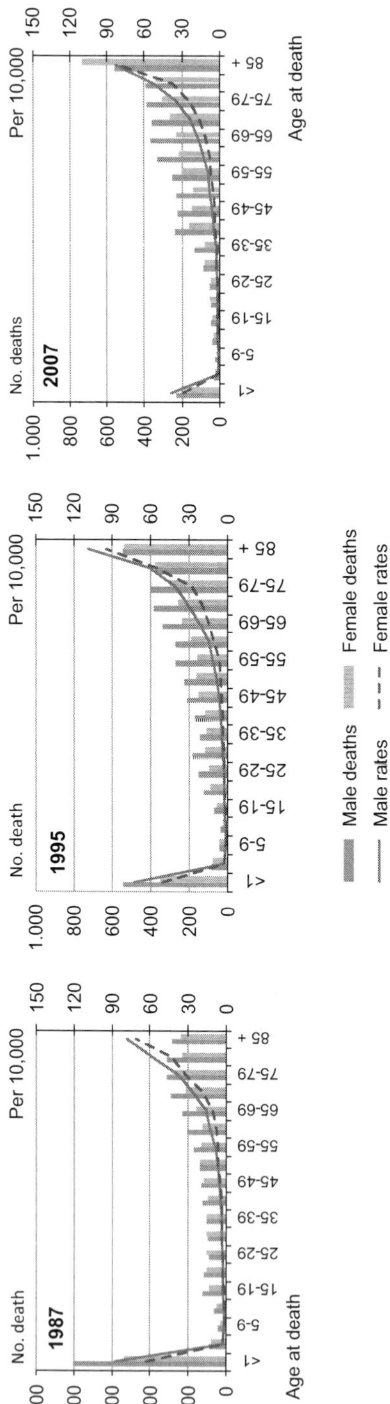

Fig. 11.11 Number of deaths and age-specific death rates of Other Causes in 1987, 1995 and 2007, Cuba. (Source: Calculations based on data from Public Health Ministry of Cuba)

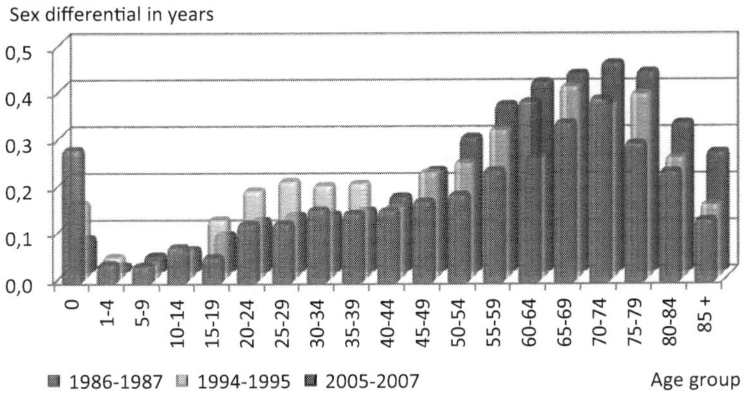

Fig. 11.12 Decomposition of Sex Differential in life expectancy at birth, by age. (Source: Calculations based on data from the National Statistic Office, Cuba)

a significant increase in the contributions of young adult ages (15–19 to 35–39 age groups). As we saw previously, in Fig. 11.8, in this period male mortality from external causes increased, but this was not the case for females, hence the abrupt increase in contributions observed in this period and not in the previous or the following one.

For the last period 2005–2007 (red bars), the differential in life expectancy was 4.01 years, slightly higher than in the previous period. Infant mortality continued to drop in importance, and the female advantage became concentrated even more at older ages, especially at ages 70–74. For age-group 85 and above the contribution is double that of the first period.

The overall reading of Fig. 11.12 is that female life expectancy has been higher than that of males for all 3 years in the study, and the major contributions to the sex-gap in life expectancy shift to the right as infant and childhood mortality lose their importance. However, there is also an important increase in contributions at young adult ages as a result of the increase in male mortality for the period 1994–1995. This could be related to the economic crisis and the deterioration in living conditions that shocked Cuban society after 1989.

We now split these contributions according to the corresponding causes of death implicated in the changes in life expectancy. This means that each bar will be divided according to the weight of each cause with respect to: the total difference in the sex gap and the total difference in time by each sex. Data used to build graphs 13, 14 and 15 are in Annex sections 8 to 14. The results should be interpreted with caution, given that the detailed information we are using for the analysis (splitting by cause of death) could lead to some inconsistencies, for instance, the irregularity by age of the contributions (bars nearby often didn't follow a consistent increase or decrease), especially when the sexes are analysed separately.

Figure 11.13 presents the decomposition for the years 1987, 1995 and 2007. For the year 1987, it shows a predominantly greater female survival for almost all age groups. The few disadvantages (negative contributions), especially at adult ages (35–54), are due to cancer and diabetes, as well as a strong negative effect of cancer,

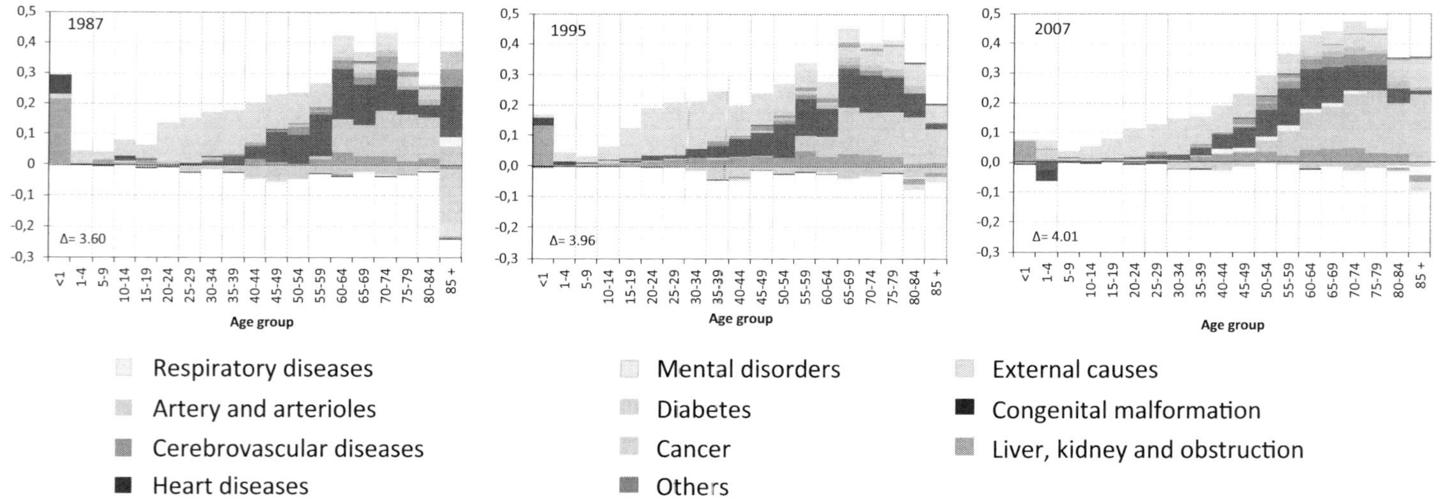

Fig. 11.13 Decomposition of the difference in Life Expectancy at birth between females and males by causes of death and age, 1987, 1995 and 2007. (Source: Calculations based on data from the National Statistic Office and the Public Health Ministry of Cuba)

at 85 years and over. On the other hand, females are doing better in terms of survival than males, especially for other causes at age 0 (at that time, still significant gains are found at this age); external causes, heart diseases and cancer. For 1995, some differences with respect to the previous period can be observed: firstly, the growth of the contribution due to external causes; secondly, the share of infant mortality is considerably reduced in size; and thirdly, for all age groups there were some causes with small negative contributions (males advantage over females), which are concentrated at adult ages. For 2007, the contrast with respect to the other 2 years is the concentration at older ages of the majority of contributions, the reduction in the infant mortality effect and the reduction in external causes at younger ages.

Taking a general overview of the period shown in Fig. 11.13, we see that the importance of infant mortality declined over time; external causes increased in 1995 but then declined again, but still remained the foremost cause of death at young ages and adults before age 50, for the entire period. Females' advantages are mainly due to cancer, external causes and heart diseases. At older ages, cancer leads the higher gains in women's survival, followed by heart diseases, and respiratory diseases. Male advantage is mainly concentrated in their lower mortality from cancer at younger adult ages (30–49), and from diabetes at older ages.

11.5.2 Time Differential in Life Expectancy at Birth

The second part of the analysis will allow us to illustrate the behaviour of each sex separately, between two periods: 1987–1995 and 1995–2007. Starting with males (Fig. 11.14), they improved their life expectancy at birth by 3.26 years over the 20 years of the study (1987–2007). Only 0.2 of that gain was achieved in the first period 1987–1995. During this period, important improvements of infant mortality due to congenital malformation and other causes took place.

At young ages there were almost no signs of improvements; on the contrary, for age groups 1–4, 20–29 and 35–50, there was actually a decline. At older ages the intensity of the effects was greater, but also with an overall negative contribution to the indicator. In fact, the ages between 55–59 and 75–79 experienced both the highest improvements and deteriorations in the same age groups, with heart diseases and cerebrovascular diseases leading the negative contributions.

There was a greater improvement in male survival during the period 1995–2007 and life expectancy at birth increased by 3.06 years. This was due to improvements at almost all ages and from almost all causes of death. The reduction in external causes contributed most to the positive changes at younger ages, while at older ages these were mainly due to heart diseases and cerebrovascular diseases and, to a lesser extent, diabetes and external causes. At older ages, deterioration (negative contribution) was mainly due to cancer and mental disorders.

For females, life expectancy at birth increased by 3.68 years over the entire period and the trends were similar to those for males. In the first period (1987–1995) there was little improvement, around half a year, and the major advances took place in the second period (1995–2007), with more than 3 years of improvement (Fig. 11.15).

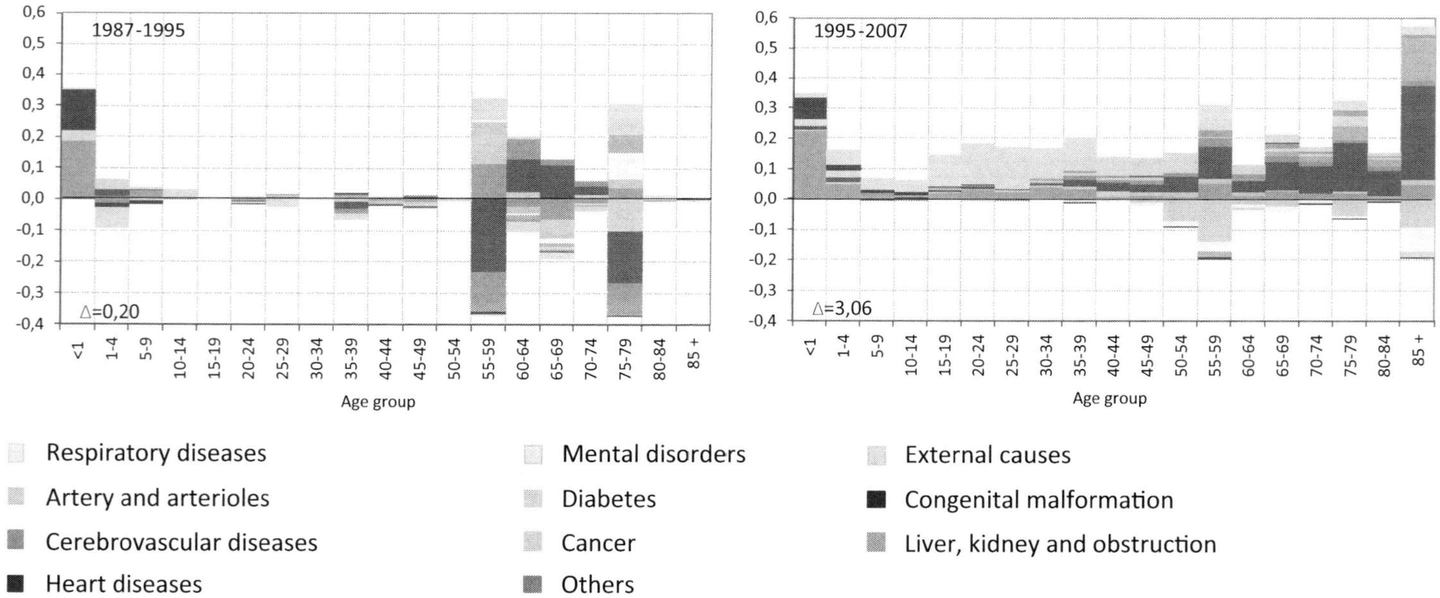

Fig. 11.14 Decomposition of the difference in male life expectancy at birth between 1987–1995 and 1995–2007, by age and causes of death, Cuba. (Source: Calculations based on data from the National Statistic Office and the Public Health Ministry of Cuba)

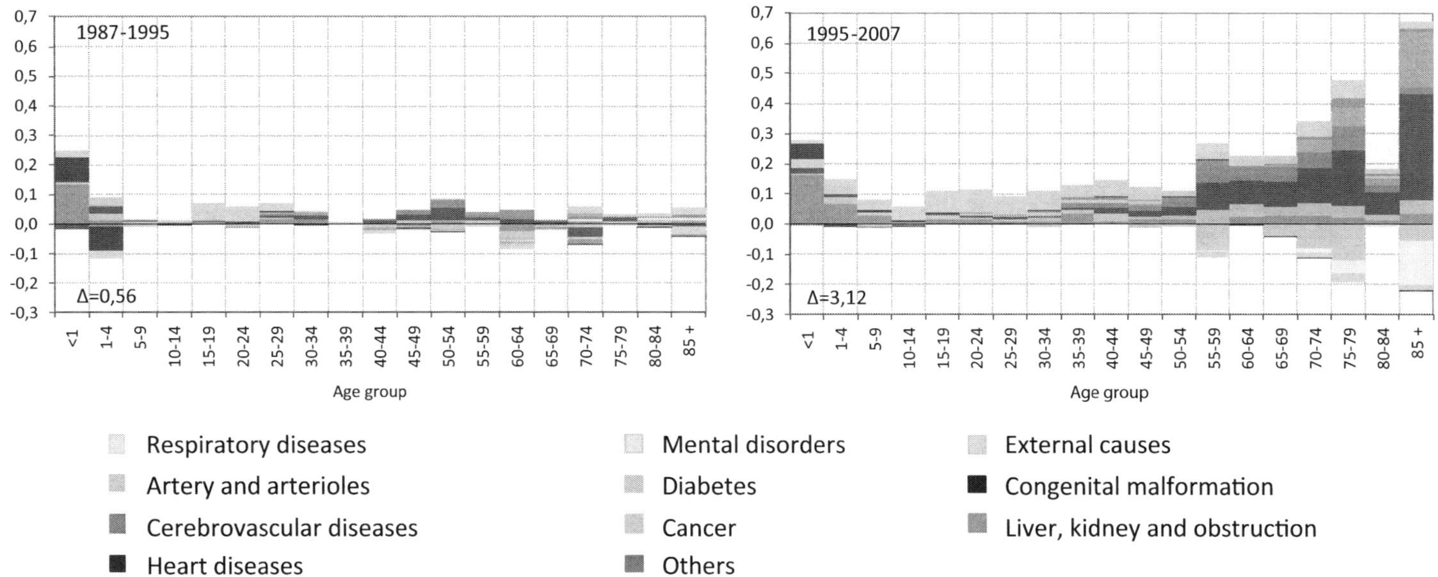

Fig. 11.15 Decomposition of the difference in female life expectancy at birth between 1987–1995 and 1995–2007, by age and causes of death, Cuba. (Source: Calculations based on data from the National Statistic Office and the Public Health Ministry of Cuba)

During the first period the female improvement was more than double that for males (0.56 compared with 0.20); in the second period both show almost the same progress, which was only 0.06 of a year higher for females (3.12 and 3.06 respectively).

In the first period infant mortality showed improvements (reductions in other causes and congenital malformation) as did mortality at younger adult ages, from age 15 to 34, largely owing to the reduction in external causes. Mortality at ages 1–4 made an overall negative contribution, while at older ages, there was a concentration of both losses and of increments in life expectancy. Positive shares were mainly due to heart and cerebrovascular diseases, and external causes.

The second period shows greater improvements, with a gain of 3.12 years in life expectancy. Females improved their survival on account of all causes of deaths, except for cancer, mental disorders, and respiratory diseases at ages older than 55 (excluding age groups 60–64 and 80–84). Slightly negative contributions were also found at younger ages (0 to 14) due to: cancer; congenital malformation; other causes; cerebrovascular diseases; liver, kidney and obstruction and arteries and arterioles.

11.6 Conclusions

One of the great successes of society in the twentieth century has been the control of infectious and parasitic diseases, leading to a decline in mortality and a remarkable increase in life expectancy especially in the first half of the century. However, sex differences in life expectancy also widened, meaning that the mortality decline did not affect both sexes in the same way. As has been argued in previous studies, survival is affected by biological factors, but also by behavioural and sociological differences. These differences have been decreasing over time, leading to a reduction or stagnation in the sex gap, especially over the last three decades.

As we have shown in this study, Cuban life expectancy at birth has been increasing since the beginning of the twentieth century, reaching 80 years of life expectancy for females and 76 years for males at the last available record (2005–2007). This has been possible as a result of the changes experienced by the Cuban population: a rapid progression into the demographic transition (it stands now at the last stage, with low levels of mortality and fertility); and by the changes inherent in the epidemiologic transition, showing in Cuba a mixture of mortality patterns and a co-existence of endogenous and exogenous causes of death among the leading causes of death in the country.

However, unlike other countries, in Cuba this increase in life expectancy has not been translated into a growing mortality difference between males and females. In the 20 years analysed here, this is particularly true for the first period (1987–1995) in which life expectancy increased around half a year for females, and even less for males; in the subsequent period (1995–2007) both sexes increased their life expectancy by more than 3 years.

In this research, we have focussed our attention on the impact of changes in the mortality patterns on male and female life expectancy in Cuba. We summarise our findings concerning the improvements in survival over time by looking at the three aspects analysed: age; causes of death; and sex. Results by *specific age-group* contributions show that despite the fact that mortality is now concentrated at older ages (50 per cent of years gained are due to mortality reductions above age 60), mid-adult mortality is still important, particularly for 1987 and 1995. Furthermore, even though infant mortality shows very low and decreasing contributions, other causes remain important in this age group, indicating deaths which could have been prevented.

In terms of *causes of death*, there are four main causes of death which contribute the most to the higher female survival compared to that of males: heart disease, external causes, cancer and cerebrovascular diseases. However, males do enjoy an advantage with respect to some causes, mainly diabetes, and cancer at younger adult ages.

When comparing *within* each sex, females show higher gains for both periods. For 1987–1995 these were mainly due to a decrease in infant mortality, while the small gains at other ages were counterbalanced by losses at age group 1–4 and age 40 and over. In the following period (1995–2007), females experienced higher gains of life expectancy. In this period, both higher positive and negative contributions were found, and these were substantially greater at 55 years and over. In this case, females experienced losses at older ages mainly due to cancer, mental disorders and respiratory diseases.

Males' advantage in the first period of analysis is concentrated in childhood and between ages 55 and 80. The gains in survival at older ages were accompanied by opposite effects that exceeded the positive contributions. For other ages, there were only changes towards a slight deterioration. The second period shows an important increase in male survival. Almost all ages showed positive contributions, in particular for: other causes in childhood; external causes at young adult ages, and heart diseases at older ages. Negative contributions were found principally for cancer at old ages.

Our results suggest that there is a mix of mortality patterns in Cuba, where most deaths are attributable to chronic or degenerative diseases, but there are a sizeable proportion of avoidable deaths (for instance external causes, respiratory diseases or diabetes). Although effects by sex are different, with females having higher survival, this difference is less than might otherwise be expected. The evidence suggests that life expectancy can still increase for the Cuban population, particularly by reducing the impact of external causes, respiratory diseases, heart diseases and other causes.

The differences between the periods are clear. The first one was the period when increases in life expectancy were at their lowest. The second period shows a recuperation of the positive trend in life expectancy. During the economic crisis, male survival was seriously constrained while females kept their advantage of half of a year; in the recovery period, males recovered faster than females, almost catching up with them.

11.7 Annex

11.7.1 Annex 1. Groups of causes of death used in the analysis, according to ICD-10 and ICD-9

Group of Causes of death	CIE-9	CIE-10
01 Cancer	140–208	C00-C97
02 Diabetes mellitus	250	E10 E14
03 Mental disorders (including Alzheimer)	290	F01-F03
	310	G30
04 Heart diseases	393–429	I05-I52
05 Cerebrovascular diseases	430–438	I60-I69
06 Artery and arterioles	440–444	I70-I79
	447–448	
07 Respiratory disease (including Influenza)	490–496	J40-J47
08 Liver, Kidney and Obstruction	550–553	K40-K46
	560	K56
09 Congenital Malformation	740–759	Q00-Q99
10 External causes (Accidents, Violent deaths and Suicide)	800–949	V01-X59
		Y85-Y86

Harmonization elaborated with data from the Public Health Ministry, Cuba http://www.sld.cu/sitios/dne/verpost.php?blog=http://articulos.sld.cu/dne&post_id=260&tipo=1&opc_mostrar=2_&n=dx. Consulted on April, 2011

11.7.2 Annex 2. Number of deaths and age-specific death rates of Heart Diseases. Cuba, 1987, 1995 and 2007

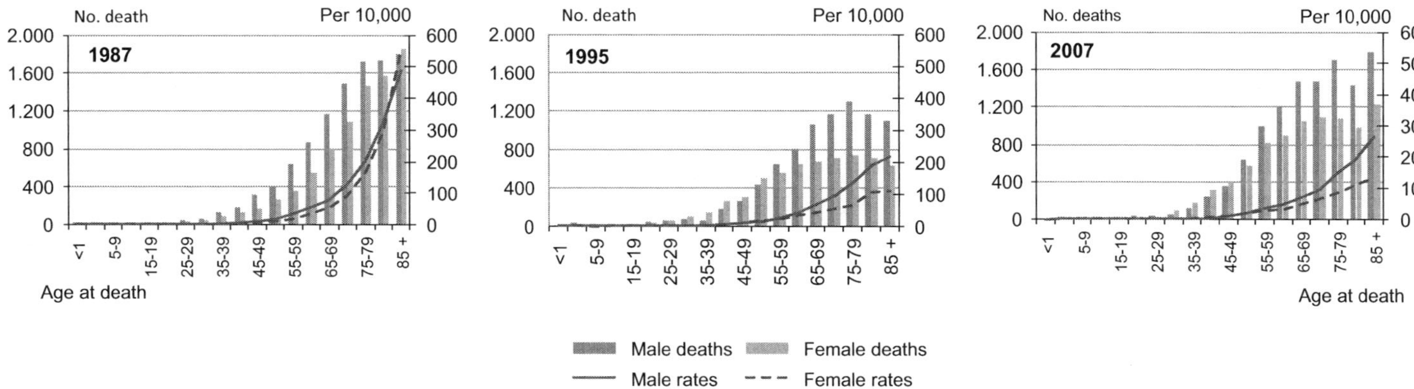

Source: Calculations based on data from Public Health Ministry of Cuba.

11.7.3 Annex 3. Number of deaths and age-specific death rates of Liver, Kidney and Obstruction. Cuba, 1987, 1995 and 2007

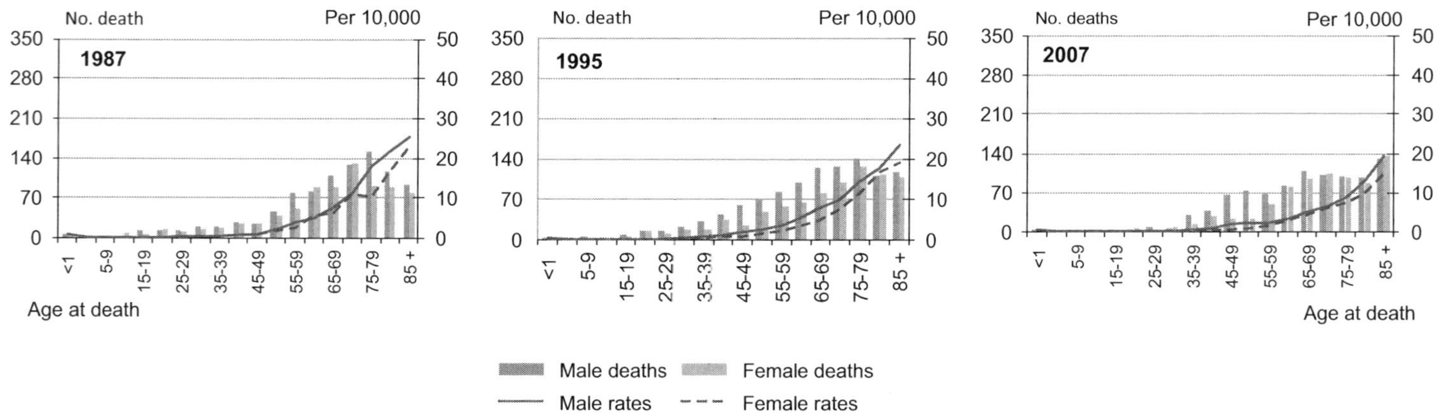

Source: Calculations based on data from Public Health Ministry of Cuba.

11.7.4 Annex 4. Number of deaths and age-specific death rates of Cerebrovascular Diseases. Cuba, 1987, 1995 and 2007

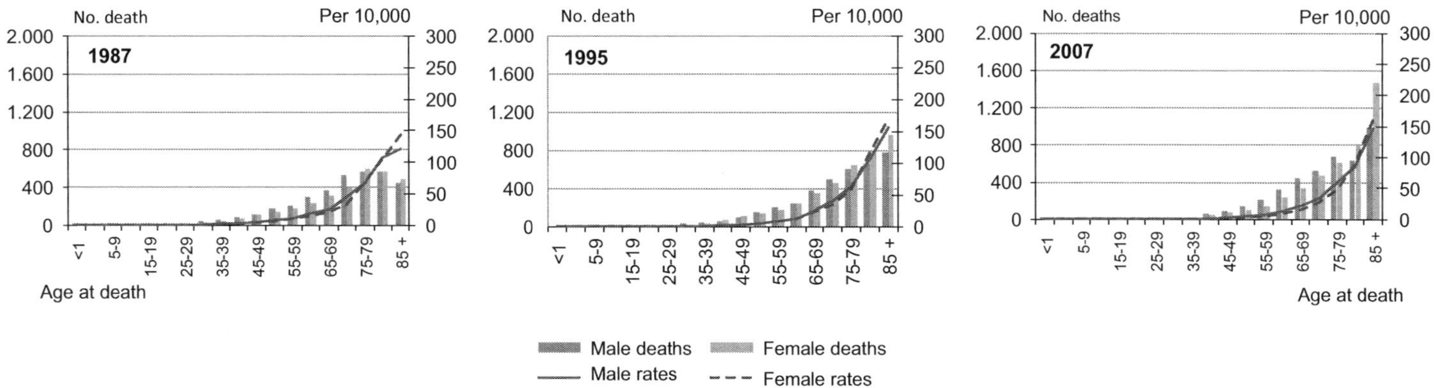

Source: Calculations based on data from Public Health Ministry of Cuba.

11.7.5 Annex 5. Number of deaths and age-specific death rates of Artery and Arterioles. Cuba, 1987, 1995 and 2007

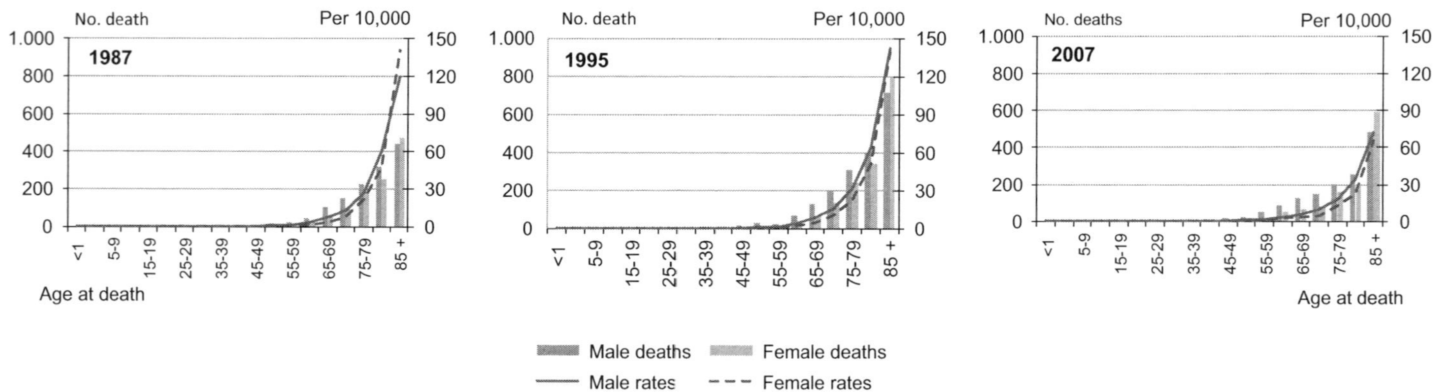

Source: Calculations based on data from Public Health Ministry of Cuba.

11.7.6 Annex 6. Number of deaths and age-specific death rates of Congenital Malformation. Cuba, 1987, 1995 and 2007

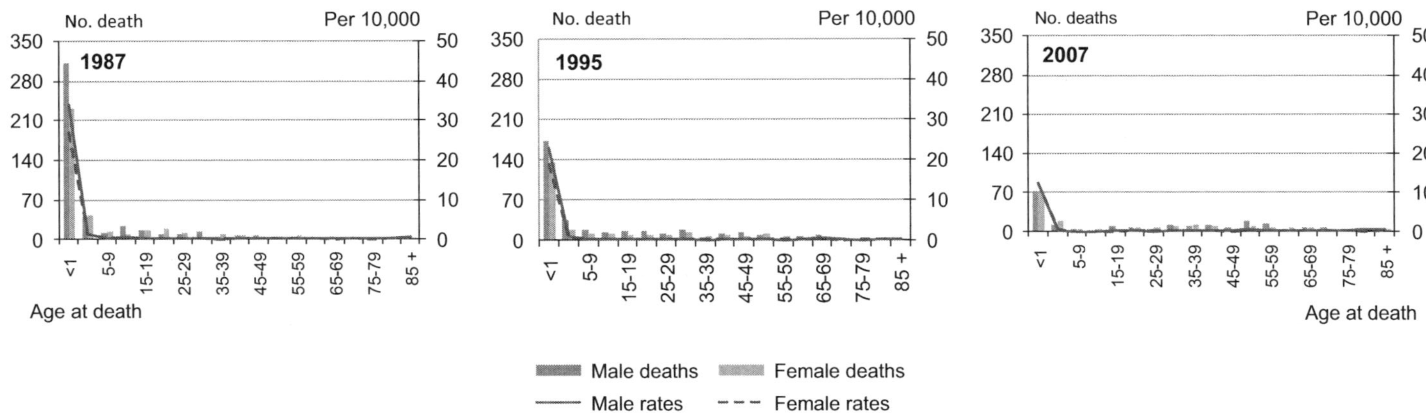

Source: Calculations based on data from Public Health Ministry of Cuba.

11.7.7 Annex 7. Number of deaths and age-specific death rates of Mental Disorders. Cuba, 1987, 1995 and 2007

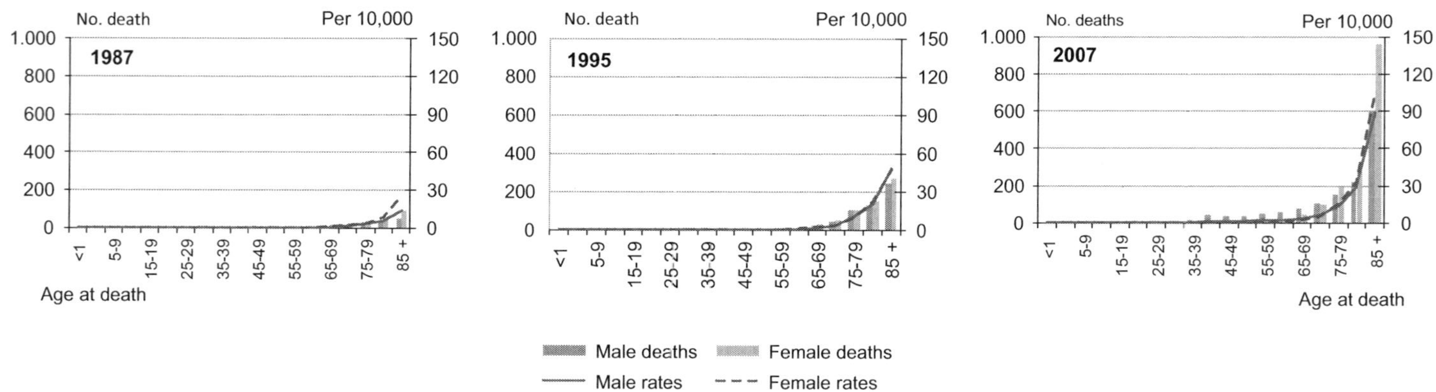

Source: Calculations based on data from Public Health Ministry of Cuba.

11.7.8 Annex 8. Decomposition of the difference in Life Expectancy at birth between females and males by causes of death and age, 1987

Cause specific component of the sex differential 1987

Age groups	Other Causes	Cancer	Diabetes Mellitus	Mental Disorders	Heart Diseases	Cerebrovascular D.	Artery/ Arterioles	Respiratory Dis.	Liver/ Kidney/Obst	Congenital Malf.	External causes
< 1	0.21337	−0.00223	0.00000	0.00000	0.00179	0.00094	0.00000	0.01489	−0.00042	0.06131	−0.00472
1–4	0.00202	0.00482	0.00000	0.00000	0.00029	0.00000	0.00000	0.00144	−0.00015	−0.00298	0.03432
5–9	0.01124	−0.00090	0.00000	0.00000	0.00189	0.00189	0.00000	0.00088	−0.00116	−0.00260	0.02513
10–14	0.00478	0.00759	0.00107	0.00000	0.00426	0.00154	0.00000	−0.00013	−0.00391	0.00730	0.05358
15–19	0.01402	−0.00032	−0.00377	0.00052	0.00433	−0.00218	0.00000	−0.00191	0.00348	−0.00034	0.04030
20–24	0.00526	0.00634	0.00042	0.00000	−0.00070	0.00081	0.00090	−0.00377	−0.00195	−0.00421	0.12226
25–29	−0.00788	−0.00594	−0.00465	0.00000	0.00471	−0.00131	0.00133	−0.00464	0.00135	−0.00265	0.14556
30–34	−0.00169	−0.01132	−0.00153	0.00001	0.00970	0.00679	0.00056	0.00354	0.00288	0.00442	0.14288
35–39	−0.00416	−0.01717	−0.00067	0.00000	0.02828	0.00481	−0.00003	−0.00304	0.00100	−0.00290	0.14229
40–44	0.01720	−0.03592	−0.00385	0.00000	0.04288	0.00632	0.00247	−0.00783	0.00111	0.00012	0.13157
45–49	0.00856	−0.02704	−0.01286	0.00064	0.09710	0.00414	0.00189	−0.01615	0.00056	0.00126	0.11644
50–54	0.00198	−0.02796	−0.02003	0.00064	0.09355	0.02554	0.00702	0.00220	0.00529	0.00066	0.09960
55–59	0.01858	0.00978	−0.02587	0.00000	0.13657	0.00994	0.00286	−0.00100	0.01288	−0.00096	0.07792
60–64	0.04050	0.10790	−0.03215	0.00151	0.16318	0.03022	0.01209	0.02225	−0.00403	−0.00002	0.04682
65–69	0.02633	0.10350	−0.02515	−0.00255	0.13498	0.02032	0.01772	0.02671	0.00785	0.00110	0.03174
70–74	0.02773	0.14918	−0.03469	−0.00361	0.13575	0.04268	0.02050	0.02949	0.00034	−0.00029	0.02640
75–79	0.01269	0.15257	−0.03006	−0.00116	0.08192	−0.00275	0.01201	0.02867	0.01797	0.00029	0.02633
80–84	0.02055	0.13443	−0.01863	−0.00441	0.04153	0.00097	0.01797	0.03106	0.00710	−0.00026	0.00805
85 +	−0.01691	−0.17377	0.05957	0.03161	0.16492	0.05966	0.05389	−0.04378	−0.00577	−0.00066	0.00512
										Sex Δ 1987	3.60

Source: Calculations using the Decomposition Method, based on data from Public Health Ministry of Cuba and National Statistic Office, Cuba

11.7.9 *Annex 9. Decomposition of the difference in Life Expectancy at birth between females and males by causes of death and age, 1995*

Cause specific component of the sex differential 1995

Age groups	Other Causes	Cancer	Diabetes Mellitus	Mental Disorders	Heart Diseases	Cerebrovascular D.	Artery/ Arterioles	Respiratory Dis.	Liver/ Kidney/Obst	Congenital Malf.	External causes
< 1	0.13341	− 0.00017	0.00000	0.00000	− 0.00614	0.00000	0.00000	− 0.00410	0.00151	0.02349	0.00876
1–4	0.00032	− 0.00048	0.00000	0.00000	0.00004	− 0.00084	0.00000	0.00203	− 0.00005	0.01180	0.03001
5–9	− 0.00161	0.00605	− 0.00003	0.00000	− 0.00098	0.00178	0.00000	− 0.00058	0.00082	0.00284	0.01872
10–14	0.00831	0.01081	0.00000	0.00000	0.00274	− 0.00113	0.00000	− 0.00014	− 0.00302	0.00038	0.03839
15–19	0.00838	0.00290	− 0.00122	0.00000	0.00620	0.00172	0.00000	0.00091	0.00042	0.00378	0.10013
20–24	0.01497	0.00462	− 0.00010	0.00000	0.01041	− 0.00058	0.00000	− 0.00330	− 0.00070	0.00340	0.15676
25–29	0.02182	− 0.00221	0.00210	0.00000	0.00996	− 0.00094	0.00000	− 0.00058	0.00169	0.00081	0.17243
30–34	0.02719	− 0.01223	0.00161	0.00040	0.02193	0.00082	0.00000	− 0.00196	0.00161	0.00161	0.15545
35–39	0.02062	− 0.04069	0.00625	0.00185	0.03551	0.00638	− 0.00060	− 0.00154	0.00877	− 0.00117	0.16527
40–44	0.02713	− 0.03415	0.00424	0.00051	0.05928	− 0.00555	0.00309	− 0.00826	0.00490	0.00161	0.09663
45–49	0.03053	− 0.01378	0.00241	− 0.00045	0.07714	− 0.00049	0.00293	0.00328	0.01671	0.00338	0.10325
50–54	0.02849	− 0.02492	− 0.00075	0.00044	0.11240	0.00785	0.00632	0.00338	0.00974	− 0.00123	0.10351
55–59	0.05055	0.04738	− 0.01974	0.00224	0.12199	0.01132	0.00495	0.00707	0.01225	− 0.00265	0.07986
60–64	0.02981	0.06718	− 0.02285	− 0.00115	0.09339	− 0.00031	0.01342	0.00461	0.01465	0.00079	0.05477
65–69	0.04042	0.15213	− 0.04061	− 0.00229	0.12914	0.01183	0.02599	0.03039	0.01771	0.00160	0.04165
70–74	0.03845	0.13806	− 0.03616	− 0.00163	0.12328	0.01647	0.01750	0.04203	0.00929	0.00087	0.01824
75–79	0.03014	0.14545	− 0.02123	0.00238	0.11628	0.00650	0.02086	0.06970	0.00640	− 0.00060	0.01644
80–84	0.00856	0.15344	− 0.03808	− 0.00322	0.07920	− 0.01866	0.02449	0.06790	0.00162	0.00004	− 0.01920
85 +	0.01336	0.10683	− 0.02159	0.00182	0.01994	− 0.01406	0.00331	0.05395	0.00437	0.00002	− 0.01360
										Sex Δ 1995	3.96

Source: Calculations using the Decomposition Method, based on data from Public Health Ministry of Cuba and National Statistic Office, Cuba

11.7.10 *Annex 10. Decomposition of the difference in Life Expectancy at birth between females and males by causes of death and age, 2007*

Cause specific component of the sex differential 2007

Age groups	Other Causes	Cancer	Diabetes Mellitus	Mental Disorders	Heart Diseases	Cerebrovascular D.	Artery/ Arterioles	Respiratory Dis.	Liver/ Kidney/Obst	Congenital Malf.	External causes
< 1	0.06817	0.00000	0.00000	0.00000	−0.00296	0.00111	0.00000	−0.00243	−0.00025	−0.00189	0.00842
1–4	0.00953	0.03225	0.00000	0.00000	−0.02835	0.00380	0.00000	0.01042	0.00000	−0.03512	0.01911
5–9	0.00760	0.00656	0.00000	0.00000	0.00088	−0.00005	0.00000	0.00186	−0.00099	−0.00027	0.01718
10–14	0.00365	0.00761	0.00000	0.00000	−0.00176	0.00077	0.00000	−0.00090	0.00072	−0.00266	0.03855
15–19	0.00346	0.00044	−0.00130	0.00000	0.00109	0.00053	0.00119	0.00225	0.00179	0.00348	0.06481
20–24	−0.00392	0.00880	−0.00010	0.00077	0.00828	−0.00010	0.00077	0.00511	−0.00337	−0.00041	0.09227
25–29	0.00616	0.00438	−0.00208	0.00088	0.01256	0.00425	0.00088	−0.00214	0.00601	−0.00309	0.09167
30–34	0.00135	−0.02335	0.00298	0.00359	0.01817	0.00024	0.00000	0.00289	−0.00070	0.00134	0.11526
35–39	0.01945	−0.02030	−0.00080	0.00490	0.02382	0.00378	0.00174	0.00125	0.00587	−0.00078	0.09157
40–44	0.02645	−0.02635	0.00313	0.01531	0.04766	0.00256	0.00103	−0.00120	0.00384	0.00038	0.08733
45–49	0.03309	−0.01512	0.00117	0.01384	0.06682	0.00794	0.00341	0.00274	0.01871	0.00131	0.08239
50–54	0.03612	0.03464	0.00333	0.01194	0.09132	0.02083	0.00335	−0.00482	0.01988	0.00324	0.06748
55–59	0.02291	0.08252	−0.00495	0.01807	0.12302	0.02588	0.01355	−0.00302	0.00787	0.00323	0.06809
60–64	0.04337	0.12194	−0.02253	0.01530	0.13384	0.03128	0.01273	0.01451	0.00280	−0.00020	0.05185
65–69	0.04418	0.14245	−0.01683	0.01220	0.12083	0.03692	0.01852	0.01818	0.00532	0.00011	0.04137
70–74	0.04736	0.18423	−0.02778	0.00708	0.08690	0.03455	0.02774	0.04426	0.00244	0.00133	0.03761
75–79	0.03207	0.20807	−0.01803	−0.00581	0.08590	0.03709	0.01570	0.05130	0.00380	0.00065	0.01632
80–84	0.03003	0.16843	−0.01245	−0.00753	0.04893	−0.00989	0.02402	0.07051	0.00626	0.00134	−0.00211
85 +	0.00385	0.22282	−0.01507	−0.02876	0.01212	−0.02412	0.01207	0.09434	0.00746	0.00051	−0.03010
										Sex Δ 2007	4.01

Source: Calculations using the Decomposition Method, based on data from Public Health Ministry of Cuba and National Statistic Office, Cuba

11.7.11 Annex 11. Males, decomposition of the difference in life expectancy at birth between 1987–1995, by age and causes of death, Cuba

Males cause specific component of the time differential 1987–1995

Age groups	Other Causes	Cancer	Diabetes Mellitus	Mental Disorders	Heart Diseases	Cerebrovascular D.	Artery/ Arterioles	Respiratory Dis.	Liver/ Kidney/Obst	Congenital Malf.	External causes
< 1	0.18458	−0.00087	0.00000	0.00000	−0.00366	0.00129	0.00000	0.03147	0.00142	0.13108	0.00290
1–4	0.00673	−0.00148	0.00000	0.00000	0.02318	0.00000	0.00000	0.03340	−0.01140	−0.01564	−0.06482
5–9	0.02383	0.00005	−0.00236	0.00000	0.00659	−0.00285	0.00000	−0.00049	−0.00285	−0.00904	0.00652
10–14	0.00532	0.00194	0.00053	0.00000	0.00079	0.00063	0.00000	0.00063	−0.00032	0.00195	0.01765
15–19	0.00007	−0.00003	−0.00001	0.00001	0.00000	−0.00003	0.00000	−0.00003	0.00001	−0.00007	−0.00059
20–24	−0.00695	0.00064	−0.00128	0.00000	−0.00427	0.00105	0.00049	−0.00153	−0.00100	−0.00259	0.00479
25–29	0.00234	−0.00092	−0.00304	0.00000	0.00146	0.00430	0.00068	0.00393	0.00037	−0.00052	−0.01920
30–34	−0.00016	0.00000	0.00009	0.00000	−0.00005	−0.00026	−0.00002	−0.00030	−0.00006	−0.00002	−0.00030
35–39	−0.00018	−0.00916	0.00563	0.00226	−0.02457	−0.01162	−0.00317	−0.00417	0.00842	0.00063	−0.01287
40–44	−0.00541	−0.00612	−0.00132	−0.00016	−0.00105	0.00506	−0.00039	−0.00130	−0.00207	−0.00085	0.00300
45–49	−0.00972	−0.00019	−0.00526	0.00018	0.00580	0.00376	−0.00057	−0.00567	−0.00494	−0.00128	−0.00208
50–54	−0.00122	−0.00090	−0.00079	0.00001	0.00044	0.00213	−0.00012	−0.00030	−0.00024	−0.00007	−0.00072
55–59	0.11302	0.09319	0.04308	0.00718	−0.23101	−0.09812	−0.00320	0.06681	−0.02809	−0.00605	−0.00226
60–64	−0.02585	0.02280	−0.02289	−0.00283	0.10597	0.06298	−0.01432	0.01000	−0.00554	−0.00175	−0.03391
65–69	−0.06441	−0.03993	−0.02433	−0.01283	0.11069	0.01506	−0.01259	−0.00997	−0.00259	−0.00358	−0.02396
70–74	−0.01307	0.01341	0.00153	−0.00589	0.02590	0.01389	−0.00660	−0.00628	0.00271	−0.00039	−0.00729
75–79	0.03834	−0.10328	0.02888	0.08388	−0.16453	−0.06113	0.05548	0.04639	−0.04141	−0.00272	0.05419
80–84	0.00061	−0.00218	0.00090	0.00424	−0.00058	−0.00044	0.00127	0.00101	−0.00111	0.00004	0.00401
85 +	−0.00039	−0.00052	−0.00004	−0.00045	−0.00078	−0.00044	−0.00029	0.00022	0.00002	0.00000	−0.00043
										Δ 1987–1995	0.20

Source: Calculations using the Decomposition Method, based on data from Public Health Ministry of Cuba and National Statistic Office, Cuba

11.7.12 *Annex 12. Males, decomposition of the difference in life expectancy at birth between 1995–2007, by age and causes of death, Cuba*

Males cause specific component of the time differential 1995–2007

Age groups	Other Causes	Cancer	Diabetes Mellitus	Mental Disorders	Heart Diseases	Cerebrovascular D.	Artery/ Arterioles	Respiratory Dis.	Liver/ Kidney/Obst	Congenital Malf.	External causes
< 1	0.22458	0.00267	0.00000	0.00000	0.01172	−0.00339	0.00000	0.02352	0.00016	0.07144	0.01196
1–4	0.04867	0.00637	0.00000	0.00000	0.01746	−0.00132	0.00000	0.01954	0.00103	0.02044	0.04835
5–9	0.01040	−0.00435	0.00073	0.00000	−0.00109	0.00273	0.00000	0.00109	0.00364	0.00929	0.03789
10–14	−0.00251	0.00022	0.00000	0.00000	0.00521	0.00110	0.00000	0.00255	−0.00301	0.01442	0.03876
15–19	0.01949	0.00439	0.00008	0.00000	0.00675	0.00024	−0.00111	0.00255	0.00278	0.00517	0.10489
20–24	0.02952	−0.00114	0.00244	−0.00057	0.00817	0.00110	−0.00057	−0.00008	0.00512	0.00307	0.13518
25–29	0.02327	−0.00097	0.00557	−0.00063	0.00349	−0.00219	−0.00063	0.00382	−0.00009	0.00195	0.13266
30–34	0.03611	0.00284	0.00455	−0.00327	0.00965	0.00352	0.00000	0.00420	0.00576	0.00148	0.10084
35–39	0.03433	−0.00625	0.00780	−0.00452	0.01947	0.01500	−0.00213	0.00991	0.00829	−0.00127	0.10779
40–44	0.00807	0.01535	0.00331	−0.01180	0.02731	0.00933	0.00178	0.00431	0.00756	0.00212	0.05813
45–49	0.01259	−0.01041	0.00779	−0.01072	0.02863	0.01149	0.00173	0.01002	0.00205	0.00335	0.05563
50–54	0.00812	−0.07441	0.01294	−0.01729	0.05423	0.01028	0.00179	0.00168	0.00068	−0.00386	0.06511
55–59	0.05305	−0.14131	0.01500	−0.03211	0.10230	0.03269	−0.01662	0.00156	0.02402	−0.00831	0.08172
60–64	0.00958	−0.01842	0.01249	−0.01045	0.03600	0.00574	0.00334	−0.00792	0.01326	0.00079	0.03095
65–69	0.02553	−0.02555	0.00258	−0.01615	0.09469	0.02089	0.01474	0.00804	0.01832	0.00160	0.02674
70–74	0.01801	−0.00278	−0.00171	−0.00914	0.09147	0.01551	0.01572	0.00740	0.00899	−0.00033	0.01550
75–79	0.02023	−0.05563	0.00660	−0.00980	0.16177	0.00668	0.04401	0.03469	0.01794	−0.00139	0.03360
80–84	0.00568	−0.00218	0.00482	−0.00631	0.08153	0.01588	0.02201	0.00855	0.00355	−0.00025	0.00938
85 +	0.04997	−0.09302	0.01326	−0.07994	0.31253	0.01818	0.14263	−0.01708	0.00858	−0.00109	0.02639
										Δ 1995–2007	3.06

Source: Calculations using the Decomposition Method, based on data from Public Health Ministry of Cuba and National Statistic Office, Cuba

11.7.13 *Annex 13. Females, decomposition of the difference in life expectancy at birth between 1987–1995, by age and causes of death, Cuba*

Females cause specific component of the time differential 1987–1995

Age groups	Other Causes	Cancer	Diabetes Mellitus	Mental Disorders	Heart Diseases	Cerebrovascular D.	Artery/ Arterioles	Respiratory Dis.	Liver/ Kidney/Obst	Congenital Malf.	External causes
< 1	0.13502	0.00166	0.00000	0.00000	−0.01611	0.00000	0.00000	0.00267	0.00440	0.08244	0.02357
1–4	0.01368	0.02329	0.00000	0.00000	0.02084	0.00368	0.00000	0.02608	−0.01015	−0.07895	−0.02700
5–9	−0.00414	0.00745	−0.00054	0.00000	−0.00094	0.00014	0.00000	−0.00135	0.00108	0.00299	0.00586
10–14	0.00574	0.00183	0.00000	0.00000	−0.00039	−0.00051	0.00000	0.00065	0.00059	−0.00152	0.00413
15–19	0.00251	0.00211	0.00120	0.00000	0.00404	0.00261	0.00000	0.00098	−0.00179	0.00046	0.05792
20–24	−0.00303	−0.00053	−0.00323	0.00000	0.00402	0.00057	0.00000	−0.00270	−0.00067	0.00337	0.05235
25–29	0.01675	0.00094	0.00140	0.00000	0.00912	0.00791	0.00000	0.00333	0.00157	0.00293	0.02502
30–34	0.01554	0.00039	−0.00177	0.00022	0.01153	0.00543	0.00062	0.00230	0.00148	−0.00247	0.00616
35–39	0.00008	−0.00043	0.00007	0.00000	0.00065	0.00027	0.00004	−0.00009	0.00002	0.00005	0.00039
40–44	−0.00378	−0.01216	0.00221	0.00000	0.00958	0.00283	−0.00027	−0.00309	−0.00166	−0.00073	−0.01027
45–49	−0.00863	0.01246	−0.00397	−0.00069	0.02060	0.01110	−0.00053	−0.00033	0.00222	−0.00228	−0.00005
50–54	0.00749	−0.01790	0.00478	0.00000	0.04316	0.02493	−0.00236	−0.00441	0.00117	−0.00356	0.00274
55–59	0.00251	0.00918	0.00048	0.00039	0.00836	0.01247	0.00137	−0.00375	0.00203	−0.00013	−0.00583
60–64	−0.02677	−0.01806	−0.01040	−0.00532	0.01593	0.01287	−0.00713	−0.01167	0.01928	−0.00028	−0.00777
65–69	−0.00700	0.00270	−0.00688	−0.00172	0.00763	−0.00135	−0.00042	−0.00188	0.00210	−0.00045	−0.00242
70–74	0.00752	−0.01337	0.00039	0.00732	−0.03160	0.00736	0.01363	−0.00575	−0.01509	−0.00075	0.02072
75–79	0.00221	0.00456	0.00027	−0.00256	0.01442	0.00421	−0.00021	0.00688	−0.00050	−0.00007	−0.00376
80–84	0.00532	0.00291	0.00439	0.00578	−0.00630	0.00395	0.00184	−0.00453	0.00014	−0.00003	0.01300
85 +	0.01058	−0.00103	0.00106	0.00982	−0.01019	0.01197	−0.00052	−0.02533	−0.00186	−0.00006	0.02077
										Δ 1987–1995	0.56

Source: Calculations using the Decomposition Method, based on data from Public Health Ministry of Cuba and National Statistic Office, Cuba

11.7.14 Annex 14. Females, decomposition of the difference in life expectancy at birth between 1995–2007, by age and causes of death, Cuba

Females cause specific component of the time differential 1995–2007

Age groups	Other Causes	Cancer	Diabetes Mellitus	Mental Disorders	Heart Diseases	Cerebrovascular D.	Artery/ Arterioles	Respiratory Dis.	Liver/ Kidney/Obst	Congenital Malf.	External causes
< 1	0.16304	0.00334	0.00000	0.00000	0.01852	−0.00282	0.00000	0.03028	−0.00201	0.05161	0.01155
1–4	0.06494	0.02288	0.00000	0.00000	0.00957	0.00137	0.00000	0.02584	0.00137	−0.00889	0.02012
5–9	0.02917	−0.01099	0.00110	0.00000	0.00193	−0.00027	0.00000	0.00550	0.00193	0.00633	0.03494
10–14	−0.00638	−0.00119	0.00000	0.00000	−0.00148	0.00335	0.00000	0.00094	0.00209	0.00754	0.04413
15–19	0.01792	0.00213	0.00030	0.00000	0.00119	−0.00157	0.00000	0.00483	0.00531	0.00561	0.07231
20–24	0.01563	0.00148	0.00287	0.00000	0.00592	0.00180	0.00000	0.00772	0.00381	−0.00028	0.07528
25–29	0.01047	0.00458	0.00259	0.00000	0.00467	0.00190	0.00000	0.00311	0.00318	−0.00108	0.05989
30–34	0.01083	−0.00956	0.00752	−0.00015	0.00561	0.00374	0.00000	0.01188	0.00433	0.00143	0.06421
35–39	0.03419	0.01071	−0.00021	0.00000	0.01089	0.01182	0.00079	0.01212	0.00584	−0.00092	0.04275
40–44	0.00737	0.02515	0.00253	0.00000	0.01785	0.01772	0.00003	0.01132	0.00727	0.00120	0.05274
45–49	0.01486	−0.01258	0.00801	0.00046	0.01806	0.02175	0.00228	0.01128	0.00286	0.00181	0.03844
50–54	0.01529	−0.00056	0.01418	−0.00216	0.02699	0.02131	−0.00124	−0.00665	0.01104	0.00133	0.02029
55–59	−0.00427	−0.08477	0.04588	−0.00334	0.09129	0.05963	−0.00145	−0.01837	0.01482	0.00292	0.05138
60–64	0.02298	0.01831	0.02302	0.00220	0.07866	0.04198	0.00172	−0.00206	0.00432	−0.00003	0.03247
65–69	0.02915	−0.03414	0.02750	−0.00034	0.08429	0.04710	0.00660	−0.00493	0.00480	−0.00002	0.02603
70–74	0.02889	−0.08206	0.03892	−0.01544	0.11558	0.05311	0.04329	−0.01448	0.01005	−0.00125	0.05295
75–79	0.02070	−0.12186	0.04217	−0.04256	0.18149	0.07752	0.06663	−0.03049	0.02807	0.00027	0.05899
80–84	0.01449	−0.00190	0.01685	−0.00853	0.07478	0.02162	0.02314	0.00801	0.00569	0.00024	0.01780
85 +	0.03344	−0.05624	0.04815	−0.14420	0.35051	0.02224	0.18390	−0.01824	0.01045	−0.00065	0.02244
										Δ 1995–2007	3.12

Source: Calculations using the Decomposition Method, based on data from Public Health Ministry of Cuba and National Statistic Office, Cuba

References

Aja, A. (2000). La emigración cubana hacia Estados Unidos a la luz de su política inmigratoria. Working Paper, *Colección: Centro de Estudios de Migraciones Internacionales—CEMI/UH*, La Habana, Cuba. http://biblioteca.clacso.edu.ar/ar/libros/cuba/cemi/laemig.pdf. Zugegriffen: 2. Okt. 2012.

Aja, A. (2002). La emigración cubana. Balance en el Siglo XX. Working Paper, *Colección: Centro de Estudios de Migraciones Internacionales—CEMI/UH*, La Habana, Cuba. http://biblioteca.clacso.edu.ar/ar/libros/cuba/cemi/laemig.pdf. Zugegriffen: 2. Okt. 2012.

Albizu-Campos, J. C. (2002). *Mortalidad y supervivencia en Cuba en los noventa*. La Habana: Centro de Estudios Demográficos- Universidad de La Habana.

Albizu-Campos, J. C. (2003). *La esperanza de vida en Cuba en los 90*. La Habana: *Centro de Estudios Demográficos- Universidad de La Habana*.

Annandale, E., & Hunt, K. (2000). Gender inequalities in health: research at the crossroads. In Annandale, E. & Hunt, K. (Eds.) Gender Inequalities in Health (pp. 1–35). Buckingham: Open University Press. (http://www.mcgrawhill.co.uk/openup/chapters/0335203647.pdf)

Bongaarts, J., & Feeney, G. (2002). How long do we live? *Population and development Review, 28*(1):13–29. (http://onlinelibrary.wiley.com/doi/10.1111/j.1728-4457.2002.00013.x/pdf)

Centro de Estudios de Población y Desarrollo. (2008). Envejecimiento de la Población Cubana. La Habana: Oficina Nacional de Estadísticas.

Chackiel, J. (2004). *La dinámica demográfica en América Latina. Población y Desarrollo, Series, 52* (CEPAL).

Christensen, K., Doblhammer, G., Rau, R., & Vaupel, J. (2009). Ageing populations: The challenges ahead. *The Lancet, 374*.

Fernández, J. M. (2006). Principales Causas de mortalidad general en Cuba. Año 2004. *Revista Habanera de Ciencias Médicas, 5*(2). (La Habana, Cuba).

González, F., & Ramos, O. (1996). *Cuba: Balance e indicadores demográficos estimados del período 1900–1959*. La Habana: Centro de Estudios Demográficos (CEDEM), National Statistic Office.

Hernández, R. (1986). *El Proceso de La Revolución Demográfica en Cuba*. La Habana: Editorial Ciencias Sociales.

López, L. M., Albizu-Campos, J. C., & Gran, M. A. (2005). Evolución del diferencial por sexo de la esperanza de vida al nacer. (Cuba, Siglo XX). *Revista Cubana de Salud Pública, 31*(3):182–191. (http://scielo.sld.cu/pdf/rcsp/v31n3/spu03305.pdf)

Meslé, F., & Vallin, J. (2004). The health transition: Trends and prospects. In G. Caselli, J. Vallin, & G. Wunsch (eds), *Demography: Analysis and synthesis, Vol. II*. France: INED.

Nathanson, C. (1984). Sex differences in mortality. *Annual Review of Sociology, 10*:191–213. (http://www.annualreviews.org/doi/pdf/10.1146/annurev.so.10.080184.001203)

Oeppen, J., & Vaupel, J. (2002). Broken limits to life expectancy. *Science, 296*:1029–1031.

Oficina Nacional de Estadísticas. (2007). *Anuario Demográfico de Cuba, 2006*. La Habana: Oficina Nacional de Estadísticas.

Oficina Nacional de Estadísticas. (2008). *Esperanza de vida Cuba y provincias, 2005–2007. Cálculos por sexo y edades*. La Habana: Oficina Nacional de Estadísticas.

Oficina Nacional de Estadísticas. (2009). *Anuario Demográfico de Cuba, 2008*. La Habana: Oficina Nacional de Estadísticas.

Oficina Nacional de Estadísticas. (2010). *Panorama Económico y Social. Cuba 2009*. La Habana: Oficina Nacional de Estadísticas.

Oficina Nacional de Estadísticas. (2011). *Anuario Demográfico de Cuba, 2010*. La Habana: Oficina Nacional de Estadísticas e Información.

Omran, A. B. (1971). The epidemiological transition. A theory of the epidemiology of population change. *Milbank Q., 83*(4):731–757 (2005).

Riverón, R., & Azcuy, P. (2001). Mortalidad Infantil en Cuba 1959–1999. *Revista Cubana de Pediatría, 73*(3):143–157. (http://scielo.sld.cu/scielo.php?script=sci_arttext&pid=S0034-75312001000300001&lng=es&nrm=iso)

Rogers, A., & Hackenbert, R. (1987). Extending epidemikologic transition theory: A new stage. *Social Biology, 34*.

Shkolnikov, V. M., Valkonen, T., Begun, A. Z., & Andreev, E. M. (2001). Measuring inter-group inequalities in length of life. Genus, LVII (3–4): 33–62. (http://www.jstor.org/stable/29788701)

Torreira, R., & Buajasan, J. (2000). Operación Peter Pan, un caso de la guerra psicológica contra Cuba. La Habana: *Editora Política*.

Trovato F. (2005). *Narrowing sex differential in life expectancy in Canada and Austria: Comparative analysis* (pp. 17–52). Vienna Yearbook of Population Research.

UNICEF. (1995). *Cuba, Transición de la Fecundidad. Cambio social y conducta reproductiva*. La Habana: CEDEM, ONE, MINSAP, FNUAP.

Chapter 12
Variable Scales of Avoidable Mortality Within the Russian Population

T. P. Sabgayda, V. G. Semyonova, A. E. Ivanova and V. I. Starodubov

Abstract Socio-political changes over the past 30 years have led to important changes in the mortality of the Russian population. The largest variations were observed in death rates due to preventable causes, which depend on the conditions and way of life of the population as well as on the quality of health care. We show that now that mortality rates are declining, government measures to protect public health are more important for improving the demographic situation than efforts to increase the income of the population. Expenditure on the protection of public health is greatest in regions with a high level of economic development, but they do not necessarily lead to the reduction of mortality from preventable causes. Avoidable mortality depends not only on the level of poverty in a region, but also on other factors: climate, the economic way of life, the level of property stratification of the population and the intensity of regional economic development. The analysis of the heterogeneity of avoidable mortality in Russia is of interest not only for Russian researchers. Data on mortality in Russia may be used as a testing ground for studying the various factors that influence mortality. The wide range of changes in mortality on different scales permits us to analyze trends which are weaker and less noticeable in countries with a smaller population.

Keywords Russia · Avoidable deaths · Mortality trends · Regional differences · Gender differences

Life expectancy at birth in Russia in 2010 was 63.03 years for males and 74.87 years for females, almost 10 years less for men and 5 years less for women than in Central and East Europe. Compared with West European countries, the lag is more than 15 years for men and 10 years for women.

T. P. Sabgayda (✉) · V. G. Semyonova · A. E. Ivanova
Department of Health Statistics, Federal Research Institute for Health Organization and Informatics of Ministry of Health of the Russian Federation, 11, Dobrolubov str., Moscow 127254, Russia
e-mail: tsabgaida@mail.ru

V. I. Starodubov
Academy of Medical Sciences, Federal Research Institute for Health Organization and Informatics of Ministry of Health of the Russian Federation, 11, Dobrolubov str., Moscow 127254, Russia

J. Anson, M. Luy (eds.), *Mortality in an International Perspective*, European Studies of Population 18, DOI 10.1007/978-3-319-03029-6_12,

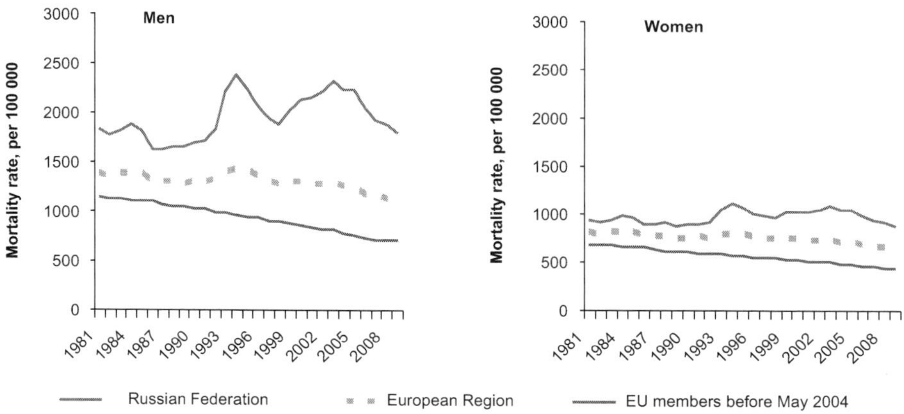

Fig. 12.1 Trends in mortality of men and women in Russia and the European Union before and after May 2004. (Website WHO 2009)

During the last three decades there have been two pronounced peaks in the mortality of the Russian population: in 1994, due to the changing socio-political situation, and in 2003, due to the formation of new economic relations (Fig. 12.1). It has been argued that at the end of the twentieth century the mortality of the Russian population was more closely related to the country's public health policy than to the quality of health care (Andreev et al. 2003). A positive trend in life expectancy in recent years also developed due to the country's social and political recovery (Ivanova and Semyonova 2008). As a result, mortality has declined in Russia more rapidly than in any other European country. Between 2003 and 2010 the mortality rate among Russian men declined by 30.4 % and for women by 30.8 %. In the EU countries over this period, male and female mortality declined by 15.9 % and 14.5 %, respectively (Website WHO 2009). Nonetheless, and despite the increase in Russian life expectancy over the past 5 years, its value in 2010 was still lower than it was in the mid-1980's.

Recently, there has been a slowdown in the rate of growth in life expectancy of the Russian population. In 2006–2007 the average annual increase was 1.23 years for men and 0.78 years for women, in 2008–2009 these figures were 0.66 and 0.40 years, respectively and in 2010–2011 (preliminary data) they were 0.22 and 0.11 years. The economic and financial crisis of 2008–2009 and extreme weather conditions in 2010 do not explain the slowdown in the decrease of mortality in Russia. These factors also affected European countries but the rate of growth in life expectancy remained constant. The question arises, why, despite the improving socio-economic conditions in Russia has the mortality decline slowed down? Is this phenomenon universal for all regions of the country or not?

The life expectancy gap between the different regions coincides almost exactly with the lag between life expectancy in Russia and Western Europe. These regional life expectancy differences Russia are due to variations in socio-economic, climatic, cultural and ethnic composition of the population (Prohorov 1998). In 2010 the gap

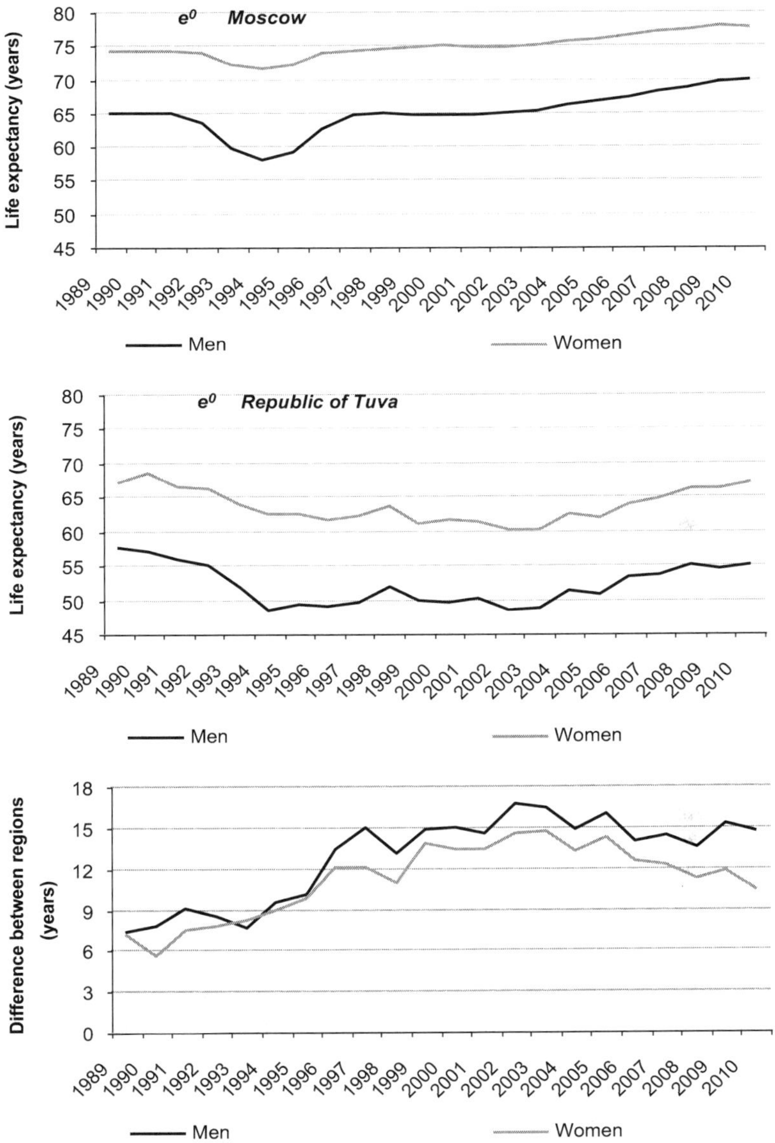

Fig. 12.2 Life expectancy e^0 of men and women in the city of Moscow and Republic of Tuva and difference between these regional characteristics

between life expectancy in the Republic of Tuva and the city of Moscow was 14.7 years for males and 10.4 years for females. Regional disadvantages are also reflected in the fact that these differences in life expectancies increase when mortality rises and are reduced when mortality declines (Ivanova 2009). Figure 12.2 compares changes in mortality rates in Moscow (a region with one of the highest life expectancies in the country) and in the Republic of Tuva (one of the regions with the lowest life expectancy). The regional gap grew till the last mortality peak, in 2003, since which time the gap has narrowed, especially for women's life expectancy.

However, the patterns of change in mortality in the regions are not all the same. For the country as a whole the gap in life expectancy at birth between men and women in 2010 was 11.8 years, down from 13.1 years in 2003. In Moscow, the gap in life expectancy between men and women declined from 9.8 years in 2003 to 7.7 years in 2010, while in the Republic of Tuva it increased slightly—from 11.4 to 12.1 years, respectively. These characteristics of the variation in the average death rate are the complex sum of essentially heterogeneous regional mortality trends.

12.1 Justification of the Choice of Research Method

Mortality trends in Russia have recently improved in response to social and political stability as well as new public health policies. A primary indicator of health system performance is avoidable mortality, that is, total mortality from causes that are preventable through the intervention of health care institutions (Rutstein et al. 1976). Given the current state of medical knowledge, there are a number of causes from which people should no longer die. For developed countries, during the second half of the last century, rates of avoidable mortality declined more rapidly than did those of unavoidable mortality (in other words, the health care systems worked effectively) (Korda and Butler 2006; Treurniet et al. 2004). In this paper we focus on variations in changes in rates of avoidable mortality.

The analysis of avoidable mortality was initially recommended for use in countries with a high level of technological development (Rutstein et al. 1976). Later it was found that this methodology can be used for the assessment of health care systems at any level of socio-economic development (Charlton and Velez 1986; Logminiene et al. 2004; Nolte et al. 2000). In the countries of the European Union the contribution of avoidable mortality to the total death rate ranges from 10 to 30 %, while in countries with weaker economies it is 40 to 50 % (Westerling 2001). The different mortality trends of men and women are related to gender differences in the way health policy influences the risk of death from preventable causes (Westerling 2003). In regions with a lower socio-economic level, the level of avoidable mortality is relatively higher (Westerling et al. 1996), as also is the case with low social status population groups (Lagasse et al. 1990; Pampalon 1993) and populations with low levels of education (Marshall et al. 1993). Levels of avoidable mortality also vary by ethnic characteristics of the population (Woolhandler et al. 1985). On the one hand these properties of avoidable mortality help explain its variations in the Russian Federation. On the other hand, during the period of socio-economic improvement, these properties also underlie the heterogeneity of its dynamics.

12.2 Data, Methods and Study Design

The changes in the level and structure of avoidable mortality in all regions of Russia since 1989 till 2010 were analyzed. Data for 2010 were taken without regard to the population census in order to ensure consistency with data for the previous period. In total, the analysis included 80 regions of the Russian Federation. Autonomous districts were excluded because their population is not large and the indicators of mortality are hence unstable.

The program STATISTICA 6.1 StatSoft, Inc. (2003) was used for calculation of the Pearson correlation coefficients. The Spearman's rank correlation coefficients were calculated using Microsoft® Office Excel 2003. The Spearman correlation coefficient ρ was computed using n (number of regions), M_i and L_i (their ranks for two characteristics) as well as their average values (Myers and Well 2003):

$$\rho = \frac{\sum_{i=1}^{n} (M_i - \overline{M}) * (L_i - \overline{L})}{\sqrt{\sum_{i=1}^{n} (M_i - \overline{M})^2 * \sum_{i-1}^{n} (L_i - \overline{L})^2}}.$$

Estimates of avoidable mortality were made in accordance with the European approach, under which avoidable mortality refers to deaths due to 34 causes and 4 classes of causes (Holland 1988). In practice, the preventability of 38 causes of death from the European list in Russia is possible only for age groups 5–64 (Mikhailova and Ivanova 2006). The official data of the State Statistics Committee were analyzed. In Russia, all deaths are subject to mandatory registration. Physicians code the cause of death in accordance with the international classification ICD-10. The standardized death rates were calculated using the factual automated information system "FAISS-Potential" (Ermakov et al. 1999). With its help the standardized death rates from preventable causes for the population aged from 5 to 64 years were calculated and summarized. The Scandinavian ("European") population age structure was used as standard (Doll 1976).

Preventable causes are divided into 3 groups according to three levels of disease prevention (Holland 1997). The first group includes the causes of death which can be prevented by measures for primary prevention of disease (Table 12.1). This group includes the causes largely determined by lifestyle. Alcohol consumption and smoking are risk factors for vascular disorders of the brain, for chronic liver disease, for malignant neoplasm of different topologies in the digestive tract, respiratory tract, bladder and liver. The first group also includes injuries and poisoning. Mortality in this group is largely influenced by law enforcement, and economic and social measures such as road safety and measures to reduce crime.

The second group includes the causes of death which can be prevented by secondary prevention, that is, by early diagnosis of diseases. This group includes malignant neoplasms of breast and uterus, and malignant neoplasms of the skin.

The third group includes the causes of death which depend on the quality of treatment and medical care. Changes in mortality from this group of causes are

Table 12.1 Groups of preventable causes of death. (WW Holland 1997)

Causes of death	ICD-10 code
Group 1	
Malignant neoplasms of lip, oral cavity and pharynx	C00–C14
Malignant neoplasms of esophagus	C15
Malignant neoplasms of liver and intrahepatic bile ducts	C22
Malignant neoplasms of larynx	C32
Malignant neoplasms of trachea, bronchus and lung	C33, C34
Malignant neoplasms of other and ill-marked locations of the respiratory and chest	C30, C31, C37–C39
Malignant neoplasms of bladder	C67
Malignant neoplasms of other and not refined urinary organs	C65, C66, C68
Subarachnoid hemorrhage	I60
Intracerebral and other intracranial hemorrhage	I61–I62
Cerebral infarction	I63
Stroke, not specified as hemorrhage or infarction	I64
Other cerebrovascular diseases	I67–I69
Alcoholic liver disease (alcoholic: cirrhosis, hepatitis, fibrosis)	K70
Fibrosis and cirrhosis (excluding alcohol)	K74
Other liver disease	K71–K73, K75–K76
CLASS XIX. Injury, poisoning and certain other consequences of external factors	S00–S09, T00–T98
Group 2	
Malignant melanoma of skin	C43
Other malignant neoplasms of skin	C44
Malignant neoplasm of breast	C50
Malignant neoplasms of cervix	C53
Malignant neoplasms of other and updated parts of uterus	C54, C55
Group 3	
Malignant neoplasm of prostate	C61
Malignant neoplasm of other male genital organs	C60, C62, C63
Hodgkin's disease	C81
Non-Hodgkin's lymphoma	C82–C85
Leukemia	C91–C95
Chronic rheumatic heart disease	I05–I09
Hypertonic disease	I11–I13, I10, I15
Gastric ulcer	K25
Duodenal ulcer	K26
Diseases of the appendix	K35–K38
Hernia	K40–K46
Cholelithiasis	K80
Cholecystitis	K81
CLASS I. Certain infectious and parasitic diseases	A00–A99, B00–B99
CLASS X. Respiratory diseases	J00–J99
CLASS XV. Complications of pregnancy, childbirth and the postpartum period	O00–O99

associated with the efficacy of the public health system and the completeness of medical measures, such as transportation to hospitals, the adequacy of medical and surgical care, timely care etc.

In this paper we present an analysis of different kinds of heterogeneity in avoidable mortality in Russia. Variation in avoidable mortality is considered from four aspects: the level of avoidable mortality in different periods of social and economic reforms in Russia (1989–2010 years), territorial differences in mortality level (2010), gender differences in mortality levels and differences in trends in avoidable mortality (2003–2010). In this way we aim:

- To estimate the contribution of avoidable mortality to the regional differences in life expectancy;
- To estimate the contribution of avoidable mortality to the distinction of death rates between regions with different socio-economical situations;
- To characterize the factors influencing regional variations in mortality.

12.3 Results

The level of avoidable mortality In 2010, avoidable mortality was 526.2 per hundred thousand among men and 175.1 among women. Figure 12.3 shows the dynamics of avoidable mortality among men and women in Russia, divided into three groups according to the three levels of prevention (standardized rates per 100,000 inhabitants). At present, the level of avoidable mortality in Russia is 2.5 times higher than in the countries of European Union. At its peak, in 1994, the difference was more than 8 times. This excess is determined primarily by preventable causes of the first group, mostly related to external causes. In 2010, the first group of causes of death accounted for 79.7 % of avoidable mortality among males and 68.2 % among females. Mortality due to untimely identification of disease (group 2) was responsible for 0.46 % of avoidable mortality among men and 16.2 % among women. Deaths attributed to poor quality of medical care (group 3) account for 19.9 % of avoidable mortality among men and 15.5 % among women.

Since the end of the Soviet period avoidable mortality rates grew by 69.8 % among males and 53.1 % among females up to the first peak in mortality of the Russian population (1989–1994) and by 57.5 % and 51.5 % respectively up to the second peak in mortality (1989–2003). In parallel with the economic recovery after 2003, the level of avoidable mortality fell to its 1998 level over 4 years, whereas the increase in mortality was observed over 5 years. During the period of 1989–2010, the level of avoidable mortality as a whole grew by 10.5 % among males and by 10.3 % among females. The greatest short-time variations in mortality were observed for preventable causes of groups 1 and 3.

Overall, however, for the period under analysis, the mortality of men changed to a greater extent for preventable causes of groups 2 and 3 and the mortality of women for causes of groups 1 and 2. Table 12.2 shows the magnitude of increasing avoidable and unavoidable mortality for different periods and for the period under review as a whole (in percentages). The "Shock therapy", launched in 1992 by the Gaidar government led to the first peak of mortality. The growth in mortality of men and women due to preventable causes of groups 1 and 3 was greater than that due

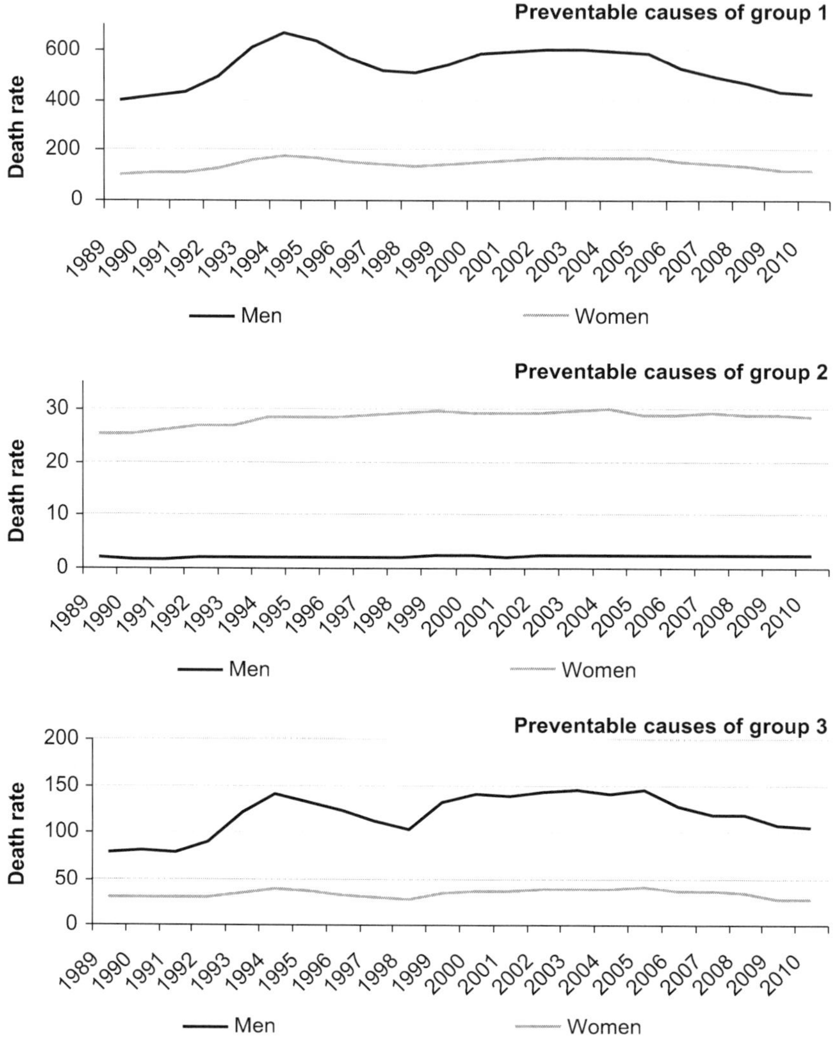

Fig. 12.3 Avoidable mortality (standardized rates, per 100,000 inhabitants) among men and women in Russia in 1989–2010 years. The causes of death can be prevented by: group 1—measures for primary prevention of disease; group 2—early diagnosis of diseases; group 3—adequate quality of treatment and medical care

to causes of group 2. The "default" of the economy that occurred in 1998 led to the second peak of mortality. Here too there was a greater increase in mortality of the Russian population due to causes of groups 1 and 3 than to causes of group 2. In both cases male mortality increased most for causes which depend on the quality of medical care. The leading causes during the first peak in female mortality were preventable by measures of primary prevention and during the second peak by the

Table 12.2 The magnitude of increases in avoidable (group 1—the causes of death that can be prevented by measures of primary prevention of disease; group 2—by early diagnosis of diseases; group 3—by adequate quality of treatment and medical care) and unavoidable mortality in the Russian Federation for different periods (per cent)

Mortality	1989–2010	1989–1994	1998–2003	2003–2010
Males				
Group 1 of avoidable deaths	5.9	68.4	19.8	– 30.4
Group 2 of avoidable deaths	50.0	18.8	10.0	9.1
Group 3 of avoidable deaths	33.9	78.2	41.9	– 27.8
Total avoidable deaths	10.6	69.8	23.5	– 29.8
Unavoidable deaths	36.1	71.1	40.4	– 21.7
Females				
Group 1 of avoidable deaths	14.6	70.1	26.4	– 30.8
Group 2 of avoidable deaths	11.8	11.0	1.0	– 3.7
Group 3 of avoidable deaths	– 6.5	28.9	40.5	– 29.4
Total avoidable deaths	10.3	53.1	24.5	– 27.2
Unavoidable deaths	24.6	74.3	31.2	– 25.5

quality of medical care. When the mortality rate declined the changes in death from causes of group 1 and group 3 were approximately the same for both sexes. Deaths from preventable causes of group 2 (due to late detection of malignant tumors) have decreased since 2003 among women, but have increased among men. In general, during the post-Soviet period, relatively small changes in male mortality from causes of group 2 (which are determined by the timely initiation of treatment) have led to a significant change in mortality.

Avoidable mortality in Russia is predominantly determined by causes preventable by measures of primary prevention. However, its dynamics shows that the socio-economic upheavals over the past 20 years have had the greatest impact on the level of mortality among women. Among men, the greatest changes have been in mortality from causes which are determined by poor quality of medical care. *Ex facte*, this contradicts the known data about the extremely high level of alcohol consumption and smoking among Russian men. However, at the same time, deaths of females, particularly those under 40 years of age, during the crisis (before 2003) grew faster than did male mortality. The extremely high growth rates of female mortality were observed for alcohol-related causes. This reflects a decrease in gender differences in the distribution of behavioral risk factors in Russia (Semyonova et al. 2010).

Over the analyzed period, 1989–2010 as whole, unavoidable mortality increased more than avoidable mortality: by 36.1 % among males and by 24.6 % among females. During the two periods of increasing mortality the number of unavoidable deaths has increased to a greater extent than has avoidable ones, whereas they have decreased less during the period of declining mortality. As a result, variations in the growth of life expectancy at birth, eliminating preventable causes of death, for the period 1989–2010 years are not as large as might be expected.

The larger increases in unavoidable compared with avoidable mortality suggests that for the post-Soviet period, the social and political upheavals influenced the

Table 12.3 The gains in life expectancy with elimination of preventable causes of death for three groups (group 1—the causes of death can be prevented by measures for primary prevention of disease; group 2—by early diagnosis of diseases; group 3—by adequate quality of treatment and medical care) and in total (in years). The share of these gains in life expectancy (per cent) at different years

Indicators	1989	1994	2003	2010
Males				
Gains in life expectancy with elimination of:				
Avoidable death causes of group 1	3.62	5.36	4.77	3.55
Avoidable death causes of group 2	0.01	0.01	0.01	0.01
Avoidable death causes of group 3	0.60	0.60	0.65	0.65
Total avoidable deaths	4.23	5.97	5.43	4.21
Life expectancy (years)	64.05	57.72	58.76	63.03
Share in life expectancy, per cent	*6.2*	*9.4*	*8.5*	*6.3*
Females				
Gains in life expectancy with elimination of:				
Avoidable death causes of group 1	0.91	1.53	1.52	1.12
Avoidable death causes of group 2	0.18	0.19	0.19	0.19
Avoidable death causes of group 3	0.21	0.22	0.24	0.25
Total avoidable deaths	1.30	1.94	1.95	1.56
Life expectancy (years)	74.42	71.20	71.87	74.87
Share in life expectancy, per cent	*1.7*	*2.7*	*2.6*	*2.0*

mortality of the Russian population to a greater extent than the activities of the health institutions. Many studies have shown that mortality depends on economic factors and, in particular, is influenced by the level of income (Duleep 1995; Judge 1998; Mackenbach and Looman 1994). The poverty rate in Russia, which in 1991 amounted to only 4 %, reached 35 % in the first quarter of 1993 and 21 % in the fourth quarter of 1994 (Gordon and Klopov 2000). With the reduction or mitigation of market factors (sharp fall in real incomes; extremely big differentiation of income) the poverty level was reduced in 1996–1997. However, the financial crisis of 1998, deepening the gap between the price of labor and its cost, the lack of real social guarantees for the growth of unemployment, forced unpaid leave and delayed payment of wages led to a sharp increase in the level of poverty in Russia (Lebedeva 1999). In 1999, more than half of the population lived below the poverty line and in 2005 the poverty rate declined to a quarter (Balatsky and Saakyants 2006). By 2007, the poverty rate in Russia had fallen to 13.4 % of the population (Website Sotsialny atlas rossiyskih regionov 2009). So the pattern of change in poverty is similar to the pattern of avoidable mortality.

Table 12.3 presents estimates of gains in life expectancy eliminating preventable causes of death for three groups and in total. The contributions of preventable deaths to life expectancy are also calculated (the sum of the life expectancy at birth and its gain when eliminating preventable causes). Male life expectancy fell by 9.4 % due to deaths from preventable causes in 1994 and by 6.3 % in 2010. The contribution of avoidable mortality to reducing female life expectancy at birth is less significant; it declined since 1994 to 2010 by one third, whereas in men the contribution declined by a half. So at present, the contribution of avoidable mortality to life expectancy at birth is still larger than in 1989.

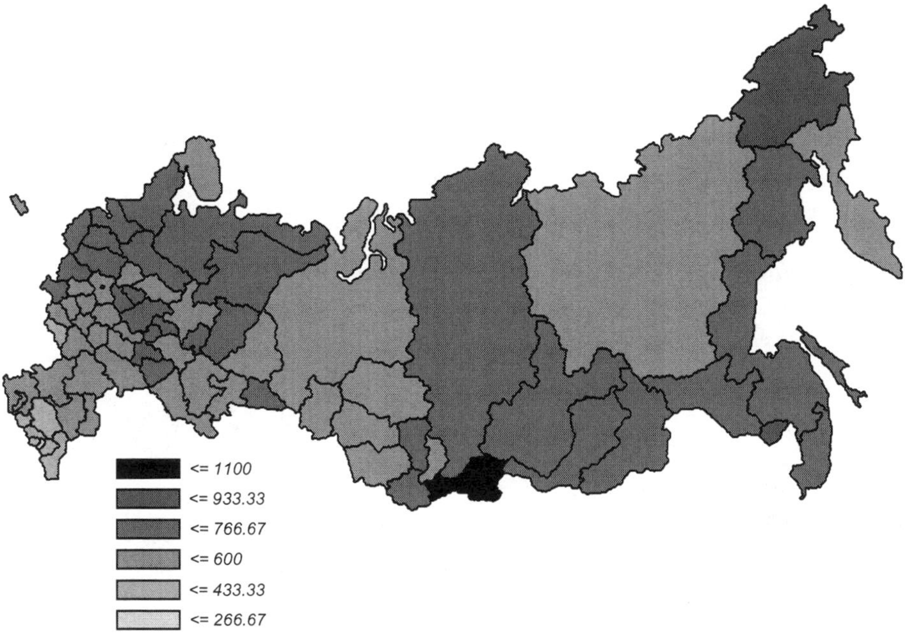

Fig. 12.4 Avoidable mortality among males in different regions of the Russian Federation (standardized rates, per 100,000 inhabitants), 2010

Regional variations in mortality The level of preventable deaths is close to the average performance in less than half of the Russian territory. Figure 12.4 shows a map of Russia with the levels of avoidable mortality for males in 2010. There is an increase in mortality from south to north in the European part of country, which coincides with the regional distribution of life expectancy as well as with the socioeconomic development of the territories. The Republic of Tuva is the leader in terms of avoidable mortality for males, but the Chukotka autonomous district and the Jewish autonomous region also had high levels of male avoidable mortality. The lowest level of avoidable mortality in the population is in the Republic of Ingushetia, but the quality of the collection of death data there does not meet acceptable standards. Among the regions with reliable information the lowest mortality rate is registered in the city of Moscow.

The level of avoidable mortality for males is three times greater than for females and the patterns of spatial variation in avoidable mortality among males and females are not the same. The levels of male avoidable mortality are close to the national level in 41.1 % regions, the levels of female avoidable mortality in 53.3 % regions. Figure 12.5 shows regional variations of avoidable mortality among females in 2010. There is an increasing mortality gradient from South to North and from South-West to North-East, which coincides with the climatic living conditions more than with the socioeconomic development of the territories. The Chukotka autonomous district and the Republic of Tuva are leaders in terms of avoidable mortality for females. The

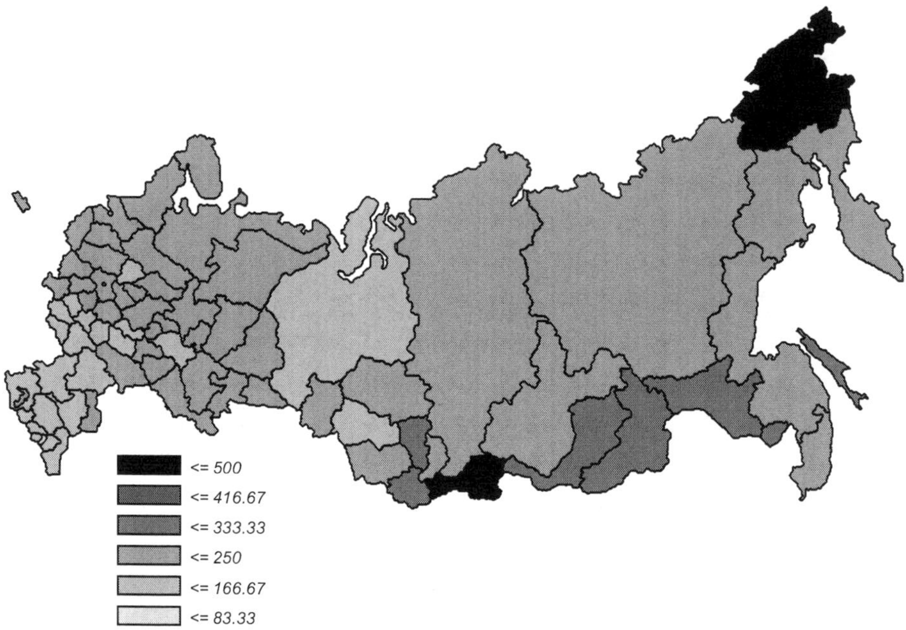

Fig. 12.5 Avoidable mortality among females in different regions of the Russian Federation (standardized rates, per 100,000 inhabitants), 2010

lowest level of avoidable mortality among women is also registered in the Republic of Ingushetia and in Moscow city.

In 2010, the level of avoidable mortality varied by a factor of 4.2 (between the values for Moscow and Republic of Tuva, varying respectively from 256.2 to 1097.7 for males and from 113.7 to 473.8 for females). The level of unavoidable mortality rates in these same regions differed by 1.3 and 1.6 times (varying respectively from 321.6 to 423.8 for male deaths and from 129.2 to 209.7 for female deaths). In 2003, with a higher mortality rate, the relations between Moscow and Republic of Tuva were similar: avoidable mortality differed by a factor of 4.1 for males and 5.8 for females, whereas unavoidable mortality differed only by a factor of 1.3 and 1.6 respectively. We may thus consider the identified relationships as a stable phenomenon, meaning that most of the regional differences in mortality (80 %) are determined by the preventable component.

Table 12.4 shows the variability in the level of avoidable mortality and the share of preventable causes in the total number of deaths among men and women aged 5–64 years in the different regions of the Russian Federation. It does not take into account the southern republics which do not have reliable data. Male mortality has the greatest observed variations for preventable causes of the first group (the mortality of which is due to living conditions and behavioral risk factors). Female mortality has the greatest observed variations for preventable causes of the third group (managed by the quality of medical care).

Table 12.4 The highest and the lowest regional values of (1) levels of avoidable mortality (standardized rates, per 100,000 inhabitants) of three groups[a] and (2) share of preventable causes in the total number of deaths among men and women aged 5–64 years in Russian Federation (per cent), 2010

Indicators	Males	Females
(1) *Avoidable mortality levels*		
Total in RF	526.2	175.1
Max (region)	1097.7 (Republic of Tuva)	473.8 (Republic of Tuva)
Min (region)	154.8 (Moscow city)	113.7 (Moscow city)
Causes of group 1 in RF	419.2	119.5
Max (region)	882.4 (Republic of Tuva)	364.0 (Republic of Tuva)
Min (region)	195.0 (Moscow city)	65.8 (Moscow city)
Causes of group 2 in RF	2.4	28.4
Max (region)	4.0 (Tambov region)	37.9 (Republic of Altai)
Min (region)	0.0 (Republic of Kalmykia)	11.4 (Republic of Sakha)
Causes of group 3 in RF	104.6	27.2
Max (region)	213.6 (Republic of Tuva)	84.0 (Republic of Tuva)
Min (region)	59.1 (Moscow city)	15.0 (Lipetsk region)
(2) *The share of three groups of preventable causes among total deaths cases (per cent)*		
All groups in RF	55.7	52.7
Max (region)	75.3 (Republic of Tuva)	71.9 (Republic of Tuva)
Min (region)	43.7 (Moscow city)	44.8 (Lipetsk region)
Causes of group 1 in RF	44.4	35.8
Max (region)	61.5 (Republic of Tuva)	55.7 (Republic of Tuva)
Min (region)	33.2 (Moscow city)	26.6 (Moscow city)
Causes of group 2 in RF	0.25	8.9
Max (region)	0.53 (Republic of Adygeya)	15.2 (Republic of Dagestan)
Min (region)	0.05 (Republic of Kalmykia)	2.8 (Republic of Sakha)
Causes of group 3 in RF	11.1	8.1
Max (region)	15.4 (Kurgan region)	12.7 (Republic of Tuva)
Min (region)	5.8 (Republic of Sakha)	4.4 (Republic of Marij El)

[a] Group 1—the causes of death can be prevented by measures for primary prevention of disease; group 2—by early diagnosis of diseases; group 3—by adequate quality of treatment and medical care

Due to variations in the level of socio-economic development, the proportion of preventable causes of death in the total mortality in each region is different and does not correlate with the level of avoidable mortality. For the country in general, deaths from avoidable causes for ages 5–64 years was 60.0 % of all deaths in 1994 and 54.9 % of all deaths in 2010. Since 2010, fewer than half of all deaths at ages of 5–64 years in some regions of Russia can be classified as avoidable, whereas before this was true only in Moscow. The largest proportion of avoidable deaths is in the Republic of Tuva and accounted for about three-quarters of all losses.

In terms of their impact on mortality reduction, the leading causes of mortality in all regions are determined by living conditions and behavioral risk factors (causes of the first group). In all regions male mortality from these causes constitute no less than a third of all deaths. The share of this group of causes in different regions varies by a factor of almost two for males and three for females. The public health system is responsible for causes of the second and the third groups, premature deaths as a consequence of late diagnosis and poor treatment. Such causes may account for up to one sixth of total deaths among males and up to third among females, highlighting the poor quality of medical institutions in some regions.

Excluding the Caucasian Republics, the highest life expectancies for men and women in 2010 were observed in Moscow (69.83 and 77.64), and the lowest in the Chukotka autonomous district (52.35 and 62.72). The increase in male life expectancy when eliminating avoidable mortality ranged from 1.94 years in Moscow to 8.31 years in the Republic of Tuva. The contributions of these losses to male life expectancy are 2.78 and 15.08 % respectively. Life expectancy for females is less dependent on preventable causes. The increase in their life expectancy when eliminating avoidable mortality varies from 0.99 years in Moscow to 4.24 years in the Chukotka autonomous district, or 1.28 and 6.76 % respectively.

The spatial variation in these parameters corresponds to changes in mortality levels. We converted the values of regional avoidable mortality, values of gains in life expectancy eliminating preventable causes of death and their shares in life expectancy to appropriate ranks (Annex 1). For male mortality the Spearman's rank correlation coefficient[1] of the level of avoidable mortality with the increase in life expectancy is 0.96 and with the contribution of this increase in life expectancy is 0.97; for female mortality both are 0.98 ($N = 82$, $p < 0.001$). These results suggest that the patterns of spatial variation of avoidable and unavoidable mortality are similar. In several regions, there is a small shift between rank positions of the value of increase in life expectancy and rank positions of its share in life expectancy. For example, in the Kamchatka region (now Kamchatka Territory) the rank positions of the increase in life expectancy when eliminating avoidable mortality for males and females are 18 and 49 respectively, and the rank positions of the contribution of these increments in life expectancy are 21 and 51 respectively; in the Smolensk region the values are 55 and 60 versus 60 and 61.

The variations in mortality structure for males and females are not the same: the Spearman rank correlation coefficient between male and female mortality is 0.92; between the values of increases in their life expectancy eliminating avoidable mortality is 0.91, and between contributions of these increases in life expectancy is 0.91. We calculated the differences between the rank position of regions on values of increases in their life expectancy when eliminating avoidable mortality and the rank position of its contribution to life expectancy. The sum of absolute values of these differences is 142 points for men and only 62 points for women. This means that regional variations in avoidable and unavoidable deaths for women are more concordant than for male mortality.

Relationship between the levels of avoidable mortality and population poverty Table 12.5 shows the Pearson correlation coefficients of mortality and indicators of poverty, calculated in two ways: using death rates for Russia for the period 1989–2010 and using the values of regional rates in 2010 (Website of Rosstat. Regions

[1] Own calculation.

Table 12.5 The correlation coefficients between avoidable and unavoidable mortality and life expectancy of the Russian population with the value of cash income[a], and the headcount index[b], calculated for the average index for Russia in the dynamics[c] and for regional indicators (Website of Rosstat. Regions of Russia. Socio-economic indicators—2011), 2010 (statistically significant coefficients in *bold*)

Indicators	Dynamical analysis				Regional analysis			
	Average per capita income ($N=17$)		The share of poor ($N=22$)		Average per capita income ($N=82$)		The share of poor ($N=82$)	
	Male	Female	Male	Female	Male	Female	Male	Female
Avoidable deaths of group 1	_– 0.69_**	_– 0.52_*	_0.70_**	_0.62_**	0.004	0.07	_0.25_*	_0.31_**
Avoidable deaths of group 2	0.26	0.16	– 0.16	_0.45_*	_– 0.24_*	– 0.19	– 0.09	0.01
Avoidable deaths of group 3	– 0.24	– 0.13	_0.54_**	0.35	_– 0.22_*	0.19	_0.34_**	_0.23_*
Total avoidable mortality	_– 0.63_**	– 0.47	_0.68_**	_0.60_**	– 0.04	0.08	_0.28_**	_0.30_**
Unavoidable mortality	– 0.07	– 0.41	_– 0.45_*	_0.60_**	0.09	_0.23_*	0.005	0.07
Life longevity	_0.62_**	_0.76_**	_– 0.69_**	_– 0.67_**	0.016	– 0.014	– 0.07	– 0.06

Group 1—the causes of death can be prevented by measures for primary prevention of disease; group 2—by early diagnosis of diseases; group 3—by adequate quality of treatment and medical care

* The level of significance equal to 0.95; **The level of significance equal to 0.99

[a] Average per capita income (per month, now in rubles, until 1998—in thousand rubles)

[b] The number of people with incomes below the subsistence level (percentage of total population)

[c] Average figures for RF for the period 1989–2010 (calculations with per capita incomes—for the period 1994–2010)

of Russia. Socio-economic indicators 2011b, c). The dynamic analysis of changes for the period 1994–2010 reveals a relatively high degree of association of poverty with life expectancy and the level of avoidable mortality from the causes of the first group. That means that the way of life of the population is closely linked with the level of welfare. The regional analysis found an association of avoidable mortality with the headcount index but not with the size of cash income. Regions with higher percentages of poor people have higher mortality due to poor quality of care (causes of group 3).

With regard to unavoidable mortality and longevity in general, our data did not allow us to separate out the influence of different factors on health status, which was reflected in the results of correlation analysis. There is no correlation between the level of unavoidable mortality and the share of the poor, but there was a direct correlation between female mortality and the average per capita income. This, apparently,

Table 12.6 Average per capita income[a] and the share of poor inhabitants[b] in regions with the lowest and the highest levels of avoidable mortality (standardized rates, per 100,000 inhabitants), 2010 (Website of Rosstat. Regions of Russia. Socio-economic indicators—2011)

Regions	Avoidable mortality		Income indexes	
	Male	Female	The share of poor (per cent)	Average per capita income
Regions with the lowest level of avoidable mortality				
Karachaevo-Cherkessian Republic	411.5	129.8	16.5	8.7
Republic of North Ossetia	409.8	107.4	11.5	9.8
Khanty-Mansijsk autonomous district	392.5	133.3	7.4	32.9
St. Petersburg	387.5	149.8	11.0	17.6
Kabardino-Balkarian Republic	372.9	117.0	15.5	8.6
Belgorod region	372.8	119.3	10.3	12.8
Republic of Dagestan	290.2	91.8	10.1	11.0
Moscow	256.2	113.7	11.8	34.2
Republic of Ingushetia	154.8	50.4	27.8	5.5
Regions with the highest level of avoidable mortality				
Republic of Tuva	1097.7	473.8	32.9	7.9
Jewish autonomous region	832.4	285.3	23.6	10.9
Chukotka autonomous district	827.5	452.1	13.5	32.1
Republic of Buryatia	766.0	282.3	21.3	11.3
Sakhalin region	755.9	268.0	11.5	24.6
Kemerovo region	755.0	257.3	10.0	14.4
Pskov region	754.9	244.0	16.1	10.3
Zabaikalsk territory	732.8	273.5	19.9	11.0
Amur region	728.9	262.9	22.2	11.9

[a] Average per capita income (per month, thousand rubles)
[b] The number of people with incomes below the subsistence level (percentage of total population)

is a reflection of the influence of the level of socialization of society. The results of the dynamic analysis show that life expectancy in Russia grows in line with the growth of per capita income and reduced headcount, but this is not the case with the regional analysis. This inconsistency may be explained by the additional factor of social stratification that influences the mortality rate and is not equally manifested in different regions: in the poorest regions there are also few people with excess earnings. For countries with more equal distribution of poverty, it has been shown that the level of mortality does depend on the scale of variation in income distribution (Wilkinson 1992).

The analysis does not show the same relationships for the three groups of avoidable causes of death when the average indices for Russia and the regional indicators are used. This indicates a substantial heterogeneity of the socio-economic situation in different regions of the country, as well as the territorial differentiation of the factors affecting the mortality of men and women. The regional rank positions for levels of avoidable mortality and indicators of poverty are also not always the same. We compared opposing groups of regions, that is regions with the smallest and the largest values of the indicators. Table 12.6 shows the indicators of population poverty in the regions with the lowest and the highest levels of avoidable mortality. Low levels of avoidable mortality are observed in economically highly developed regions (e.g. Moscow city and Khanty-Mansijsk autonomous district, which are leaders in terms of per capita income).

On the other hand, in the Caucasian Republics avoidable mortality is below the national level. Some of these are among the ten regions with the lowest per capita income (Republic of Ingushetia, Republic of Karachaevo-Cherkessian, Republic of Kabardino-Balkarian) and the share of the poor there are above the average. In the Republic of Dagestan the poverty rate is less than the national rate, while the value of per capita income is the highest among all the southern republics of Russia. The relatively good mortality situation in these regions is only partially explained by the poor quality of the statistical data. As a whole, the southern area of Russia is characterized by higher life expectancy (i.e., a low mortality among populations of working age and a higher proportion of children in the population), than the territories with an industrial type of social development. In regions with a high level of avoidable mortality the per capita cash income ranged from the lowest (Republic of Tuva, ranked 82) to the highest (Chukotka autonomous district and Sakhalin region, rank positions 4 and 6, respectively). Because of the uneven distribution of income among the population, the "number of people with incomes below the subsistence minimum" reflects regional differences in living standards better than does the "average per capita incomes".

We next analyzed the differences in life expectancy through elimination of preventable causes for opposing regional groups. To analyze the heterogeneity of the socio-economic situation in different regions of the country we looked at extreme values of life expectancy, levels of avoidable and unavoidable mortality, the proportion of poor people, the values of per capita income, and the levels of the consolidated regional budgets on health, physical culture and sports. For different groups we calculated average values of gains in life expectancy in these cases as well as their contribution to the life expectancy of males and females.

Table 12.7 shows these assessments for the nine regions with the lowest and the nine regions with the highest values of avoidable mortality. The table also presents the assessments for groups of regions with different values of life expectancy and indicators of poverty. In regions with the highest life expectancy (including Moscow, Saint-Petersburg, the southern Republics, Republic of Tatarstan and the Belgorod region) the contribution of preventable male deaths to life expectancy is greater than the contribution in the regions with the lowest level of avoidable mortality. For females these contributions are equal. These two groups differ by the Republic of Tatarstan and Khanty-Mansijsk autonomous district, while the southern Republics of the Caucasus, Belgorod region, Moscow and St. Petersburg are included in both groups. The climate of the Caucasus region is the most favorable in Russia and moreover, the southern Republics have only just begun the transition from an agricultural to an industrial economy, while Moscow and St. Petersburg have a developed industrial economy. That is, climatic conditions and the economic way of life now determine the level of avoidable mortality equally with the level of regional economic development in Russia.

Table 12.7 The gains in life expectancy of males and females through elimination of preventable causes (e^0 losses) and their contribution to life expectancy (share in e^0) in groups of regions with the lowest and the highest values of indicators (Website of Rosstat. Regions of Russia. Socio-economic indicators—2011)

Characteristics of groups of regions	e^0 losses years due to avoidable deaths		Share of the losses in e^0 (per cent)	
	Male	Female	Male	Female
Life expectancy: the highest	2.7	1.0	4.0	1.3
The lowest	5.9	2.8	10.3	4.0
Avoidable mortality: the lowest	2.6	1.0	3.8	1.3
The highest	6.2	2.8	10.7	4.0
Unavoidable mortality: the lowest	2.9	1.1	4.4	1.4
The highest	4.8	2.2	8.2	3.2
Proportion of poor people: the lowest	3.9	1.4	6.2	1.9
The highest	4.7	2.1	7.8	2.9
Per capita income: the lowest	4.1	1.6	6.7	2.2
The highest	4.3	1.9	7.2	2.7
Consolidated regional budgets on health, physical culture and sports in 2005–2010:				
The highest	3.4	1.4	5.4	1.9
The lowest	5.0	2.2	8.5	3.2

The varying contributions of preventable causes of death between groups with extreme values of life expectancy is more than that between groups with extreme values of unavoidable mortality. Among the economic factors, the greatest influence on the contribution of avoidable mortality to life expectancy is expenditure on health, physical education and sports in the regions. Such spending in the Russian regions is proportional to the size of the gross regional product (Pearson correlation coefficient = 0.99, $N = 82$, $p < 0.001$) and inversely proportional to the level of male avoidable mortality (correlation coefficients = − 0.35 for males and − 0.20 for females, $N = 82$, $p = 0.002$ and $p = 0.072$). That is, government public health measures are now more effective in reducing mortality than is the growth of income of the population.

Trends in avoidable mortality in opposing groups of regions During the socio-economic cataclysms in the country an increase in avoidable mortality was observed, whereas for the last 5 years, during the global economic crisis but in a stable political and social situation, avoidable mortality has decreased rapidly. As a result, from 2003 to 2010 life expectancy for Russian men rose by 4.3 years and for women by 3.0 years. At the same time, the level of avoidable mortality declined by more than a quarter. As in Europe, the rate of decline in avoidable mortality in Russia is greater than the rate of decline in unavoidable mortality. This leads to a gradual reduction in the contribution of preventable causes to the total number of deaths. However, this is a slow process. The proportion of preventable deaths was greatest in 1992 for males (62.6 %) and in 1999 for females (57.2 %). In 2003 they were 58.9 % and 56.5 %, respectively. By 2010, their share fell to 55.7 % of all deaths for males and 52.7 % for females.

Table 12.8 Average, maximum and minimum values of the increment of the level of avoidable and unavoidable mortality of males and females in the Russian Federation (per cent), average increment in the groups of regions for 2003–2010

Kind of mortality causes	Rate of decline since 2003–2010 (per cent)	
	Males	Females
In general, Russia		
Total avoidable mortality	29.8	27.2
Max (region)	45.5 (Kaliningrad region)	45.4 (Republic of Tuva)
Min (region)	0.9 (Chukotka)	– 19.5 (Chukotka)
Avoidable deaths of group 1[a]	30.4	30.8
Max (region)	45.2 (Kaliningrad region)	45.9 (Republic of Tuva)
Min (region)	1.4 (Chukotka)	– 27.6 (Chukotka)
Avoidable deaths of group 2	– 9.1	3.7
Max (region)	100.0 (Magadan region)	55.3 (Republic of Sakha)
Min (region)	– 375.1 (Republic of Buryatia)	– 63.6 (Chukotka)
Avoidable deaths of group 3	27.8	29.4
Max (region)	56.2 (Republic of Khakassia)	64.2 (Yaroslavl region)
Min (region)	– 5.9 (Samara region)	– 13.1 (Samara region)
Unavoidable mortality in RF	20.2	16.3
Max (region)	39.1 (Leningrad region)	36.9 (Leningrad region)
Min (region)	– 43.6 (Chukotka)	– 31.0 (Chukotka)
Regions with the lowest level of avoidable mortality		
Avoidable mortality	26.1	27.7
Unavoidable mortality	24.0	18.5
Regions with the highest level of avoidable mortality		
Avoidable mortality	21.8	22.3
Unavoidable mortality	10.0	11.5

[a] Group 1—the causes of death can be prevented by measures for primary prevention of disease; group 2—by early diagnosis of diseases; group 3—by adequate quality of treatment and medical care

Table 12.8 shows the changes in the level of avoidable deaths from 2003 to 2010 (decrease), as well as of unavoidable deaths, expressed as a percentage of the values of 2003. The table also shows the average values of changes in avoidable mortality in the top and bottom groups of Russian territories, composed of the 9 above-mentioned regions with the highest levels of avoidable mortality and the 9 regions with the lowest levels. The country level of avoidable mortality declined for this period by more than a quarter, but in some areas it declined by almost a half.

In the Chukotka autonomous district, the rate has not changed for male mortality and has increased for female mortality. The analysis of the three groups of preventable causes of death for males shows that Group 1 deaths decreased in all regions, Group 3 deaths grew in the Samara and Saratov regions and Group 2 deaths increased in 36 regions of Russia. Female mortality increased in the Chukotka autonomous district due to causes of Group 1, in the Samara region due to causes of Group 3 and in 21 regions due to causes of Group 2. Unavoidable mortality has grown in four regions among males and in three regions among females. The coincidence of the results for male and female mortality indicates a problem of early diagnosis of disease in a large number of regions, and a problem of quality of medical care in the Samara region.

In territories with lower levels of mortality both avoidable and unavoidable mortality decreased to a greater extent than in regions with high death rates. In regions with low mortality, the avoidable and unavoidable causes of death among males have declined to about the same extent. In regions with high mortality avoidable male deaths decreased to a greater extent than unavoidable deaths. Among women, avoidable mortality decreased to a greater extent than unavoidable ones, regardless of the level of mortality. The qualitative difference in the organization of public health in various regions of Russia expresses itself not only in the level of avoidable mortality, but also in the trajectory of its change. So, the question arises: to what extent does the reduction in preventable mortality depend on the amount of funds spent on public health?

The yearly expenditure per capita on health, physical education and sports in Russia amounted to 4.89 thousand rubles (€ 122.2) during the period 2005–2010. At the regional level this expenditure ranged from 1,890 rubles in the Republic of Dagestan to 20.1 thousand rubles in the Khanty-Mansijsk autonomous district (Website of Rosstat. Regions of Russia. Socio-economic indicators 2011a), a tenfold difference. We compared the dynamics of avoidable mortality in areas with the smallest and largest volumes of these expenses for the period 2003–2010. The first cluster includes seven regions with an annual expenditure of less than € 300 per person (2.3 thousand rubles), the second cluster includes eight regions with an annual expenditure of more than € 1,000 (12.6 thousand rubles). Table 12.9 shows the regional indicators of economic well-being of the population of the regions from these two clusters.

Local expenditure on public health is determined more by regional politics than by the level of economic development. Thus, among the seven regions with low health outlays, only three are listed among the 20 most subsidized regions of Russia (Republics of Dagestan, Kabardino-Balkarian Repablic and Republic of Ingushetia), while another three such regions are among the eight regions with highest spending (Magadan region, Chukotka autonomous district and Republic of Sakha) (Gorod 2011). In addition, in both clusters there are regions with a large share of poor inhabitants. The biggest difference between the clusters is in the indices of gross regional product per capita. This allows us to characterize the latter as "rapidly-developing" and the first cluster may be labeled as "slow-developing".

Table 12.10 shows the rates of decline of avoidable mortality from 2003 till 2010 for these clusters. Both avoidable and unavoidable mortality rates are higher in the rapidly developing regions than in slow-developing regions. Male and female avoidable mortality in the slowly-developing regions decreased to a greater extent than in the rapidly-developing regions. In both clusters male avoidable mortality declined more slowly than unavoidable mortality, whereas among females avoidable mortality declined faster than the unavoidable mortality. The relationships between mortality and levels of expenditure on public health in the regions correspond to previous findings that mortality reduction is faster in areas with an initially lower level of mortality. Unavoidable mortality is also, paradoxically, subject to feedback

Table 12.9 Indicators of economic well-being of the inhabitants of regions from two clusters: regions with the lowest and the highest levels of expenditure per capita on health, physical education and sports, 2010 (Website of Rosstat. Regions of Russia. Socio-economic indicators—2011)

Regions	The gross regional product per capita (thousand rubles)	The share of poor[a] (per cent)	Average per capita income (thousand rubles monthly)	Expenditure on public health[b] (yearly thousand rubles per person)
Claster 1: slowly developing				
Kostroma region	116.7	19.1	9.4	2.5
Kursk region	145.0	11.5	11.4	2.7
Vladimir region	122.0	19.9	9.6	2.3
Tambov region	111.9	11.2	11.3	2.3
Dagestan	78.3	10.1	11.0	1.9
Kabardino-Balkaria	65.7	15.5	8.6	2.2
Ingushetia	38.1	27.8	5.5	2.1
Average	*96.8*	*16.4*	*9.5*	*2.3*
Claster 2: rapidly developing				
Moscow	804.7	11.8	34.2	9.0
St. Petersburg	310.6	11.0	17.6	10.4
Magadan region	255.2	17.0	19.7	15.5
Sakhalin region	650.3	11.5	24.6	13.1
Chukotka	615.3	13.5	32.1	6.6
Sakha (Yakutia)	320.8	19.6	18.7	9.0
Khanty-Mansi AD[c]	849.2	7.4	32.9	20.1
Yamal-Nenets AD[c]	849.2	6.6	38.1	16.7
Average	*581.9*	*12.3*	*27.2*	*12.6*

[a] The number of people with incomes below the subsistence level (percentage of total population)
[b] Consolidated expenditure on health, physical education and sport in the region, averaged over the period 2005–2010
[c] The gross regional product per capita took for Tumen region

depending on the amount of money spent on public health. A significantly greater reduction in unavoidable mortality was observed in slow-developing regions than in the rapidly-developing regions for both sexes, which may be interpreted in terms of a correlation between the intensity of the diseases of civilization and regional economic development.

Currently the proportion of avoidable mortality in rapidly-developing regions is less than in the slow-developing regions. However, this advantage merely reflects the high level of unavoidable mortality, not more effective measures of primary prevention, higher quality of care or early detection of pathology. The leading causes of deaths in both clusters are causes of the first group, which depend on living conditions and behavioral risk factors among the population. In regions with a higher level of spending on health, physical education and sport this mortality rate is significantly higher than in regions with lower spending. Male mortality due to these causes in fast-developing regions declined more slowly that in slow-developing regions. Male mortality decreased more successfully when it was at a lower level. A higher level

Table 12.10 Mortality rates (standardized rates, per 100,000 inhabitants) for males and females of regions with low (Cluster 1, slow-developing regions) and high (Cluster 2, fast-developing regions) levels of spending on health, physical education and sports[a] (Website of Rosstat. Regions of Russia. Socio-economic indicators—2011)

Mortality rates	Male		Female	
	Cluster 1	Cluster 2	Cluster 1	Cluster 2
Unavoidable mortality				
Level in 2010	*368.9*	*461.8*	*126.1*	*188.2*
Rate of decline since 2003–2010 (per cent)	23.3	10.8	21.4	7.1
Avoidable mortality				
Level in 2010	*439.5*	*549.4*	*137.2*	*206.0*
Share in the total number of deaths (per cent)[b]	55.5	53.6	52.3	51.3
Rate of decline since 2003 to 2010 (per cent)	26.9	20.5	27.7	20.6
Avoidable deaths of group *1*[c] in 2010	*349.2*	*460.0*	*90.1*	*147.9*
Share in the total number of deaths (per cent)[b]	43.8	44.3	32.9	35.7
Rate of decline since 2003 to 2010 (per cent)	30.2	20.4	30.4	32.9
Avoidable deaths of group *2* in 2010	*2.3*	*1.6*	*27.0*	*25.0*
Share in the total number of deaths (per cent)[b]	0.3	0.2	11.2	7.3
Rate of decline since 2003 to 2010 (per cent)	– 42.9	0	12.7	6.8
Avoidable deaths of group *3* in 2010	*88.0*	*87.8*	*20.2*	*33.1*
Share in the total number of deaths (per cent)[b]	11.4	9.1	8.2	8.4
Rate of decline since 2003 to 2010 (per cent)	31.2	19.2	36.3	18.3

[a] Consolidated expenditure on health, physical education and sport in the region, averaged over the period 2005–2010

[b] For population 5–64 aged

[c] Group 1—the causes of death can be prevented by measures for primary prevention of disease; group 2—by early diagnosis of diseases; group 3—by adequate quality of treatment and medical care

of spending on health did have a small effect on female mortality, but only on the first group of causes of death.

It is possible that a high level of spending on health resulted in the timely detection of skin cancer among males. In regions with lower spending, male mortality due to the second group of causes increased during the period under review, while it remained the same in regions with high spending. In 2010, the level of this group of causes among males, and its share of overall mortality, were higher in the regions with low expenditures than in the regions with high expenditures. Levels of female mortality in both clusters were close, but the reduction in the number of deaths was greater in the slow-developing regions. The presence of multidirectional changes in male and female mortality permit us to infer that the observed situation is the result of variations in people's behavior under different conditions of regional economic development, but not of the work of health facilities for early detection of diseases.

The lack of dependence of the quality of medical performance on the amount of money spent on public health protection is evident in mortality trends for preventable causes of the third group. For these, too, mortality in slow-developing regions declined faster than in the rapidly-developing regions. The steepest declines in male mortality occurred in areas with initially high levels of mortality. As a result, in 2010 the male death rate in the first cluster caught up with the mortality level in the second cluster. Female mortality was much greater in the second than in the first cluster for the entire period, but there was a more pronounced reduction in mortality rates in the regions of the first cluster. In other words, the mortality rate for those causes which depend directly on the quality of medical care, decreased more intensively in regions where the levels of spending on health, physical education and sports are smaller! This could mean that in regions with lower levels of spending, which we identified as "slow growing", the old social traditions which act to protect the population's health were more effective than in the economically more active regions.

The results indicate that the amount of spending on health, physical education and sport do not affect the mortality rate under current Russian conditions. Perhaps the distribution of these funds for practical measures does not meet the criteria of optimality, and perhaps funds are too small and have not yet reached a critical level to affect the health of the population.

12.4 Conclusion

Variations in mortality of the Russian population in the last 30 years have been due to socio-political changes in the country. The rate of increase in mortality after the deterioration in the political situation is greater than its decline as the living conditions of population improve. The largest oscillations were in mortality due to preventable causes of death, which depend on the living conditions and way of life of the population. At present, these causes constitute 44.4 % of all deaths among males aged 5–64 years and 35.8 % of all female deaths. There were also significant variations in mortality for 1989–2010, for causes of death which are the result of inadequate health care. Relatively small short-time changes in the rate of male mortality due to causes which are dependent on the timely initiation of treatment, led to a significant increase in mortality for the whole post-Soviet period.

The larger increase in unavoidable, compared with avoidable, mortality during the post-Soviet period suggests that the social and political upheavals had a greater influence on the mortality of the Russian population than did the activities of health institutions. The coincidence of the patterns of changes in avoidable and unavoidable deaths indicates a *de facto* absence of effective health facilities to reduce the mortality rate for the period under review. The availability of such measures affects male mortality more than it affects female mortality. The results indicate that now, in the period of declining mortality rates, government public health measures and policies are more important for the demographic situation than efforts to increase the income of the population.

The contribution of avoidable deaths to the life expectancy for females is much smaller than it is for males. However, the contribution of losses of female life expectancy due to preventable causes of death declined by one third from 1994 to 2010, whereas for male life expectancy it declined by a half. Mortality which is controlled by primary prevention measures increased among females more than it did among males. This demonstrates the rise in the prevalence of behavioral risk factors among females.

The dynamics of mortality in Russia are the sum of essentially heterogeneous regional mortality trends. The proportion of preventable deaths varies between regions and does not correlate with the level of non-preventable mortality. Both avoidable and unavoidable mortality decreased in regions with lower mortality to a greater extent than in regions with high mortality. Male avoidable and unavoidable deaths decreased by approximately the same extent in regions with low mortality; in regions with high mortality male avoidable deaths decreased to a greater extent compared with unavoidable one. Female avoidable mortality decreased to a greater extent than the unavoidable deaths, regardless of its level. The regional variations in avoidable and unavoidable deaths of women are more concordant than for male mortality.

The analysis of preventable deaths has helped not only in estimating the magnitude of the problem, but also to identify the most pressing issues in health systems, by way of the interregional comparisons. The weaknesses of this approach lies in the need to combine several similar regions for the analysis of some preventable causes of death, which are associated with just a small number of such deaths in each area (this is particularly true of the autonomous districts). The level and structure of mortality can be used as a sign of the division of the Russian territories in terms of social and economic welfare. It permits us to identify regions which are homogeneous in the context of socio-economic conditions of the population. In this case, it is necessary to keep in mind the limited duration of the observations, due to non-uniform changes in living conditions in different parts of Russia.

Different forms of correlation analysis give different levels of correlation between poverty and preventable causes of death. This implies the existence of significant heterogeneity of the socio-economic situation in different regions, as well as the territorial differentiation of the factors affecting the mortality of men and women. Higher mortality due to poor quality of care was observed in regions with higher percentages of poor people. Apparently, the quality of care is associated indirectly with poverty through the development of industrial society as a whole, as well as through the ability of people to pay for medical services and to purchase medicines and medical supplies. The analysis of avoidable mortality in the regions revealed their dependence not only on the level of poverty, but also on other factors: climate, economic way of life, the level of property stratification of the population and the intensity of regional economic development. Such results allow us to classify the Russian territory based on the level and structure of avoidable mortality for types which are similar to levels of socio-economic well-being.

In Russia, the biggest consolidated expenditure on protection of public health is in the regions with a high level of economic development, but these expenditures do not stimulate the reduction of mortality from preventable causes. Avoidable and unavoidable mortality decreased more intensively in regions where the levels of spending on health, physical education and sports are small. The absence of regional differences in the proportion of avoidable deaths, which depends on the timeliness of detection of malignant tumors, can raise the question about the quality of diagnosis of this pathology as a cause of death in Russia. Mortality, which depends on the quality of health care, is determined more by the socio-political situation in the country in general than by the level of regional health care expenses.

The results of the analysis of heterogeneity of avoidable mortality in Russia are of interest not only for Russian researchers. Data on mortality in Russia may be used as a testing ground for studying the various factors that influence mortality. *The level of avoidable mortality* is extremely high (more than half of all deaths in people aged less than 65) and *varies substantially across Russia*. The factors influencing mortality are common worldwide. But in Russia these factors are more pronounced for several reasons. The most important of these are the large size of the Russian territory, the fundamentally different living conditions in different regions of the country and the high level of social inequality. Consequently, access to health care is not equal in the regions due to geographical, economical, social and cultural heterogeneity and the scale of variation of avoidable mortality in Russia is much greater than in other European countries. The wide range of changes in mortality on different scales permits us to analyze these trends, which are weak in countries with a smaller population size.

12.5 Annex 1

The ranks of Russian regions on avoidable mortality, gains in life expectancy in case of elimination of avoidable mortality and their shares in life expectancy, 2010

No	Russian regions	Avoidable mortality		Gains in life expectancy		Share of the gains	
		Men	Women	Men	Women	Men	Women
1	Altay territory	31	39	33	43	31	44
2	Amur region	74	75	74	76	73	76
3	Arkhangelsk region	49	41	50	38	51	38
4	Astrakhan region	35	35	28	35	28	37
5	Belgorod region	6	8	7	7	7	7
6	Bryansk region	61	37	60	40	59	39
7	Chechen Republic	3	4	2	2	2	2
8	Chelyabinsk region	41	49	51	56	49	55
9	Chukotka autonomous district	80	81	81	82	81	82
10	Chuvashi Republic	64	51	62	45	62	43

No	Russian regions	Avoidable mortality		Gains in life expectancy		Share of the gains	
		Men	Women	Men	Women	Men	Women
11	Irkutsk region	71	73	71	73	72	73
12	Ivanovo region	56	62	45	57	50	57
13	Jewish autonomous region	81	79	75	77	76	78
14	Kaliningrad region	30	63	46	63	40	63
15	Kaluga region	39	42	36	48	38	46
16	Kamchatka territory	24	54	18	49	21	51
17	Karachaevo-Cherkessian Republic	11	9	14	8	13	8
18	Kemerovo Region	77	74	78	74	78	74
19	Kabardino-Balkarian Republic	7	6	6	4	6	5
20	Khabarovsk territory	69	65	63	65	66	66
21	Khanty-Mansijsk autonomous district	9	10	12	20	12	19
22	Kirov region	45	36	47	31	44	30
23	Kostroma region	40	47	40	39	41	41
24	Krasnodar territory	15	21	16	15	14	15
25	Krasnoyarsk territory	51	60	57	58	58	58
26	Kurgan region	59	52	61	62	61	60
27	Kursk region	28	20	15	23	17	24
28	Leningrad region	65	69	65	70	63	70
29	Lipetzk region	29	12	29	10	33	11
30	Magadan region	55	59	41	64	45	64
31	Moscow region	20	28	23	33	24	34
32	Murmansk region	17	34	11	29	15	32
33	Nizhni Novgorod region	53	55	43	47	46	49
34	Novgorod region	70	66	66	71	70	72
35	Novosibirsk region.	34	27	25	26	23	26
36	Omsk region	23	31	26	30	25	29
37	Orel region	26	25	32	27	32	28
38	Orenburg region	44	44	49	50	47	48
39	Penza region	25	15	34	21	35	21
40	Perm territory	67	67	72	66	71	65
41	Primorsky territory	52	70	53	69	52	69
42	Pskov region	76	72	73	68	74	68
43	Republic of Komi	58	64	54	61	56	62
44	Republic of Marij El	68	53	69	46	67	47
45	Republic of Adygeya	33	32	35	22	30	22
46	Republic of Altai	73	80	77	80	77	80
47	Republic of Bashkortostan	22	30	42	37	37	35
48	Republic of Buryatia	79	78	80	78	79	77
49	Republic of Dagestan	4	2	4	3	4	3
50	Republic of Ingushetia	1	1	1	1	1	1
51	Republic of Kalmykia	27	23	19	24	19	23
52	Republic of Karelia	62	57	52	51	55	50
53	Republic of Khakassia	43	71	56	72	53	71
54	Republic of Mordovia	19	11	21	12	22	13
55	Republic of Sakha (Yakutia)	46	45	70	55	69	56

No	Russian regions	Avoidable mortality		Gains in life expectancy		Share of the gains	
		Men	Women	Men	Women	Men	Women
56	Republic of North Ossetia	10	3	10	6	8	4
57	Republic of Tatarstan	16	13	20	11	18	10
58	Republic of Tuva	82	82	82	81	82	81
59	Rostov region	14	19	8	19	10	20
60	Ryazan region	42	29	37	34	39	33
61	Sakhalin region	78	76	76	75	75	75
62	Samara region	57	58	58	59	57	59
63	Saratov region	38	38	30	36	29	36
64	Smolensk region	63	61	55	60	60	61
65	Stavropol territory	12	14	9	13	9	12
66	Sverdlovsk region	47	46	48	54	43	52
67	Tambov region	36	24	24	17	26	16
68	Tomsk region	32	33	38	32	36	31
69	The City of Moscow	2	5	3	5	3	6
70	The City of Sankt-Petersburg	8	18	5	14	5	14
71	Tula region	48	50	39	52	42	53
72	Tver region	72	68	68	67	68	67
73	Tyumen region	13	16	22	28	20	27
74	Udmurtian Republic	60	48	67	44	64	45
75	Ulyanovsk region	50	40	59	41	54	40
76	Vladimir region	54	56	44	53	48	54
77	Volgograd region	18	22	17	18	16	18
78	Vologda region	66	43	64	42	65	42
79	Voronezh region	21	17	27	16	27	17
80	Yamalo-Nenets autonomous district	5	7	13	9	11	9
81	Yaroslavl region	37	26	31	25	34	25
82	Zabaikalsk territory	75	77	79	79	80	79

References

Andreev, M. E., Nolte, E., Shkolnikov, V. M., Varavikova, E. A., & McKee, M. (2003). The evolving pattern of avoidable mortality in Russia. *International Journal of Epidemiology, 32,* 437–446.

Balatsky, E. V., & Saakyants, K. M. (2006). Indeksy sotsialnogo neravenstva (The indices of social inequality). *Monitoring obschestvennogo mneniya (Monitoring of public opinion), 2* 122–128.

Charlton, J. R. H., & Velez, R. (1986). Some international comparisons of mortality amenable to medical intervention. *British Medical Journal, 292,* 295–300.

Demographic Yearbook of Russia. (2009). Federal State statistics service. http://www.gks.ru/bgd/regl/B09_16/IssWWW.exe/Stg/01-07.htm.

Doll, R. (1976). Comparison between registries. Age-standardized rates. In J. A. H. Waterhouse, C. S. Muir, P. Correa, & J. Powell (Eds.), *Cancer incidence in five continents*, Vol. III (IARC Scientific Publications No. 15) (pp. 453–459). Lyon: International Agency for Research on Cancer.

Duleep, H. O. (1995). Mortality and income inequality among economically developed countries. *Social Security Bulletin, 58*(2), 34–50.

Ermakov, S. P., Antonyuk, V. V., Gavrilova, N. S., & Evdokushkina, G. N. (1999). Factographic automated information reference system (FAISS-"Potential"). In K. Peter (Ed.), *Proceedings of*

the international collaborative effort on automating mortality statistics, Volume 1 (pp. 99–1252, 191–192). Hyattsville (NCHS): DHHS Publication No.(PHS).
Gordon, L. A., & Klopov, E. V. (2000). Sotsialnye effekty i struktury bezrabotitsy v Rossii [Social effects and structure of unemployment in Russia]. *Sotsiologicheskie issledovaniya (Sociological Studies), 1,* 25.
Gorod. (2011). [20 of the most subsidized regions of Russia] 20 samyh dotatsionnyh regionov Rossii. *Electronic Journal "Gorod-812 [The City-812]"* 05/12/2011; No. 41. http://www.online812.ru/2011/11/02/006/.
Holland, W. W. (Ed.). (1988). *European Community Atlas of Avoidable Death.* (Commission of EC Health Services Research Series No. 3). Oxford University Press.
Holland, W. W. (1997). *European Community 'Atlas of Avoidable Death'.* Commission of the European Communities Health Services Research Series Oxford Medical Publications.
Ivanova, A. E. (2009). Tendentsii i prichiny smerti naseleniya Rossii [Trends and causes of death in Russia]. In V. G. Osipov & L. L. Ribakovsky (Eds.), *Demograficheskoe razvitie Rossii v XXI veke* (pp. 110–131) [Demographic Development of Russia in the XXI Century]. Moscow (in Russian).
Ivanova, A. E., & Semyonova, V. G. (2008). Prioritetnye problemy sokrascheniya smertnosti [Priority of reducing mortality]. In V. G. Osipov & S. V. Ryazantsev (Eds.), *Demograficheskie perspektivy Rossii* (pp. 359–372) [Russia's demographic prospects]. Moscow (in Russian).
Judge, K. (1998). Income distribution and life expectancy: A critical appraisal. *British Medical Journal, 311,* 1282–1285.
Korda, R. J., & Butler, J. R. (2006). Effect of healthcare on mortality: Trends in avoidable mortality in Australia and comparisons with Western Europe. *Public health, 120*(2), 95–105.
Lagasse, R., Humblet, P. C., Lenaerts, A., Godin, I., & Moens, G. F. G. (1990). Health and social inequities in Belgium. *Social Science and Medicine, 31,* 237–248.
Lebedeva, L. F. (1999). Problemy izmereniya i dinamika urovnya bednosti (mirovoy opyt i osobennosti Rossii) [Measurement problems and the dynamics of poverty (World experience and especially in Russia]). http://www.iskran.ru/russ/works99/lebedeva1.html.
Logminiene, Z., Nolte, E., McKee, M., Valius, L., & Gaizauskiene, A. (2004). Avoidable mortality in Lithuania: 1991–1999 compared with 1970–1990. *Public health, 118*(3), 201–210.
Mackenbach, J. P., & Looman, C. W. N. (1994). Living standards and mortality in the European Community. *Journal of Epidemiology and Community Health, 48,* 140–145.
Marshall, S. W., Kawachi, I., Pearce, N., & Borman, B. (1993). Social class differences in mortality from diseases amenable to medical intervention in New Zealand. *International Journal of Epidemiology, 22,* 255–261.
Mikhailova, Yu. V., & Ivanova, A. E. (Eds.). (2006). *Predotvratimaya smertnost v Rossii I puti ee snizheniya* (in Russian) (p. 308). Moscow: CNIIOIZ. English edition: Mikhailova, Yu. V., & Ivanova, A. E. *Avoidable mortality in Russia and ways of its reduction* (trans).
Myers, J. L., & Well, A. D. (2003). *Research design and statistical analysis* (2nd ed., p. 508). Lawrence Erlbaum.
Nolte, E., Shkolnikov, V., & McKee, M. (2000). Changing mortality patterns in East and West Germany and Poland: I. Long-term trends. *Journal of Epidemiology and Community Health, 54,* 890–899.
Pampalon, R. (1993). Avoidable mortality in Quebec and its regions. *Social science & medicine (1982), 37,* 823–831.
Prohorov, B. B. (1998). *Prikladnaya antropoekologiya [Applied anthropoecology]* (p. 312). Moscow: MNEPU (in Russian).
Rutstein, D. D., Berenberger, W., Chalmers, T. C., Child, G. C., Fischmen, A. P., & Perrin, E. B. (1976). Measuring the quality of medical care. *The New England Journal of Medicine, 294,* 582–588.
Semyonova, V. G., Antonova, O. I., Evdokushkina, G. N., & Gavrilova, N. S. (2010). Poteri naseleniya Rossii v 2000–2008, obuslovlennye alkogolem: Masshtaby, struktura, tendentsii [Loss of Russia's population in 2000-2008 due to alcohol: Size, structure, trends]. *Social aspects*

of public health, 14(2). http://vestnik.mednet.ru/content/view/188/30 (in Russian; electronic edition).

Treurniet, H. F., Boshuizen, H. C., & Harteloh, P. P. M. (2004). Avoidable mortality in Europe (1980–1997): A comparison of trends. *Journal of Epidemiology and Community Health, 58,* 290–295.

Website of Rosstat. Regions of Russia. Socio-economic indicators. (2011a). Expenses of consolidated budgets of the Russian Federation in 2005-2010. http://www.gks.ru/bgd/regl/b11_14p/IssWWW.exe/Stg/d03/23-05.htm.

Website of Rosstat. Regions of Russia. Socio-economic indicators. (2011b). The number of people with incomes below the subsistence minimum. http://www.gks.ru/bgd/regl/b11_14p/IssWWW.exe/Stg/d01/05-11.htm.

Website of Rosstat. Regions of Russia. Socio-economic indicators. (2011c). The average per capita income of the population. http://www.gks.ru/bgd/regl/b11_14p/IssWWW.exe/Stg/d01/05-02.htm.

Website Sotsialny atlas rossiyskih regionov. (2009). English edition: Social atlas of Russian regions (trans). http://www.socpol.ru/atlas/overviews/household/index.shtml.

Website WHO. (2009). http://www.who.int/gho/en/index.html.

Westerling, R. (2001). Commentary: Evaluating avoidable mortality in developing countries—An important issue for public health. *International Journal of Epidemiology, 30*(5), 973–975.

Westerling, R. (2003). Decreasing gender differences in "avoidable" mortality in Sweden. *Scandinavian Journal of Public Health, 31*(5), 342–349.

Westerling, R., Gullberg, A., & Rosen, M. (1996). Socioeconomic differences in 'avoidable' mortality in Sweden 1986–1990. *International Journal of Epidemiology, 25*(3), 560–567.

Wilkinson, R. (1992). Income distribution and life expectancy. *British Medical Journal, 304,* 165–168.

Woolhandler, S., Himmelstein, D. U., Silber, R., Bader, M., Harnly, M., & Jones, A. A. (1985). Medical care and mortality: Racial differences in preventable deaths. *International Journal of Health Services: Planning, Administration, Evaluation, 15,* 1–22.

Chapter 13
Long-term Mortality Changes in East Asia: Levels, Age Patterns, and Causes of Death

Zhongwei Zhao, Edward Jow-Ching Tu and Jiaying Zhao

Abstract One of the most significant events in recent history has been the worldwide demographic transition. This transition started with mortality decline in some European countries around the beginning of the nineteenth century. While mortality reduction started late in most East Asian populations, their life expectancies have increased faster than those observed in Europe. In recent years, Japan and Hong Kong have achieved the highest life expectancy and led the mortality decline in the world. These changes raise many important research questions and have significant implications. This chapter examines long-term mortality changes in East Asia and compares them with those observed in England and Wales, France and Sweden. Its discussion particularly concentrates on changes in age-specific mortality rates and their contribution to the increase of life expectancies in recent history. To explain these changes and their patterns, the chapter also analyses changes in major causes of death and their impacts on mortality decline across different age groups. On the basis of its major research findings, the chapter concludes with a brief discussion of several factors and their contribution to the rapid mortality transition in East Asia in recent decades.

Keywords East Asia · Mortality trends · Epidemiologic transition · Cause of death · Age-specific mortality

Z. Zhao (✉)
Australian Demographic and Social Research Institute (Coombs Building),
Research School of Social Sciences, College of Arts and Social Sciences,
The Australian National University, Canberra, ACT 0200, Australia
e-mail: zhongwei.zhao@anu.edu.au

E. Jow-Ching Tu
National Centre for Epidemiology and Population Health,
Building 62, College of Medicine, Biology & Environment,
Australian National University, Canberra,
ACT 0200, Australia

J. Zhao
Room 210, Academic House, 34 Marcus Clarke Street,
Canberra City, ACT 2601, Australia

J. Anson, M. Luy (eds.), *Mortality in an International Perspective*,
European Studies of Population 18, DOI 10.1007/978-3-319-03029-6_13,

13.1 Introduction

One of the most significant events in recent history has been the worldwide demographic transition. This change has been so important to 'the creation of the modern world' that some scholars argue that the modern process of development cannot be understood unless the demographic transition is put on the centre-stage (Dyson 2010, p. viii). The demographic transition started with mortality decline in some European countries around 1800. In England and Wales, France and Sweden, life expectancies at birth rose from around 35 years in 1800–1809 to about 50 years at the end of the nineteenth century, and further increased to approximately 70 years in 1950 (Livi-Bacci 2007). Similar changes were also recorded in most western countries in the second half of the nineteenth century and the first half of the twentieth century. It is largely based on these experiences that the classic demographic transition and epidemiological transition theories were developed (Notestein 1945; Omran 1971).

Mortality decline in most East Asian populations began in the early or mid-twentieth century, but their life expectancies have increased faster than those in Europe. Japan and Hong Kong have led the mortality decline in recent years, with the highest life expectancy in the world (United Nations 2011). Mortality in South Korea and Taiwan has also reached a very low level. Rapid mortality transition in East Asia raises a number of questions. What is the route of mortality decline in East Asian populations? To what extent has mortality decline, especially its decline in major age groups, in these populations differed from that observed in North and West Europe in the past? Why could many of these populations improve their mortality so rapidly in comparison with other parts of the world in recent decades? Have changes in major causes of death in East Asia conformed to the patterns observed previously in western industrial countries? What are their contributions to the rapid increase in longevity? Finally, in what ways could East Asia's experience of lowering mortality enrich our knowledge of epidemiological transition and contribute to the theoretical advancement in the study of mortality? Despite their potential theoretical implications and the great significance of mortality decline in East Asia, many of these questions have not been systematically studied from a global perspective.

This chapter examines some of these questions. Following this introduction, section two compares long-term mortality changes in East Asia with those observed in England and Wales, France and Sweden. The selection of these European populations is largely due to the fact that they all possess reliable mortality data for a very long period and that their mortality decline has in many ways exemplified the major characteristics of the classic epidemiological transition described by Omran (1971). After that, section three describes changes in age-specific mortality rates over the past half century and their contribution to the overall mortality decline. In section four, we examine changes in major causes of death and their impact on the increase of life expectancies. Finally, we discuss our major research findings and make some concluding remarks in the last section.

Data used in this study are drawn primarily from the following sources: the Human Mortality Database constructed at the Max Planck Institute for Demographic

Research and University of California at Berkeley; World Population Prospects: 2010 Revision published by the United Nations, and mortality data collected by the World Health Organization. In addition, death records and demographic data collected from Hong Kong and Taiwan are used. The death records are provided by the governments of Hong Kong and Taiwan, and the population data are largely taken from official publications such as *Taiwan-Fukien Demographic Fact Book*.

In the discussion of long-term mortality changes, we include all East Asian populations, but only some of them are included in more detailed investigations of changes in age-specific mortality rates and changes in major causes of death due to data availability. We use conventional demographic methods to analyse and compare long-term mortality changes in study populations. Decomposition techniques developed by Arriaga (1984) are used to examine the contribution of changes in both age-specific mortality rates and major causes of death to the improvement in life expectancies in these populations.

13.2 Mortality Decline in East Asia and Selected European Populations

Available evidence suggests that the worldwide mortality transition started in North and West Europe about 200 years ago. As shown in Fig. 13.1, mortality fluctuated notably in England and Wales, France and Sweden in the second half of the eighteenth century, although their life expectancies at birth were different. This began to change around 1800 when the trend of mortality decline became clearer. This change continued and the improvement in mortality was particularly notable between 1870 and the mid-twentieth century. By the end of this period, life expectancies were already around 70 years in these populations. Similar changes, though slightly later in general, also took place in other parts of North and West Europe, North America, and some countries in Oceania, where life expectancies were also close to 70 years in the mid-twentieth century. According to the United Nations, mortality in these countries decreased to an even lower level during the last six decades. Their life expectancies increased to about 80 years in 2005–2010 (United Nations 2011).

In comparison with these countries, the mortality transition started later in East Asia. Available studies suggest that in Japan mortality decline did not begin until perhaps the last quarter of the nineteenth century. Figure 13.2 shows that in the first half of the twentieth century, Japan's life expectancy rose notably, although this was shattered by the Second World War (Jannetta and Preston 1991; Tsuya and Kurosu 2004; Zhao and Kinfu 2005). Mortality remained high in other parts of East Asia at the end of the nineteenth century. In Korea, Taiwan, and some cities in Mainland China, a long-term mortality decline started in the early twentieth century and this change was also affected strongly by wars and social upheavals during this period (Banister 1987; Barclay et al. 1976; Campbell 2001; Chen 1946; Engelen et al. 2011; Kim 1986; Kwon 1977; Mirzaee 1983; Zhao 1997, 2007a). By the early 1950s, life expectancy for the East Asian population as a whole was only around 46 years, lower

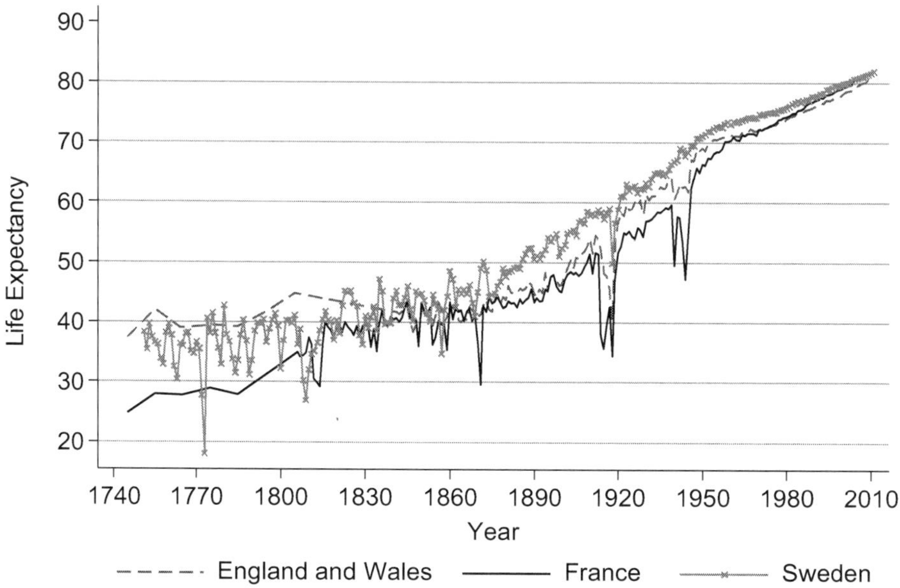

Fig. 13.1 Changes in life expectancies in England and Wales, France and Sweden since the mid-eighteenth century. (England and Wales: 1745–1805 from Wrigley et al. 1997, 1841–2009 from Human Mortality Database; France: 1745–1785 from Blayo 1975, 1806–1815 from Vallin and Mesle 2001, 1816–2010 from Human Mortality Database; Sweden: 1751–2010 from Human Mortality Database)

than the world average. Even in Japan where the lowest mortality in East Asia was recorded, the life expectancy was 62 years and markedly lower than the average for the European population, which was 66 years (United Nations 2011).

Since the early 1950s, East Asia has experienced the most rapid mortality decline observed in major regions of the world. According to estimates made by the United Nations, life expectancy increased 28 years in East Asia in the past six decades and reached 74 years in 2005–2010. In contrast, the average life expectancy for the world population rose only 20 years over the same period. By the 1970s, life expectancies in Japan and Hong Kong had already caught up with that in North and West Europe. In recent years, mortality in Japan and Hong Kong has been among the lowest in the world. Mortality in Macau has been largely similar to that in Hong Kong in the past 30 years. Rapid mortality reduction has also been observed in South Korea and Taiwan. Their life expectancies are now around 80 years, very close to the average recorded in North and West Europe. The life expectancy in Mainland China has been lower than the five East Asian populations mentioned above, but its mortality also went through an extraordinary decline, especially during the third quarter of the twentieth century. At present, life expectancy in Mainland China is close to 75 years. As far as their mortality levels are concerned, Mongolia and North Korea have been falling behind

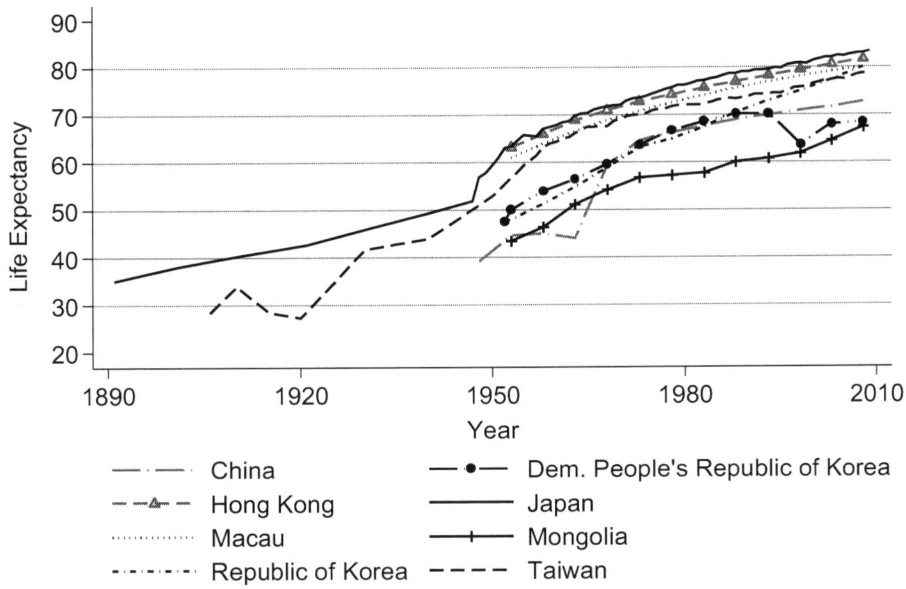

Fig. 13.2 Changes in life expectancies in East Asian populations in recent history. (China:1946–1949 from Zhao and Kinfu 2005, 1950–2010 from United Nations; Dem. People's Republic of Korea: 1950–2010 from United Nations; Hong Kong: 1950–2010 from United Nations; Japan: 1891–1941 from Zhao and Kinfu 2005; 1947–2009 from Human Mortality Database; Macau: 1950–2010 from United Nations; Mongolia:1950–2010 from United Nations; Republic of Korea: 1925–1949 from Zhao and Kinfu 2005, 1950–2010 from United Nations; Taiwan: 1895–1955 from Mirzaee 1986; Taiwan 1957–2009 from Ministry of the Interior, Taiwan)

other East Asian populations. Their current life expectancies are around 69 years, according to the *World Population Prospects: 2010 Revision* (United Nations 2011).

It is noteworthy that the reduction in mortality or the increase in life expectancy has not been constant in either the three selected European countries or East Asia. To further examine this change, mortality statistics computed annually or for a relatively short period are often needed. Such data, however, are difficult to find, especially for the early period of our investigation. In addition, there were considerable fluctuations in mortality before life expectancies reaching 50 years. For these reasons, there are some difficulties in determining how long it took for the life expectancy to increase from 30 to 40 years or from 40 to 50 years. After life expectancies reached 50 years, mortality decline generally became steadier, and measuring the speed of mortality changes became easier. To reduce the uncertainty mentioned above, we computed the five-year smoothed life expectancy for the study population, which is used to indicate the time when the population achieved a life expectancy of a certain level. These results, especially changes after life expectancies reached 50 years, are largely consistent with those recorded annually. In the case where available data could not show the year in which the life expectancy in the population reached exactly 40 or

50 years, the year when the life expectancy was closest to 40 or 50 years is selected as a proxy.

In most of the study populations, there were long-term and notable fluctuations in mortality before life expectancies reached 40 years. The increase in life expectancy from 40 to 50 years took a relatively long time (around four decades) in the three European populations, though it was completed in two to three decades in Japan, South Korea and Taiwan. In contrast, the increase of life expectancy from 50 to 60 years and from 60 to 70 years was faster. In the three European countries, the 20-year increase of life expectancies took about five decades to accomplish, which occurred largely in the first half of the twentieth century. In most East Asian populations, life expectancies reached 50 years after the Second World War, and it took less than three decades for them to rise to 70 years. The increase in life expectancy from 70 to 80 years has been more difficult to achieve in comparison with its increase from 50 to 60 years or from 60 to 70 years. This increase took around half a century to complete in the three European countries. While it was faster, a similar increase still took some 30 years to achieve in Hong Kong and Japan.

13.3 Changes in Age-Specific Mortality Rates and Their Contributions to the Increase in Life Expectancy

The previous section showed that mortality decline in several East Asian populations has been faster in comparison with that in the three European countries. This raises a number of questions. Did mortality decline in these populations exhibit similar patterns? For example, when life expectancy in these eastern and western populations rose by the same number of years, did their age patterns of mortality change in a similar way? If not, how did contributions to life expectancy from mortality reductions in major age groups vary across populations or at different stages of their mortality decline? These questions are examined in this section.

13.3.1 Variations in Mortality Decline in Major Age Groups

Mortality decline did not take place simultaneously in all age groups during the process of mortality transition. Generally, mortality fell first among children aged 1–14, who experienced the most significant mortality reduction in the early stage of mortality transition, as observed in England and Wales, France, Hong Kong, and Taiwan. But in Sweden and Japan, a rapid decline in infant mortality was also recorded at the same time when mortality was falling among children aged 1–14. In other sub-population groups, mortality reduction was closely related to people's age. Population aged 15–44 generally experienced an earlier and faster mortality decline, followed by those aged 45–64, and then those aged 65–84 and over. This is largely because infectious diseases were gradually eradicated or controlled during the earlier stages of the epidemiological transition. This change had a stronger impact on mortality decline among children and young adults than among infants or older people, who were more likely to be affected by congenital or degenerative conditions. Because of what has been said above, a significant shift in the distribution of deaths has taken place in the process of mortality transition.

While the decline in age-specific mortality in East Asian populations generally followed the patterns observed in North and West Europe in the past, they differed notably in two respects. First, in almost all age groups, mortality declined faster in the selected East Asian populations. In the three European populations, for example, it took more than 75 years for the probability of death to fall from around 300 per thousand to around 100 per thousand in the population aged 15–44, but the reduction of a similar magnitude took around 30 years to complete in Taiwan. Second, in comparison with those recorded in the three European populations, the time lag or the interval between the times when mortality started falling at younger ages and that at older ages were also notably shorter in the East Asian populations, where simultaneous mortality reductions were increasingly observed in different age groups. For example, in the three European populations, after mortality decline started among people aged 1–14, it generally took a century or even longer for a notable mortality reduction (about a 10 % reduction from its previous level) to be recorded among people aged 65–84. But in Japan and Taiwan, this lag was shorter and around 50 years.

Variations in the speed of mortality decline across different ages can be further examined from Table 13.1, which shows mortality changes in five major age groups over four phases of mortality decline. The four phases are divided according to changes in life expectancy at birth, which has been calculated using the methods discussed in Sect. 13.2.

It is noteworthy that when life expectancy increased from 40 to 80 years, changes in age-specific mortality have followed a rather similar pattern in most of the populations. When life expectancy increased from 40 to 50 years and from 50 to 60 years, the most rapid mortality decline was observed among children aged 1–14, with a few exceptions. The probability of death in this age group fell by 25–54 % and 50–61 % in these two phases of mortality changes, respectively. However, in Japan the decline of infant mortality was faster than that of children aged 1–14 when its life expectancy at birth increasing from 40 to 50 years. In England and Wales the decline of infant mortality was also slightly faster than child mortality when its life expectancy at birth increased from 50 to 60 years. During these phases of mortality transition, mortality decline among those aged 45 and above was generally slow. When the life expectancy increased from 60 to 70 years, the most rapid mortality reduction was still recorded among children aged 1–14. During this period, mortality also fell by 58–70 % and 41–64 % among infants and people aged 15–44. In contrast, the probability of death declined by 21–37 % among those aged 45–64, and the reduction was even smaller among those aged 65–84.

When the life expectancy increased from 70 to 80 years, a notable mortality decline took place in all major age groups and the magnitude of the decline was generally related to age. During this phase of mortality improvement, while the largest reduction was still recorded among infants except in Taiwan, mortality decline sped up considerably among those aged 45–64 and those aged 65–84. Their reductions

Table 13.1 Percentage decline of probability of death in major age groups at different phases of mortality changes. (Data Sources: See Figs. 13.1 and 13.2)

Changes in e_0 (years)	Population	q_0	q_{1-14}	q_{15-44}	q_{45-64}	q_{65-84}
40–50	England and Wales	12.11	49.09	39.48	8.72	0.72
	France	26.15	53.89	32.29	10.45	1.01
	Sweden	27.63	33.57	26.99	33.62	8.82
	Hong Kong	–	–	–	–	–
	Japan	52.51	32.29	15.81	10.75	1.37
	Taiwan[a]	23.32	25.42	31.73	18.76	–
50–60	England and Wales	51.34	49.64	32.86	24.97	2.73
	France	45.85	54.15	27.87	11.78	4.90
	Sweden	42.20	60.74	17.61	17.61	4.93
	Hong Kong	–	–	–	–	–
	Japan	38.74	55.27	46.38	25.33	8.30
	Taiwan	–	–	46.90	23.38	– 0.65
60–70	England and Wales	60.85	83.45	61.82	23.29	7.29
	France	57.62	74.98	63.66	32.67	11.23
	Sweden	62.52	77.82	63.74	20.51	1.41
	Hong Kong	69.57	82.68	40.69	22.69	23.27
	Japan	60.32	75.62	57.01	26.63	4.41
	Taiwan	–	–	45.69	36.50	10.82
70–80	England and Wales	80.88	76.81	44.49	52.88	34.52
	France	86.76	78.64	45.17	45.45	39.29
	Sweden	85.86	85.80	64.32	50.32	33.19
	Hong Kong	80.81	67.72	59.85	54.00	28.37
	Japan	80.81	72.44	59.09	50.23	36.67
	Taiwan	63.99	75.91	36.22	36.61	31.42

– data unavailable

[a] For Taiwan the last age group is 65 +. This group is used as a proxy for age group 65–84. In the panels where life expectancy increased from 40 to 50 years, from 50 to 60 years, and from 60 to 70 years, for Taiwan, age group 0–4 is used as a proxy for age group 0, and age group 5–14 is used as a proxy for age group 1–14. Data Sources: See Figs. 13.1 and 13.2

varied between 37 and 54 % and between 28 and 39 %, respectively. It is important to keep in mind that in Table 13.1, the statistics are presented by phases of mortality change. When annual mortality changes have been calculated, the decline in the probability of death in most of the East Asian populations was faster than that in the three European countries, because it took a shorter period to gain the same increase in life expectancy in East Asia.

13.3.2 *Mortality Changes in Different Age Groups and Their Contributions to the Improvement in Life Expectancies at Birth*

While the speed of mortality decline at a given age is a major factor determining its contribution to the increase of life expectancy, the latter is also related to the absolute level of mortality reduction and at which age this reduction takes place.

Table 13.2 Contribution of the decline in age-specific mortality to the increase in life expectancies by phases of mortality improvement. (Data Sources: See Figs. 13.1 and 13.2)

Changes in e_0 (years)	Age group	England and Wales	France	Sweden	Hong Kong	Japan	Taiwan[a]
40–50	0	11.34	24.90	23.66	–	56.90	26.89
	1–14	51.72	43.71	34.90	–	23.88	25.47
	15–44	31.67	26.39	17.50	–	12.44	31.46
	45–64	4.42	4.04	16.50	–	5.34	13.77
	65–84	0.81	0.98	7.32	–	1.38	2.42
	85+	0.03	– 0.02	0.12	–	0.06	–
50–60	0	42.41	41.25	30.17	–	19.06	58.97
	1–14	26.57	26.38	47.40	–	28.81	4.44
	15–44	14.97	20.80	10.28	–	34.49	23.70
	45–64	12.85	6.35	7.60	–	11.08	11.29
	65–84	3.31	5.05	4.42	–	6.29	1.94
	85+	– 0.11	0.19	0.15	–	0.27	– 0.33
60–70	0	28.07	25.60	27.11	27.34	24.84	47.85
	1–14	26.29	15.77	24.90	22.30	24.28	6.99
	15–44	25.60	31.78	37.24	10.90	29.74	16.05
	45–64	11.80	16.34	8.69	11.75	13.89	18.32
	65–84	7.88	10.06	2.01	27.35	7.07	10.38
	85+	0.36	0.45	0.05	0.36	0.19	0.42
70–80	0	17.03	20.19	16.34	12.92	13.68	8.72
	1–14	4.78	5.32	7.35	4.27	5.94	8.74
	15–44	8.79	10.81	16.73	14.64	14.38	12.28
	45–64	27.46	22.46	22.52	30.38	23.86	21.12
	65–84	38.42	37.23	34.10	33.31	38.97	42.81
	85+	3.53	3.99	2.96	4.48	3.17	6.34

– data unavailable

[a] In the panel where life expectancy increased from 40 to 50 years, for Taiwan the last age group is 65 +. This group is used as a proxy for age group 65–84. In the panels where life expectancy increased from 50 to 60 years, and from 60 to 70 years, for Taiwan, age group 0–4 is used as a proxy for age group 0, and age group 5–14 is used as a proxy for age group 1–14

It is for this reason that we have decomposed the contribution to increasing life expectancy made by falling mortality in major age groups at different phases of mortality transition. According to the results presented in Table 13.2, the increase in life expectancy was generally accompanied by a shift in its major contributors: from being driven predominately by the mortality reduction at younger ages to being driven largely by falling mortality in adult and old populations. When the life expectancy in these populations rose from 40 to 50 years and from 50 to 60 years, the largest contribution (varying between 48 and 81 %) to these improvements was made by mortality reduction among children under age 15. The relatively small contribution (48 %) recorded in Japan when life expectancy rose from 50 to 60 years was closely related to its large contribution of 81 % made when the life expectancy improved from 40 to 50 years. Because a significant mortality improvement was made mainly at younger ages during this phase of the mortality transition, life expectancy at age 65 showed only a small increase (1 or 2 years in general), although life expectancy at birth rose by 20 years.

When the life expectancies improved from 60 to 70 years, the contribution made by the mortality reduction among people aged 15–44 increased. In most of the listed populations, mortality reduction among people under age 45 made more than 70 % contribution to the increase in life expectancy. In contrast, when their life expectancies rose from 70 to 80 years, most of the contribution was made by the mortality reduction among people aged 45–84 years, those aged 65–84 years in particular. The mortality decline in these two age groups contributed 57–66 % of the increase in their life expectancies. For this reason, a more notable increase (4.5–5.7 years) in life expectancy at age 65 was also recorded at the phase when the life expectancy at birth rose from approximately 70 to about 80 years. This was attributable to the fact that while mortality at younger ages continued to fall significantly, it had already reached a very low level. Such a reduction could not make a large contribution to the increase in life expectancy in this and future times.

13.4 Recent Changes in Major Causes of Death

The previous section showed marked variations in the time and speed of mortality decline at different ages and in their contributions to the increase in life expectancy at birth. These results raise a further question about the mortality transition: what are the major factors that led to these variations? To answer this question, it is important to examine changes in major causes of death and their contributions to mortality improvement.

Omran developed the theory of epidemiological transition in 1971. According to him, the process of epidemiological transition and mortality decline can be divided into three phases: 'the Age of Pestilence and Famine', 'the Age of Receding Pandemics', and 'the Age of Degenerative and Man-Made Disease'. In the first phase mortality was high and was caused largely by infectious and parasitic diseases. In the second phase the impact of these diseases lessened gradually. As a result, mortality fell. In the third phase degenerative diseases became the primary killer. Mortality further declined and then stabilised at a relatively low level (Omran 1971, pp. 737–738). Since Omran published his theory, notable epidemiological changes have taken place in the world. Based on the examination of these new developments, several scholars, including Omran himself, further developed or revised the classic epidemiological transition theory. Olshansky and Ault pointed out that mortality decline did not stop at 'the Age of Degenerative and Man-Made Diseases'. There was a fourth stage of the epidemiological transition: 'the Age of Delayed Degenerative Diseases'. During this phase, mortality caused by degenerative diseases continued to fall and life expectancy further increased (Olshansky and Ault 1986). Countries with low mortality are now experiencing these changes. We would very much like to systematically examine changes in causes of death over the entire period when mortality fell from a high to a low level. But, because of data availability, our discussion has to concentrate on major changes in causes of death since the mid-twentieth century.

Before 1950, infectious diseases remained a major killer in many parts of the world and led to high or relatively high mortality. This was also the case in East Asia. In Japan and some other East Asian populations, although mortality had started to fall, infectious diseases still caused a significant number of deaths in the first half of the twentieth century. Eradicating these diseases played a crucial part in the early mortality decline in the selected populations (Campbell 2001; Engelen et al. 2011; Omran 1971; Zhao 2007a). By the early 1950s, life expectancies were between 50 and 60 years in Hong Kong, Japan and Taiwan, and they further increased to around 80 years in 2010. During the past six decades, changes in major causes of death in these and the three European populations showed notable similarities.

As shown in Tables 13.3 and 13.4, age standardised death rates for infectious diseases were already lower than 0.5 per thousand in the three European populations in the 1950s. In contrast, they were still relatively high and close to 2 per thousand in the three East Asian populations. By 2005 they were all below 1 per thousand and accounted for 1–3 % of the overall mortality. These results indicate that the classic epidemiological transition was completed many decades ago in all these populations, and the mortality impact of infectious diseases was rather small in the past half century.

During this period, cardiovascular diseases (CVD) were the major killer in most of the study populations and for most of the time. In the 1950s, standardised death rates attributable to CVD were 2.5–5.0 per thousand in the six populations. In the late 1970s, their contribution to the overall mortality seemed to have reached, or been close to, the peak, which was followed by a notable decline. Their levels fell to 1.0–1.6 per thousand in 2005, with relatively high mortality rates recorded in England and Wales and Sweden, where CVD mortality contributed 33–37 % of the overall mortality. In the four other populations, they constituted 21–28 % of the total.

Standardised mortality rates of respiratory diseases were relatively high in England and Wales, Hong Kong, Japan and Taiwan in the 1950s, while they had already dropped to less than 1 per thousand in France and Sweden. During the next half century, they all declined notably and varied between 0.3 and 0.6 per thousand in 2005. Their contributions to overall mortality were relatively high in England and Wales, Hong Kong and Japan, ranging from 12 to 17 %. In the other three populations, they were lower and ranged between 5 and 9 %.

In the 1950s, standardised mortality rates of neoplasms were higher than 1 per thousand in all study populations except Taiwan. They all exhibited some increases in the next three or four decades and only showed some decrease since the mid-1980s, though a similar reduction has not yet been witnessed in Taiwan. In the first decade of the twenty-first century, deaths caused by various types of neoplasms accounted for 27–34 % of the overall mortality in these populations.

Injuries and poisoning were also among the major causes of deaths. During most of the period under investigation, their standardised mortality rates were 0.3–0.9 per thousand. But, they have shown some decreases during the last 10–20 years. Despite that, they still accounted for 5–11 % of the overall mortality in these populations in 2005.

Table 13.3 Age-standardised mortality rates by major causes of death in six populations. (Data Sources: England and Wales, France, Sweden, Hong Kong, Japan: (WHO Mortality Database); Taiwan: 1955–1970 (WHO Mortality Database), 1971–2005 (Ministry of the Interior))

	1950	1960	1970	1980	1990	2000	2005
Infectious diseases							
England and Wales	0.44	0.10	0.06	0.04	0.03	0.04	0.06
France	0.69	0.25	0.12	0.09	0.07	0.10	0.08
Sweden	–	0.09	0.07	0.04	0.04	0.05	0.06
Hong Kong	–	1.11	0.56	0.20	0.19	0.09	0.10
Japan	2.08	0.53	0.27	0.10	0.07	0.08	0.08
Taiwan	–	1.02	0.58	0.34	0.25	0.14	0.10
Neoplasms							
England and Wales	1.60	1.62	1.69	1.71	1.70	1.45	1.39
France	1.44	1.57	1.55	1.64	1.59	1.49	1.40
Sweden	–	1.43	1.40	1.44	1.31	1.24	1.21
Hong Kong	–	1.10	1.39	1.54	1.52	1.38	1.28
Japan	1.15	1.34	1.35	1.33	1.29	1.26	1.17
Taiwan	–	0.83	1.05	1.21	1.27	1.47	1.46
CVD							
England and Wales	4.81	4.42	4.09	3.54	2.66	1.87	1.54
France	3.20	2.89	2.58	2.20	1.53	1.23	1.05
Sweden	–	3.97	3.42	3.22	2.52	1.88	1.55
Hong Kong	–	2.45	2.27	1.99	1.50	1.12	0.94
Japan	3.04	3.68	3.61	2.62	1.68	1.09	0.99
Taiwan	–	2.71	2.77	2.76	2.15	1.23	1.09
Respiratory diseases							
England and Wales	1.06	0.94	1.23	1.01	0.60	0.77	0.58
France	0.90	0.73	0.48	0.36	0.32	0.26	0.24
Sweden	–	0.50	0.40	0.34	0.36	0.29	0.25
Hong Kong	–	1.57	1.24	1.09	0.92	0.65	0.63
Japan	1.22	0.82	0.70	0.49	0.55	0.46	0.45
Taiwan	–	1.00	0.88	0.77	0.61	0.47	0.49
Injuries and poisoning							
England and Wales	0.40	0.45	0.40	0.35	0.30	0.25	0.25
France	0.60	0.69	0.80	0.76	0.64	0.49	0.41
Sweden	–	0.58	0.60	0.55	0.44	0.32	0.34
Hong Kong	–	0.42	0.51	0.44	0.30	0.25	0.25
Japan	0.66	0.71	0.62	0.44	0.38	0.40	0.38
Taiwan	–	0.64	0.72	0.88	0.85	0.62	0.54
Taiwan	–	0.64	0.72	0.88	0.85	0.62	0.54
Other diseases							
England and Wales	1.61	1.23	0.89	0.82	0.91	0.80	0.90
France	3.88	2.80	2.04	1.55	1.21	1.14	1.11
Sweden	–	1.31	0.93	0.79	0.82	0.80	0.81
Hong Kong	–	3.16	2.05	1.33	0.82	0.60	0.56
Japan	6.25	3.39	1.88	1.10	0.74	0.54	0.51
Taiwan	–	5.77	3.48	2.21	1.85	1.80	1.65

Standardized mortality rates are calculated using the five-year-age-sex structure of the WHO standard population (Ahmad 2001)
– data unavailable

Table 13.4 Percentage distribution of age-standardised mortality by major causes of death in six populations. (Data Sources: See Table 13.3)

	1950	1960	1970	1980	1990	2000	2005
Infectious Diseases							
England and Wales	4.44	1.12	0.71	0.47	0.54	0.81	1.23
France	6.42	2.79	1.62	1.32	1.25	2.08	1.92
Sweden	–	1.15	0.97	0.67	0.68	1.07	1.45
Hong Kong	–	11.35	7.01	3.02	3.60	2.12	2.69
Japan	14.40	5.07	3.19	1.61	1.49	2.11	2.19
Taiwan		8.55	6.07	4.15	3.55	2.45	1.85
Neoplasms							
England and Wales	16.12	18.47	20.19	22.87	27.40	27.93	29.48
France	13.47	17.55	20.51	24.80	29.67	31.53	32.60
Sweden	–	18.16	20.55	22.53	23.90	27.06	28.68
Hong Kong	–	11.17	17.33	23.40	29.01	33.86	34.02
Japan	8.01	12.81	16.03	21.82	27.31	32.77	32.69
Taiwan	–	6.92	11.11	14.84	18.19	25.70	27.36
CVD							
England and Wales	48.50	50.46	48.88	47.42	42.94	36.11	32.76
France	29.88	32.38	34.06	33.32	28.51	26.13	24.37
Sweden	–	50.35	50.08	50.43	45.94	41.00	36.67
Hong Kong	–	24.98	28.25	30.21	28.55	27.35	24.89
Japan	21.13	35.17	42.83	43.19	35.75	28.52	27.65
Taiwan	–	22.66	29.18	33.84	30.84	21.48	20.51
Respiratory Diseases							
England and Wales	10.70	10.77	14.73	13.53	9.64	14.90	12.26
France	8.40	8.20	6.28	5.50	6.03	5.59	5.56
Sweden	–	6.36	5.91	5.33	6.54	6.31	5.99
Hong Kong	–	16.04	15.46	16.56	17.62	15.98	16.72
Japan	8.47	7.84	8.25	8.10	11.66	12.09	12.53
Taiwan	–	8.34	9.33	9.39	8.80	8.23	9.11
Injuries and poisoning							
England and Wales	4.05	5.13	4.84	4.68	4.77	4.73	5.20
France	5.64	7.71	10.61	11.55	11.86	10.42	9.64
Sweden	–	7.32	8.80	8.68	7.97	7.09	8.01
Hong Kong	–	4.26	6.40	6.72	5.67	6.05	6.65
Japan	4.60	6.76	7.38	7.23	8.07	10.54	10.73
Taiwan	–	5.32	7.64	10.78	12.12	10.75	10.21
Other diseases							
England and Wales	16.19	14.06	10.65	11.02	14.70	15.53	19.08
France	36.19	31.36	26.92	23.50	22.68	24.24	25.91
Sweden	–	16.66	13.68	12.37	14.97	17.47	19.20
Hong Kong	–	32.20	25.55	20.10	15.55	14.63	15.03
Japan	43.38	32.35	22.34	18.06	15.72	13.96	14.21
Taiwan	–	48.22	36.68	26.99	26.51	31.39	30.96

– data unavailable

Table 13.5 Contributions of changes in cause-specific mortality to the improvement in life expectancy at birth, 1955–2005. (Data Sources: See Table 13.3)

Populations	Changes in e_0	Increase in e_0 (years)	Contribution made by					
			Infectious Disease	Neo-plasms	CVD	Injury and poisoning	Respira-tory diseases	Other diseases
England and Wales	70.53–79.45	8.92	0.38	0.69	4.58	0.44	1.06	1.78
France	68.28–80.53	12.25	0.85	0.44	3.58	0.83	1.09	5.45
Sweden	72.40–80.75	8.35	0.23	0.63	4.35	0.64	0.46	2.05
Hong Kong[a]	60.50–81.72	21.23	3.74	0.54	3.91	0.65	4.06	8.33
Japan	64.97–82.44	17.48	2.31	0.74	4.34	1.17	1.20	7.72
Taiwan[b]	62.91–77.68	14.77	2.58	– 0.65	2.88	– 0.29	2.02	8.23

[a] For Hong Kong the starting year is 1956
[b] For Taiwan the starting year is 1958

Mortality due to causes that were not included in the above five groups varied notably among the six populations. This may be caused partly by variations in both the quality of death records and the practice of coding causes of death in these populations. In 2005, standardised mortality rates attributable to these causes varied between 0.5 and 1.7 per thousand, with the highest rate recorded in Taiwan. Deaths attributable to these causes accounted for 15–31 % of the overall mortality, with 26 % for France and 31 % for Taiwan, respectively.

Table 13.5 shows that life expectancies rose by 8.4–12.3 years in the three European populations and 14.8–21.2 years in the three East Asian populations over the period between the mid-1950s and 2005. In the European populations the increases were mainly attributable to the decrease in mortality caused by CVD and diseases included in the group of 'others', which accounted for more than 70 % of the total improvement in life expectancy. In England and Wales and Sweden, the decrease in mortality due to CVD led to an increase of 4.6 or 4.4 years in life expectancy, respectively. In France, the decline of mortality caused by diseases grouped as 'others' resulted in a 5.5-year increase in life expectancy. Less than 30 % of the improvement in life expectancies was attributable to mortality decline in the four other groups of diseases.

In Hong Kong and Taiwan, the decline of mortality attributable to diseases classified as 'others', respiratory diseases, CVD, and infectious diseases all made notable contributions to the remarkable increase in their life expectancies. In Japan, the contribution made by the decline of mortality attributable to respiratory diseases was slightly smaller, and the decrease of mortality caused by diseases classified as 'others', CVD and infectious diseases contributed to more than 70 % in the increase in its life expectancy. During this 50-year period, the decrease in mortality caused by diseases grouped as 'others' played the most important role in improving survival. It led to an increase of 8.3 years, 8.2 years and 7.7 years in life expectancy in Hong Kong, Taiwan and Japan, respectively.

To further examine the impact of changes in cause-specific mortality on the improvement of survival, we have compared their contributions to mortality decline

Table 13.6 Contributions of changes in cause-specific mortality to the improvement of survival when life expectancy rose from around 70 to approximately 80 years. (Data Sources: See Table 13.3)

Populations	Period	Changes in e_0	Contribution made by					
			Infectious Disease	Neo-plasms	CVD	Injury and poisoning	Respira-tory diseases	Other diseases
England and Wales	1954–2007	70.34–79.98	0.45	0.79	5.04	0.44	1.00	1.91
France	1959–2004	70.12–80.22	0.56	0.43	3.18	0.80	0.89	4.23
Sweden	1951–2002	71.41–80.16	0.59	0.60	3.71	0.50	0.50	2.84
Hong Kong	1971–1998	71.18–80.04	0.96	0.56	2.31	0.50	1.66	2.88
Japan	1964–1995	70.05–80.05	0.68	0.50	4.04	0.76	0.27	3.74
Taiwan	1974–2007	70.30–78.23	1.05	− 0.51	3.31	0.82	1.36	1.90

during the time when life expectancies rose from around 70 years to approximately 80 years in these populations. According to the results presented in Table 13.6, the main driving force for rising life expectancies at this phase of the transition was the significant reduction in mortality caused by CVD and diseases classified as 'others' in England and Wales, France, Japan and Sweden, while the decline of mortality caused by respiratory diseases also made a notable contribution to the increase in life expectancies in Hong Kong and Taiwan.

13.5 Concluding Remarks

On the basis of the analysis presented in previous sections, we now further comment on the major findings of this study and address the following questions: What can we learn from the mortality decline in East Asian populations? In what ways could their experience of lowering mortality enrich our knowledge of the epidemiological transition in the world?

Mortality transition arrived late in East Asia. Long-term mortality decline did not start until the late nineteenth century in Japan and until the early twentieth century in some other populations, and it was also interrupted by the wars and social upheavals taking place in several countries in the first half of the century. Since the 1950s, however, East Asia has experienced a very rapid mortality decline. Its life expectancy increased 28 years between 1950–1955 and 2005–2010. Very low, or the lowest, mortality has been recorded in several East Asian populations in recent years.

The acceleration of mortality transition taking place in most East Asian populations was not a simple compression of the time or the process of mortality decline experienced by many North and West European populations in the past. Such a compression has indeed been observed in many East Asian populations, where a mortality decline of the same magnitude took a shorter period to accomplish in most age groups in comparison with that recorded in selected European populations. However, aside from this compression, the acceleration of the mortality decline in East Asia was also closely related to the fact that simultaneous mortality reductions were increasingly observed in different age groups in East Asian populations.

The increasing simultaneity in mortality decline at different ages and the compression of the mortality decline, or the compression of the time required for the mortality decline, were both related to the changes that took place in the process of the epidemiological transition. In the classic epidemiological transition experienced by the selected European populations, controlling and eradicating major infectious diseases were often achieved gradually and took a long time to complete (Omran 1971, 1983; Riley 2001; Szreter 2003). In this phase, fighting major degenerative diseases was not yet on the agenda and it was also prevented by limited medical knowledge and the lack of effective treatments. It is largely for these reasons that mortality decline was slow during this period and usually showed a long delay at older ages. This changed significantly in the first half of the twentieth century, and especially after the Second World War. In the mid-twentieth century a wide range of effective prevention methods, medicines and treatments were already available and used in conquering various kinds of infectious diseases. Progress in preventing and treating some degenerative diseases was also made at the time and in the decades that followed. Since the late 1950s, medical science and knowledge have advanced significantly. Many new methods, equipments and techniques have been developed and used in preventing, detecting and treating cardiovascular diseases and neoplasms (Beckmann 2006; Ford et al. 2007; Laatikainen et al. 2005; Tunstall-Pedoe et al. 2000). All these led to increasingly simultaneous reductions in mortality that was caused by infectious diseases, degenerative diseases and diseases of other kinds. This contributed to the rapid decline in age-specific mortality and the increasing simultaneity of such changes, which together brought about the 'accelerated model' of epidemiological transition (Omran 1971).

The accelerated epidemiological transition observed in some East Asian populations was of course related to the fact that their transitions took place at a later time or a different stage of development in comparison with that witnessed in the selected European populations. The late starters did have the advantages that they could learn from the experiences of other countries and that they could use the latest knowledge and technologies to prevent and treat various kinds of diseases. But the successful story of lower mortality in Japan, Hong Kong, Macau, South Korea, Taiwan and perhaps Mainland China may also be attributable to the following facts. These populations have all experienced rapid economic growth in recent decades and people have enjoyed high or relatively high standards of living. They have good or reasonably good health care systems and facilities. Many of these countries and areas had and still have relatively egalitarian social policies. They all emphasize the importance of education including health education and disease prevention. Educational levels in these populations have been relatively high. In addition, they are all highly organized societies, where the role of government interventions and policies in promoting public health has been more effective than in many other populations. The importance of some of these factors for improving population health has been discussed by Caldwell (1986) and other scholars (Frenk et al. 1991).

Aside from what was mentioned above, the successful experience of Japan is particularly noteworthy. The country has led the mortality decline in the world in recent decades. This is revealed by the fact that in 2005, age-standardised mortality rates varied between 3.58 and 5.34 per thousand in the six selected populations. Japan had the lowest standardised mortality and its mortality rates for neoplasms, CVD and diseases classified as 'others' were also the lowest or the second lowest among these populations. In Hong Kong, the level of mortality and its causal structure were very similar to those observed in Japan. Successively lowering mortality caused by these diseases, which is closely related to their early detection and effective prevention, has been the main reason why these populations achieved the highest life expectancy in the world (Hamzelou 2012). Examining such experiences could provide very useful lessons for countries that are trying to further improve their life expectancies in the fourth stage of the epidemiological transition.

Another noteworthy lesson learnt from this and other studies (Zhao 2003, 2007b) is that frequent changes in age patterns of mortality have often been observed in the process of the mortality transition. While regional variations in mortality patterns might have existed in the past when many populations lived in isolation and their mortality fluctuated around a high level, recent cross-population variations in age patterns of mortality were often related to the time and phase of the mortality transition. There is hardly any population that has maintained the same age pattern of mortality throughout the period when its life expectancy rose from a low to a high level. The same is also true for changes in sex differentials in mortality, although they are not discussed in this chapter. Understanding the nature and characteristics of these changes is of considerable importance for improving our knowledge about the mortality transition.

Acknowledgments The study is partly supported by the research grants for the projects "Mortality transition in Hong Kong and its major theoretical and policy implications" (RGC, HKUST6001 PPR 2), Hong Kong University of Science and Technology and "The study of the long-term relationship between mortality, climatic conditions and air pollution" (RGC, RPC10HSS01), Hong Kong University of Science and Technology.

References

Ahmad, O. B., Boschi-Pinto, C., Lopez, A. D., Murray, C. J., Lozano, R., & Inoue, M. (2001). *Age standardization of rates: A new WHO standard, in GPE Discussion Paper Series*. Geneva: World Health Organization.

Arriaga, E. E. (1984). Measuring and explaining the change in life expectancies. *Demography, 21*(1), 83–96.

Banister, J. (1987). *China's changing population*. California: Stanford University Press.

Barclay, G. W., Coale, A. J., Stoto, M. A., & Trussell, T. J. (1976). A reassessment of the demography of traditional rural China. *Population Index, 42*(4), 606–635.

Beckmann, E. C. (2006). CT scanning the early days. *British Journal of Radiology*, 79: 5–8.

Blayo, Y. (1975). La mortalité en France de 1740 a 1829. *Population* (*French Edition*), *30,* 123–142.

Caldwell, J. C. (1986). Routes to low mortality in poor countries. *Population and Development Review, 12*(2), 171–220.

Campbell, C. (2001). Mortality change and the epidemiological transition in Beijing, 1644–1990. In T. Liu, J. Lee, D. S. Reher, O. Saito, & F. Wang (Eds.), *Asian population history*. Oxford: Oxford University Press.

Chen, T. (1946). *Population in modern China. Chicago*: University of Chicago Press.

Dyson, T. (2010). *Population and development: The demographic transition*. London: Zed Books.
Engelen, T., Shepherd, J. R., & Yang, W. S. (2011). *Death at the opposite ends of the Eurasian Continent: Mortality trends in Taiwan and the Netherlands 1850–1945*. Amsterdam: Aksant.
Ford, E. S., Ajani, U. A., Croft, J. B., Critchley, J. A., Labarthe, D. R., Kottke, T. E., Giles, W. H., & Capewell. S. (2007). Explaining the decrease in U.S. deaths from coronary disease, 1980–2000. *New England Journal of Medicine, 356*(23), 2388–2298.
Frenk, J., Bobadilla, J. L., Stern, C., Frejka, T., & Lozano, R. (1991). Elements for a theory of the health transition. *Health Transition Review, 1*(1), 21–38.
Hamzelou, J. (2012). Global health report card. *New Scientist, 216*(2896–2897), 6–7.
Jannetta, A. B., & Preston, S. (1991). The centuries of mortality change in Central Japan: The evidence from a temple death register. *Population Studies, 45,* 417–436.
Kim, T. H. (1986). Mortality transition in Korea: 1960–1980. PhD Dissertation, Australian National University.
Kwon, T. H. (1977). *Demography of Korea: Population change and its components 1925–66*. Seoul: Seoul National University Press.
Laatikainen, T., Critchley, J., Vartiainen, E., Salomaa, V., Ketonen, M., & Capewell, S. (2005). Explaining the decline in coronary heart disease mortality in Finland between 1982 and 1997. *American Journal of Epidemiology, 162*(8), 764–773.
Livi-Bacci, M. (2007). *A concise history of world population* (4th ed.). Oxford: Blackwell Publishing.
Max Planck Institute for Demographic Research and University of California at Berkeley. (2011). The human mortality database. http://www.mortality.org/. Accessed 11 Aug 2011.
Ministry of the Interior (published annually). *Taiwan-Fukien Demographic Fact Book*. Taipei: Ministry of the Interior.
Mirzaee, M. (1983). *Trends and determinants of mortality in Taiwan*. Ann Arbor: University Microfilms International.
Notestein, F. W. (1945). Population—The long view. In T. W. Schultz (Ed.), *Food for the world*. Chicago: University of Chicago Press.
Olshansky, S. J., & Ault, A. B. (1986). The fourth stage of the epidemiologic transition: The age of delayed degenerative diseases. *The Milbank Quarterly, 64*(3), 355–391.
Omran, A. R. (1971). The epidemiological transition: A theory of the epidemiology of population change. *Milbank Memorial Fund Quarterly, 49,* 509–538.
Omran, A. R. (1983). The epidemiologic transition theory. A preliminary update. *Journal of Tropical Pediatrics, 29,* 305–316.
Riley, J. C. (2001). *Rising life expectancy: A global history*. New York: Cambridge University Press.
Szreter, S. (2003). The population health approach in historical perspective. *American Journal of Public Health, 93*(3), 421–431.
Tsuya, N. and Kurosu, S. (2004). Mortality and household in two Ou villages, 1716–1870. In T. Bengtsson, C. Campbell, J. Lee et al., *Life under Pressure, Mortality and Living Standards in Europe and Asia, 1700–1900* (pp. 253–292). Cambridge USA: The MIT Press.
Tunstall-Pedoe, H., Vanuzzo, D., Hobbs, M., Mähönen, M., Cepaitis, Z., Kuulasmaa, K., & Keil, U. (2000). Estimation of contribution of changes in coronary care to improving survival, event rates, and coronary heart disease mortality across the WHO MONICA Project populations. *Lancet, 355*(9205), 688–700.
United Nations (2011). *World Population Prospects: 2010 Revision*. http://esa.un.org/wpp/Excel-Data/mortality.htm. Accessed 20 Aug 2011.
Vallin, J., & Meslé, F. (2001). Tables de mortalité Française pour les XIX et XX siècle et projections pour le XXI siècle. Données statistiques, INED(4).
World Health Organization. WHO Mortality Database. http://www.who.int/healthinfo/morttables/en/. Accessed 20 Aug 2011.
Wrigley, E. A. et al (1997). *English population history from family reconstitution*. Cambridge: Cambridge University Press.

Zhao, Z. (1997). Demographic systems in historic China: Some new findings from recent research. *Journal of the Australian Population Association, 14*(2), 201–232.

Zhao, Z. (2003). On the Far Eastern pattern of mortality. *Population Studies, 57,* 131–147.

Zhao, Z. (2007a). Changing mortality patterns and causes of death. In Z. Zhao & F. Guo (Ed.), *Transition and challenge: China's population at the beginning of the 21st century* (pp. 160–176). New York: Oxford University Press.

Zhao, Z. (2007b). Interpretation and use of the United Nations 1982 model life tables: With particular reference to developing countries. *Population (English Version), 62,* 89–115.

Zhao, Z., & Kinfu, Y. (2005). Mortality transition in East Asia. *Asian Population Studies, 1*(1), 3–30.

Index

J. Anson, M. Luy (eds.), *Mortality in an International Perspective*,
European Studies of Population 18, DOI 10.1007/978-3-319-03029-6,

Printed by Publishers' Graphics LLC
MLSI140326.15.13.11